# PARADOX PROGRAMMER'S GUIDE

## PAL by Example

# PARADOX PROGRAMMER'S GUIDE

## PAL by Example

Alan Zenreich

James M. Kocis

ScottForesman
ProfessionalBooks
*An Imprint of* ScottForesman

To Lauren. Scott. Joshua. Cassandra. Jeffrey. Kerry.

Cover photo courtesy of Image Bank

Computer screen image courtesy of Borland International

Quattro and Quattro Pro, Sidekick, Reflex, Paradox, Sprint, and The Paradox Engine are registered trademarks of Borland International. Lotus is a trademark of the Lotus Development Corporation. DOS and OS/2 are trademarks of Microsoft Corporation. ScriptView is a trademark of Farpoint Systems. ParaLex is a trademark of Zenreich Systems. PlayRight is a trademark of The Burgiss Group.

**Library of Congress Cataloging-in-Publication Data**
Zenreich, Alan.
    Paradox programmer's guide : PAL by example / Alan Zenreich, James M. Kocis.
       p.     cm.
    ISBN 0-673-38827-1
    1. PAL (Computer program language)  2. Paradox (Computer program)
I. Kocis, James M.    II. Title.
QA76.73.P18Z46  1990
005.75′65—dc20

90-8043
CIP

ISBN 0-673-38827-1

# Acknowledgments

Many people contributed to this effort, but none more than Richard Schwartz and Robert Shostak, the pair of Docs whose foresight and diligence first created Paradox. Many thanks as well to the Paradox Development team, past, present and future, whose hard work keeps Paradox healthy and thriving. Special thanks to the Borland team, including Nan Borreson, Tony Lee, Rick Gretter, Uri Geva, Kevin Gallagher and Debbie Rivers and to Borland alumni Tom Swegles, Brad Jung, Celeste Robinson and Derc Yamasaki. For technical review of the manuscript, medals of honor go to Matthew J. Oliver and Douglas Rosen.

WaitPlus would not be what it is without assistance from dozens of beta testers; likewise, our knowledge of Paradox would not be what it is without the crew on CompuServe. Special thanks to friends Michael Ax and Andrew Appell for their input on WaitPlus; to Kevin Smith of Softbite International, one of the finest instructors on the planet; and to Mark Pauker, the father of the Data Entry Toolkit.

Finally, thanks to Stephen Louis Kocis for suggesting this collaboration and to Amy Davis for steadfast support of it.

# Foreword

If you develop or plan to develop Paradox applications, you'll find this book invaluable. As well as being a comprehensive reference, the *Paradox Programmer's Guide* teaches you a development style and philosophy that lets you create professional applications with substantially less effort than traditional database programming.

The crux of this philosophy, in a word, is laziness! By availing yourself of the powerful form, report, and query construction features built into Paradox, you can develop the "guts" of your application without writing a single line of code. What then remains is to glue it all together using the high-level constructs of PAL, the Paradox Application Language.

The authors, Jim Kocis and Alan Zenreich, are not only masters of the Zen of Paradox programming but also have a knack for communicating their understanding in a most PALatable, entertaining manner. These gentlemen have cultivated their own exquisite sense of "laziness" through years of experience writing Paradox tools and applications and through close communication with Richard Schwartz, me, and other members of the Paradox development team.

Among the fruits of this experience is a host of useful information about the workings (and not workings!) of Paradox and PAL that you will find here and probably nowhere else. The subtleties of procedure swapping, error handling, disk and memory management, and the data entry toolkit, for example, are all covered with copious illustrations. As a bonus, source code and documentation are included for WaitPlus, the authors' own set of tools for advanced programming.

Highly recommended.

Rob Shostak

PAL is not simply another programming language. It is an extension of the Paradox database environment. PAL is best understood by first understanding Paradox as an interactive problem-solving tool. Paradox provides a set of very high-level tools for querying, reporting, multiuser operation, and multitable manipulation. For you as a developer to get maximal leverage from these tools, you have to think differently about the development process. All the interactive capabilities of Paradox are available from PAL. All the functionality, all the tools, all the user display interaction, and all problem solving approaches are derived from interactive Paradox.

Jim and Alan's book captures the essence of this philosophy. The book explains not just the mechanics of the PAL commands and functions, but stresses how to use Paradox and PAL most efficiently to build applications—how to leverage the power of the product. This book is a virtual encyclopedia for PAL: it covers both basic application paradigms and very advanced control over the environment. I'm sure that this book will stimulate many new and creative uses of Paradox and PAL!

Richard Schwartz

# Contents

# PART FOUR

**645**

# PARADOX PROGRAMMER'S GUIDE

## PAL by Example

# Part One

# Chapter 1

## Preliminaries

## 1.1  ABOUT THIS BOOK

The Paradox Application Language (PAL) is the programming language of Paradox, a relational database management system for the PC. PAL extends the reach and control of interactive Paradox by supplementing menu choices with powerful functions, commands, and a special set of procedures called "The Data Entry Toolkit." This book was written to help both novice and experienced PAL programmers use PAL more efficiently.

We start from the perspective of a user untrained in programming, but trained and experienced in interactive Paradox. For new users, a little help from PAL can go a long way. The Paradox {InstantRecord} and {QuerySave} commands encourage use and exploration of programming by saving your keystrokes to text files. With a little help, new users learn to combine and edit these *scripts*, and they're programming before they know it. Included with Paradox3 is a utility called "The Personal Programmer," which helps those unfamiliar with programming create applications. We do not cover this utility in this book, in part because we assume that readers of this book want to learn to write PAL programs from scratch.

To experienced programmers, PAL offers many paths to the same destination and the costs/benefits of different routes are rarely intuitive. Throughout the book, examples of PAL code will help clarify the reasons we prefer a particular method.

As Paradox changes, so does PAL. Techniques that may have made sense in the second release of Paradox have been supplanted by much simpler techniques in release 3. This doesn't mean that programming with Paradox3 is simpler; in fact, it is more complex. Yet there are things that can be done with release 3 that we would not have attempted in release 2. We expect that this trend will continue as Paradox evolves.

3

"This manual assumes at least a basic understanding of programming concepts; we will not teach you how to program here."

Page 1 of the PAL User's Guide

This book is meant to complement the Paradox documentation. The PAL manual is a reference work that guides those already familiar with programming. On occasion we will quote from the Paradox manuals directly; at other times, we'll refer you to them for further information or instruction. Though we'll point out errors and omissions in the documentation, we regard the manuals that accompany Paradox as among the most thorough and clearly written guides we've encountered. And although a great deal of effort has been made to assure the accuracy and completeness of the information *we* present, we expect that this book will have errors as well.

*PAL by Example* is the book that we wished we had when we set out to learn programming with Paradox. There are other books that include PAL, but few, we felt, that were written with a full grasp of the differences between PAL and other database programming languages. PAL is different from other database programming languages because Paradox is different from other database programs. PAL draws strengths from Paradox's strengths. Wherever a user can venture in Paradox, PAL can too, so it isn't limited to the manipulation of data in tables—PAL can be used in any system mode, from queries to forms to reports to graphing. This book was written to help you exploit these differences to your advantage.

## 1.2 HOW TO USE THIS BOOK

*This book is in four parts.*

- It begins with a narrative section that introduces those familiar with Paradox to PAL. It uses simple examples to illustrate how to record keystrokes, write and edit scripts, and create and use procedures and procedure libraries.
- The second part is an examples section, grouped by topic, that illustrates the use of nearly all PAL commands and functions. The examples present comparative coding techniques and detailed information on the effects of these techniques.
- The third section includes an introduction to the Data Entry Toolkit and an application development tool called WAITPLUS. Written in PAL for this book by the authors, WAITPLUS handles most routine complex multitable data entry and editing sessions with relative ease.
- The fourth part describes Paradox 3.5, problems and solutions, and performance tuning tips. Refer to this section for updated information on Paradox 3.5 memory management.

How you use this book will depend on your level of knowledge of Paradox and of programming in general. Programming books are rarely read from front to back. Programming is about problem solving; if you're interested in a particular topic, you might start reading from the index. If you're new to both Paradox and PAL, we recommend that you read the narrative to give you some insight into what makes Paradox different. If you're a programmer with experience in other languages, this section may help bring you up to speed more quickly. For those already familiar with PAL, this first section may largely be a review.

The second section is example-based and assumes a working knowledge of procedures and procedure libraries. It is a reference work, with examples of the use of PAL functions and commands grouped together. Read this section and borrow its code for use in your applications.

The third section is almost entirely PAL code. Like the Data Entry Toolkit, the application tool called WAITPLUS is more than the sum of its parts. Although you can use fragments of WAITPLUS to augment your applications, it's perhaps best used in its entirety, supplemented with your own custom procedures. With the design of tables and forms in place, WAITPLUS can be used as a core of procedures that can greatly simplify application development in PAL.

## Multiuser Issues

Several PAL topics relate specifically to programming Paradox for local area networks. We have elected to integrate multiuser topics directly into the examples section (Part II) rather than to discuss these network issues separately. The line between single user and multiuser programming isn't always clear. For example, "CoEdit" mode, designed expressly for sharing tables on a network, provides great benefits when used on single user systems as well. For another example, table locking, originally intended only to facilitate network use, allows semaphore locking in single user systems.

## 1.3 UPGRADE

"The King is dead. Long live the King."

Each major release of Paradox has brought substantial improvements. The third release, Paradox3, presents many, many advantages over prior releases. If you are serious about doing PAL programming, do not pass Go, do not collect $200, go directly to your telephone and upgrade from releases 1.0 or 2.0. It will save you hundreds of hours. This book is written from the perspective of Release 3.0, which introduced features that will enable you to greatly simplify both interactive use of Paradox and programming.

## 1.4 OTHER SOURCES OF INFORMATION

For the first time, Paradox3 was shipped with a file called README on the installation disk. It is easy to overlook because it is not copied onto your hard disk during installation. Read it, for it contains valuable last-minute information on changes to Paradox. As with most Borland products, this README file will most likely accompany future versions as well. The Borland Database Forum (BorDB) of Compuserve is a user-based source of information, discussion, and help on Paradox and PAL.

## 1.5 CONVENTIONS AND TYPOGRAPHY

This book will refer to the many versions of Paradox by the executable file name:

Paradox 2.0 as *Paradox2*
Paradox 3.0 as *Paradox3*
Paradox 386 as *PDOX386*
Paradox OS|2 as *PDOXOS2*

Paradox Menu choices are represented in curly braces, like this selection for modify: {Modify}. If a table name is requested as a menu choice, it too is in curly braces.

```
{Tools} {Rename} {Table} {Ordrs} {NewOrdrs} {OK}
```

Paradox keystrokes are represented by the name of the key.

```
[F1] Help
```

The example code in this book is in single-spaced type, set off from the rest of the text. Most of the time PAL is insensitive to upper- or lowercase, though not always. We will point out when the case of a word can be expected to make a difference.

## 1.6 PBE NOTATION

Note for experienced programmers: This book also introduces a method of variable and procedure naming based on a style known as "Hungarian Notation," developed by Charles Simonyi of MicroSoft Corporation. Our variation on this naming style uses a suffix to denote the type of variable or value returned from a procedure. For example, variables that are alphanumeric end with an "a"; thus a customer's name might be assigned to a variable named "CustName.a." A procedure that determines whether an entry is for a current customer (returning a True or False, a logical constant) might be named "IsCustomer.l()". We explain this style and the reasoning behind its use more fully in Chapter 5, Language Elements.

## 1.7 WHY A NEED FOR PAL?

"I know someone who's extremely capable with Lotus 1-2-3 who tried Paradox and didn't find it easy at all. I thought Paradox was supposed to be easy to use."

We were walking up Eighth Avenue after a lunch at John's Pizzeria (charcoal-fired ovens crisping thin crust pies). Our editor from Scott Foresman was sounding a familiar note. Since 1-2-3 is considered easy to use, there is the danger that any product that lays claim to being easy to use should be rated on the same scale.

"Paradox is easy to use," replied Alan. "Databases are difficult."

Another paradox.

Paradox is extremely powerful and maintains a consistent, understandable, and intuitive design. But . . . it ain't easy—no database is. Databases are difficult because people want them to do difficult things, maintaining whole systems of information rather than tending to bits and pieces. Databases are difficult because people have complex expectations about what a database should deliver. These expectations give rise to programming.

For those new to databases, Paradox may seem simple at first—create a table, store some data in it, keep it up to date, print it out when it's needed. The ease with which Paradox lets you get things done is rewarding. A sense of accomplishment pushes you farther. Simple queries are followed by more complex requests. You begin to read the User's Guide more closely. Your knowledge grows. Eventually you're pulled into making Paradox perform for you. That's called programming.

Other database management systems are known to create a barrier between the user and the developer—very little of the experience gained by interactive use can be carried over into programming. In contrast, PAL is in essence an "automated" Paradox user. The more you know about the way Paradox behaves interactively, the closer you come to understanding how to program in PAL. The gap that at first may appear large diminishes over time; a leap becomes a step.

The developers of Paradox took great pains to make this so. For example, queries done the "Paradox way" are internally optimized each time they are run. "Heuristic Query Optimization" frees the developer from having to predict changing database characteristics and "hard code" only one solution. By relying on Paradox to handle many internal decisions, programming is simplified. (As with any generalization, there are exceptions to the rule of relying on the internal workings of Paradox to most efficiently accomplish a task. We will show some of them later.) For developers, Paradox is becoming popular because of its easy end-user support and maintenance, unrivaled multiuser implementation, excellent prototyping environment, and short development cycle.

Though PAL is an inviting language in which to learn to program, it is by no means a simple language. PAL presents challenges to any programmer, regardless of skill level. Experienced programmers encountering PAL for the first time may be tempted to follow their instincts and, unfortunately, may miss out on the advantages of programming "The Paradox Way." Old habits die hard.

## 1.8 PROGRAMMING "THE PARADOX WAY"

What is programming "The Paradox Way"? That's what this book is about. Paradox attempts to debunk the myth that complex database problems require programming solutions. Here's an example. You have two tables, "Products" and "Orders," and you'd like a list of all current orders. Simple enough—but while you're at it, you'd like to do a little inventory management and have Paradox flag items you need to reorder. For these reorder items only, you'd like to include the current quantity in stock and a short description.

A simple matter of programming, right? Here are two different solutions.

```
CREATE "Answer"
"Order #" : "N",
"Order Quant" : "N",
"Stock Quant" : "N",
"Stock #" : "N",
"Description" : "A23"
VIEW "Answer"
VIEW "Products"
Right
VIEW "Orders"
```

```
CoEditKey
SCAN
  MOVETO "products"
  LOCATE [Orders->Stock #]
  MOVETO "Answer"
  IF NOT IsBlank ([Order #]) THEN
    Down
  ENDIF
  [Order #] = [Orders->Order #]
  [Order Quant] = [Orders->Quant]
  IF RETVAL AND ( [Orders->Quant] >= [Products->Quant] *.25) THEN
    [Stock #] = [Orders->Stock #]
    [Description] = [Products->Description]
  ENDIF
  MOVETO "Orders"
ENDSCAN
Do_It!
ClearAll
SORT "Answer"
```

Here's a single Paradox query that accomplishes the same result.

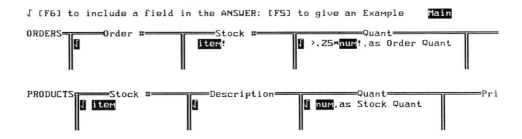

The resulting "Answer" table could look as follows:

```
Viewing Answer table: Record 1 of 15                        Main  ▲═

ANSWER╤═Order #═╤Order Quant╤Stock #═╤════Description════╤Stock Quan╤
     1║  1180   ║     2      ║        ║                   ║           ║
     2║  1442   ║     2      ║        ║                   ║           ║
     3║  1574   ║     1      ║        ║                   ║           ║
     4║  2280   ║     1      ║  130   ║ Stretch VW Beetle ║     3     ║
     5║  3351   ║     1      ║        ║                   ║           ║
     6║  3885   ║     5      ║  244   ║ Mink handkerchiefs (13 ║ 14   ║
     7║  4492   ║     3      ║        ║                   ║           ║
     8║  5119   ║     1      ║  235   ║ Diamond-filled bathtub ║ 1    ║
     9║  6235   ║     1      ║  890   ║ Matching panthers ║     3     ║
    10║  6975   ║     3      ║        ║                   ║           ║
    11║  7643   ║     1      ║        ║                   ║           ║
    12║  8070   ║     8      ║        ║                   ║           ║
    13║  8933   ║     1      ║        ║                   ║           ║
    14║  9226   ║     1      ║        ║                   ║           ║
    15║  9554   ║    15      ║        ║                   ║           ║
```

This "problem" and its query solution come straight out of the *Paradox3 User's Guide* (page 106), not, as might be expected, from the *PAL User's Guide*. This problem is a request that can be solved interactively with a single query.

## 1.9 BEAUTY AND THE BEAST

This example illustrates a brute-force solution typical of database programming languages, and an elegant, but perhaps not so elementary, query solution. The query solution is faster and doesn't involve a line of programming. It is a model of programming "The Paradox Way." In this case the message is clear: avoid programming. It turns out that the main difficulty with this problem is framing the question.

This brings us to another truthful contradiction, another paradox. Avoiding programming is one of the tenets of programming "The Paradox Way." The fewer lines of code that need to be written and maintained, the better. If a query can be used to accomplish a task, it usually (but not always) pays to use it. If a report can be designed with the necessary grouping bands to sort data, there's no need to sort it first. If a multitable form can be used to locate and manipulate related records, Paradox encourages you to design and use it. Avoiding programming takes practice and requires vigilance. Rather than asking "How do I do this with PAL?" the better approach is to first ask "Can I do this without resorting to PAL?"

This example also brings out the dual personalities of PAL: PAL as both the beauty and the beast. Through brute force programming, the beast can be made to do anything (though perhaps not always with grace, and at times getting pretty ugly). And there are many times when nothing but the raw power of PAL can get the job done. But there is another side to PAL, one that relies on the power of queries and structural objects you create with interactive Paradox—reports, forms, validity checks, settings. Learning to efficiently program with Paradox means, in part, learning to distinguish when you need Paradox and when you need PAL.

## 1.10 WHY PROGRAM AT ALL?

If Paradox is so capable of bypassing programming to achieve results, why program at all? Clearly, the lure of programming in Paradox is a gain in efficiency. Tasks that repeat and repeat beg for automation. As the size and complexity of a database system design grow, programming becomes not a luxury, but a necessity. Programming becomes the means to an end that allows complex systems to be as simple as they can be.

## 1.11 KNOW PARADOX!

The underlying premise of this book is that you already understand the workings of interactive Paradox. While we hope that this book will help you better understand interactive Paradox, that is not our main goal. The warning, sounded loud and clear, is in the first pages of the PAL User's Guide, and we will echo it here:

> "If you've programmed applications with other databases, it would be natural to assume that you could jump in and start writing PAL programs without understanding Paradox. After all, PAL is just another database programming language, right? Wrong . . . We can't emphasize this enough: The better you understand Paradox, the better you'll understand PAL."

Good PAL Programming is synonymous with efficient manipulation of the Paradox workspace. Writing good PAL code means writing programs that work with the structural advantages of Paradox, and the results are programs that are reliable, compact, easy-to-maintain, and efficient. Programs that merely happen to be written in PAL and that don't take advantage of the Paradox environment are often slow, clumsy, and hard to maintain.

A programming language bridges the gap between you and a machine. Because it cannot intuit, a computer follows your instructions and not necessarily your intent. "Paralanguage," a linguistic term that refers to the signals in speech not contained in words—intonation, stress, emotional overtone, the speaker's identity—is absent from programming. Thankfully, programming is free from the ambiguities of the spoken word; programs must be declarative and unambiguous. And although they are designed to expect the unexpected, most programming languages require you to work within strict rules to achieve your intent. Subtle differences in expression usually make for entirely different results.

To the beginner anxious to start programming with PAL, plunge in and make mistakes. You'll learn a lot of rules in no time at all. Do things at the risk of being wrong, but keep a back-up of your data. Persist. Whether you are new to programming or just simply new to PAL, this programming language may spoil you because of the level of productivity it can help you reach in a very short time.

## 1.12 LEARNING FROM MISTAKES

We use PAL almost every day. If those who have made the greatest number of mistakes are theoretically those most capable of avoiding future mistakes, we should be well-equipped. Oh, have we made mistakes! Thousands of them. Big ones, little ones. Inconsequential. Monumental. Through curiosity and invention we have made mistakes that have taken hours or days to find or fix. At times we have labored long and hard to discover that we had unearthed a bug in Paradox. Much of this book presents techniques that help you avoid mistakes big and small. We will continue to make mistakes of all kinds and learn from them.

## 1.13 KEEP IT SIMPLE

Nothing is more important in programming than the rule *"Keep It Simple."* If things get too complex, break them up into pieces small enough to understand. Avoid cleverness. Mark Pauker, the programmer who created the Data Entry Toolkit, stresses this concept: "While teaching undergraduates in programming, I actively discouraged correct, but clever solutions. When it came to grading papers, 'Very Clever, minus 10' was my reaction to programs that could be simpler by being less clever. Students caught on very quickly." A lot of thinking goes into programming. There are almost always many solutions to a problem. Clever solutions are usually cryptic solutions. Stick to the ones that are most direct.

# Chapter 2

# PAL Basics Are Paradox Basics

This chapter is a review of the capabilities of interactive Paradox as a prelude to programming. If you feel well versed in interactive Paradox, we suggest you skim, but not skip, this chapter. This chapter uses Paradox terminology, and introduces some PAL terminology.

## 2.1 PARADOX IS EVOLVING

Paradox 1.0, introduced in the fall of 1985, was designed to store data in a fixed-length record format and featured sophisticated memory management, a capable report generator, built-in validity checking, the first micro-based implementation of query-by-example, and a powerful programming language. Paradox 2.0, introduced in the spring of 1987, added functionality by including true local area network multiuser capability, more programming commands, an improved code generator called "The Personal Programmer," and the Data Entry Toolkit, a series of PAL procedures that extend control during data entry and editing.

Paradox 3.0, introduced in January of 1989, features expanded query operations, graphics, greater control of the use of color, more efficient memory utilization and greatly enhanced multitable operations.

## 2.2 SPECIAL VERSIONS

For owners of PCs based on the 80386 microprocessor, Borland introduced Paradox 386 in early 1988. This special version uses an embedded extension of DOS that permits access to 16Mb of contiguous memory, and makes significant performance gains when used with tables of 10,000 records or more. Paradox OS|2 is based on the first release of IBM/Microsoft's OS|2 standard edition, the character-based multitasking operating system that works in the protected mode of the 80286 and 80386 chips. In addition to being able to address the 16Mb of memory that OS|2 supports, Paradox OS|2 can support multiple "sessions" running at once. In December 1989, Borland announced "Paradox Engine," designed to allow C programmers to tap into the Paradox table structure.

## 2.3 THE PARADOX SYSTEM DESIGN

Paradox was designed to hide complexity from the user. Without sacrificing control, Paradox will hide unnecessary detail from the user wherever and whenever possible. Yet Paradox and PAL combine to make a very large language, with hundreds of allowable menu choices, commands, and functions, along with dozens of operators and special rules. This by itself makes for complexity.
Despite its size and complexity, Paradox is made up of two basic elements:

- A set of structural definitions for storing data and information.
- A set of tools (programs) that manipulate data.

## 2.4 PARADOX OBJECTS

The structures created within Paradox are called **Objects** and are stored as DOS files.

| Object | Description | Example |
|--------|-------------|---------|
| .DB | Table (database) | Customer.DB |
| .F* | Form | Customer.F3 |
| .R* | Report | Customer.R1 |
| .VAL | Validity Checks | Customer.VAL |
| .SET | Settings | Customer.SET |

| Object | Description | Example |
|--------|-------------|---------|
| .PX | Primary Index | Customer.PX |
| .X## | Secondary Index | Customer.X04 |
| .Y## | Secondary Index | Customer.Y04 |
| .G | Graph Settings | ApplePie.G |
| .SC | Script | Mainmenu.SC |
| .LIB | Procedure Library | Paradox.LIB |

The ## in secondary index filename extensions corresponds to the hexadecimal number of the field indexed (Hex FF = 255, the maximum number of fields). The * following .F and .R refers to the form and report numbers, 1 to 14.

Paradox objects are usually built through the use of the menu commands, but can also be built under program control, or created as by-products of Paradox operations. A group of related Paradox files with a table at its center is called a **Family.** Each of the family member types has a different filename extension automatically assigned by Paradox (e.g., Reports = R followed by a number). Family objects are married to the structural definition of the table. If you delete a field from a table by modifying the table's structure, the field will be deleted from that table's forms and reports, and reference to it eliminated in other related files. Paradox is able to keep track of file modifications with the use of a date and time stamp within each family object, so it knows which objects are current.

- Validity Checks help enforce the content, form, and source of information added to tables.
- Settings dictate how tables display data.
- Forms and Reports are particularly powerful structures, allowing you to achieve results through the interactive use of Paradox that require programming with most other data bases.

Two family objects, the **standard** report and **standard** form, will be created on the fly if they don't exist. The standard form and report, though simple in design, can be redesigned for more elaborate effects. With release 3.0, forms and reports play a critical role in the manipulation of data, serving as gateways to data in other tables. Secondary indexes, also known as **QuerySpeedUp** files, may be created and deleted by Paradox automatically. Index files can also be created explicitly by using the PAL INDEX command.

Since a table knows about and has access to all of the structures in its family, Paradox will usually display an error message if you make any attempt to use a family member that has been modified outside of Paradox or is otherwise out of sync with the date/time stamp of the rest of the family.[1] These rules apply to family objects only. Paradox program files are called **scripts,** are not included in the definition of a family, and with one exception (library creation), do not have rules dictating file creation or modification.

## 2.5 MENU CATEGORIES AND SPECIAL FEATURES

All Paradox objects can be built by creating and manipulating their structures through interactive use through the Paradox menu structure. Menu selections can be divided into two broad classes:

- Menu selections that manipulate Paradox objects. These selections can also delete Paradox objects.
- Menu selections that create Paradox objects. These are relatively few in number, and most of the objects created are tables. A list of the commands that create Paradox objects follows.

| | |
|---|---|
| Tables: | Fully listed on pages 19–20. |
| Report Specifications: | {Report} {Design} |
| | {Tools} {Copy} {Report} |
| Form Specifications: | {Form} {Design} |
| | {Tools} {Copy} {Form} |
| Graph Specifications: | {Image} {Graph} {Save} |
| Secondary Indexes: | {Tools} {QuerySpeedUp} |
| Validity Checks: | Edit {Valchecks} |
| Settings: | {Image} {KeepSet} |
| Scripts: | {Scripts} {BeginRecord} |
| | {Editor} {Write} |
| | {QuerySave} |

In addition to the features accessed through menu choices, Paradox provides:

- Query-by-Example
- Graphics
- PAL Commands and Functions
- The PAL Programming Environment
- Specialized Utilities (FLIMPORT, TUTILITY, Hardware Device drivers)
- Paradox RUNTIME (purchased separately)

## 2.6 SYSTEM CONFIGURATION

You can customize your Paradox configuration four ways:

- During installation, you define the manner in which characters are sorted. The resulting file, PARADOX.SOR, is read upon initial startup.
- From the DOS prompt, optional command line parameters can override a few of the configuration defaults.

- Via the "Custom" script, which should be played to set global configuration parameters.
- A specially named script, "Init.sc," can be played automatically by Paradox upon start-up.

## 2.7 THE "CUSTOM" SCRIPT

The Paradox Custom Configuration Program, the "Custom" script, allows you to modify system defaults. If Paradox3 is installed in the \Paradox3 directory, you run this special program within Paradox by choosing {Scripts} {Play} \paradox3\custom. The file the custom script modifies is the Paradox configuration file, (Paradox3.CFG), which is read by Paradox upon initial startup and sets or changes parameters for global settings such as:

> Monitor Type
> Default Colors
> Query Order
> Report Defaults
> NetworkType
> External Script Editors

Identical PAL scripts may produce entirely different results with different configurations. A query may produce a differently structured table if the default query order is set to ImageOrder rather than TableOrder. A financial report that relies on blanks being treated as zeroes will most likely produce different figures if run on a system that does not count blanks as zeroes. Fortunately, for a few of the more critical aspects, PAL provides functions that report on the current condition of these configuration defaults. IsBlankZero() and QueryOrder() are PAL functions that can save you time and trouble (see the Examples section for specific information on these PAL functions).

## 2.8 COMMAND LINE PARAMETERS

Typing "Paradox3" at the DOS prompt simply brings up Paradox in its interactive mode with its default configuration set by the custom script. Command line parameters, that is, optional words and symbols that follow the word "Paradox3" on the DOS command line, override the configuration as specified in the configuration file. Here are a few examples:

- Set monitor type to black and white (of special use with Compaq monochrome units):

  ```
  Paradox3 -B&W
  ```

- Set expanded memory use to zero (to substitute other disk caches, or to
  avoid expanded memory conflicts):

  ```
  Paradox3 -emk 0
  ```

- Play a script automatically upon startup:

  ```
  Paradox3 scriptname
  ```

## 2.9 THE "INIT" SCRIPT

A special Paradox program is looked for in the current directory (or, on networks,
in the user's private directory) upon start-up. If this script file, INIT.SC, is found
when you load Paradox, this initialization script will run and will also allow you
to set aspects of the Paradox configuration. The INIT.SC file will be discussed
more fully in Chapter 3, Avoiding Keystrokes.

## 2.10 PARADOX MODES

Paradox starts out in the Main mode, where the main menu is accessible through
the [F10] key. There are 11 other modes that are subsystems of the "Main" mode.
Here is a listing of all 12 Paradox modes and a brief description of what they do.

| | |
|---|---|
| Main | Tables can be viewed and all other subsystems are accessible. |
| Create | Table structures can be created. |
| Report | Formatted information can be sent to the screen, a file, or a printer. |
| Edit | Data in tables can be modified while maintaining a transaction log, with partial or total rollback. |
| CoEdit | Data in tables can be simultaneously edited on nodes of a network, with one-record rollback capability. |
| DataEntry | Tables can be added to through batch entry. |

| | |
|---|---|
| Restructure | Tables can be modified in structure. |
| Sort | Data in a table can be sorted. |
| Form | Screen forms for data entry and manipulation can be designed. |
| Script | Programs (scripts) can be written, edited, or played. |
| Password | Allow and enable protection of data and scripts. |
| Graph | Data in tables can be viewed and plotted graphically. |

## 2.11 TABLES

The basic structural element within Paradox is the **table.** Tables store data in fixed length records in fields of type:

| Type | Length |
|---|---|
| "A" Alphanumeric | Width in bytes (width 1–255) |
| "D" Date | 4 bytes |
| "$" Dollar | 8 bytes |
| "N" Number | 8 bytes |
| "S" Short Number | 2 bytes, number or integer (−32767 to 32767) |

Tables can either be keyed or unkeyed. A key both establishes the order in which records are stored and prevents duplicate key-value records. Tables can have up to 255 fields. The maximum overall width of an unkeyed table is 4000 bytes; for a keyed table it is 1350 bytes. Tables are particularly efficient structures and Paradox was designed to use them well. We define two broad classes of tables, internal and external. You create and maintain external tables; Paradox creates and maintains internal tables as by-products of your interaction. The {Create} command allows you to create a Paradox table explicitly. Other user-created tables are temporary tables resulting from queries and menu commands. Here's a complete list of Paradox menu choices that create tables:

| Tablename | Sources of Creation |
|---|---|
| Answer | {Ask} |
| Changed | Changeto Query |
| | {Tools} {More} {Add} {Update} |
| Crosstab | {Image} {Graph} {Crosstab} |
| Deleted | Delete Query |
| Entry | {Modify} {DataEntry}[2] |
| | {Tools} {More} {FormAdd} |
| Family | {Tools} {Info} {Family} |
| Inserted | Insert Query |

| Tablename | Sources of Creation |
|---|---|
| Keyviol | {Modify} {Restructure} |
| | {Modify} {DataEntry}[3] |
| | {Modify} {MultiEntry} |
| | {Tools} {More} {Add} |
| | {Tools} {More} {MultiAdd} |
| | {Tools} {More} {FormAdd}[4] |
| List | {Tools} {Info} {Inventory} |
| | {Tools} {More} {FormAdd} |
| | {Tools} {Info} {Who} |
| Password | {Tools} {More} {Protect} |
| Problems | {Modify} {Restructure} |
| | {Tools} {ExportImport} {Import} |
| Struct | {Create} |
| | {Modify} {Restructure} |
| | {Tools} {Info} {Structure} |

These special table names are reserved for use by Paradox and they are called temporary with good reason—they may disappear when you least expect it. For example, the "Password" table is created, used during password assignment, and deleted automatically once password assignment is completed. If you create a table called "Password," don't expect to keep it; it will be deleted upon changing the current directory or exiting Paradox, or when you assign passwords to a table. All temporary tables are deleted by Paradox when changing tables.

Use this to your advantage. Many Paradox operations that you perform, both interactively and through programming, call for the creation of intermediary tables. You may query a table, get an ANSWER table, and then want to use ANSWER to perform additional operations. Instead of renaming ANSWER to "Temp," and then later deleting "Temp," rename this ANSWER table to LIST, or FAMILY, or ENTRY1, ENTRY2, ..., thus saving you the bother of keeping track of the tables you need to delete or overwrite later. However, if you use one of these names to either create a table or rename an existing table, do it intentionally with the knowledge that it will disappear unless renamed.

## 2.12 TEMPORARY TABLES ON NETWORKS

A different set of rules apply when running Paradox on a local area network. During network installation of Paradox, you create a separate subdirectory for each user designated as that user's private directory. Paradox will use the private directory as a special working directory where all temporary tables, both external and internal, are created and deleted. Only a single user may be logged into a particular private directory; thus there can only be one ANSWER, LIST, or

STRUCT table. Temporary tables in a user's private directory will appear as if they were stored in the current working directory (identified with {Tools}{More} {Directory}). If you rename an ANSWER table to a nonreserved table name, the newly named table and its family are moved from the private directory to the current working directory.

Say for example, you are using Paradox on a network and your private directory is F:\USER\SCOTT, the working directory is F:\USER\DATA, and the "Customer" table is in the current directory (it is officially "F:\USER\DATA-\CUSTOMER.DB"). When you do a query on the Customer table, the ANSWER table will be created in the F:\USER\SCOTT subdirectory, but it will appear in the current directory listing, when you {View} the table. If you rename the ANSWER table "Cust1," the now permanent table "Cust1" will be physically moved to the F:\USER\DATA subdirectory.

Conversely, if you have a private directory set and you rename a permanent table to a temporary table name, that table will be moved to your private directory. For example, if you rename "Cust1" using {Tools}{Rename}{Table} to "LIST," the table and all of its family will be moved to F:\USER \SCOTT.

## 2.13 LOCKING

On networks, Paradox allows for simultaneous use of tables by more than one user through table and record *locking* mechanisms. Many users can be editing the same table if they all use the *CoEdit* mode (introduced in Paradox2). CoEdit monitors every user's activity on a table at the record level—it imposes *record locks* while a user is changing a record. Paradox doesn't allow you to change a record when it is locked by any other user. Other table-level activities require locks to be placed on the entire table. Copying a table to a new table, for instance, requires *full locks* to be placed on both the source and the target tables.

Paradox's locking mechanisms also keep users informed about who has placed a lock on a Paradox object. Whenever you try to access a table or a record in use by another user, Paradox places a message on your screen stating the name of the user who has placed the lock. In addition, the *autorefresh* feature allows you to keep abreast of changes in a table made by other users by automatically rewriting your screen image at regular intervals.

## 2.14 INTERNAL TABLES

Internal tables are tables created, maintained, and at times deleted by Paradox. Internal tables either hold and maintain data with a restricted use or hold data temporarily. For example, a "keyed" table creates an internal table with a ".PX" filename extension as an index. This password-protected internal table cannot be modified through interactive Paradox (nor would you want it to be modified). Paradox uses internal tables extensively and may make and delete dozens of internal tables during routine operations. Here are a few ways internal tables are used:

- In edit mode, a table named with the current table name and an extension of ".ED" is created. This transaction log table is deleted once the edit session is completed.
- The "Password" table is created and deleted after password assignments have been made for a table.
- Temporary tables are used when creating reports with groups for sorting.
- Paradox index files are a special form of table.
- When editing or writing scripts with the Paradox script editor, a temporary table called ZZZXZZZZ.DB is created.

## 2.15 RESTRUCTURING TABLES TO GAIN SPACE AND EFFICIENCY

Heavily edited tables may become laden with the space of deleted records, for although the information in the physical records has been removed, the disk space formerly consumed by the record is not removed, but simply made available for new records. Obsolete records consume disk space and may slow performance. There are several ways to reclaim the space that deleted records leave behind, but the simplest is to use the {Modify} {Restructure} command, select the table, make no changes to the STRUCT table, and press [DO-IT]! A restructure of a table copies the old table record by record, discarding deleted records and thus creating a smaller file. This restructuring operation requires about twice the existing table's disk space to complete.

Keyed tables will benefit less from this restructuring. Unkeyed tables maintain records in their order of entry, unless modified with the {Sort} command; keyed tables maintain their records in key value order. In heavily edited keyed tables, new records may occupy places left available by deleted records or by gaps left when a new record is inserted. When restructuring keyed tables, all indexes are automatically rebuilt as well.

## 2.16 DAMAGED TABLES

In the case of damaged tables, you can use an auxiliary utility program provided on the installation disk, TUtility.exe. TUtility, which stands for Table Utility, allows you to verify that a table's structure is intact and rebuild damaged tables if necessary. Use of TUtility on a table will delete all related index files, so a table's primary index must be rebuilt by restructuring the table, and any secondary indexes, through the use of {Tools} {QuerySpeedup} or the PAL INDEX command (see below).

When you restructure a table or use TUtility, all column rotation settings in the table's .SET file are deleted and must be rebuilt by rotating the columns into place and using {Image} {KeepSet}.

## 2.17 .PX PRIMARY INDEX

A **primary index** is a file created and maintained by Paradox when a table is keyed. To key a table, place an asterisk next to the field type of the first field when creating or modifying the table's structure. The first field in the structural definition of a keyed table is called the **primary key field.** Additional fields can be added to the primary index by placing asterisks next to consecutive field types starting with the second field in the structure. A key consisting of more than one key field is called a multifield or concatenated primary index. Primary indexes are the only type of index in Paradox that provides for multifield keys. Additional fields in the primary index serve as tie-breakers, allowing for duplication in the first field or fields of a record.

A keyed table physically maintains records in key field order.

```
Restructuring Bookord table                                    Restructure

STRUCT      Field Name        Field Type      ┌─── FIELD TYPES ───
    1   Cust              N*             A_: Alphanumeric (ex: A25)
    2   Date              D*                 Any combination of
    3   Item #            S*                 characters and spaces
    4   Vol               A3                 up to specified width.
    5   Quant             N                  Maximum width is 255
    6   Emp #             N
                                          N: Numbers with or without
                                             decimal digits.

                                          $: Currency amounts.

                                          D: Dates in the form
                                             mm/dd/yy, dd-mon-yy,
                                             or dd.mm.yy
                                          ────────────────────────
                                          Use '*' after field type to
                                          show a key field (ex: A4*).
```

Keyed tables have a maximum record size of 1350 bytes, roughly one-third of the allowable 4000 byte record size for nonkeyed tables. When a table is keyed, each record must have a unique set of values in its key fields. There are many advantages to using keyed tables wherever possible, and one of the most important reasons is to provide increased speed during queries and searches.

In many Paradox operations, keyed tables are treated differently than unkeyed tables. For example, you cannot sort a keyed table except to a new table. Adding records to a keyed table with {Tools} {More} {Add} requires you to identify the additional records as {NewEntries} or records that will {Update} existing records.

## 2.18 SECONDARY INDEXES (QUERY SPEEDUP)

Secondary indexes are also called QuerySpeedup files; these are used by Queries, Zooms, and the PAL LOCATE function. These SpeedUp files may be generated, used, and deleted automatically by Paradox as the result of a query. They can also be created explicitly when a query is on the workspace with the menu selection {Tools} {QuerySpeedup} or PAL INDEX command. A {QuerySpeedup} will attempt to create indexes on all of the selected fields not part of the primary key. They are of two types:

- Maintained, where modifications to the index are made (1) upon leaving a changed record in CoEdit mode and (2) after Do-It! in Edit mode. Maintained indexes are only possible with keyed tables.
- Batch maintained, where any modification to a table with an up-to-date index marks the index file as out-of-date. This method does not require that the table have a primary key.

Which method of indexing is in place depends first upon a setting in the configuration file that can be changed by playing the "custom" script and selecting {PAL} {MaintainIndexes}. The default value ensures that secondary indexes are not maintained. Maintained indexes can also be explicitly created for keyed tables with the PAL INDEX command through the MAINTAINED option, which overrides a nonmaintained setting in the configuration file for that index only. A secondary index consists of two files, one with an extension of .X##, and one with an extension of .Y##. The ## is a hexadecimal number from 01 to FF (decimal 0 to 255) representing the field position in the table's structure.

## 2.19 .VAL VALIDITY CHECKS

Validity checks (ValChecks) are powerful restrictions on the content and form of data entered interactively in Paradox. They have no effect on data entered through the use of table-oriented menu commands such as {Tools} {More} {Add},

Insert or Changeto queries, or data that exist in the table before the ValCheck is placed.

There are six categories, and all work in the edit, coedit, or dataentry modes:

| | |
|---|---|
| Low Value | The lowest numeric, date, or alpha value allowed. |
| HighValue | The highest numeric, date, or alpha value allowed. |
| Default | The value entered by Paradox if the cursor passes through this field without the user entering a value. |
| TableLookup | A value that matches the first field of a keyed table designed for Lookup. Two types are supported: JustCurrentField and AllCorrespondingFields. Lookup help can be specified as FillNoHelp, which doesn't allow you to browse in the lookup table, or HelpAndFill, which does. |
| Picture | Restrict the field type further with representations of allowable data types. |
| Required | Require the user to enter a value in this field if the cursor gets to it. |

The TableLookup validity check is extremely useful, provided that you can structure your tables to take advantage of it. Pictures help keep entries consistent and greatly simplify programming by establishing restrictions that automatically apply during data entry.

## 2.20 .SET SETTINGS

The {Image} {KeepSet} command saves the current display image settings of {ColumnSize}, {Format}, {Move}, and {PickForm} to a file with the extension ".SET." Whenever the table is viewed, the settings file controls these display characteristics. The settings file may be deleted with {Tools} {Delete} {KeepSet}.

## 2.21 FORMS

On a simple level, {Form} enables you to design screens that provide a view into your data in Paradox tables. Whereas tableview only allows columnar fields to be sized, rotated, and formatted, forms allows you to place data anywhere on the screen with formatting and provides a nearly character-by-character choice of style attributes, including color, inverse video, underlining, and blinking. You can design up to 15 forms per table, and each form can contain 15 screens (or in Paradox terms, 15 "pages"). Each screen must have a regular field placed on it.[5]

## 2.22 DATABASE DESIGN AND FORM DESIGN

Show me your flowcharts and conceal your tables, and I shall continue to be mystified. Show me your tables, and I won't usually need your flowcharts; they'll be obvious.
—Frederick P. Brooks, Jr. *The Mythical Man-Month*

One of the major goals of relational database design is to create small tables that can be linked while sharing a minimum of data. Paradox3 has simplified the more difficult aspects of relational database design with multitable forms. This innovation turns the lowly data entry form into the tie that binds data together. Through one master table form, data in up to five keyed detail tables can be viewed, edited, or manipulated. If all of the modification of a table is done through the form, the form forces tables to maintain the most critical relational database design element: "referential integrity." At its core, referential integrity is the maintenance of logical associations (links) between tables. By working only through properly designed forms, one can make and maintain all necessary links automatically. Although this methodology imposes some restrictions on the use of data, it allows for simplicity of design in many applications.

A Paradox3 form is defined by its contents as either single table or multitable. A multitable form is a *master* form. Embedded tables within the master form are called *detail* tables. The embedded tables on the master form are drawn from forms designed in the detail tables. The size of the detail table's form that is placed on the master form is determined by the intersection of the lowest and rightmost characters on the form; this is referred to as the form's *natural* size. You can embed up to five different detail tables per master table form. Fields and tables may be placed in regular or display-only format and with *multirecord* forms, scrolling regions can display as many as 22 records per page. Only one master record may display on a form at a time if the form has linked embedded detail tables. Calculated fields, which can draw off fields in any table and be a combination of fields, values, and mathematical operators, are by nature display only. Calculated fields can be purely numeric, using simple arithmetic operators; date calculations, involving addition or subtraction and any combination of numeric operations; or a concatenation of fields.

## 2.23 A SPECIAL RULE FOR FORM DESIGN

In Paradox3, a special rule must be applied when designing multitable forms: if you plan to view the tables through the form from a different default directory, design all multitable forms *outside* the table's native directory. As you might expect, Paradox records the names of the embedded tables in the master table's form. If you design the form in the table's directory, which we will refer to as the table's "native" directory, only the name of the table is recorded, not the full path specification. If you design multitable forms outside of the table's native directory, Paradox will record the full path specification of the embedded tables in the multitable form. The result is that a form designed outside the table's native directory can be used to look at the embedded tables using the form from any directory. Without using this method, you cannot view a table with embedded forms outside its native directory.

## 2.24 MULTITABLE LINKS

The form not only establishes the view, but also defines strict rules about how data can be manipulated. Of particular interest is that data in a linked table viewed through a multitable form are treated almost as a table unto itself; this is called a *restricted view* of the table. The form plays another critical role in database design. Depending on the number of key fields that are embedded in a detail form, the relationship between the master and the detail becomes:

- One-to-one ("1-1 group"). This is accomplished by having as many key fields in the embedded table's structure as exist in the master table, and omitting the placement of those fields from the detail table's form.
- One-to-many ("1-M group"). This is accomplished by having more key fields in the embedded table's structure than in the master's, and then omitting the placement of the master table's key fields from the detail table's form.
- Many-to-many ("group"). In this case, there is duplication of key values in both tables. The group relationship is formed by omitting some, but not all, of the key fields on the detail form linked to fields with duplicate field values in the master table.
- Many-to-one ("group"). The detail table has fewer key fields than the master. This is accomplished by placing all of the key fields in the embedded form of the detail table.

The link for 1-1 groups and 1-M groups creates a special editing rule: once an editing session has begun using a master table's form, no changes can be made in tableview to any of the tables linked through the form. These tables are referred to as "link-locked." No such rule applies for many-to-many or many-to-one forms.

Properly designed databases allow for economy and simplicity. The process of properly designing tables is called "normalization." Although the topic of data normalization is beyond the scope of this book, here are a few common guidelines:

- Keep tables small. One often-quoted recommendation is to try to keep the number of fields in a Paradox table less than 20. However, this is misleading because efficiency has to do with how fast Paradox is able to handle records, and this is based not only on the number of fields, but on their types as well. We discuss this more completely in the discussion on the SETMAXSIZE command in the examples section.
- Try to key tables whenever possible.
- Eliminate repeating fields.

## 2.25 REPORTS

> Information is the lessening of uncertainty.
>
> *Information Processes*

Printed reports help transform data into something sensible—information. When you design a report in Paradox, you create a report specification (report "spec") that becomes part of a table's family. A report spec is of no use without its table. The report spec contains only references to field names—it doesn't contain the table's field names themselves. This bonding of report to table permits Paradox to quickly eliminate references to fields that have been either modified in length or changed in type in all report specifications when you modify the structure of a table.

In Paradox3, multitable reports are based around a many-to-one or a one-to-one structure. A multitable report is created on a detail table and lookup links are established via key fields. You first link tables by identifying key fields in the lookup table with {Field} {Lookup} {Link}. Once a link is made, the fields in the lookup table can be accessed in the {Field} {Place} menu by first selecting the lookup table's tablename (e.g., [Customer->]). Fields in lookup tables are treated as regular fields and so can be used in any kind of calculation. If you want to delete the lookup table from the report, you must first remove all references to it from the report by using the {Field} {Lookup} {Unlink} command. Multitable reports may contain bonds to multiple tables.

## 2.26 TABULAR AND FREE-FORM

There are a few distinctions between the Paradox features available for the two types of reports, tabular and free-form:

| **Tabular** | **Free-Form** |
|---|---|
| Field Rotation | Field and Line Squeeze |
| Resizing of Columns | Labels |
| Suppression of Repeated Fields | |
|   Within Groups | |

Report design is a subjective art with few hard and fast rules. The "Report" mode allows you to assemble and test reports piece-by-piece. When you are prototyping, it pays to {Output} the report to the {Screen} often, saving both time and paper. While you're working on the report specification, it is also a good idea to save it to disk often. The [Ctrl Break] key, which can be used to interrupt screen output, will also cancel report design if accidentally hit when the screen returns to the report spec.

Iterative report design is the nature of the beast. You'll rarely get it right the first time.

Paradox reports on tables in record order, from the top of the table down. If you want to change the order in which records appear, you insert group bands around the data in the report specification. If group bands exist, the table is sorted prior to output. If several groups exist, the outermost group is the primary sort key, and the rest of the sort is by group band order, and finally, structure order. Paradox will begin printing as soon as one complete group has been sorted, while it continues to sort the rest of the records. Groups can be created on a number of records, and on ranges, for example substrings of fields (e.g., all customers can be grouped by the first letter of the last name field or numeric or date groupings). Summary reports detail information on groups of records. Record counts, sums, averages, minimums, and maximums are supported. Calculations can be made for regular as well as summary fields, and calculations involving alphanumeric fields can create concatenated fields.

The use of summary operators within calculated fields is often overlooked.

## 2.27 REPORT LIMITATIONS

The Paradox report generator is by design sequential. Because of this top-down, record-oriented approach, Paradox cannot calculate an individual record's values as a percentage of a group unless the table contains a field (or a linked field in a lookup table) in which the group's summary value has been placed. With

Paradox3, reports can draw information from several tables without the user having to create intermediary tables. With earlier releases of Paradox, there was need for more empty tables whose sole purpose was to hold report specifications. There is less of a need to do this in Paradox3.

Use of variables in report specifications can be achieved through multitable report design.

## 2.28 QUERIES

A query, the Paradox User's Guide tells us, is simply a "question you ask about the data stored in Paradox tables." Yet queries embody the principal power behind Paradox and allow data in tables to become not only accessible but intelligible. In essence, a Paradox query is a visual metaphor that is interpreted and transformed into a low-level programmatic construct. This visual metaphor, called Query-by-Example, allows even the most complex questions about data in tables to be asked without programming. The query forms abide by a strict set of rules that preclude asking questions that cannot be answered. Most importantly, a query defines the goal, *but not the method*, of achieving the answer. This is a critical difference between Paradox and other database programs. The Paradox query process is a search for the most direct route to the answer. Unlike most other database languages, a Paradox query relies on current conditions, not assumptions about current conditions, to achieve the result in the shortest time. Querying in Paradox is a dynamic process that often relies on multiple levels of intermediary results to achieve an answer.

There are two fundamentally different types of queries: those that produce an answer table and those that modify existing data. Both types are initially performed in the same manner. Paradox begins queries by asking resource questions:

How big are the tables? Are they indexed? Will the indexes help? Which fields are included? What are the selection criteria? How much data needs to be extracted? Are secondary indexes available? Are they maintained? What are the table links? ■

A judgment may be made to create an intermediary table. Followup questions address intermediate results.

What is the structure of this new table? How many records does it contain? Should it be sorted? ■

Optimization of certain operations may require building indexes on the fly. They are built and used, and so it goes, with Paradox always seeking the shortest route.

The order in which you place table query forms on the workspace has no effect on this optimization. There is only a predetermined order of operation in queries when you use the "inclusion" operator to create an "outer join." We will discuss the types of joins in a few pages. Nowhere is the Paradox design principle of "hiding complexity" more apparent than in queries.

## 2.29 QUERY EXAMPLES

When you think a query can't possibly be used to accomplish a result, think again. Experiment. Play. Push them to the limit. Though there are things they cannot do, queries are one of your best allies in programming with Paradox because of their simplicity, reliability, and speed. Paradox queries are not, however, always simple. There are 75 examples of queries in the Paradox3 User's Guide, and most of them frame hypothetical situations by beginning with the word "Suppose." Among these examples you can usually find one that is similar to nearly any operation you are trying to perform. The following section is a narrative describing the essential elements of queries. It is meant to complement the examples in the User's Guide.

## 2.30 QUERY LIMITATIONS

There are things queries cannot do and some operations that are best done without queries. Queries have no ability to manipulate substrings of fields. For example, you cannot split an alphanumeric field value by the position of a character with a query. You also cannot apply many financial and mathematical functions in queries. Queries have limits: there can be only 255 characters in a query field and 22 rows on a query form. There are other reasons why you might be unable or unwilling to use queries.

- Queries on large tables can require even larger amounts of disk space to run. The rule of thumb is that your free disk space should be two-and-a-half times the size of the largest table involved in a query. Thus, if you have a 10Mb table, you may need 25Mb of free storage to produce the result.
- Queries sometimes produce "Answer," "Inserted," "Deleted," and "Changed" tables that may be unnecessary or impractical.
- In network situations, many queries place or attempt to place what may be unacceptable locks on tables.

## 2.31 THE MECHANICS OF QUERYING

Queries use three principal operations:

| | |
|---|---|
| Choosing Tables | (Join) |
| Choosing Records | (Selection) |
| Choosing Fields | (Projection) |

## 2.32 CHOOSING TABLES

When you {Ask} about a table, a query form is put on the workspace. A query consists of all of the query forms on the workspace that have special operators, example elements, or literals. Blank query forms are ignored. For tables to be joined, they must have common data. To join them, a query form must be put on the workspace for each table. An "example" element must be placed in the query form's fields which have common data. The example element is first indicated by pressing the [F5] key, which puts the next set of letters and numbers in inverse video. Example elements can consist only of combinations of letters and numbers—no punctuation or special characters are allowed. Example elements are not case sensitive. The fields used to join them do not have to have the same name, but their types must be "compatible."

- Alpha is compatible with an alpha field of any length. If one field is shorter than the field it is linked to, an incomplete linking may result if values in the wider alpha link field exceed the width of the narrower alpha link field.
- Date fields are compatible only with other date fields.
- Number, $, or Short Number are compatible with each other, but values of over 32,767 for number or $ may create incomplete answer tables when linked with a short number.

## 2.33 JOIN TYPES

Joining can be accomplished in one of three ways listed here, but it is commonly done the first way.

- **Natural Join.** The answer table contains only selected records that exactly match example element links. This type of link is called an "exclusive" link.

- **Assymetrical Outer Join.** The answer table contains all of the selected records in the table that contains the inclusion operator (!) after an example element.
- **Symmetrical Outer Join.** The answer table contains all the selected records from all tables. The inclusion operator must follow an example element in each table's query form.

## 2.34 CHOOSING FIELDS

Checking a field creates a field of similar type in the ANSWER table. You select a field with either a Checkmark or a Checkplus. By design, a query with a checkmark [F6] in a single field will produce an ANSWER table with only unique values, sorted in ascending order. Checkmarking several fields will continue this pattern, producing ANSWER tables with nonrepeating occurrences of the combination of Checked fields. The query first selects all the records in the field that meet the selection criteria, then sorts the result and eliminates duplicates. Paradox3 introduced a variation on the Check called CheckDescending [Shift F6], which reverses the sort order on the field in which it is applied.

CheckPlus [Alt F6] simplifies the query process. A Checkplus in any field in a query form produces an ANSWER table including all the records that meet the selection criteria. Duplicate records are kept and the ANSWER table is in record order; it isn't sorted by the query process. CheckPlus queries are therefore faster than Check queries.

In Paradox3, the order in which fields in the answer table appear depends on a configuration parameter set in the CUSTOM script. There are two ways of ordering fields: ImageOrder and TableOrder. TableOrder follows the underlying structural order of fields. ImageOrder creates an answer table in the order of fields as displayed. If you rotate fields on a query form using Paradox configured for ImageOrder, the answer table will reflect this rotation.

## 2.35 SPECIAL FIELD OPERATORS

- BLANK specifies a field in a record that has no entry.
- LIKE is an extended pattern operator that can perform inexact matching.
- NOT in front of an example, literal string, or keyword looks for anything but the entry.
- TODAY used in a date field represents the system date.

## 2.36 NEW FIELDS—THE CALC OPERATOR

New fields can be created in the answer table by using the CALC query operator. The word CALC followed by example elements, literals, mathematical symbols, and reserved query words can create new columns of data with new field names. A CALC expression can be in any field in the query form and the new field or fields will be created as the last field or fields in the answer table. CALC can be used to:

- Concatentate alphanumeric fields using the "+" operator and example elements and/or literals.
- Perform mathematical operations on numeric, dollar, or short number fields. If a calculation is performed on these fields, the following rules apply:

  $\$ * N = \$$
  $\$ * S = \$$
  $N * S = N$

- Perform date arithmetic. The TODAY operator can be used to represent the system date. Dates subtracted in a calculation create a numeric field. Dates cannot be added to dates, but numbers can be added to or subtracted from dates, which results in a date field value.
- Create new fields with the same type as an existing field by combining the reserved query operators CALC BLANK.
- In Paradox3, the AS operator enables you to rename the result of any field in the Answer table.

Combinations of CALC operators can lead to some interesting results. For example, you can create an empty column called "Total" with a dollar type by using "CALC BLANK as Total" with any dollar field, or you can create an empty date field called "New Date" with "CALC BLANK as New Date" in any date field.

## 2.37 RECORD SELECTION

By far the most complicated part of formulating queries is choosing records, which is known as "selection."

Selection is achieved by the Check and CheckPlus operators alone if no other criteria are supplied. As previously noted, Check eliminates duplicate records and sorts the "Answer" table, while CheckPlus includes every record and leaves

"Answer" unsorted. Literal characters in query fields must match the field type and are always case sensitive. Example elements can also serve as selection criteria.

Punctuation and special characters play a very important role in queries.

- A comma separates conditions in the same field that must be simultaneously satisfied—the logical AND condition.
- Range operators ($>$, $<$, $>=$, $<=$) work on fields of all types. The order of precedence is determined by the sort order Paradox is configured to work with. The default sort order is ASCII, whereby $0 < 1 < A < a <$ international characters $<$ graphic characters. Range operators are especially useful with date fields.
- The concatenation operator ($+$) can be used to combine alphanumeric fields.
- Mathematical symbols ($+$, $-$, $/$, $*$) can be used in CALC queries on numeric, dollar, or short number fields.
- Parentheses can and should be used to group the order of precedence in mathematical CALC queries.
- Inexact matching of records is achieved with pattern operators—the @ sign and two periods in a row (..). These are also known as wildcards. The @ substitutes for a single character, and the .. substitutes for any set of characters. When wildcards are used, the search is independent of case. Patterns used on date fields must match the current date format in the display image.
- Quotation marks can be used in any field to enclose literals that contain special characters. This includes numeric fields in which you want to specify a decimal point as part of the search.
- The backslash is used to specify literals that contain quotes. Enclose the entire string in quotes and precede each quote within a quote with a backslash.

Range and pattern operators cannot be mixed. (Not allowed, for example, is LIKE Me..).

---

## 2.38 "OR" CONDITIONS

---

Queries that evaluate mutually exclusive conditions simultaneously are looking for the answers to different questions. "Either this or that or . . . " questions (logical OR) can be answered in either of two ways with Paradox3. In prior versions, OR conditions had to be specified in separate lines of a query. With Paradox3, the new OR operator placed between conditions results in queries that are smaller, easier to code, and faster. However, the conditions evaluated must be in the same field. When selection is based on mutually exclusive conditions in different fields, multiline queries are still necessary. The OR operator cannot be used with example elements.

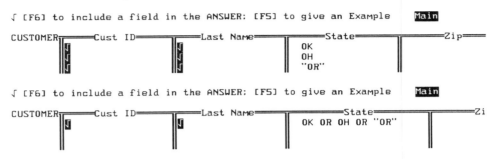

## 2.39 OTHER USES OF EXAMPLE ELEMENTS

Example elements are not only used to join tables, but to help select records as well. As noted, example elements are restricted to upper- and lowercase letters and numbers and are case insensitive. Example elements used in single table record selection can be used to represent a value that then defines a subset.

## 2.40 SPECIAL OPERATORS

There are four reserved query operators that create tables as by-products of the query. Three of them, Find, Insert, and Delete, are placed in the leftmost column under the table name in the query form. The fourth, Changeto, is field oriented and can be placed in any field or combination of fields. These special operators work on the table as a whole. None of these special query operators allow the use of checkmarks.

## 2.41 FIND

FIND queries consist of the word "Find" in the leftmost column and literal characters or example elements in one or more query images. A FIND query locates all the records that meet the record selection criteria. If a record is found that meets the criteria, the table will be placed on the workspace and the cursor will briefly flash at and remain on the record number of the matching record. If the table is already on the workspace, the cursor will simply flash in the record number column of the match. In addition, FIND will create an "Answer" table that consists of all the records that meet the condition. FIND queries can be performed across tables with example elements. The "Answer" table will contain only fields from one table—the table with the FIND operator.

## 2.42 INSERT AND DELETE

An INSERT query enables you to add records from tables of dissimilar structures by placing example elements in the source table that correspond to example elements in a destination table. The INSERT query will produce a table called "Inserted." If you need to reverse the INSERT, you can use {Tools} {More} {Subtract} {Inserted} {<source table>}. A DELETE query removes records that meet the selection criteria and places them in a table called "Deleted." If you need to add them back, you can use {Tools} {More} {Add} {Deleted} {<Target table>}.

## 2.43 CHANGETO

CHANGETO is a field-based operator that changes the contents of a field in every record that meets the overall selection criteria. The query may not contain any checkmarks. A CHANGETO query produces a table called "Changed" while updating the original table with the new field contents. Changeto queries are quite versatile:

- You can blank a field of selected records with CHANGETO BLANK.
- You can replace or add to alpha fields with literals and/or example elements.
- You can perform mathematical operations on numeric, short number, and dollar fields.

## 2.44 SUMMARY OPERATORS

Summary operators used with the CALC operator produce numerical statistics of values in fields in records that meet the selection criteria. If no criteria are supplied, summary operators work on all records.

- COUNT creates an answer table with a calculated total on the number of occurrences of records that match the selection criteria. The default total is based on a count of the unique records. If you want all records included in the count, use CALC COUNT ALL.
- MAX creates an answer table with the value of the record with the maximum value of all the records that meet the selection criteria.
- MIN creates an answer table with the minimum value of all the records that meet the selection criteria.
- AVERAGE creates an answer table with the average of all unique values that meet the selection criteria.

## 2.45 SET QUERIES

Set queries were introduced with Paradox3 and offer power beyond the original scope of QBE. A set query enables you to define a query within a query, to look at a *subset* of records, to make comparisons with those records, and to select records that compare to the records in the defined set. Set queries can help answer very complex questions of your data in one operation.

Creating a set query involves three steps:

- **Set Definition.** The selection, by literals and example elements placed in query fields, of the range of records that are to constitute the subset of records of the table.
- **Set Comparison.** There are two parts: (1) selection of fields with check-marks (the checkmarks must be on different query lines than the set definition) and (2) the use of a set operator (exactly, no, every, only) or a mathematical summary operator (sum, count, average, min or max) that enables the system to compare the selected subset and the selected records. A special operator, Groupby [Shift F6], enables you to group summary operations on fields without displaying their values in the Answer table.
- **Set Linking (Optional).** Normal linking, through example elements, to other tables for other related record information.

Set queries can perform extraordinarily complex operations without programming. Set queries are of great benefit to your programming, but they require you both to frame your questions carefully and to rigorously test your results before depending on them in your programs.

## 2.46 CHAPTER SUMMARY

Paradox is powerful and easy to use on an interactive level. Although it is easy to learn, it is not easy to know all of Paradox equally well. Programming in Paradox is built on a foundation of knowledge gained by interactive use. The more you use Paradox and the more you ask of it, the better you'll understand its limitations and appreciate its capabilities.

This chapter has covered the major aspects of Paradox system design, but there are other important areas as well. Graphics, not described here, is a world unto itself, having great power to transform data in tables into charts and graphs. Other aspects, including multiuser issues, will be covered in detail in later chapters.

## NOTES

1. Copying an old report specification (.R#) with the DOS COPY command to an existing table is an example. When restoring from a back-up copy of a table, make sure that the directory to which you're restoring is free of the back-up table's family objects. Problems may arise if a mix of old and new appear in the same directory.
2. Can also create Entry1, Entry2 etc.
3. Can also create KeyViol1, KeyViol2, etc.
4. Can also create KeyViol1, KeyViol2, etc.
5. The "wallpaper" script, written by Rick Alber, is a model of programming efficiency due to the way several forms were designed. This script is available in the Borland Database Forum (BorDB) of Compuserve or from Borland.

# Chapter 3

# Avoiding Keystrokes

This chapter begins to introduce elements of the PAL programming environment, with a special emphasis on use of Paradox facilities that help cut down on keystrokes.

A keyboard is an operational bottleneck. At times, no matter how fast you type, your PC is always ahead, waiting. In its most basic form, a Paradox program, or *script*, helps you avoid keystrokes by hitting keys for you, thus speeding your work. This chapter describes what a script is and introduces several methods by which Paradox will write scripts without requiring you to type a line of code.

First, however, we will provide an introduction to some basic PAL terminology.

## 3.1 PARADOX AND THEATER

"The play's the thing. . . ."

—*Hamlet*, II, ii

The Paradox term for a program, script, was chosen with care. Like a playwright's work, a Paradox script is a series of statements that are read word-by-word and line-by-line, interpreted, and acted upon. Under script control, Paradox is the actor, reading and carrying out these instructions step-by-step. This comparison of Paradox programming to theater is used throughout the PAL manual to help convey the visual nature of Paradox programming. We reintroduce it here.

## 3.2 THE WORKSPACE AND THE CANVAS

By interactively using Paradox, you become the actor. You set the stage by making menu choices. You direct Paradox, changing modes to modify or report on data in tables. You see the results of this interaction on the screen. Under script control, your screen takes on a new role—hiding activity rather than displaying it. Paradox uses two terms for the screen in these two roles: the Paradox workspace and the PAL canvas. Here's the description of the workspace from the Paradox User's Guide:

> Workspace—A metaphorical plane where images of tables, queries, forms, and/or design specifications are placed so they can be worked on. Different parts of the workspace may be brought into view as required. The display screen presents a view onto the workspace below the menu area.

The menu area consists of the top two lines of the screen, where Paradox displays menu choices and their explanations. This metaphorical plane is your link to the action. When you use Paradox interactively, almost all of your work on Paradox tables happens on the workspace. Under script control, however, Paradox is the actor, and you are its audience. All activity that normally takes place on the Paradox workspace is hidden from view by the PAL *canvas*.[1] From the PAL User's Guide:

> Canvas—The screen you see during the playing of a PAL script. When a script begins, the canvas is initialized with the scene present on the Paradox workspace. While the script is being played, the canvas hides the workspace unless the script explicitly calls for the user to view it.

Unless your scripts call for the workspace to be revealed, it will be hidden throughout script play.

## 3.3 CREATING SIMPLE SCRIPTS

Theater is about performance, and so is script writing. By creating and running a script, Paradox can perform tasks unattended or assist users in performing complicated routines. A script, a text file with the filename extension ".SC," may be one line or a thousand. Each script line can hold up to 132 characters. The simplest scripts are often the most useful, and Paradox provides two convenient methods for creating simple scripts:

- {Scripts} {QuerySave}—A menu command that saves the current query images in script form.
- Instant Script Recording—A menu command (or alternately, a keystroke, [Alt F3]) that translates your keystrokes into Paradox scripts.

Once captured in a script, your keystrokes never have to be typed again. If you want to modify a script, you can edit it using the built-in Paradox script editor or any other ASCII text editor. To get Paradox to recreate your keystrokes, you *play the script*. The {Scripts} {Play} command allows you to type in or select the name of a script and play it. Another choice, the {Scripts} {RepeatPlay} command, allows you to repeat the playing of a script any number of times.

## 3.4 QUERYSAVE

Because getting the right answer depends on asking the right question, getting Paradox queries to give you what you want from your tables is usually a trial-and-error process, often requiring dozens of attempts to produce the answer you need. Recreating a complex query not only takes time, but also courts error. The {Scripts} {QuerySave} command allows you to take a snapshot of the current query image and translate it into a special script format. With a query on the workspace, you select {Scripts} {QuerySave}, and you are prompted for a script name. If you supply a script name that already exists, you will be asked to confirm this script name by selecting {Replace}. A QuerySave script is equivalent to a single Paradox statement, and it can be used to recreate the actual query, thus avoiding keystrokes. Like a photo negative, the script-based query becomes the model for the actual query. When you want to recreate the query, you simply play the script that you assigned to the {QuerySave}.

A comparison of the two formats highlights the similarities and differences between the query image and its QuerySave counterpart.

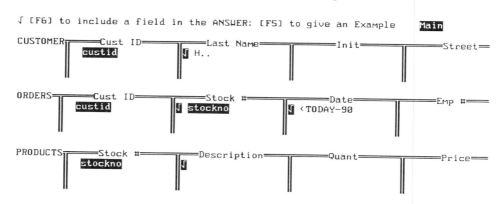

```
Changing script C:\paradox3\sample\q2                          Script
....+...10....+...20....+...30....+...40....+...50....+...60....+...70....+...80
Query

  Customer | Cust ID | Last Name |
           | _custid | Check H.. |
           |         |           |
           |         |           |

  Orders | Cust ID |    Stock #     |        Date        |
         | _custid | Check _stockno | Check <TODAY-90 |
         |         |                |                 |
         |         |                |                 |

  Products | Stock # | Description |
           | _stockno | Check      |
           |          |            |
           |          |            |

Endquery
```

## 3.5 QUERYSAVE TIPS

- The script form of a saved query begins with the word QUERY and ends with the word ENDQUERY. Each of these words is on a line by itself and is separated from the body of the query with a blank line. You must leave these entirely blank lines in the script. Deleting them will produce a script error when played. PAL regards the lines between the words QUERY and ENDQUERY as a single statement.
- If your query includes a temporary table ("Answer," "Changed," etc.), use the QuerySave command *before* you press [DO-IT!]. In queries where these tables are changed or modified, their query images are cleared from the workspace as part of the query process. For example, if your query creates an "Answer" table from an "Answer" table, the query image of the first "Answer" table will be cleared when the new answer table appears.
- Playing a query saved with the {QuerySave} command merely puts the query on the workspace. Once on the workspace, you must press [DO-IT!] to perform the query. To have the script perform the query, edit the script with the QuerySave and type the Do_It! command after the query.
- In script form, the two extra lines of split vertical bars (I) indicating field position, with nothing between them, can be deleted. They are designed to more precisely depict a query image in script format, but their existence or absence in script form has little effect, offering a slight speed up in their script play if they are deleted. If you use the {Scripts} {Showplay} command for a query with these embedded rows of extra vertical bars, you'll hear two beeps.

- Though the vertical bars do not have to line up for the query to execute properly, it is a good idea to keep them lined up so that you can tell at a glance the field with which each checkmark, example element, or literal is associated.
- If the last table name doesn't have any associated fields, it may be eliminated as well (use [Ctrl y]).

A single keystroke in constructing a query can make a dramatic difference in the outcome. For this reason, the PAL manual encourages you to use only queries created by the QuerySave command. This is safe, but not necessarily efficient. For example, here are two methods of representing a query that simply checks all of the fields in a wide table.

```
Changing script C:\paradox3\sample\q3                          Script

....+...10....+...20....+...30....+...40....+...50....+...60....+...70....+...80

Menu {Ask} {Customer} "Check"           ;is equivalent to checking all
                                        ;the fields in the Customer table:

Query

Customer | Cust ID | Last Name |  Init  | Street | City  | State  |
         | Check   | Check     | Check  | Check  | Check | Check  |
         |         |           |        |        |       |        |
         |         |           |        |        |       |        |

Customer |  Zip    | Country | Credit |
         | Check   | Check   | Check  |
         |         |         |        |
         |         |         |        |

Endquery
```

Both have the same effect. The first relies on a checkmark placed under the name of the table in the query image, which will checkmark all fields in the table. The second example, a QuerySave script, may also look right and execute properly, but it may also make you wonder if you've checked all of the table's fields. In this instance, the first is also more reliable. If new fields are added to the table, the query still performs as intended. The second example assumes that the names of the fields in the tables will not change in position or name.

Saved queries are a great convenience, allowing you to reliably capture even the most complex queries in script form. Saved queries, coming as they do from query forms on the workspace, have an advantage in conforming to query rules. Yet alternative query-building techniques can at times be more flexible and concise.

## 3.6 INSTANT SCRIPTS

InstantRecord [Alt F3] is a Paradox function key assignment that begins and ends script recording. When you press [Alt F3], PAL becomes an observer, "watching" your keystrokes and translating them into equivalent PAL commands. When you press [Alt F3] a second time, Paradox writes the collected PAL commands to a Paradox script file named "Instant."

Let's do an example. As mentioned in the last chapter, restructuring a table can help economize on disk space by eliminating deleted records. Restructuring a table called "Orders" requires the following steps:

**Step 1**
Press:          [F10] (Menu)
**Step 2**
Select:         {Modify}
                {Restructure}
**Step 3**
Type:           Orders
**Step 4**
Press:          [Enter]
**Step 5**
Press:          [F2]

If you press [Alt F3] InstantRecord before these menu selections, and then [Alt F3] just after this operation completes, you will record their PAL equivalents in a script called "Instant." During script recording, an "R" will appear in the upper right corner of your screen. The "R" will clear after you finish recording. You select menu choices in the usual way.

## 3.7 USING THE PARADOX EDITOR TO VIEW A SCRIPT

To view how the keystrokes are translated into script form, you'll need to edit the script called "Instant." This is done with the {Scripts} {Editor} {Edit} command.

**Step 1**
Press:          [F10] (Menu)
**Step 2**
Select:         {Scripts}
                {Editor}
                {Edit}

**Step 3**
Type:        Instant
**Step 4**
Press:        [Enter]

At this point, the mode indicator changes to "Script" and your one line of script appears beneath a status line.[2]

```
Changing script C:\paradox3\sample\instant                        Script
....+...10....+...20....+...30....+...40....+...50....+...60....+...70....+...80
Menu {Modify} {Restructure} {Orders} Do_It!
```

Each command is considered a PAL statement. Instant script recording enables you to capture whole sections of commands exactly as you would type them to write a program—a great time saver. The script contains just the one line above with one significant difference. The [F2] key is recorded with an underscore rather than a dash; it is changed to its keystroke equivalent: Do_It! Whenever you record the [DO-IT!] key, [F2], the hyphen is replaced by an underscore. When you type the Do_It! command in a PAL script, always use the underscore to separate the two words.[3]

The editor is a stripped-down word processor for script writing and editing. All text in scripts is line oriented, and so, unlike a word processor, the script editor doesn't wrap words at the end of a line—you end a line by pressing [Enter]. Here are a few other hints.

- When you first are brought into the Paradox Script editor, you are placed in the overtype mode, where all the characters that you type replace existing characters. The insert mode, which allows you to add text without deleting existing text, is toggled on and off with the [Ins] key.
- Cursor movement keys behave in much the same manner as in form or report design.
- The function keys perform as you might expect, with [F1] accessing Paradox help, [F2], the [Do-It!] key, saving the script and returning to Paradox, and [F10] bringing up the script editor menu:

```
Read Go Print Help DO-IT! Cancel
Read a script into the current script
```

- {Read} enables you to copy the contents of an existing script into the current script below the cursor. This feature is essential for combining scripts.
- {Go} saves the script, exits the script mode, and plays the script upon returning to main mode.

- {Print} attempts to print the script to the default printer. If the printer is not ready, selecting {Print} will produce an error.
- {Help} gives you access to Paradox help.
- {Do-It!} saves the script and returns you to the main mode.
- {Cancel} cancels script editing and returns you to the main mode.

Without making changes, play the script by selecting {Go}. You'll see the message "Playing Instant . . ."

## 3.8 THE WORKSPACE BECOMES INVISIBLE

> "Well! I've often seen a cat without a grin," thought Alice; "but a grin without a cat! It's the most curious thing I ever saw in all my life!"

With the exception of some disk activity, nothing will appear to happen until the restructured table appears on your screen when script play stops. The reason: Paradox attempts to finish script play in the shortest possible time. Screen activity takes time. Since the script never *requires* use of the screen, the screen doesn't change during script play. Rather than displaying work in progress, Paradox presents you with the result of its work at the end of script play.

This example illustrates the difference between the Paradox workspace and the Paradox canvas. The canvas only "exists" under script control. When script play is begun, the script paints the canvas with the images present on the workspace. If nothing is on the workspace but the menu, and the script doesn't explicitly change the canvas (as was the case in this example), nothing will appear to change for the duration of the script. In fact, during script play, the menu that appears on the screen isn't the menu at all—it is an *image of the menu on the canvas*. When script play ends, the canvas is lifted, and the workspace, in whatever state your script leaves it, is revealed.

What happens behind the scenes? Behind the canvas, the workspace is racing with activity. Menu selections are being made at breakneck speed, the system mode indicator is changing as subsystems are loaded and used, and messages are flashing in the lower right. Since Paradox uses a script to play your keystrokes, it works as fast as it can. While learning Paradox programming, one of the most useful things you can do is to watch the backstage action. Paradox allows you to observe activity on the workspace during script play in a number of ways. One method calls for slowing down the action and turning on the backstage lights—the {Scripts} {ShowPlay} command.

**Step 1**
Press:        [F8] (to clear the image)

**Step 2**
Select:       {Scripts}
              {ShowPlay}
**Step 3**
Type:         Instant
**Step 4**
Press:        [Enter]
**Step 5**
Select        {Slow}

The {ShowPlay} command reveals all workspace activity and introduces a delay between instructions. The canvas is "lifted" when necessary—it is only shown when used. This animated view of a script enables you to see Paradox act on your instructions like an "automated" user in slow motion. You'll probably find that the {ShowPlay} command is best used with the {Fast} selection.

## 3.9 HOW KEYSTROKES ARE TRANSLATED

Paradox "watches" your keystrokes when you record a script and translates each into a:

- Braced Menu Selection    {Modify}
- Command                  CtrlPgDn
- String                   "not CA"

Paradox will translate a menu selection into a single word in braces with an initial capital letter. The PAL manual refers to this as a *braced menu selection*. A menu selection is always regarded as a single command. No matter how many times you press [Right], [Left], [Home], or [End] in a menu while recording a script, only the actual selection is recorded. In the preceding example, when you typed in the table name "Orders," it was translated to {Orders}. Keystrokes that aren't part of menu selections are either special key commands or quoted strings. All special key commands are recorded in "InterCaps," in which the first letter of each word-like syllable is capitalized. Quoted strings are literal characters put between quotation marks and appear almost exactly as you would type them. The following are lists of the keys that Paradox interprets as commands as they would appear in a recorded script.

   As you record, write, edit, and read scripts, you quickly become familiar with these names for keys.

# 3.10 KEYSTROKE COMMANDS

### Cursor Movement

| | |
|---|---|
| Backspace | Enter |
| CtrlBackspace | FieldView |
| CtrlBreak | Home |
| CtrlEnd | Ins |
| CtrlHome | Left |
| CtrlLeft | PgDn |
| CtrlPgDn | PgUp |
| CtrlPgUp | ReverseTab |
| CtrlRight | Right |
| Delete | Tab |
| Ditto | Up |
| Down | Zoom |
| End | ZoomNext |

### Query

| | |
|---|---|
| Check | Example |
| CheckDescending | GroupBy |
| CheckPlus | |

### Special

| | |
|---|---|
| DeleteLine | Help |
| DOS | InstantPlay |
| DOSBIG | InstantReport |
| GraphKey | VertRuler |

### Workspace

| | |
|---|---|
| ClearAll | GraphKey |
| ClearImage | KeyLookUp |
| CoEditKey | LockKey |
| CrossTabKey | Menu |
| Do_It! | Refresh |
| EditKey | ReSyncKey |
| Esc | Rotate |
| DownImage | Undo |
| FormKey | UpImage |

## 3.11 A KEY ISN'T A KEY ISN'T A KEY

To Paradox, every key you press is an instruction. What each keystroke does depends on the state of the Paradox workspace. Here are some examples:

- Pressing [Home] in a table moves the cursor to the first record while remaining in the current field. Pressing [Home] while designing a report moves the cursor to the first line of the report in the current column.
- While in tableview, [CtrlRight] attempts to move one screen to the right. However, if you are using FieldView, [CtrlRight] will attempt to move the cursor one word to the right.
- [CtrlPgDn], a key that attempts to move to the next record while remaining in the current field in formview, will beep in tableview.
- You can't use [ZoomNext] if you haven't identified a value to [Zoom] to in the current column. Attempting to use [Zoom] while designing a form only produces beeps.

If you are unsure about how a key works in a particular context or a particular Paradox mode, stop what you're doing and test it. Chapter 8, "Visualizing and Controlling the Workspace" provides examples of how to determine the current Paradox mode. In addition, the Examples Section more fully explains how each of these keystrokes is used.

## 3.12 SUCCESS DOESN'T GUARANTEE CONTINUED SUCCESS

Knowing what a key will do in a certain context isn't based on intuition. We once again state the cardinal rule of PAL programming: Know Paradox! If your scripts contain references to commands out of context, the results are usually unpredictable. And just because you save keystrokes with InstantRecord doesn't mean that they will be able to be played back. Here's an example:

You've just finished restructuring a table by keying it. During the restructuring, Paradox created a table called KEYVIOL which contains all of the records with duplicate key values. You corrected these records and added them back to the main table. However, the table called KEYVIOL still exists. Now you decide to restructure your "Orders" table by playing the "Instant" script. ■

```
Menu {Modify} {Restructure} {Orders} Do_It!
```

This script will now fail to restructure the table. Why? Because the Paradox environment has changed in a very subtle way. A table named KEYVIOL exists in the current directory.[4] Because of KEYVIOL, the menu choices that led to proper execution before will no longer be valid. If you use {Scripts} {ShowPlay} to view the playing of the script under these conditions, you will see that an additional menu appears:

```
Cancel   Ok
Do not overwrite existing Problems or KeyViol tables.
```

Once the script reaches this point, paradox will ignore all commands until a selection is made from this menu or until script play ends. Since the Do-It! command doesn't satisfy this condition and it is the last command in the script, table restructuring does not proceed.

## 3.13 INSTANTPLAY

InstantPlay is a Paradox command key assigned to [Alt F4]. When you press [Alt F4], a script named "Instant" will be looked for in the current (or the private) directory. If it exists, Paradox will play it. The "Instant" script, though not temporary in the same manner as temporary tables (which are deleted when changing directories or exiting Paradox), is overwritten the next time you press [Alt F3]. The same rule applies as with temporary tables: if you want to save the script named "Instant," rename it.

## 3.14 SETKEY

A special Paradox command, SETKEY, enables you to redefine standard Paradox key conventions or assign specific keys to tasks, much like keyboard macros. The SETKEY command has one limitation: the entire assignment has to be on one line.

Here's a common complaint: "I'd prefer if the cursor would move to the first field with a press of the [Home] key, and to the first record with the [CtrlHome] combination. And I'd also like a similar swapping of assignments for [End] and [CtrlEnd]." You can write a script that swaps these Paradox key defaults very easily.

**Step 1**
Press:        Menu
**Step 2**
Select:       {Scripts} {Editor} {Write}
**Step 3**
Type:         Mykeys
**Step 4**
Type the four script lines below:

```
SETKEY "Home" CtrlHome
SETKEY "End" CtrlEnd
SETKEY "CtrlHome" Home
SETKEY "CtrlEnd" End
```

**Step 5**
Press:        [F10]
**Step 6**
Select        {Go} to save and play the script.

All SETKEY assignments will now be in effect. Keep in mind that the remapping of keys through the SETKEY command only works in interactive Paradox; it has no effect during the playing of a script.

Reassigning keys is just one of the ways that SETKEY is useful. You can also set keys to replace several keys at once or play entire scripts. Here's another sample—assigning the [Zoom] key to automatically clear a previous entry when pressed:

```
SETKEY "Zoom" Zoom CtrlBackspace
```

And another, assigning the playing of a script to a key:

```
SETKEY "F11" Play "Paralex"
```

SETKEY is a very powerful command, which you can use to help cut down on keystrokes, or with which you can "remap" the functionality of your entire keyboard. For a more complete discussion of it, turn to the SETKEY command in the Examples section.

## 3.15 CHAPTER SUMMARY

Capturing keystrokes in a script gives you shortcut access to PAL, but an instant script has no decision making capability—it merely follows commands. Should something unexpected arise, a recorded script will fail miserably. But these two techniques, recording scripts and querysave, enable you to get the framework of scripts in place quickly. Keyboard macros can be assigned through the special PAL SETKEY command. These techniques aren't for beginners only—they are general-purpose tools used by advanced PAL programmers as well because they save time and trouble.

## NOTES

1. The theatrical term (not used by Paradox) is *scrim*, a stretched canvas sheet used to obscure the backstage action.
2. Pressing [F10] when a menu is already present has a peculiar effect: capturing the keystroke as the "Esc" key. If a table is on the workspace and the menu isn't visible, pressing [F10] will produce the word "Menu." Likewise, pressing [CtrlBreak] will record as many Esc's as necessary to clear the menu from the screen.
3. The dash, used in PAL for subtraction, will interpret Do-It! as the variable "Do" minus the variable "It".
4. Or in private directory, if assigned.

# Chapter 4

## Script Writing Fundamentals

This chapter is an introduction to writing simple PAL scripts.

## 4.1 ABBREVIATED MENU COMMANDS

Recorded scripts follow keystrokes exactly as you would type them. Here's a one-line script in recorded format that brings a table called "Orders" onto the workspace and places Paradox in the edit mode.

```
Menu {Modify} {Edit} {Orders}
```

Here's a PAL shortcut:

```
EDIT "Orders"
```

The menu choices have been shortened to two words with the use of a PAL *Abbreviated Menu Command*, EDIT. The name of the table, ORDERS, is no longer a braced menu selection; it is between quotation marks. When you play this "shortcut" script, it will follow the recorded menu choices in the recorded version above. This is easily seen by using the {Scripts} {ShowPlay} option. The abbreviated menu command is a shortcut for you, not for Paradox.

Abbreviated menu commands are a class of commands that provide a script substitute for ordinarily long menu choice sequences. In Paradox 3.0, there are 27 PAL abbreviated menu commands. Knowing and using these shortcut commands can help you simplify scripts, making them shorter and more readable. But take care, for in many cases there is a dramatic difference between the recorded version and the shortened command version. Here are four ways of ending an {Edit} session.

- End by pressing [F2]:

    ```
    Do_It!
    ```

- End by selecting menu choices:

    ```
    Menu {Cancel} {Yes}
    ```

- Or use an abbreviated menu choice that doesn't ask for nor require a confirmation (the confirmation is automatic):

    ```
    CANCELEDIT
    ```

- Use the command CTRLBREAK.

## 4.2 FOREWARNED IS FOREARMED!

Abbreviated menu choices should be used deliberately, because they generally do things one way, whereas Paradox might offer you a choice. A list of the menu commands that make decisions for you follows later in this chapter. A knowledge of what these abbreviated menu commands will not do is almost as important as a knowledge of what they will do. There are times when only the recorded script format will accomplish what you want. Here's an example. The following one-line script adds records from the "NewData" table to the table named "OldData":

```
Menu {Tools} {More} {Add} {NewData} {OldData}
```

With unkeyed tables, this can be expressed more simply with an abbreviated menu command:

```
ADD "NewData" "OldData"
```

Although this command works as well with keyed tables, it makes an assumption about the way the records are added from one table to a second, keyed table. By definition, every record in a keyed table is unique. When you add records from one table (source) to a keyed table (target):

```
Menu {Tools} {More} {Add} {SourceTable} {TargetTable}
```

Paradox will prompt you with an additional menu:

`{NewEntries} {Update}`

{NewEntries} screens the incoming data for records with key field matches in the target table. If records with identical keys exist, these records are rejected and placed in a temporary table called KEYVIOL (Key violations). The {Update} option works differently, replacing records with matching key fields in the target table. The matching records from the original table are deleted and placed in a temporary table called "Changed." When using the ADD menu shortcut with a keyed table, you are choosing between these two methods. The ADD command uses {Update}, and will thus replace records in the target table with matching records in the source table. If you need to screen incoming records, you must use the recorded form, not the shortened form.

`Menu {Tools} {More} {Add} {sourcetable} {targetable} {NewEntries}`

In making the transition from recorded scripts to scripts that you write, abbreviated menu commands can make scripts smaller and simpler. A list of selected abbreviated menu commands follows. This list contains only those commands that also shortcut menu selections. In general, these abbreviated menu commands eliminate steps that confirm the deletion of existing files or records. Since PAL commands can only be issued under script control, the assumption is that you know what they do. If you're unsure, caution is advised—check before you use them. In this listing, source, target, and table-name all represent standard Paradox table names.

## 4.3 ABBREVIATED MENU COMMANDS

| Abbreviated Menu Command | Menu Equivalent | What It Does |
|---|---|---|
| ADD "source" "target" | {Tools} {More} {Add} {source} {target} {Update} | Updates keyed tables, replacing existing records with key matches |
| CANCELEDIT | {Cancel} {Yes} | Cancels edit session without confirmation |
| COPY "source" "target" | {Tools} {Copy} {Table} {Source} {Target} {Replace} | If the target table exists, replaces it |

| Abbreviated Menu Command | Menu Equivalent | What It Does |
|---|---|---|
| DELETE "tablename" | {Tools} {Delete} {Table {Tablename} {OK} | Deletes table without confirmation |
| EMPTY "tablename" | {Tools} {More} {Empty} {tablename} {Ok} | Empties table of records without confirmation |
| EXIT | {Exit} {Yes} | Exits Paradox without confirmation |
| RENAME "source" "target" | {Tools} {Rename} {Table} {Source} {Target} {Replace} | Renames source to target, even if target exists |
| REPORT "tablename" "R" | {Report} {Output} {tablename} {R} {Printer} | Sends report to printer, not screen or file |
| SETDIR "directory" | {Tools} {More} {Directory} {directory} {Ok} | Okays change of directory and confirms the deletion of temporary tables |
| SETPRIVDIR "directory" | {Tools} {Net} {SetPrivate} {directory} {Ok} | Okays change of private directory and confirms the deletion of temporary tables |
| SETUSERNAME "username" | {Tools} {Net} {UserName} {username} {Ok} | Okays change of user name |
| SORT "tablename" ON "fieldname" | {Modify} {Sort} {source} {target} {Replace} | Replaces target if table by same name exists |
| COPYFORM "source" "#" "target" "#" sourcenumber | {Tools} {Copy} {Form} {SameTable} \| {DifferentTable} {source} {#} {target} {#} {Replace} | Replaces target if table by same name exists |
| COPYREPORT sourcetable sourcenumber targettable targetnumber | {Tools} {Copy} {Report} {SameTable} \| {DifferentTable} {source} {#} {target} {#} {Replace} | Replaces target if table by same name exists |

## 4.4 QUOTED STRING RULES

The first example of an abbreviated menu command we showed was:

```
EDIT "Orders"
```

The table name, Orders, was placed between a pair of quotation marks (""). Anything in a PAL script between quotation marks is called a quoted string, or more simply, a string.[1] Strings in scripts follow a few special rules. When comparing one string to another, a capital letter "A" (ASCII character 65) is not equivalent to a lower case "a" (ASCII character 97). A comparison of strings means a comparison of capitalization. Within strings, special characters, extended ASCII characters, and control sequences can be specified by using the backslash (\):

- To display a quotation mark within a string, you must precede each quotation mark within the quoted string with a backslash character.

```
"\"Who's on First?\" said Costello"
```

- Here's an example of this rule's use in a PAL command that searches for a value with a period in it. This example uses the pattern operator (..) to precede and follow the literal character we'd like to search for, the period. Because the period is within a quoted string, the quotation marks surrounding it must be preceded by backslashes:

```
LOCATE PATTERN "..\".\".."
```

- To display a backslash within a string, you must double up the backslash. This is particularly important when identifying file names with their full path designation. To designate a file named C:\PARADOX3 \SAMPLES\CUSTOMER in a script, you will need to specify the quoted string:

```
"C:\\PARADOX3\\SAMPLES\\CUSTOMER"
```

- All ASCII characters can be represented in strings by preceding a three-digit ASCII code with a backslash. This is most important for ASCII codes of less than 32 and greater than 127 characters. For example, to display the checkmark character, use:

```
"\251"
```

When sending output directly to a printer, four additional backslash combinations are important.

- \t represents the tab character.
- \f represents the form feed character.
- \r represents the carriage return character.
- \n is called the *newline* character, which is a combination of a carriage return and a line feed.

When present in quoted strings, these special characters can help control where information gets printed on a page or a text file. Note: Dates are not usually represented as strings in Paradox—they are special date constants. The item 22-Feb-1990 may look like a string, but dates are used without quotation marks.

# 4.5 FUNCTION KEY REPRESENTATIONS

Quoted strings are also used to designate the function keys and function keys in combination with the [Shift], [Ctrl], and [Alt] keys. There are 40 key combinations supported:

- [F1] through [F10] are represented by "F1" through "F10."
- [Shift F1] through [Shift F10] are represented by "F11" through "F20."
- [Ctrl F1] through [Ctrl F10] are represented by "F21" through "F30."
- [Alt F1] through [Alt F10] are represented by "F31" through "F40."

# 4.6 INTERACTING WITH THE USER

Thus far you've seen scripts that have a single purpose and are intended to run uninterrupted from beginning to end. Programming in this manner helps you automate tasks that Paradox can perform alone. This type of script is ideally suited for discrete tasks: for example, querying a table, followed by sorting, followed by the printing of a report. No user intervention is requested nor usually required.

But data bases require user interaction. Records constantly need to be added to, edited, and deleted from your tables—tasks that Paradox doesn't normally perform by itself. A single actor on a stage can perform only monologues, but two actors allow for the possibility of a dialogue. By consciously introducing a second actor into a PAL script—the user—the nature of programming changes and a dialogue must occur in which both PAL and the user are informed about their roles.

## 4.7 WAIT UNTIL..

Let's expand the one-line script with which this chapter began by introducing a simple and powerful command that restricts user keystrokes: the WAIT command. While we're at it, let's break the script up into four lines:

```
EDIT "Orders"
WAIT TABLE UNTIL "F2"
Do_It!
ClearImage
```

When this script is played, the "Orders" table is displayed. The WAIT command lifts the PAL canvas, revealing the table on the Paradox workspace, and gives a measure of control to the user. How much control is dictated by the special key designation that follows the UNTIL clause; in this case the quoted string that represents the [F2] key. For this script, PAL will literally "wait in the current mode (edit) until the [F2] key is pressed." When PAL is waiting during edit, interactive editing rules apply. The user can insert, modify, and delete records, use fieldview, zoom to records, and make use of tablelookup functions. All other function key assignments are rendered inoperable; their keyboard assignments are "mapped-out" of user control. Short of interrupting the script, there is only one way out: by pressing [F2]. As soon as [F2] is pressed, PAL resumes total control and continues with the commands that follow. In this example, Do_It! saves the editing session, the table image is cleared, and script play ends. The screen displays the workspace as it was before this script was played.

## 4.8 PROMPT

The WAIT command restricts user interaction. Since we have not explicitly allowed its use, the [F10] key only beeps when pressed during the WAIT. Unless a user trained in interactive Paradox is informed of the restrictions, panic might arise. "Where's the menu? What am I supposed to do?" or worse "How do I get out of this?"

You can begin a dialogue with the user with an optional part of the WAIT command. The PROMPT option uses the top two lines of the screen (which are not part of the Paradox workspace) to display a message to the user. The word PROMPT is followed by the message as a quoted string.

```
EDIT "Orders"
WAIT TABLE
PROMPT "Edit the table.  Press [F2] when done."
UNTIL "F2"
Do_It!
ClearImage
```

The PROMPT can use both lines above the workspace with a maximum width of 80 characters on each line (if you exceed 80 characters, the excess is ignored). If you do use two lines, the two strings must be separated with a comma.

```
EDIT "Orders"
WAIT TABLE
PROMPT "Editing the Orders Table.",
       "Press [F2] when done."
UNTIL "F2"
Do_It!
ClearImage
```

```
Editing the Orders Table.
Press [F2] when done.
```

| ORDERS | Order # | Cust ID | Stock # | Quant | Dat |
|---|---|---|---|---|---|
| 1 | 2280 | 4277 | 130 | 1 | 4/22/ |
| 2 | 3351 | 3266 | 519 | 1 | 12/16/ |
| 3 | 8070 | 6125 | 632 | 8 | 6/04/ |
| 4 | 6235 | 2779 | 890 | 1 | 8/01/ |
| 5 | 1442 | 9004 | 519 | 2 | 10/27/ |
| 6 | 5119 | 7008 | 235 | 1 | 3/04/ |
| 7 | 9554 | 3266 | 558 | 15 | 7/27/ |
| 8 | 6975 | 6666 | 519 | 3 | 6/24/ |
| 9 | 8933 | 9226 | 422 | 1 | 2/28/ |
| 10 | 1180 | 3128 | 519 | 2 | 5/31/ |
| 11 | 4492 | 5341 | 244 | 3 | 12/24/ |
| 12 | 9226 | 1784 | 983 | 1 | 1/14/ |
| 13 | 7643 | 6954 | 519 | 1 | 4/30/ |
| 14 | 1574 | 2177 | 632 | 1 | 11/22/ |
| 15 | 3885 | 9004 | 244 | 5 | 4/22/ |

# 4.9 WHITE SPACE

White space is a term for the area within a program listing that contains no instructions. White space consists of tab characters and embedded spaces. PAL ignores all white space in your scripts. In this example we have chosen to indent the second line of the prompt command for no other purpose than to make it more easily understood by human beings. Paradox strips out the white space and interprets this script as:

```
EDIT "Orders" WAIT TABLE PROMPT "Editing the Orders table."," Press [F2] when done."
UNTIL "F2" Do_It!
```

This may be thoroughly confusing to the casual reader, but it is perfectly obvious to Paradox. Throughout this book, we will format the layout of a script with generous doses of white space, indenting whole sections of code to make it more easily understood. In addition, as we make progressive refinements to scripts, the changes will be highlighted in boldface type.

## 4.10 TRAPPING MULTIPLE KEYS

The WAIT command is a program control structure that rules the Paradox environment until the user presses a designated key; the WAIT command traps keystrokes, excluding specific keys and allowing others to pass through. The example above only allows the user to press [F2], but any number of key assignments can cause the WAIT condition to end. The UNTIL is followed by a list of names for Paradox keys separated by commas:

```
EDIT "Orders"
WAIT TABLE
PROMPT "Editing the Orders Table.",
       "Press [F2] when done."
UNTIL "F2", "Esc"
Do_It!
ClearImage
```

The representation of special key commands in the UNTIL clause must also consist of quoted strings. Thus, in this example, the [Esc] key is represented by the string "Esc". Pressing [F2] or [Esc] will have the same effect—ending the edit mode and completing script play. If the [Esc] key were represented as an unquoted string, Esc, it would be interpreted as a command and Paradox would act on it as a keystroke rather than waiting for it.

## 4.11 ANOTHER WAY TO REPRESENT KEYS

Thus far you have seen two ways to represent keys. When you want the effect of the key in a script, you use the name of the key: Enter, Do_It!, Esc. When you want the name of the key represented, the name is put in quotes: "F2" "Esc." Names of function keys that have special key commands have aliases: thus "F2" is also known as "Do_It!", "F1" is also "Help", etc. These representations are mnemonic: it is easy to associate the name of the key with the Paradox key assignment.

Not all keys are given names by Paradox. Yet within PAL, you need to be able to represent any key or key combination. Paradox has a third and complete method of identifying keys—through numbers. Each key or key combination is assigned a number. These key assignments, unfortunately, are less than memorable. Standard character keys are assigned their number as positive integers that match their ASCII character code. These are called the standard ASCII key codes. For example, 65 is the capital letter A, 97 is the lowercase a, and 251 is the checkmark. Cursor movement and special [Shift], [Ctrl], and [Alt] key combinations are assigned negative integers. These are called IBM extended key codes. There is duplication here as well. Key −60 is Do_It!, −81 is PgDn, −84 is "F11".

Most importantly, these integers constitute the complete IBM keyboard set and so allow you to designate keys that do not have names assigned by Paradox. Key −30, for example, is simply [Alt A]; −127 is [Alt 8]. Some key combinations do not have representations in the IBM keyboard set (for example [AltUp]), and so have no key assignment. The PAL User's Guide presents a complete listing of these codes.[2]

These key codes simply map a keystroke to a number, and so can be used in a script wherever a key assignment is required. In our previous example, the UNTIL clause in the WAIT command could be revised as follows to trap for the Do_It! or Esc keys.

```
VIEW "Orders"
WAIT TABLE
PROMPT "Editing the Orders Table.",
       "Press [F2] when done."
UNTIL -60, 27
Do_It!
```

Alas, what was intuitive is now cryptic. It is clear that this method should only be used when you are trapping for a keystroke that has no assigned Paradox key name. Whenever you have a choice, use the Paradox special key command name or function key designation; it will make your code much more understandable.

## 4.12 WAIT VARIATIONS

The WAIT command has three variations:

WAIT TABLE
WAIT RECORD
WAIT FIELD

All work exactly as you might expect. They are in this order increasingly restrictive. WAIT TABLE restricts user interaction to the current table. WAIT RECORD restricts user interaction to the current record. WAIT FIELD restricts activity to the current field within the current record. All of these WAIT conditions halt when a designated key is pressed. For more information on all of these commands, turn to the Examples Section.

## 4.13 RETVAL—THE RETURNED VALUE

The key that triggers the end to a WAIT condition has special significance. This keystroke is passed back to PAL and is assigned a special name, RETVAL, which stands for the returned value. The value returned by a WAIT condition is always a single key and is always assigned in the form that you designated. Thus if your script is

```
WAIT TABLE UNTIL "F2", "Esc"
```

and the user pressed [Esc], "Esc" is assigned to RETVAL; if the user pressed [DO-IT!], "F2" is assigned to RETVAL. This distinction is important when later checking the value of RETVAL. If instead your script was:

```
WAIT TABLE UNTIL "f2", "esc"
```

the returned value will be assigned to either "f2" or "esc". If you have duplicate keys in the UNTIL listing, the last one in the list will be assigned to RETVAL:

```
WAIT TABLE UNTIL "f2", "esc", -60
```

Since −60 is an alternate key designation for [DO-IT!] and it is the last designation for [DO-IT!] on the UNTIL list, if you press [F2] to end this WAIT, RETVAL will be set to the number −60.

## 4.14 VARIABLES

At the conclusion of a WAIT, PAL assigns a value to a name; in this case, the name RETVAL. If you reinvoke the WAIT condition by again playing this script, the key that ended the latest WAIT condition will be assigned to RETVAL. Since the value of RETVAL can change, it is called a *variable*. Variables are names that are assigned a value. RETVAL is a special variable; it is one of only three of what

Paradox terms *system variables,* and it has a special importance in program flow and control. We will discuss Paradox system variables more thoroughly in Chapter 5, Language Elements.

"There are no small parts . . . only small actors."

Assigning values to names is a fundamental part of programming. Variables have a lifespan, and during their life they may act out bit parts in a variety of roles. Although a variable occupies memory, the memory that it occupies can be selectively released, obliterating all traces of its existence. In addition, like fields, all variables in Paradox have an associated type that defines how the variable can be manipulated. The variable types roughly correspond to the allowable types of fields in a table definition. Paradox will automatically assign the type of a variable according to the value that you supply:

- Alphanumeric, which is also given a width corresponding to the number of characters assigned
- Numeric
- Date
- Currency
- Short Number (integers from −32767 to 32767)

The last two types can only be defined by assigning the variable from a field of like type or with the PAL ACCEPT command. In addition, variables introduce two special types that are only available through PAL:

- *Logical*, the values True or False.
- *Array*, a sequentially numbered set of *elements* that are identified by a single name followed by a number in square brackets. The number is called an *array subscript*. For example, you might have an array called Order.r with values assigned to Order.r[1], Order.r[2], Order.r[3], etc. Each element in an array can hold a different type of a variable, though an array element cannot hold another array. An array can have up to 15,000 elements. An array subscript can also involve a calculation; for example Order.r[n+1]. In this event, [n+1] is called a *subscript expression.* Arrays are particularly useful for manipulating entire records of a table at once.

Many programming languages attach special significance to the type of a variable, placing restrictions on what you can and cannot do with them once they are assigned. For example, many programming languages won't allow you to assign a variable with an alphanumeric type to a variable already assigned to a number, a number to an integer, or a date to a logical. When reassigning variables, Paradox generally doesn't care what type a variable presently holds. Thus, in the WAIT condition above, RETVAL can be assigned to one type by one statement ("F2" is type "A2") and another type by the next (−60 is type "N").

In addition, variables have what is known as a *scope*, which is the domain of their existence. We will discuss the scope of variables in the chapter entitled "Procedures."

## 4.15 PROGRAM FLOW

The simplest of programs normally flow as if under the pull of gravity: from the top of a script to the bottom, with every statement executed in sequence. If something unexpected occurs, a program that depends on this linear execution will usually fail. To make a program more robust, it should be equipped to expect the unexpected.

Controlling program flow is at the heart of programming. Here is our little script:

```
EDIT "Orders"
WAIT TABLE
PROMPT "Editing the Orders Table.",
       "Press [F2] when done."
UNTIL "F2", "Esc"
Do_It!
ClearImage
```

This script offers little of the power of Paradox; the user is being short-changed. With interactive Paradox, an editing session can be accepted or cancelled. Here we've locked the changes in—both [F2] and [Esc] post any changes to the table. Ideally, this program should allow two ways out—with [Esc] cancelling the edit session and with [F2] saving the changes. This can only be done if a distinction is made between these two keys. The critical word is "if."

## 4.16 IF STATEMENTS

```
EDIT "Orders"
WAIT TABLE
PROMPT "Editing the Orders Table.",
       "Press [F2] when done or [Esc] to cancel."
UNTIL "F2", "Esc"
IF RETVAL = "Esc" THEN
  CANCELEDIT
ELSE
  Do_It!
ENDIF
ClearImage
```

The programming device or programming *construct*:

```
IF condition THEN
  do this
ELSE
  do that
ENDIF
```

is called an IF statement and it produces *conditional execution*. In an IF statement, the ELSE clause is optional, but here it is needed. An IF must have a corresponding ENDIF.

IF statements direct program flow according to the result of a logical test. In this example a comparison is made between the variable assigned to RETVAL and the quoted string "Esc." The logical test is accomplished with the equals sign (=), which is used here as a *comparison operator*. If the two sides of the equals match, the WHILE condition is true and the statements that follow it are executed. In our example, if the value of RETVAL and the string "Esc" do not match, the user must have pressed [F2], the condition must be false, and the statements following the ELSE will be executed. Since these two are mutually exclusive conditions, this logical test will always work.

The comparison test must be exact: the strings "Esc" and "ESC" are not the same. Whenever you make a string comparison, make sure that the strings you are comparing have a chance to be the same. If they don't, the comparison is useless, because it will always fail.

There are two kinds of program flow control structures in Paradox:

- Conditional execution (avoidance)
- Looping (repetition)

This example shows only conditional execution, which allows a portion of a program to execute when certain conditions are met and skips the remainder. Looping is the repeated execution of a portion of a program. Both of these methods are critical to what is termed *structured programming* design.

Although this script now offers the user a choice, the choice isn't a particularly good one. The reason is clear: cancelling an edit session is a pretty drastic action to take by simply hitting [Esc]—dozens or hundreds of changes can be undone in the press of a key. In the next few pages, we will introduce problems and follow them with solutions. Experienced PAL programmers, please bear with us. Let's revise this script to add a little more fine-tuned control.

## 4.17 THE SHOWMENU COMMAND

The SHOWMENU command allows you to mimic the workings of the Paradox bounce-bar menu.

```
EDIT "Orders"
WAIT TABLE
PROMPT "Editing the Orders Table.",
       "Press [F2] when done or [Esc] to cancel."
UNTIL "F2", "Esc"
IF RETVAL = "Esc" THEN
  SHOWMENU
    "DoNotCancel" : "Save editing changes",
    "Cancel" : "Cancel edit."
  TO cancel.a
  IF cancel.a = "Cancel" THEN
    CANCELEDIT
  ELSE
    Do_It!
  ENDIF
ELSE
    Do_It!
ENDIF
```

```
DoNotCancel  Cancel
Save editing changes
```

| ORDERS | Order # | Cust ID | Stock # | Quant | Dat |
|--------|---------|---------|---------|-------|------|
| 1 | 2280 | 4277 | 130 | 1 | 4/22/ |
| 2 | 3351 | 3266 | 519 | 1 | 12/16/ |
| 3 | 8070 | 6125 | 632 | 8 | 6/04/ |
| 4 | 6235 | 2779 | 890 | 1 | 8/01/ |
| 5 | 1442 | 9004 | 519 | 2 | 10/27/ |
| 6 | 5119 | 7008 | 235 | 1 | 3/04/ |
| 7 | 9554 | 3266 | 558 | 15 | 7/27/ |
| 8 | 6975 | 6666 | 519 | 3 | 6/24/ |
| 9 | 8933 | 9226 | 422 | 1 | 2/28/ |
| 10 | 1180 | 3128 | 519 | 2 | 5/31/ |
| 11 | 4492 | 5341 | 244 | 3 | 12/24/ |
| 12 | 9226 | 1784 | 983 | 1 | 1/14/ |
| 13 | 7643 | 6954 | 519 | 1 | 4/30/ |
| 14 | 1574 | 2177 | 632 | 1 | 11/22/ |
| 15 | 3885 | 9004 | 244 | 5 | 4/22/ |

The SHOWMENU command has three elements:

- The word SHOWMENU
- Quoted strings separated by a colon (:) representing menu choices and explanations. A comma is between menu choices. To work most simply, each menu choice (the left side of the colon) should begin with a different letter.
- The word TO followed by a variable name. Unlike the WAIT command, which automatically assigns the key that ended the WAIT to a predefined

variable, RETVAL, the SHOWMENU command requires you to explicitly assign the user's menu selection to a variable you define.

Because SHOWMENU behaves exactly like a Paradox menu, the captured variable, cancel.a, should first be tested for "Esc". Often overlooked, trapping for "Esc" after a SHOWMENU is one of the most important things you can do to keep your applications flowing smoothly. If the user doesn't press [Esc], and selects one of these choices, the variable named cancel.a is assigned to either the string "DoNotCancel" or "Cancel". The IF statement is a string comparison in which the contents of cancel.a are tested against "Cancel". Only if these two strings match is the edit session cancelled.

## 4.18 NESTING

This test is accomplished with an IF statement within an IF statement, and demonstrates what is termed program control nesting. You can nest as many levels of conditional tests as you need. Again we liberally use white space in the listing; we've indented the second IF to more clearly depict program flow.

Our SHOWMENU script as written nicely guards against accidentally striking the [Esc] key, but it forces the user into ending the edit session any time the [Esc] key is pressed. What is needed is a way to allow the user to resume editing if [Esc] is pressed. This is done by forcing the main body of the script to repeat by enclosing it in a loop.

## 4.19 A WHILE LOOP

```
EDIT "Orders"
WHILE True
  WAIT TABLE
  PROMPT "Editing the Orders Table.",
       "Press [F2] when done or [Esc] to cancel."
  UNTIL "F2", "Esc"
  IF RETVAL = "Esc" THEN
    SHOWMENU
      "DoNotCancel" : "Save editing changes",
      "Cancel" : "Cancel edit."
    TO cancel.a
    IF cancel.a = "Esc" THEN
      LOOP
    ENDIF
```

```
    IF cancel.a = "Cancel" THEN
      CANCELEDIT
      QUITLOOP
    ENDIF
  ELSE
    Do_It!
    QUITLOOP
  ENDIF
ENDWHILE
```

The WHILE command is a very powerful program control structure. WHILE and ENDWHILE force the repetition of all commands they enclose as long as the condition that follows the word WHILE is true or until special commands that exit the loop are encountered. The word WHILE must always be followed by a logical condition—one that will evaluate True or False.

## 4.20 LOGICAL CONSTANTS: TRUE AND FALSE

The word True used in this context is not a string: it is a special language element called a *logical constant*. With it, you are defining the condition to be True, assuring that the loop will always force execution of the statements that follow it. A common mistake beginning PAL programmers make is to use the quoted string "True" when they mean the logical constant True. There are only two logical constants: True and False.

## 4.21 HOW THE WHILE LOOP WORKS

In this example, WHILE True and ENDWHILE enclose all but the first command, forming a loop around the WAIT TABLE and SHOWMENU commands. There are only two points that allow you to exit the loop. These are those points where the PAL command QUITLOOP is encountered. When program flow forces the next instruction to be QUITLOOP, PAL quite literally quits this loop, and continues executing the script after the ENDWHILE. Because there are no statements that follow the ENDWHILE here, script play ends. If the LOOP command is encountered first, the WHILE condition is evaluated and found true, and all the commands following it are reexecuted.

The script's program flow is now highly controlled. From the user's perspective, script play begins with the ORDERS table in edit mode. The WAIT TABLE command allows the user to edit the table and a two-line prompt displays instructions at the top of the screen, above the table. If the user presses [F2] to complete the edit session, the UNTIL "F2" clause of the WAIT TABLE condition is satisfied, the changes are saved, and the loop is exited, ending script play. If the user presses [Esc], a SHOWMENU appears as a safety net, displaying a Paradox-style menu offering two choices. If the user chooses "DoNotCancel", editing resumes through the LOOP command, which reevaluates the WHILE condition (which will always be true) and again executes the commands that follow it. If the user selects "Cancel" after hitting [Esc], the editing session is canceled and the loop is exited, ending script play.

## 4.22 INFINITE LOOPS

We have presented a special case of the WHILE command in which the condition evaluated by the WHILE is always true. Unless you provide an exit point that succeeds, the program will loop indefinitely—an infinite loop.

```
WHILE True
 <statements>
 IF condition THEN
   <statements>
   QUITLOOP
 ENDIF
ENDWHILE
```

In the event that the IF condition that you test is never true, the WHILE loop will never end. Whenever you program with a looping control structure, make sure you leave yourself an out.

## 4.23 CHAPTER SUMMARY

In making the transition from script recording to script writing, you can and should use recorded scripts as the basis for your programs. But script writing requires a different level of knowledge about Paradox than simply recording keystrokes does. In this chapter, you've been introduced to fundamental tools of script writing in PAL: program constructs that allow user interaction (WAIT and SHOWMENU); program control structures that direct a script's action (IF and WHILE); nesting of control structures; and special rules for representing strings and keys. In addition, several fundamental programming elements were introduced: variables; a special Paradox system variable named RETVAL; logical conditions; and the logical constants true and false.

## NOTES

1. Strings are also sometimes referred to as "alphanumeric constants."
2. There are two typographical errors in Appendix B of the Release 3.0 PAL manual that might lead to a bit of confusion. The key code −15 is represented as Enter: it should be ReverseTab. Key code 127 is listed as CtrlLeft; it should be CtrlBackspace.

# Chapter 5

# Language Elements

This chapter introduces additional elements of the language called PAL.

## 5.1 BEEP AND THEN WAIT A SECOND

Anything a user can do, PAL can do faster (but not perhaps smarter).

Repetition is part of life, but senseless repetition is what programming helps avoid. Any computer program, however small, attempts to reduce human effort by performing repetitive tasks accurately without complaining. "Sound a tone and wait a second" can be easily expressed in PAL:

```
BEEP
SLEEP 1000
```

BEEP and SLEEP are PAL commands that sound a tone on the computer's speaker and momentarily halt the action of a Paradox program. BEEP is an output command. One thousand counts of SLEEP equal one second. These commands can't be found within the Paradox menu structure—they can only be used through PAL. Though PAL scripts can manipulate the workspace as if it were an automated Paradox user, special PAL features reach beyond the normal boundaries of user interaction. There are over 150 PAL commands in Paradox3, but you've already been introduced to 56 of them as the special key commands you saw in Chapter 3, Avoiding Keystrokes.

## 5.2 EXPRESSIONS

An expression is an argument to a PAL command or function. From the manual:

"An expression is a single value, or a set of one or more elements that evaluate to (return or result in) a value."

A value can only be of one type. In this example, the SLEEP command requires an expression that equals a value between 1 and 30,000. The 1000 could also be expressed as:

```
SLEEP (100*10) ;or
SLEEP (10e3) ;or
SLEEP (delay.s) ;where delay.s has been assigned the value 1000
```

Expressions can be relatively simple or quite complex. An expression can include almost all PAL language elements: constants, including alphanumeric strings; variables and arrays; operators; field specifiers; and functions. Here, for example, is an expression used in the PROMPT option under a WAIT RECORD:

```
WAIT RECORD PROMPT
"Editing record "+STRVAL(RECNO())+" of " +STRVAL(NRECORDS(Table()))+ "in the " +
  Table()+" table."
UNTIL "F2"
```

This combination of language elements equates to a single value, a string. For example:

```
"Editing record 12 of 333 in the Orders table."
```

Different element types within an expression at times may, and at other times may not need to be converted to be compatible. Here, the RECNO() and the NRECORDS() functions return numeric values and hence need to be converted with the STRVAL() function, which converts nonalphanumeric types to a string.

There is some confusion as to when you need to make type conversions.[1] Here are two equivalent expressions. The first uses a comma to separate elements of the expression. This is referred to as an *ExpressionList*.

```
MESSAGE "The value of Z is ",(x+y)
```

The second example first converts the value of (x+y) to a string, and then uses a plus sign to *concatenate* the two strings. The result is a single string.

```
MESSAGE "The value of Z is "+STRVAL(x+y)
```

The next example won't work because you can't add an integer to an alphanumeric type without type conversion of the value of the RECNO() function.

```
MESSAGE "Processing is " + INT(RECNO()/x*100)  + "% complete."
```

You can make this work correctly by using commas and an ExpressionList, or by converting all values into a string.

```
MESSAGE "Processing is ", INT(RECNO()/x*100)," % complete."
MESSAGE "Processing is "+STRVAL(INT(RECNO()/x*100))," % complete."
```

## 5.3 FIELD SPECIFIERS

Field specifiers are shorthand references to the contents of fields. All are enclosed by a pair of square brackets.

| Field Specifier | Field Description |
|---|---|
| [] | Current field in current image. |
| [#] | Current record number in current image. |
| [field] | Named field in current image. |
| [table→] | Current field in the named table. |
| [table→field] | Named field in the named table. |
| [table(n)→] | Current field in nth image in named table. |
| [table(n)→field] | Named field in nth image of named table. |
| [table(Q)→] | Current field in query image of named table. |
| [table(Q)→field] | Named field in query image of named table. |

## 5.4 MORE ON FUNCTIONS

The WHILE command, introduced in the last chapter, was used to continuously repeat program statements until user interaction caused a QUITLOOP to be encountered. The word WHILE is immediately followed by a condition that must be true for the instructions within the WHILE loop to repeat. If ever the condition is false, the program skips all statements until it reaches an END-WHILE, and continues executing at the statement following the ENDWHILE. In the example, we used a common programming technique and *defined* the WHILE condition as true, forcing the exit from the loop at another location.

The following script fragment uses a WHILE loop in a slightly different fashion, checking at each pass whether a condition, the result of a PAL *function*, is true. As long as the condition is true, the commands following the WHILE repeat.

Occasionally a user needs waking up (for example, when a printer isn't ready to print). Here's a small program that instructs Paradox to "Beep every quarter second until the user presses a key: "

```
WHILE NOT CHARWAITING()   ;no keyboard interaction?
   BEEP                   ;then beep
   SLEEP 250              ;pause 1/4 of a second
ENDWHILE                  ;and repeat
```

A command performs an explicit action; copying a table, moving the cursor, sounding a beep. In contrast, a PAL function performs an operation or calculation and *returns a value.*

Functions are one of the fundamental building blocks of PAL: there are 139 functions in nine broad categories; Date and Time, Information, Input/Output, Mathematical, Statistical, String Manipulation, System Status, and Workspace and Canvas Status. Although the Examples Section of this book provides specific application of each function, we will introduce many of them in the course of this narrative.

## 5.5 CHARWAITING

The PAL input/output function, CHARWAITING(), determines if a key has been pressed by checking the keyboard buffer where characters are stored before Paradox acts on them. If a key has been pressed, CHARWAITING() returns the value True. In this example, the full condition of the loop is WHILE NOT CHARWAITING(). What does the word NOT do?

## 5.6 LOGICAL OPERATORS

You've encountered NOT before, as a special query operator. The word NOT, when used in a query followed by an example element or string, selects records that don't match these values. The use of the PAL word NOT shown here is as a *logical operator* and it has the effect of reversing logical conditions. If something is true, preceding the condition with the logical operator NOT makes it false. If the condition is false, preceding it with NOT forces it to be true. The condition NOT CHARWAITING() is true until someone presses a key. In this example, when a key is pressed, the beeping stops.

There are two other logical operators, the word AND, which combines logical conditions and the word OR, which makes logical conditions nonexclusive. When a statement involves two conditions linked by the word AND:

```
condition1 AND condition2
```

both conditions have to be true for the combined conditions, the *expression*, to be true. As a reminder, an expression is any combination of PAL language elements that creates a single value. If two conditions are linked by the word OR:

```
condition1 OR condition2
```

the expression is true if either condition is true (or if both are true).

## 5.7 COMMENTS

Something else is different about the script above that uses NOT CHARWAIT-ING. Each statement is followed by a short explanation of what the line does. This explanation, or *comment*, is separated from the PAL instructions by a semicolon. A comment is any text to the right of a semicolon in a PAL script. Comments can be placed anywhere; like white space, PAL will simply ignore all comments when running the script.

## 5.8 CAPTURING ERRANT KEYSTROKES

Though it may not at first seem important, what happens to the keystroke that stops the beeping? "Who cares?" might be the usual response. However, if this little program is a *code fragment*, part of a much larger script, you need to care. If, for example, the next portion of this script displays a menu, the keystroke that stops the beeping will be passed through to the menu. Depending on the keystroke, the user will either hear a beep or an inadvertent menu selection will be made. If a report is ready to print, Paradox may pause printing. To head off these possibilities, the keystroke must be captured and rendered harmless.

```
WHILE NOT CHARWAITING( )
  BEEP
  SLEEP 250
ENDWHILE
n = GETCHAR( ) ;grab any character
```

This statement removes the keystroke from the keystroke buffer, ending the program. It consists of a variable name, *n*, the assignment operator, =, and the GETCHAR() function.

## 5.9 ASSIGNMENT

In the previous chapter, you saw how the WAIT TABLE command automatically assigned the name of the key used to end the WAIT to a variable called RETVAL. You also used the SHOWMENU command, which assigned the selected menu choice to a variable you named. The equals sign plays two roles in PAL. The first time you used the equals sign, it was as a *comparison operator*. (IF RETVAL = "Esc"). The second role is that of a PAL command called the *assignment operator*, in which a variable name (or, as you will see, a field) is assigned to a value. The assignment operator works by giving the value on the right of the equals sign to the name on the left.

## 5.10 GETCHAR( )

The value on the right in this instance is determined by a second PAL input/output function. GETCHAR() is designed to capture a single keystroke from the user. The value that GETCHAR() returns is always a number: the key code of the key that is pressed. For example, pressing the spacebar will return the key code 32; pressing [Enter] will return 13. Here GETCHAR() works with an explicit variable assignment. When this statement is completed, the character that was in the keyboard buffer has been captured, and its key code assigned to the variable named *n*. All PAL functions work in tandem with a command; they are useless alone. Commands, in contrast, are often self-sufficient.

## 5.11 RELEASING MEMORY

The code fragment that alerted the user by beeping has a small flaw. The key that was trapped and stored as a variable occupies memory and memory is a precious commodity with Paradox. Let's complete the script by adding a single command:

```
WHILE NOT CHARWAITING()
  BEEP
  SLEEP 250
ENDWHILE
n = GETCHAR()
RELEASE VARS n
```

This next statement is the PAL command RELEASE VARS, which is followed by the variable name n. VARS stands for variables, and it is always plural, even, as is in this case, if you are releasing only one variable. The RELEASE VARS command helps you keep a clean house, where variables are swept away once they're no longer useful. Although you don't need to free the memory occupied by this variable, what is more important is that you have no need to keep it. Variables can clutter up memory, which can slow or interfere with performance. The general rule to apply: to get rid of unneeded variables, RELEASE them.

## 5.12 PRECEDENCE

**Precedence** is the ordering of operations. The rules of precedence clarify which operations are performed first, next, and last. Although perhaps not obvious, an important aspect in deciphering the statement:

```
n = GETCHAR()
```

is the question of precedence. This statement involves two operations, a function and an assignment. Which is evaluated first? The precedence of an operation depends on the players involved. The rules of precedence in this example dictate that the function is executed first and the assignment to the variable is made second (it wouldn't make much sense otherwise). Here is another example:

```
1 + 2 * 3
```

If evaluated from left to right by position, the result is 9. Yet because of the rules of precedence, the result is 7. The multiplication operator (*), has a higher precedence than the addition operator (+). The rules of precedence coincidentally evaluate this expression from right to left. The rules of precedence have a profound effect on the results of your scripts. Let us take a look at them.

## 5.13 UNARY MINUS

Like the equals sign, the minus operator (−) has several roles. First, it serves as a mathematical subtraction operator, allowing you to subtract both numbers and, following special rules, dates. Secondly, the minus operator is used for negation, when it is also known as the *unary* minus. The unary minus makes a positive value negative and a negative value positive. The unary minus has a higher precedence than other mathematical operators. Understanding its use reconciles what otherwise would look like a conflict of operations:

```
2* -3
```

which equals −6.

## 5.14 ORDER OF PRECEDENCE

The Paradox3 PAL manual omits the description of the unary minus in its ordering of precedence.

**TABLE 5.1**
Rank of the PAL Manual's Precedence against
the Real Precedence

| | | |
|---|---|---|
| 1 | ( ) | ( ) |
| 2 | */ | − (Unary minus) |
| 3 | + − | */ |
| 4 | = <> < <= > = | + − |
| 5 | NOT | = <> < <= >= |
| 6 | AND | NOT |
| 7 | OR | AND |
| 8 | | OR |

Where operations of equal precedence are involved, for example:

```
3 * 4 / 5
```

the operations are evaluated from left to right. In the table above, the equals sign is used as a comparison operator and it has a higher precedence than it does when used as the assignment operator. This brings up an interesting and often useful technique—the combination of assignment and comparison in one statement. Here's an example that makes an assignment based on a comparison of dates:

```
IsDateSame.l = ( 25-Jan-90 = 1/25/90 )
```

The first equals sign is used in assignment. Yet the second equals sign is used as a comparison operator, and so it has a higher precedence. The dates are equal and so IsDateSame.l = True. This can substitute for several lines of code, with the general form:

```
variable.l = ( condition1 = condition2 )
```

The parentheses are optional, because comparison has a higher precedence than assignment, but we will always use parentheses for the sake of clarity. This statement is equivalent to:

```
IF condition1 = condition2 THEN
  variable.l = True
ELSE
  variable.l = False
ENDIF
```

## 5.15 USE PARENTHESES!

Parentheses have the highest priority. The cardinal rule of precedence: *When in doubt, use parentheses! For example, the logical operators rank as shown: (1) NOT, (2) AND, and (3) OR. Therefore, the expression:*

```
condition AND NOT condition1 OR condition2
```

is by the rules of precedence:

```
(condition AND (NOT condition1)) OR condition2
```

The NOT condition is evaluated first, the AND condition second, and the OR condition last. If you meant instead:

```
condition AND NOT (condition1 OR condition2)
```

use parentheses and write it this way to begin with. The liberal use of parentheses will help avoid confusion and guarantee precedence in the order that you intend.

## 5.16 COMPARISON RULES

As a reminder, comparison operators always result in a value of True or False. When used as a comparison operator, the = sign tests for equivalence (is the left equal to the right?). The opposite of the = sign when used as a comparison operator is <>, meaning not equal to. The other comparison operators should be familiar from queries:

- \> greater than
- \< less than
- \>= greater than or equal to
- \<= less than or equal to

Comparison operators work on data of all types, but different data types follow different rules of comparison. Date types and numeric types proceed from low to high. Thus 1/12/89 < 3/31/92 and 100 > 99.99999 <1.45e15. The logical value False is less than the logical value True.[2] The alphanumeric order of comparison is not fixed, but depends on the default sort order chosen in the CUSTOM script. The default, ASCII, is in the order of 1 < A < Z <z.

## 5.17 NAMES, NAMES, NAMES

As a user of Paradox, you've had the opportunity to attach names to hundreds of things: tables, fields, reports, and forms, just to name a few. You probably also have discovered how the names and phrases you've supplied are important.

- Table names, limited to eight characters, create the family name, which is supplied to all family objects. Naming tables with unique first letters makes it easy to select a table interactively.
- Field names are automatically used for a variety of objects, including free form and tabular reports, and the standard form. Accurately named fields convey field contents. Warning: be careful to omit mathematical operators from field names. A field with a name like "Notes–>Due" is allowable but bound to create trouble.
- Descriptions play an important role in selecting reports and forms. Copying one report to another also copies the description. (It's always a good rule to edit duplicate descriptions—naming and maintaining accurate descriptions can help you keep the number of files you have to keep track of down to a minimum.)

It is often difficult to name Paradox objects accurately. With programming, the naming of names becomes even more important.

## 5.18 RESERVED WORDS

A reserved word is a word (and a few special symbols) to which Paradox and PAL attach special meaning. Commands and optional parts of commands, functions, logical constants, and special query operators are all words reserved for use by Paradox. If you attempt to use them in a script in a manner other than that allowed, a script error will result.

## 5.19 VARIABLE NAMING RESTRICTIONS

Variable names must not duplicate Paradox reserved words, must begin with a letter, and can be up to 132 characters in length. Subsequent characters in variable names can include letters, digits, a period, a dollar sign, an exclamation point, or an underline. Variables are case-independent; thus RETVAL, retval and rEtvAl are regarded as the same name. There is seldom a need for a variable name longer than 20 characters.

> "If you were to break up a program, put it into a grinder, and then sort the pieces, you would find that the bulk of the program is in names. If you just write, "apples + oranges," the name "apples" is six characters, the operation "+" is one character, the name "oranges" is seven characters, for a total of fourteen characters. Only one character, the plus sign, had to do with the operation. So to me it seemed logical that to make an impact or improve things, I would try to improve the greatest bulk—and that was the names."
>
> —Charles Simonyi, "Programmers at Work"

As Charles Simonyi suggests in the quote above, one of the best things you can do to keep things simple is to pay very close attention to how you name things. Naming a variable is not like naming a child; you can always change the name of a variable. Yet the longer you wait to give a variable an appropriate name, substituting something temporary in the interim, the deeper you dig yourself into a hole. Take extra time to name variables. The PAL manual gives some insight into why this is so important:

> You should be careful to make sure that the information you're manipulating is in the form you want it to be. This is especially important since PAL performs automatic

type conversion in many of its operations. . . . Many PAL commands and functions only work when you pass them data of a specific type. The ACOS (arc cosine) function, for instance, will produce a script error if you pass it a nonnumeric variable such as the string "two". How do you ensure that you're working with the right type of data if the variable automatically follows the type of the data assigned to it? There are two ways to prevent a data type error:

Use the TYPE function to explicitly check the type of the variable before passing it to the function.

Make sure that the variable never contains anything but a number in the first place. One method of facilitating this is to name all variables in a predictable pattern like:

   a_varname alphanumeric (string) variable
   n_varname numeric variable
   d_varname date variable
   l_varname logical variable
   c_varname currency ($) variable

Of course, naming your variables in this way won't keep Paradox from converting variables automatically and sticking a date value into a logical variable, but it will help verify your scripts. If you see a date variable being assigned a value, you can verify that it is a date value . . . There are many other naming conventions that you might want to use instead . . . (but the) important point is not that you name variables exactly as described here, but that you use a consistent system that lets you quickly and correctly identify what type of data the variable contains.

We agree, but unfortunately, the PAL manual fails to practice what it preaches: the examples of the functions, commands, and the sample stocks application have no consistent naming method. The Data Entry Toolkit code affords a better example of consistent naming, but even it does not identify the type of the variable as recommended.

The idea behind this technique, that the name of the variable should convey information about the variable itself including type, is a variation on a method invented by Charles Simonyi, one of the chief software designers for Microsoft. Mr. Simonyi, who is from Hungary, has been incorporating a system of variable naming in all of the software he has developed since the early 1970s. This system of naming is known as "Hungarian" notation,[3] and in languages with more complex data types than Paradox, its use becomes even more critical.

Some people think that if they can read each of the words in a code, then the program is readable. In fact, readability is in that sense unimportant. Nobody takes a listing, goes up to a podium, and reads a program out loud. It's comprehension that counts. The fact that you can just read the words and pronounce them is useless. When people see a listing in Hungarian, they find these words difficult to pronounce, so they think it isn't readable. But in fact, it's easier to comprehend and easier to communicate because of the association between the name and the properties."
—Charles Simonyi

We have surveyed programmers far and wide, and discovered that there are several concerns that the PAL manual does not address that can make the use of a system of naming even more important. A naming system can:

- Avoid potential conflict with PAL reserved words, past, present, and future. PAL is a young language, and though perhaps stabilizing, PAL is evolving. Particular emphasis has been placed on maintaining compatibility with prior releases. As Paradox changes, PAL grows and changes. It stands to reason that a good name for a variable is also a good name for a PAL reserved word. Devising and using a system of naming that avoids all future conflicts with reserved words is preferred over retrofitting existing scripts to accommodate new PAL reserved words.
- Differentiate between reserved words and words of a particular programmer's invention or use. From a standpoint of program documentation, third party examination of PAL programs is made simpler.
- Make learning PAL easier. PAL should be accessible. Using a system of naming helps demystify PAL, making it easier to learn.

## 5.20 PAL BY EXAMPLE (PBE) NOTATION

In response, we have adopted the following method of naming variables.

- If a variable is trivial—for example, if it is used and then immediately released or it is used as a counter in a loop, it is named by a single letter designating its type according to the rules below. If more than one of the same type is needed, the letter is followed by consecutive integers starting with 1 (e.g., n1, n2, n3).
- All other variables are identified by a name, a period, and a letter. We have modified the types suggested in the PAL manual to include

a for alphanumeric (string)
n for numeric
d for date
l for logical
c for currency
s for short number
r for array
v for a type that may vary.

We have opted for the use of suffixes rather than prefixes. Suffixes tend to be less obtrusive and allow you to group variable names alphabetically. In addition, we chose the period because the underscore presents problems with query statements, where it is taken to represent an example element whenever it is found. (Almost more importantly, the period is easier to type than the underscore.)

```
FormView.l = IsFormView()
HelpOn.l = True
IsNetWork.l = ( NetType()<>"SingleUser")
Text.a = "abcd"
Birthday.d = 1/23/80
n = GETCHAR() ;returns numeric
ACCEPT "A50" TO choice.a
SHOWMENU ...TO Choice.a
Selection.a = MenuChoice()
CustomerID.s = [Cust ID]
Invoice.d = [Invoice Date]
Invoice.n = [Invoice #]
Invoice.c = [Amount]
COPYTOARRAY Record.r
MaxBalance.v = CMAX("Invoice","Balance Due")
;because CMAX can return n, s, c or "Error"
```

## 5.21 ARRAYS

An array is a series of related variable assignments that can be made at one time. An array has a single name followed by an element number in square brackets. The number can be from 1 to 15,000. Every array has a size, and every array element that is assigned has a type. If you reassign an array element to a different type, the array element takes on the new type without restriction.

A PAL array is known as a one-dimensional array, for each variable within the array is associated with only one dimension element. This structure is particularly useful for the record-oriented environment of a table, and PAL provides two specialized commands that enable you to manipulate the contents of whole records, COPYTOARRAY and COPYFROMARRAY.

You can declare an array with a pal command:

```
ARRAY r[10]
```

The number in brackets is called an *array subscript*. You can also declare an array of an ambiguous size by using a variable:

```
ARRAY r[size.s]
```

Or an array with an expression:

```
ARRAY r[x+2]
```

(in this case, x+2 is known as a *subscript expression*).

Here's an example of the declaration and filling of an array:

```
Array weekday.r[7]

Weekday.r[1] = "Lundi"
Weekday.r[2] = "Mardi"
Weekday.r[3] = "Mecredi"
Weekday.r[4] = "Jeudi"
Weekday.r[5] = "Vendredi"
Weekday.r[6] = "Samedi"
Weekday.r[7] = "Dimanche"
```

Each of these seven array elements is alphanumeric, with a length equal to its string length.

# 5.22 COPYTOARRAY AND COPYFROMARRAY

With the cursor on a record in a table, the PAL command:

```
COPYTOARRAY arrayname.r
```

declares and creates an array that mirrors the structure of the table and assigns the current values in those fields to the array elements. The first element in the arrayname.r is the name of the table from which the array was created. A special rule applies when referencing the subscripts of an array created with CopyToArray. You can identify the subscripts of the array not only by number, but by the name of the field as well.

Thus if you had a table called "Deposits" with fields:

| Deposits | Acct No. | Date | Amount | Transaction Type |
|---|---|---|---|---|
| 1 | 123 | 1/2/89 | 450.00 | Deposit |
| 2 | 346 | 1/2/89 | 333.00 | Withdrawal |

the command CopyToArray on record #1 would create a five element array with the following contents and types:

```
Deposits.r[1] = "Deposits"
Deposits.r[2] = Deposits.r["Account No"] = 123
Deposits.r[3] = Deposits.r["Date"] = 1/2/89
Deposits.r[4] = Deposits.r["Amount"] = 450.00
Deposits.r[5] = Deposits.r["Transaction Type"] = "Deposit"
```

Referencing array elements by element name is slower than using the array element subscript. (See CopyToArray in the examples section for more specific information.) The CopyFromArray command, which assigns the elements in an array to a table, assumes that you are viewing a table of a compatible structure and are modifying the table in edit, coedit, or dataentry modes.

Since the assignment of an array is an assignment to only one variable name, arrays are cleared by releasing the name:

```
RELEASE VARS Deposits.r
```

## 5.23 THE TYRANNY OF PROGRAMMING

Programming is a humbling activity, a never-ending reminder of our poor typing, sticky fingers, and plain goofs. Here are some common PAL syntax error messages:

- "Syntax error: Missing )." If you open a parentheses in PAL, close it.
- "Syntax error: Missing ] in field specifier." If you open a square bracket "[", close it.
- "Syntax error: Missing right quote." Quotes usually come in pairs, but not always. Quotes are paired with backslashes if you want the quote to be within a quote. "\"Right\" said Abbot."
- "Unrecognized command." Watch out for spelling.

As noted, PAL, a language that is largely case insensitive, is occasionally very case sensitive. Here's an example.

```
MOVETO 1                        ;move to the first image
WHILE IMAGETYPE()= "query"
CLEARIMAGE                      ;clear it
ENDWHILE
```

The code attempts to clear only query images from the Paradox workspace. Though there is nothing wrong syntactically with this routine, it will fail because of one letter. The ImageType() function in Paradox returns a string: "Display" for tables, "Query" for query images, and "None" if no images are present. All string comparisons in PAL are case sensitive. We've asked PAL to compare "Query" with "query". The comparison will fail.

## 5.24 OTHER SYNTAX RESTRICTIONS

PAL is somewhat free-form in the way you can write statements. Ordinarily, white space in scripts has very little meaning except between commands. As always, there are a few exceptions to this rule.

Any variable name followed by square brackets on the same line is interpreted by PAL to be an element in an array. Here are two statements on one line:

```
EDIT tablename.a  [ID] = 5
```

This is really meant to be two statements, but because of the way array elements are assigned, it is interpreted as:

```
Edit tablename.a[ID] = 5
```

The spaces between the tablename.a variable and the [ID] field are stripped away, instructing PAL to first make a comparison between an array element and a value, and then edit the result. A statement written in this manner will always cause a script error. If you mean to assign 5 to the field [ID], put it on a separate line.

```
Edit tablename.a
[ID] = 5
```

The RETURN command, which controls program flow by leaving the current script or procedure, allows for an optional parameter that is returned to the calling program. The following example attempts to return a variable named "ENDIF," thus leaving the IF conditional incomplete.

```
IF RETVAL THEN RETURN ENDIF
```

If the RETURN is placed on the end of a line, it will work as expected:

```
IF RETVAL THEN
 RETURN
ENDIF
```

The SETKEY command must be on one line. Here is a proper SETKEY statement that calls the PlayRight script editor with [Shift F1]:

```
SETKEY "F11" RUN "PR PI"
```

If this statement is broken into two lines, its intended effect is lost.

```
SETKEY "F11"
RUN "PR PI"
```

The first line resets [Shift F1] key assignment to nothing. The second line runs the DOS command string that follows, "PR PI", immediately rather than at the press of a key.

## 5.25 CHAPTER SUMMARY

This chapter has introduced many of the missing language links in PAL; functions, mathematical and logical operators, comments, assignment, precedence, and syntax restrictions. In addition, with "PBE notation," it has introduced a systematic way of naming variables. In a later chapter, "Procedures," this notation is carried one step further. The next chapter introduces the tools of the programming environment.

## NOTES

1. These examples were used incorrectly in the Paradox3 PAL manual as examples for the ?, ??, and MESSAGE commands. Adding to this confusion is a third example illustrating the use of MESSAGE with the RECNo () function (which decidedly will not work).
2. This follows the usual convention of False = 0 and True = 1 found in most programming languages.
3. The term "Hungarian notation" is also a play on the phrase "It's Greek to me." In some of the more complex languages, some programmers say, listings written with Hungarian notation look as though they might as well be written in Hungarian.

# Chapter 6

## The PAL Menu

An often overlooked feature of PAL is that the PAL menu can be called up with a key, [Alt F10],[1] in almost every Paradox system mode, allowing you direct access to PAL tools. This special menu is not only for use by PAL programmers, though. In addition to allowing you to record and play scripts and assist in debugging, the PAL menu has a powerful {Value} command that can be used as a calculator or to help you to determine the state of the Paradox environment. This chapter introduces the PAL menu and script debugging.

## 6.1 THE PARADOX TOOLBOX

The right tools make all the difference.

At times, writing a script to do a little task seems like more trouble than its worth. Yet if you're in the middle of designing a report, putting ValChecks into a table, designing a form, or modifying records in a table, a little PAL can go a long way.

One of the best investments you can make in learning programming in Paradox is getting to know the PAL Menu and its alter ego, the PAL Debugger. Whenever you're using Paradox interactively, pressing [Alt F10] brings up the PAL menu. Unlike all other Paradox menus, the number and selection of menu choices that are available through the PAL menu change, and depend on:

- whether or not a script is currently being recorded, and
- whether or not a script is being debugged.

## 6.2 BEGINRECORD

Here's an example. InstantRecord, [Alt F3], allows you to record keystrokes into an "instant" script, which can be played back with [Alt F4], InstantPlay. Yet "Instant.sc" is by nature temporary—it is overwritten any time you use [Alt F3] again. If you want to save a script you've recorded with [Alt F3], you must rename it. An easier way to record keystrokes you want saved is through the PAL menu.

**Step 1**
Press:        [Alt F10]

The PAL menu shows:

```
Play RepeatPlay BeginRecord Debug Value Miniscript
```

**Step 2**
Select:        {BeginRecord}
**Step 3**
Type:        Test
**Step 4**
Press:        [F10]
**Step 5**
Select:        {Tools}
                 {More}
                 {Directory}
**Step 6**
Press:        [Enter]
**Step 7**
Select:        {Ok}
**Step 8**
Now press:    [AltF10]

and you will see that the PAL menu shows only:

```
Cancel EndRecord
```

**Step 9**
Select:        {EndRecord}

When you are recording a script, there are only two choices on the PAL menu. By recording scripts through the PAL menu, which allows you to name a script before you begin recording, your saved keystrokes can be made safe from being recorded over with [Alt F3].

The PAL menu allows you to:

- {Play} play a script in the middle of something else while editing a table, while defining graphs, or while within the script editor, the forms generator, or the report generator
- {BeginRecord} record a script at any time while editing a table, creating a validity check, or placing fields in a report.
- {Value} determine the current values of variables or array elements. Use PAL functions to report on the state of the Paradox environment. Test for valid expressions before using them in scripts.
- {Debug} steps through a script statement by statement.
- {MiniScript} write and execute a one-line script.

## 6.3 VALUE

The {Value} command allows you to type in any expression, including field assignments, the names of any variables you have assigned, PAL functions, and mathematical operators and strings, and display PAL's interpretation of that expression. {Value} is equivalent to a one line script:

```
RETURN <expression>
```

You can use {Value} as a simple calculator. For example,

**Step 1**
Press:      [Alt F10]
**Step 2**
Select:     {Value}
**Step 3**
Type:       TODAY()+90
**Step 4**
Press:      [Enter]

The value of a date 90 days from today will be shown in the lower right corner of your screen in MESSAGE format. In a like manner you can use any combination of valid PAL functions to calculate a value.

## 6.4 MINISCRIPTS

If you have "quick and dirty" tasks to perform on a table, a *miniscript* might help. A miniscript is a one-line script entered from the PAL menu. Here's an example: a simple miniscript that might save a lot of work. You've got names and addresses in a table in upper case, and you'd like to put them into what Paradox terms "proper" case, with initial capital letters.

Get into the edit or coedit mode and move into the field you want in proper case.

| | |
|---|---|
| **Step 1** | |
| Press: | [Alt F10] |
| **Step 2** | |
| Select: | {Miniscript} |
| **Step 3** | |
| Type: | SCAN [] = FORMAT("CC", LOWER ( [] )) ENDSCAN |
| **Step 4** | |
| Press: | [Enter] |
| **Step 5** | |
| Press: | [DO_IT!] to save your changes. |

The script will execute, and upon conclusion, reveals the Paradox workspace with the field in proper case. With a little help from miniscripts, an experienced PAL programmer can perform near-miracles with raw data.

## 6.5 THE PAL DEBUGGER

Debugging is the process of removing errors from a program. Paradox has an integrated debugging facility in which the script and Paradox are seamlessly linked. The features of the PAL debugger are among the best kept secrets in Paradox.

When you begin writing and playing scripts, you quickly learn that PAL is intolerant of syntax errors. By selecting {Debug} from the {Cancel} {Debug} menu, you are given access to the PAL debugger. When the debugger is activated, the Paradox workspace is revealed (the "canvas" is lifted), the name of the current script and line number of the error is displayed, the source of the error is marked with the blinking debugger cursor, and a message gives you an indication of the error (e.g., "Not a possible menu choice"). Another message states "Type Control-Q to Quit."

While debugging, the PAL menu now displays nine choices:

```
Value Step Next Go MiniScript Where? Quit Pop Editor
```

The new commands in this array of menu selections are:

- {Step} rereads the current instruction and attempts to re-execute it.
- {Next} passes over the current instruction with no attempt to execute it.
- {Go} saves and plays the script again.
- {Quit} halts debugging.
- {Pop} "pops" up one level in a "nested" script.
- {Editor} stops debugging, clears the workspace, and loads the current script into the editor.
- {Where?} graphically depicts the location of the current command within nested scripts or procedures.[2]

```
Edit the table. Press [F2] when done.
```

| ORDERS | Order # | Cust ID | Stock # | Quant | Dat |
|---|---|---|---|---|---|
| 1 | 2280 | 4277 | 130 | 1 | 4/22/ |
| 2 | 3351 | 3266 | 519 | 1 | 12/16/ |
| 3 | 8070 | 6125 | 632 | 8 | 6/04/ |
| 4 | 6235 | 2779 | 890 | 1 | 8/01/ |
| 5 | 1442 | 9004 | 519 | 2 | 10/27/ |
| 6 | 5119 | 7008 | 235 | 1 | 3/04/ |
| 7 | 9554 | 3266 | 558 | 15 | 7/27/ |
| 8 | 6975 | 6666 | 519 | 3 | 6/24/ |
| 9 | 8933 | 9226 | 422 | 1 | 2/28/ |
| 10 | 1180 | 3128 | 519 | 2 | 5/31/ |
| 11 | 4492 | 5341 | 244 | 3 | 12/24/ |
| 12 | 9226 | 1784 | 983 | 1 | 1/14/ |
| 13 | 7643 | 6954 | 519 | 1 | 4/30/ |
| 14 | 1574 | 2177 | 632 | 1 | 11/22/ |
| 15 | 3885 | 9004 | 244 | 5 | 4/22/ |

```
                                        Syntax error: Unrecognized command
Script: INSTANT  Line:  11                 Type Control-Q to Quit
            ▶ QUIP
```

While debugging, these keystroke shortcuts enable you to execute debugger commands without resorting to the PAL menu:

| Debugging Key | PAL Menu command |
|---|---|
| [Ctrl E] | {Editor} |
| [Ctrl G] | {Go} |
| [Ctrl P][3] | {Pop} |
| [Ctrl N] | {Next} |
| [Ctrl S][3] | {Step} |
| [Ctrl W] | {Where?} |

The best way to get to know the PAL debugger is to use it. The examples disk that comes with Paradox contains a script ("Debugtst.sc"), designed to be used with a short tutorial on the debugger. We strongly recommend that you take the time to use this tutorial (pages 128–134, release 3.0, PAL User's Guide).

## 6.6 THREE CURSORS

While debugging, your screen has three active cursors. The *debugger cursor* is on the inverse video *debugger line* at the bottom of the screen and it blinks if it is before a statement that invoked an error. The debugger cursor is arrow shaped and will only move as you use the debugging commands {Next}, {Step}, or {Pop}.

The second cursor is rarely seen—the canvas cursor. It displays only with commands that echo the canvas to the screen.

Another cursor, the normal *workspace cursor*, is still active while you are debugging and can be controlled as in interactive Paradox. In fact, because script play is suspended during debugging, the entire Paradox workspace can be manipulated as usual. While debugging, you have complete control over interactive Paradox—you can and should manipulate the workspace:

- if your script failed to place a table on the workspace (use the menu to view it);
- if the workspace cursor is in the wrong field or record (move it to the right one);
- if the script error is "Assignment cannot be made in this context" (the system mode may be "Main" rather than edit; simply press [F9] to change the mode to edit).

## 6.7 ADDITIONAL TOOLS

Another debugging tool is essential: a pencil. Every time you use a workspace or PAL command to permit your script to execute properly, write down the current line number and the action you used to get past the error. Restart script play with the {Go} command, [Ctrl G]. When you get through the script, you'll have a series of script changes that you can fix all at once. This technique enables you to debug a greater portion of your script without having to {Play} and {Debug} from the beginning with each test.

## 6.8 MINISCRIPTS IN THE DEBUGGER

If you forget to assign a variable in a script, you can make the assignment by using a miniscript from within the debugger. This is accomplished in two install-ments. First use the PAL menu to create a miniscript:

**Step 1**
Press:        [Alt F10]
**Step 2**
Select:       {Miniscript}
**Step 3**
Type:         n = 999        ;for example
**Step 4**
Press:        [Enter]

This creates a one-line script on the debugger line:

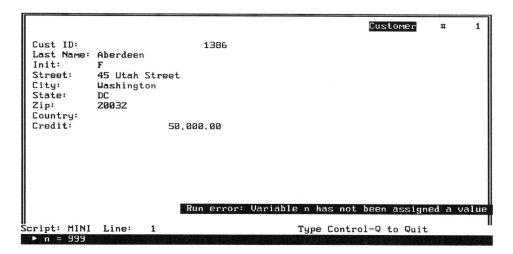

```
                                                        Customer    #     1
  Cust ID:                      1386
  Last Name: Aberdeen
  Init:      F
  Street:    45 Utah Street
  City:      Washington
  State:     DC
  Zip:       20032
  Country:
  Credit:             50,000.00




                         Run error: Variable n has not been assigned a value
Script: MINI  Line:   1                     Type Control-Q to Quit
 ▶ n = 999
```

Secondly, {Step} through this command using the PAL menu, executing it with:

**Step 1**
Press:     [Alt F10]
**Step 2**
Select:    {Step}    (or more simply, [Ctrl S])

The variable will now take on the value. With the variable assigned, you can resume script play:

**Step 3**
Press:       [Alt F10]
**Step 4**
Select:      {Go}

## 6.9 SAVEVARS

Because program flow often depends on the state of a few variables, you can use the PAL menu command {Value} to display the contents of your variables one by one, or you can use the SAVEVARS command in a miniscript to let you examine all current variables in one script listing. Here is its syntax:

```
SAVEVARS {ALL | VarNameList }
```

Either the ALL parameter or a comma-separated list of the names of the variables you want saved follows the word SAVEVARS. For example, if the script you are debugging has made assignments to four variables you are interested in:

```
custid.s = 253
invoice.d = 11/23/89
invoice.c = 423.59
Newcust.l = True
```

**Step 1**
Press:       [Alt F10]
**Step 2**
Select:      {Miniscript}
**Step 3**
Type:        SAVEVARS custid.s, invoice.d, invoice.c,
             Newcust.l
**Step 4**
Press:       [Enter]

The command appears on the debugger line.

**Step 5**
Press:       [Alt F10]

**Step 6**
Select:        {Step}

When you press {Step}, the command will be executed. SAVEVARS ALL creates a simple text file, called "SAVEVARS.SC," which lists all of your variable assignments. A typical SAVEVARS script might look like this:

```
;Variables saved with Savevars
custid.s = 253
invoice.d = 11/23/89
invoice.c = 423.59
Newcust.l = True
```

The SAVEVARS command serves two purposes.

The first purpose is simple. By executing it as a miniscript or embedding it within a script, you can use SAVEVARS to save the state of one, several, or all current variables in a script. This technique is especially useful if you are using an external editor to write and edit scripts.[4]

Secondly, because SAVEVARS results in a script, this script can be played, restoring variables to their former status:

```
PLAY "Savevars"
```

Like "INSTANT.SC," "SAVEVARS.SC" is somewhat temporary. Subsequent calls to the SAVEVARS command will overwrite the file "SAVEVARS.SC." With network use, "SAVEVARS.SC" is written to the user's private directory. See the Examples Section for additional examples of the use of SAVEVARS.

# 6.10 THE DEBUG COMMAND

Falling into the PAL debugger as a result of a script error isn't often intentional. And although you can place a syntax error in a script to intentionally invoke an error to get to the debugger, there's a better way. The PAL DEBUG command is used to invoke the debugger at will, stopping script play and loading the line after the DEBUG in the debugger line. Simply place it in your script where you want the debugger to be called:

```
<Statements>
DEBUG
IF RETVAL = "Esc" THEN
   QUIT
ENDIF
<Statements>
```

In this example, the debugger would load with the line:

```
IF RETVAL = "Esc" THEN
```

## 6.11 THE BACK DOOR, [CTRL BREAK]

Although the PAL menu lets you {Debug} a script from its beginning and the DEBUG command allows you to invoke the debugger at a certain point within your script, quite often you'll want to get into the debugger through the "back door." The back door has intentionally been left open so that you can get in at any time: simply press [Ctrl Break] at a point at which you want to examine your script line by line in the debugger. Depending on the statement your script is executing, the {Cancel} {Debug} menu will come up either right away or after the next designated keypress. This back door to PAL scripts during script play can only be locked by password protecting your scripts. When you use {Tools} {More} {Protect} and protect your script with a password,

- your script will be encrypted and made safe from examination or changes by curious users, and
- no one will be able to interrupt script play with [Ctrl Break], unless the script's password has been issued.

You will probably want to wait until your scripts are thoroughly debugged before encrypting them. Encrypted scripts can only be edited directly through {Scripts} {Editor} {Edit}, which will prompt you for your password. Upon receiving the correct password, Paradox converts the encrypted script to simple ASCII text, which allows the script to be edited by any text editor.

## 6.12 CHAPTER SUMMARY

The PAL Menu provides instant access to PAL from within any environment, enabling you to use PAL functions and commands while editing tables, reports, or forms. Two of the most useful commands, {Value} and {Miniscript}, enable you to explore and change the current state of variables and system conditions during debugging. Both the number and selection of menu choices available when you press [Alt F10] to get into the PAL menu can change. When debugging, you can either use the PAL menu for certain commands or bypass them with keystroke shortcuts.

Time spent learning these tools is well spent, for as with any set of tools, you need to use the right one for the right job. The range of uses for the PAL menu in developing Paradox applications is limitless. Get in the habit of reaching for the PAL menu when you need simple tasks accomplished; it will save you a lot of effort.

## NOTES

1. The PAL menu is not available when you are in Paradox Help, Lookup Help, or FieldView or if the field has invalid data.
2. With procedures, {Where?} also shows the values of private variables.
3. In ParadoxOS/2, [Ctrl P] is [Alt P] and [Ctrl S] is [Alt S], because OS/2 reserves these control keys.
4. One of the sacrifices you make when using an external script editor is that you no longer have access to the PAL menu. If you need to know the state of any variables while editing scripts with an external editor, you must use the SAVEVARS command before loading the editor.

# Chapter 7

# The Canvas

The PAL Canvas is a view into Paradox that exists only during script play. Once script play ends, the canvas disappears and leaves behind the workspace as the script left it. Controlling activity on the PAL canvas helps you define interaction with the user. This chapter introduces commands, functions, and techniques that allow you to control the PAL canvas.

## 7.1 THE CANVAS IS FOR THE USER

Even simple scripts can perform complex tasks—tasks which may take a long time to process. As noted, when you play a script, the screen doesn't change; it is frozen with the image of its initial condition. Any change made to the screen will happen only when instructed by an explicit PAL command. To the uninitiated, a screen frozen under script control for an extended period of time may seem unnatural: "Something must be wrong." On a local area network, where the file server may be doing all the work, a lack of disk activity on the local drive may add to the confusion: "Nothing is happening. The PC must be locked up." Panic may set in and disaster can follow.

The PAL canvas is a message center; it is the link between the user and the action in your PAL scripts. The canvas allows you to alternately hide and expose activity on the workspace, controlling, to a degree, the level of user involvement.

## 7.2 ECHO

Though suppressing workspace activity is the default condition of script play, you can control it with the ECHO command:

| | |
|---|---|
| ECHO FAST | Slight delay between statements |
| ECHO SLOW | Long delay |
| ECHO OFF | Default, hide workspace |
| ECHO NORMAL | Shortest delay between statements |

A script that begins:

```
ECHO NORMAL
<Statements>
```

will make the canvas transparent from the outset and display all workspace activity throughout script play. Though it is the fastest of the three, even ECHO NORMAL takes time, and you'll find that script play slows down. The ECHO command is best used

- for debugging, so that you can watch the progress of a script.
- selectively, with an ECHO OFF matching every ECHO NORMAL.

An easy way to keep the user informed about the workspace is to take a snapshot and display it on the canvas. This is done by simply turning ECHO on and off in succession:

```
ECHO NORMAL    ;Reveal the workspace
ECHO OFF       ;Hide the workspace
SYNCCURSOR     ;Synchronize the position of the cursor
```

The ECHO command is entire-screen oriented. PAL offers you a variety of tools to control screen activity on a character-by-character basis.

## 7.3 DISPLAY CHARACTERISTICS

Like most of the current software written for the PC, Paradox is character-based and uses the built-in IBM standard and extended character set on a standard-size screen. A standard screen accommodates 80 characters on each of 25 lines—a total of 2000 characters. In all character-based systems, the shape of a character is constant. For example, the capital letter "Q" will always look the same, being controlled by the character set definition in video ROM. Each screen position is controlled by two bytes—one byte to display the character and an extra byte that controls the character's attributes. Most monochrome monitors can display characters in low and high intensity, reverse video, blinking, and underlining. On color displays, changing the attribute byte also sets the color of the foreground (the color of the character) and background (the color around the character).

If the foreground color and the background color are the same, a character cannot be seen. This feature, though not used often, is useful in prompting a user for a password. With the background and foreground colors the same, the password can be typed, but not seen.

## 7.4 THE CANVAS GRID

If you were to plot these 2000 positions starting in the upper left of the screen with coordinate 0,0, the last position would be 24,79. This is how Paradox interprets screen position along a top-down coordinate grid.

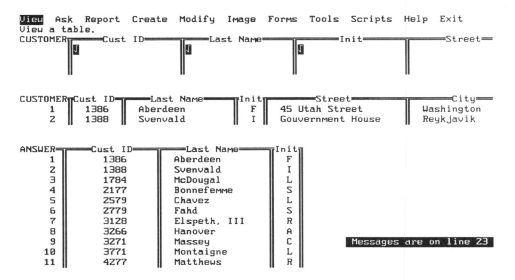

Although you can use the entire canvas in any manner you choose, Paradox sets an example by using three standard screen areas:

- The top two lines (from 0,0 to 1,79), comprise the menu and prompt area. Four commands that begin with the word "SHOW" and the PROMPT command use these top two lines. The SHOW commands, SHOWMENU, SHOWTABLES, SHOWFILES, and SHOWARRAY, are based on a similar syntax and create a Paradox-style, bounce-bar menu.
- The Paradox workspace begins on the third line (2,0) and includes the rest of the screen (24,79).

• A special command, MESSAGE, places a message on the screen in the lower right corner of the workspace. The content of the MESSAGE displays in inverse video or in a special system color flush right with the end of line 22.[1] A MESSAGE is transient and will restore the screen to the former underlying conditions after it finishes displaying. MESSAGE is usually used in conjunction with another command, like SLEEP.

These standard areas coincide with the way Paradox uses the screen, and these few commands allow you to easily substitute your menus, prompts, or messages as if they were built into Paradox. The WAIT command forces the Paradox workspace to the screen during script play. During a WAIT TABLE, RECORD, or FIELD, the canvas is transparent, revealing the workspace. At almost all other times during script play, the view that PAL presents is that of the canvas. The PROMPT option of the WAIT command and all the SHOW commands use only the top two lines of the screen; they don't normally overwrite the workspace.

The following section briefly describes some of the commands and functions that deal with the canvas. The examples section provides more detailed descriptions and examples.

## 7.5 CLEAR

The CLEAR command clears the canvas. There are three variations:

```
CLEAR      ;Clears the entire screen.
CLEAR EOL  ;Clears from the cursor position to the end of the current line.
CLEAR EOS  ;Clears from the cursor position to the end of the screen in a
           ;rectangular block.
```

CLEAR is usually one of the first commands in any script because it removes the image of the Paradox workspace from the canvas. CLEAR does NOT reposition the cursor.

## 7.6 THE CURSOR

While using Paradox interactively, activity centers around the cursor. Whether editing a table, changing a form, or creating a graph, the position of the cursor tells you a lot about what you can and cannot do. Under script control there are two independent cursors—the normal workspace cursor and the *canvas cursor*.

## 7.7 ?, ??,@—POSITIONING THE CURSOR

The canvas cursor can be controlled with two characters that are also commands: the ? and the @. The question mark is primarily used to display information to the user. It can also be used to print. Here's its syntax:

```
? <ExpressionList>
```

The question mark drops the cursor down to the beginning of the next line. If the cursor is on the last line, it moves up to the first line. If a valid expression or list of expressions follow the question mark, these expressions will be displayed on the PAL canvas, and the cursor will end up one character past the last character in the last expression. Two question marks in a row start display at the current cursor position.

```
?? <ExpressionList>
```

An ExpressionList is a series of values separated by commas; the type of the values in an ExpressionList can be mixed. A single question mark can stand alone on a line. The double question mark requires an ExpressionList or a script error will occur. To better control positioning, you need to be able to place the canvas cursor at any screen location. The next PAL canvas command directs the cursor to a coordinate on the canvas:

```
@ Row, Column
```

By PAL grid coordinates, the origin, 0,0, is the upper left of the screen and the lower right is 24,79. Used in combination, the @ and the ?? commands position and display text on the screen.

```
@ 12, 40 ?? "This message begins at the center of the screen, but wraps to the next line."
```

## 7.8 TEXT/ENDTEXT

If you have long sections of descriptive text that you want to display on the canvas, an easier way is with the TEXT command. Portions of your scripts that are between the words TEXT and ENDTEXT will display as a block. The TEXT and ENDTEXT key words must be on lines by themselves.

```
PROC splash()
  @ 3,0
  TEXT
```

```
  ENDTEXT
ENDPROC
```

A related command, SETMARGIN, establishes a temporary margin against which all TEXT and ? statements start. Any text displayed with ?? will ignore the SETMARGIN position.

```
SETMARGIN number    ;Sets the left margin at number
SETMARGIN OFF       ;The margin is reset to 0
```

## 7.9 CURSOR DISPLAY

The canvas cursor can be turned off entirely with the CURSOR command:

```
CURSOR OFF      ;Turns canvas cursor off
CURSOR NORMAL   ;Turns cursor on
CURSOR BAR      ;Makes cursor thicker than normal
CURSOR BOX      ;Makes cursor a rectangular box
```

Note: the workspace cursor is always on. When you issue a WAIT command, the workspace cursor is revealed. The reason is clear: it is almost impossible to edit a table without a cursor. The only time that your scripts require a cursor on the canvas is when they incorporate an ACCEPT command or issue the RUN command.

## 7.10 SYNCCURSOR

In alternating between the canvas and the workspace, the canvas cursor and the workspace cursor are usually not at the same location. The SYNCCURSOR command allows you to synchronize their positions.

## 7.11 CANVAS

The canvas can be turned off as well, with the CANVAS command:

```
CANVAS ON      ;Default, any display to canvas happens immediately
CANVAS OFF     ;Turns display to canvas off
```

This command is intended to be able to build display images on the canvas and then "blast" them to the screen in one shot.

## 7.12 STYLE

The canvas display attributes can be controlled with a PAL command called STYLE, which sets the attribute byte character by character. The effects of the STYLE command will only be seen with ?, ??, ACCEPT, and the TEXT commands.

```
STYLE              ;Default, clears all styles in effect
STYLE BLINK        ;Blinks
STYLE INTENSE      ;High intensity
STYLE REVERSE      ;Inverse video
```

or combinations, such as

```
STYLE BLINK, REVERSE      ;Combinations are separated by commas
STYLE ATTRIBUTE number    ;A number from 0 to 255
```

STYLE is in effect until PAL reaches another STYLE command or until script play ends. INTENSE on a monochrome screen is brighter than normal; REVERSE is inverse video; BLINK makes each character blink.

## 7.13 PAINTCANVAS

Like STYLE, the PAINTCANVAS command allows you to selectively set the attributes of an area or a border around an area and optionally fill the area with a string. Unlike STYLE, the PAINTCANVAS command affects characters already on the screen.

```
PAINTCANVAS REVERSE BLINK Row1, Column1, Row2, Column2
PAINTCANVAS BLINK Row1, Column1, Row2, Column2
PAINTCANVAS INTENSE Row1, Column1, Row2, Column2
PAINTCANVAS ATTRIBUTE number Row1, Column1, Row2, Column2
PAINTCANVAS FILL String Row1, Column1, Row2, Column2
PAINTCANVAS FILL String BACKGROUND Row1, Column2, Row2, Column2
```

## 7.14 THE FORMAT FUNCTION

All of the canvas activity we have been describing has been the result of PAL commands. A very important PAL function, FORMAT, enables you to change the appearance of values. For example, here's a script fragment that displays the date:

```
CLEAR
@0,0 ?? "Today's date is ",TODAY()
n = GETCHAR()
```

Here's a short script that displays the date in as many ways as Paradox permits using the FORMAT function:

```
CLEAR
@24,0
FOR n FROM 1 to 11
   a = "d"+STRVAL(n)
   ? "Today's date is ", FORMAT(a,TODAY()), " with date format", n, "."
ENDFOR
?
? "Press Any Key To Continue"
n = GETCHAR()
```

Here is its output on the 20th of May, 1989:

```
Today is 5/20/89 with date format 1.
Today is May 20, 1989 with date format 2.
Today is 5/20 with date format 3.
Today is 5/89 with date format 4.
Today is 20-May-89 with date format 5.
Today is May 89 with date format 6.
Today is 20-May-1989 with date format 7.
Today is 5/20/1989 with date format 8.
Today is 20.05.89 with date format 9.
Today is 20/05/89 with date format 10.
Today is 89-05-20 with date format 11.

Press Any Key To Continue
```

The FORMAT function is used to change the display characteristics of PAL expressions. The way the values appear depends on their type. This script loops through the 11 formats that you can use for an expression that evaluates to a date type. See Part II for a complete listing of the FORMAT function.

## 7.15 CHAPTER SUMMARY

The PAL canvas is a view of the screen that exists only under script control—once script play ends, the canvas disappears, revealing the Paradox workspace. PAL canvas commands help you control interaction with the user by enabling you to create and change screen images. During script play, manipulation of Paradox objects takes place behind this scrim on the Paradox workspace (or off the workspace entirely). The next chapter, Visualizing and Controlling the Workspace, focuses on what happens behind the canvas during script play.

## NOTES

1. MESSAGE is meant for a maximum of 80 characters and does not support word-wrap; the message wraps backward character by character and will move up if it is longer than 80 characters.

# Chapter 8

# Visualizing and Controlling the Workspace

Keeping track of the activity on the workspace is critical to controlling Paradox during script play. This chapter introduces some of the tools that can help you control the workspace.

"Workspace—A metaphorical space where all Paradox operations take place."

## 8.1 THE CROWDED WORKSPACE

In interactive Paradox, nearly everything that happens to your data happens on the workspace. The same is true when Paradox works under program control. Here's a four-line script:

```
CLEAR              ;clear canvas
CLEARALL           ;clear workspace
CoEdit "Customer"
WAIT TABLE UNTIL "F2"
```

This simple script clears the canvas, clears the workspace, and does a simple WAIT TABLE in CoEdit mode. This sets Paradox in motion, checking for Paradox objects in the "Customer" family.
   Paradox checks for:

- Customer.SET, the settings file, and displays the table according to the settings or defaults (if there are no settings);

- Customer.PX, to see if the table is keyed. If it is, Paradox opens this primary index file;
- Maintained secondary indexes, or all files that match Customer.X## and Customer.Y##.
- Customer.VAL and puts validity checks in place. When using validity checks, other tables may be referenced through tablelookups, which need not be on the workspace.

So what appears to be one file on the workspace is usually the work of many. With several images, the Paradox workspace becomes even more complex. Here are some examples of information that may be important when attempting to control Paradox with a script:

- There is only one workspace cursor. No matter how many images are on the workspace, only one image contains the workspace cursor and that image is the *current image*.
- Every image, whether display or query, maintains a *current position* with a corresponding *row number* and *column number*. *When moving between images, the workspace cursor moves to the current position within the image.*
- There are two types of images: *Query* and *Display* images. Tables displayed in either tableview or formview are Display images. Every Query image must conform to strict rules that make it a valid query.
- Though the row number is equivalent to the *record number* within a display image, the *row number* of a query image is simply the line that the cursor is on (query images don't have record numbers). The *column number* of the current position is the current field within the image.
- When using a multitable form in Paradox3, a single image may become multiple images by relationships to linked or unlinked tables not explicitly placed on the workspace. In Edit or CoEdit mode, by virtue of the constraints referential integrity imposes on these related images, the tables may be *link-locked* and therefore may not behave like independent tables.
- Within a display image, record numbers of detail records in a multitable form are likely to be different than their absolute record numbers in the full-detail table.

## 8.2 "FLYING BLIND"

When script play begins, the visual nature of interactive Paradox is lost, and you're in effect "flying blind." A query created under script control won't show on the screen. An answer table will only display if you tell it to. If an error occurs and an error message appears on the workspace, you won't see the message. If you attempt to assign field values to a table that is link-locked, the assignment simply won't work and you may not know that it didn't work.

Program control in Paradox means controlling activity on the workspace, which, to be successful, depends on a clear picture of the ever-changing workspace. PAL gives you gauges to let you know where you are and what's going on, and controls to help you pilot Paradox while flying blind. Through PAL status functions and workspace commands, nearly any question about the Paradox workspace that needs to be answered can be answered. This section introduces tools and techniques for understanding, visualizing, and controlling the Paradox workspace.

## 8.3 SYSMODE( )

At the beginning of a Paradox session, the workspace is clear, available memory is at a maximum, and the system mode is "Main." The SYSMODE() function returns a string representing the current mode of 12 system modes. It is usually compared against a string or assigned to a variable.

```
IF SYSMODE() = "CoEdit" THEN
     <statements>
ENDIF
```

SYSMODE() will return a string with one of the following. As a reminder, since string comparisons are always case-sensitive, SYSMODE() will never report "Coedit"; it may report "CoEdit".

```
"CoEdit" "Create" "DataEntry" "Edit" "Form" "Graph" "Main" "Password" "Report"
 "Restructure" "Script" "Sort"
```

Each mode represents a Paradox subsystem, each with its own menu. Keeping track of the system mode enables you to make decisions about what is and what is not possible on the workspace. For example, if you are in the "CoEdit" mode and press [Menu], you can't {Cancel} your editing session, you can only choose {DO-IT!} to end it. The SYSMODE() function lets you know what to expect.

## 8.4 IMAGENO( ) AND IMAGETYPE( )

As tables are viewed, edited, or queried, images appear on the screen and are assigned a positive integer corresponding to their position from the topmost image. The IMAGENO() function returns the image's current number. To make the topmost image the current image, you can issue a simple PAL command:

```
MOVETO 1 ;since 1 is topmost image, this makes it current
```

The IMAGENO() of an image is dynamic—for example, as you add a Query image, the number assigned to each display image will increase by one because Query images are inserted above Display images. A Query image added to the workspace becomes the last Query image. For example if you have two Query images and a Display image on the workspace and you add a Query image, the IMAGENO() for the new Query image is 3. As you view additional tables, each in turn is assigned an image number. As mentioned above, images on the workspace are either tables, called Display images, or queries, called Query images. IMAGETYPE() returns one of two strings: "Display" or "Query" if an image is present, or "None" if no images are present.

In multitable forms, images are numbered according to their chronological order of placement when the form was designed. If a detail table from a multitable form is placed on the workspace prior to its appearance in the multitable form, it will retain the original image number assignment. The total number of images on the workspace can be determined with the NIMAGES() function.

```
IF NImages() = 0 THEN
  ;Is equivalent to IF Imagetype() = "None"
  <do something>
ENDIF
```

## 8.5 UPIMAGE, DOWNIMAGE, AND CLEARIMAGE

A few general workspace commands work like their function key counterparts. The UpImage and DownImage commands perform like their namesakes, the [F3] and [F4] keys. The ClearImage command, like the [F8] key, clears the current image from the screen and renumbers the images present from the top down.

## 8.6 CLEARALL, SETDIR, AND RESET

Tables on the workspace reflect data in memory, and changes made to data in tables are not necessarily saved to disk immediately. There are a few commands that affect not only images on the workspace, but also changes made to tables in memory and, subsequently, on disk as well.

In interactive Paradox, pressing the [ClearAll] key clears all images from the workspace and writes the changes made in any table to disk, clearing memory in the process. Like the [ClearAll] key [Alt F8], the CLEARALL command clears all images of any type from the workspace, but does not change information in memory or on disk.[1]

SETDIR, the abbreviated menu command for {Tools} {More} {Directory}, affects the workspace much like the [ClearAll] key. SETDIR, followed by a directory name, clears all images from the workspace, flushes all changes to disk, returns the system mode to "Main," and deletes all temporary tables.

A more powerful PAL command, RESET, clears all images from the screen, writes changes to disk, clears memory, deletes all temporary tables, revokes passwords that have been cleared with the UNPASSWORD command, and clears all locks from tables. With large tables or complex applications involving hundreds or thousands of changed records, all of this disk and memory activity takes time. The more changes, the longer the time.

The time these commands take to execute is more pronounced with the use of expanded memory or the larger memory address space available with Paradox OS|2 and Paradox386.

With Paradox accessing tables on a floppy disk, the distinction between data in memory and data on disk becomes more critical. Before removing a floppy disk that has been accessed by Paradox, you must issue a command such as SETDIR that flushes all changed memory blocks to disk. If you don't, you'll be staring at an unwelcome message: "Unexpected condition: File Read. Leaving Paradox."

## 8.7 Window( )

Paradox messages that appear on the workspace are invisible to the user under script control. The Window() function enables you to grab the contents of any message that appears on the workspace.

```
IF WINDOW( ) = "Match not found" THEN
  Return False
ENDIF
```

It's often used to pass the message along to a user or interpreted to help change program direction.

## 8.8 MENUCHOICE( )

When a menu is displayed, MenuChoice() returns the currently highlighted choice as a string in proper case (such as "View," "Ask," or "Report") or the word "Error" if a menu is not displayed.

```
MENU {ValCheck} {Define} Enter {LowValue} Lowvalue.a = MENUCHOICE()
CtrlBreak          ;clears menu
? "The low value for this field is ",Lowvalue.a,"."
```

MENUCHOICE() also returns the value of any type-in prompt.

## 8.9 HELPMODE( )

HelpMode() is one of four "minor" mode status functions.[2] If help is active, the function returns a string that represents the type of help available.

```
"Help" ;for Paradox help
"LookupHelp" ; for TableLookup help
"None" ; if help is not active.
```

## 8.10 TABLE-ORIENTED FUNCTIONS

Table-oriented functions report on images on the workspace; table-oriented commands influence how those images are displayed on the workspace.

## 8.11 TABLE( )

The Table() function returns the name of the current table or the table referenced by the current query image as a string. If the first character of the string is a letter, that letter is capitalized (e.g., the first letter may be an uppercase drive specifier).

```
IF TABLE() = "Customer" THEN ;This is true for a table in
 ; the current directory.
 ; is different from

IF TABLE() = "CUSTOMER" THEN        ;This will never be true
```

If the table is in the current directory, no path is prefixed with the TABLE() function. If the table is in another directory, the full path of the table, but not the drive specifier, is returned. If the table is in another drive, the drive specifier is included as well.

## 8.12 ISFORMVIEW( )

IsFormView() returns True when a table is displayed in FormView and False when it is in TableView. This command is particularly useful with multitable forms, which automatically place multiple tables on the workspace when in FormView only.

```
;want image in formview
IF IMAGETYPE() = "Display" THEN ;can only toggle display images into form
 IF NOT ISFORMVIEW() THEN
    FORMKEY
 ENDIF
ENDIF
```

The number of tables on the workspace may change dramatically when a multitable form is placed in TableView. A multitable form can display up to six tables; when flipped to TableView with the FORMKEY command, there may be only one table on the workspace.

## 8.13 FORM( )

The name of the current form can be determined with the Form() function, which returns "F," "1"-"14," or "None" if no form is present.

```
IF FORM() <> "None" THEN
 MESSAGE "Now using ",TABLE()," with form ",FORM()
ENDIF


IF IsFormView() = False
; is equivalent to: IF Form() = "None" ;which is not as explicit as IsFormView,
; therefore not preferred
```

## 8.14 COLNO( )

Every table is divided into columns. Each column is assigned a column number, starting with the leftmost column in the image (in a display image, the record number column). The fourth field in a table is in the fifth column. Caution: The result of using the COLNO() function on an image can be misleading, because the column number reported is sensitive to the rotation of columns within an image and the column number reported will not always be the same value for the same field name. For example, the first field of the "Customer" table, the [Cust ID] field, when rotated to the 10th field in the table, will report a value of 11.

While creating a report or form or editing a script, COLNO() returns the column at the cursor.

## 8.15 ROWNO( )

The ROWNO() function returns a value from 1 to 22 representing the current table row. When you first view a table, row numbers coincidentally correspond to record numbers, but in fact bear no relation to the record number. If 3 of 50 records are being displayed and the cursor is on the second line from the top of the image, ROWNO() returns 2, regardless of the record number. Within a regular form, ROWNO() always returns 1; within a multirecord region of a form, ROWNO() returns a value of from 1 to 22.

This function can also be used in the script editor, or the form or report modes.

## 8.16 RECORD ORIENTED

All record numbers are dynamic: They may change when records are inserted or deleted. The current record number in tableview can be represented either as the value returned by the RECNO() function or the special symbol [#].

With Paradox3, there is a difference between what we will term "absolute" and "relative" record numbers. Absolute record numbers are always reported by the record number symbol [#]. In tableview, the RECNO() function will always report the same value as [#]. However, in a linked detail table in multitable form, RECNO() will report a value relative to the first record in the restricted view—a relative value.

Record numbers of records in other images on the workspace can be referenced by their tablename and a pointer symbol followed by the pound sign: "->#." For example, if the "Orders" table is on the workspace, the current record number within it is [Orders->#].

## 8.17 NIMAGERECORDS( )

The number of records in the current image, whether in tableview or formview, can be determined with the NIMAGERECORDS() function.

```
IF LINKTYPE() <> "None" THEN
 PROMPT "Editing "+STRVAL(RECNO())+" of "+STRVAL(NIMAGERECORDS())+" Linked records."
ENDIF
```

In CoEdit mode, the NIMAGERECORDS function reports a minimum value of one record in a detail table of a multitable form.

## 8.18 ATFIRST( ) AND ATLAST( )

These functions simply tell you if you are at the first or last record in the image. Whether in a normal or a restricted view of a table, the ATFIRST() function returns True if the current record is the first record (one with a RECNO() of 1). Likewise, ATLAST() returns True if it is the last record in the current image in tableview or if it is the last record in the restricted view of a detail table of a multitable form.

## 8.19 BOT( ) AND EOT( )

While moving through records with the SKIP, MOVETO, or LOCATE commands, an additional test is necessary. The BOT() function tests whether one of these movement commands would move the cursor past the beginning of the table; EOT() tests for a move past the last record in the current image. Both respect the restricted view of a detail table in a multitable form. Both functions return a value of True or False.

```
;Scan backwards
WHILE NOT BOT()
  SKIP -1
ENDWHILE
```

## 8.20 FIELD-ORIENTED FUNCTIONS

### 8.20.1 [ ]

As was noted in the chapter titled "Language Elements," the contents of a field in an image can be represented a variety of ways. The current field is represented by the field name in square brackets. If the "Employee ID" field is the current field in the current table, it can be represented by empty square brackets [ ]. Thus, if the cursor is in the [Employee ID] field, instead of using an assignment such as:

```
[Employee ID] = 124
```

you could simply write:

```
[] = 124
```

Values in other fields can be represented by their field names in square brackets—for example [Cust ID]. Fields in other tables on the workspace can be referenced by preceding their field identifiers with the name of their table followed by a representation of an arrow using the dash and the "greater than" signs—for example, [Invoice−>Cust ID]. The current field in the invoice table is simply [Invoice−>]. If the image is a query image, a "Q" in parentheses must follow the name of the table—for example:

```
[Customer(Q)->]
```

Assignment cannot be made to fields in other than the current table if the form is link-locked. You must move to the other image and then make the assignment. For a complete listing of these field assignments, turn to page 75.

### 8.20.2 FIELD( ), FIELDTYPE( ), and FIELDSTR( )

Three field functions return strings. FIELD() reports the field name as it appears as a string in the structure of the table. The maximum field-name width is 25 characters. The value of a field of any type can be returned as a string with the FIELDSTR() function. A field's type can be determined with the FIELDTYPE() function, which returns a string of:
"D"
"N"
"S"
"$" or

"A###"
where the ### is an integer from 1 to 255.

### 8.20.3 ISFIELDVIEW( )

Another of the minor modes, FieldView, which allows character-by-character scrolling in fields, can be determined with the IsFieldView() function, which returns True or False. Pressing [Enter], [Esc], or [Help] in FIELDVIEW may have unintended effects in a WAIT condition. See page 196, Part Two, which overcomes some of these effects.

## 8.21 QUERY-ORIENTED FUNCTIONS

Although Query images have much in common with Display images, there are a few special Query commands that allow you to build query statements on the fly. Query images abide by a stricter set of rules than do Display images. Field assignments using field specifiers will work in Query images, but if the assignment is unsuccessful, subsequent attempts to move off the field will be unsuccessful until the Query field is valid.

Five commands work like their function key counterparts in Query images.

Check
CheckPlus
CheckDescending
GroupBy
Example

### 8.21.1 CheckMarkStatus

A special function reports on the status of the first four of these commands. If a field is identified with one of the field selection symbols, CHECKMARKSTATUS() returns a string of:

```
"Check"
"CheckPlus"
"CheckDescending"
"GroupBy"
```

If a field in a Query image isn't selected, CHECKMARKSTATUS() will return a null string, " "

## 8.22 REPORTS AND FORMS WORKSPACE FUNCTIONS

There are a few functions that can report information about the workspace in the report generator and the form subsystem. Some of these functions also work outside these subsystems.

### 8.22.1 CURSORCHAR(), CURSORLINE(), ROWNO(), and COLNO()

The report and forms mode are rather free-form in nature. That is, the cursor can generally roam all across the workspace, unimpeded by the column restrictions found in tables. Here navigating about the workspace depends on knowing which row the cursor is in with ROWNO(), and which column with COLNO(). The character at the cursor can be determined with the CURSORCHAR() function. The CURSORLINE() function returns the entire line at the cursor. Both CURSORCHAR() and CURSORLINE() return a null string (" ") if the character or line at the cursor is blank.

### 8.22.2 NPAGES( ), PAGENO( ) and PAGEWIDTH( )

While navigating through the report specification under script control, you can get a sense of its boundaries with the PAGEWIDTH() and NPAGES() commands

```
Totalwidth.n = NPAGES() * PAGEWIDTH()
```

The current page of a report or a form has a page number. This can be useful in restricting access to forms:

```
IF ISFORMVIEW() AND editpagetwo.l = FALSE THEN
  IF PAGENO()=2 THEN ;restrict access to 2
    PgDn ;move to next record
  ENDIF
ENDIF
```

### 8.22.3 BANDINFO( )

Within the report generator, BANDINFO() gives you additional vertical position information by reporting which of the report bands noted by the cursor is in proper case:

"Report Header"
"Report Footer"
"Form Band, Field Squeeze, Line Squeeze"

### 8.22.4 IsInsertMode( )

Depending on the status of the mode indicator for the status of the Insert key in forms, reports, and scripts, the ISINSERTMODE function returns True or False. The Ins command toggles the mode.

```
IF NOT ISINSERTMODE() THEN
   INS ;toggle it on
ENDIF
```

### 8.22.5 VERTRULER

VERTRULER is the only specialized command in the report or script modes that has a purely visual effect on the workspace. It is only useful as a command in a script that displays the report generator. You cannot have a script edit a script, and thus the VERTRULER command will only work from a miniscript played within the script editor.

## 8.23 CHAPTER SUMMARY

To program the Paradox workspace, the functions and commands introduced in this chapter provide a means of evaluating conditions and changing program flow based on them. This chapter is a summary; details about syntax and examples of their use are found in the examples section.

## NOTES

1. This is not true for multiuser Paradox. We describe a routine for clearing all query images on page 446.
2. The other minor mode status functions are IsInsertMode(), IsFormView(), and IsFieldView().

# Chapter 9

# Procedures

Surround a script with two simple statements and it becomes a procedure. Once you play a script that defines a procedure, the procedure remains in memory as long as script play continues (or until you explicitly RELEASE it). Whereas scripts have to be reinterpreted every time you want them to play, procedures, once read into memory, can then be called like built-in PAL functions and commands. This chapter introduces procedures.

## 9.1 SCRIPT PARSING

When you play a script, you are instructing PAL to read, interpret, and execute the script statement by statement: read, interpret, execute; read, interpret, execute. The reading and interpreting of a script is known as *parsing*. If a syntax error causes the script to halt, PAL stops dead in its tracks and presents you with the Cancel/Debug menu. Unless you correct the condition that led to the error, or skip over the current statement with the PAL debugger, Paradox will never get to the next statement. So during script play, each PAL statement is not only independent—it is blind to the existence of a predecessor or successor. Once it executes, a PAL script statement is simply discarded. If you repeatedly play a script, Paradox must reread and reinterpret the entire script at every pass, unaware that it executed the same statements a moment before.[1]

## 9.2 PROCEDURES

Procedures are designed to work differently, parsing a series of statements at once, and storing these parsed statements in available memory before execution. By defining a script (or a portion of a script) as a procedure, you separate reading and interpretation from execution. These separate steps are termed procedure definition and procedure *calling*. While in memory, a procedure can be called exactly like a PAL function. Most importantly, as long as the procedure is in memory, you can call it as many times as you need without it being reread and reinterpreted from the script.

The main objective of creating procedures is to more closely bind your application code with native Paradox code, making natural, logical extensions to PAL that fit your application's needs. In this chapter we will introduce the definition and calling of procedures within scripts. In the next chapter, you will see how procedures can be more efficiently stored and called from special files, called procedure libraries.

## 9.3 PROCEDURE DEFINITION

You write, edit, and debug procedures in regular script files. A script, or a portion of a script, becomes a procedure definition by enclosing it within two commands:

- At the beginning of the procedure, the word PROC,[2] followed by a procedure name, followed by an optional parameter list inside a matched pair of required parentheses;
- at its end, the word ENDPROC.

Here is its generalized form:

```
PROC procname([VarNameList])
 <statements>
ENDPROC
```

PROC and ENDPROC control program flow and define a procedure's scope; they do not invoke the procedure. We will describe the rules for procedure naming in a few pages. When PAL encounters the word PROC in a script, it immediately suspends execution. Each statement within the procedure is then read and interpreted. If the statement conforms to PAL syntax, the interpreted instruction is placed in consecutive order in memory. If an error is encountered, the Cancel/Debug menu is presented as if the script were executing. When ENDPROC is encountered, the procedure definition is considered complete.

## 9.4 CALLING PROCEDURES

Once in memory, a procedure can be called by name from a script or another procedure.

```
PROC DoSomething()
<Statements>
ENDPROC

<Statements>
DoSomething()
<Statements>
```

Most importantly, a procedure thus defined can be called as many times as necessary without having to be reread or reinterpreted.

## 9.5 PROCEDURE PARSING

The script parsing feature of procedures can be used as an integrated spelling checker for PAL. Not only are obvious errors caught, like misspelled commands or missing quotation marks or brackets, but program flow is checked as well. A message like "ENDPROC not expected" may mean that there is a missing ENDIF, ENDWHILE, ENDFOR, or ENDSCAN. There may be several of these missing. Yet if the procedure is successfully loaded into memory, that is, if PAL is able to work its way from PROC to ENDPROC, the code between is syntactically correct. With one rare exception,[3] making a script a procedure means that the code will never crash with a "Syntax error" message. No such claim can be made of even the smallest of scripts: though a script plays a thousand times, there is no guarantee that it is free of syntax errors. Here's a simple example:

```
Menu {ask} TABLE()
Check
Do_It!
IF NOT IsEmpty("Answer") THEN
  QUIT "Here are the unique records"
ENDIF
QUIP "There are no records found in the answer table"
```

This script branches past an obvious syntax error as long as the resulting "Answer" table has records. If the selected table always has records, the word "QUIP" should never be encountered. If instead this code fragment is made into a procedure, the procedure will stop being interpreted when the unknown "QUIP" command is encountered:

```
Proc GetUniqueRecords.u()
  Menu {ask} TABLE()
  Check
  Do_It!
```

```
    IF NOT IsEmpty("Answer") THEN
      QUIT "Here are the unique records"
    ENDIF
    QUIP "There are no records found in the answer table"
ENDPROC
```

## 9.6 USING PROC/ENDPROC TO DEBUG SCRIPTS

In complex scripts, errors of syntax may be well hidden, nested within IFs within ELSEs within IFs. Because of its need to examine every character in a script for proper syntax construction, a procedure is a powerful debugging tool. Simply bracket any script with PROC Test() and ENDPROC:

```
PROC Test()
<statements>
ENDPROC
```

Then play the script. Syntax errors will trigger the Cancel/Debug menu. Correct errors, one-by-one, by repeatedly playing the script and making corrections until it plays without an error. Because scripts as procedures aren't executed, but merely read and interpreted, debugging scripts in procedure format is faster than debugging scripts in script form. Once a script passes this syntax acid test of making it a procedure, you can revert the procedure to its script form by simply deleting the PROC and ENDPROC statements from the script.[4]

## 9.7 PROCEDURE NAMING RULES

Like variable names, procedure names must start with a letter, be followed by letters or numbers, and can include three special characters: the underscore, the dollar sign, and the period. Unlike script names, which are restricted to eight characters, the PAL manual states that procedure names may be up to 132 characters in length. However, undocumented restrictions make procedure names that are longer than 31 characters unreliable. Here's a 31-character procedure name:

```
PROC BeepAnnoyinglyUntilAUserWakesUp()
```

It turns out that this inadvertent length restriction on procedure names is really no restriction at all—31 characters should be plenty for even the most imaginative names you devise. The general rule: make a procedure name as long as it should be to clearly express its purpose, but no longer than it needs to be. If you name procedures carefully, your application code will be easier to understand, maintain, and document.

As with our naming of variables, we have incorporated a system of naming procedures that serves a number of purposes. Explaining this system of naming is intertwined with another important aspect of procedures, returning values.

## 9.8 RETURNING VALUES

Like a PAL function, a procedure can return a single value to the script or procedure that called it. This is done with an optional part of the RETURN command:

```
PROC procname()
  <statements>
  RETURN Expression
ENDPROC
```

In a procedure, the returned value is automatically assigned to the special system variable, RETVAL. When the procedure returns to the calling script, this new value is available for use. The value returned can be of type:

- Logical Constant (True or False)
- Alphanumeric
- Currency
- Date
- Number
- Short Number (integer)

It's easy to have procedure names that can resemble PAL function names. Unless you've memorized the names of all of the functions or devised a naming convention that avoids conflicts, your procedure naming can get you into trouble. Thus we adapted the convention we use to name variables in procedure naming. All our procedure names begin with a name that reflects its purpose and ends with a suffix distinguishing the type of returned value.

```
procname.a()     ;alphanumeric
procname.c()     ;currency
procname.d()     ;date
procname.l()     ;logical
```

```
procname.n()    ;numeric
procname.s()    ;short (integer)
procname.v()    ;type may vary
```

If the procedure doesn't return a value, it is given a type ".u" for "unassigned":

```
procname.u()    ;unassigned
```

Here are some examples of procedures named this way:

```
GetUserID.s() ;returns a short number for an ID
CalcInvoiceAmt.c() ;returns $ value of invoice
IsHelpOn.l() ;returns True or False
```

Naming procedures in this manner offers several notable advantages:

- Eliminates conflicts with all present and future PAL reserved words, greatly reducing the effort of coding conversions when a new paradox version appears.
- Cuts down on variable type mismatches. If you see assignment like:

```
UserID.a = GetUserID.s()
```

  where an attempt is made to assign an alphanumeric ID with a procedure that generates a short number, the differing types can be more easily seen and corrected.
- Makes the procedure's purpose more easily understood.

For a more complete discussion of this naming technique, turn to the chapter entitled "Language Elements."

## 9.9 PROCEDURE PARAMETERS

When defining or calling procedures, the procedure name, like a PAL function name, must be followed by parentheses. The parentheses may be empty, for example:

```
PROC GetUserID.s()
```

or the parentheses may contain names of variables separated by commas, termed *formal parameters*. These optional parameter variable names allow you to pass values to the procedure and enable you to make a procedure widely useful.

Here's an example of how parameters might be used:

```
PROC GetUserID.s (IdTable.a, Field.a)
  View IDTable.a
  MOVETO FIELD Field.a
  UserId.s = []
  CoEditKey
  [] = [] + 1
  Do_It!
  CLEARIMAGE
  RETURN UserId.s
ENDPROC
```

The values substituted for these parameters can then be used throughout the procedure. In this example, when the procedure "GetUserID.s" is called, PAL will expect it to be followed by two values in parentheses.

```
NewEmpID.s = GetUserID.s ("NewIDs", "Employee")
```

With this example, the table "NewIDs" is viewed and the "Employee" field, containing the next employee ID number, is assigned to UserID.s. The current ID value is then incremented by one, and the value assigned to the variable UserID.s is returned and assigned to NewEmpID.s.

The actual values passed to the procedure are called *arguments* to the procedure. In this example, the parameters are IDTable.a and FieldName.a, and the arguments are "NewIDs" and "Employee." Arguments to a procedure must equate to a single value; they may be constants, functions, variables, array elements, or combinations of these operators. Arrays, which by nature identify several or many array elements, cannot be procedure arguments. To add a final layer of complication, in the above example, each of the parameters can be assigned before the call to variable names, and then the variable names passed as arguments:

```
Table.a = "NewIDs"
Field.a = "Employee"
NewEmpID.a = GetUserID.s(Table.a, Field.a)
```

Because actual values are given to the procedure, this process is termed **call by value.**[5] One of the most important aspects of this technique is that the value or values passed are unchanged by the procedure. In this example, at the end of the procedure call, Table.a is still "NewIDs" and Field.a is still "Employee," though NewEmpID.a has been given a new value.

Being able to pass parameters to a procedure means that you can design procedures that are more generally useful—more generic. There is no theoretical limit to the number of parameters you can pass to a procedure.

## 9.10 REUSING PROCEDURE NAMES

There are some restrictions when reusing procedure names within the course of one script. The PAL manual states:

"You can't define a procedure without releasing it first. Once a procedure is defined, PAL ignores all subsequent PROC commands for the same procedure name."

Procedure names should be unique to a session.[6] Once a procedure name is used, you cannot redefine the procedure to do something else unless you explicitly release it from memory with the RELEASE PROCS command:

```
RELEASE PROCS {ALL | ProcNameList}
```

The ALL option releases every procedure in memory. A ProcNameList is a list of procedure names, without their parentheses or parameters, separated by commas:

```
RELEASE PROCS DoSomething.1, Test.1, LoopTimingTest.v
```

## 9.11 ADVANTAGES

One of the principal benefits of making a script into a procedure is increased execution speed. In scripts that are long, complex, or involve repeated looping, the difference can be quite dramatic. To give you an idea, here's a simple test—an otherwise useless script that counts from 1 to 10,000:

```
CLEAR ;Clear the canvas
? TIME() ;Note the time
FOR n FROM 1 TO 10000      ;Begin FOR loop
  n = n ;Make an assignment
ENDFOR
? TIME() ;Recheck & display the time
n = GETCHAR() ;Leave on screen until a key is pressed
```

Run this script, and note the time difference in seconds. Changing the script into a procedure is a matter of adding three lines:

```
PROC LoopTimingTest.u() ;Test takes no arguments
CLEAR
? TIME()
```

```
FOR n FROM 1 TO 10000
 n = n
ENDFOR
? TIME()
n = GETCHAR()
ENDPROC
LoopTimingTest.u()   ;call the PROC
```

This test should show over a 60% improvement in total time of execution. When played, each command in the nonprocedurized version has to be reinterpreted each time through the loop. Once the procedure version is in memory, it simply executes 10,000 times. The greater the number of commands in a loop, the greater the time difference between script and procedure execution.

## 9.12 KEEP PROCEDURES SMALL

Procedures, like scripts, should be modular in design and serve a singular purpose. When you keep them small, procedures are easier to understand and debug. Yet unlike a script, many procedures can be stored in a single script file, allowing you to cut down on the number of script files that an application requires. Because a typical application without procedures may involve dozens of scripts, the same application may be contained in a few scripts, each containing multiple procedure definitions.

## 9.13 VARIABLES WITHIN SCRIPTS

Every variable you assign in a script occupies memory. If a script uses a variable, the value of the variable remains in memory until:

- it is released with the RELEASE VARS command,
- it is overwritten with another assignment of the same name, or
- the Paradox session ends.

Variables defined in scripts are known as *global* variables because they are universally available to the Paradox environment. One of the advantages to a global variable is that its value can be used whenever and wherever needed. Yet managing global variables takes work—both careful observation of what a variable does, and accurate tracking of how and when it may interfere with another assignment or operation.

- Though global variables are easy to reuse, reusing them can often lead to confusion. What was just a date variable may now contain an alphanumeric string.
- Assigning and reassigning the same names for variables that are trivial, such as counters in a loop, allow you to reuse memory rather than cluttering it up needlessly. However, you must keep track of which counters are currently active.
- A misplaced assignment can wreak havoc on an application. Consistent variable naming can help avoid conflicts between variables, but releasing a variable once it's no longer needed is a good solution to many concerns. However, releasing variables depends on knowing when a variable is no longer needed, which isn't always easy to determine.

## 9.14 VARIABLES WITHIN PROCEDURES

Through procedures, PAL provides a means of greatly reducing or eliminating the work involved in managing variables. There are two techniques that rely on optional parameters to the PROC command, and one technique that is implicit in the PROC command's design:

- Variables can be declared as *PRIVATE* to the procedure.
- Procedures can be made self-contained units, shut off from the rest of an application, with the *CLOSED* option.
- Formal parameters to a procedure are automatically PRIVATE to the procedure.

## 9.15 PRIVATE VARIABLES

Private variables restrict the domain, that is, the range of a variable's travels; and its life, the length of its existence. This is done with the optional PRIVATE declaration.

```
PROC procname()
 PRIVATE VarNameList
 <statements>
ENDPROC
```

The word PRIVATE immediately follows the procedure name. *VarNameList* is a comma-separated list of variables that are to be declared private. All variables in the list will be released automatically once the procedure ends. All variables not declared in the list, but used in the procedure, are by default global.

## 9.16 DYNAMIC SCOPING OF VARIABLES

Procedures that call procedures, like segments of a telescope, are separate yet interrelated. A private variable's sphere of influence is restricted to the procedure in which it is declared *and all procedures called by it.* This concept, known as *dynamic scoping of variables,* has many implications. For instance, a variable that has been declared PRIVATE to a procedure is "public" to all procedures called within the scope of the procedure with the private declaration. For example, the following procedure has a single private variable, LightColor.a:

```
PROC GreenLight.u()
  PRIVATE LightColor.a
  LightColor.a = "Green"
  CLEAR
  ? LightColor.a
  SLEEP 2000
  ChangetoYellow.u()
ENDPROC
```

When this procedure, GreenLight.u() makes a call to a second procedure, ChangetoYellow.u(), the variable LightColor.a is available to and can be changed by it:

```
PROC ChangetoYellow.u()
  ? "Still "+LightColor.a
  LightColor.a = "Yellow"
  ? LightColor.a
  SLEEP 2000
  ChangetoRed.u()
ENDPROC
```

And the process goes on and on. When the third procedure, ChangetoRed.a(), is invoked, it too has access to the variable declared private in the topmost procedure. You can easily see this by introducing the DEBUG command into the middle of the final procedure definition, and then calling the topmost script:

```
PROC ChangetoRed.u()
  LightColor.a = "Red"
  ? LightColor.a
  DEBUG ;this will invoke the debugger when called
  SLEEP 2000
ENDPROC
GreenLight.u()
```

When DEBUG is encountered, procedure execution is suspended, awaiting your control with the PAL debugger commands. The Where? key, [Ctrl w], will display the following:

```
Script LIGHTS

 Proc  GreenLight.u()
  LightColor.a = Red

  Proc  ChangetoYellow.u()

   Proc  ChangetoRed.u()

    **Debugger**

     (You are here)
```

```
                                        Press any key to continue...
 Script: LIGHTS  Line:  22              Type Control-Q to Quit
        ▶ SLEEP 2000
```

All variables declared as private to a procedure will be revealed in the {Where?} screen of the debugger.

## 9.17 FORMAL PARAMETERS ARE PRIVATE

Formal parameters to a procedure are temporary variables as well. Formal parameters are assigned for the duration of the procedure call and released when the PROC completes. This means that you don't have to declare the variables passed to a procedure as PRIVATE. Thus with a previous example,

```
GetUserID.a(Table.a, Field.a)
```

the two formal parameters, Table.a and Field.a, are variables whose lifetimes are limited by the call to the procedure. Once the procedure ends, these variables are released. In addition, as with private variables, the values of formal parameters are available to procedures called by the procedure in which they are declared. Thus, Table.a and Field.a are available to procedures that GetUserID.a calls. Only when GetUserID.a finishes are Table.a and Field.a released from memory.

## 9.18 TRACKING MEMORY: MEMLEFT( )

The MEMLEFT() function is a measure of the available working memory within Paradox—that which the PAL manual refers to as the "central memory pool." Tracking the value that MEMLEFT() returns enables you to measure how procedures use and restore memory. You can determine the value of MEM-LEFT() at any time through the PAL Menu:

**Step 1**
Press:      [Alt F10]
**Step 2**
Select:     {Value}
**Step 3**
Type:       MEMLEFT()
**Step 4**
Press:      [Enter]

The amount of memory in Kb will be displayed in the lower right of your screen. In theory, releasing a procedure and all the variables that it used should return the amount of memory the procedure used to the central memory pool, freeing the memory for other procedure calls. Yet no matter how carefully you manage memory by releasing unneeded variables and procedures, executing large or complicated applications usually decreases the available memory as the application is used.

## 9.19 CLOSED PROCS

The CLOSED option of the PROC command, introduced in Paradox3, helps recover all the available memory used by procedures and variables. When you follow the PROC declaration with the CLOSED option, Paradox treats the procedure as a world unto itself:

```
PROC CLOSED procname( )
<statements>
ENDPROC
```

Shutting a procedure off from the rest of an application means:

- All variables declared and used in a CLOSED procedure are automatically private.

- All procedures read into memory and called by the CLOSED procedure are automatically released when this level of procedure ends.
- If you have global variables that are necessary for the operation of any portion of the CLOSED procedure, they must be declared with another PROC option that applies only to CLOSED procedures, the USEVARS option.

```
PROC CLOSED PrintInvoice.u()
 USEVARS Custid.s, Invoice.d
 <statements>
ENDPROC
```

Although up to six levels of closed procedures are supported, the PAL manual recommends that:

> "Within each major module, regular procs should be used to structure the code that does the actual work."

We will discuss the use of CLOSED procedure more thoroughly in the next chapter, "Procedure Libraries."

## 9.20 ERROR HANDLING

Expecting the unexpected is what error handling is about. There are three classes of errors in PAL:

- Syntax errors are errors in the use of elements of the language—a misspelled command, a missing comma or parentheses. By making a script a procedure, you eliminate the possibility of a syntax error remaining in your code.
- The second class of programming errors in PAL are errors of logic and there is no easy way to eliminate them. Examples of logic error are: a WHILE loop without a QUITLOOP, RETURN, or EXIT; a calculation based on the wrong fields or an incorrect constant; a procedure that calls itself without end (faulty use of recursion).
- The third class of errors can't be eliminated; they can only be anticipated and handled when encountered. These are called run errors and they are induced by events or conditions external to the script. A disk drive might suddenly be full or accidentally write-protected; a table might be password protected and no password issued; a lock might be in effect that restricts the ability of a script to perform as designated; a user might have deleted a table. In short, there are dozens of reasons why a valid script might suddenly fail because of a run error.

## 9.21 ERRORPROC

Careful coding can prevent many errors, but there always seems to be one last bug. PAL doesn't allow you to recover from a syntax error; that is, you can't step over the command that caused a syntax error in the PAL debugger. You must edit the script that induced the error to proceed. Yet PAL includes a mechanism to allow you to anticipate and recover from run errors, enabling your code to "expect the unexpected." This mechanism consists of two elements:

- A system variable called ERRORPROC, which designates the name of a procedure to be invoked in the event of a run error.
- The procedure itself, with which you can evaluate the run error through three special functions, attempt to change the condition that caused the error, and return to the script or procedure that caused the error to occur with a value that instructs Paradox whether to stop or how to continue.

The variable, ERRORPROC, is the second *system variable* we've introduced. RETVAL, the first, was introduced in "Script Writing Fundamentals," and is set by a variety of commands under a wide array of circumstances. In contrast, ERRORPROC has to be set by you by direct assignment.

```
ERRORPROC = "ErrorProc.n"
```

Though you can reassign it whenever you want, only one procedure can be designated as the ERRORPROC at a time.

Not only can the nature of the error condition be determined, but the statement in the script or procedure that produced the error can be retried or skipped. The result may allow play to continue as if no error had been encountered. Thus ERRORPROC can control script play by its returned value, one of the integers 0, 1, or 2:

| Value | | Purpose |
|---|---|---|
| 0 | {Step} | Retry the statement in the script that caused the error. |
| 1 | {Next} | Skip the statement that caused the error; execute the next one. |
| 2 | Default | Display the {Cancel} {Debug} menu. |

## 9.22 ERROR FUNCTIONS

Three functions, ERRORMESSAGE(), ERRORUSER, and ERRORCODE(), are at the heart of any procedure that attempts to recover from a run error.

- ERRORMESSAGE() returns the text that is put on the workspace when the error is encountered. Under script control, the canvas usually hides this error message. The value of this function is usually passed to the user to give an indication of the problem that caused the error.
- ERRORUSER() is only active with Paradox running on a network and it only reports on locking errors. ERRORUSER() reports the name of the user who has placed a lock on the Paradox object your script is attempting to use.
- ERRORCODE() corresponds to an error code number. They are listed under the examples section under "ERRORCODE."[7]

An example of a general-purpose ERRORPROC is listed in WWPUTIL2.SC.

## 9.23 MAKING ERRORPROC AVAILABLE

The procedure designated by ERRORPROC must always have been read into memory at least once before being called so that Paradox will know where to find it even if it has been swapped out to make room for another procedure. Paradox is not able to read and interpret another line of code if an error has been induced; it can, however, use a procedure already stored in memory. We will discuss this special requirement more in the next chapter, "Procedure Libraries."

## 9.24 IN CASE OF EMERGENCY, BREAK GLASS

Invoking ERRORPROC is a drastic programming recourse. It is saying: "Something went wrong with my script that I couldn't have anticipated." From the manual:

> "As a matter of good coding style, it is not recommended that you rely too much on error procedures. Instead, you should avoid script errors by testing for error conditions (such as drives or printers that are not ready, or tables that are locked) by explicitly using the appropriate commands or functions."

Underscoring its use as a last resort, each time a script invokes ERRORPROC *in a loop*, Paradox3 loses 200 bytes of working memory (as measured by MEMLEFT()).[8] This unfortunate fact has an important corollary: make sure the procedure you designate as your ERRORPROC has been well tested. Losing memory by invoking ERRORPROC can be particularly disastrous if your ERRORPROC isn't error free, thus invoking itself recursively. Your application will soon run out of memory and crash.

## 9.25 WHEN YOU NEED A SCRIPT

Thus far you've seen that a procedure can only be made available by playing a script that contains its definition. Thus you can have a script that branches at the topmost level, playing scripts that define procedures, like this:

```
Choice.a = ""
WHILE Choice.a <> "Esc"
  SHOWMENU
    "Customers" : "Customer info",
    "Credit" : "Credit info",
    "Inventory" : "Inventory info"
  TO Choice.a
  SWITCH
    CASE Choice.a = "Customers" :
      PLAY "Custs" ;loads cust procs
      Customer() ;calls cust proc
      RELEASE PROCS ALL ;release
    CASE Choice.a = "Credit" :
      PLAY "Credit" ;loads credit procs
      Credit() ;calls Credit proc
      RELEASE PROCS All ;release
    CASE Choice.a = "Inventory" :
      PLAY "Invent" ;loads Inventory procs
      Inventory() ;calls Inventory proc
      RELEASE PROCS All ;release
  ENDSWITCH
ENDWHILE
```

When a script plays another script, the first script is suspended until the second script finishes playing or terminates script play altogether. Since procedures exist in memory only during script play, when script play ends, all procedures are automatically released and the memory they occupied again becomes available. If you are working with relatively small scripts, this approach works fine.

Yet playing a top-level script that defines all the procedures that you need in an application, or that in turn plays scripts that define procedures, can be made vastly simpler with the use of the Procedure Libraries, the subject of the next chapter. With the use of procedure libraries, you'll need only a single script that calls your first procedure.

## 9.26 CHAPTER SUMMARY

This chapter focused on the mechanics of creating PAL procedures, which provide the benefits of modularity, speed, and syntax checking for scripts. A special procedure designated by the system variable ERRORPROC can improve the reliability of your code by providing a last-chance recovery mechanism. Although these benefits can dramatically improve the quality of your PAL applications, the true power of procedures is only made available through the use of Procedure Libraries.

## NOTES

1. In Paradox3, making a script play over and over is most easily accomplished with the {Scripts} {RepeatPlay} menu choice.
2. Thus procedures are also known as "Procs."
3. The use of the EXECUTE and EXECPROC commands, which execute a string as a command, can lead to syntax errors at run time.
4. There is no guarantee that your script will run, however. Errors that are induced by hardware and software conditions at time of execution—*run errors*—are not trapped by this preparsing.
5. The other way of passing parameters, call by reference, passes a memory address of a variable, and a procedure call can change the variable in memory. Paradox uses only call by value.
6. In version 2.0 of Paradox, procedure names that duplicated previously assigned procedure names sometimes had difficulty in releasing, even after repeated RESET commands.
7. The error codes in the release 3.0 PAL manual are incomplete on page 86 and partially incorrect on page 411.
8. As of this writing, it appears that if ERRORPROC is triggered directly from within a loop (not from something invoked by a script or procedure), 200 bytes are consumed on each pass. Outside a loop, ERRORPROC has no direct effect on MEMLEFT(). The memory is returned once the loop is exited.

# Chapter 10

# Procedure Libraries

A procedure library is a file that stores procedures in a preparsed, memory-ready format. Procedures can, in effect, be "borrowed" from libraries. This chapter introduces procedure libraries.

## 10.1 WHY A PROCEDURE LIBRARY?

Thus far we've shown that the principal advantage of your writing "procedurized" code has been speed—speed pure and simple. Once in memory, a procedure can be called repeatedly by name and executed rapidly. Another tangible benefit is less obvious—since every script line in a procedure must pass the test of use by the PAL parser, your PAL procedures are free of syntax errors. In contrast, PAL scripts written to be played at run time may have untested IF, ELSE, or CASE clauses, and thus may have syntax errors. Syntax errors will present a user with the "Cancel/Debug" prompt and bring an application to an unexpected and screeching halt.

Once declared and parsed, a procedure remains available in an application until script play ends or until it is released from memory. The RELEASE PROCS command frees defined procedures from memory:

```
RELEASE PROCS GetUserName.u, LocateUser.u
```

If a script needs to use a procedure after it has been released from memory, the script that contains the procedure must again be played. Reading a PROC back into memory by again playing its script not only takes extra time, but because of memory constraints, may not always be possible. These rules make using procedures by playing scripts from within an application awkward.

Using procedure libraries not only helps solve these problems, but is the not-so-obvious solution to many PAL programming woes.

142

Throughout this book we have emphasized a simple rule: "Let Paradox do the work." Perhaps nowhere is this rule more important than with procedure libraries. Paradox libraries have been designed to let you let Paradox do the work.

- With release 1.1, Paradox introduced the "AUTOLIB" system variable, which loads undeclared procedures automatically;
- With Paradox2, the use of procedure swapping and expanded memory further encouraged their use;
- With Paradox3, the addition of the "AUTOLIB" path and more sophisticated internal memory management makes their use even easier.

The gradual refinement in the way Paradox handles procedures called from libraries is far more than a simple endorsement of their use; it is a proclamation stating: "This is programming the Paradox way." This chapter will explore PAL procedure libraries: what they are and how they are created, maintained, and used.

## 10.2 WHAT IS A PROCEDURE LIBRARY?

A Procedure Library is a file that contains PAL procedures stored in memory-ready form. The preparsed form of these procedures allows for efficiency in both storage and execution. If stored within libraries, your procedures can be made to execute nearly as fast and as naturally as built-in PAL functions. When filled with a series of procedures and specially designated with the AUTOLIB command, a PAL procedure library can behave like a user-created Paradox program overlay file.

As the need for a library in your home begins with a single book, the need for a PAL procedure library begins with one commonly used procedure. As an example of this, the following PROC creates a message in the upper left of the screen:

```
PROC Working.u(Message.a)
  a1,0 CLEAR EOL
  ?? Message.a
  a0,0 CLEAR EOL
  ?? "Working"
  STYLE BLINK
  ?? "...."
  STYLE
  a0,0
ENDPROC
```

You've seen elements of this procedure before. "Working.u" simply places a message on the canvas above the workspace. The more generic a procedure, the wider the possibilities for its use, and the more likely a candidate it is for inclusion into a library. Like phrases from a treasured book, frequently used procedures become part of your programming lexicon. A procedure library makes referencing this extended vocabulary easy.

## 10.3 CREATING A LIBRARY

As with a table, where you must create its structure before entering data, you must create the structure of a library before you can store procedures in it. The CREATELIB command takes either a DOS filename, as a quoted string, for example:

```
CREATELIB "Utility"
```

or a variable already assigned to a legitimate library file name:

```
LibName.a = "C:\\Paradox3\\Utility"
CREATELIB LibName.a
```

CREATELIB lacks the safety net afforded by other file creation activity in interactive Paradox, and automatically overwrites an existing library with the same name in the same location on a disk. The CREATELIB command makes a 2224-byte file with a filename extension of ".LIB." This small file is a "header" (a table of contents), which by default can track 50 procedures entries. Though a library may contain up to 300 procedures, you must create libraries larger than 50 procedures with the needed capacity using the optional SIZE parameter:

```
CREATELIB "Utility" SIZE 300
```

If you're using Paradox2, keep the library sizes as small as possible to avoid memory problems.

## 10.4 STORING A PROCEDURE IN A LIBRARY

To store a procedure in a library, the procedure must first be in memory. Then, the command

```
WRITELIB <Library Name> <Procedure Name>
```

appends the procedure to the library and updates the library file header. The following is a script that creates the "Utility" library, reads the "Working.u" procedure into memory, and writes it to the library:

```
CREATELIB "Utility" ;creates utility.lib


PROC Working.u(Message.a) ;defines it in memory
  [body of procedure as above]
ENDPROC


WRITELIB "Utility" Working.u ;writes Working to utility.lib
```

The WRITELIB command appends the parsed PROC to the library along with the full path name of the script that created it. Note that the name of the procedure in the WRITELIB command does not have parentheses. Because this is a complete script, once play ends, the PROC is released from memory.

Here's another useful utility procedure we'll add to our library. This one clears all of the Query Images on the workspace:

```
PROC ClearQueryImages.u()
  IF SYSMODE() = "Main" THEN
    IF NIMAGES()<> 0 THEN ;any images on workspace?
      MOVETO 1 ;go to first image
      WHILE IMAGETYPE() ="Query"
        ClearImage ;clear it if it's a query image
      ENDWHILE
    ENDIF
  ENDIF
ENDPROC
```

## 10.5 WRITING MULTIPLE PROCEDURES TO A LIBRARY

There are two common methods of getting procedures into a library.

With one method, you read all procedures into memory first. You then write all of the procedures to the library in one fell swoop at the end with a WRITELIB followed by a list of the procedure names separated by commas:

```
CREATELIB "Utility"
PROC Working.u(Message.a)
    <statements>
ENDPROC

PROC ClearQueryImages.u()
    <statements>
ENDPROC


WRITELIB "Utility" Working.u, ClearQueryImages.u
```

You can write as many procedures as memory allows, limited only by the maximum SIZE of the library. Although this first method nicely groups the procedure names at the end, the grouping becomes a liability when attempting to move blocks of code intact from one application to another. Another disadvantage becomes evident with long scripts, which write many procedures to the library at once. Because all procedures must be in memory for the WRITELIB to work, adding "just one more proc" to the middle of a large script may exceed memory limits.

The preferred method for writing procedures to libraries (used by both the Personal Programmer and portions of the Data Entry Toolkit demo), offers several advantages. You first assign the name of the library to a variable, and then use a repeated pattern of define, write, and release.

```
LibName.a = "Utility" ;assign library name to variable
CREATELIB LibName.a ;create library

PROC Working.u(Message.a) ;define
 <statements>
ENDPROC
WRITELIB LibName.a, Working.u ;write
RELEASE PROCS Working.u ;release

PROC ClearQueryImages.u() ;define
    <statements>
ENDPROC
WRITELIB LibName.a ClearQueryImages.u ;write
RELEASE PROCS ClearQueryImages.u ;release
```

The advantages are twofold:

- Your code is much more transportable. Both the assignment of a library name to a variable and the block orientation of the procedure (define, write, and release) allows any procedure to be pulled out of a script and snapped into another application with ease. Within a new application, the variable LibName.a can take on a new library name by simply reassigning it to a new library name at the top of the script.
- There is minimal chance of running out of memory because there is only one procedure in memory at a time.

## 10.6 DEBUGGING PROCEDURES IN LIBRARIES

If a run error causes a procedure called from a library to be interrupted, the familiar "Cancel/Debug" menu will appear. Debugging procedurized code called from libraries involves debugging the script that created the library entry:

- Since every library entry contains the full path name of the script that created it, the script will be looked for automatically by Paradox with [Ctrl E]. If the script exists and is unchanged, the script will be loaded at the line number that caused the error.
- If the script that created the library entry has been changed, Paradox will be unable to load the script and will display a message noting that the script has been changed. Finding the error that triggered the initial "Cancel/Debug" menu requires an up-to-date library entry: first, the script that created the library entry must be played to update the library, and second, the script that called the procedure that induced the run error must be played to induce the error again. The procedure will then debug as expected.
- If the script you used to create a library entry can't be found, script debugging comes to a stop. The error is often something simple. A message like: "Could not find script D:\PARADOX3\UTILITY.SC containing text of procedure Working.u" may indicate an incorrect drive specifier or a missing subdirectory name.

Last-minute debugging of applications that use procedures can be made much easier if you re-create your Paradox libraries on the PC on which the application will run, thereby assuring that procedures are to be found on drives and in subdirectories that exist.

## 10.7 SCRIPT SIZE AND DEBUGGING

Although PAL procedures allow you to keep program modules small, it's often of great benefit to group 20, 50, or 100 procedures into a single file. Not only does this cut down on the number of files in a subdirectory, but it also makes finding procedures easy. It's not unusual for these modular procedures to end up in a single script of 1000 lines or more.

A word of caution about large scripts and the PAL Debugger:

- When working interactively with the debugger, scripts of more than 1000 lines can slow stepping through the debugger to a crawl while Paradox attempts to locate successive lines in a procedure.
- From time to time, with very large scripts, Paradox can actually appear to lose its place in the display line of the debugger.

For easy debugging, keep script files that write procedures to under 1000 lines.

## 10.8 MANAGING LIBRARY SIZE

The file size in bytes of a library file depends not only on the SIZE option in the CREATELIB command and the length of each procedure, but also on the number of times each procedure has been written to the library.

The WRITELIB command appends procedures to a library. If a procedure already exists, it isn't deleted—the library header information is simply updated with the new location. All outdated copies of procedures remain in the library and its file size grows. While developing and refining an application, you may write procedures to their libraries dozens of times.

From time to time, the library should be recreated from scratch to trim its file size. Typically this is done by writing a *calling* script that first recreates the library, and then plays a series of scripts that define, write, and release the procedures in the library. We commonly preface script names that write to libraries with a "w." Here's one called "wUtility.SC":

```
;Script: wUtility

LibName.a = "Utility" ;assign library name
CREATELIB LibName.a ;create library

MESSAGE "Writing wUtil1"
PLAY "wUtil1" ;define, write & release procs

MESSAGE "Writing wUtil2"
PLAY "wUtil2" ;define, write & release procs

MESSAGE "Writing wUtil3"
PLAY "wUtil3" ;define, write & release procs

INFOLIB LibName.a ;display and capture result
```

Since the CREATELIB command overwrites existing files, there's no need to delete an existing library.

## 10.9 THE INFOLIB COMMAND

INFOLIB is a PAL command that gives you the names and sizes of all procedures stored in a library. The INFOLIB command takes one argument, the name of the library, and creates a table called "LIST." If the library is empty, the "LIST" table will be empty as well. The last line of the wUtility script

```
INFOLIB LibName.a
```

creates the following table.

```
Viewing List table: Record 1 of 2                          Main
LIST            =Procedure=                    =Size=
        1 ║ WorkingMessage.u      ║          ║  624  ║
        2 ║ ClearQueryImages.u    ║          ║  349  ║
```

The [Size] field indicates the amount of memory the procedure will need to load. Because memory constraints should always be of concern, you should keep procedures as small as possible. A rule of thumb is to attempt to keep your largest procedures to about 10K. If necessary, split larger procedures into procedures that call other procedures.

Though there are no stated restrictions on the length of a procedure name stored in a library, the [Procedure] field in the LIST table is 31 characters wide. Although 31 characters should be sufficient to accurately name a procedure, additional warnings are in order.

- Procedure names longer than 31 characters cannot be reliably read from a library.
- Attempting to write a procedure name longer than 35 characters to a library can bring Paradox to an unexpected halt.

## 10.10 A LIBRARY PACKING UTILITY

With the LIST table and the size of the library file in bytes, you can determine if the size of the library can be reduced by removing outdated procedure code. As a rough estimate, the file size of the library should equal the size of the library header plus the sum of the [Size] column in the LIST table produced by the INFOLIB command. In libraries with less than 50 procedures, the formula to approximate the size of a library file is:

```
2224 + CSUM("List", "Size")     ;"List" is produced with the "INFOLIB" command
```

The Paradox CSUM (Column Sum) function totals numeric fields in columns. In our example, the expected size of our "Utility" library should be:

```
2224 + 973 = 3197 bytes
```

The DOS directory listing indicates a file size of 3288 bytes, close enough not to warrant restructuring.

What follows is a procedure that "restructures" a procedure library, eliminating outdated procedure code, much as the {Modify} {Restructure} command may be used to reduce the file size of a Paradox table. "PackLib.u()" takes as its argument the name of the library.

**Listing 10.1: Library Packing Utility**

```
PROC PackLib.u(LibName.a)
  PRIVATE templib.a
  IF ISFILE(LibName.a+".lib") THEN
    RESET
    RUN "RENAME "+LibName.a+".lib templib.lib"
    INFOLIB "TempLib"
    RIGHT
    NRecords.n = NRECORDS("List")
    IF NRecords.n < 50 THEN
      CREATELIB LibName.a
    ELSE
      CREATELIB LibName.a SIZE NRecords.n
    ENDIF
    @ 0,0
    CLEAR
    ?? "Working"
    ; The next line creates a temporary variable that greatly
    ; simplifies the coding of the EXECUTE command below.
    templib.a = "Templib"
    SCAN
      ?? "."     ; Indicate progress of scan with a dot each time through.

      EXECUTE "READLIB Templib.a "+[]+ " WRITELIB LibName.a "+[]+" RELEASE PROCS "+[]
;e.g. READLIB "Templib" Working.u WRITELIB "Utility" Working.u RELEASE PROCS Working.u
    ENDSCAN
    RESET
    RUN "DEL TempLib.lib >NUL"
  ELSE
    QUIT "Library \""+LibName.a+"\" does not exist."
  ENDIF
ENDPROC
```

This procedure uses an often-overlooked aspect of libraries: once a procedure is read from a library and is in memory, the procedure may be written to any other library. "PackLib.u" renames the original library file to a file called templib.lib, creates a new empty library with your original library name, and then reads procedures one-by-one from templib.lib and writes them into the new file. When it is finished, the temporary library file is deleted. This eliminates outdated code. Once all of the procedures have been duplicated, the temporary library file is copied back to the original name of the library by using the DOS COPY command. Finally, the temporary library is deleted.

By evaluating and using the number of records in the "List" table, this procedure also creates the minimum size library required. Beyond the minimum of 50, "PackLib.u" creates a library with exactly enough room for all your procedures. If you attempt to add an additional PROC, Paradox will give you an error message stating that the library is full. Additional procedures can be added by explicitly creating the library with a greater SIZE than "required."

## 10.11 READING PROCEDURES FROM LIBRARIES

There are two methods you can use to call procedures from a library, one "manual" and one "automatic." The manual method uses the READLIB command to explicitly place procedures in memory:

```
READLIB "Utility" Working.u, ClearQueryImages.u
```

The READLIB command is followed by the name of the library and a list of procedures in the library separated by commas. Once read in with READLIB, you can call the procedure at any time during script play. Now that the procedures Working.u and ClearQueryImages.u are in memory, the single line:

```
Working.u("Processing your request")
```

will call the procedure and execute it. If the procedure is no longer needed, it should be released from memory:

```
RELEASE PROCS Working.u
```

With Release 2.0, Paradox included a feature termed "Virtual Memory Management" (VMM), which makes the explicit reading and releasing of procedures less necessary. VMM allows any number of procedures to be read into memory, recognized, and if necessary, temporarily swapped out of memory.

## 10.12 PROCEDURE SWAPPING

With procedure swapping, procedures are read into memory in the sequence specified by READLIB as usual. If the amount of memory necessary to hold these procedures exceeds available memory (or a special memory "setswap" point to be discussed in the next chapter), the procedures will be:

- swapped out in their entirety to Expanded Memory, if it is available; or,
- cleared from memory, to be reread from the disk when necessary.

With procedure swapping, the order of procedures specified by the READLIB command (or commands) is significant, for Paradox uses a "Least Recently Used" (LRU) algorithm to dictate which procedures are to be swapped out. At the start of an application, the last procedure you specify with the READLIB command will be the first one available. The last procedure read will always be in memory when the application starts. As an application uses and reuses procedures, they will migrate to and from conventional memory, expanded memory, or disk in an order specified by memory constraints and the frequency of their use.

For example, if an application from the "Utility" library calls the "Main-Menu.a()" procedure first, the READLIB should be structured as follows to assure that the top level menu is available first:

```
READLIB "Utility" Working.u, ClearQueryImages.u,..., Mainmenu.a
```

Procedure swapping lets Paradox do some of the work, but using the READLIB command is cumbersome—you must make sure that the proper procedures are in memory when needed. And you must make certain that there is enough memory for the next needed procedure to load. Simpler still would be an automated system for loading and releasing procedures, much in the same manner that Paradox loads subsystems from its overlay files when needed. This method would couple procedure swapping with an automated READLIB command, which would "know" which procedure your application needed next. This automatic procedure-reading method was introduced with Paradox 1.1 and uses a system variable called "AUTOLIB."

## 10.13 AUTOLIB

The third Paradox system variable[1] is called AUTOLIB and is used to designate a library from which procedures can be loaded automatically. AUTOLIB is short for "AutoLoad Library" and controls one of the most powerful aspects of PAL programming—letting Paradox manage procedures. Its proper use can make your PAL programs flow seamlessly, with efficient memory utilization and with little work.

AUTOLIB in its simplest form is a variable that is set to a single library name. Here's an example. The command:

```
AUTOLIB = "Utility"
```

assigns "Utility" to AUTOLIB, and instructs Paradox to search for undefined procedures it encounters in an application in the "Utility" library. AUTOLIB supplements explicit READLIB commands. With this assignment made, any procedure stored in "Utility.lib" can be accessed without a READLIB. If the procedure is not found in memory or "Utility.lib," a script error will result.

```
Without AUTOLIB                With AUTOLIB set to "Utility"
--------------------------     -----------------------------
READLIB "Utility" Working.u    Working.u("Processing request")
Working.u("Processing request")
```

With release 3.0, the AUTOLIB command looks and performs much like the DOS PATH command. Library entries in AUTOLIB in Release 3.0 are separated by commas, no spaces are permitted, and all backslashes must be doubled. Each portion of the AUTOLIB "path" must end with a library name. Here are two examples of a release 3.0 AUTOLIB assignment:

```
AUTOLIB = "UtilLib,Paradox,MainLib"
AUTOLIB ="C:\\Paradox3\\UtilLib,C:\\Paradox3\\Paradox,D:\\MainLib"
```

The first library specified in the list is searched first, and if the called procedure is not found, the second library is searched, and so on. The more libraries designated by the AUTOLIB path, the longer the search process. Sequentially ordered, smaller procedure files allow you to devote a minimum of memory to managing library size.

## 10.14 MAKING AUTOLIB PRIVATE

Because AUTOLIB is simply a variable, it can be made PRIVATE to a procedure and automatically released when the procedure ends, returning AUTOLIB to its prior status. For example:

```
PROC MainMenu.u()
  PRIVATE choice.a
  AUTOLIB = "C:\\Paradox3\\Salesjnl"  ;the initial library assignment

  WHILE True
    SHOWMENU
      "SalesJournal" : "Run the Sales Journal",
      "Reports" : "Run Reports"
    To Choice.a
    SWITCH
      CASE Choice.a = "Esc" :
        RETURN
      CASE Choice.a = "SalesJournal" :
        SalesJournal.u()
      CASE Choice.a = "Report" :
        ReportMenu.u()
    ENDSWITCH
  ENDWHILE
ENDPROC
```

```
PROC ReportMenu.u()
  PRIVATE AUTOLIB
  AUTOLIB = "C:\\Paradox3\\Reports"  ; Assigned to a new library
  ReportStuff.u()
ENDPROC   ; When proc ends, returns AUTOLIB to old value.
```

Initially set to "SALESJNL" in the c:\Paradox3 directory, AUTOLIB is reassigned with the PRIVATE designation to "REPORTS" in the c:\Paradox3 directory. Once the Report menu is exited, AUTOLIB returns to "SALESJNL." A variation on this technique is to reassign the order of the AUTOLIB path so that the procedure search is made more efficient. For example:

```
AUTOLIB = "Lib1,Lib2,Lib3"
```

may be reset to a different order when accessing procedures more common in "lib3":

```
AUTOLIB = "Lib3,Lib1,Lib2"
```

Explicit subdirectory naming may be used as well:

```
AUTOLIB="c:\\path3\\Lib3,d:\\path2\\Lib2,c:\\path1\\Lib1"
```

allowing the AUTOLIB path to function across directories and drives if necessary.

## 10.15 A SPECIAL LIBRARY: PARADOX.LIB

Paradox.lib is the name of the default "Autoload" library. If AUTOLIB has not been assigned a value (or its value has been eliminated with RELEASE VARS AUTOLIB), Paradox allows one last procedure resource, a library in the current directory called "Paradox."

When you create and use a procedure library called "Paradox," you needn't assign AUTOLIB. However, if your application changes the current directory, the assignment of Paradox.lib, being looked for in the current directory, is lost. The solution is to assign the system variable AUTOLIB to the full path name of the Paradox.lib file before changing directories. In the following example, all procedures up to this point have been called with "Paradox.lib" in the current directory. These two lines make the transition to a different directory while maintaining the original library as the "Autoload" library:

```
AUTOLIB = DIRECTORY()+"Paradox" ;adds "Paradox" to current directory
SETDIR "C:\\Paradox3\\NewDIR" ;sets the new directory
```

If an application has only one procedure library, create it with the name "Paradox.lib."

## 10.16 WHERE PROCEDURES ARE LOOKED FOR

Each procedure name called within an application should be unique. Once a procedure has been called, Paradox knows where to find it; if you have two procedures with the same name in two different libraries in one application, only the first one will be used. Make your procedure names unique.

In summary, Paradox looks for procedures called by applications in the following order:

- Conventional memory. Procedures must have been explicitly defined, read with the READLIB command, or made available to be read into memory by assigning the AUTOLIB variable.
- Expanded memory. Procedures explicitly read into memory with READLIB or automatically read with AUTOLIB or PARADOX.LIB may be temporarily "swapped out" to expanded memory, to be swapped back in when needed.
- On disk, ready to be read back into memory. If memory constraints have forced an already-used procedure out of memory, the location of the procedure on disk in the original library file remains referenced in memory.
- On disk, in the library assigned by the system variable, AUTOLIB, or if AUTOLIB is unassigned, in a library called PARADOX.LIB in the current directory. If the procedure called does not reside in any of these locations, and the procedure is invoked, a script error will result.

## 10.17 DISTRIBUTING PROCEDURIZED CODE IN LIBRARIES

Libraries offer another advantage as well for developers who distribute their applications—protection of source code. Although Paradox cannot "play" procedures from a library, a calling script can start an application from a library.

```
;Script: Go.sc
AUTOLIB = "C:\\Paradox3\\Sales"
MainMenu.a()
```

In this example, the procedure "MainMenu.a" takes over from this calling script and defines the workings of the application. The library file, "Sales.lib," stored in parsed form, is safe from probing by curious users. These few program files and any additional tables and their families, coupled with a copy of Paradox Runtime, make a complete turnkey system.

## 10.18 A WORD ON ERRORPROC

When using AUTOLIB, handling run time errors with ERRORPROC[2] requires special attention. Paradox can invoke the procedure you designate to handle run errors with ERRORPROC only if the Paradox "knows" where the procedure is located; that is, if the ERRORPROC procedure has been *explicitly read from a library or purposefully invoked* at least once before the run error. Thus you can't rely on AUTOLIB to load ERRORPROC after a run error has occurred. The solution is to explicitly read the ERRORPROC when you start your application:

```
ERRORPROC="OopsPrint.u"          ;sets procedure to be called on a run error
AUTOLIB="Utility"    ;Sets the Autolib
READLIB "Utility" OopsPrint.u
```

No other explicit READLIBs are normally necessary in the entire application. If you follow this special rule, ERRORPROC will behave as expected.

## 10.19 ERRORPROC, AUTOLIB, AND CLOSED PROCS

CLOSED procedures present another special case with ERRORPROC and AUTOLIB. Because procedures that have been declared CLOSED treat all variables as private, both AUTOLIB and ERRORPROC have to be passed to the CLOSED procedure through the USEVARS option. The ERRORPROC again has to be read. If AUTOLIB refers to one library (it is not an AUTOLIB path), you can use the following:

```
PROC CLOSED procname()
 USEVARS AUTOLIB, ERRORPROC
 READLIB AUTOLIB ERRORPROC
 <Statements>
ENDPROC
```

An alternate approach, which loads an Errorproc from an AUTOLIB in the path format, is described in the WaitPlusSetup.1 procedure in the WWPCore2 script in Part III.

## 10.20 CHAPTER SUMMARY

When Luke Skywalker was about to make his bombing run on the Death Star, he had his craft's computer controls locked on the location of the shaft that led to the main reactor. At the last moment, the voice of Obi Wan Kenobi echoed "Trust the Force, Luke," and advised him to give up the controls. Luke, of course, turned the computer off, trusted in the Force, blew the Death Star to smithereens, and sent Darth Vader tumbling into space.

Though there is little that can be termed "natural" in programming, giving up control is hardly natural. Yet Paradox asks us time and time again to give up control with the promise of a gain in efficiency. "Trust in Paradox," it tells us, "here are the tools." What the designers of Paradox are saying couldn't be clearer: "Use Procedures. Put your procedures in libraries. Call your procedures with autoloading libraries."

This chapter has covered one of the most important tools for gaining PAL programming efficiency—libraries. Libraries are the natural extension of application programming using procedures, giving them organization and easy and secure access. With auto-loading of procedures from libraries and procedure swapping, Paradox is left to manage its most important resource—memory—while greatly simplifying programming. In the next chapter, "Managing Memory and Disk Resources," we will explore additional reasons to let Paradox do the work.

## NOTES

1. RETVAL and ERRORPROC are the other two system variables.
2. Discussed in the last chapter, "Procedures."

# Chapter 11

# Managing Memory and Disk Resources

Paradox is hardware exploitive, pushing whatever resources you give it to the limit to give you the best performance possible. Although we have been emphasizing that you should let Paradox do as much of the work as possible, you shouldn't give up control completely. There are many things you can do to help Paradox make the most of your hardware resources. There is more information on these topics in Chapters 20 and 21.

## 11.1 MEMORY AND DISK SPACE

Think of Paradox as an information factory. Data gets shipped in, processed, and shipped out in an automated stream of operations. Timing is everything. Memory is the factory's floor space and every piece of equipment that's put into the production line has to be on the floor at the right moment. Things often get a bit crowded, so Paradox is continually rearranging memory, shuttling in and out infrequently called routines when necessary.

The resource that's most often in critical supply with Paradox is memory and the general rule is simple: the more memory the better. Paradox3 requires 512K of memory to run, but the most important measure of memory is how much is available to your applications.

The PAL MEMLEFT() function returns the amount of memory available for Paradox operations. The current value of MEMLEFT (in Kb) can be determined from the PAL menu.

> **Step 1**
> Press:      [Alt F10]
> **Step 2**
> Select:     {Value}

**Step 3**
Type in:    MEMLEFT()
**Step 4**
Press:      [Enter]

Adding memory works wonders with Paradox. Equipping a PC with 640K boosts MEMLEFT() and eases memory constraints. On a network, 640K is rarely enough with the increased overhead of the network operating system. Adding and using memory above 640K as expanded memory can have a dramatic effect on performance. Under script control, the use and availability of memory becomes even more important.

Less frequently, but often enough to warrant attention, the Paradox resource in short supply is disk space. The second part of this chapter is devoted to disk management.

Paradox's use of these two interdependent resources, memory and disk space, is complex. Unlike most programs for the PC that simply use memory, Paradox actively manages memory, and further provides you tools to help you manage memory.

## 11.2 EXPANDED AND EXTENDED MEMORY

Paradox will automatically take advantage of available expanded memory that conforms to the Lotus-Intel-Microsoft expanded memory specification. The manner in which Paradox uses this memory depends on a variety of hardware and software considerations:

- The amount of expanded memory available.
- Monitor type: Color or Monochrome.
- Type of expanded memory: EMS or EEMS.
- Configuration Settings. The "Custom" script's settings under {Defaults} {EMS} allows you to dictate the percentage of available EMS used for disk caching.
- Paradox Command Line Parameters. The -emK parameter described in Chapter 14 of the Paradox3 User's Guide (page 288) overrides configuration settings. The undocumented -emP 0 parameter disables the Paradox disk cache, enabling you to substitute a more versatile commercial disk cache (e.g., Super PCKwik).

The description of how Paradox handles expanded memory is in several places in the Paradox3 guides. Chapter 14 of the Paradox User's Guide contains a section "How Paradox Uses Memory." Chapter 15 of the PAL User's Guide,

"Performance and Resource Tuning," contains additional information on memory.

## 11.3 SETSWAP

Procedure swapping in Paradox is enabled with the PAL command:

```
SETSWAP number
```

where the number is an integer, usually in the tens of thousands, representing the number of bytes of memory to maintain during script play. Paradox2 introduced the concept of procedure swapping.

If an application uses procedures found in libraries (as opposed to being defined explicitly at run time), and you specify a SETSWAP point, Paradox will automatically manage the memory used for those procedures. Paradox uses a least recently used (LRU) algorithm to swap procedures in and out of memory to make room for other procedures. As this name implies, procedures that have been read in or used from libraries are classified according to frequency of use. If there is more than one procedure in memory, one is always the *least recently used* procedure; it will be swapped out first. If you are using expanded memory, Paradox will store swapped procedures there; if not, procedures will simply be reread from their libraries when needed again.

This generally frees the programmer from worrying about memory constraints placed by the hardware being used. We say "generally" because there are times when you must monitor available memory and act accordingly. There is confusion aplenty about the SETSWAP mechanism—page 183 of the Paradox 3.0 PAL manual states:

> "For example, each image on the workspace takes about 2K of memory. If you know that a later procedure will display five images, you could use SETSWAP 10000 to reserve 10K for these images."

This information is incorrect. The very existence of images on the workspace means that the memory necessary for placing them on the workspace has already been accounted for. Here are a few guidelines regarding the SETSWAP command:

- Unless you specify a SETSWAP point, procedures will not be swapped.
- Setting a SETSWAP point below 10,000 bytes is pretty much the same as not having set a SETSWAP at all.

- Setting the SETSWAP point too high can cause Paradox to perform a lot of unnecessary swapping.

The many factors that will inhibit procedure swapping are discussed in the next section, "Procedure Swapping."

Paradox decides whether or not it has to swap procedures on a statement by statement basis,[1] gauging available memory as measured by the MEMLEFT() function. If swapping occurs, Paradox determines *which* procs are swapped, and *where* they go (they either go to EMS memory, or are simply "forgotten," to be reread later). If memory is below the SETSWAP point, Paradox swaps out enough procedures to reach it. Once Paradox swaps out all the procedures it can, MEMLEFT() will continue to decrease.[2]

The SETSWAP command is used to tell Paradox how much memory to reserve for your application's operations: it sets a memory "low water mark." If memory dips below this critical level, procedures in memory will begin to be swapped out. In theory, Paradox needs a value of SETSWAP only large enough to accommodate the memory requirements of the next PAL statement. Unfortunately, this is where theory and practice diverge.

Memory management was refined with Paradox3. Some of the more critical memory issues in Paradox2 are often no longer a concern with Paradox3. Many applications that exhibited memory problems under Paradox2 run well under Paradox3. For example, the CREATELIB SIZE command influenced the amount of *contiguous* memory Paradox2 needed to read any procedure from a library. With Paradox2, it was common practice to set the SETSWAP point very high because the memory had to be contiguous. This is no longer necessary with Paradox3.

## 11.4 HOW MUCH SETSWAP?

How much SETSWAP is enough? We have discovered few hard and fast rules. Some PAL statements (BEEP, for example) use almost no memory. Complex commands may require large chunks of memory. The same command issued under differing circumstances may have dramatically different memory requirements. An example is one of the simplest commands: Do_It! When executing a query, Do_It!, may require 50,000 bytes, while ending an edit session with Do_It! may require comparatively little.

A low water mark of about 4K of memory is reserved by Paradox to attempt to tell you that there is a memory problem. The result: A very low swap point is the same as no swap point at all. Combine this value with the need for at least a few thousand bytes of memory for general use, and you come to a minimum swap threshold of about 10,000 bytes. Anything below 10,000 is useless.

Experience indicates that most large applications require a SETSWAP of around 30,000; a lower SETSWAP often only delays, but does not eliminate, memory problems. Many PAL applications work fine with SETSWAP set to 20,000. Unless you are executing a very large query or are working with complex multitable forms, you may never need to set SETSWAP greater than 15,000 (roughly the largest amount of memory a single statement should use). No one is quite sure why a higher swap point is sometimes needed to provide a safety margin.

Only by experimentation can you determine the minimum SETSWAP point that allows your procedures to run effectively. Setting SETSWAP too high simply means that Paradox will swap procedures more often than necessary and slow overall performance. Setting the swap point too low usually results in a "Not enough memory to complete operation" error, resulting in a Cancel/Debug prompt.

## 11.5 CHANGING SETSWAP

Once you set it, the SETSWAP point isn't fixed—you can change it at any time. By resetting SETSWAP on a task-by-task basis, you can improve overall performance by maintaining as low a SETSWAP as possible.

Say, for example, that SETSWAP is currently at 20,000 bytes, there are procedures in memory available for swapping, and you need roughly 50,000 bytes to execute a multitable query. You place the query images on the workspace. Your current MEMLEFT() shows 30,000 bytes. What happens when you include the following?

```
SETSWAP 50000
SETSWAP 20000
DO_IT!
```

When Paradox executes the first SETSWAP command, it raises the swap point to 50,000 bytes. Before executing the second SETSWAP, Paradox sees that the current memory (30,000 bytes) is already below the new swap point and it swaps out enough procedures to bring the MEMLEFT() back to at least the swap value.[3] Then and only then will Paradox execute the next statement, SETSWAP 20000, which resets the swap point to 20,000 bytes. MEMLEFT() should still be about 50,000 bytes, ready for the next command. Finally, as Paradox prepares to execute the DO_IT! command, available memory is above the swap point, with plenty of memory to execute the query.[4]

Reducing SETSWAP does not recall swapped-out procedures. The only way procedures can be "swapped back" into active memory is if they are again called, either through their explicit use or the resumption of a swapped-out procedure on the calling chain.

# 11.6 PROCEDURE SWAPPING

If you write procedure to libraries, Paradox is able to swap procedures into and out of memory whenever needed, subject to a few restrictions. An application program typically has a top level procedure, which in turn calls subordinate procedures, each of which can call other procedures. The flow of these procedure calls is called the *calling chain*. A visual representation is shown with the [Ctrl W] or {Where?} PAL menu choice while debugging.

If Paradox finds that there is not enough free memory available, it will swap out of memory enough of the least recently used procedures to make room for the next PAL statement. A few things are worth noting:

- As a reminder, you must define a SETSWAP point to activate the swapping mechanism.
- The current procedure cannot be swapped out.
- When swapped procedures are needed again, Paradox swaps them back into memory.
- There are a few syntax restrictions that inhibit swapping of certain, or all procedures.

# 11.7 WHAT TO DO TO ALLOW SWAPPING

Rather than trying to remember all of the possible things that inhibit procedure swapping, simply remember the two proper ways to activate a procedure:

- As a standalone call, for example

```
ShowSplashScreen.u()
```

- By assigning the returned value of a proc to a variable:

```
l = CheckPrinter.l() ; in this case the procedure returns a logical value
```

## 11.8 WHAT INHIBITS SWAPPING

All other syntax that includes a call to a procedure will inhibit the swapping of the procedure that contains the offending (but permissible) syntax. For example if you write:

```
IF CheckPrinter.l() THEN
  REPORT "Customer" 1
ENDIF
```

the procedure will execute, but the entire procedure that uses this call cannot be swapped out. If you eliminate the test of the logical condition, swapping will be able to occur. The proper way to code the condition is:

```
l = CheckPrinter.l()
 IF l THEN
   REPORT "Customer" 1
ENDIF
```

This is true for all commands that depend upon a test of logic, including WHILE, SCAN, and FOR loops, and also applies to calls to procedures as part of a command, such as:

```
VIEW GetTableName.a()
```

A less than obvious syntactical problem is:

```
l = NOT ExitProc.l()
```

where an assignment operator, in conjunction with NOT, a logical operator, disables swapping. In addition, although you can assign the returned value of a procedure to a variable, you cannot assign it to a field and still permit swapping of the calling procedure. So,

```
[Customer ID#] = GetCustomerID.n()
```

will not allow swapping, but

```
n = GetCustomerID.n()
[Customer ID#] = n
```

works just fine.

These are examples of what you should not do with procedures if you want to maintain full use of the Paradox swapping mechanism. As you can see, it is easier to remember the two things that you can do, rather than learning and avoiding all the things you shouldn't do.

## 11.9 EXECUTE, SETKEY, MINI, VALUE DISABLE SWAPPING

The SETSWAP command is only active while you are under script control—it is not a global variable that hangs around when script play ends. Consequently you wouldn't have an init.sc that says Setswap 30000.

As of Paradox 2.01, there is another factor that can totally disable procedure swapping. The disabling factor is calling a procedure directly from any internal Paradox script (namely Mini, Value, KeyMacro, or Execute). If any of these scripts plays another script, which in turn runs a procedure, the swapping behaves normally. In PAL programming, it is usually the EXECUTE that is improperly used to call another procedure. When you use EXECUTE, PAL creates a one-line script in the calling chain. Thus

```
EXECUTE "myProc.u()"
```

disables swapping as long as this one line script called "EXECUTE" is on the calling chain. Here, the EXECPROC command should be used instead.

Many PAL programmers have trouble when they try to run a procedure directly through a SETKEY assignment:

```
SETKEY "F11" autolib="myprocs" MainMenu.u()
```

The problem is that calling a procedure directly from a key macro also disables the swapping mechanism. Fortunately, the workaround is simple. Create a script that can be played from a SETKEY:

```
;MainMenu.sc
  autolib="myprocs"
  MainMenu.u()
```

Now have the setkey assignment call the script:

```
SETKEY "F11" PLAY "MainMenu"
```

## 11.10 THE SWAPDEMO SCRIPT

The script that follows demonstrates the idiosyncrasies of the swapping mechanism and the accompanying figures are a graphic representation of some of the screens the script produces if you play it and follow its directions. Toward the end of each portion of the demo, we set an absurdly high SETSWAP point to force all procedures out of memory that can be swapped out. The SWAPDEMO script uses three coding techniques. We've structured it so that you will have to run the script once for each menu choice.

```
;---------------------------------------------------------------
PROC swapdemo.u()          ; This proc can be swapped.
  PRIVATE choice.a
  CURSOR OFF
  CLEAR
  a 3, 0
  TEXT
This script demonstrates how various coding styles affect the way
Paradox swaps procedures.

Rather than try to remember all the ways that swapping can be inhibited,
it is easier to remember that procedures may be swapped if used as a
standalone call, or assigned to a variable (if the proc returns a value).
All other ways of calling a procedure will inhibit the swapping of the proc
that did the calling.  As a reminder, the current proc can never be swapped
out. You'll need to run this script three times to see each example used.

This code will take you into the PAL debugger. Follow the instructions
presented in the debugger line (they will appear as variable assignments.)

While in the debugger a few special keys are used:

        [Ctrl S]  executes the next statement.      {Step}
        [Ctrl W]  displays the calling chain screen. {Where}
        [Ctrl G]  continues script play.            {Go}

When viewing the [Ctrl W] screen, pay particular attention to whether
or not procedures are swapped out, and if so, which ones.
  ENDTEXT
  SHOWMENU
    "SwapAll" : "Demo code that allow full swapping of procedures",
    "Inhibit" : "Show a proc that cannot be swapped, although others can",
    "Disable" : "Show how EXECUTE'ing a proc totally disables swapping",
    "Quit"    : "Return to Paradox"
  TO choice.a
  SWITCH
    CASE choice.a = "SwapAll" : a1.u()
    CASE choice.a = "Inhibit" : a2.u()
    CASE choice.a = "Disable" : a3.u()
  ENDSWITCH
  MESSAGE "SwapDemo over, press any key"
  n = GETCHAR()
ENDPROC
```

```
WRITELIB libname.a swapdemo.u
RELEASE PROCS     swapdemo.u


; Define three different variations of a single procedure (a1,a2,a3)
; with three different effects on swapping.
;------------------------------------------------------------------
PROC a1.u()               ; This proc *can* be swapped.
  PRIVATE l
  MESSAGE "Now running procedure a1.u"
  SLEEP 1000

  l = b.l()               ; Simple variable assignment.

  IF l THEN
    MESSAGE "This message displayed because b.l returned True"
    SLEEP 1000
  ENDIF
ENDPROC
WRITELIB libname.a a1.u
RELEASE PROCS a1.u


;------------------------------------------------------------------
PROC a2.u()               ; This proc *cannot* be to be swapped because
                          ; of call to b.l().
  PRIVATE l
  MESSAGE "Now running procedure a2.u"

  SLEEP 1000

  IF b.l() THEN           ; Making a call to a proc part of a logical
                          ; condition inhibits swapping.

    MESSAGE "This message displayed because b.l returned True"
    SLEEP 1000
  ENDIF
ENDPROC
WRITELIB libname.a a2.u
RELEASE PROCS a2.u
;------------------------------------------------------------------
PROC a3.u()               ; This proc won't let anything swap at all as long
  PRIVATE l               ; as the EXECUTE is in the calling chain.

  MESSAGE "Now running procedure a3.u"
  SLEEP 1000

  EXECUTE "l = b.l()"    ; EXECUTE'ing a proc disables swapping entirely.

  IF l THEN
    MESSAGE "This message displayed because b.l returned True"
    SLEEP 1000
  ENDIF
ENDPROC
WRITELIB libname.a a3.u
RELEASE PROCS a3.u


;------------------------------------------------------------------
; Define a proc that returns a logical value
```

```
PROC b.l()
  MESSAGE "Now running procedure b.l"
  SLEEP 1000
  c.u ()                  ; Call the c.u procedure.
  RETURN True             ; Pass a value back to the calling procedure.
ENDPROC
WRITELIB libname.a b.l
RELEASE PROCS b.l

; Finally, a proc that calls the debugger and prompts you to continue.
;-----------------------------------------------------------------------
PROC c.u()
  MESSAGE "Now in procedure c.u, follow instruction in the debugger"
  SLEEP 1000
  DEBUG
  a="Press [Ctrl W] now to see calling chain, then press [Ctrl S] to step"

  SETSWAP 500000          ; Absurdly high swap point, continue stepping.

  MESSAGE "Now SETSWAP is at 500,000"
  a="Press [Ctrl W] again to see swapped procs, then continue stepping"
  a="Press [Ctrl G] to continue normal script play"
ENDPROC
WRITELIB libname.a c.u
RELEASE PROCS c.u

;-----------------------------------------------------------------------
;Run the demo
AUTOLIB = "SwapDemo"
SwapDemo.u()
```

**Figure 11.1**

## 11.11 OTHER MEMORY AND PERFORMANCE FACTORS

Setswap is the most explicit form of PAL memory management. Give Paradox all the memory you can. Don't use memory resident utilities if you can help it. Other factors that influence the use of memory have already been discussed in some detail. Many are design issues: keep the size of your procedures small; keep overall table width as small as possible; use keyed tables; use AUTOLIB to load procedures; use coding techniques that don't disable procedure swapping. There is more information on these topics in Chapters 20 and 21.

## 11.12 DISK RESOURCES

A Paradox table is like a stack of blocks, with space for the same number of records in each block. The size of a block in a table is fixed at the time of table creation at 1K, 2K, 3K, or 4K in size. Six bytes are reserved at the end of each block for Paradox's internal use.

Each record in a table is of a fixed length and the number of bytes for each record can be calculated by adding up the space required for each field:

| | |
|---|---|
| Alphanumeric | 1 byte per character |
| Date | 4 bytes |
| Number | 8 bytes |
| Short number | 2 bytes |
| Currency | 8 bytes |

Paradox automatically selects what it considers to be the optimum block size when you create a new table, based on whether a table is keyed and the length of the record in bytes. Unkeyed tables will be given the smallest block size that can contain a single record. Keyed tables will be given the smallest block that can contain three records. This is the reason there is a 1350-byte limit on the length of keyed records (roughly 4096/3 = 1365.33, which was reduced to 1350).

Thus if your table is unkeyed and a record is 509 bytes in length, the block will be 1024 bytes (1K) with 6 bytes taken by Paradox. This leaves 1018 bytes, so two records will fit exactly into each block. If the record is 510 bytes, the block size will still be 1K, but only one record will fit in each block, and four records in 4094 bytes, resulting in 50 percent wasted space. If the table is keyed and a record is 509 bytes, the block size for three records 509*3+6=1532 will be 2K, and you'll get three records per block, or six records in 4096 bytes, with only 25%

wasted space. This simple math leads to very dependable determinations that can have a dramatic effect on performance (but more on that later).

Another factor enters when determining the maximum number of records that a table can hold—its maximum size. By design, the number of blocks that Paradox can keep track of is a fixed value: the "block counter" is an integer (short number). Thus a Paradox table can track a maximum of 65,536 blocks (64K). If the records are unkeyed, and each is 512 bytes, Paradox by default will be able to keep track of the integer value of (1024/512) multiplied by the maximum number of blocks, 65,536, for a total of 131,072 records. When the record length is 513 bytes, since only one record will fit in per 1K block, Paradox will be able to track only half that number of records.

The SETMAXSIZE command enables you to force Paradox to use a block size that accomodates more records than usual without fussing over this block division. You set the maximum size of the table to 64, 128, 256, or 512 megabytes.

Once Paradox has created a table, it knows its block size and how to maintain it. However, if it needs to recreate the table, for example, via a restructure, Paradox will use the normal block algorithms unless you use SETMAXSIZE to define a table with a size greater than Paradox would normally allow.

Some important rules:

- Paradox can read records from a table created with a higher block size than is currently set, but may not be able to write to them.
- Restructuring a table that has more records than Paradox would normally automatically allow will probably truncate the overflow records, but this is unconfirmed and we haven't tested it.
- Theoretically, simply editing an existing table should pose no problem, because Paradox reads the file header for the block structure. However, the PAL User's Guide issues the following grave warning: "Writing to a table with a different block size than the one under which it was created risks corrupting the data."

The warning is confusing and we're not sure if it is correct. Although the information on SETMAXSIZE says that "By default, the largest table can be 64 megabytes," we aren't so sure. For example, according to these guidelines, Paradox should have no trouble creating and tracking a 120-megabyte table with 60,000 records, each 2000 bytes wide without use of SETMAXSIZE. On the other hand, Paradox cannot track 70,000 records of that length by default, since they would require more than 64K blocks. Since SETMAXSIZE sets the minimum block size that Paradox will use when creating tables, if you had issued SETMAXSIZE 256 before creating this table, Paradox would be forced to use a 4K block. The maximum number of records able to be tracked would be close to 130,000.

So, the SETMAXSIZE command sets the minimum block size that Paradox will use when allocating blocks to a table. SETMAXSIZE 64 uses a 1K minimum block; 128 uses a 2K minimum block; 256 uses a 3K minimum block; and 512 sets a 4K minimum block. The default, SETMAXSIZE 64, lets Paradox do what it does naturally.

SETMAXSIZE does not affect the block size of existing tables; only newly created tables are affected. However, since Paradox often creates new tables in queries and restructures, you have to be careful when manipulating tables that have been set up with a SETMAXSIZE larger than the default (64K) and make sure that you enforce the override when necessary.

For example, if you had issued a SETMAXSIZE 256 when creating the table outlined above, you would need to make sure that the same SETMAXSIZE value was in effect when querying the records if it were likely that the number of records in the "Answer" table would exceed the number of blocks that Paradox would automatically choose for the "Answer" table. On the other hand, if the table is to be simply updated in Edit, CoEdit, etc., you would not need to SETMAXSIZE each time you entered Paradox.

If the table needs to be restructured, you could issue a SETMAXSIZE 256 just before the restructure and a SETMAXSIZE 64 after the restructure to get things back to normal.

This "Block Math" leads to a final critical point not directly related to SETMAXSIZE that can have a dramatic effect on table design and performance. In an unkeyed table, unless a record length goes into 1K evenly, there is always wasted space in Paradox's fixed length record. Thus you may be able to speed performance by shortening a record by a few bytes, and cut down on wasted space. In the example above, if you shorten an unkeyed record length of 510 to 509 bytes by restructuring the table and lopping off a single byte, two records will fit into the same amount of disk space as one did. In keyed tables, the same logic applies. If the length of a keyed record is 340 bytes, it will require a 2K block ($3*340+6=1026$). If you reduce the length of the record by only one byte, to 339, three records will fit in a single 1K block ($3*339+6=1023$ bytes). Since Paradox reads and writes records in blocks, the more records you can fit in a smaller block, the faster record access will be. Note: Paradox 3.5 defaults to a minimum block size of 2K.

## 11.13 OTHER DISK FACTORS

Other factors influencing disk performance are more obvious. For example, try to keep the number of files in the working directory of application to a minimum. Normal Paradox operations like sorting, querying, and reporting can create dozens or even hundreds of temporary files. With access to files dependent on DOS access, the fewer files created in a directory, the better. On networks, .LCK files will be made in the data directory. A well-documented warning is worth repeating here: always use a RESET before removing a floppy disk from which Paradox files have been accessed.

## 11.14 CHAPTER SUMMARY

SETSWAP and SETMAXSIZE are two explicit commands that influence memory and disk behavior, and thereby performance. Paradox386, which uses 16M of contiguous address space, doesn't suffer the same kinds of memory constraints Paradox3 does (as of this writing, Paradox386 is based on the Paradox2 release). With tables of 10,000 records or more, the performance advantages of PDOX386 are quite dramatic.

Though the disk caching provided by Paradox is effective, by no means is it of the quality that commercial disk caching products provide. An offering by MultiSoft called Super PCKwik is popular as a disk-cache substitute. In the way of expanded memory managers, QEMM and QEMM386 by Quarterdeck and 386-to-the-Max by Qualitas are popular as well. Both of the 386 products provide expanded memory simulation on the extended memory of 386. We have found that most disk-based expanded memory simulators on non-386 machines either don't work or work poorly, degrading Paradox performance. There is more information on these topics in Chapters 20 and 21.

## NOTES

1. A statement is equivalent to a single STEP in the PAL debugger.
2. Variables and images on the workspace cannot be swapped.
3. At this point, MEMLEFT() may be 50,000 or more, depending on the number of bytes freed by swapping out the last procedure.
4. Using a higher SETSWAP does not result in faster query processing: either the query will work or it won't.
5. This is also true for MINI and VALUE scripts called from the PAL menu.

# Part Two

# Chapter 12

# Input and Output

## 12.1 INTERACTING WITH THE USER

Programming means making many, many decisions: some critical, some seemingly arbitrary. Among the most critical are decisions about program logic—if nothing else, your scripts should accurately capture and present data. In many ways, creating program logic is easy because it is measurable—a record, a calculation, or a statistic about your data is either right or wrong. And as there are usually many ways to get the right answer, there are many ways to get the user to it.

The screen presents the most tangible evidence of your work, because what a user sees often leaves a stronger impression than what is hidden. No matter what level of attention you devote to the work your program does behind the scenes, how clever an algorithm, or how elegant a query, if the set of screen instructions that the program provides—its "user interface"—is ill-conceived or poorly executed, the user, and subsequently the data, will suffer. If your system is logically correct, but presents itself as ugly, illogical, or confusing, it may never be used. (On the other hand, no amount of screen pyrotechnics can make up for flaws in program logic.) This section presents PAL functions and commands that allow you to create and direct interaction with the user.

Though designing a user interface is a subjective art, its basics are universal. Give users clear directions and keep them informed. Hide unnecessary detail and leave the appreciation of your programming technique to other programmers. If possible, keep screens uncluttered. Use color for emphasis, not for color's sake. Keep up a screen dialogue, but don't ramble or shout.

What other things contribute to "interface" style?

- Do users type in values or pick them from menus and lists?
- Do you provide help? How?

- Is the screen frozen during background processing or does it keep the user informed?
- How do you handle run errors? (Do you alert the user? Allow system messages to show through?)

PAL functions and commands favor writing applications with a "Paradox interface." Though there is a trend (initiated by IBM's System Application Architecture (SAA)) towards using pulldown menus, millions of users are comfortable with Paradox- and Lotus-style bounce-bar menus. They are easy to understand and were designed to be easy to code and change. Other PAL commands provide direct ways of imitating the well-thought-out Paradox interface. The PAL MESSAGE command allows you to display messages as Paradox would. Many built-in facilities like [Zoom] and {TableLookup} Val-Checks are part of Paradox interaction under PAL.

When stuck on a question of design, we generally look to Paradox as the model. In most situations, [Esc] or [F10] {Cancel} gets you out of a Paradox menu choice or system mode; we generally follow the same rule. When Paradox needs more information from the user (for example, when sorting a table or creating Passwords), it usually presents a table or record to fill in. This technique offers many advantages, allowing you freedom to move from field to field and use Paradox features like [Ditto] as you would normally; ValChecks can dictate the limits of acceptable values.

Paradox provides you built-in tools to mimic its approach, and programming "the Paradox way" requires that you use these tools efficiently. Our emphasis will be on the use of the tools Paradox provides.

This chapter is divided into seven sections:

Getting Data From the User
Alerting the User
Presenting Menus
Displaying the Workspace
Controlling the Canvas
Controlling Graph Output
Controlling Printed Output

## 12.1.1 Getting Data from the User

The ACCEPT command is used to prompt the user for a value of a specified type. The syntax includes a broad array of options to check the value the user types in.

### ACCEPT: Accept a Value from the User

```
ACCEPT Type [MAX maxvalue] [MIN minvalue] [REQUIRED]
[LOOKUP tablename] [DEFAULT defaultvalue]
[PICTURE picturevalue] TO Varname
```

| | |
|---|---|
| Type | String evaluating to valid data type. |
| MAX maxvalue | Maximum value allowed. |
| MIN minvalue | Minimum value allowed. |
| PICTURE picturevalue | String evaluating to a valid picture. |
| REQUIRED | If nonblank value is required. |
| LOOKUP tablename | Input must appear in first column of a table. |
| DEFAULT defaultvalue | Default value to display. |
| TO | |
| Varname | Name of variable to be assigned when [Enter] is pressed. The variable is not assigned if [Esc] is pressed. |

Returns:

| | |
|---|---|
| A Variable | Variable varname is set to input. |
| RETVAL = True | Gets set to True if a selection is made. |
| RETVAL = False | Set to False if user pressed [Esc] or [Ctrl-Break]. |

The script pauses until the user types in a value and presses [Enter] or [Esc] ([CtrlBreak] is treated as an [Esc]). If the user ends an entry by pressing [Enter], the variable designated by the "To varname" parameter is assigned the value entered from the keyboard.

One of the most common PAL programming errors we encounter is an error of omission: not trapping for [Esc] after an ACCEPT. Users inevitably press [Esc] to get out of what they're doing. ACCEPT was designed to handle this probability, but PAL relies on you to test for this condition. When [Esc] is pressed after an ACCEPT, the system variable RETVAL is set to False, but the varname specified will not be assigned. If the varname was previously assigned and not released, it will retain its old value. You must check the status of RETVAL immediately after each ACCEPT.

```
IF RETVAL = False THEN
   RETURN
ELSE
```

ACCEPT's optional parameters permit extensive error trapping. Number and date formatting is automatic when specifying type "N," "S," "$," or "D." FieldView does not work, nor does Lookup Help for lookup functions. If multiple ACCEPT statements are required, it usually pays to build tables for data entry instead of using ACCEPTs. Tables and forms allow the user to move around in a true Paradox table, while creating the illusion of a form with multiple ACCEPTs usually requires a lot of code. On the other hand, ACCEPT gives total control over the placement and style of data entry elements, and can be used in any Paradox mode.

If your scripts issue a CURSOR OFF, you'll need to turn the cursor back on so that the user can see the cursor position during the accept. See the notes on the CURSOR command.

```
@1,0 CLEAR EOL
??"Or Press Esc to cancel"
@0,0 CLEAR EOL
?? "Enter your name: "
CURSOR NORMAL
ACCEPT "A25" TO name.a
CURSOR OFF
; now continue using or evaluating the result of the ACCEPT
```

Two examples below prompt a user for a password and verify the entry against a table with a first field that contains valid passwords. The first example works harder than it should, and this is corrected in the second example.

Another little trick used in the code is setting the STYLE ATTRIBUTE to 0, black on black, so the value typed in does not appear on the screen.

### Listing 12.1: ACCEPT.L1

```
WHILE TRUE
  @1,0 CLEAR EOL
  ??"Or Press Esc to cancel"
  @0,0
  ?? "Enter your authorization code: "
  STYLE ATTRIBUTE 0        ; black on black
  CURSOR NORMAL
  ACCEPT "A8" REQUIRED
  TO password.a
  STYLE                    ; reset to normal style for all subsequent text
  CURSOR OFF               ; only need CURSOR NORMAL for ACCEPT and RUN commands
  IF RETVAL=FALSE THEN     ; user pressed esc
    EXIT   ; exit paradox, back to DOS
  ENDIF
  VIEW "PWORDS"
  MOVETO [codes]
  LOCATE password.a
  CLEARIMAGE
  IF NOT RETVAL THEN       ; same as retval=false
    MESSAGE password.a, " is not a valid entry"
  ELSE
    QUITLOOP               ; entry was ok, so quit the loop and continue
  ENDIF
ENDWHILE
; rest of script would use variable password.a where appropriate
```

In contrast, the second example shows how you can greatly simplify the task of validating passwords by using the LOOKUP option of ACCEPT to verify data with values in the first field of a specified table. If the user attempts to enter data not contained in this other table, a message appears: "Not one of the possible values for this field." This message is a Paradox message—you don't have to provide it. The same code may be rewritten:

**Listing 12.2: ACCEPT.L2**

```
@ 1, 0 CLEAR EOL
??"Or Press Esc to cancel"
@ 0, 0 CLEAR EOL
?? "Enter your authorization code: "
STYLE ATTRIBUTE 0           ; black on black
CURSOR NORMAL
ACCEPT "A8" REQUIRED  LOOKUP "Pwords"  ; LOOKUP restricts values to those
                                       ; found in the first field of "Pwords"
TO password.a
STYLE                       ; reset to normal style for all subsequent text
CURSOR OFF                  ; only need CURSOR NORMAL for ACCEPT and RUN commands
IF RETVAL=FALSE THEN        ; user pressed esc
  EXIT                      ; exit paradox, back to DOS
ENDIF
; rest of script would use variable password.a where appropriate
```

On a network, the LOOKUP option places a write lock on the lookup table for the duration of the ACCEPT. If ACCEPT cannot place a write lock (because someone else has either a Full Lock or a Prevent Write Lock on the table) within the currently set retry period, a run error will occur and Paradox will trigger an ERRORCODE() = 3 and set ERRORUSER() to the name of the user who is preventing the write lock.

You can use an errorproc procedure to inform the user of the conflict and possibly take corrective action. Another approach is to try to place an explicit write lock before the ACCEPT command and remove the lock after the ACCEPT.

As a reminder, PAL attempts to place a write lock on any table when using functions that access data from a column: CMIN, CMAX, CAVERAGE, CSUM, CNPV, CVAR, CSTD, CCOUNT, IMAGECMIN, IMAGECMAX, IMAGECSUM, IMAGECAVERAGE, and IMAGECCOUNT. See the listed commands as well as LOCK and UNLOCK for more examples.

The next script uses ACCEPT to let you jump ahead any number of records in a table image, with a default value halfway between the cursor position and the end of the table. The PICTURE clause restricts the entry to whole numbers. The code requires a response but defaults to one half the distance between the current record and the last record. It uses NIMAGERECORDS() instead of NRECORDS() so it can work correctly in embedded forms.

**Listing 12.3: ACCEPT.L3**

```
@1,0 CLEAR EOL
?? "Currently on Record ",RECNO()," of ",
NIMAGERECORDS(TABLE()),". Press [Esc] to quit."
```

```
@0,0 CLEAR EOL
??"How many records to move forward? (MAX ",NIMAGERECORDS(TABLE())-RECNO(),")  "
CURSOR NORMAL

ACCEPT "N" MAX (NIMAGERECORDS(TABLE())-RECNO()) PICTURE "#[*#]" REQUIRED
DEFAULT INT( (NIMAGERECORDS(TABLE())-RECNO()) /2 )
TO choice.n

CURSOR OFF
IF RETVAL THEN
  MOVETO RECORD RECNO()+choice.n
ENDIF
```

We've already looked at the effects of the user making a selection and at what happens when the user presses [Esc]. There is another possibility—what happens when the user presses [CTRLBREAK] in response to an ACCEPT?

Normally, pressing [CtrlBreak] interrupts script play and brings you to a {Cancel}/{Debug} menu. With password protected scripts, [CtrlBreak] has no effect unless the password has been issued. If you are going to protect your top level script, some additional notes are in order.

If [CtrlBreak] is pressed during an ACCEPT command two things happen:

1. Retval is sent to True
2. The variable normally assigned by the ACCEPT is set to the current value in the field when [CtrlBreak] is pressed.

The latter of the two effects is particularly problematic because the [CtrlBreak] keypress overides any and all validity checking. Some examples:

1. ACCEPT "A5" REQUIRED to choice.a
   a. If the user presses [CtrlBreak] and the field is blank, choice.a=""
2. ACCEPT "A5" PICTURE "&&&&&" to choice.a
   a. If the user presses [CtrlBreak] and only three characters (ABC) have been filled in, choice.a="ABC"
3. ACCEPT "N" LOOKUP "Customer" to choice.n
   a. If the user presses [CtrlBreak] while an invalid customer code is in the field, choice.n is set to that code.
4. ACCEPT "D" REQUIRED to choice.d
   a. If the user presses [CtrlBreak] while an invalid or incomplete date is on the screen, the results can be unpredictable because of the way Paradox handles blank and incomplete dates.

| User Types in | Choice.d Is Set to | |
|---|---|---|
| nothing | blankdate() | ; valid blank date |
| 1/1/90 | 1/01/90 | ; valid date |
| 1/45/90 | 2/14/90 | ; invalid date wraps forward |

| 1/1 | 1/01/7765 | ; incomplete date |
| 1 | 12/31/–30400 | ; incomplete date |
| 15– | 3/16/7875 | ; incomplete dd-MON-yy format |

So, if you are going to be running protected scripts, you will need to do some additional errorchecking to make sure that the value returned by an ACCEPT command actually does what you need it to do.

Also remember that turning off [CtrlBreak] in the Paradox's Custom Configuration program does not have any effect in PAL scripts. It only keeps interactive users from doing things like clearing all images off the workspace by pressing [CtrlBreak].

The next two functions are input functions, and deal with individual keystrokes. The first, GETCHAR(), is used to grab a keystroke from the user and it returns the Paradox keycode. Every keystroke that gets typed is first put into the keystroke buffer.

### GETCHAR: Get a Keystroke from the Keyboard Buffer

```
GETCHAR ()
```

Returns:

A Number    The number of the next character in the keyboard buffer.
            A positive number if an ASCII character. A negative
            number if an IBM extended character.

If the buffer is empty, GETCHAR() produces a pause in script processing and the program waits for the next press of a key. If there is a character waiting, the key is removed from the buffer.

### CHARWAITING: Is There a Keystroke Pending?

```
CHARWAITING ()
```

Returns:

True     There is a keystroke pending.
False    The keyboard buffer is empty.

CHARWAITING asks a question of the system: "Is there a keystroke pending in the keyboard buffer?" Here's one example of its use that restricts the user's ability to type ahead of the program's ability to process.

**Listing 12.4: CHARWAIT.L1**

```
PROC clearkeyboard.u()
  PRIVATE n
  WHILE CHARWAITING()    ; as long as there is a key in the keyboard buffer
    n=GETCHAR()          ; grab the character
  ENDWHILE
ENDPROC
```

When you display a message, you usually need to give the user time to read the
text. Typically, a simple statement can follow the message:

```
MESSAGE "Read this message, then press any key."
n = GETCHAR()
```

However, if the user types ahead of the program, a key already stored in the
keyboard buffer might satisfy the GETCHAR() and clear the message before it
could be read. So here's a procedure that clears the keyboard buffer and beeps at
the user until any key is pressed.

**Listing 12.5: GETCHAR.L1**

```
;  Beeps until operator presses any key, formal parameter delay.n sets sleep
;  time between beeps.  That way the beeping can be made more (or less) urgent.
;  Used to get operator's attention when necessary.
;
;   Example:
;   MESSAGE "This is some text.  Press any key to continue"
;   Beeper.u (1000)

PROC beeper.u(delay.n)
  PRIVATE n                      ; n any characters in the buffer

                                 ; First CLEAR buffer if necessary
  WHILE CHARWAITING()            ; user might be typing ahead of the program
    n=GETCHAR()                  ; grab keystroke from buffer assign to n
  ENDWHILE

  IF delay.n > 30000 THEN
    delay.n = 1000               ; if more than 30000, set delay.n to one second
  ENDIF

  WHILE NOT CHARWAITING()        ; waits for keystroke from operator
    BEEP BEEP                    ; two quick beeps to alert operator
    SLEEP delay.n                ; pauses for the amount specified by delay.n
  ENDWHILE

  n=GETCHAR()                    ; retreives the operator keystroke.
                                 ; necessary so it doesn't get passed on to
                                 ; program
ENDPROC
```

GETCHAR() is used extensively by the Data Entry Toolkit to retrieve each character whose key is pressed. See the chapter "The Data Entry Toolkit" for a complete explanation of the versatility of GETCHAR(). In addition, look at the listings under the discussion of ECHO later in this chapter.

## 12.1.2 Alerting the User

### BEEP: Produce a Beep

```
BEEP        Sounds the speaker
```

The BEEP command sounds a short beep through the computer's speaker. The beep sounded is slightly lower in tone than Paradox's keyboard beep. There is no control over the duration or tone of the beep. After finishing a query, you might want to alert the user to a lack of records in the answer table:

```
BEEP BEEP
MESSAGE "No records meet your specifications, press any key"
n = GETCHAR()
```

### SLEEP: Pause Script Execution for a Period of Time

```
SLEEP Number
```

Number    Numeric expression between 0 and 30,000 representing the number of milliseconds for the script to pause.

SLEEP 1000 makes script processing pause for one second. Note that SLEEP is also a keyword in the RUN command, where it pauses after running a DOS command so the user can see the results of the DOS program.

## 12.1.3 Presenting Menus

PAL has two types of menu tools available. The SHOW commands define Paradox style menus and the PopUp procedures in the Data Entry Toolkit present vertical menu choices. All of the Paradox SHOW menus produce bounce-bar menus on the top two lines of the screen. Bounce-bar menus offer simplicity of design and ease of use.

The bounce-bar menus in Paradox display instantly and they appear above the Paradox workspace. The second line provides up to 80 characters for a detailed description of each menu choice. The menus disappear after use; there is no need to update the PAL canvas.

These menus are extremely simple to use. If you define menu choices with unique first letters, simply pressing the letter will activate the choice. This is consistent with the way Paradox works: {Tools} {More} {Directory} can be issued at the keyboard by simply pressing the letters "TMD." If the menu contains more than one choice with the same first letter, pressing the letter will let the user select from only those applicable choices.

In addition, all of the menu commands are available from any Paradox mode. Most SHOW commands have little memory overhead. PAL has four types of SHOW menus:

- SHOWMENU lets you design menu choices and descriptions.
- SHOWARRAY takes choices and descriptions from two arrays that you predefine. (This lets you define the menu choices "on the fly.")
- SHOWTABLES presents a menu of all of the tables in a subdirectory.
- SHOWFILES presents a menu of files that match a specification.

With all of these commands, when a user makes a menu choice, a variable is set to that choice. If the user presses [Esc], the variable is set to "Esc." We'll discuss each SHOW menu in turn and then present a procedure to sort a table that uses several of the SHOW commands together. There are additional examples of SHOWMENUs combined with full screens of text with the descriptions under the TEXT command.

### SHOWMENU: Display a Menu of Predefined Choices

```
SHOWMENU MenuItemList [DEFAULT defaultvalue] To Varname
```

| | |
|---|---|
| MenuItemList | Comma separated list of choices and descriptions. |
| DEFAULT | Highlight a specific menuchoice. |
| defaultvalue | Value to be highlighted on the menu. |
| To | |
| Varname | Variable to be assigned when choice is made |

When writing the MenuItemList, it is important to remember that each choice is separated from its description by a colon, and that all but the last descriptions end with a comma. SHOWMENU in its simplest form:

**Listing 12.6: SHOWMENU.L1**

```
SHOWMENU
  "Files":"Play the files script",
  "Report":"Play the report script",
  "Utility":"Play the utility script"
TO choice.a
  ; now let's decide on a course of action based on the user's choice
```

```
SWITCH
  CASE choice.a = "Files":
    PLAY "File"            ; plays the file menu script
  CASE choice.a = "Report":
    PLAY "Report"          ; play the report script
  CASE choice.a = "Utility":
    PLAY "Utility"         ; play the utility script
  CASE choice.a = "Esc" :
    QUIT                   ; exit back to Paradox
ENDSWITCH
```

When played, the SHOWMENU would display:

```
Files  Report  Utility
Play the files script
```

with the Files choice highlighted. This example executes the menu only once; when a choice is made, the appropriate script is played. You usually want the called scripts to return back to this menu, where pressing [Esc] allows you to exit. This requires a loop. This next procedure uses a loop and a default choice to highlight the last menu choice made.

**Listing 12.7: SHOWMENU.L2**

```
PROC mainmenu.u()
  choice.a = "Files"   ; initialize the default choice
  WHILE TRUE    ; begin the loop
    CLEAR   ; clear the screen
    SHOWMENU
      "Files":"Play the files script",
      "Report":"Play the report script",
      "Utility":"Play the utility script"
      DEFAULT choice.a
    TO choice.a
    ; now let's decide on a course of action based on the user's choice
    SWITCH
      CASE choice.a = "Files":
        PLAY "File"             ; plays the filemenu script
      CASE choice.a = "Report":
        PLAY "Report"
      CASE choice.a = "Utility":
        PLAY "Utility"
      CASE choice.a = "Esc" :
        QUIT                         ; exit back to Paradox
    ENDSWITCH
    ; now the menu will repeat again because it goes back to the top of the loop
  ENDWHILE
ENDPROC

; now execute the menu

mainmenu.u()
```

Now when the user picks "Report," the script plays "Report.sc," and then redisplays the menu, this time highlighting "Report." Unfortunately, subsequent scripts may overwrite existing variables. If in the script above, the "Report.sc" sets choice.a to "Customer," the DEFAULT option won't work properly when play continues. There are several ways to handle this:

1. Add a line to explicitly reset the variable.

```
CASE choice.a = "Report":
  PLAY "REPORT"
  choice.a = "Report"  ; assure that the variable doesn't change
```

2. Use procedures and define variables as PRIVATE to their procedures.

```
CASE choice.a = "Report":
  reportmenu.u() ; typically residing in a library specified by autolib.
```

When the following procedure executes, Choice.a in the ReportMenu.u procedure is PRIVATE and does not affect the Choice.a variable in the main menu loop.

**Listing 12.8: SHOWMENU.L3**

```
PROC reportmenu.u()
  PRIVATE choice.a        ; private variable won't affect other procs above it
  choice.a = "Customer"   ; initialize the default choice
  WHILE TRUE   ; begin the loop
    CLEAR  ; clear the screen
    SHOWMENU
      "Customer":"Print the customer report",
      "Invoice":"Print the invoices"
      DEFAULT choice.a
    TO choice.a
    SWITCH
      CASE choice.a = "Customer":
        REPORT "Customer" 1   ; print customer.r1
      CASE choice.a = "Invoice":
        REPORT "Invoice" 3
      CASE choice.a = "Esc" :
        RETURN              ; back to the menu that called it
    ENDSWITCH
  ENDWHILE
ENDPROC
```

A menu inside a procedure lets Paradox handle the lifetime of variables (and other related memory issues). There is an additional SHOWMENU trap to look out for. Look at the following code carefully:

**Listing 12.9: SHOWMENU.L4**

```
WHILE TRUE
  SHOWMENU
    "view":"View a table",
    "report":"Report on a table"
  TO choice.a
  SWITCH
    CASE choice.a = "view":
      viewmenu.u ()
    CASE choice.a = "report":
      reportmenu.u ()
    CASE choice.a = "Esc":
      RETURN
    OTHERWISE :
      BEEP
      MESSAGE "Error: You pressed ", choice.a
      SLEEP 2000
  ENDSWITCH
ENDWHILE
```

You might expect that this SHOWMENU would work just fine, and it does. The SWITCH does not; in fact, neither procedure will execute. Paradox *automatically* capitalizes the first letter of each menu choice string in a showmenu (even if you code them in lowercase). The CASE comparisons, which are written to match the menu choices, are in lowercase. The SWITCH statement won't work correctly—"view" does not equal "View." So the corrected switch would have to look like this:

**Listing 12.10: SHOWMENU.L5**

```
SWITCH
  CASE choice.a = "View":
    viewmenu.u ()
  CASE choice.a = "Report":
    reportmenu.u ()
```

You can also allow for more flexibility in SHOW commands by using variables in place of quoted strings. There is little penalty for storing menu choices and their descriptions as variables (except the little memory they use). Although SHOWARRAY may be better suited to accomplishing this purpose, variables in SHOWMENU can be very handy.

The next example uses PAL functions to place the current year into a SHOWMENU choice, and calculates the procedure to execute with EXECPROC.

**Listing 12.11: SHOWMENU.L6**

```
WHILE TRUE
  SHOWMENU
```

```
     "1969" : "Do the 1969 analysis",
     "1979" : "Do the 1979 analysis",
     STRVAL(YEAR(TODAY())) : "Do current year analysis"
  TO choice.a

    SWITCH
      CASE choice.a = "Esc":
        RETURN
      OTHERWISE:
        EXECPROC "analysis" + choice.a + ".u"
        ; EXECPROC executes a procedure whose name is passed as a parameter.
        ; This code assumes that a script has already defined procedures called
        ; analysis1969.u ()
        ; analysis1979.u ()
        ; and a simliarly named proc for the current year
        ;   i.e., analysis1989.u()
        ; and they are already in memory, or in a library accessible to AUTOLIB
    ENDSWITCH
ENDWHILE
```

The menu displays 1969, 1979, and the current year.

### SHOWARRAY: Display a Menu Based on Values in a Pair of Arrays

```
SHOWARRAY Array1 Array2 [DEFAULT Choice] To Varname
```

| | |
|---|---|
| Array1 | Name of array with menu choices. |
| Array2 | Name of array with menu descriptions. |
| DEFAULT | Optional default highlight. |
| Choice | The item to highlight. |
| To | |
| Varname | Name of variable to be assigned with the choice made. |

Returns:

| | |
|---|---|
| A String | The choice that the user made, or "Esc" if the user pressed [Esc]. |

Sets:

| | |
|---|---|
| RETVAL = True | If user actually makes a selection by pressing Enter. |
| RETVAL = False | If user presses Esc. |

SHOWARRAY lets you create menus that can be easily changed at your whim, or that reflect choices that are appropriate at any given moment.

### Listing 12.12: SHOWARRA.L1

```
ARRAY  choice.r [4]            ; define the choices array
choice.r [1] = "Lucy"
choice.r [2] = "Ricky"
```

```
choice.r [3] = "Fred"
choice.r [4] = "Ethel"

ARRAY  desc.r [4]
desc.r [1] = "Zany redhead"
desc.r [2] = "Cuban bandleader"
desc.r [3] = "Tightwad landlord"
desc.r [4] = "Friend and accomplice"

SHOWARRAY
  choice.r   desc.r
TO choice.a
```

would display the following menu:

```
Lucy  Ricky  Fred  Ethel
Zany redhead
```

It is important to remember these three restrictions:

1. The two arrays *must* be defined with the same number of elements
2. Each element *must* be assigned
3. Each element *must* be a string value

We'll demonstrate creating the arrays dynamically at the end of this section.

### SHOWFILES: Display a Menu of Files That Match a Specification

```
SHOWFILES [NOEXT] DOSPath Prompt To Varname
```

| | |
|---|---|
| NOEXT | Optionally, do not show file extensions |
| DOSPath | String for directory to search including file wildcard specifications. |
| Prompt | Message to appear on the top line of the screen. |
| To | |
| Varname | Name of variable to assign with the choice made. |

Returns:

| | |
|---|---|
| A Value | A string of the choice made from the menu, exactly as it appears on the menu. "Esc" if the user presses [Esc], or "None" if no files are found for the specification. |

Sets:

| | |
|---|---|
| RETVAL = True | If user actually makes a selection by pressing Enter. |
| RETVAL = False | If [Esc] is chosen. |

The SHOWFILES command doesn't always list all the files specified. Often, a RESET is helpful when SHOWFILES seems to be returning an incomplete list because Paradox-created files may not yet be written to disk. Always use SHOWTABLES instead of SHOWFILES "*.db" if you want to show a menu of tables for two reasons:

1. tables may still be in memory and may not yet be written to disk, and
2. tables may be in a private directory, yet still accessible to the user.

The following code fragment presents a menu of all Quattro spreadsheets. If the user makes a selection, it runs Quattro with the selected worksheet. After exiting Quattro, the run command returns to Paradox.

**Listing 12.13: SHOWFILE.L1**

```
SHOWFILES noext        ; do not show the WKQ extension
  "\\Quattro\\*.WKQ"   ; file specifications
  "Select the Quattro worksheet to use"
TO choice.a

IF choice.a <> "Esc" AND choice.a <> "None" THEN
  RUN BIG "Q " + "\\Quattro\\" + choice.a
ENDIF
```

## SHOWTABLES: Display a Menu of Tables Found in a Directory

```
SHOWTABLES DosPath Prompt To Varname
```

| | |
|---|---|
| DosPath | String specifying DOS directory. |
| Prompt | String that will appear at the top of the screen. |
| To | |
| Varname | Name of variable to assign if the user makes a menu selection. |

Returns:

| | |
|---|---|
| A Value | A string of the choice made from the menu, exactly as it appears on the menu. "Esc" if the user presses [Esc], "None" if no tables are found. |

Sets:

| | |
|---|---|
| RETVAL = True | If user actually makes a selection by pressing Enter. |
| RETVAL = False | If [Esc] is chosen |

The SHOWTABLES command displays a menu with choices for the tables you would normally get with:

```
{Tools} {Info} {Inventory} {Tables}
```

(except the Tools approach often includes the LIST table just created).

Both techniques include PRIVATE tables and files not yet written to the disk. The next example presents a list of tables for the c:\Paradox3\samples subdirectory, and if the user makes a selection, the table is placed on the workspace.

**Listing 12.14: SHOWTABL.L1**

```
SHOWTABLES
  "c:\\Paradox3\\sample"     ; trailing backslashes are optional
  "Select a table to view, or Press [Esc] to cancel"
TO choice.a
SWITCH
  CASE choice.a = "None" :  ; no tables found, menu wasn't displayed at all
    MESSAGE "There were no tables found"
    SLEEP 3000
  CASE choice.a = "Esc" :
    MESSAGE "Cancelled"
    SLEEP 2000
  OTHERWISE:
    VIEW choice.a           ; view the table selected
ENDSWITCH
```

It is worth reiterating that you shouldn't use SHOWFILES *.DB because it doesn't have the sophistication necessary to deal with private directories. The only disadvantage to SHOWTABLES is that you can't show a subset of available tables. If you need to do this, you can use {Tools} {Info} {Inventory} {Tables} to create a temporary LIST table, delete any records of table names that do not match your specifications, SCAN the table, and set up two arrays for a SHOWARRAY menu.

For example, to show a menu of tables that meet a particular wild-card match, you could use the following procedure. Unlike SHOWTABLES, the ShowTablePattern.a procedure can only be called from MAIN mode.

**Listing 12.15: SHOWTABL.L2**

```
PROC showtablepattern.a (directory.a, pattern.a)
  ; directory.a      ; DOS subdirectory
  ; pattern.a        ; Paradox style wildcard pattern  i.e. "B.."
  ; RETURNS          ; Like SHOWFILES, this proc returns a table name,
  ;                    "None" , if no files match the specifications or
  ;                    "Esc", if the user cancels, or
  ;                    "Error" if the syntax is invalid.

  PRIVATE
  choice.r,          ; array of tables found
  desc.r,            ; descriptions
  choice.a           ; selection made
```

```
       IF DIREXISTS(directory.a) <> 1 THEN    ; directory does not exist, or invalid
         RETURN "Error"
       ENDIF

       Menu {Tools} {Info} {Inventory} {Tables}
       SELECT directory.a    ; this produces a "List" table with names of tables found

       Clearimage
       MENU {Ask} {List}
       moveto [name]
       Check
       TYPEIN  pattern.a
       DO_IT!

       IF WINDOW() <> "" then    ; there was an error in the pattern syntax
         CLEARALL
         RETURN "Error"
       ENDIF

       IF ISEMPTY("Answer") then
         CLEARALL    ; the query and its answer table
         RETURN "None"
       ELSE  ; we are viewing the answer table
         ARRAY choice.r  [NRECORDS("Answer")]  ; table names
         ARRAY desc.r  [NRECORDS("Answer")]     ; description
         SCAN
           choice.r [RECNO()] = [name]            ; name of table for this record
           desc.r  [RECNO()] = "Select the " + [name] + " table"   ; description
         ENDSCAN
         CLEARALL
         SHOWARRAY  choice.r  desc.r
         TO choice.a
         RETURN choice.a    ; a table name, or the string "Esc"
       ENDIF
     ENDPROC


       ; Now to use the procedure to present a menu of all tables beginning with the
       ; letter C and view the selected table:

       table.a = showtablepattern.a ("c:\\Paradox3\\Toolkit\\","C..")

       SWITCH
         CASE table.a = "Esc":
           MESSAGE "Canceled"
           SLEEP 2000
         CASE table.a = "None":
           MESSAGE "No tables found"
           SLEEP 2000
         CASE table.a = "Error":              ; in this demo, we know that C.. is ok.
           MESSAGE "Error in pattern"
           SLEEP 2000
         OTHERWISE:                            ; view the table
           VIEW table.a
       ENDSWITCH
```

This lets the user select from "Cust" and "Carriers", or whatever other tables begin with "C", and assign their choice to table.a. If the user actually made a selection, the table would be placed on the workspace; if not, the appropriate message is displayed. Note that the pattern.a parameter can be any valid PAL query syntax. For example:

```
"C.."            Tables starting with C
"NOT C.."        Tables that don't start with C
">L"             Tables greater than L
"Like Samson"    Samson, Sammy, Sonny, etc.
```

Finally, the last example ties three of the SHOW commands together, allowing the user to select a table from a predetermined directory, pick a field to sort by, and choose the direction of the sort. It then presents an "Answer" table, sorted appropriately. Using menus allow users to simply point and shoot.

**Listing 12.16: SHOWDEMO.L1**

```
; This procedure centers a text line used for display later on

PROC centertext.u (row.n, text.a)
  ; row.n       ; screen row
  ; text.a      ; any string of text

  @ row.n, 0
  ?? FORMAT("W80,AC", text.a)    ; display the text centered on the screen
ENDPROC


PROC sort2answer.l (directory.a)
  ; directory.a     ; DOS directory name
  ; RETURNS         ; True if sort was successful,
  ;                 ; False if user canceled

  PRIVATE
  table.a,          ; table selected from menu
  field.a,          ; field selected from menu
  order.a,          ; sort order selected
  fields.r,         ; array of field names
  desc.r            ; array of field descriptions

  CURSOR OFF        ; turn off the cursor, so it doesn't blink at us
  CLEAR             ; clear the screen
  CLEARALL          ; clear the workspace
  IF ISTABLE("Answer") THEN
    DELETE "Answer" ; we don't want Answer table in list
  ENDIF

  ; Use SHOWTABLES to show a menu of all tables in the subdirectory

  centertext.u (4, "Please select a table from the list above")

  SHOWTABLES
    directory.a    "Tables available in " + directory.a
  TO table.a
```

```
      IF table.a = "Esc" OR table.a= "None" THEN  ; [Esc], or no tables found
        RETURN FALSE
      ENDIF

      ; let's prepare a SHOWARRAY menu of fields for the table

      centertext.u (4, "Working..... preparing menu of field names")
      MENU {Tools} {Info} {Structure}
      SELECT table.a    ; creates a "Struct" table of field names

      ARRAY fields.r [nrecords("Struct")]  ; array with room for each field name
      ARRAY   desc.r [nrecords("Struct")]

      ; now scan the table and place the field names and descriptions into
      ; the two arrays that will be used with SHOWARRAY.
      SCAN
        fields.r [recno()] = [field name]
        desc.r [recno()] = "Sort table by " + [field name]  ; description
      ENDSCAN
      DELETE "Struct"   ; remove the structure table
      centertext.u (4, "Select a field to sort by")

      ; show the menu of available field names

      SHOWARRAY
        fields.r  desc.r
      TO field.a      ; name of field chosen
      IF field.a = "Esc" THEN
        RETURN FALSE
      ENDIF

      ; next present a SHOWMENU that lets the user decide on sort order

      centertext.u (4, "Select sort order")
      SHOWMENU
        "Ascending"  : "Sort in ascending order by " + field.a ,
        "Descending" : "Sort in descending order by " + field.a
      TO order.a
      IF order.a = "Esc" THEN
        RETURN FALSE
      ENDIF

      ; finally, sort the selected table to a new table called "Answer"
      IF order.d = "Ascending" THEN
        SORT table.a ON field.a TO "Answer"
      ELSE
        SORT table.a ON field.a D TO "Answer"   ; D specifies Descending
      ENDIF
      MOVETO FIELD field.a     ; place cursor in the selected field
      RETURN TRUE              ; everything went well
    ENDPROC

    ;----------------------------
    ; now to use the procedure:

    l= sort2answer.l ( DIRECTORY() )    ; show tables for the current directory
    IF l THEN
      RETURN "Here is your Answer table"
```

```
ELSE
  RETURN "Sort canceled"
ENDIF
```

## 12.1.4 Displaying the Workspace

### WAIT: Show User a Table until a Specified Keystroke Is Pressed

```
WAIT {Table | RECORD | FIELD} [PROMPT ExpressionList] [MESSAGE
Expression] UNTIL KeycodeList
```

| | |
|---|---|
| WAIT | Begin the wait. |
| TABLE | User can move through all records. |
| RECORD | User is limited to current record. |
| FIELD | User is limited to current field. |
| PROMPT | Display Prompt1 and Prompt2 on top of screen. |
| ExpressionList | Prompt1,Prompt2 for first and second lines. |
| MESSAGE | Display a message until any key is pressed. |
| Expression | Message to display. |
| UNTIL | |
| KeyCodeList | List of keycodes that will exit the WAIT condition. |

Sets:

RETVAL      To the key pressed in the UNTIL clause.

The WAIT command is the most common way of letting the user interact with Paradox tables. All the WAIT variations "lift" the PAL canvas, exposing the underlying table on the workspace. The WAIT session ends when one element of a specified list of keys is pressed. Since a WAIT returns a single value, a SWITCH statement is usually used to direct action based on the selection. When the WAIT session ends, the PAL canvas is repainted with the workspace.

WAIT is useful on all levels, from simple access to a table, to complex subsystems like WAITPLUS. WAIT comes in three forms:

WAIT TABLE, WAIT RECORD, and WAIT FIELD

The PROMPT option of the WAIT commands, which displays one or two lines of messages at the top of the screen, may be overridden by the stand-alone PROMPT command. The MESSAGE option puts an inverse video message in the lower right at the beginning of the WAIT until a key is pressed.

    We recommend always trapping for two Paradox special keys that allow you to temporarily leave Paradox: [Ctrl O], "DOS," and [Alt O], "DOSBIG." As a reminder, these keys suspend the Paradox environment and invoke a DOS shell. We trap "DOS" and "DOSBIG" in every WAIT interaction, for it's both disorienting to the user and dangerous to your application to allow them to slip by. We also prefer to use the names of Paradox special keys whenever possible, because they make the code easier to understand. However, certain keycodes don't have Paradox aliases. For example, although [Ctrl F] can be represented as 6 or "FieldView" [Ctrl C] can only be represented as the number 3.

The following code adds a bit of muscle to WAIT, trapping for these unwanted keys and demonstrating that the Zoom key ([Ctrl Z]) needs special handling. See the ZOOM command for a more complete procedure for handling Zoom in a WAIT. This example of WAIT lets the user view a table in TableView, edit individual records, or go into FieldView. It only begins to trap for record locking in CoEdit mode. Any LookupHelp can be accessed when editing a record by pressing [F1]. This example also doesn't handle key violation checking and doesn't allow the user to use FormView or delete any records.

**Listing 12.17: WAIT.L1**

```
VIEW "Customer"
WHILE TRUE          ; the wait table loop
  WAIT TABLE
    PROMPT "Viewing "+STRVAL(NRECORDS(TABLE()))+" in the "+TABLE()+" table",
    "[Esc] when done, [F9] edits current record"
  UNTIL "Esc","Zoom","F9","Dos","DosBig","FieldView", "F35"   ; "F35" is [Alt F]
  SWITCH
    CASE RETVAL="Esc" :   ; user pressed Esc, let's clear the table and quit the loop
      CLEARIMAGE
      QUITLOOP
    CASE RETVAL="FieldView" or RETVAL=6:
      FIELDVIEW
      WHILE TRUE    ; the WAIT Field Loop
        WAIT FIELD PROMPT
          "Press \017\217 when done with field view"  ; \017\217 shows up as <┘
          MESSAGE "Currently in FieldView"
        UNTIL "Enter","Dos","DosBig"
        IF RETVAL="Enter" THEN
          ; end the field view
          QUITLOOP ; quit the wait field loop and drop through the switch
        ENDIF
      ENDWHILE
    CASE  RETVAL="F9":  ; user wants to edit the record
      COEDITKEY          ; go into CoEdit mode
      LOCKRECORD         ; attempt to lock the record
      IF NOT RETVAL THEN   ; if lock was unsuccessful then
        DO_IT!  ; end coedit mode
        MESSAGE "Record is currently locked by ",ERRORUSER()
        BEEP
        SLEEP 2000
        LOOP  ; go back to the top of the WAIT table loop
      ENDIF
      WHILE TRUE       ; wait record loop
```

```
            WAIT RECORD
              PROMPT "Edit this record and press [F2] when done",
              "or [Esc] to cancel changes to record"
            UNTIL "F2","Esc","Dos","DosBig", "FieldView", "F35"
            SWITCH
              CASE RETVAL="F2":
                ; if necessary do some errorchecking here for fields that
                ; must be filled out etc.
                UNLOCKRECORD ; post the record to the table
                ; might need to do additional checking for key violations
                DO_IT!
                QUITLOOP
              CASE RETVAL="Esc":
                UNDO
                DO_IT!
                QUITLOOP
              CASE RETVAL="FieldView" or RETVAL="F35":
                FIELDVIEW
                WHILE TRUE
                  WAIT FIELD PROMPT
                  "Press \017\217 when done with field view" ;\017\217 shows up as <┘
                  MESSAGE "Currently in FieldView"
                  UNTIL "Enter","Dos","DosBig"
                  IF RETVAL="Enter" THEN
                   QUITLOOP ; quit the loop and drop thru the switch
                  ENDIF
                ENDWHILE
            ENDSWITCH
          ENDWHILE
    ENDSWITCH
ENDWHILE
```

The next example is simpler. It uses Edit mode and gives the user freeform access to any table with a specified form. it also allows records to be deleted after confirmation.

**Listing 12.18: WAIT.L2**

```
PROC waitdemo.u(table.a,form.a)
  ; table.a is the name of the table to view
  ; form.a is the name of the form to use

  PRIVATE choice.a
  EDIT table.a
  PICKFORM form.a
  WHILE TRUE
    WAIT TABLE
      PROMPT "Editing "+UPPER (table.a)+"  [F2]-Save&Quit",
      "[Esc]-CancelEdit [Del]-DeleteRecord  [F7]-FormToggle  [Ctrl-F]-FieldView"
    UNTIL  "F2","Esc","Del","F7","F35","FieldView", "Dos","DosBig"
    SWITCH
      CASE RETVAL="F2":
        DO_IT!
        CLEARALL
        RETURN
      CASE RETVAL="Del":
```

```
        SHOWMENU
          "Cancel":"Do not delete this record",
          "OK":"Ok to delete this record"
        TO choice.a
        IF choice.a = "OK" THEN
          DEL
        ENDIF
      CASE RETVAL="Esc":
        SHOWMENU
          "Edit":"Return to edit mode, do not cancel changes",
          "CancelEdit":"Ok to cancel all changes to this table and quit"
        TO choice.a
        IF choice.a = "CancelEdit" THEN
          CANCELEDIT
          CLEARALL
          RETURN
        ENDIF
      CASE RETVAL="F7":
        FORMKEY           ; simply toggle the form
      CASE RETVAL="FieldView" OR RETVAL="F35":
        FIELDVIEW
        WHILE TRUE
          WAIT FIELD
            PROMPT "Edit field and press \017\217 to continue",
            "Use cursor keys to move around in the field"
          UNTIL "Enter"
          IF RETVAL="Enter" THEN
            QUITLOOP
          ENDIF
        ENDWHILE
    ENDSWITCH
  ENDWHILE
ENDPROC


; now you could test the code by invoking:

WaitDemo.u("\\Paradox3\\Samples\\Customer", 1)
```

See an important description of how the UNTIL clause is evaluated in "Script Writing Fundamentals."

## ECHO: Lift the PAL Canvas so User Can See the Workspace

```
ECHO [NORMAL | OFF | FAST | SLOW]
```

NORMAL     Show current state of the workspace in real time.
OFF     Stop showing the workspace; show the canvas.
FAST     Show the workspace, but insert a delay between commands.
SLOW     Show the workspace, but insert a long delay between commands.

ECHO is used to rewrite the canvas with a scene of the underlying workspace. ECHO NORMAL refreshes the screen continuously, as fast as your PC can. ECHO FAST is equivalent to {Scripts} {ShowPlay} {Fast}, and inserts a delay between PAL statements to display what is going on step-by-step. ECHO SLOW inserts a long delay between each keystroke (you can feel yourself aging). ECHO OFF returns script play to the default state, leaving an image of the current workspace on the PAL canvas. In Paradox Runtime, the echo commands have no effect and must be replaced with the RefreshCanvas() procedure from the Data Entry Toolkit.

To refresh the canvas with a picture of the underlying workspace, use two variations of ECHO in succession:

ECHO NORMAL
ECHO OFF

Here's another example of ECHO that provides a partial remedy for a Paradox deficiency: Text fields have a limit of 255 characters. The Memo.1() procedure allows the user to type up to 23 lines of free-form notes, and then places each line into the ENTRY table. Although somewhat rudimentary, this simple technique is effective, making use of the Form mode and ECHO NORMAL as a memo pad. When the user presses [F2], the text will be transferred into the records of the "Entry" table.

```
Designing memo, Press [F2] when done, [F10] for menu
─────────────────────────────────────────────────────────────────
This is a test of the memo.l procedure that presents a rudimentary way of
using the Forms design area as a place to type free form text.

The cursor follows most of the same rules for [Ins] and [Del] as a text editor.
When [F2] is pressed the text is saved to a table called "Entry".
```

**Figure 12.1**
ECHO.FG1

```
Viewing Entry table: Record 1 of 5                                Main
                            ─Memo─
   This is a test of the memo.l procedure that presents a rudimentary way of
   using the Forms design area as a place to type free form text.

   The cursor follows most of the same rules for [Ins] and [Del] as a text edi
   When [F2] is pressed the text is saved to a table called "Entry".
```

**Figure 12.2**
ECHO.FG2

Here's the procedure:

**Listing 12.19: ECHO.L2**

```
PROC memo.l()
  PRIVATE
    n,                    ; numeric counter and getchar variable
    choice.a,             ; showmenu choice
    lastcol.n,            ; column position indicator
    memo.r                ; array that will hold screenful of data

  CREATE "Entry"          ; first create a table called entry
    "Memo":"A80"          ; with one A80 field

  {Forms} {Design} {ENTRY} {1} {}    ; go directly into form design on form 1
  ; now replace the normal Paradox prompt with a special message and a
  ; solid line.
  PROMPT "Designing memo, Press [F2] when done, [F10] for menu",
         FILL("\196",80)    ; 80 character solid line
  WHILE TRUE
    ECHO NORMAL           ; let the user see the workspace
    n = GETCHAR()         ; get a character from the user.
                          ; Remember that GETCHAR returns a number
    SWITCH
      CASE n = (-60):        ; user pressed [F2]
        QUITLOOP
      CASE n = (-68):        ; user pressed [F10]
        ECHO OFF
        SHOWMENU
          "DO-IT!":"Save memo and prepare report",
          "Cancel":"Cancel this memo"
        TO choice.a
        ECHO NORMAL
        SWITCH
          CASE choice.a = "Esc":
            ECHO NORMAL       ; will loop back to the top
          CASE choice.a="Cancel":
            CTRLBREAK         ; cancels the form design
            RETURN FALSE
          CASE choice.a="DO-IT!":
            QUITLOOP          ; stop getting characters from the user
        ENDSWITCH
      CASE n = 15 or n = -24:   ; Dos and DosBig
        BEEP
      OTHERWISE:                ; process the keystroke
        lastcol.n = COLNO()    ; find out the column number
        KEYPRESS n
        IF lastcol.n = 80 THEN
          DOWN                 ; move the cursor down one line, as it just
                               ; wrapped back to the beginning of the same line
        ENDIF
    ENDSWITCH
  ENDWHILE
  ECHO OFF                     ; let the user see only the canvas
  CLEAR
  @0,0 ??"Working loading Entry table"
```

```
HOME ; move to the first line of the form
ARRAY memo.r [23]              ; define an array to hold the screen lines
FOR n FROM 1 TO 23
  memo.r [n] = CURSORLINE()  ; assign each line to an array element
  IF n <> 23 THEN
    DOWN
  ENDIF
ENDFOR
CTRLBREAK                      ; move out of form design
EDIT "ENTRY"
MOVETO [memo]
FOR n FROM 1 TO 23
  [] = memo.r[n]
  DOWN
ENDFOR
DEL  ; the extra record appended by the last down
; now start with the last record and delete all of the records that have no
; text in them.  It will stop when it comes to a record with text.
WHILE [] = SPACES(80)        ; strip out the trailing spaces caused by any
  DEL                         ; blank lines below the last line of text
ENDWHILE
DO_IT!
HOME    ; you are now viewing the ENTRY table. It is available for standard
        ; reporting routines and can be renamed to save it.
ENDPROC
```

The procedure can be invoked:

```
l = Memo.l()
IF l THEN   ; the ENTRY table would be on the workspace
  InstantReport
ELSE
  MESSAGE  "Memo cancelled"
  SLEEP 2000
ENDIF
```

## PROMPT: Replace the Top Two Lines of the Workspace with a Custom Prompt

```
PROMPT Prompt1, Prompt2
```

Prompt1     String to display at the top of the screen.
Prompt2     String to display at the second line of screen.

The PROMPT command allows you to replace the default top two lines of workspace when no menu is being displayed and the workspace is viewed by either a WAIT, DoWait, or ECHO command. It has no effect on the PAL Canvas.

```
prompt1.a = "Editing " + TABLE()
```

```
prompt2.a = "Press F2 to end session"
PROMPT prompt1.a, prompt2.a
```

In a WAIT condition the stand-alone version of the PROMPT command over-rides the PROMPT option, which is part of the WAIT syntax. See the code listing under ECHO for an example of how to use PROMPT on the workspace.

## 12.1.5 Controlling the Canvas

Even experienced PAL programmers seem to have difficulty distinguishing when they are writing to the canvas and when they are manipulating the workspace. The rule is simple. Under Script control, a WAIT interaction is the only direct manipulation of the Paradox workspace; everything else is done on the canvas.

### CLEAR: Clears All or Part of the Canvas

```
CLEAR [{EOL} | {EOS}]
```

| | |
|---|---|
| CLEAR | Clears entire screen, from (0,0) to (24,79) |
| CLEAR EOL | Clears from the cursor position to the end of the line. |
| CLEAR EOS | Clears a rectangular block from the cursor position to the end of screen (24,79). |

The CLEAR command clears all or part of the PAL canvas. It is often confused with CLEARIMAGE or CLEARALL, which have nothing to do with the canvas. These commands remove tables from the underlying Paradox workspace.

The following example is handy in letting the user know that something is going on. Working.u() takes a message as a parameter and displays the word "Working" followed by blinking dots on the first line of the screen. If you invoke working.u(" "), the second line of the screen will be cleared; however, Working.u ("Preparing report, please wait") places the message on the second line under-neath the word "Working. . . ." Using this simple procedure and occasionally updating the message can go a long way towards making your users comfortable.

### Listing 12.20: CLEAR.L1

```
PROC working.u (message.a)
   a 0,0 CLEAR EOL      ; clear to the end of the line
   ??"Working"
   STYLE BLINK          ; begin blinking characters
   ??"...."             ; place a string of dots
   STYLE                ; end blinking characters
   a 1,0 CLEAR EOL
```

```
  ?? message.a      ; display the message.a string
ENDPROC
```

The next example shows how you can use a loop to clear a group of lines from row 5 to row 10.

**Listing 12.21: CLEAR.L2**

```
FOR n FROM 5 TO 10
  @ n, 0
  CLEAR EOL
ENDFOR
```

Typically, when starting an application, you would want to start with a "clean slate." The next code demonstrates a few lines from a startup script.

**Listing 12.22: CLEAR.L3**

```
CLEAR             ; Clears PAL canvas, as otherwise it would default to the
                  ; current Paradox workspace
MESSAGE "Working" ; while the rest of the cleanup proceeds
RESET             ; Assures current workspace is clear, removes all explicit
                  ; locks possibly also add
RELEASE VARS ALL  ; to remove any previous variables
RELEASE PROCS ALL ; to remove any previous procedures
SETDIR DIRECTORY() ; to remove all temporary tables as if you just got here
                  ; from another directory
```

See also PAINTCANVAS.

### MESSAGE: Displays a Message on the MESSAGE Line

```
MESSAGE Expressionlist
```

ExpressionList    A list of PAL expressions separated by commas.

If the ExpressionList is longer than one line, Paradox will wrap lines until the entire message is displayed. MESSAGE is usually followed by a SLEEP or GETCHAR() to make sure the user sees the message.

An ExpressionList is a comma-separated list of expressions. Though each expression must equate to a single value, the list can be as long as you like. No type conversion is necessary as long as you separate valid expressions with commas.

```
MESSAGE "Today is ", TODAY(), " you have ", DRIVESPACE(SUBSTR(DIRECTORY(),
1,1))), " bytes of disk space left"
```

The PAL manual states that any calculations should be converted to strings and concatenated; however we have not found this to be the case with the MESSAGE, PRINT, ?, or ?? commands.

**Listing 12.23: MESSAGE.L1**

```
x = 2
y = 9
MESSAGE "X=", x, " Y=", y, " Z=", ABS(INT(x-(y+SQRT(3+y))))+7
n = GETCHAR()

; The previous four lines work just fine, so messages like:

MESSAGE "Invoices billed today are due by ", TODAY()+30, " !"

; seem TO work ok, but if there is any potential for problems, you can
; replace the line with one concatenated string:

MESSAGE "Invoices billed today are due by " + STRVAL(TODAY()+30) + " !"
```

There is another typo in the 2.0 manual that really confuses the issue:

**Listing 12.24: MESSAGE.L2**

```
VIEW "Stock"
MOVETO FIELD "Quan in Stock"  ; could have also used MOVETO [Quan in Stock]
x=NRECORDS("Stock")
SCAN FOR ISBLANK([])
  []=0  ; replace the blank with a zero
  MESSAGE "Processing is "+INT(RECNO()/x*100)+"% complete"
ENDSCAN

; The code above is impossible because you cannot add a number to a string.
; The correct MESSAGE line should have either been:

MESSAGE "Processing is ",INT(RECNO()/x*100),"% complete"

; or alternately

MESSAGE "Processing is "+STRVAL(INT(RECNO()/x*100))+"% complete"
```

MESSAGE is also a keyword in a WAIT TABLE, RECORD, or FIELD syntax whereby a message will appear until the first keystroke is pressed.

## ? ??: Display Characters on Screen

```
{?? | ?} Expressionlist
```

> ??    Displays characters at the current cursor coordinates.
> ?     Positions cursor at the first column of the next line of canvas (subject to SETMARGIN constraints).

In version 3.0 the ? command positions the cursor at the leftmost margin as defined by SETMARGIN. If the cursor reaches the bottom line on the screen, the next ? will move to the top line. ? may be used on a line by itself to display a blank line. Text that is longer than one line will wrap to the next available line.

**Listing 12.25: QUEST.L1**

```
CLEAR
@0,0             ; position the cursor in the upper left hand corner
?? "Working"
?                ; skips a line
? "Please wait" ; will print on row 2, the third screen line
n = GETCHAR()
```

Syntax Trap:

**Listing 12.26: QUEST.L2**

```
CLEARALL
CLEAR
@0,0
?
"MR"
n = GETCHAR()    ; wait for a keystroke

;will actually make the {Modify} {Restructure} MENU choices because the
;"MR" will be taken as literal keystrokes whereas

CLEARALL
CLEAR
@0,0
? "MR"           ; will place "MR" at line 1 column 0
n = GETCHAR()    ; wait for a keystroke
```

The expressionlist is separated by commas without regard to datatype, even if there are calculations on the line.

```
@ 0, 0
?? "Current memory is ",MEMLEFT()," bytes"
n = GETCHAR()
```

The next few commands and functions deal with the cursor on the PAL canvas.

### @: **Position the Cursor on the Canvas**

```
@ Row, Column
```

Row        Screen row from 0 to 24.
Column     Screen column from 0 to 79.

```
@ 13, 15 ?? "This text will begin display at row 13 column 15"
```

The current row and column coordinates of the cursor can be evaluated with the ROW() and COL() functions. The next example shows how to place the next line of text beginning at coordinates 3 lines down and 5 characters over from where the cursor currently resides:

```
@ ROW() + 3, COL() + 5
?? "This text is offset from the old cursor position by 3 rows and 5 columns"
```

The COL() and ROW() functions deal only with the PAL canvas, not the underlying workspace. If you need to know the cursor position on the workspace, you can usually use SYNCCURSOR to move the cursor on the canvas to the corresponding coordinates on the workspace.

### COL: What Is the Current Column of the Cursor on the Canvas?

```
COL ()
```

Returns:

A number — Current column of cursor on PAL canvas. 0–79, with 0 being the left-hand margin and 79 the right-hand margin.

### ROW: What Is the Current Row of the Cursor on the Canvas?

```
ROW ()
```

Returns:

A number — The cursor row on the PAL canvas (0–24).

### SYNCCURSOR: Synchronize the Canvas Cursor with the Workspace Cursor

```
SYNCCURSOR
```

The SYNCCURSOR command places the canvas cursor where the underlying workspace cursor would appear. It's often used with the command combination that copies the workspace to the canvas.

```
ECHO NORMAL
ECHO OFF
SYNCCURSOR
```

### CURSOR: Determines How the Cursor Will Be Displayed

```
CURSOR [NORMAL | OFF | BOX | BAR]
```

| | |
|---|---|
| NORMAL | Default. |
| OFF | No cursor on workspace. |
| BOX | Shape is box. |
| BAR | Thicker than normal. |

Having a useless cursor blinking on the PAL canvas was cured by the addition of CURSOR OFF to version 2.0. In most applications there is little need for the canvas cursor except during two commands, ACCEPT and RUN. You should generally issue CURSOR OFF at the beginning of your application and only turn the cursor on with CURSOR NORMAL with a RUN or an ACCEPT statement.

Only one variable (day.v) is used in the procedure that follows. Reusing variables in this manner is efficient, but can be confusing. The procedure returns the day of the week corresponding to a birthdate.

**Listing 12.27: CURSOR.L1**

```
;CURSOR OFF at beginning of application:

PROC showbirthday.u()
  PRIVATE day.v
  @1,0 CLEAR EOL
  ??"Or Press Esc to cancel"
  @0,0 CLEAR EOL
  ?? "Enter your birthdate: "
  CURSOR NORMAL
  ACCEPT "D" REQUIRED TO day.v
  CURSOR OFF

  IF RETVAL THEN    ; user made a choice
    day.v = DOW(day.v)
    SWITCH
      CASE day.v = "Tue": day.v = "Tuesday"
      CASE day.v = "Wed": day.v = "Wednesday"
      CASE day.v = "Thu": day.v = "Thursday"
      CASE day.v = "Sat": day.v = "Saturday"
      OTHERWISE : day.v = day.v+"day"
    ENDSWITCH
    MESSAGE "You were born on a ",day.v,". Press any key"
    day.v = GETCHAR()
  ENDIF
ENDPROC
```

### CANVAS: Display or Hide Updates to the Canvas

```
CANVAS
```

ON      Show canvas updating in real time.
OFF     Canvas can be built in background.

The CANVAS command allows you to build a screen in the background and blast it onto the canvas all at once. Normally Paradox updates a portion of the PAL canvas each time you write to it with a ?, ??, TEXT, or MESSAGE command.

The next example displays an ASCII character chart on the screen. The chart appears on the screen, line by line, as the display is updated. As each screen fills, the user presses any key to get the next screen full of codes. Part of one of the screens is displayed in the next figure.

```
CHR(51) = "3"
CHR(52) = "4"
CHR(53) = "5"
CHR(54) = "6"
CHR(55) = "7"
CHR(56) = "8"
CHR(57) = "9"
CHR(58) = ":"
CHR(59) = ";"
CHR(60) = "<"
CHR(61) = "="
CHR(62) = ">"
CHR(63) = "?"
CHR(64) = "@"
CHR(65) = "A"
CHR(66) = "B"
CHR(67) = "C"
CHR(68) = "D"
CHR(69) = "E"
CHR(70) = "F"
CHR(71) = "G"
CHR(72) = "H"
CHR(73) = "I"          [Esc] to exit, or any other key to continue
CHR(74) = "J"
CHR(75) = "K"
```

**Figure 12.3**
**CANVAS.FG1**

Now for the code:

**Listing 12.28: CANVAS.L1**

```
PROC chrlist1.u ()
  PRIVATE n, n1
```

```
a 0,0
CLEAR
FOR n1 FROM 1 TO 255

   ?? " CHR(", n1, ") = \"", CHR(n1) , "\""

   ; would display something like CHR(65) = "A"
   ; note the backslash preceding the literal quotation marks.

   ; now check to see if this is the last row on the screen,
   ; or the very last number
   IF ROW()=24 OR n1=255 THEN
     MESSAGE "[Esc] to exit, or any other key to continue"
     n = GETCHAR()
     IF n = 27 THEN
       RETURN
     ENDIF
     a 0, 0
     CLEAR
   ELSE
     ?  ; move down a line
   ENDIF
 ENDFOR
ENDPROC
chrlist1.u ()
```

In this next version the canvas is turned off during writing to the screen, so an entire screen of numbers pops up at once.

### Listing 12.29: CANVAS.L2

```
PROC chrlist2.u ()
  PRIVATE n, n1
  a 0,0
  CLEAR
  MESSAGE "Working"
  CANVAS OFF      ; turn off the canvas
  FOR n1 FROM 1 TO 255

    ?? " CHR(", n1, ") = \"", CHR(n1) , "\""

    ; would display something like CHR(65) = "A"
    ; note the backslash preceding the literal quotation marks.

    ; now check to see if this is the last row on the screen,
    ; or the very last number
    IF ROW()=24 OR n1=255 THEN
      MESSAGE "[Esc] to exit, or any other key to continue"
      CANVAS ON       ; let the user see the new canvas
      n = GETCHAR()
      IF n = 27 THEN
        RETURN
      ENDIF
      MESSAGE "Working"
      CANVAS OFF
      a 0, 0
```

```
     CLEAR
    ELSE
      ?  ; move down a line
    ENDIF
  ENDFOR
ENDPROC
chrlist2.u ()
```

## SETMARGIN

```
SETMARGIN {OFF | Number}
```

OFF      Uses left edge of screen for ? and Text.

Number    Number of characters to offset ? and TEXT displayed from the left edge of the screen.

Normally Paradox treats column 0 as the left margin for ? and TEXT commands. However, the SETMARGIN command overrides the default and establishes a new left margin. This can be used, for example, in coding popup help screens as demonstrated in the discussion of PAINTCANVAS.

## TEXT

```
TEXT ENDTEXT
```

TEXT      Treat the following words as text.

ENDTEXT   End the text section.

The TEXT and ENDTEXT commands define a block that displays text. The text begins displaying at column 0 on the PAL canvas unless SETMARGIN is used, in which case the TEXT will start at the specified column.

The examples that follow demonstrate a way of defining procedures that combine SHOWMENUs with full-screen help. When the menu is first displayed, the screen shows a description of each choice from the appropriate TEXT statement in the helpmenu.u procedure. The main screen is shown as Figure 12.4 on the next page.

If the Utility choice is made, a submenu is displayed as shown on page 212. The code for the help menu is shown on page 213.

```
Tables  Reports  Utilities  Help  Quit
Menu of Tables to view or edit

      {View}  menu lets you view tables
    {Report}  menu lets you output reports
 {Utilities}  menu lets you output reports
      {Help}  toggles help screen on and off
      {Quit}  exits this program and returns you to DOS




              To make a selection press the first letter of the choice,
                 or use <- and -> to highlight choice, then press <┘.

Level 1 M                              Main Menu
```

**Figure 12.4**
TEXT.FG1

```
┌──────────────────────────────────────────────────────────────┐
│ DateChange  Setup   User   Info   Help                         │
│ Change system clock                                            │
│                                                                │
│ Utilities are part of the maintenance of the program and its datafiles. │
│    {Report}  menu lets you output reports                      │
│    {DateChange} Allows you to change the computer's system date.  This │
│              program gets its date information from the computer's clock. │
│              If the clock is wrong, or if you need to change the date, use │
│              this option.                                       │
│    {Setup}   Sets defaults for Company Name, Tax rate, etc.    │
│    {User}    Sets individual user configuration, including defaults for │
│              user name, printer data, and memory swap point.   │
│    {Info}    Shows table usage and status.  Also shows disk and memory usage. │
│    {Help}    Toggles help screen on and off.                   │
│                                                                │
│                                                                │
│           To make a selection press the first letter of the choice, │
│              or use <- and -> to highlight choice, then press <┘ . │
│                                                                │
│  Level 2 MU              Utilities Menu              Esc=↑Level │
└──────────────────────────────────────────────────────────────┘
```

**Figure 12.5**
TEXT.FG2

### Listing 12.30: TEXT.L1

```
PROC menuhelp.u(menucode.a)
   menucode.a=UPPER(menucode.a)   ; so that we don't have to worry about
                                  ; case sensitivity.  "mu" or "Mu" or "MU"
     @21,0   ; place cursor instructions near bottom of screen
   TEXT
               To make a selection press the first letter of the choice,
                  or use <- and -> to highlight choice, then press <—' .
   ENDTEXT

   @4,0    ; start text on the fifth line down
   SWITCH
     CASE menucode.a="M":              ; The main menu help screen
       TEXT
       {Tables} menu lets you view tables
       {Report} menu lets you output reports
    {Utilities} menu lets you output reports
         {Help} toggles help screen on and off
         {Quit} exits this program and returns you to DOS
       ENDTEXT
     CASE menucode.a="MT":             ; The Table menu help screen
       TEXT
  This is where help for the Table menu will go
       ENDTEXT
     CASE menucode.a="MR":             ; The report menu help screen
       TEXT
  This is where help for the Report menu will go
       ENDTEXT
     CASE menucode.a="MU":             ; The utilities menu help screen
       TEXT
  Utilities are part of the maintenance of the program and its datafiles.

     {DateChange} Allows you to change the computer's system date.  This
                  program gets its date information from the computer's clock.
                  If the clock is wrong, or if you need to change the date, use
                  this option.
         {Setup} Sets defaults for Company Name, Tax rate, etc.
          {User} Sets individual user configuration, including defaults for
                  user name, printer data, and memory swap point.
          {Info} Shows table usage and status.  Also shows disk and memory usage.
          {Help} Toggles help screen on and off.
       ENDTEXT
   ENDSWITCH
ENDPROC
```

### Listing 12.31: TEXT.L2

```
PROC menuM.u()      ; main application menu
                    ; subordinate menus are named similarly, i.e, the menu that
                    ; menuM.u() calls for Tables is menuMT.u(), etc.

   PRIVATE choice.a, helpon.l
   CURSOR OFF
```

```
helpon.l=TRUE
WHILE TRUE          ;-- menu loop
  CLEAR     ; clear the canvas
  @ 24, 0  ; position cursor at the bottom of the screen
  STYLE REVERSE
  ??" Level 1 M                    Main Menu                        "
  STYLE
  IF helpon.l THEN
    menuhelp.u("M")        ; place the text of the menu help here
  ENDIF
  @2,0  ??FILL("—",80)    ; draw a line under the menu placed next
  @0,0
  SHOWMENU
    "Tables": "Menu of Tables to view or edit",
    "Reports": "Menu of available reports",
    "Utilities": "Utilities and system maintenance",
    "Help":"Toggle menu help",
    "Quit": "Leave the system"
  TO choice.a

  SWITCH
    CASE choice.a = "Esc":
      MESSAGE "If you want to leave system, select Quit from the menu"
      BEEP
      SLEEP 2000
    CASE choice.a = "Tables":
      MESSAGE "Table menu still under development"
      SLEEP 2000
      ; the actual code would include a call to a table menu like:
      ; menuMT.u()        ; view menu of available tables
    CASE choice.a = "Report":
      MESSAGE "Report menu still under development"
      SLEEP 2000
      ; the actual code would include a call to a report menu like:
      ; menuMR.u()        ; view menu of available reports
    CASE choice.a = "Utilities":
      menuMU.u()          ; a similarly coded utilities menu currently in place
    CASE choice.a = "Quit":
      SHOWMENU
        "No": "Do not leave the program.",
        "Yes": "Leave the program, return to DOS."
      TO choice.a
      IF choice.a="Yes" THEN
        CLEAR
        EXIT
      ENDIF
    CASE choice.a = "Help":
      helpon.l= NOT helpon.l
      ; toggles helpon.l so menu help is or is not displayed
  ENDSWITCH
ENDWHILE
ENDPROC
```

## STYLE: Controls the Color, Intensity and Blinking Attributes of Subsequent Text

```
STYLE {[Blink [,] [INTENSE [,]] [REVERSE]}|{[Attribute]}
```

| BLINK | Causes subsequent ?, ?? and TEXT to display in blinking characters. |
| INTENSE | Display in intense. |
| REVERSE | Display in inverse video. |
| ATTRIBUTE | Second form of command, not used with BLINK, INTENSE, or REVERSE. |
| Number | Number from 0 to 255 representing the color combination to use as defined in Appendix A of the PAL manual. |

The STYLE command sets the color and attributes for *subsequent* characters placed on the canvas. It does not affect existing screen text (see PAINTCANVAS). STYLE alone on a line resets the default style. The next procedure demonstrates a table of attributes in the appropriate colors.

**Listing 12.32: STYLE.L1**

```
PROC styledemo.u ()
  CURSOR OFF
  CLEAR
  STYLE INTENSE
  @3,0 ??format("W80,ac","PAL Attribute table")
  STYLE
  attrib.n = 0
  FOR row.n FROM 5 TO 14              ; for 9 rows of numbers
    FOR col.n FROM 0 TO 15           ; 15 columns of numbers
      @ row.n, 8 + (col.n * 4)       ; position the cursor
      STYLE ATTRIBUTE attrib.n       ; change the attribute
      ??format("w4,ar", attrib.n) ; display the number as a 4 character
                                     ; wide string, aligned right
      IF attrib.n = 127 THEN         ; if we are finished, demo blinking text
        @20,0 STYLE BLINK,REVERSE
        ?? FORMAT("W80,ac","Press any key to exit")
        BEEP
        STYLE
        ?? FORMAT("W80,ac","\024  Blinking and reversed \024")  ; \024 = up arrow
        n = GETCHAR()
        RETURN
      ENDIF
      attrib.n = attrib.n + 1        ; increment the attribute counter
    ENDFOR
  ENDFOR

ENDPROC

styledemo.u ()    ; run the proc
```

Obviously, we can't show the colors here, but you can see the layout of the screen below (each number appears in a different color):

```
PAL Attribute table

  0   1   2   3   4   5   6   7   8   9  10  11  12  13  14  15
 16  17  18  19  20  21  22  23  24  25  26  27  28  29  30  31
 32  33  34  35  36  37  38  39  40  41  42  43  44  45  46  47
 48  49  50  51  52  53  54  55  56  57  58  59  60  61  62  63
 64  65  66  67  68  69  70  71  72  73  74  75  76  77  78  79
 80  81  82  83  84  85  86  87  88  89  90  91  92  93  94  95
 96  97  98  99 100 101 102 103 104 105 106 107 108 109 110 111
112 113 114 115 116 117 118 119 120 121 122 123 124 125 126 127




                    Press any key to exit
                  ^ Blinking and reversed ^
```

**Figure 12.6**
**STYLE.FG1**

### PAINTCANVAS: Paint an area of the screen with a color

```
PAINTCANVAS [BORDER] [FILL String] {[BLINK] [INTENSE]
[REVERSE] | [ATTRIBUTE number | BACKGROUND} Row1, Column1, Row2, Column2
```

| | |
|---|---|
| BORDER | Only affects a one-character-wide border around the coordinates. |
| FILL | Fills the area with a string. |
| String | Character to be used in the border. |
| BLINK | Makes area blink. |
| INTENSE | Shows area in intense color. |
| REVERSE | Shows area in reverse video. |
| ATTRIBUTE number | Sets area to a specific color. |
| BACKGROUND | Leaves color and style of the area unchanged, but only affects the FILL string. |
| Row1 | Row for upper-left-hand corner of the rectangle. |
| Column1 | Column for upper-left-hand corner of the rectangle. |
| Row2 | Row for lower-right-hand corner of the rectangle. |
| Column 2 | Column for lower-right-hand corner of the rectangle. |

Unlike the STYLE command, which affects characters yet to come, PAINTCAN-VAS colors or styles affect an area of the canvas whether or not you have placed any text on screen. Any text placed subsequent to the PAINTCANVAS command is displayed in the default style or whatever attributes are currently set by the STYLE command.

If you want to combine the monochrome attributes, separate the commands with commas. For example, to put whatever is on the screen at 5,6 to 10,16 in blinking inverse video, use:

```
PAINTCANVAS REVERSE, BLINK 5, 6, 10, 16
```

PAINTCANVAS is particularly useful for coding pop-up menus and help text. By combining PAINTCANVAS with CANVAS OFF and CANVAS ON, you can quickly draw screens.

**Listing 12.33: PAINTCAN.L1**

```
CANVAS OFF                  ; turn the canvas off to build the screen
SETMARGIN 15                ; set the left screen margin
@ 10, 15
TEXT
This box pops up at line 10
in the same color attribute
chosen for the text in Paradox help
screens. A border of spaces
surrounds the text in the same
color as the message window.
ENDTEXT

PAINTCANVAS ATTRIBUTE SYSCOLOR(13) 10, 15, 15, 52  ; color the text

;place a border of spaces around the text in the message color
PAINTCANVAS BORDER FILL " " ATTRIBUTE SYSCOLOR(3) 9, 14, 16, 53

SETMARGIN 0                 ; reset default screen margin
CANVAS ON                   ; display the screen
MESSAGE "Press any key"
n = GETCHAR()
```

There is considerably more work in coding this effect for versions earlier than Paradox3:

**Listing 12.34: PAINTCAN.L2**

```
STYLE ATTRIBUTE 63       ; cyan text
@ 10, 15 ?? "This box pops up at line 10       "
@ 11, 15 ?? "in the same color attribute       "
@ 12, 15 ?? "chosen for the text in Paradox help  "
@ 13, 15 ?? "screens. A border of spaces       "
@ 14, 15 ?? "surrounds the text in the same    "
@ 15, 15 ?? "color as the message window.      "

; although there are several ways of placing the side borders, well do it
; by explicitly placing the spaces as border characters.

STYLE ATTRIBUTE 4                    ; red color
a = "\219"                           ; the solid block ASCII character

@ 9, 14 ?? FILL (a, 40)              ; place the top border
@ 10, 14 ?? a   @ 10, 53 ?? a        ; place a space on each side of the text for each row
@ 11, 14 ?? a   @ 11, 53 ?? a
@ 12, 14 ?? a   @ 12, 53 ?? a
```

```
@ 13, 14 ?? a    @ 13, 53 ?? a
@ 14, 14 ?? a    @ 14, 53 ?? a
@ 15, 14 ?? a    @ 15, 53 ?? a
@ 16, 14 ?? FILL (a, 40)          ; the bottom border
STYLE  ; reset the style
MESSAGE "Press any key"
n = GETCHAR()
```

The code in PAINTCAN.L1 executes much faster than the code in PAINTCAN.L2 does because the TEXT command is very fast and CANVAS OFF speeds up the screen updating.

### SYSCOLOR: What Colors Have Been Assigned to Various Paradox Elements?

```
SYSCOLOR (Number)
```

| Number | From the list of screen elements: | |
|---|---|---|
| **General:** | | |
| 0 | TopTwoLines | Top two screen lines and menu selection. |
| 2 | CurrentSelection | Current menu selection. |
| 4 | Annotation | Description of current menu selection. |
| 5 | ModeIndicator | Mode indicator at upper-right corner. |
| 8 | WorkSpace | Empty workspace areas. |
| 19 | QueryElements | Checkmarks and example elements. |
| **Image Display:** | | |
| 6 | NoncurrentImage | Noncurrent image(s) on workspace. |
| 9 | CurrentImage | Current image on workspace. |
| **Field Display:** | | |
| 11 | FieldView | FieldView cursor, or edit marker when record is locked. |
| 17 | FieldValues | Field values in table and form view. |
| 18 | NegativeValues | Negative values of currency or number fields. |

**Message/Status Display:**

| 3 | Messages | Messages displayed in lower right, also in the current line in the debugger. |
| 16 | DebuggerStatus | Status of the PAL debugger. |

**Help/Protection Generator:**

| 12 | Border | Border of system forms. |
| 13 | NormalText | Text of system forms. |
| 15 | Highlight | Reverse-video text. |
| 21 | RegularText | Help index text. |
| 22 | Lines | Graphic and bold characters of the help index. |
| 23 | Bold | Reverse video of the help index. |

**Report:**

| 24 | VerticalRuler | Vertical ruler and page width marker in reports and PAL editor. |
| 25 | BandLines | Band lines in the report generator. |

**Form:**

| 7 | FormArea | Edge marker of area in form design. |
| 27 | ReverseVideo/HI | High intensity and reverse video in form design on B&W monitors. |
| 28 | ReverseVideo | Reverse video mapping in form design on B&W monitors. |
| 29 | HighIntensity | High intensity in form design on B&W monitors. |

Returns:

| A Number | The color attribute of the screen element as defined with CUSTOM.SC |

Paradox3 allows you to control color combinations for 24 different Paradox screen elements. For example, the default MESSAGE color displays white letters on a red background on a color monitor. The SYSCOLOR value is constant, because it denotes a screen element, not a screen color. The colors themselves reflect the default colors chosen. The color combination used for messages is always represented by SYSCOLOR(3). With default colors in place, n = SYSCOLOR (3) sets n, the ATTRIBUTE, to 79. If you want to display some text on the screen in the same color as the user selected for the Paradox messages:

**Listing 12.35: SYSCOLOR.L1**

```
@ 0,0
STYLE ATTRIBUTE SYSCOLOR(3)
?? FORMAT("W80,AC","This is a centered string, in the message color")
?? FORMAT("W80,AC","Press any key to continue")
STYLE   ; reset the style back to normal
```

Substituting one of the numbers corresponding to a different screen element displays the MESSAGE in that color.

### SETNEGCOLOR: Override the Color Settings for Negative Numbers and Currency

```
SETNEGCOLOR {CURRENCY | NUMERIC | BOTH} {ON | OFF}
```

| | |
|---|---|
| CURRENCY | Affects $ data type only. |
| NUMERIC | Affects N and S data types only. |
| BOTH | Affects all negative values. |
| ON | Uses negative colors values defined by Custom.SC. |
| OFF | Does not change values for negative values. |

The SETNEGCOLOR command overrides (or resets) the default settings defined in the custom script for color display of negative values. It applies only to values in tables—values in a form's calculated fields, whether positive or negative, always display in the form area's color.

### MONITOR: What Kind of Monitor Are We Using?

```
MONITOR ()
```

Returns:

| | |
|---|---|
| A string | The type of monitor currently in use. |

"Color"    For a color monitor.
"Mono"     For a monochrome monitor.
"B&W"      For a composite monitor or a color monitor configured to run
           without the color attributes.

MONITOR enables you to display text with different STYLE ATTRIBUTEs based
on those that display best on particular monitor types. Paradox picks up the
monitor type from three possible sources. In order of availability they are
obtained:

1. from the command line override (B&W -COLOR or -MONO) for example:

   ```
   C:> PARADOX3 -B&W
   ```

2. from the current Paradox3.CFG file (modifiable through Custom.sc), or
3. if no .CFG file is found, when Paradox goes directly to the hardware

Special Note for PDOXOS2 Users: Since OS | 2 uses the "&" character to string
commands together, the ampersand is omitted. The black and white override is
invoked in OS | 2 with: PDOXOS2-BW. However, MONITOR() still returns
B&W" in PDOXOS2 to maintain consistency between versions.

## 12.1.6 Controlling Graph Output

Graphing, introduced in Paradox3, is used to help make sense out of otherwise
confusing data. Seeing numbers in graphic form often makes it much easier to
spot trends that otherwise go unnoticed. PAL scripts can modify graph settings
in much the same way as PAL can change anything else in the workspace.
Remember that like reports, graphs may be sent to the screen, a printer, or a file.

### GRAPHTYPE: What Is the Current Graph Type?

```
GRAPHTYPE ()
```

Returns:

A string    The current graph type available, e.g., "Bar", "Combined",
            "Line", "Marker", "Pie", "RotatedBar", "StackedBar", "3DBar",
            or "XY".

The GRAPHTYPE function returns the current graph type. The settings for the current graph type {Image} {Graph} {Modify} {Type} can be changed by pressing the first letter of the type without first clearing the field. See GRAPHKEY.

The next example lets the user select a graph type from a SHOWMENU and then updates Paradox to make that choice by checking to see if the current graph type needs changing. The routine must be called from Main mode.

**Listing 12.36: GRAPHTYP.L1**

```
SHOWMENU
  "Pie"          : "Pie chart",
  "Bar"          : "Bar Graph",
  "RotatedBar"   : "Rotated bar graph",
  "StackedBar"   : "Stacked bar chart",
  "3dBar"        : "Three dimensional bar chart",
  "Line"         : "Line graph",
  "Marker"       : "Marker graph",
  "Combined"     : "Use combined lines and markers",
  "XY"           : "XY scatter graph"
TO choice.a

IF choice.a <> "Esc" THEN
  IF choice.a <> GRAPHTYPE() THEN
    ; only need to modify graph type if different than current setting
    MENU {Image} {Graph} {Modify}
    KEYPRESS SUBSTR( choice.a, 1,1)  ; only need the first character
    ; or alternately
    ; CTRLBACKSPACE
    ; TYPEIN choice.a
    DO_IT!
  ENDIF
ENDIF
```

### GRAPHKEY: Presses the [Ctrl F7] Key to Output Graph

```
GRAPHKEY
```

The GRAPHKEY command can only be used to send the current graph to the screen. Use {Image} {Graph} {ViewGraph} {Printer} if you want to send the graph to the printer.

### 12.1.7 Controlling Printed Output

Though the Paradox report generator is capable of assembling almost any type of report, there are times when you may need to send data to the printer without using a report specification. This section describes PAL commands and functions that help create printed output directly.

### SETPRINTER: Select the Printer Port

```
SETPRINTER PrinterPort
```

> PrinterPort    The name of the port to use for printer output, e.g., "LPT1", "LPT2", "LPT3", "COM1", "COM2", or "AUX".

Whichever port is selected will be the port tested by PRINTERSTATUS() and controlled by OPEN PRINTER and CLOSE PRINTER. SETPRINTER "LPT2" is the same as {Report}{Printer}{Override}{Port}{LPT2}. If you want to override the setup strings embedded in Paradox reports, you can use:

```
;override.a = "COM1"
MENU {Report} {Printer} {Override} {SetupString}
SELECT Override.a
```

### PRINTERSTATUS: Check Whether the Printer Is Ready

```
PRINTERSTATUS ()
```

Returns:

> True     If printer is on-line and ready.
> False    If the printer is unavailable.

The PRINTERSTATUS() function reports only on the current output port. Though usually LPT1, the default port can be changed with the SETPRINTER command or MENU {Report} {Setprinter} {Override} {Port}. If your printer is on-line and ready, PRINTERSTATUS() will return True immediately. If it isn't ready, DOS may take some time to return False. The delay is the time DOS takes to retry the printer until it finally gives up and tells Paradox that the printer is off-line.

On many networks, printing is sent to a print queue, and so, although the printer may not be ready to accept data, PRINTERSTATUS() will almost always return the value True. In addition, PRINTERSTATUS will always return the value True when there is a spooler in place or when using PDOXOS2 (OS/2's background printing includes its own spooler).

There have been some reports of PRINTERSTATUS not working properly with some HP LaserJet II printers with Serial cable connections. In addition, PRINTERSTATUS will always return a True if you check a port that does not physically exist, so be careful.

The example below ensures that the printer is ready. If it isn't, it gives the user the option to quit. CheckPrinter.l() returns True if ready or False if the user chose to quit.

### Listing 12.37: PRINTERS.L1

```
PROC checkprinter.l ()
  ; RETURNS a True if printer is ready
  ;            False if printer is offline and user chooses Quit

  PRIVATE choice.a
  STYLE REVERSE
  @24,0
  ?? FORMAT("W80,ac","Checking Printer...") ; display a message
  STYLE
  WHILE NOT PRINTERSTATUS()                    ; if printer is not ready
    STYLE REVERSE
    @24,0
    ?? FORMAT("W80,ac","Printer is not ready, press any key for options..")
    STYLE
    BEEP
    BEEP
    ; or see CHARWAITING discussion for beeper.u procedure
    ; beeper.u (1000)                          ; annoy the operator
    @24,0  CLEAR EOL                           ; remove message
    SHOWMENU
      "Continue":
      "Turn on printer, then make this choice to continue printing report",
      "Quit":"Do not print report"
    TO choice.a
    SWITCH
      CASE choice.a <> "Continue":
        @24,0 CLEAR EOL                        ; clear the last line of the screen
        RETURN FALSE
      OTHERWISE:  ; try again
        STYLE REVERSE
        @24,0
        ?? FORMAT("W80,ac","Checking printer.....")
        STYLE
    ENDSWITCH
  ENDWHILE
  @24,0  CLEAR EOL
  RETURN TRUE                                  ; then go on to print the report
ENDPROC

; Now to use the procedure to print the standard report for the customer table

l = CheckPrinter.l ()
IF l THEN
  REPORT "Customer" "R"
ENDIF
```

## OPEN PRINTER: Open the Printer for Output

```
OPEN PRINTER
```

## CLOSE PRINTER: Close the printer

```
CLOSE PRINTER
```

The OPEN PRINTER and CLOSE PRINTER commands are particularly useful on networks where outputting to printer can generate a header page. Each PRINT statement, for example, is considered a separate print job and is followed by its own end-of-file marker. In some versions of Paradox, problems arise with a HP LaserJet II in an IBM character set, because the Ctrl Z (end of file) marker prints as a character, an arrow. Using OPEN PRINTER suppresses the arrow. We've had difficulty in embedding an "\f" FormFeed as part of a PRINT statement after a printer has been opened with OPEN PRINTER. PRINT "\f" seems to work only after the CLOSE PRINTER, and therefore generates its own end-of-file marker. The next code fragment is a simple way to print all the values in the current record in a display image.

**Listing 12.38: OPENPRIN.L1**

```
COPYTOARRAY record.r
IF PRINTERSTATUS() THEN      ; almost always true on a network because of QUEUE
  OPEN PRINTER
  PRINT "Table: ",record.r[1],"\n"  ; remember that first element is table name
  FOR n FROM 2 TO ARRAYSIZE(record.r)
    PRINT "Field #" + STRVAL(n-1) + ": " + record.r[n] + "\n"
    ; the "\n" is a newline character
  ENDFOR
  CLOSE PRINTER
ELSE
  MESSAGE "Printer not ready, press any key"
  BEEP
  n = GETCHAR()
ENDIF
```

### INSTANTREPORT: Prints the .R Standard Report for the Current Table

```
INSTANTREPORT
```

The INSTANTREPORT key command is equivalent to pressing [Alt F7] to send the standard report for the current table to the printer. In REPORT mode, while designing a report, INSTANTREPORT is the equivalent of:

```
MENU {Output} {Printer}
```

### REPORT: Sends a Report to the Printer

```
REPORT Tablename Reportname
```

| | |
|---|---|
| Tablename | Name of table (string). |
| Reportname | Name of report, "R" or "1" thru "14", or 1 thru 14. |

All of the following syntaxes perform the same action:

```
1) REPORT "Customer" 2
2) REPORT "Customer" "2"
3) table.a = "Customer"
   rpt.n = 2
   REPORT table.a rpt.n
4) {Report} {Output} {Customer} {2} {Printer}
```

Note that REPORT only outputs to the printer. If you want to output Customer Report #2 to the screen, you need to use: MENU {Report} {Output} {Customer} {2} {Screen}. Reports sent to files on disk must also use the appropriate Paradox menu choices. Here's one way to print multiple copies of a report:

**Listing 12.39: REPORT.L1**

```
@1,0 ?? "Or Esc to cancel"
@0,0 ?? "How many copies of the customer report would you like to print? "
ACCEPT "S" REQUIRED DEFAULT 1
TO choice.s
IF NOT RETVAL THEN         ; the user pressed [Esc]
  RETURN
ENDIF

FOR n FROM 1 TO choice.s
  ; place some code here to check if the printer is ready
  REPORT "CUSTOMER" 1    ; send the Customer.R1 report to the printer
  PRINT "\f"             ; purely optional, formfeed ejects a blank page
                        ; between reports
ENDFOR
```

The following example sends a report to a printer or screen. It could be expanded to output to a file or a range of pages by adding more parameters and additional error checking. The procedure calls the checkprinter.l() procedure from the description of PRINTERSTATUS().

**Listing 12.40: REPORT.L2**

```
PROC outputreport.l (table.a,report.v,output.a)
  ;table.a    ; the table name
  ;report.v   ; "R" or a number from 1 to 14
  ;output.a   ; "Printer" (or any thing starting with "P") to output to printer
  ;            "Screen" (or any thing starting with "S") to output to screen
  ;            "" a blank string will present a menu for Printer/Screen choices

  ;Returns     True if the report was output, False if canceled for any reason
  ;            (report doesn't exist, [Esc] pressed, etc.).

  PRIVATE
  choice.a,    ; menu choice
```

```
    filename.a,  ; file name
    n,           ; used by GETCHAR()
    l            ; used by check printer

    ;-- check for report existence --- (optional) ------------------------------
    IF report.v = "R" THEN
      filename.a = table.a + ".R"
    ELSE
      filename.a = table.a + ".R" + STRVAL(report.v)
    ENDIF

    IF NOT ISFILE(filename.a) THEN
      MESSAGE filename.a + " not found. Press any key to return"
      BEEP BEEP BEEP
      n = GETCHAR()
      RETURN FALSE
    ENDIF
    ;----------------------------------------------------------------------------
    IF output.a = ""  THEN  ; no screen or printer specified on commandline
      BEEP
      SHOWMENU
        "Printer":"Send report to the printer",
        "Screen":"Send report to the screen",
        "Quit":"Cancel report"
      TO output.a
      IF output.a= "Esc" OR output.a="Quit" THEN
        RETURN FALSE
      ENDIF
    ENDIF

    output.a = LOWER(SUBSTR(output.a, 1, 1)) ;-- allows p or s from command line

    IF output.a = "p" THEN
      l = checkprinter.l () ; do whatever routine you need to make sure
      ; l = True if printer is online and ready
      IF NOT l THEN       ; user chose Quit
        RETURN FALSE
      ENDIF
    ENDIF

    SWITCH    ; show the appropriate message
      CASE output.a="s":
        STYLE REVERSE
        @23,0
        ??format("W80,ac","Preparing screen report. It will pause at each screenful")
        ??format("w80,ac","To cancel press Ctrl-Break at screen pause")
        STYLE
        MENU {REPORT} {Output} SELECT table.a SELECT report.v {Screen}
      CASE output.a="p":
        STYLE REVERSE
        @23,0 ??format("W80,ac","Printing report...to pause or cancel press any key")
        ??format("w80,ac","then follow on-screen instructions")
        STYLE
        REPORT table.a report.v
    ENDSWITCH
    RETURN TRUE  ; report was output
ENDPROC
```

The procedure could be invoked by issuing:

```
1 = OutputReport.1 ("Customer","R","Printer")
```

## REPORTTABLES: Does a Report Use Lookup Tables? If So, Which Ones?

```
REPORTTABLES TableName ReportName ArrayName
```

| | |
|---|---|
| TableName | Name of table that contains the report. |
| ReportName | A string "R" or "1"–"14", or a number 1–14. |
| ArrayName | Name of array to be created and loaded if lookuptables are found. |
| Sets RETVAL | |
| True | If report contains embedded tables. |
| False | If report does not contain embedded tables. |

REPORTTABLES and FORMTABLES are hybrid command/functions. They not only set RETVAL, but if RETVAL is True, they construct an array. As illustrated in the next example, REPORTTABLES can be used to determine if all the tables necessary to output a report are available. The procedure, OkReportRights.u, also looks to see if you are on a network and attempts to place a Prevent Full Lock on each of the tables in the report. If a table can be locked successfully, it then makes sure that you have at least read-only rights to each table.

### Listing 12.41: REPORTTA.L1

```
PROC okreportrights.l(table.a, report.v)
  ; table.a    ; name of table
  ; report.v   ; name of existing report  "R", "1" - "14"  or 1 - 14
  ; RETURNS    ; True if all tables for report are available, False otherwise

  ; Note that this proc places a Prevent Full Lock on all of the report tables
  ; and only releases the locks if one of the tables is not available.
  ; *** It is the programmer's responsibilty to remove these locks later,
  ; after the report is run.***

  PRIVATE
    lookup.r,          ; array of lookup tables found
    lookups.n,         ; number of lookups found
    n,                 ; counter variable
    ok.l,              ; ok flag
    lockedlookups.n,   ; number of lookup tables locked
    isnetwork.l        ; are we on a network

  ok.l = True    ; initialize variable
  isnetwork.l = NETTYPE()<>"SingleUser"
  ; first, let's see if anyone has placed a full lock on the table
```

```
    IF isnetwork.l THEN
      LOCK table.a PFL      ; try to prevent anyone from placing a full lock
      IF NOT retval THEN
        MESSAGE ERRORUSER(), " has a full lock on ", table.a, " Press any key"
        n = GETCHAR()
        RETURN FALSE
      ENDIF
    ENDIF

    ; next see if table is encrypted and if we have at least read only rights
    IF NOT TABLERIGHTS(table.a, "ReadOnly") THEN
      MESSAGE "You have insufficient rights to read ", table.a, " Press any key"
      n = GETCHAR()
      UNLOCK table.a PFL  ; remove the explicit lock
      RETURN FALSE
    ENDIF

    IF NOT ISMULTIREPORT(table.a, report.v) THEN
      ; we don't have to bother with checking out any lookup tables
      RETURN True
    ENDIF

    ; if we got to this point, there must be lookup table to check.
    ; now see which tables are looked up by the report, and list the names
    ; of the tables in array lookup.r
    REPORTTABLES table.a report.v lookup.r

    lookups.n = ARRAYSIZE(lookup.r)       ; the number of lookup tables found
    lockedlookups.n = 0    ; number of lookup tables locked
    ; step through each array element and try to lock the table and check rights
    FOR n from 1 to lookups.n
      IF isnetwork.l THEN          ; make sure no one else has a full lock on lookup
        LOCK lookup.r[n]  PFL      ; try to place a prevent full lock on the table
        IF NOT retval THEN
          MESSAGE ERRORUSER(), " has locked ", lookup.r[n], ".  Press any key"
          n = GETCHAR()
          ok.l = FALSE             ; it was not ok to continue
          QUITLOOP                 ; don't look any further
        ENDIF
        lockedlookups.n = n        ; count number of tables successfully locked
      ENDIF
      IF NOT TABLERIGHTS(table.a, "ReadOnly") THEN
        MESSAGE "You have insufficient rights to read ", lookup.r[n], ". Press any key"
        n = GETCHAR()
        ok.l = FALSE
        QUITLOOP
      ENDIF
    ENDFOR
    IF isnetwork.l and NOT ok.l THEN
      ; let's unlock all the tables potentially locked
      UNLOCK table.a PFL
      IF lockedlookups.n > 0 THEN
        ; need to unlock any locks successfully placed
        FOR n from 1 to lockedlookups.n
          UNLOCK lookup.r[n] PFL
        ENDFOR
```

```
     ENDIF
   ENDIF
   RETURN ok.l    ; true if tables were locked successfully, False otherwise
ENDPROC
```

See the FORMTABLES command for another example of REPORTTABLES.

### ISMULTIREPORT: Does a Report Use Lookup Tables?

```
ISMULTIREPORT (TableName, ReportName)
```

TableName     Name of table that contains the report.
ReportName    A string "R" or "1"–"14", or a number 1–14.

Returns:
A logical value value True if report uses lookup tables, False otherwise.

The ISMULTIREPORT function can be used to determine whether or not you need to go through the trouble of checking REPORTTABLES to determine if lookup tables are present. If ISMULTIREPORT returns the value False, the report uses only one table. See the example under REPORTTABLES.

### PRINT: Send Text to the Printer or File

```
PRINT [FILE FileSpec]
```

FileSpec     A valid DOS file name.

The PRINT command outputs text to the printer or a file. It offers character-by-character control of printed output. When PRINT FILE is used, if the file exists, text is appended; otherwise it creates a new file.

If you need to output data in a way that a predefined report can't handle, the PRINT command may be the best choice. Unlike Paradox reports, the PRINT command may be used in any Paradox mode and gives you total control over the contents and placement of the output, including margins and pagebreaks.

PRINT is often used in conjunction with FORMAT(), SPACES(), FILL(), and the special literal characters "\f", "\n", "\t", "\r", "\"", and "\\". See OPEN PRINTER for a simple example of outputting a record's contents to the printer. See also the OopsPrint.u() error procedure in the WWPUTIL2.SC script of the WaitPlus section for code that outputs both to the printer and to a file.

### PRINTER: Send Screen Output to the Printer

```
PRINTER {ON | OFF}
```

ON    Echo screen output to printer.
OFF   Stop printed output.

PRINTER ON causes subsequent ?, ??, and TEXT commands to be output to the printer as well as to the display.

The PRINTER command is of limited utility except during debugging and documentation, when you might want to have all screen output also go to the printer. Usually the PRINT command or predefined Paradox report specifications are preferred. See also OPEN PRINTER, CLOSE PRINTER, and SET-PRINTER for associated notes.

# Chapter 13

# Program Control

Recorded scripts simply play from beginning to end without stopping or changing direction. Programs you devise generally require program control structures, which are commands that direct program flow according to existing conditions. Program control structures play a critical role in making your scripts work for you. At times you may find that a procedure consists mainly of program control structures, which perform error checking and elaborate tests. At the heart of these programs may be a single action. Conditions, including the state of variables, system mode, values of fields, available drive space or memory, and calculations, are evaluated with the help of functions and other commands.

This section presents further details on commands and functions that help you control script play.

## 13.1 FIELD AND VARIABLE ASSIGNMENT

### = : Assignment Operator

=

The equals sign assigns a value to a variable, field, or array element. It is used in both comparison and assignment. In assignment, it assigns the value on the right to the variable or field on the left. In comparison, it evaluates the equality of the conditions to its right and left. If the equals sign is used more than once in a statement, the result is a logical constant, True or False, from the comparison made on the right.

```
n = 1                        ; Assigns 1 to the variable n.

r[1] = "A"                   ; Assigns "A" to the first element of array r.

[Invoice date] = TODAY()     ; Assigns today's date to the invoice date field

paidup.l = [Balance due] = 0 ; Assigns TRUE to paidup.l if the contents of
                             ; [Balance due] is zero, FALSE otherwise.
```

In determining if you are currently on a network, two approaches lead to exactly the same result:

**Listing 13.1: EQUALS.L1**

```
;this IF construct
IF NETTYPE()="SingleUser" then
  isnetwork.l = FALSE
ELSE
  isnetwork.l = TRUE
ENDIF

; can be replaced by a single line of code:
isnetwork.l = NETTYPE() <> "SingleUser"
```

Because of the resemblance of field specifiers and array subscripts, array element names and field assignments should be kept on separate lines. The next code fragment causes a run error:

**Listing 13.2: EQUALS.L2**

```
[Code]="AAA"
a1="BBB"
a2=a1    [Code]=a1+a2  ; these two statement combined are interpreted incorrectly.
```

An error message displays "Variable CODE has not been assigned a value." Paradox ignores all white space on the same line between array names and their subscripts and thus evaluates "a1 [code]" as an array element with an array subscript of a variable named code: "a1[code]". The solution is simply to move the second statement onto a line of its own:

**Listing 13.3: EQUALS.L3**

```
[Code]="AAA"
a1="BBB"
```

```
a2=a1
[Code]=a1+a2
```

### ISASSIGNED: Has a Value Been Assigned to a Variable?

```
ISASSIGNED (String)
```

    String     Variable name or array element.

Returns:

    True     If the variable or array element is assigned.
    False    If the variable or array element is not currently assigned.

The ISASSIGNED function evaluates whether a value has been assigned to a single variable or array element. If a script attempts to determine the value of an unassigned variable, a script error will occur. If you're unsure whether a variable or array element has been assigned a value, test it first with ISASSIGNED.

**Listing 13.4: ISASSIGN.L1**

```
RELEASE VARS ALL        ; let's start clean
n = 15                  ; a number
a = ""                  ; a blank string
ARRAY Temp.r [15]       ; define an array structure
Temp.r [2] ="ABCD"      ; assign the second array element

l = ISASSIGNED (a)              ; sets l = True
l = ISASSIGNED (n)              ; sets l = True
l = ISASSIGNED (n1)             ; sets l = False
l = ISASSIGNED (temp.r [1])     ; sets l = False
l = ISASSIGNED (temp.r [2])     ; sets l = True
l = ISASSIGNED (temp.r)         ; causes a script error because Paradox
                                ; is be expecting an array subscript
```

ISASSIGNED is particularly valuable when trying to make a duplicate copy of an array. (See the example in the EXECUTE function.)
    Here's an example. To copy the entire contents of one array into another, you must first create an array of equal size, and then proceed through each array element to assure that it has been assigned a value.

**Listing 13.5: ISASSIGN.L2**

```
size.n = ARRAYSIZE (old.r)
ARRAY new.r [ size.n ]  ; create new array with the same
; # of elements as old array
```

```
; Now step through each of the elements of old.r and check if the
; element is assigned, and if so, assign the corresponding element in new.r.

FOR n FROM 1 TO size.n
  IF ISASSIGNED( old.r [n] ) THEN
    new.r [n] = old.r [n]
  ENDIF
ENDFOR
```

When evaluating array elements with ISASSIGNED, you must refer to array subscripts by number even if the array was created with the COPYTOARRAY command (which normally allows you to reference array elements by field name). The following script produces "Run Error: Expecting a value of numeric type" for the array element Temp.r["Last Name"]. The fix is to first evaluate temp.r[2]. The first element in an array created by the COPYTOARRAY command is always the name of the table. The record's first field value is the second array element.

**Listing 13.6: ISASSIGN.L3**

```
CREATE "Test"                           ; create a one field "Test" table
  "Last Name" : "A10"
EDIT "Test"                             ; open a blank record
COPYTOARRAY temp.r                      ; temp.r ["Last name"] = ""
DO_IT!
RESET
IF ISASSIGNED(temp.r["Last Name"]) THEN    ; will cause run error
  MESSAGE "Script will never get to this point even though element is assigned"
ENDIF
```

In Paradox2, if you tried to evaluate an array element without specifying a subscript, it would lock up the computer. Fortunately, this bug was fixed in Paradox3. If your code is intended to run on this version, you should be aware of the problem.


### ISBLANK: Is a Value Assigned, but Blank?

```
ISBLANK (Expression)
```

Expression     Any expression.

Returns:

True     If the expression is blank.
False     If the expression is not blank.

### Listing 13.7: ISBLANK.L1

```
l = ISBLANK("")          ; sets l = TRUE , the string is blank
l = ISBLANK("ABCD")      ; sets l = FALSE, the string is not blank
l = ISBLANK(" ")         ; sets l = FALSE,  the string has spaces, so it is not blank
l = ISBLANK(TRUE)        ; sets l = FALSE, logical value is not blank
l = ISBLANK(4/22/84)     ; sets l = FALSE, date value is not blank
l = ISBLANK(BLANKDATE()) ; sets l = TRUE, BLANKDATE() is always blank
l = ISBLANK(BLANKNUM())  ; sets l = TRUE, BLANKNUM() is always blank
```

The ISBLANK function can be used to eliminate a need to test for data types. For example, if you want to find out if there is a value in the current field in a table, you could use one of two approaches; each sets l to True if the field is blank:

### Listing 13.8: ISBLANK.L2

```
a = SUBSTR(FIELDTYPE(), 1, 1)   ; get first character of the current field type
SWITCH
  CASE a = "A" and [] = "" : l = True
  CASE a = "D" and [] = BLANKDATE()  : l = True
  CASE (a = "N" or a = "S") and [] = BLANKNUM()  : l = True
  OTHERWISE: l = False
ENDSWITCH

; the code above can be easily replaced by:

l = ISBLANK( [] )
```

Using ISBLANK on an unassigned variable will cause a script error. If you are unsure if the variable has been assigned, test it.

### Listing 13.9: ISBLANK.L3

```
SWITCH
  CASE NOT ISASSIGNED( test.v ):
    MESSAGE "Variable test.v  has not been assigned"
  CASE ISBLANK( test.v ) :   ; must already be assigned to get to this point
    MESSAGE "Variable test.v is type ", TYPE(test.v), " and is blank"
  OTHERWISE:
    MESSAGE "Variable test.v is type ", TYPE(test.v), " and equals ", test.v
ENDSWITCH
SLEEP 3000                   ; let user see message
```

## TYPE: What Is the Data Type of an Expression?

```
TYPE (Expression)
```

Expression      Any PAL expression

Returns:

"An"    If expression is alphanumeric, where n is the length of the expression. For example, TYPE("ABCD")="A4". This truncates values greater than 255 characters in length to 255 characters.
"N"     Number.
"$"     Currency.
"S"     Short Number.
"D"     Date.
"L"     True or False.

The TYPE function always returns a string. If the expression is not valid, TYPE produces a script error. The type of a field, variable, array element, or any valid expression is at times critical to the task at hand, with the success or failure of a statement depending on a single value's type conversion. Although the PAL manual suggests that conversion from one type to another is largely automatic, you should rarely rely on PAL to convert types.

Short number and currency data types cannot be explicitly declared, but may result from calculations based on fields in a table, or values assigned as the result of an ACCEPT command. Though the currency data type always visually rounds off to two decimal places, it maintains the same mathematical precision equal as numeric data types.

**Listing 13.10: TYPE.L1**

```
a = TYPE("Paradox")                    ; sets a = "A7"    length of the string
a = TYPE("Pair " + "of ducks" )  ; sets a = "A13"
a = TYPE(1234)                   ; sets a = "N"
a = TYPE(1234 + 4567)            ; sets a = "N"      6912
a = TYPE(7/4/1776)               ; sets a = "D"
a = TYPE(4-jul-1776 + 7)         ; sets a = "D"      11-Jul-1776
a = TYPE(4-jul-90 - 2-jul-90)    ; sets a = "N"      2 days between the dates
a = TYPE(True)                   ; sets a = "L"          Logical True
a = TYPE(4=2)                    ; sets a = "L"      Logical True

; The following examples assume assigning two values from a table's fields.
c = [Invoice amount]   ; a field defined as a $ field
s = [Customer#]        ; a short number field

; Any manipulation of a currency field remains currency.

a = TYPE(c)            ; sets a = "$"
a = TYPE(c + 12.23456) ; sets a = "$"

; Any manipulation of a short number with any other number results in a full number.

a = TYPE(s)            ; sets a = "S"
a = TYPE(s + 1)        ; sets a = "N"
a = TYPE(s + s)        ; sets a = "N"
```

```
; Any valid manipulation of a short number with a date results in a date.

a = TYPE(s + 4/22/84)  ; sets a = "D"
```

### LEN: What Is the Length of an Expression?

```
LEN (Expression)
```

Expression      Any valid PAL expression of any data type.

Returns:

A number      An integer representing the number of characters in the expression.

The LEN function evaluates the length in characters of any PAL expression as if it were converted to a string. It automatically converts values of any type to strings.

**Listing 13.11: LEN.L1**

```
n = LEN ("ABCD")      ; sets n = 4
n = LEN ("AB"+"CD")   ; sets n = 4
n = LEN (3)           ; sets n = 1
n = LEN (-3)          ; sets n = 2
n = LEN (1/12/90)     ; sets n = 7
n = LEN (1/1/90)      ; sets n = 7, it is considered 1/01/90 if format is MM/DD/YY
n = LEN (1-Jan-90)    ; sets n = 7, for the same reason
n = LEN (True)        ; sets n = 4
n = LEN (False)       ; sets n = 5
n = LEN (3=2)         ; sets n = 5, the length of False
```

See the SUBSTR function for an example of the use of LEN.

### SAVEVARS

```
SAVEVARS {VarList | ALL}
```

Varlist      Names of variables to be saved, separated by commas.
ALL      Save all variables in effect.

The SAVEVARS command writes specifically named or all current variables to a script file called "Savevars." This script is in a form that can later be played to reinstate the current variables. The SAVEVARS command is most often used during debugging. Individual variables can be saved by explicitly naming them and separating multiple variable names with commas. The SAVEVARS ALL command only saves variables "known" within the scope of the current procedure or script. With regular procedures, SAVEVARS will save global variables and all private variables. Used within a CLOSED procedure, SAVEVARS saves only those variables known within the current scope of the procedure, and those designated with the USEVARS option. As of this writing, the SAVEVARS ALL command will not save the contents of the system variable RETVAL. If you want to save the value of RETVAL, issue: SAVEVARS RETVAL.

"Savevars.sc" is one of three private scripts (the others are "Instant" and "Init") that are written to the current directory, or if assigned, to the private directory. Private directories were designed primarily for use on a network. Since every user on a network has the potential to create these scripts at any time, writing them to a user's private directory avoids all contention with other users. If you are using an external script editor, you should expect to load and save these files from the private directory. Unlike temporary Paradox tables, private scripts are not deleted when the Paradox session ends.

The SAVEVARS command automatically overwrites an existing "Savevars.sc" file. If you want to keep the current "Savevars" script, rename it. The following code fragment illustrates what is saved by a SAVEVARS command:

**Listing 13.12: SAVEVAR.L1**

```
table.a = "Customer"      ; define a string variable
balance.n = 12345         ; a number
extra.a = "This is an extra variable"
ARRAY test.r [25]         ; define an array
test.r[3] = 7/04/1776     ; load third element of the array
RETVAL = True             ; Set the system variable
RELEASE VARS extra.a      ; removes the extra.a variable from memory
SAVEVARS ALL              ; save the remaining variables
RELEASE VARS ALL          ; remove all the rest of the variables
```

This will produce the following "Savevars.sc" file:

**Listing 13.13: SAVEVAR.L2**

```
; Variables Saved Using Savevars Command
balance.n = 12345
Array test.r[25]
test.r[3] = 7/04/1776
table.a = "Customer"
```

## 13.1.1 System Variables

You've been introduced to the three special *PAL System Variables*: RETVAL, AUTOLIB and ERRORPROC. RETVAL, the *Returned Value* of an action or procedure, is set by many PAL commands and functions. AUTOLIB and ERRORPROC are variables that you must set that help avoid a lot of work managing procedures and error trapping.

### RETVAL: The Returned Value of a Procedure, LOCATE, SHOWMENU, LOCK, etc.

RETVAL

| | |
|---|---|
| Expression | The returned value of a procedure. |
| True | LOCATE was successful. |
| False | LOCATE failed to find a record. |
| True | User pressed [Enter] for an ACCEPT. |
| False | User pressed [Esc] or [CtrlBreak] while in an ACCEPT. |
| True | LOCK was successful. |
| False | Another user prevented the locking of one or more tables. |
| True | LOCKRECORD was successful in CoEdit. |
| False | Another user has locked a record, or record is already locked by you. |
| True | If UNLOCKRECORD or UNLOCK was successful. |
| False | If unlocking failed for any reason (e.g., the record was not originally locked, or there was a key violation). |
| True | If REPORTTABLES or FORMTABLES finds embedded or linked tables. |
| False | If REPORTTABLES or FORMTABLES finds that a form or report has only one embedded or linked table. |
| False | If user presses [Esc] in a SHOWMENU, SHOWFILES, SHOWTABLES, or SHOWARRAY. |
| True | With Paradox3, if the user makes a selection in one of the SHOW menus. Prior to version 3.0, does not set RETVAL at all if a selection is made. |
| Keycode or String | Result of satisfying an UNTIL clause in a WAIT TABLE, RECORD, or FIELD. There are some rules about the way RETVAL is assigned within a WAIT condition. See the WAIT command for full details and example code. |

The AUTOLIB system variable designates a procedure library or a series of libraries in which Paradox will look for invoked procedures currently not in memory. AUTOLIB frees the programmer from explicitly loading and releasing procedures from libraries. See the Procedure Libraries chapter.

### AUTOLIB: What Library (or Libraries) Should Be Searched for Procedures?

```
AUTOLIB = "Libname" or "Lib1,Lib2,..LibN"
```

| | |
|---|---|
| "Libname" | Library name (a string). |
| "Lib1,Lib2, . . Libn" | Commas separated list of libraries to search. |

There are no spaces between library names in the AUTOLIB string of multiple libraries.

**Listing 13.14: AUTOLIB.L1**

```
autolib = "Utility"    ; will search utility library
autolib = "Utility,Toolkit,Report"  ; will search each of the three until proc is found
; The next variation causes Paradox to search UTILITY.LIB file in the current directory
; when the autolib was defined, failing that, it searches the MAIN.LIB file in the same
; directory as the current script.
autolib = DIRECTORY() + "Utility," + SDIR() + "Main"
```

### ERRORPROC: What Error Procedure Should Be Executed?

```
ERRORPROC = Procname
```

Procname    The name of a procedure to execute if a run error occurs.

First discussed in the chapter on Procedures, an "Error Procedure" is designed to form a last-chance barrier between the user and the "Cancel/Debug" prompt in a PAL application. You name the error procedure and generally base its design on three functions: ERRORCODE, ERRORMESSAGE, and ERRORUSER. ERROR-PROC is simply the name of a variable that is assigned a string naming the current error procedure.

```
ERRORPROC = "MyErrorHandler.n"
```

If a run error occurs in your application, Paradox checks to see if a variable named ERRORPROC has been set to a value and if it knows its location. If it has been set to a procedure and the procedure can be found, Paradox will attempt to execute it.

An error procedure should be designed to return one of three values, 0, 1, or 2. If it returns 0, Paradox will retry the statement that caused the error. If it returns 1, Paradox will ignore the statement and go on to the next statement. Finally, if it returns a value of 2 (or no value at all), Paradox will bring up the normal "Cancel/Debug" prompt. A few restrictions apply:

- The error procedure must not have any formal parameters.
- The procedure must have been explicitly read into memory at least once during the scope of the current highest level procedure (usually with a READLIB at the beginning of your program). Unless the procedure has been read or executed once, it will not be able to be found. If you rely on it to read automatically from a library designated by AUTOLIB, it will not be able to be invoked at the time of the run error.

There is a way to read an errorproc into memory, providing that it exists in your AUTOLIB (or AUTOLIB path), even if you don't know the name of the specific library. The technique involves setting a variable as a flag and then explicitly calling the errorproc procedure (found by autolib, because this is not a run error). The errorproc must then look for the flag variable, and, if the variable is set, simply return to the calling proc. This forces the errorproc into memory but does not take any corrective action. An example and full commentary of this technique is found in the WaitPlusError.V procedure found in WWPCORE2.SC in the WaitPlus section.

- If you used CLOSED procedures, you must use READLIB to read in the error procedure each time a separate CLOSED procedure is invoked. Even if it has been invoked in another level of the procedure, and the name passed along with the statement USEVARS ERRORPROC, the error procedure will not be invoked. A closed procedure, by design, "forgets" the location of other procedures loaded before the closed procedure was started.
- The error procedure itself cannot be a CLOSED procedure.
- Error procedures cannot trap for insufficient memory or insufficient stack space errors (if there is not enough memory to execute the instruction, there aren't enough resources to invoke the error procedure).

The procedure that follows, Oops.n(), is a fairly generic error procedure. In this case it is augmented with a table specific command at the end. The SWITCH evaluates ERRORCODE and/or ERRORMESSAGE to try to determine the cause of the problem. If possible, it takes corrective action (e.g., it removes write-protection from a table if this caused an error and sets a flag to re-protect it later if necessary).

Though the Oops.n() procedure demonstrates trapping for a few common errors, it also has a safety valve in the OTHERWISE condition, invoking a more comprehensive procedure called OopsPrint.u(). The code for OopsPrint.u() is listed in the WWPUTIL2.SC script in the WaitPlus chapter. OopsPrint.u sends a complete time stamped status report to the printer (if on line) and to a file called "Errorlog.sc." It is designed so that you can easily keep track of recurring errors and is enough of an error procedure all by itself. The call to OopsPrint.u() under Oops.n() illustrates how a main error procedure can call subordinate procedures.

Your own error procedures might have special instructions about a number to call in the event of a run error, or information about taking corrective action (e.g., if the errorcode was 41, "Not enough disk space," you might let the user free up some disk space and try to continue the script).

**Listing 13.15: ERRORPRO.L1**

```
Proc Oops.n()
 ;returns a number, if it returns anything at all
 PRIVATE errorproc      ; Errorproc itself is kept private in case of an error in the
                        ; erroproc code.  This way, any error in this proc will not
                        ; call itself recursively.
 SWITCH
    CASE ERRORCODE()=8:  ; OBJECT VERSION MISMATCH; wrong sort order
       CLEAR
       @ 4,0
       ?"Your table has a version mismatch!"
       ? ERRORMESSAGE()   ; will show the exact errormesage including the table name
       ?"Your current SortOrder is ", SORTORDER()
       ?"SortOrders are discussed in the Advanced Topics chapter of the"
       ?"Paradox users manual."
       Message "Press any key to quit"
       n = GETCHAR()
       RESET
       QUIT                ; or perhaps EXIT
    CASE ERRORCODE()=6:  ; Run error because the table is damaged
       CLEAR
       @ 4,0
       ? "A table is damaged !!  You must repair or remove the table"
       ? ERRORMESSAGE()
       MESSAGE "Press any key go back to Paradox"
       n = GETCHAR()
       RESET
       QUIT                ; or perhaps EXIT

       ; The next case attempts to correct an error where a table was
       ; write protected and a call to EDIT the table flags an errorcode 35,
       ; invalid menu choice.  Combining ERRORCODE and ERRORMESSAGE allows you
       ; determine the exact problem, correct it, and retry the command by
       ; returning 0.
    CASE ERRORCODE()=35 AND MATCH(ERRORMESSAGE(),"..is write-.."):
       ; couldn't complete  "EDIT" table.a  statement
       CtrlBreak            ; return to main menu
       ; now unprotect the table
       {Tools} {More} {Protect} {Write-protect} SELECT table.a {Clear}
       wasprotected.l = True  ; writeprotected flag, the main code could
                              ; ressurrect the write protection later if needed
       RETURN 0             ; retry the offending EDIT table.a statement

       ; Other cases can go here, as they are tripped across, however there should always
       ; be an OTHERWISE to alert users of unanticipated errors, and as shown below,
       ; catalog the errors.
    OTHERWISE:               ; unknown error, let's print it to file and printer.
```

```
      BEEP
      OopsPrint.u()            ; print out the error. Listing in WWPUTIL2.SC
      ; by default, at this point the {Cancel}{Debug} menu will appear
   ENDSWITCH
ENDPROC
```

## 13.1.2 Field Specifiers

Paradox allows you to refer to fields in tables in a number of ways. You can usually retrieve or input information from any point on the workspace. An exception is assignment in multitable forms, which is restricted to the current table.

**Listing 13.16: FIELDSPE.L1**

```
n = []  ; Assigns the current field value to the variable n
[] = n  ; Assign the contents of n to the current field value

; Next increment the balance due field by the value of the invoice total
; in the current record
[Customer->Balance Due] = [Customer->Balance Due] + [Invoice total]
```

### FIELD ASSIGNMENT: What Is the Value of a Specified Field?

```
[]
```

Returns:

    A Value    The current field contents. The field must be empty or complete—a partially filled in date field will return a script error or incorrect information. The FIELDSTR() function can be used to return even a partially filled field as a string.

```
[Fieldname]
```

    Fieldname    Name of the field in this table.

Returns:

    A Value    of the field whose name is specified.

```
[TableName->FieldName]
```

    TableName    Name of table on the workspace.
    FieldName    Name of field in the table.

Returns:

A Value      The contents of the field.

`[Tablename(Q)->Fieldname]`

TableName      Name of a table whose query image is on the workspace.
FieldName      Name of a field in that image.

Returns: A string the value of the selected field in the query image.

`[Tablename(Q)->]`

Tablename      Name of table whose query image is on the workspace.

Returns:

A String      The string value of the current field of the query image. All query fields are treated as strings.

`[Tablename->]`

TableName      The name of a table already on the workspace.

Returns:

A Value      The value for the current field in the image.

## 13.1.3 Arrays

Arrays are structures that contain a number of variables with the same variable name, and are designated by an array subscript in square brackets. Arrays can be created in three ways in Paradox:

- by explicitly declaring an array with the ARRAY command (values in the array are created by direct assignment)
- by using COPYTOARRAY to create an array with values that include the table name and each field's values
- by using FORMTABLES or REPORTTABLES to create an array of embedded or lookup tables

## ARRAY: Declare an Array Structure

```
ARRAY Arrayname[number]
```

Arrayname    A valid variable name.
Number       Number of elements to be allowed. Creates a new array with a specified number of unassigned elements.

The ARRAY command names and sizes an array. Each element in the array is identified by an integer called an array subscript. The next example loads the names of the days of the week into an ARRAY and then uses a FOR loop to step through each element to display each element to the screen. The technique is easily adapted to arrays created through the COPYTOARRAY command to output the values of a record.

**Listing 13.17: ARRAY.L1**

```
ARRAY days.r[7]  ; seven element array
; now load the array with names of days
days.r[1]="Monday"
days.r[2]="Tuesday"
days.r[3]="Wednesday"
days.r[4]="Thursday"
days.r[5]="Friday"
days.r[6]="Saturday"
days.r[7]="Sunday"

; If we wanted to print the array on the screen we could step
; through the array one element at a time:

@0,0
CLEAR
FOR n FROM 1 TO 7
  ? days.r[n]
ENDFOR
MESSAGE "Press any key"
n = GETCHAR()
```

Until an array element is assigned a value, it is considered unassigned. Once assigned, however, you cannot unassign an individual array element without clearing the entire array. You can reassign any element that already contains a value to a value of any other type. If you need to blank out the values of individual array elements, be consistent and assign "" for array strings, BLANK-NUM for a number, and BLANKDATE for a date. If you issue:

```
RELEASE VARS Days.r
```

it will release all of the values in the array named Days.r.

### ARRAYSIZE: What Is the Size of an Array?

```
ARRAYSIZE (Arrayname)
```

> Arrayname     Valid name of an already assigned array.

Returns:

> A Number     Number of elements in the array as defined in ARRAY Arrayname[Size] command, regardless of the number of elements that have actually been assigned.

ARRAYSIZE is the number of elements in an array specified by an ARRAY command. For example, ARRAY test.r[10] defines an array with room for 10 elements. The statement n = ARRAYSIZE(test.r) sets n = to 10. See the ISASSIGNED function at the beginning of this chapter for an example of code that copies an array.

PAL has two powerful ARRAY commands especially designed for handling entire records at a time: COPYTOARRAY and COPYFROMARRAY.

### COPYTOARRAY: Copy the Contents of the Current Record into an Array

```
COPYTOARRAY Arrayname
```

> Arrayname     Not quoted; a valid variable name. Copies current record values to an array with one more element than the number of fields.

COPYTOARRAY can only be used when the workspace cursor is on a record in a Display image. This includes the "Struct" and "Password" tables. The size of the array created is one larger than the number of fields in the table, equal to NFIELDS (TABLE()) + 1. The first element is a string containing the table name.

### COPYFROMARRAY: Copy the Entire Contents of an Array into the Current Record

```
COPYFROMARRAY Arrayname
```

> Arrayname     Not quoted; a valid variable name. Replaces the values of the current record with those from the array.

COPYFROMARRAY only works when the cursor is on a record in a display image in "Edit," "CoEdit," or "DataEntry" modes. The special nature of query images, the "Struct" (when restructuring a table), and "Password" tables do not allow its use. COPYFROMARRAY attempts to copy the values in the array elements into the current record of the current table. Paradox treats the values entering from COPYFROMARRAY as if they were typed in. All validity checks except one apply—the {Picture} clause.

You can use COPYFROMARRAY to copy all the fields from one record into a table with more fields than the original, provided that the target table contains the same structure as the source table, with any new fields tacked onto the end of the table. We will discuss COPYFROMARRAY into detail tables of multitable forms in a few more pages.

The code that follows uses COPYTOARRAY to move single records from one table to another. The next example lets the user point to records in the "Customer" table and move them, one at a time, to the "CustHist" table.

**Listing 13.18: COPYTOAR.L1**

```
VIEW "CUSTHIST"                ; archive file of outdated records same structure as customer
COEDIT "CUSTOMER"              ; active customer records
IMAGERIGHTS READONLY           ; don't let the user change the CUSTOMER table
PICKFORM 1
WHILE TRUE                     ; wait table loop
  WAIT TABLE
    PROMPT "Move to a record to archive and press [F2] to move it to the CustHist table",
           "or press [Esc] to exit table"
  UNTIL "F2","Esc","Dos","DosBig", "Zoom"
  SWITCH
    CASE RETVAL="Zoom" :
      zoom.l()                 ; traps for zoom related problems.
                               ; See the ZOOM command and WaitPlus for details
    CASE RETVAL="Esc" :
      DO_IT!
      CLEARALL
      QUITLOOP
    CASE RETVAL="F2":
      MESSAGE "Moving record to CUSTHIST table"
      COPYTOARRAY  original.r    ; get all the field values
      UPIMAGE ; same as MOVETO "Custhist"
      END
      DOWN
      COPYFROMARRAY original.r   ; add record to table
      UNLOCKRECORD               ; posts the record
      DOWNIMAGE                  ; or ; MOVETO "customer"
      FORMKEY
      DEL                        ; remove the original record
    OTHERWISE:
      BEEP                       ; for "Dos" and "DosBig"
  ENDSWITCH
ENDWHILE
```

If an array has been created using COPYTOARRAY, you can refer to array elements by field name (as opposed to by element number). This technique is slower, but more flexible than referencing elements by number. If, for example, you restructure a table by inserting new fields at the beginning of the table, existing code that refers to array elements by number will cause problems. From the programmer's standpoint, field names are also more explicit. Code that references array elements by field names, like:

```
IF record.r["CustID"] = "A-100" THEN...
```

is a lot easier to maintain and understand than code referencing field numbers, like:

```
IF record.r[6] = "A-100" THEN...
```

This is especially true when you modify the field order. Though referring to array elements by field name is a great advantage, it comes at the expense of a few potential problems and some performance penalty.

Paradox requires access to the table structure to determine the field number for a given field name. This can be particularly slow on a network, because Paradox needs to check for table access.

If the table is in the current directory when the COPYTOARRAY is issued, the first element of the array does not contain the table's path. This is a problem only if you later change directories and attempt to access the array by element name—Paradox will have no idea where to find the original table. A solution to this problem is to explicitly place the directory name into the first element of the array. For example, to view a one-record "Config" table and copy the record into an array that can be used from any directory:

**Listing 13.19: COPYTOAR.L2**

```
VIEW "CONFIG"
COPYTOARRAY config.r
config.r[1] = DIRECTORY()+config.r[1]
```

With the directory name before the table name, you can reference the array field names wherever you want.

Password-protected tables present another problem. If you view a password-protected table by issuing the password, and then use COPYTOARRAY on a record and clear all passwords, you will not be able to access elements by name because Paradox needs the password to provide an alias for the field number. You will get a "Table is password protected" error message. So it's necessary to maintain the password in memory if you plan to access the elements by name.

In Paradox3, attempting to use COPYFROMARRAY in a linked table will cause a script error because values cannot be assigned to the linked fields. This is a cause for great consternation. Thus we've devised a procedure to handle detail tables:

```
CopyFromArray3.u ( arrayname.a, RequiredCheck.l)
```

This procedure simulates a COPYFROMARRAY, but is flexible enough to work in any kind of table—linked or master. The code and commentary for CopyFromArray3.u() are included in the WWPUTIL2.SC in the WaitPlus chapter.

# 13.2 PROCEDURE AND LIBRARY MANAGEMENT

Write PAL code as procedures into libraries and let Paradox do the resource juggling.

### PROC: Define a Procedure and Place It into Memory

```
PROC [CLOSED] ProcName ([VarNameList1]) [USEVARS VarNameList2]
[PRIVATE VarNameList3] ENDPROC
```

| | |
|---|---|
| ProcName | Name of the procedure. |
| CLOSED | Maximum recovery of memory. |
| VarNameList1 | Names of formal parameters. |
| USEVARS | Use the following list of global vars. |
| VarNameList2 | Names of global variables for closed procedures. |
| PRIVATE | Keep the following list of vars private. |
| VarNameList3 | Names of variables to keep private. |
| Returns: | |
| A Value | If the RETURN command is used to pass a value from the procedure. As a byproduct, RETVAL is set to the same value as that returned by the procedure. |

Although procedure names can be up to 132 characters long, keep them to 31 or fewer characters. See details under the RELEASE PROCS command. The PROC command is the declaration for a PAL procedure, an encapsulated script that behaves like a subroutine or a customized "function." The CLOSED option treats the procedure as a world unto itself. There are examples of procedures all throughout this book, but none of them are CLOSED procedures. We chose this approach because:

- Closed procedures must reside in libraries. You cannot define a closed procedure and then call it without writing it to a library. We wanted you to be able to test code fragments without going through this step.
- You can easily change almost any regular procedure to a CLOSED procedure.
- Closed procedures are best used as the top level procedure of major subsystems in your code. You can only nest CLOSED procedures six levels deep. You must also make extensive use of USEVARS to bring in variables the system might need. Special care must be taken with your error procedures (see ERRORPROC for more details).
- We have found that our code runs well with regular procedures; closing the procedures has not improved performance in our testing, so we rarely use them. However, other users report that closed procedures have lessened memory problems.

### CREATELIB: Create an Empty Library to Hold Procedures

```
CREATELIB LibraryName [SIZE Number]
```

| LibraryName | Name of library as a string. |
| SIZE | Default size is 50; however, sizes of up to 300 are allowed. |
| Number | Number of procedures to allow. |

CREATELIB sets up a procedure library into which procedures can be written with the WRITELIB command. The number of procedures that you can store in a library is limited by the defined size. The default is 50 procedures. You can declare a library size of up to 300 procedures with the SIZE option. Paradox3 includes a path for the AUTOLIB, which makes it easier to keep several smaller libraries under control.

When a library is created, an existing library with the same name is overwritten. Although libraries are not actually considered Paradox objects, they should not be deleted while shelled out to DOS, because this has been known to cause an inelegant exit out of Paradox.

Every time you write a procedure into a library, the library size grows. If you redefine a procedure and rewrite it to a library, the old version of the procedure is flagged as obsolete and the new procedure is tacked onto the end of the library. Though obsolete procedures still consume disk space, they are otherwise ignored. During the developmental cycle, you should have a master script that creates the library and plays the scripts that write all procedures into the library, as demonstrated in the Procedures chapter.

### WRITELIB: Write a Procedure or Procedures into an Existing Library

```
WRITELIB LibName ProcList
```

LibName    The name of the library already created (a string).
ProcList    Comma-separated list of names of procedures to write into the library.

When writing multiple procedures into a library, parentheses and formal parameters are left off, procedure names are separated by commas, and the procedure names are not quoted strings. Making the library name a variable allows more flexibility than hard coding it into a procedure does. You should RELEASE the procedure immediately after the WRITELIB command so that it makes room for the next procedure to be read. See the chapter on Procedure Libraries.

### READLIB: Reads Procedure(s) from a Library

```
READLIB Libname [IMMEDIATE] Proclist
```

Libname    The name of the library, no .lib extension.
IMMEDIATE    Does not account for insufficient memory.
ProcList    Comma-separated list of procedure names to read. Do not enclose list of procedures in quotes.

The READLIB command reads a procedure or series of procedures from a library. READLIB is essential to read in an error procedure, or to force a procedure into memory. We have been stressing all along that you avoid using READLIB. Use AUTOLIB to locate procedures. Any procedure that has been read or used by the script will always be found, even if it is not in the current AUTOLIB and even if it has been swapped out and AUTOLIB temporarily changed to something else.

**Listing 13.21: READLIB.L1**

```
CLEAR
MESSAGE "Loading program"
AUTOLIB = "utility"
ERRORPROC = "oops.n"
READLIB AUTOLIB oops.n      ; force the errorproc into memory
mainmenu.u()                ; call the main menu, stored in the library
```

We have never found a need or reason to use the IMMEDIATE parameter. If used, it seems to be a problem waiting to happen. Without using IMMEDIATE, procedures load and swap just fine.

## INFOLIB: Create a List Table with Procedures Found in a Library

```
INFOLIB LibraryName
```

LibraryName       Name of library; a string, without the ".LIB" extension.

The INFOLIB command creates a table that lists the procedures and their size in a library. The next example shows a list of procedures in a library, along with general library statistics.

**Listing 13.22: INFOLIB.L1**

```
PROC InfoLib.l(libname.a)
  ; libname.a is the library name, without .LIB extension
  PRIVATE
    procs.a,          ; string value of the number of proc found
    procsize.a,       ; string value of the size of all procs combined
    libsize.a         ; string value of the size of the library file
  RESET  ; need to flush buffers for accurate file sizes
  If NOT ISFILE(libname.a + ".LIB") THEN
   MESSAGE libname.a + " cannot be found.  Press any key"
   n = GETCHAR()
   RETURN FALSE        ; let proc specify that it was unsucessful
  ENDIF
  INFOLIB libname.a   ; places a list table on the workspace
  IF ISEMPTY("LIST") THEN
   MESSAGE libname.a + " does not contain any procedures.  Press any key"
   n = GETCHAR()
   RETURN FALSE        ; let proc specify that it was unsucessful
  ENDIF
  ; now let's find some statistics
     procs.a = STRVAL(NRECORDS("list"))      ; get the number of records
  procsize.a = STRVAL(CSUM("list","Size")    ; get the total proc size
   libsize.n = STRVAL(FILESIZE(libname.a + ".lib") ; get the file size

   ; now show the table with some overall statistics about its contents and size
   WHILE TRUE
     WAIT TABLE
     PROMPT "[Esc]-Done. "+UPPER(libname.a)+" has " + procs.a + " procs",
            "totaling " + procsize.a + " bytes of " + libsize.a + " LIB size"
     UNTIL "Esc","Dos","DosBig"
     IF retval = "Esc" THEN
       Clearall
       RETURN TRUE
     ENDIF
   ENDWHILE
ENDPROC
```

## RELEASE: Remove Procedures or Variables from Memory

```
RELEASE PROCS {Procedurelist|ALL}
RELEASE VARS  {Varlist|ALL}
```

| | |
|---|---|
| PROCS | Release procedures explicitly. |
| Procedurelist | Comma-separated list of procedures to release. |
| VARS | Release variables explicitly. |
| Varlist | Comma-separated list of variables to release. |
| ALL | May be used with PROCEDURES or VARS to release all defined procedures OR variables. |

The RELEASE PROCS command, the complement to the READLIB command, clears the named procedures from memory. RELEASE PROCS is mainly used immediately after writing a procedure to a library, thereby freeing the memory for the next procedure to be written. In general, it is preferable to let Paradox handle the loading and releasing of variables and procedures with AUTOLIB. Unless your code writes procedures "on the fly" instead of getting them from libraries, there is no need to explicitly release procedures.

Along the same lines, the RELEASE VARS command only applies to global variables. Private variables cannot be explicitly released—they simply dissolve when the procedure that declared them as private ends. RELEASE VARS ALL is often used at the beginning of a script to "clean up" the memory environment to avoid conflicts. Ideally, all variables should be kept private to their respective procedures, either by declaring them as PRIVATE, or by using CLOSED top-level procedures.

While writing and debugging your scripts, you should issue a SAVEVARS ALL to reveal any variables that you failed to keep private. If leftover variables are found, you can either make them PRIVATE, or put a RELEASE VARS command in your code to remove them. You must use RELEASE VARS RETVAL if you want to rid memory of RETVAL; it is not affected by RELEASE VARS ALL.

The next example is a start-up script that initializes the system and passes control to procedures stored in libraries.

**Listing 13.23: RELEASE.L1**

```
;Let's start the script as clean as possible:
CLEAR                     ; clears the canvas
MESSAGE "Working"
RELEASE VARS ALL          ; remove any global variables
RELEASE PROCS ALL         ; shouldn't be necessary, but is sometimes helpful
RESET                     ; clears the workspace
startmem.n = MEMLEFT()    ; get starting memleft()  ; a global variable
IF startmem.n < 50000 THEN
  BEEP
  QUIT "You don't have enough memory to run this application"
ENDIF
AUTOLIB = "Utility"
ERRRORPROC = "Oops.n"
READLIB AUTOLIB Oops.n    ; explicitly read in the errorproc
mainmenu.u() ; a proc that has all variables private, or is a closed proc that
             ; USEVAR's the global startmem.n for a display screen about memory
             ; now let's clean up the only global variable set.
RELEASE VARS startmem.n   ; the only global variable
```

In a followup to the notes on long procedure names, if you are simply defining a procedure on the fly, you can use very long names:

```
PROC ThisIsAnExampleOfAnExtraordinarilyLongProcName.u()
```

As of this writing, there is one Syntax Trap: You should not explicitly release long procedure names—doing so will often dump you out of Paradox:

```
RELEASE PROCS ThisIsAnExampleOfAnExtraordinarilyLongProcName.u
```

## 13.3 PROGRAM FLOW CONTROL

### PLAY: Plays a Script

```
PLAY Scriptname
```

Scriptname     Name of script to play (a string).

The PLAY command runs a script as a subroutine of the current script. When the script that is played ends, or a RETURN is encountered, control returns to the original script that played it. If the second script contains a QUIT or EXIT, script play will halt entirely. Although it is usually preferable to put your code into procedure libraries, there are times when PLAY is very useful. See the section on procedure libraries on how to use the PLAY command to create libraries from scratch.

Another use for PLAY is to conditionally play an initialization script for an application. This developer's tool allows a back-door approach to script testing and debugging. The main script for an application might look like:

**Listing 13.24: PLAY.L1**

```
AUTOLIB="Utility"
ERRORPROC="OOPS.u"
IF NOT ISFILE(AUTOLIB+".lib")
  QUIT AUTOLIB + ".lib cannot be found"
ENDIF
READLIB AUTOLIB oops.u                  ; must read in to take effect
setswap.n = 30000
IF ISFILE(SDIR()+"initapp.sc") THEN     ; might want to replace SDIR() with PRIVDIR()
  PLAY SDIR()+"initapp"                  ; perhaps changes setswap.n
ENDIF
SETSWAP setswap.n                        ; possibly overridden by INITAPP.SC
mainmenu.u()                             ; call the main menu
EXIT                                     ; Typically a "turn-key" application
                                         ; script exits Paradox when done
```

An initialization script found in the main script's subdirectory might override some of the first script's defaults or do some special processing.

**Listing 13.25: PLAY.L2**

```
;INITAPP.SC

setswap.n = 35000  ; let's override the 30000 byte normal setswap for this application
PASSWORD "shhh"     ; perhaps this file is only on the developer's machine
CLEAR
TEXT
;Put up some message here, or ask for special passwords, etc.
ENDTEXT
;Any special processing can also go here to override the normal defaults
```

### INSTANTPLAY: Plays INSTANT.SC

```
INSTANTPLAY
```

The INSTANTPLAY command is much the same as pressing [Alt F4] on the keyboard. It will play a script called INSTANT.SC that resides in the current directory or, if set, the user's private directory. INSTANTPLAY does not have to be called from main mode. The following shows a quick test of INSTANTPLAY and how you can use PRINT FILE to create a script on the fly:

**Listing 13.26: INSTANTP.L1**

```
IF ISFILE(PRIVDIR()+"INSTANT.SC") THEN
  ; remove any existing script
  {Tools} {Delete} {Script} {instant} {Ok}
ENDIF
; now lets create a new script
PRINT FILE PRIVDIR()+"INSTANT.SC"   ; create the script in the private directory
"Message \"This was played by instant script\"\n",  ; \n is a line feed
"BEEP SLEEP 2000"

INSTANTPLAY                          ; will play the script just defined
```

### SDIR: In Which Directory Was the Current Script Found?

```
SDIR ()
```

Returns:

A String     The name of the directory of the current script being played.

The SDIR() function returns the directory name of the current script being played and is particularly useful if the script directory is different from the working directory. For example, say the "wAppLib" script creates and writes a library to the current directory:

```
;the current script directory is c:\Paradox3\scripts"
SETDIR "C:\\Paradox3\\Sample"
PLAY SDIR()+"wAppLib"          ;will create the library in c:\Paradox3\sample
```

There are a couple of odd aspects to the script directory. The EXECUTE command within a script creates a "virtual" script in the current directory; the script never exists on disk, only in memory. Let's assume you have a script called SDIRDEMO.sc in the c:\demo directory with the following lines of code:

### Listing 13.27: SDIR.L1

```
MESSAGE "The SDIRDEMO script exists in the " + SDIR() + " directory"
BEEP
SLEEP 5000
EXECUTE "MESSAGE \"Execute script exists in \" +SDIR()"
; executes the following command
; MESSAGE "Execute script exists in " + SDIR()
BEEP
SLEEP 5000
```

Now if you move to the c:\Paradox3\Sample subdirectory and issue {Scripts} {Play} {C:\DEMO\SDIRDEMO}, the script will display this message for 5 seconds:

The SDIRDEMO script exists in the c:\demo directory

Then it displays this message:

Execute script exists in c:\paradox3\sample\

This is easily seen in the PAL debugger with the {Where?} selection. The same holds true for Mini and Value scripts created by the PalMenu. However, only EXECUTE has any practical effect on SDIR(), since the other scripts are not part of an application program.

### {Scripts} {RepeatPlay}: Play a Script a Number of Times

```
{Scripts} {RepeatPlay} SELECT scriptname SELECT NumberOfRepeats
```

ScriptName       Name of script to play (a string).

NumberOfRepeats   Number of times script should repeat, or "C" for continuous.

Normally, repeated playing of a script is done with a PLAY statement within a FOR or a WHILE loop. Paradox3 introduced the {Scripts} {RepeatPlay} menu choice to help interactive users play scripts repetitively for tasks like unattended printing of multiple copies of reports. {RepeatPlay} is particularly handy for users who create scripts by only recording keystrokes, and it offers some of the advantages of a controlled loop.

### {Scripts} {ShowPlay}: Show the Progress of a Script and Insert Pauses

```
{Scripts} {ShowPlay} SELECT ScriptName { {Fast}|{Slow} }
```

ScriptName    Name of script to play (a string).
{Fast}        Insert a brief pause between statements.
{Slow}        Insert a long pause between statements.

The {Scripts} {ShowPlay} choices are almost equivalent to issuing an ECHO command to lift the canvas and see through to the workspace. However, if you have a password-protected script and issue: ECHO FAST PLAY "Demo" the script will play properly, whereas {ShowPlay} {Demo} {Fast} will ask you for the password before proceeding.

### DEBUG: Trip the PAL debugger

```
DEBUG
```

When placed in a script, the DEBUG command trips the PAL debugger. It can be used to set break points for code inspection and to trap for errors during the development cycle. For example, if a query doesn't seem to work as planned, use DEBUG to test it:

**Listing 13.28: DEBUG.L1**

```
PLAY "Query1"          ; some query save image
DO_IT!
IF WINDOW()<>"" THEN   ; Paradox had some problem with the query
  MESSAGE "There was some error in the query, it did not execute, press key"
  BEEP BEEP
  n = GETCHAR()
  DEBUG                ; see exactly what is going on.....
ENDIF
; rest of the script continues here
```

If you have a remote section of code that is not giving you the results that you expect, place the DEBUG command at the suspect location in the script. When it reaches the DEBUG while running the script, play stops, and you can step through the debugger manually. You'll often need to press a key to reveal the cursor if the canvas is displayed instead of the workspace.

### SETKEY: Reassign the Function of a Key

```
SETKEY KeyCode ScriptStatements
```

The SETKEY command saves keystrokes by allowing you to assign PAL commands or functions to one key. Its use is restricted to interactive Paradox. For example if you regularly view a "Customer" table in Form #3, you could include a line in an INIT.SC to redefine the [Ctrl C] key to place the table on the workspace with the following:

```
SETKEY 3 VIEW "Customer" PICKFORM 3
```

A SETKEY assignment must fit on a single script line. (As of this writing, in the "Weird but True" category: If your editor supports line lengths longer than 132 characters, you can create as long a SETKEY as you want. You do, however, have to make sure your commands skip the 175 character, and the 350th, and the 525th.) An easier way is to assign a key to play a script:

```
SETKEY 3 Play "ViewCust"
```

SETKEY is also useful when setting up tables, reports, and forms in Paradox interactively. You might want to use a couple of SETKEYs to avoid dealing with the PAL menu.

**Listing 13.29: SETKEY.L1**

```
SETKEY "F11" char.a = CURSORCHAR()   ; [SHIFT F1] grabs current character
SETKEY "F12" TYPEIN char.a           ; [SHIFT F2] places the literal character anywhere
SETKEY "F13" line.a = CURSORLINE()   ; [SHIFT F3] grabs line
SETKEY "F14" TYPEIN line.a           ; [SHIFT F4] types in the line literals
SETKEY "F15" calc.a = MENUCHOICE()   ; [SHIFT F5] grabs any menuchoice
SETKEY "F16" TYPEIN calc.a           ; [SHIFT F6] lets us see calc before pressing ENTER
```

### EXECUTE: Execute a String as a PAL Script

```
EXECUTE CommandString
```

| | |
|---|---|
| CommandString | String containing valid PAL syntax. Disables procedure swapping. |

The EXECUTE command converts a string to an executable PAL statement as if it were typed in by the user at the PAL Menu {MiniScript} prompt. The Command-String equates to a single string, with literal quotes prefaced by a backslash and backslashes doubled. Though constructing proper EXECUTE statements can get a little confusing (especially with embedded quotation marks), the results are usually well worth the effort. As noted above, each EXECUTE statement is listed as a separate script on the calling chain with the {Where?} menu selection in the debugger. In Paradox version 1, EXECUTE was used extensively to construct the equivalent of the MOVETO FIELD command introduced in version 2.0.

EXECUTE still has many uses. Say, for example, that with several tables on the workspace, you want to move to any field under script control and both the field and table names are variables. EXECUTE makes this possible in one statement:

```
EXECUTE "MOVETO [" + table.a + "->" + field.a + "]"
;e.g.  MOVETO [Customer->Customer ID#]
;this is the same as
;MOVETO table.a
;MOVETO FIELD field.a
```

Using EXECUTE has the potential to change the script directory for the duration of the call. EXECUTE creates a one-line script in memory that is treated as script played from the current directory. Therefore, during the portion of the script that runs under the EXECUTE, a call to the SDIR() function, which returns the current script directory, will always return the current directory. Also remember that using EXECUTE to invoke a procedure totally disables the swapping mechanism until the EXECUTE is released, so the technique should be used with discretion.

The following example uses EXECUTE appropriately to create a generic procedure that copies the entire contents of one array into a new array.

### Listing 13.30: EXECUTE.L1

```
PROC DuplicateArray.u(source.a, target.a)
  ; source.a  the name of original array, a string  i.e., "old.r"
  ; target.a  the name of new array, a string i.e., "new.r"
  PRIVATE n,
        size.n                                  ; size of source array
    ; get the array size      i.e., size.n = ARRAYSIZE(old.r)
  EXECUTE "size.n = ARRAYSIZE(" + source.a + ")"
    ; create the new array     i.e., ARRAY new.r [size.n]
  EXECUTE "ARRAY " + target.a + "[size.n]"
    ; step through each element of the array
  FOR n FROM 1 to size.n
      ; next see if element has been assigned    i.e.,  l = ISASSIGNED(old.r[n])
    EXECUTE "l = ISASSIGNED(" + source.a + "[n])"
        ; copy the value to the proper new array element
```

```
    IF l THEN
      ; copy the value to the new array element i.e., new.r[n] = old.n[n]
      EXECUTE target.a + "[n] = " + source.a + "[n]
    ENDIF
  ENDFOR
ENDPROC
```

In the chapter "Procedure Libraries," you'll find a demonstration of a complex EXECUTE that "packs" a library. Also, note the discussion of EXECUTE on swapping under "Memory Management."

## EXECPROC: Execute a Procedure Whose Name Is Contained in a String

```
EXECPROC Procedurename
```

> Procedurename        Name of procedure to execute as a string.

EXECPROC is a special command that executes a procedure with no formal parameters. The procedure name must be a string or string variable. Because it doesn't have to parse a parameter list, EXECPROC is very fast. The following listings show two methods of calling similarly named procedures from a library, and demonstrates how EXECPROC can make code more compact. Though there's nothing wrong with the first method, the second is faster.

**Listing 13.31: EXECPROC.L1**

```
PROC HelpCustomer.u()
  PRIVATE n
  CLEAR
  @0,0
TEXT
  A few lines of descriptive text for customer table
  would go here
ENDTEXT
  MESSAGE "Press any key"
  n = GETCHAR()
  CLEAR
ENDPROC

; Now for a menu of help topics:
PROC TableHelpMenu.u()
  WHILE TRUE
    CLEAR
    SHOWMENU
      "Customer":"Help for the customer table",
      "Vendor":"Help for the vendor table",
      "Product":"Help for the Product table"
    TO choice.a
```

```
        SWITCH
          CASE choice.a = "Esc":
            RETURN   ; to whatever proc called it
          CASE choice.a = "Customer":
            HelpCustomer.u()
          CASE choice.a = "Vendor":
            HelpVendor.u()
          CASE choice.a = "Product":
            HelpProduct.u()
        ENDSWITCH
      ENDWHILE
    ENDPROC
```

Here's a simplified alternative using EXECPROC:

**Listing 13.32: EXECPROC.L2**

```
;Revised menu of help topics:
PROC TableHelpMenu.u()
  WHILE TRUE
    CLEAR
    SHOWMENU
      "Customer" : "Help for the customer table",
      "Vendor"   : "Help for the vendor table",
      "Product"  : "Help for the Product table"
    TO choice.a
    SWITCH
      CASE choice.a = "Esc":
        RETURN                           ; to whatever proc called it
      OTHERWISE:
        EXECPROC "Help" + choice.a +".u"  ; e.g. EXECPROC "HelpVendor.u"
    ENDSWITCH
  ENDWHILE
ENDPROC
```

See the SHOWMENU command for another way of creating help about menu choices.

### RETURN: Return Control from a Script or Procedure, Optionally Passing Back a Value

```
RETURN [Expression]
```

Expression     PAL expression that is to be passed back to the procedure or script that called the routine.

Returns:

The Expression to the calling script or procedure.

Sets:

> RETVAL    To the expression if RETURN Expression is issued from within a procedure.

RETURN immediately exits a script or procedure and returns control to the script or procedure that called it. If no higher level script or procedure is found, RETURN resumes interactive Paradox, or in the case of Paradox Runtime, exits to DOS. Procedures allow the best use of RETURN, as procedures are optionally allowed to return a value.

Syntax Trap: The RETURN command must be the last statement on a line, unless it is passing an optional expression parameter. Thus the following line of code will cause a script error:

```
IF 1 THEN RETURN ENDIF
```

Paradox attempts to return a variable called ENDIF. The workaround is to keep the RETURN on a line by itself:

```
IF 1 THEN
  RETURN
ENDIF
```

When using RETURN in a procedure, you can only return one value, not an array. There are two workarounds to this problem. The following code shows a way of getting two values from the last record in a table. The procedure returns a string with the characters | | (two vertical bars) separating the first field value from the second. This method requires that you process the returned value:

**Listing 13.33: RETURN.L1**

```
PROC GetLastRecordValues.a (table.a, field1.a, field2.a)
  ; table.a   the name of table
  ; field1.a  the name of first field to check, a string
  ; field2.a  the name of second field to check, a string
  ; RETURNS a string where the first value is separated from the second by a ||
  PRIVATE a
  IF ISEMPTY(table.a) THEN
    RETURN "||"      ; no values found
  ENDIF
  VIEW table.a
  END
  MOVETO FIELD field1.a
  a = STRVAL([])
  MOVETO FIELD field2.a
  a = a + "||" + STRVAL([])  ; use the || characters as a separator
  CLEARIMAGE
  RETURN a
ENDPROC
```

Here's an example of its use—getting two fields from an "Orders" table:

**Listing 13.34: RETURN.L2**

```
string.a = getlastrecordvalues("Orders","Order number","Order date")

; Which might set string.a = "12345||6/12/88"

; Then use a match to separate the values, looking for the || characters
; as the dividing point.

l = MATCH(string.a, "..||..", ordernumber.a, orderdate.a)
; now convert back to the proper data types
ordernumber.n = NUMVAL(ordernumber.a)
orderdate.d = DATEVAL(orderdate.a)
```

Even though it's a bit sneaky, another method of returning more than one value works quite well. Although RETVAL is generally a regular variable, it can also be defined as an array. To demonstrate using RETVAL to return an array:

**Listing 13.35: RETURN.L3**

```
RELEASE VARS ALL       ; for demo purposes, make sure no variables are around
RELEASE VARS RETVAL    ; must be explicitly released

PROC retvaldemo.r ()   ;note that we will be simulating the
                       ;returning of an array

  ARRAY retval [5]      ; define retval as an array
  retval[1]="A"         ; load each element
  retval[2]="B"
  retval[3]="C"
  retval[4]="D"
  retval[5]="E"
  RETURN               ; you would *not* want to do a
                       ; RETURN retval
                       ; as a script error would result,
                       ; expecting the subscript of the array.
ENDPROC

; You cannot use  r = retvaldemo.r() because as far as Paradox is concerned,
; retvaldemo.r() did not return any value at all.  So instead,

retvaldemo.r ()  ; execute the procedure and create the retval array
SAVEVARS RETVAL  ; retval array is saved to SAVEVARS.SC
```

With this procedure, you are really setting a global variable for RETVAL. If you needed this information in another array name we could transfer it fairly easily:

```
ARRAY newarray.r [arraysize(RETVAL)]     ; create the new array
FOR n FROM 1 TO ARRAYSIZE(RETVAL)
  newarray.r [n] = retval[n]             ; load each corresponding value
ENDFOR
```

Since RETVAL is such a widely used variable, it's important that you grab the information from RETVAL before RETVAL gets reset by something else.

### RUN: Run a DOS (or OS/2) Program and Then Return to Script Play

```
RUN [BIG] [SLEEPNUMBER] [NOREFRESH] [NORESTORE] DOSCOMMANDS
```

| | |
|---|---|
| BIG | 500K |
| NOREFRESH | Leaves canvas in view while suspended. |
| NORESTORE | Leaves DOS result on screen until PAL resumes. |
| SLEEP number | Delay upon finish of command run by DOS. |
| DOSCOMMANDS | A string containing the DOS command to be executed. |

The RUN command executes a DOS command as if typed from the keyboard, and then returns to Paradox when the command is completed. RUN remembers the current state of the workspace and resumes with the next line in the script. On a 640K system, RUN leaves about 200K available for DOS programs. RUN BIG makes about 500K available by storing the suspended Paradox environment to disk, or expanded memory, if present. If expanded memory is present, RUN BIG executes nearly as quickly as RUN.

Paradox3 introduced two new options to the RUN command, NOREFRESH and NORESTORE.

- NOREFRESH keeps the current PAL canvas on the screen while Paradox is suspended. If the DOS command has no screen output, then the user will not even be aware that Paradox has been suspended. If the DOS command does have screen output, it will simply overwrite the PAL canvas. Most word processors and spreadsheets clear the screen before displaying their program.
- NORESTORE keeps the PAL canvas from being automatically restored when returning from the RUN command. That is, the DOS screen output will remain until the PAL script ends, explicitly writes to the screen, or displays the workspace (which would cause a screen update).

The SLEEP parameter lets you produce a delay of up to 30 seconds between the completion of the DOS command and resuming script play. This allows you to pause on the last display screen created by the program that you ran. The sleep time can be between 0 and 30000 milliseconds (thousandths of a second).

    RUN SLEEP 5000 "DIR /W"

Paradox shells out to DOS, executes the DOS DIR command, displays the directory, and gives the user five seconds before returning to Paradox.

Since Paradox lacks the ability to store more than 255 characters in a field, you can use Paradox to run other programs that can. You can then link these into a Paradox application by using the run command tied to filenames.

For example, say you have a table of 30 customers, each with a unique entry in an eight-character [Customer ID] field. You also have an editor or word processor present—in this case SPRINT. The task here is to show users the records in the "Customer" table, then let them select a customer, temporarily exit Paradox, and run SPRINT to load a file with the same name as the customer ID#. When the user exits SPRINT, they will be placed back into the original table. This example assumes that SPRINT is in the DOS path.

**Listing 13.37: RUN.L1**

```
VIEW "CUSTOMER"
WHILE TRUE
  WAIT TABLE
    PROMPT  "Viewing Customers.  Press [F2] to edit or create customer document"
    "or [Esc] to exit table."
  UNTIL "F2", "Esc", "Dos","DosBig"
  SWITCH
    CASE RETVAL = "F2" :
      CLEARIMAGE   ; remove the table
      QUITLOOP
    CASE RETVAL="F2":
      MESSAGE "Loading document for customer ", [customer id#]
      RUN BIG norefresh norestore  "SP " + STRVAL([customer id#])
  ENDSWITCH
ENDWHILE
```

So if the user is on Customer ID# A3245, Paradox will issue the DOS command "SP A2345," which will edit the "A2345.SPR" text file, or create one if it is not already present. Even with the BIG option of the RUN command, there is still about 100K of memory overhead, so very large programs may not run.

## DOS: Suspends Script Play, Exits to DOS (or OS/2) until EXIT Is Typed at DOS Prompt

DOS

Same as [Ctrl O] or {Tools} {More} {ToDos}.

The DOS command creates a DOS shell, saving the current Paradox environment in conventional memory. Since Paradox uses about 400K, on a PC equipped with 640K the DOS command frees 150K of RAM, enough to run small programs or DOS commands. Deleting Paradox objects when shelled out to DOS can cause an inelegant exit from Paradox upon returning. To return to Paradox, type EXIT and the workspace will be restored exactly as it was when the DOS command was issued.

See also the DOSBIG, RUN, and RUN BIG commands.

It's good to be reminded that you must type "Exit" at the DOS prompt to return from the commands that shell out to DOS.

**Listing 13.38: DOS.L1**

```
REM pdox3.bat
CLS
ECHO loading paradox3
PROMPT Current directory is $p$_ Type EXIT to return TO Paradox $g
PARADOX3
PROMPT $P$G
```

When the user shells out, the prompt will appear something like:

Current directory is C:\Paradox3\Toolkit
Type EXIT to return to Paradox >

The cursor will be placed just beyond the >. When the user exits Paradox entirely, the prompt should be reset back to its default.

## DOSBIG

Suspends script play, exits to DOS (or OS/2) until EXIT is typed at DOS prompt, but maximizes memory available to operating system.

```
DOSBIG
```

The DOSBIG command, the same as [Alt-O] in interactive Paradox, exits temporarily to DOS, saving the current Paradox environment on a disk file, PARADOX3.RUN, or to expanded memory. Paradox retains use of about 100K. On a 640K machine, DOSBIG leaves 500K of free memory, enough to run major programs like word processors or spreadsheets.

When it shells out, Paradox displays a warning about deleting Paradox objects. The warning not to delete Paradox objects should be taken very seriously. When EXIT is typed, the workspace will be restored. See also the DOS, RUN, and EXIT commands.

## SESSION: Invoke Another OS/2 Session

```
SESSION [FOREGROUND] OS/2Command
```

FOREGROUND    Causes OS/2 session to start in the foreground. By default, SESSION starts a background session.

PDOXOS2 runs under OS | 2, a multitasking operating system. The SESSION command allows multiple "copies" of PDOXOS2 to be running simultaneously, while sharing the core Paradox code. Multitasking has many purposes. You can create background sessions that control applications that span many sessions. For example, under PDOXOS2 you can provide reports processing while work continues in the foreground. SESSION allows you to load tasks as records into a shared REPORTS table, and monitor their completion.

```
CoEditing Reports table: Record 1 of 3                    CoEdit

REPORTS┬Status┬───────Table────────┬Report┐
     1 │      │    Customer        │    3  │
```

On a network, other users can add to the queue by adding to the controlling table.

```
CoEditing Reports table: Record 3 of 3                    CoEdit

REPORTS┬Status┬───────Table────────┬Report┐
     1 │  √   │    Customer        │    3  │
     2 │      │    Invoice         │    R  │
     3 │      │    Orders          │   12  │
```

The next listing is a code fragment that invokes another SESSION if the "Reports" table has records.

**Listing 13.39: SESSION.L1**

```
IF NOT ISEMPTY("Reports") THEN
  Session "PdoxOS2 -MULTI DOREPORT"
ENDIF
```

The DOREPORT script, which is run by the other PDOXOS2 sessions, looks at the table, prints the first report pending, and finally deletes the record from the table. Optionally, the routine could attempt to print all reports pending.

**Listing 13.40: SESSION.L2**

```
; DOREPORT.SC
IF ISEMPTY("Reports") THEN     ;no reports to work on
  EXIT
ENDIF

VIEW "Reports"
SCAN FOR [status] = ""
  COEDITKEY
  LOCKRECORD
  ; if attempt to lock the record was unsucessful, then another user or
```

```
; session is taking care of this record
IF RETVAL THEN
  ; no need to test PRINTERSTATUS() because OS/2 spooler would always return
  ; TRUE anyway
  table.a = [Table]          ; get the name of the table
  report.a = [Report]        ; get the name of the report
  [status]="\251"  ; "√"     ; flag report as being done
  DO_IT!
  REPORT [table] [report]
  ; now let's locate and delete the record from the table
  LOCATE "\251", table.a, report.a
  IF retval THEN
    COEDITKEY
    DEL
  ENDIF
  QUITLOOP      ; or alternately, delete this line and let the routine
                ; print out all the reports that still need work
  ENDIF
ENDSCAN
CLEARIMAGE
EXIT        ; EXIT PdoxOS2 session
```

The SESSION command defaults to an OS/2 session running in the background. RUN and SESSION operate differently. The RUN command suspends Paradox, runs a DOS or OS2 program, and then returns control to the next line of a script. The SESSION command spawns a child PDOXOS2 session that runs independently of its parent session. This second SESSION can terminate after the first. When a background session terminates, it simply dissolves; no further action is necessary. Foreground sessions terminate by returning to the OS | 2 program selector or task manager screen.

### QUIT: End Script Play and Return to Paradox

```
QUIT [Expression]
```

> Expression     Optional message to display on the Paradox message window when script play ends.

The QUIT command halts script play and returns to interactive Paradox. In runtime, QUIT exits to DOS. QUIT has an often overlooked option—a string to display after the script ends:

**Listing 13.41: QUIT.L1**

```
IF NOT ISTABLE ("CUSTOMER") THEN
  MESSAGE "Customer table is missing or has the wrong sort order.  Press any key"
  BEEP
  n = GETCHAR()
  QUIT "Please replace or repair the Customer table and retry the script"
ENDIF
```

Syntax Trap: Like the RETURN command, QUIT must be the last command on a line unless it is passing back an optional expression.

## EXIT: End Script and Paradox Session, Return to Operating System

```
EXIT
```

The EXIT command leaves Paradox, saves all nontemporary objects, and returns to DOS. It must be issued from main mode. The following procedure presents a menu so the user can select an exit option, returning a string of the choice made. Of course if the choice is EXIT or QUIT, the returned value cannot be evaluated because the script is over.

**Listing 13.42: EXIT.L1**

```
PROC GetOutMenu.a()
  ; RETURNS choice made so later code could evaluate action taken
  ;
  PRIVATE choice.a, confirm.a
  SHOWMENU
    "Exit" : "End current Paradox session",
    "Quit" : "End current Script, return to interactive Paradox",
    "ToDos" : "Shell out to DOS temporarily, then return to script",
    "DosBig" : "Shell out to DOS with more memory than ToDos, then return to script"
  TO choice.a
  SWITCH
    CASE choice.a = "Esc":                ; don't do anything, but let OTHERWISE work
    OTHERWISE: ; get confirmation
      SHOWMENU
        "No":"Cancel request for "+ choice.a,
        "Ok":"Choice request for "+ choice.a
      TO confirm.a
      SWITCH
        ; note that we eveluate confirm.a before getting to choice.a
        CASE confirm.a <> "Ok":
          choice.a = "Esc"                ; reset the choice
        CASE choice.a = "ToDos":          ; if we got to this point, confirm.a was OK
          DOS  ; user would type EXIT at DOS prompt to return
        OTHERWISE:
          EXECUTE choice.a                ; DOSBIG, EXIT, or QUIT
      ENDSWITCH
  ENDSWITCH
  RETURN choice.a
ENDPROC
```

We chose "ToDos" and "DosBig" as menu selections that present unique first letters.

# 13.4 CONDITIONAL EXECUTION

As discussed in "Script Writing Fundamentals", there are two ways of controlling script flow: conditional branching and looping. Branching executes commands or redirects the program based on a set of conditions being True. The branching commands are IF and SWITCH and each has its own strengths.

## 13.4.1 Branching

### IF: Do Something if a Condition Is True

```
IF Condition THEN Commands1 [ELSE Commands2] ENDIF
```

| | |
|---|---|
| Condition | Set of conditions that evaluate to True. |
| Commands1 | Set of PAL statements to execute if condition is True. |
| Commands2 | Set of PAL statements to execute if condition is False. |

The IF construct executes commands based on a condition being True. The condition *must* be True for the Commands1 statements to be performed.

**Listing 13.43: IF.L1**

```
IF TODAY() < 1/1/88 THEN
  MESSAGE "Your system clock must be incorrect, press any key to EXIT Paradox"
  n = GETCHAR() ; wait for a key
  EXIT
ENDIF
```

The IF statement may contain an ELSE condition, which is similar to the OTHERWISE condition in a SWITCH statement:

**Listing 13.44: IF.L2**

```
CLEARALL
MENU
{Ask} {Invoices}
MOVETO [customer id#]
CHECK
[balance due]=">0, calc sum all"   ; calcs total balance due per customer id#
DO_IT!
IF ISEMPTY("Answer") THEN
  MESSAGE "No customers currently have an outstanding balance, press any key"
  BEEP
  n = GETCHAR()
```

```
ELSE
  INSTANTREPORT                    ; assumes printer is online and ready
ENDIF
CLEARALL
```

Nested IF statements are permitted, but often a SWITCH is more direct:

**Listing 13.45: IF.L3**

```
WHILE TRUE
  CLEAR
  SHOWMENU
    "A":"Do the A proc",
    "B":"Do the B proc",
    "C":"Do the C proc",
    "D":"Do the D proc"
  TO choice.a                ; Now we'll show an series of nested IFs that is
                             ; needlessly complicated

  IF choice.a="A" THEN
    a.u()
  ELSE                       ;Must not be A
    IF choice.a="B" THEN
      b.u()
    ELSE                     ;Must not be B
      IF choice.a="C" THEN
        c.u()
      ELSE                   ;Must not be C
        IF choice.a="D" THEN
          d.u()
        ELSE                 ;Must not be D, must be "Esc"
          QUITLOOP
        ENDIF
      ENDIF
    ENDIF
  ENDIF
ENDWHILE
```

A better approach would be:

**Listing 13.46: IF.L4**

```
WHILE TRUE
  CLEAR
  SHOWMENU
    "A":"Do the A proc",
    "B":"Do the B proc",
    "C":"Do the C proc",
    "D":"Do the D proc"
  TO choice.a
  ; now show a case statement equivilant
  SWITCH
    CASE choice.a="Esc":  QUITLOOP
    CASE choice.a="A":    a.u()
    CASE choice.a="B":    b.u()
```

```
      CASE choice.a="C":    c.u()
      CASE choice.a="D":    d.u()
    ENDSWITCH
ENDWHILE

;the SWITCH can even be simplified further:
SWITCH
   CASE choice.a="Esc":
      QUITLOOP
   OTHERWISE:
      EXECPROC choice.a+".u"
ENDSWITCH
```

Multiple logical conditions must evaluate to True to execute.

**Listing 13.47: IF.L5**

```
IF a.l AND b.l AND c.l THEN
   ; will only execute if a.l=true and b.l=true and c.l=true

IF a.l AND (b.l OR c.l) THEN
   ; will only execute if a.l=true and either b.l=true or c.l=true

IF NOT a.l AND (b.l OR NOT c.l) THEN
   ; will only execute if a.l=False and either b.l=true or c.l=False

;As you see, many permutations are possible, sometimes often confusing.


; Now for a few lines of code to let only those with a master password
; print a report on an encrypted customer table.

IF TABLERIGHTS("CUSTOMER","All") AND NOT ISEMPTY("Customer") THEN
   REPORT "Customer" 1
ELSE
   BEEP
   MESSAGE "You have insufficient rights, or customer table is empty, Press any key"
   n = GETCHAR()
ENDIF
```

An IF statement only looks as far as the first condition that completes the statement:

**Listing 13.48: IF.L6**

```
RELEASE VARS ALL  ; force all variables out of memory
l1 = TRUE
IF l1 OR l2 THEN
   MESSAGE "l1 is true, and this message shows even though l2 is not assigned"
   SLEEP 3000'
ENDIF

;On the other hand, the next few lines will cause a run error:
RELEASE VARS ALL  ; force all variables out of memory
```

```
l1 = TRUE
IF l2 OR l1 THEN
  MESSAGE "This message would never show because a cancel/debug would take over."
          ; Error would be :"Variable l2 has not been assigned a value"
ENDIF
```

The following illustrates IF conditions and proper procedure swapping syntax.

**Listing 13.49: IF.L7**

```
; If your procedures are stored in libraries, do not write:
IF CheckPrinter.l() THEN
  REPORT "Customer" "R"
ENDIF

; because it will disable some of the swapping mechanism.
; Instead write:

l = CheckPrinter.l()
IF l THEN
  REPORT "Customer" "R"
ENDIF
```

## SWITCH: Execute the Commands Following the First True Condition, Ignore All Other Cases

```
SWITCH CASE CaseList [OTHERWISE]: Commands ENDSWITCH
```

| | |
|---|---|
| SWITCH CASE | Begins the switch. |
| CaseList | Is any number of conditions in the following form: CASE Conditions : Commands Where first set of conditions that are True will be executed, and all other CASEs are ignored. |
| OTHERWISE | If none of the CASE statements evaluate to True, the commands following the OTHERWISE are executed. |
| Commands | Commands to execute if all other cases are False. |

All commands in a SWITCH are optional. A CASE may opt to do nothing, but should at least do something. PAL evaluates each CASE in succession until it finds a condition that is true, executes commands for that condition, then executes the statement after ENDSWITCH.

**Listing 13.50: SWITCH.L1**

```
PROC SpellDOW.a(date.d)
  ; date.d  any valid date
  ; RETURN the day of the week spelled out, or "Error" if date doesn't exist
  PRIVATE  day.a
```

```
; let's do a little errorchecking for an invalid date
IF DATEVAL(STRVAL(date.d))="Error" THEN
  RETURN "Error"
ENDIF

day.a=DOW(TODAY())                          ; find day of week
SWITCH
  CASE day.a = "Tue" : day.a = "Tuesday"
  CASE day.a = "Wed" : day.a = "Wednesday"
  CASE day.a = "Thu" : day.a = "Thursday"
  CASE day.a = "Sat" : day.a = "Saturday"
  OTHERWISE : day.a = day.a + "day"         ; everything else ends in "day"
ENDSWITCH
RETURN day.a
ENDPROC
```

## 13.4.2 Loops

The looping commands repeat sections of code until a condition is satisfied. PAL has three types of loops: WHILE, FOR, and SCAN. Each has its strong points, but like branching constructs, they all can often be interchanged or combined.

### WHILE: Do Something as Long as a Condition Is True

```
WHILE Condition [Commands] ENDWHILE
```

| WHILE | Start a loop if condition is True. |
|---|---|
| Condition | A condition that evaluates to True. |
| Commands | Commands to be executed within the loop. |

WHILE executes a series of PAL commands as long as a condition is met. The condition is evaluated at the top of the loop and the loop is exited when the condition is no longer True. If you need to force an immediate exit from the loop, use a QUITLOOP or RETURN command.

**Listing 13.51: WHILE.L1**

```
; An example that strips out trailing spaces from a string,
; demonstrates that a loop does not necessarily have to contain explicit
; commands, note that there are no lines internal to this loo

string.a = "Hello there     "

; The next loop keeps reassigning all but the last space to string.a and
; exits the loop when there are no more spaces
WHILE MATCH(string.a, ".. ", string.a)
ENDWHILE
```

```
; Similary, the next routine deletes all records in California;
; The code exits the loop implicitly when LOCATE sets retval = False

EDIT "Customer"
MOVETO [state]
RETVAL=TRUE  ; initialize variable so at least one pass will be made thru loop
WHILE RETVAL
  LOCATE NEXT "CA"
  IF RETVAL THEN
    DEL
  ENDIF
  ; if retval was false then we will drop thru loop automatically
ENDWHILE
DO_IT!
```

A procedure call as part of a logical condition disables the swapping of procedures. Instead, use a WHILE True to start and continue looping, and a QUITLOOP to end it.

**Listing 13.52: WHILE.L2**

```
WHILE CheckPrinter.l()
  ; a printing routine
ENDWHILE

; Is syntactically valid, but it inhibits procedure swapping.
; Instead, use the following:
WHILE TRUE     ; loop will continue until exited explicitly
  l = CheckPrinter.l()
  IF NOT l THEN
    QUITLOOP
  ENDIF
  ; a printing routine
ENDWHILE
```

FOR loops automatically initialize and increment a counter. We often see code that works too hard by using WHILE loops with internal counters. Quite often, the FOR command is more appropriate:

**Listing 13.53: WHILE.L3**

```
CLEAR
n = 1   ; initilaize a variable
WHILE n <= 9
  @ n, 0
  ??"This is message ", n     ; just display the line number on the screen
  n = n + 1
ENDWHILE

; when it could simply be replaced by
CLEAR
FOR n FROM 1 TO 9
  @ n, 0
```

```
  ??"This is message ",n    ; just display the line number on the screen
ENDFOR

; although this example is very rudimentary, the FOR loop automatically
; initializes and increments the variable.
```

## FOR: Execute PAL Statements a Specified Number of Times

```
FOR Varname FROM num1 TO num2 [STEP num3] [COMMANDS] ENDFOR
```

| | |
|---|---|
| Varname | Variable name to be incremented. |
| num1 | Beginning counter value. |
| num2 | Ending counter value. |
| STEP | Optional special increment. |
| num3 | Increment value (default is 1). |

The FOR command is a looping structure that has its own incremental counter and step mechanism. Here it's used to compare the contents of two arrays:

**Listing 13.54: FOR.L1**

```
; The original record was saved in the array original.r
; and the edited version is in an array called edited.r.

changed.l = False
FOR n FROM 1 TO ARRAYSIZE(original.r)
  IF original.r[n] <> edited.r[n] THEN
    changed.l = True
    QUITLOOP
  ENDIF
ENDFOR
; now go on to evaluate what to do if any of the values were changed.
```

When you restructure a table, you lose any rotations that were stored with the settings file, although all other settings remain intact. The next procedure uses a FOR loop to step through every field in a table before and after restructuring to restore field rotations.

**Listing 13.55: FOR.L2**

```
PROC PackTable.l(table.a)
; table.a is the name of table to restructure, complete with Path.
;    if working on a private table, specify the subdirectory so ISFILE can work
; RETURNS  True if table restructured successfully, FALSE otherwise
  PRIVATE n, fields.r, issetting.l
  IF NOT TABLERIGHTS(table.a, "All") THEN  ; Not enough rights to restructure
    RETURN FALSE
  ENDIF
  LOCK table.a FL
```

```
      IF NOT RETVAL THEN                          ; Someone is using the table
        RETURN FALSE
      ENDIF
      issetting.l = ISFILE(table.a + ".SET")   ; Is there a settings file?
      IF issetting.l THEN                         ; Need all columnar rotations
        ;Set up array for one more than nfields, just like a copytoarray does
        ARRAY fields.r[NFIELDS(table.a)]
        EDIT table.a                ; Need at least one record to step thru fields
        REQUIREDCHECK OFF           ; Prevent getting stuck on empty required fields
        CTRLHOME                    ; Moves to record number field
        ; Now we'll get the field names into an array in the current rotations
        FOR n FROM 1 TO ARRAYSIZE(fields.r)
          RIGHT
          fields.r[n] = FIELD()     ; The name of the field
        ENDFOR
        CANCELEDIT                  ; In case any defaults were filled in
        CLEARIMAGE
      ENDIF
      MENU {Modify} {Restructure} SELECT table.a      ; Now go on to restructure
      IF MENUCHOICE()="Cancel" THEN
        {OK}                        ;OK to overwrite Problems or Keyviol
      ENDIF
      DO_IT!  ; Perform the restructure, places table on the workspace
      IF issetting.l THEN   ; Now restore the rotations
        EDITKEY
        REQUIREDCHECK OFF
        CTRLHOME
        FOR n FROM 1 TO NFIELDS(TABLE())
          RIGHT          ; Move to the next field
          MENU {Image} {Move} SELECT fields.r[n]  ; Name of the field to place here
          ENTER          ; Tell Paradox to put the field here
        ENDFOR
        MENU {Image}
        IF VERSION()>=3 THEN SELECT "Keepset" ELSE SELECT "KeepSettings"  ENDIF
        CANCELEDIT  ; Remove any defaults valchecks that may have been placed
                    ; when we stepped through each field
      ENDIF
      CLEARIMAGE
      UNLOCK table.a FL
      RETURN TRUE
    ENDPROC
```

There are a few syntactical notes about what is and is not required as a part of the FOR command syntax. The next listing demonstrates some of the combinations.

```
; You don't necessarily have to specify a TO value. The loop will go on and on
; until the highest number Paradox can handle, pretty much an infinite loop
; although unlike WHILE TRUE loop the FOR loop automatically increments n.
    PROC fortest1.u()
      FOR n FROM 1
        MESSAGE "n=", n ," Press [Ctrl Break] to stop"
      ENDFOR
    ENDPROC
; If the variable has been initialized, you don't even have to specify a FROM!
    PROC fortest2.u()
      n=6        ; or any number
```

```
  FOR n      ; starts counting at 6 and continues
   MESSAGE "n=", n ," Press [Ctrl Break] to stop"
  ENDFOR
ENDPROC
```

## SCAN: Execute Commands at Each Record in a Table

```
SCAN [FOR Conditions] ENDSCAN
```

FOR             Only those that meet condition.
Conditions      Any PAL expression that evaluates to True.

SCAN is a simple and powerful control structure that allows you to systematically perform one or a series of commands on every record in a table. SCAN always starts at record one, and unless you exit the loop with a QUITLOOP, QUIT, RETURN, or EXIT, it finishes with the last record. The SCAN FOR option restricts the actions to records that meet specified conditions. The examples that follow were chosen because they deal with some idiosyncracies of scanning a table.

Syntax Trap: If the word following SCAN is FOR, the FOR must be part of the SCAN condition, not the FOR command. For example, if you are trying to embed a FOR loop as the first command within a SCAN:

**Listing 13.56: SCAN.L1**

```
VIEW "Customer"
SCAN  ; once for each record in a table
  FOR n FROM 1 TO 7
    ; do something else here
  ENDFOR
ENDSCAN
```

This syntax isn't valid because Paradox ignores the comment and interprets the FOR command on the next line as part of the SCAN syntax. Since the SCAN FOR must be followed by a logical condition, the PAL parser rejects "n FROM 1 TO 7". To embed a FOR loop immediately after the SCAN command, two approaches work well:

**Listing 13.57: SCAN.L2**

```
SCAN FOR TRUE  ; same as an unconditional scan
  FOR n FROM 1 TO 7
    ; do something else here
  ENDFOR
ENDSCAN

;or simply separate the SCAN from the FOR with any other valid command
```

```
SCAN   ; same as an unconditional scan
  n = 0    ; splits up the command
  FOR n FROM 1 TO 7
    ; do something else here
  ENDFOR
ENDSCAN
```

SCAN works on one record and then *automatically* moves down to the next record. Deleting records with a SCAN causes every record after a deleted record to be skipped. Here's a five-record table:

```
CUSTOMER │ Name    │ State │
       1 │ Ellen   │ NJ    │
       2 │ Scott   │ NY    │
       3 │ Alan    │ NY    │
       4 │ Brian   │ CA    │
       5 │ Jim     │ NJ    │
       6 │ Lauren  │ NY    │
       7 │ Mary    │ IL    │
```

You might think to use a SCAN to delete all the customers from "NY":

**Listing 13.58: SCAN.L3**

```
EDIT "Customer"
SCAN
  IF [state]="NY" THEN
    DEL
  ENDIF
ENDSCAN
DO_IT!
```

The resultant table will still have one record for "NY" and look like this:

```
CUSTOMER │ Name    │ State │
       1 │ Ellen   │ NJ    │
       2 │ Alan    │ NY    │
       3 │ Brian   │ CA    │
       4 │ Jim     │ NJ    │
       5 │ Mary    │ IL    │
```

The reason is simple, if not obvious. The flow is as follows:

1. Ellen is not in NY, so the record is not deleted.
2. SCAN moves down one record to Scott.
3. Scott is in NY, so the IF condition deletes it; now the cursor is on Alan.
4. SCAN moves down one record to Brian; Alan's record never gets processed.
5. The rest of the code follows the same pattern.

The general rule: Avoid changing the order of records in a scan. If you do change the order, you may have to more precisely control record movement and it's not usually worth the effort, because the same end could be accomplished in other ways. For example:

**Listing 13.59: SCAN.L4**

```
EDIT "Customer"
MOVETO [state]
LOCATE "NY"
WHILE RETVAL      ; if a match was found
  DEL
  LOCATE "NY"     ; loops up to delete the record as long as matches are found
ENDWHILE
DO_IT!


;Or a simple delete query can easily be constructed.

MENU {Ask} {Customer}
[]="Delete"   ; make this a delete query
[state]="NY"
DO_IT!

; will produce a DELETED table as a byproduct.
```

In keyed tables, the probability of changing the record order is even greater. In "CoEdit", changing key field values often causes records to be processed twice in a SCAN. If the action of the SCAN causes a record to move down in the table, when the SCAN reaches the record a second time, it processes it again. Here's an example that increments the dates in the *keyed* table called "SCANDEMO" by five days:

```
SCANDEMO   |Scandate |
           | 1/01/88 |
           | 1/02/88 |
           | 1/03/88 |
```

A SCAN would get you into trouble:

**Listing 13.60: SCAN.L5**

```
COEDIT "SCANDEMO"
MOVETO [scandate]
n = 0          ; a message counter, so we can display the status of the scan
SCAN
  [] = []+5    ; add five days to the current date in field
  n = n +1     ; increment the message counter
  MESSAGE "Pass ", n, " Working on record# ", RECNO(), " Value= ", []
ENDSCAN
DO_IT!
```

When you add 5 to 1/1/88, you get 1/6/88, which is posted to its new key position at the bottom of the table. Next, 1/2/88 is changed to 1/7/88; 1/3/88 becomes 1/8/88; etc. All the while, the SCAN remains on the first record.

Changing the key values of records with a SCAN is often easier in Edit mode. Simply changing the word "CoEdit" to "Edit" in the script above solves the problem. An alternate approach would be a CHANGETO Query. On networks, both Edit and CHANGETO queries require (and automatically place) a Full Lock on the table. The CHANGETO approach is simpler, and creates a CHANGED table with the original values intact.

**Listing 13.61: SCAN.L6**

```
; There are two ways to construct a changeto query for the table:

; Use a QuerySave (remember that an underscore character denotes an example)
QUERY

SCANDEMO | ScanDate
         | _x, CHANGETO _x+5          |
         |                            |
         |                            |

ENDQUERY
DO_IT!

; or code the query using the {Ask} menu choice and direct field assignment


MENU {Ask} {ScanDemo}
[ScanDate] = "_x, CHANGETO _x + 5"
DO_IT!
```

At times you'd like to start a SCAN at a specific record number instead of at the top of the table—perhaps you interrupted a long process and want to pick up again where you left off:

**Listing 13.62: SCAN.L7**

```
; You could code a scan to begin working on record # 6000:

SCAN FOR RECNO() >= 6000
  ; do something here
ENDSCAN

; Although the code above will work, the SCAN must step through each
; of the first 5999 records, determining if each record is applicable to
; the SCAN condition.  A MUCH MUCH faster approach is simply:

SCAN
  IF RECNO() < 6000 THEN
    MOVETO RECORD 6000
```

```
    ENDIF
    ; do something here
ENDSCAN

; In this case, the very first thing the SCAN will do is move to record 6000,
; where the SCAN will proceed normally.
```

### LOOP: Return to the Top of the Current Loop

```
LOOP
```

LOOP redirects program flow back to the first line of the current FOR, SCAN, or WHILE loop. Although LOOP is usually used as a programming convenience, it can almost always be avoided. For example:

**Listing 13.63: LOOP.L1**

```
WHILE TRUE
  CLEAR
  SHOWMENU
    "Files":"Show the files menu",
    "Reports":"Report menu",
    "Utility":"Utility menu"
  TO choice.a
  SWITCH
    CASE choice.a="Esc":
      RETURN
    CASE choice.a="Files":
      filemenu.u()  ; or some such proc
    CASE choice.a="Reports":
      MESSAGE "Report menu will be ready next month "
      BEEP
      SLEEP 2000
      LOOP  ; not necessary because ENDWHILE follows ENDSWITCH so it would loop anyway
    CASE choice.a="Utility":
      MESSAGE "Utility menu not ready yet "
      BEEP
      SLEEP 2000
      LOOP  ; not necessary because ENDWHILE follows ENDSWITCH so it would loop anyway
  ENDSWITCH
ENDWHILE
```

Or similarly, to check to see if an application has all its tables before proceeding any further:

**Listing 13.64: LOOP.L2**

```
ARRAY tables.r[5]
tables.r[1] = "Customer"
tables.r[2] = "Invoices"
tables.r[3] = "Payments"
```

```
tables.r[4] = "Vendors"
tables.r[5] = "Carriers"

FOR n FROM 1 TO arraysize(tables.r)
  MESSAGE "Checking for table: ",tables.r[n]
  IF ISTABLE(tables.r[n]) THEN
    MESSAGE "Found table ",tables.r[n]
    LOOP      ; don't go on to the next line , go back to the top of the FOR loop
  ENDIF
  MESSAGE tables.r[n]," NOT FOUND, press any key to EXIT "
  n = GETCHAR()
  QUIT      ; or perhaps EXIT
ENDFOR
```

The FOR loop could be recoded so that the loop is eliminated:

**Listing 13.65: LOOP.L3**

```
FOR n FROM 1 TO arraysize(tables.r)
  MESSAGE "Checking for table ",tables.r[n]
  IF ISTABLE(tables.r[n]) THEN
    MESSAGE "Found table ",tables.r[n]
  ELSE
    MESSAGE tables.r[n]," NOT FOUND, press any key to EXIT "
    n=GETCHAR()
    QUIT      ; or perhaps EXIT
  ENDIF
ENDFOR
```

There are times when the LOOP command is preferred to make the code more readable.

**Listing 13.66: LOOP.L4**

```
; Assuming that some variables have been set for a set of conditionas and messages:
; The next loop is syntactically correct but the ENDIF would be separated from
; the IF by 100 lines


WHILE TRUE
  IF condition.l THEN
    MESSAGE message.a ; have to remember that way down in the code, the ENDIF
                      ; would pass to the endwhile and loop
  ELSE
    ; perhaps 100 lines of code go here
  ENDIF
ENDWHILE

; So it is probably preferable to use LOOP command so that the flow of the
; program is easier to follow:

WHILE TRUE
  IF condition.l THEN
    MESSAGE message.a
```

```
    LOOP              ; condition occurred, so try loop again
  ENDIF
  ; followed by 100 lines of code that continues the processing if condition
  ; did not occur
ENDWHILE
```

In Paradox version 1.10, a bug consumed memory each time LOOP was used in scripts (not procedures). Although this bug was fixed several years ago, it pointed out that the LOOP command was by and large unnecessary, and had the benefit of changing our programming to include more efficient and elegant coding techniques.

## QUITLOOP: Exit a Loop Explicitly

```
QUITLOOP
```

QUITLOOP immediately leaves a WHILE, FOR, or SCAN loop. Script play continues at the statement following the loop. Loops can be exited in two ways: through a change in a condition (an "implicit" exit); or through one of four commands—QUITLOOP, RETURN, QUIT, and EXIT. An example of an implicit exit follows.

**Listing 13.67: QUITLOOP.L1**

```
string.a = "ABCDEFGH"
WHILE LEN(string.a)>2   ; stay in loop as long as string has more than 2 characters
  MESSAGE "string.a is now: ",string.a
  SLEEP 500
  string.a = SUBSTR(string.a,1,LEN(string.a-1))
ENDWHILE
```

When the length of string.a is two characters, the LOOP terminates. An alternate, equally correct, approach is to leave the loop explicitly with a QUITLOOP:

**Listing 13.68: QUITLOOP.L2**

```
string.a = "ABCDEFGH"
WHILE TRUE  ; stay in the loop unless otherwise specified
  IF LEN(string.a) <= 2 THEN
    QUITLOOP ; leave the loop
  ENDIF
  MESSAGE "string.a is now: ",string.a
  SLEEP 500
  string.a = SUBSTR(string.a,1,LEN(string.a-1))
ENDWHILE
```

Quite often, in breaking apart complex procedures into simpler subroutines, you'll find QUITLOOPs for loops that are no longer part of the current procedure. Listing 13.69 is later broken into two procedures, stranding a QUITLOOP.

**Listing 13.69: QUITLOOP.L3**

```
PROC loopdemo1.u(directory.a)
  PRIVATE continue.l, n
  continue.l = True
  {Tools} {Info} {Inventory} {Tables} SELECT directory.a
  SCAN
    MESSAGE "Checking Master rights for " + [name]
    IF NOT ISTABLE([name]) OR NOT TABLERIGHTS([name],"All") THEN
      continue.l = FALSE
      beep
      MESSAGE [Name], " is unavailable, Press any key"
      n = Getchar()
      QUITLOOP
    ENDIF
  ENDSCAN
  CLEARIMAGE
  RETURN continue.l
ENDPROC
```

A common error is to move one section of code into a smaller procedure and unintentionally orphan a QUITLOOP that was previously appropriate:

**Listing 13.70: QUITLOOP.L4**

```
PROC loopdemo2.u(directory.a)
  PRIVATE continue.l
  continue.l=TRUE
  {Tools} {Info} {Inventory} {Tables} SELECT directory.a
  SCAN
    CheckMasterRights.u(directory.a + [name])
  ENDSCAN
  CLEARIMAGE
  RETURN continue.l
ENDPROC

PROC CheckMasterRights.u(table.a)
  MESSAGE "Checking rights for " + table.a
  IF NOT ISTABLE([name]) OR NOT TABLERIGHTS([name],"All") THEN
    continue.l = FALSE
    BEEP
    MESSAGE [Name], " is unavailable, Press any key"
    n = Getchar()
    QUITLOOP      ; inappropriate here, because there is no loop
  ENDIF
ENDPROC
```

The two procedures shown above simply won't work. In splitting out CheckMasterRights.u as a subroutine, the QUITLOOP causes a run error because there is no loop present in the current procedure. Let's correct the code:

**Listing 13.71: QUITLOOP.L5**

```
PROC loopdemo3.u(directory.a)
  ; directory.a is directory to check
  ;             "" if current directory
  ;             if not "" name **must** have trailing backslash
  ; RETURNs True if you have access to all tables, false otherwise
  PRIVATE continue.l, n
  continue.l=TRUE
  {Tools} {Info} {Inventory} {Tables} SELECT directory.a
  SCAN
    l = CheckMasterRights.l(directory.a + [name])
    IF NOT l THEN
      Beep
      MESSAGE [Name], " is unavailable, Press any key"
      n = Getchar()
      QUITLOOP
    ENDIF
  ENDSCAN
  CLEARIMAGE
  RETURN continue.l
ENDPROC

PROC CheckMasterRights.l(table.a)
  ; table.a   table to check
  ; RETURNS True if you have master access to the table
  ;         False if table is not found (perhaps the wrong sort order) or
  ;               if you don't have All rights for the table
  MESSAGE "Checking Master rights for " + table.a
  RETURN ISTABLE(table.a) and TABLERIGHTS(table.a, "All")
ENDPROC


; You can test the procedure by issuing:

l = loopdemo3.l("\\paradox3\\toolkit\\")
```

# NOTES

1. A bug in Paradox 2.0 and 2.01 that caused the sleep parameter to work as if you had typed:

```
RUN "Dir"
Sleep 5000
```

which flashes the directory, returns to Paradox, and then pauses for 5 seconds. This has been fixed in subsequent versions.

# Chapter 14

# System Control

It seems that the more you know about things that can befall you, the more cautious you become. As you become more knowledgeable about what can go wrong in a script, your scripts grow to encompass the code needed to prevent errors. This chapter contains explanations and examples of system functions and commands that help maintain control over the Paradox environment under script play. These tools answer such questions as "Does a file or directory exist?", "How much memory is available?", "Is Paradox running on a network?", and "What accommodations have to be made to use the current version of Paradox?" By knowing about and using these tools, you can control disk and memory resources and cut down on things that go wrong.

## 14.1 FILES

### ISFILE: Does a File Exist on the Disk?

ISFILE (String)

> String    String expression containing a valid DOS file name, including the extension. If no directory is specified, the current directory is assumed.

Returns:

> True    File exists.
> False    File does not exist.

Although the ISFILE function is fairly straightforward, there are two traps to avoid. The first involves tables that exist in memory only; the second involves the use of private directories.

As the PAL User's Guide clearly points out, you should use the ISTABLE function when trying to determine whether a table exists. Therefore, use ISTABLE("ORDERS") rather than ISFILE("ORDERS.DB"). The main reason for this is that recently created or emptied tables may exist, but may not yet have been written to disk. ISTABLE() also searches the private directory for Paradox temporary tables like "Answer." ISTABLE() is discussed in the workspace chapter. For example, suppose that your current directory is C:\Paradox3\sample and you use the SETPRIVDIR command to set your private directory to C:\Paradox3\private. You could then do a query that produces an "Answer" table and look for the table with the ISFILE function:

**Listing 14.1: Isfile.l1**

```
IF ISFILE("ANSWER.DB") THEN
  MESSAGE "Answer table found"
ELSE
  MESSAGE "Answer table not found !!"
ENDIF
SLEEP 3000
```

This script will always produce the "Answer table not found !!" message because the "Answer" table is not in the current directory—it was created in the private directory. Similarly, you should use SHOWTABLES rather than SHOWFILES "*.db" to present a menu of tables in a given subdirectory.

Another side effect of using a private directory involves three scripts that are inherently private: "Init.sc," "Instant.sc," and "Savevars.sc." Once you set a private directory, Paradox will only recognize these scripts when they originate from the private directory *even if they exist in the current working directory.*

### FILESIZE: How Many Bytes Does a File Use on Disk?

```
FILESIZE (Filename)
```

Filename     String representing a valid DOS file name, with its extension. Optionally, it includes the DOS path.

Returns:

A Number     The amount of disk space consumed by the file.

The size reported by the FILESIZE function differs from the size reported by the DOS DIR command, because Paradox returns the amount of disk space used, rather than the number of bytes in the file. Filesize will vary based on the cluster size used by the particular DOS version in use. You may need to issue a RESET to get an accurate value, because Paradox may not have written a recently changed file to disk (it may still be in the memory buffers).

Keep in mind that although you may have enough room on a drive for a table, a table's family usually includes many files. The following procedure returns True if there is enough disk space to copy a script from one drive to another.

**Listing 14.2: FILESIZE.L1**

```
PROC isdiskspace.l ( file.a, drive.a )
  ; file.a    is the name of the file, complete with extension
  ; drive.a   is a single character representing the drive to check
  ; Returns True if there is enough room on the disk, False otherwise.

  RESET    ; necessary to flush buffers and assure accurate file sizes
  ; Remember that RESET clears the workspace and all explicit table
  ; locks

  ; now return True if the drivespace available is at least equal to the
  ; filesize, False if the file is bigger.

  RETURN  DRIVESPACE( drive.a ) >= FILESIZE( file.a )
ENDPROC
```

To use the procedure:

**Listing 14.3: filesize.l2**

```
l = isdiskspace ("MYCODE.SC", "A")
IF l THEN
  MENU {Tools} {Copy} {Script} {MyCode} {A:MyCode}
  IF MENUCHOICE()="Cancel" THEN
    {Replace}
  ENDIF
ELSE
  MESSAGE "Not enough room for the file"
ENDIF
```

This example checks for available disk space before deleting an existing file. You could make the procedure more accurate by checking to see whether the file you are attempting to add already exists on the disk and adding its size to the available disk space.

## 14.2 DISKS, DIRECTORIES, AND PERFORMANCE

Paradox performance depends on many factors, the most critical of which are often beyond your ability to change. Foremost among the things you *can* change to improve disk performance are two areas controlled by DOS: Your directory structure and your DOS PATH.

The Paradox3 directory must be on your DOS PATH, but by changing the relative position of this directory on the PATH, you may be able to dramatically affect performance. If it's at the end of the list, move it up. For example, PATH = C:\;C:\PARADOX3;C:\DOS.

The logical directory structure is another matter. Paradox is constantly requesting information from and providing information to DOS about the availability of files. The longer it takes DOS (or the network software) to find a file or to tell Paradox that a file doesn't exist, the slower the Paradox response time.

When not on a network, DOS slows down dramatically when a directory contains, *or at one time has contained,* a large number of files. It often pays to set up a Paradox application with separate directories for the major parts of an application:

| | |
|---|---|
| c:\MyApp | The home directory (initializes scripts). |
| c:\MyApp\Data | Main data tables. |
| c:\MyApp\Lookup | Lookup and reference tables. |
| c:\MyApp\Report | Empty tables that hold report specifications for "Answer" tables. |
| c:\MyApp\Util | Scripts and libraries. |

Using multiple directories in an application helps organize it and speed performance, yet setting up an application to work in multiple directories requires a systematic approach. In this section, we'll talk about the ins and outs of directory management in Paradox.

### DIRECTORY: What Is the Current Directory Name?

```
DIRECTORY ()
```

Returns:

A String    The current directory, including drive specifier and trailing backslash.

The DIRECTORY function returns a string designating the current directory. The drive specifier returned is always a lowercase letter (the PAL 3.0 manual is incorrect). Because the returned value is a string, all backslashes within the directory specification are doubled. Thus if you entered Paradox from the c:\paradox3 directory, the DIRECTORY function returns: "c:\\ Paradox3\\ ". As always, take care when making string comparisons.

Here's an example that uses DIRECTORY() to determine the amount of available disk space on the current drive:

```
drive.a = SUBSTR(DIRECTORY(),1,1)
MESSAGE "You have ",DRIVESPACE(drive.a)," bytes left on drive ", drive.a
```

As demonstrated in the next example, the string the DIRECTORY() function returns corresponds to the way the directory was typed in. The example deliberately uses words of mixed case and assumes you have a directory called C:\Paradox3\Sample installed on your hard disk. From the Paradox main menu:

> **Step 1**
> Select:   {Tools}
>                 {More}
>                 {Directory}
> **Step 2**
> Press:    CtrlBackSpace
> **Step 3**
> Type:     C:\
> **Step 4**
> Press:    [Enter]
> **Step 5**
> Select:   {Ok}

Notice that the message says:

> "Working directory is now c:\"

Try it by specifying the following for the directories:

```
\Paradox3
SamplE
```

The message that displays and the returned value of DIRECTORY() is exactly as you typed it: What you type is what you get. Though this can lead to confusion when making string comparisons, the remedy is to consistently evaluate the current directory based on uppercase:

**Listing 14.4: DIRECTOR.L1**

```
IF UPPER(DIRECTORY())="C:\\PARADOX3\\SAMPLE\\" THEN
  MESSAGE "Congratulations, you followed the instructions perfectly"
ELSE
  MESSAGE "You are currently logged onto ",UPPER(DIRECTORY())
ENDIF
SLEEP 2000  ; let user view the message
```

### SETDIR: Change the Current Directory

```
SETDIR DOSPath
```

    DOSPath    A valid existing DOS path directory name.

The abbreviated menu command, SETDIR, changes the working directory and, as a consequence, deletes all temporary tables. It is the functional equivalent of {Tools} {More} {Directory} SELECT DOSPath {Ok}. To quickly remove all temporary tables and remain in the current directory, use:

```
SETDIR DIRECTORY()
```

### DIREXISTS: Does a Directory Exist?

```
DIREXISTS (Dospath)
```

    Dospath    String containing the name of a path of a directory.

Returns:

    1    The directory exists.
    0    The directory does not exist.
    −1    The string is an invalid Paradox/DOS filename.

Although DOS allows extensions in a DOS directory name, Paradox does not. Thus, if you have a directory named MYTABLES.OCT, the DIREXISTS function will not recognize it, nor will Paradox be able to work within that directory. In a more startling example, if you call Paradox from the DOS prompt in a directory with a filename extension, Paradox3 will hang, and your PC will require a cold boot. Don't use directories with file name extensions with Paradox.

    DIREXISTS is useful in two cases: First to see if a directory actually exists on disk, and second, to see if a string is a valid directory or file name. The next example asks the user for the name of a directory.

**Listing 14.5: DIREXIST.L1**

```
PROC GetDirName.v(choice.a)
  ; choice.a is the default choice to display

  ; RETURNS a directory name or the logical value FALSE.
  ; The reason for not returning the word "Esc" or "Error" if user
  ; cancels is that they might have a directory called \Esc or \Error,
  ; unlikely though it may be.

  PRIVATE choice.a
```

```
WHILE TRUE
    @1,0 CLEAR EOL
    ?? "Or press [Esc] to cancel"
    @0,0 CLEAR EOL
    ?? "Enter the directory name: "
    ACCEPT "a40" PICTURE "*{\\,&,#,:,_,-,$}" REQUIRED DEFAULT choice.a
    TO choice.a
    @1,0 CLEAR EOL   ; remove the prompts
    @0,0 CLEAR EOL

    IF NOT RETVAL THEN
      RETURN FALSE
    ENDIF

    SWITCH
      CASE DIREXISTS(choice.a) = 1:   ; directory exists
          QUITLOOP
      CASE DIREXISTS(choice.a) = 0:   ; no such directory
        MESSAGE choice.a + " does not exist"
      CASE DIREXISTS(choice.a) = -1:  ; invalid name
        MESSAGE choice.a + " is not a valid directory name"
    ENDSWITCH
    BEEP
  ENDWHILE
  ; add trailing backslash if necessary to make it consistent with syntax
  ; returned by DIRECTORY()
  IF NOT MATCH(choice.a, "..\\") THEN   ; missing trailing backslash
    choice.a = choice.a +"\\"
  ENDIF
  RETURN choice.a     ; the directory name
ENDPROC
```

The picture "*{\\,&,#,:,_,-,$}" prevents the user from entering a "." in the directory name. This picture contains most of the common characters used in file and directory names, and it also lets the user press the space bar to bring up the "\" character. GetDirName.v will return a logical value of False or the alphanumeric string containing the directory name selected. The procedure might be invoked in the following manner:

**Listing 14.6: DIREXIST.L2**

```
dirname.v = getdirname.v( DIRECTORY() )   ; use current directory as a default
IF dirname.v = FALSE THEN
  MESSAGE "You pressed [Esc]"
ELSE
  MESSAGE "You selected ", dirname.v
ENDIF
SLEEP 5000  ; let them see message
```

For another example, the following code asks the user for the name of a file to output a report to disk. The procedure checks to see if the file name is valid and whether or not the report already exists.

## Listing 14.7: DIREXIST.L3

```
PROC getrptname.v(choice.a)
  ; choice.a  ; the default choice to present

  ; RETURNS a report name or the logical value FALSE.
  ; The reason for not returning the word "Esc" or "Error" if user
  ; cancels is that they might want a file called "Error.RPT", though it is unlikely.
  PRIVATE replace.a

  WHILE TRUE
    @1,0 CLEAR EOL
    ?? "Or press [Esc] to cancel.  Report will be given the extension .RPT"
    @0,0 CLEAR EOL
    ?? "Enter the report name (max 8 characters): "
    ACCEPT "a8" PICTURE "*8[{&,#,_,-,$}]" REQUIRED DEFAULT choice.a
    TO choice.a
    @1,0 CLEAR EOL  ; remove the prompts
    @0,0 CLEAR EOL

    IF NOT RETVAL THEN    ; user pressed [Esc]
      RETURN FALSE
    ENDIF

    IF DIREXISTS(choice.a) = -1 THEN
      MESSAGE choice.a + ".RPT would not be a valid file name"
    ELSE    ; name is ok
      IF NOT ISFILE(choice.a + ".RPT") THEN
        RETURN choice.a
      ELSE
        SHOWMENU
          "NewName":"Don't use "+ choice.a + ".RPT as a name, enter a new name",
          "Replace":"OK to replace old " + choice.a + " with new report",
          "Cancel":"Do not select any name"
        TO replace.a

        SWITCH
          CASE replace.a= "Esc" OR replace.a="Cancel" :
            RETURN FALSE
          CASE replace.a="Replace":
            RETURN choice.a
        ENDSWITCH
      ENDIF
    ENDIF
  ENDWHILE
ENDPROC


; Typical use is:

rptname.v = getrptname.v( "Customer" )    ; use current directory as a default
IF rptname.v = FALSE THEN
  MESSAGE "You pressed [Esc]"
  SLEEP 2000
ELSE
  MESSAGE "Preparing disk file called ", rptname.v, ".RPT "
  MENU {Report} {output} {Customer} {1} {File}
```

```
SELECT rptname.v
IF MENUCHOICE="Cancel" THEN   ; file already exists
  {Replace}
ENDIF
ENDIF
```

### SETPRIVDIR: Set the Private Directory

```
SETPRIVDIR DOSPath
```

> DOSPath     Name of DOS directory to use for private work files and private scripts.

SETPRIVDIR clears the workspace and removes all temporary tables. Unlike the SETDIR command, SETPRIVDIR insists that you supply the drive specifier.

**Listing 14.8: SETPRIVD.L1**

```
;To tell Paradox to use c:\Paradox3\privdir as the private directory.

SETPRIVDIR "C:\\Paradox3\\Privdir"
  ; or
privdir.a = "c:\\Paradox3\\privdir\\"   ; trailing backslash is optional
SETPRIVDIR privdir.a

  ;It is equivalent to the menu selections.
{Tools} {Net} {Setprivate} {c:\\Paradox3\\Privdir} {Ok}
  ; or
privdir.a = "c:\\Paradox3\\privdir\\"
{Tools} {Net} {Setprivate}  SELECT privdir.a {Ok}
```

To recap briefly, in single-user Paradox, temporary objects are kept in your working directory. On a network, they are kept in a user's private directory so that there is no conflict between temporary objects made by other users. These temporary tables are private to each user. With PDOXOS2, this concept is taken one step further—PDOXOS2 creates private directories as needed to keep private objects created by different SESSIONS separate from one another.

In single-user Paradox, SETPRIVDIR can be used to improve Paradox's performance by forcing all temporary files to be created in a separate directory.

As files are created in a subdirectory, DOS records the names of the files in the directory header file. The more files made, the larger the directory header grows and the longer it takes DOS to find a file. When a file is deleted, the size of the directory header stays the same, leaving the space available for another file name. Many Paradox operations create temporary files behind the scenes by the dozen. Although your working directory may have 60 files, Paradox may add several dozen files while doing queries, sorts, etc. Though these files are deleted as necessary, they still affect the size of the directory header.

By setting a PRIVATE directory in single user Paradox, all temporary files are created in that directory. Fewer files in the working directory mean faster access to regular data files. In addition, the size of the directory header in the working directory doesn't swell.

To the user, temporary objects in the private directory appear as if they are in the working directory. For example, to view the "Answer" Table (now physically in the private directory), you simply VIEW "Answer". All Paradox table functions are sensitive to Private Directory status, so you need not specify the path when referring to temporary objects. The PRIVTABLES command lets you tell Paradox to treat specified, nontemporary tables as if they were private objects.

On networks, where you locate a user's private directory can have a dramatic influence on performance. You may locate it either on the local drive or the file server, or change this over time. Where it should be depends on the speed of the network, speed of the local hard disk, speed of the CPU, available memory, disk caching software, network traffic, and so on.

The general rule of thumb is that the private directory belongs on the fastest drive (which depends on whatever combination of factors make one drive faster than another). Thus a network based on a 386 server with a very fast hard disk may, on a network with limited traffic, outperform a local hard drive on an XT node. It can actually take less time to get data from the server than to get it from a slow local drive.

### PRIVDIR: What Is the Private Directory Name?

```
PRIVDIR ()
```

Returns:

A String      The name of the user's private directory.
""            If no private directory has been specified by the Custom script,
              {Tools} {Net} {Setprivate} or SETPRIVDIR.

The PRIVDIR function returns a string with the name of the currently assigned private directory. Although certain functions like ISTABLE() search the Private Directory when referring to a reserved table name, not all functions have that capability. For example, if you want to find the file size of an "Answer" table, you might be tempted to use code like:

**Listing 14.9: PRIVDIR.L1**

```
RESET
MESSAGE "Answer.db is ", FILESIZE("ANSWER.DB"), " bytes in size"
SLEEP 2000
```

However, if the private directory is set to anything other than the current working directory, the "Answer" table would physically reside in the current directory and you would get a script error saying that the file could not be found. The workaround is to simply preface the table name with the private directory name:

**Listing 14.10: PRIVDIR.L2**

```
RESET
MESSAGE "Answer.db is ", FILESIZE(PRIVDIR()+"ANSWER.DB"), " bytes in size"
SLEEP 2000
```

### PRIVTABLES: Treat the Following List of Tables as Private

```
PRIVTABLES Tablelist
```

Tablelist    Names of tables to be treated as if they were private tables. Includes all tables automatically written to the user's private directory.

PRIVTABLES causes a table or list of tables to be treated as if they were private objects for a user. The tables are created in the user's private directory, and other users do not have access to them. In essence, they are treated like temporary tables (like "Answers"), though they are not deleted at the end of a session. PRIVTABLES is of somewhat limited utility, since any table can be copied to a user's private directory, where all tables are private. Another way of making a new table private is to give it a reserved table name, i.e., "Family" or "Entry," though then it will be automatically deleted when other temporary tables are deleted.

When you use PRIVTABLES to make a table private, Paradox does not actually move existing tables to the private directory, though the documentation might lead you to believe so. A PRIVTABLE table always shows up in the list of objects in the current directory, no matter what directory is current. Thus every user can work with a similarly named table if the table is in their private directory and is declared private. One advantage of this is that the application can refer to the table without using its full pathname. However, if Paradox needs to RENAME or CREATE a private table, it will write the table to the private directory.

You can use PRIVTABLES to omit the full path name for a table not in the current directory; however, the private table must physically reside in the private directory at the time of declaration, or the table must be created subsequent to the declaration.

When you declare a table PRIVATE that is not in your private directory, that table will be removed from any directory's lists and menus in which it would normally appear for the remainder of the session. In the example that follows, the working directory is "C:\" and the private directory is "C: Paradox3\ Toolkit".

**Listing 14.11: PRIVTABL.L1**

```
; PRIVTABLES will *create* tables in your physical private directory.

SETDIR "C:\\"              ; set working directory to c:\
SETPRIVDIR "C:\\paradox3\\Toolkit"  ; set private directory to \paradoxw
PRIVTABLES "PRIVTEST"     ; specify that PRIVTEST is to be a reserved name
COPY "\\Paradox3\\Sample\\Bookord" "PrivTest"
; This copying physically writes table into c:\paradox3 directory
VIEW "PrivTest"

;However, if no copy is made, Paradox will not find the table:

SETDIR "C:\\"
SETPRIVDIR "C:\\paradox3\\Toolkit"
PRIVTABLES "c:\\paradox3\\sample\\BookOrd"  ; specify that BookOrd is private
VIEW "BookOrd"
; will produce a script error saying that BookOrd is not found in
; the current dirctory
```

Because of problems with PRIVTABLES in version 2 of Paradox, you should avoid using PRIVTABLES with version 2.

There is only one purely disk-oriented command. Although rarely used, SETMAXSIZE may prove handy in some situations.

### SETMAXSIZE: Override the Way Paradox Assigns Disk Space for Tables

```
SETMAXSIZE Number
```

Number    Representing, in megabytes, the maximum size of the table: 64, 128, 196, or 256.

This is a complex topic. See the discussion of SETMAXSIZE in the chapter titled "Managing Memory and Disk Resources."

## 14.3 MEMORY RESOURCES

Paradox generally assumes the responsibility for managing memory. The virtual memory management of tables and the swapping mechanisms for procedures let the programmer concentrate on the tasks at hand rather than the mechanics of tracking memory usage. There are only a few tools for managing Paradox memory.

## MEMLEFT: How Much Memory Is Available?

```
MEMLEFT ()
```

Returns:

A Number    The amount of memory currently available to the general memory pool where variables, images, and procedures are stored.

The MEMLEFT() function returns the number of bytes of RAM available to the Paradox virtual memory manager in 2K increments. The memory represents the general memory pool available to store procedures, variables, and images. As we have emphasized, it's best to place PAL code into procedure libraries to let Paradox handle memory management during your applications, swapping procedures in and out as necessary.

A good use of MEMLEFT() is as a check on memory at the start of an application to determine if there is sufficient memory to begin the application. Users will often load memory resident programs that consume memory, causing critically balanced Paradox applications to run short of memory.

Here's an unusual example of a memory problem. An application that had been working well for over a year suddenly stopped because of insufficient memory. The application performed a few unusually large queries. The user explained that nothing had changed, and in fact, the CONFIG.SYS and AU-TOEXEC.BAT files partially confirmed this. The culprit turned out to be a newly installed 300M disk drive. The drive had a cluster size of 4096 bytes instead of the normal DOS cluster of 512 bytes. This meant that the BUFFERS=20 command in the CONFIG.SYS file wasn't taking up the usual 10,240 bytes (20 * 512) of RAM—it was taking up 81,920 bytes (4096 * 20), and consequently strangling Paradox! The CONFIG.SYS was changed so that BUFFERS=2 and all went well.

The check on memory might be:

**Listing 14.12: MEMLEFT.L1**

```
startmem.n= MEMLEFT()          ; get the amount of memory found at the start of the program
IF startmem.n < 50000 THEN     ; or substitute the correct amount
  QUIT  "There is less memory available than usual, check your▾computer"
ENDIF
swappoint.n = 30000
SETSWAP swappoint.n            ; set the SETSWAP point
```

Somewhere else in your application you might have a menu selection that displays the current status of the machine:

**Listing 14.13: MEMLEFT.L2**

```
CLEAR
@5,0
? " Disk space available: ", drivespace(SUBSTR(DIRECTORY(),1,1)), " bytes"

? "      Starting Memory: ", startmem.n, " bytes"
? "       Current Memory: ", MEMLEFT(), " bytes"
? "      Current SetSwap: ", swappoint.n, " bytes"
SHOWMENU
  "Return" : "Return"
TO choice.a
RETURN
```

Routines of this type make it much easier to support applications over long distances. A telephone call instructing the user to read the information screen shown above can help track down very elusive problems.

### SETSWAP: Set the Point at Which Paradox Will Begin Procedure Swapping

```
SETSWAP Number
```

    Number      An integer representing the number of bytes to maintain as the procedure swapping point.

Allowing Paradox to do its procedure swapping is an integral part of efficient PAL coding. The SETSWAP command is your control over the point at which Paradox will begin to swap. See the chapter on memory and disks for a detailed discussion of this critical command.

## 14.4 PARADOX CONFIGURATION INFORMATION

### NETTYPE: What Kind of Network Are You Using?

```
NETTYPE ()
```

Returns:

    A String    The name of the network currently in use.

**Network Types:**
"SingleUser"       Not on a network.
"Novell"

"3COM"
"IBM"
"Torus"
"AT&T Starlan"
"Banyan"
"MultipleSessions"     Running PDOXOS2-MULTI.
"Other"                Running on network, but type is unknown.

The NETTYPE function returns the name of the current network, or "SingleUser" if the system is being run stand-alone. At times you will simply want your code to be smart enough to know whether it is being run on a network. Error trapping is generally more complex in multiuser systems. Here's a simple procedure that returns True if file locking should be a concern:

**Listing 14.14: NETTYPE.L1**

```
PROC isnetwork.l ()
  RETURN NETTYPE() <> "SingleUser"
ENDPROC
```

IsNetwork.l() works for PDOXOS2 as well, which is detected by the NETTYPE function as "MultipleSessions." In a stand-alone application, IsNetwork.l() returns False.

## VERSION: What Version of Paradox Is This?

```
VERSION ()
```

Returns:

| | |
|---|---|
| A Number | The current Paradox version in use. |
| 1 | Paradox version 1. |
| 1.1 | Paradox version 1.1. |
| 2 | Paradox version 2.0, 2.01, 2.02, 2.03, etc. |
| 3 | Paradox version 3.0, 3.01 |
| 3.5 | Paradox version 3.5 |

As of this writing, VERSION() returns a value with only one decimal place of precision. There is no way for a PAL program to know whether it is running under version 2.0 or 2.01. Beginning with Paradox 3.0, the current version can also be accessed by pressing [Alt =], where it appears on the first line of this undocumented screen.

As new commands are introduced into PAL, backward compatibility with prior versions of application code becomes a concern. So if your scripts take advantage of Paradox3 features, you could include some error checking at the beginning of your code:

**Listing 14.15: VERSION.L1**

```
IF VERSION() < 3 THEN
  CLEAR
  BEEP BEEP
  @ 4,0
  ?? "You need Paradox3 or newer to take advantage of the new features."
  ?? "Paradox version ", VERSION(), " is currently installed."
  MESSAGE "Press any key to exit Paradox"
  n = GETCHAR()
  EXIT
ENDIF
```

For example, the CURSOR OFF command was added in version 2, so it would not be appropriate in version 1. Here are three syntactical changes that force you to do some adjusting when coding:

**Listing 14.16: VERSION.L2**

```
;The CURSOR command was introduced in 2.0. In versions prior to 2.0,
;its use causes a syntax error.  Even version 1 recognizes
;and can handle an EXECUTE though:

IF VERSION() >= 2 THEN
  EXECUTE "CURSOR OFF"
ENDIF
.........
;A menu change from 2 to 3 forces this use in code that
;can be used across versions:
MENU
{Image}
IF VERSION() >= 3 THEN
  SELECT "KeepSet"
ELSE
  SELECT "KeepSettings"
ENDIF

;or Menu {Image} "K"
..........
;Another menu change involved {Image} {Goto}, which
;was changed to accomodate {Image} {Graph}:
MENU
{Image}
IF VERSION() >= 3 THEN
  SELECT "Zoom"
ELSE
  SELECT "GoTo"
ENDIF
;...........
```

Paradox version 3.01 fixed several problems with earlier releases, but the VERSION function has no way of letting PAL know if it is running under the newer release. Since you need to do some additional error checking with the older version (i.e., SETRECORDPOSITION works around a bug in WAIT RECORD), it's nice to know that a very minor change in 3.01 allows us to recognize the version number. In versions prior to 3.01, the ISFIELDVIEW() function always returns False while in a Paradox "type-in" prompt (e.g., when requesting a table name). Fortunately, version 3.01 is sensitive to FIELDVIEW in such cases, so we wrote the following procedure (it does not tell you the version number, but if it returns True, you know that the old bugs no longer apply):

**Listing 14.17: VERSION.L3**

```
PROC IsAtLeastV301.v()
   ; RETURNS "Error"   ; if not called from main mode
   ;           True     ; if version 3.01 or newer
   ;           False    ; if version prior to 3.01
   PRIVATE l

   IF SYSMODE()<>"Main" THEN
     RETURN FALSE
   ENDIF
   {View}       ; Paradox is requesting a table name
   FIELDVIEW    ; go into fieldview
   l = ISFIELDVIEW()   ; only True if 3.01 or newer
   CTRLBREAK    ; back to the workspace
   RETURN l
ENDPROC
```

## ISRUNTIME: Is This Paradox Runtime?

```
ISRUNTIME ()
```

Returns:

|       |                                          |
|-------|------------------------------------------|
| True  | Script is running under Runtime.         |
| False | Script is using a full copy of Paradox.  |

The ISRUNTIME() function can be used to let a PAL program know if it is running under Runtime or full Paradox.

Paradox Runtime is a special version of Paradox that only runs predefined applications. Though Runtime plays your scripts and lets the user interact with the workspace under script control, there is no free-form interactive access, nor can users develop scripts of their own. If a script is running under the Runtime version of Paradox, there are a few albeit small restrictions that must be taken into account.

- Runtime does not allow a WAIT TABLE in a Query image (although WAIT works just fine in a Display image).
- Runtime ignores the command ECHO NORMAL, although there is a special code in the runtime version of the DataEntry toolkit that allows DoWait() to work under Runtime.
- Another Echo related issue: Although LookupHelp is available, Runtime is not shipped with the Paradox help files (which are not normally used by PAL scripts), so all help screens must be explicitly coded.

## 14.5 ERROR HANDLING

In programming, error handling is the art of predicting the future and making provisions for it. Though you do the best you can to expect the unexpected and guard against bugs in your applications, some will inevitably creep in anyway. They range from minor annoyances to major events. Some will cause a run error, halting the program; other errors simply provide information. Usually it's up to you to check on information that may be available. For example, if you attempt to lock a record in CoEdit and another user already has it locked, the variable RETVAL is set to False, the ERRORCODE() function returns a 9, ERRORMESSAGE() returns a message stating that the record is already locked, and ERRORUSER() returns the name of the user that has the record lock. All of this goes on without causing a run error (which would bring up a Cancel/Debug prompt).

These mechanisms allow you to test conditions and create safeguards to prevent and handle errors when they occur. Paradox generally reports errors consistently by using one mechanism—setting an Errorcode.

### ERRORCODE: What Was the Last Errorcode That Paradox Encountered?

```
ERRORCODE ( )
```

Returns:

|   |   |
|---|---|
| 0 | No Error. |
| 1 | Drive not ready. |
| 2 | Directory not found. |
| 3 * | Table in use by another user. |

| | |
|---|---|
| 4* | Full lock placed on table by another. |
| 5 | File not found. |
| 6 | File corrupted. |
| 7 | Index file corrupted. |
| 8 | Object version mismatch. |
| 9!* | Record locked by another user (file and directory error). |
| 10* | Directory in use by another user. |
| 11* | Directory is private directory of another user (file and directory error). |
| 12 | No access to directory at operating system level. |
| 13 | Index inconsistent with sort order. |
| 14 | Multiuser access denied. |
| 15 | Paradox.Net file conflict. |

**General Script Errors:**

| | |
|---|---|
| 20 | Invalid context for operation. |
| 21 | Insufficient password rights. |
| 22 | Table is write protected. |
| 23 | Invalid field value. |
| 24 | Obsolete procedure library. |
| 25 | Insufficient image rights. |
| 26 | Invalid PAL context. |
| 27 | Operation not completed. |
| 28 | Too many nested closed procedures. |

**Argument Errors:**

| | |
|---|---|
| 30 | Data type mismatch. |
| 31 | Argument out of range. |
| 32 | Wrong number of arguments. |
| 33 | Invalid argument. |
| 34 | Variable or procedure not assigned. |
| 35 | Invalid menu selection. |
| 36 | Missing command parameter. |

**Resource Errors:**

| | |
|---|---|
| 40 | Not enough memory to complete operation. |
| 41 | Not enough disk space to complete operation. |
| 42 | Not enough stack space to complete operation. |
| 43 | Printer not ready. |

**Record-oriented Errors:**

| | |
|---|---|
| 50* | Record was deleted by another user. |
| 51* | Record was changed by another user. |

52*    Record was inserted by another user.
53!    Record with that key already exists.
54!    Record or table was not locked.
55!    Record is already locked by you.
56!    Lookup key not found.

**Multitable Operation Errors:**
60    Referential integrity check.
61    Invalid multitable form.
62    Form locked.
63    Link locked.

**Note:**

Errorcodes flagged with asterisks trigger ERRORUSER(). Errorcodes flagged with exclamation points are often used without tripping a run error.

As this list might suggest, the ERRORCODE function is the workhorse of PAL's error-detecting facilities. ERRORCODE returns a positive integer if there is an error, or 0 if there is none. The values have no intrinsic meaning; they are simply assignments made to represent conditions that you must interpret. The list portrays the types of things that can be expected to go wrong. Obviously, many things can go wrong.

It is good practice to test if a record is locked by another user before attempting to edit it. The example below checks for an ERRORCODE of 55 to see that the LOCKRECORD command did not fail because the record was already locked by you. Although most of the time you can carefully determine when a record is locked, there are a few exceptions: If the user simply presses [Field-View] or moves through a field with a default value, the record is automatically locked.

**Listing 14.18: ERRORCOD.L1**

```
LOCKRECORD
IF NOT RETVAL( ) AND ERRORCODE( ) <> 55 THEN
  MESSAGE "Record is locked by ", ERRORUSER( )
ENDIF
```

In an error handling procedure (ERRORPROC), a switch to deal with anticipated run errors might be written:

**Listing 14.19: ERRORCOD.L2**

```
SWITCH
  CASE ERRORCODE() = 24 THEN
    MESSAGE "Cannot read from an obsolete or damaged library, press any key"
  CASE ERRORCODE() = 6 THEN
    MESSAGE "The file is corrupted, press any key"
  OTHERWISE:
    MESSAGE "Found errorcode ", ERRORCODE(), " ", ERRORMESSAGE(), " press any key"
ENDSWITCH
n = GETCHAR()
RESET
QUIT
```

As mentioned, not all errorcodes are the result of a script error. The next example shows a way of testing to see if the user may lock the current record in CoEdit. A record could be already locked by the user by something as innocuous as going into fieldview.

**Listing 14.20: ERRORCOD.L3**

```
LOCKRECORD  ; attempt to lock the record
; now check to see if the lockrecord failed by seeing if retval is false
; and that the record was not already locked by you ( Errorcode()=55 )
IF NOT RETVAL AND ERRORCODE() <> 55   ; someone else must have locked record
  IF ERRORUSER()="" THEN                ; no user name found anywhere
    user.a = "another user"
  ELSE
    user.a = ERRORUSER()
  ENDIF
  MESSAGE "Record is already locked by ", user.a, ". Press any key"
  ; now you would insert some code that decides what to do in this case
ENDIF
```

See the WAITPLUS scripts for other examples of using ERRORCODE.

## ERRORMESSAGE: The Contents of the Last Error Message

```
ERRORMESSAGE ()
```

Returns:

A String     The message returned by most recent run error or error condition, or "" if no error was encountered.

The ERRORMESSAGE function returns a text string that Paradox displays in the event that a script run error or an error condition occurred. When a script error occurs, you can use ERRORMESSAGE() to display the last message that Paradox displayed on the underlying workspace.

At times you may get the message "Error occurred in protected script." This could mean a variety of things: That the script that you were running had a script error; that you also did not have an errorproc that could handle the error; and/or that the source script for the routine was not present (perhaps the code was distributed as a library). However, even if you don't have access to the source code, you can still display the real error message by doing the following immediately after the script crashes. First, bring up the PAL menu:

**Step 1**
Press:                          [Alt F10]
**Step 2**
Choose:                         {Value}
**Step 3**
Carefully type in:              ERRORMESSAGE()
**Step 4**
Press:                          [Enter]

The last error message that Paradox presented to the program is displayed in the lower right of the screen. Be careful when typing ERRORMESSAGE(), because you have only one shot at getting it right. If you spell it wrong or leave out the () at the end, Paradox complains that it doesn't understand what you have typed, and that complaint will become the new ERRORMESSAGE().

As mentioned, not all errors cause a script to go into the Cancel/Debug menu. Here's another related example. The safest way to go into the CoEdit mode on a network is to first attempt to place a Prevent Write Lock (PWL) on the table. If successful, no one can prevent you from writing to the table, and other users are not able to go into Edit mode or place a Write Lock on it. However, you can't assume that a PWL will be successful; someone else may already be in Edit mode and consequently has a full lock on the table. If you want to attempt to CoEdit a table on a network, some code like this is in order:

**Listing 14.21: ERRORMES.L1**

```
LOCK "Customer" PWL    ; attempt to place a Prevent Write lock
IF NOT RETVAL THEN     ; lock failed
  MESSAGE ERRORMESSAGE()+". Cannot continue until table is released."
  n = GETCHAR()

  ; routine designed to handle denied access to the table

ENDIF

; if the program got this far, you would add code to CoEdit the table
; When you are through with the CoEdit session you would then issue

UNLOCK "Customer" PWL   ;to remove the lock placed
```

In the event another user already has use of the table, the message could read: "Table is in use by Scott. Cannot continue until table is released." The ERRORMESSAGE() function, often used with ERRORCODE() and ER-RORUSER(), can make your messages sensitive to the Paradox environment and greatly speed up debugging of obscure network problems.

### ERRORUSER: Which User Is Preventing Access to a Resource?

```
ERRORUSER ( )
```

Returns:

A String   Containing the user name whose lock on an object caused an operation to fail. Associated with Errorcodes 3, 4, 9, and 11. The name returned is the user name as Paradox sees it, set either by {Tools} {Net} {UserName}, by SETUSERNAME, or by being picked up from the network

Many error conditions are related to another user's already having control of an object you are trying to access. Some will cause run errors and halt the program, others will not. In either case, when they occur, ERRORCODE() is set, and if it is one of the following error codes, ERRORUSER() is set to the name of the conflicting user.

| ERRORCODE | Meaning |
|---|---|
| 3 | Table in use by another user. |
| 4 | Full lock placed on table by another user. |
| 9 | Record locked by another user. |
| 11 | Directory is private directory of another user. |

The most common user of ERRORUSER() is to show messages to the user that display the name of another user who is preventing access to some resource.

As of this writing, there is an unexplained oddity about the ERRORUSER() function. In many cases, ERRORUSER() is made part of a generic ERRORPROC that displays information about the status of the Paradox environment. If the error that tripped the ERRORPROC in the first place was not caused by a conflict with another user, ERRORUSER() sometimes returns "p".

### WINDOW: What Is the Current Paradox Window Message?

```
WINDOW ()
```

Returns:

A String    Containing the contents of the Paradox message window. It returns a blank string ("") if no message is present.

The WINDOW function is especially useful in trapping for errors that Paradox would normally present to an interactive user. For example, when building a query interactively, a common message is "Missing comma." These messages appear on the workspace and are thus hidden by the canvas under script control. It is easy to determine whether a query has completely valid syntax because there is no message—WINDOW() returns a blank string:

**Listing 14.22: WINDOW.L1**

```
last.a = ""   ; initialize variable
WHILE TRUE
  CLEAR  a 1,0  ?? "or press Esc to cancel"
  a 0,0  ?? "Enter the last name (or pattern) to search for: "
  ACCEPT "A20" DEFAULT last.a TO last.a
  IF NOT RETVAL THEN
    QUITLOOP
  ENDIF
  MESSAGE "Processing query"
  MENU {Ask} {customer} CHECK
  MOVETO [last name]
  TYPEIN last.a  ; could be blank
  DO_IT!
  IF WINDOW() <> "" THEN
    ; Tell the user that there was a problem with the Query syntax and give the
    ; user a chance to correct it.  Could be an illegal pattern, missing
    ; quotation marks, excess commas, etc.
    a 1,0 CLEAR EOL
    a 0,0 ?? "Query Error: ", WINDOW()
    MESSAGE "Press any key to try again"
    n = GETCHAR()
    CLEARIMAGE        ; Remove the query
  ELSE                ; Query was ok
    MOVETO 1          ; Query form is first image
    CLEARIMAGE
    IF ISEMPTY("ANSWER") THEN
      MESSAGE "No records match your specifications. Press any key to try again"
      n = GETCHAR()
    ELSE              ; Records found
      QUITLOOP        ; Will now be viewing the answer table
    ENDIF
  ENDIF
ENDWHILE
```

WINDOW() is only useful when accessed from within a script because pressing [Alt F10] to bring up the PALMENU clears the window.

### DRIVESTATUS: Can a Disk Drive Be Read Successfully?

```
DRIVESTATUS (String)
```

| | |
|---|---|
| String | Valid drive as a single letter string. |
| Returns | |
| TRUE | Drive is readable. |
| FALSE | Drive cannot be read. |

Drivestatus returns FALSE when there is no disk in a floppy drive, the drive door is open, the disk is unreadable, or the drive does not exist. There is no implicit check to see if the disk can be WRITTEN to. If the disk is write-protected, DRIVESTATUS() returns true. The problem is that if you try to copy a table to a write-protected floppy, you'll exit Paradox with a "File Create [112]" error. Here's a workaround:

```
PROC DriveReady.l( drive.a )
   ; drive.a   ; a single character string designating the drive to check
  PRIVATE ERRORPROC, driveok.l
   ; Define a temporary errorproc to cope with a specific error
  PROC DriveReadyError.n()
   IF ERRORCODE() = 41 THEN  ; No drive space or write protected
     driveok.l = FALSE  RETURN 1  ; step over the offending PRINT command
   ENDIF
  ENDPROC
  ERRORPROC="DriveReadyError.n"
  IF NOT DRIVESTATUS( drive.a ) THEN
    RETURN FALSE          ; Drive is not ready
  ENDIF
  driveok.l=TRUE  ; initialize variable
   ; Test the drive with PRINT FILE, it trips ERRORPROC, not RESOURCE ERROR
  PRINT FILE drive.a+ ":$$$$.TMP"  "Ok to delete this file"
   ; If write protected, then the errorproc would have set driveok.l = FALSE.
  IF driveok.l THEN  ; If file output to disk ok
    RUN NOREFRESH "Erase "+ drive.a + ":$$$$.TMP"  ; erase the temporary file
    ; Used the RUN so we can delete from any sysmode
  ENDIF
  RELEASE PROCS DriveReadyError.n ; remove the errorproc from memory
  RETURN driveok.l   ; true or false
ENDPROC
```

### DRIVESPACE: How Much Disk Space Is Available?

```
DRIVESPACE (String)
```

| | |
|---|---|
| String | Valid drive as a single letter string |
| Returns | |
| a number | The amount of available disk space in bytes. |

To find the number of bytes of space available on the current drive, use the substring function to get the first character of the current directory, and pass it along to the DRIVESPACE function.

# Chapter 15

# Manipulating Paradox Objects

This chapter presents general information about Paradox objects and ways you can modify them. Most of these commands and functions do not require that a table be present on the workspace, though many of the commands leave tables on the workspace. For example, if you add one table to another, the target table, and at times a "Changed" or "KeyViol" table, will be left on the workspace.

In addition, most of the commands and functions that deal with tables will not work with encrypted tables unless you present a password first. Let's say you have access to a protected table called "Secrets." Without presenting a password, you can evaluate ISTABLE("Secrets") to determine if the table exists, but you can't test for ISEMPTY ("Secrets") or NKEYFIELDS("Secrets"), or just about anything else that deals with the contents or structure of an encrypted table, until the password has been offered. If you attempt to access a table without the proper password already in place, you'll usually get a script error telling you that the table is encrypted.

It is important to note that although tables are usually manipulated via Paradox and PAL, there are other options officially sanctioned by Borland. Paradox tables may be created and updated by several external sources, each having their own uses.

1. Quattro and QuattroPro spreadsheets can read, write and query Paradox tables. Reflex 2.0 can export but not import Paradox tables.
2. Products, based on the new Paradox Engine, makes tables available to C programs as an underlying data structure.
3. SideKick for Presentation Manager uses Paradox tables for the appointment book and phone directory.
4. Paradox's FLIMPORT program (included on your Paradox diskettes) lets you create/append tables with data gathered from fixed length ASCII files.

You would probably want to use Paradox's {Export/Import} menu choices with ASCII delimited files or files in other spreadsheet or database formats.
5. Tutility is a table utility program that also comes on your Paradox disks. It is used to verify table integrity, and if problems are found TUtility can take corrective actions and rebuild Paradox tables.

## 15.1 GENERAL TABLE INFORMATION

### 15.1.1 Table Statistics

#### ISTABLE: Does a Table Exist?

```
ISTABLE (Tablename)
```

　　　Tablename　　　Name of table (string).

Returns:

　　　TRUE　　　If table exists.

　　　FALSE　　　If table does not exist, Paradox searches its own memory buffers as well as the disk.

Use this function, ISTABLE( Tablename ), rather than ISFILE (Filename), to see if a table exists. Newly created or modified tables don't necessarily exist on disk. If you don't provide an explicit drive and path, Paradox looks for the table in the current directory. In multiuser systems, all temporary tables ("Answer", "Family", etc.) are shown as if they reside in the current directory, even though they may physically reside in a private directory elsewhere. ISTABLE() also reports on tables that have been designated private with the PRIVTABLES command.

　　　The following example looks for a table called "TempCust." If found, TempCust is emptied. If TempCust is not found, it is created with the same structure as the Customer table and all forms and reports are copied to the new table.

**Listing 15.1: ISTABLE.L1**

```
IF ISTABLE("TempCust") THEN
  EMPTY ("TempCust")
```

```
ELSE
  CREATE "TempCust" LIKE "Customer"
  MENU {Tools} {Copy} {Justfamily} {Customer} {TempCust} {Replace}
ENDIF
```

### ISEMPTY: Does a Table Contain Records?

```
ISEMPTY (Tablename)
```

      Tablename     Name of table (string).

Returns:

    True     If one table has no records.
    False    If the table contains records, or is currently in Edit or CoEdit, which automatically opens a blank record in an empty table.

ISEMPTY("Customer") returns True if "Customer" has no records, False if there are records. A script error occurs if the table does not exist, or if the user does not have sufficient rights to access the table. Note that:

```
empty.l = ISEMPTY("Customer")
```

is the same as:

```
empty.l = NRECORDS("Customer") > 0
```

However, ISEMPTY is slightly faster. In CoEdit or Edit mode, the current table cannot possibly be empty because Paradox always appends a blank record to an otherwise empty table. ISEMPTY() examines the entire table—it does not report on the restricted view of a detail record in a multitable form. Instead, when in a detail table, use

```
empty.l = NIMAGERECORDS() > 0
```

The next example looks at all the tables in a subdirectory and uses EMPTY to remove records from only those tables that are not already empty. The procedure could possibly be expanded to ask for confirmation before emptying a table, but this variation is used primarily as a quick way of starting off with a clean, empty set of tables.

**Listing 15.2: ISEMPTY.L1**

```
PROC emptyall.v (directory.a)
  ; directory.a  ; Name of an existing subdirectory.
```

```
; RETURNS       The number of tables emptied, or
;              the word "Error" if the directory does not exist.

PRIVATE emptied.n  ; Number of tables actually emptied.

CLEARALL
; First check to see that the variable directory.a has a trailing backslash.
IF NOT MATCH( directory.a, "..\\") THEN
  directory.a = directory.a + "\\"  ; Append a training backslash.
ENDIF

IF DIREXISTS( directory.a ) <> 1 THEN
  RETURN "Error"    ; directory does not exist
ENDIF

; Directory is ok, so let's get a list of available tables.
MENU {Tools} {Info} {Inventory} {Tables}
SELECT directory.a
; Now we are looking at the "List" table.
MOVETO [Name]
LOCATE "List"         ; We would not want to empty "List" by mistake.
IF RETVAL THEN        ; Found.
  COEDITKEY           ;
  DEL                 ; Remove the "List" record.
  DO_IT!
ENDIF
emptied.n = 0         ; Initialize a counter of tables emptied so far.

IF NOT ISEMPTY ("List") THEN          ; Just in case "List" was the only table.
  SCAN                                ; thru the records in the list table.
    IF NOT ISEMPTY( directory.a + [Name]) THEN  ; Only if tables have records.
      MESSAGE "Emptying ", [Name]     ; Let user see that something is happening.
      EMPTY directory.a + [Name]
      emptied.n = emptied.n +1
    ENDIF
  ENDSCAN
ENDIF
DELETE "List"                         ; Clean up.
RETURN emptied.n                      ; The number of tables actually emptied.
ENDPROC
```

The procedure would be invoked:


**Listing 15.3: ISEMPTY.L2**

```
v = emptyall.v ("C:\\Paradox3\\Testdir\\")
IF v = "Error" THEN
  MESSAGE "There was an error, the directory does not exist.  Press any key."
ELSE
  MESSAGE v, " table(s) emptied.  Press any key."
ENDIF
n = GETCHAR()
```

### NRECORDS: How Many Records Does a Table Have?

```
NRECORDS (Tablename)
```

      Tablename     Name of table (string).

Returns:

      A Number     The number of records currently in the *entire* table.

NRECORDS deals with the entire table; it does not respect the restricted view of a detail table in a multitable form. So NRECORDS(TABLE()) is to NIMAGE-RECORDS as [#] is to RECNO(). The first member of each pair deals with the entire table, while the latter concerns itself only with the current image. As with ISEMPTY, if you are editing or coediting the table, NRECORDS(TABLE()) will never return 0, because a blank record is created if the table is empty.

**Listing 15.4: NRECORDS.L1**

```
IF NRECORDS("MyTable") > 0 THEN
  EMPTY "MyTable"
ENDIF

; is the same as
IF NOT ISEMPTY("MyTable") THEN
  EMPTY "MyTable"
ENDIF
```

To display some statistics about the "Customer" table:

**Listing 15.5: NRECORDS.L2**

```
RESET                              ; To assure accurate file sizes.
CLEAR                             ; Clear the canvas.
@ 0,0
?? "The Customer table has:"
? NRECORDS("Customer"), " record(s)."            ; show number of records
? NKEYFIELDS("Customer"), " keyfield(s)."        ; show number of keyfields
? "Data file is ", FILESIZE("Customer.DB"), " bytes." ; show disk size
IF NKEYFIELDS("Customer")>0 THEN                 ; show .PX size
  ? "Primary index is ", FILESIZE("Customer.PX"), " bytes."
ENDIF
MESSAGE "Press any key"
n=GETCHAR()
```

### FIELDNO: What Is the Structural Position of a Field?

```
FIELDNO (Fieldname,Tablename)
```

| | |
|---|---|
| FieldName | Name of field to evaluate (string). |
| Tablename | Name of table (string). |

Returns:

| | |
|---|---|
| A Number | The structural field number 1–255. |
| "Error" | If the table exists, but the field does not. |

FIELDNO() returns the structural field number and isn't sensitive to image rotations nor of capitalization arguments passed. If you want to find the field number of the [Address] field in the "Company" table, use:

**Listing 15.6: FIELDNO.L1**

```
field.v = FIELDNO( "Address", "Company" )
IF field.v = "Error" THEN
  MESSAGE "There is no field called Address in the Company table"
ELSE
  MESSAGE "Address is field #", field.v , " in the Company table"
ENDIF
```

The table does not have to be on the workspace. However, unlike most similar functions, FIELDNO takes the field name as the first argument, rather than the table name. To test if a field name is contained in a table:

**Listing 15.7: FIELDNO.L2**

```
PROC isfield.l ( table.a, field.a )
   ; table.a is the name of the table
   ; field.a is the name of the field
  RETURN FIELDNO( field.a, table.a ) <> "Error"
   ; True if FIELDNO() did not return the word "Error", otherwise False.
ENDPROC
```

To use the procedure, type:

```
l = isfield.l ( "Address", "Company" )
```

### NFIELDS: How Many Fields Does A Table Have?

```
NFIELDS (Tablename)
```

| | |
|---|---|
| Tablename | Name of table (string). |

Returns:

A Number      The actual number of fields in the table (not including the record number field displayed in table view).

Script Error      If the table has a full lock, or does not exist, or if the primary index is of the wrong sort order.

```
MESSAGE "The Customer table has ", NFIELDS("Customer"), " fields."
SLEEP 2000
```

See the UPPER function for other examples of NFIELDS().

## NKEYFIELDS: How Many Key Fields Does a Table Have?

```
NKEYFIELDS (Tablename)
```

Tablename      Name of table (string).

Returns:

A Number      The number of primary key fields currently found for the table.

0      Is returned under two conditions:
   1. The table was defined with no keys.
   2. The table is keyed, but is in Edit mode, and a change has been made to the table.

When any change is made to a keyed table in Edit mode, the primary index is flagged as obsolete and Paradox treats the table as if it were unkeyed until DO-IT! is pressed (or the EDITLOG INDEX command is used). This accounts for slow LOCATEs and ZOOMs on key fields while in Edit mode. When you issue a DO_IT!, EDITLOG INDEX, or EDITLOG PERMANENT command, the indexes are updated.

The next example is a procedure that determines if a field is a key field of a table:

**Listing 15.8: NKEYFIEL.L1**

```
PROC  iskeyfield.l ( table.a, field.a )
  RETURN FIELDNO( field.a, table.a) <= NKEYFIELDS(table.a)
ENDPROC

l = iskeyfield.l ("BookOrd", "Date")
; sets l = TRUE
; Because the sample BookOrd table on the Paradox samples disk has 3 keyfields,
; and the [Date] field is the second table field.
```

## 15.1.2 Table Modifications

### CREATE: Create a New Table

```
CREATE Tablename FieldNameList
CREATE Table1 LIKE Table2
```

| | |
|---|---|
| Tablename | Name of table as a string. |
| FieldNameList | String Fld1:Type1, . . . ,Fldn:Typen. |
| Table1 | New table. |
| LIKE | Borrows a structure from Table2. |
| Table2 | Existing table with existing structure to borrow. |

CREATE is an abbreviated menu command that creates a new table and automatically overwrites an existing table with the same name. CREATE optionally copies the structure of another table.

**Listing 15.9: CREATE.L1**

```
CREATE "NewTable"
"ID#" : "N*",              ; Note that commas follow all but last field type.
"Last name" : "A25",
"First name" : "A15"
```

Paradox creates and deletes dozens of tables during even routine operations like reporting and sorting. Creating tables "on the fly" with the CREATE command has an abundance of uses. Here's a technique that creates and loads a temporary table with values to link into a query.

The example finds all customers in the New England states. This example also uses a temporary table name, a common technique when you have no use for the table after the operation has ended. Paradox automatically deletes temporary tables when you change directories or leave Paradox.

**Listing 15.10: CREATE.L2**

```
CLEARALL
CREATE "ANSWER"   ; Using the name Answer because it will be deleted automatically.
"State":"A2"

; We now have an empty "Answer" table
EDIT "ANSWER"      ; Because the table is empty, cursor is in the [State] field.
"CT" DOWN          ; Place data for Connecticut, move down one record.
"MA" DOWN          ; Do the same for all the New England states.
"ME" DOWN
"NH" DOWN
"RI" DOWN
"VT"
```

```
DO_IT!                    ; Complete the edit.
CLEARIMAGE

; Now prepare the two table query
MENU {Ask} {Answer}
[State]="_xstate"    ; Set the example.

MENU {Ask} {Customer}
CHECK
[State]="_xstate"    ; Set the example.
DO_IT!               ; The Answer table produced will overwrite the old one.
CLEARALL             ; Clear the workspace.
```

If you need to create a table with the same structure as another, you can issue CREATE "NewTable" LIKE "OldTable". This is the same as:

**Listing 15.11: CREATE.L3**

```
{Create} {NewTable}
IF MENUCHOICE()="Cancel" THEN    ; If table already exists, we need to
  {Replace}                      ; confirm the overwrite.
ENDIF
MENU {Borrow} {Oldtable}
DO_IT!
```

CREATE LIKE, coupled with a {Tools} {Copy} {JustFamily} command, enables you to more quickly create an empty copy of a table and its family with less disk space than an alternate method:

```
COPY "OLDTABLE" "NEWTABLE" EMPTY "NEWTABLE".
```

## ADD: Adds Records from One Table to Another Table

```
ADD Table1, Table2
```

Table1    Name of source table (string).
Table2    Name of target table with compatible structure with the source table.

ADD, an abbreviated menu command for {Tools} {More} {Add}, requires that the tables be of compatible structures. Field names don't have to match. ADD will update a keyed target table, producing a "Changed" table. The resultant Table2 is placed on the workspace, along with the "Changed" table (if it exists).

ADD "NewData" "OldData" is the equivalent of {Tools} {More} {Add} {NewData} {OldData} if the target table "OldData" is not keyed, or {Tools} {More} {Add} {NewData} {OldData} {Update} if "OldData" is keyed. If you need to add new records to a keyed table *without* updating, you must use:

```
{Tools} {More} {Add} {Table1} {Table2} {NewEntries}
```

This will produce a "KeyViol" table if key conflicts exist. ADD can be used as an alternative to restructuring a table to reclaim disk space:

```
CREATE "TempTable" LIKE "OldTable"
ADD "OldTable" "TempTable"
{Tools} {Copy} {JustFamily} {OldTable} {TempTable} {Replace}
RENAME "TempTable" "OldTable"   ; replacing the original table
```

### SUBTRACT: Remove Records in One Table That Also Appear in Another Table

```
SUBTRACT TableName1 TableName2
```

| | |
|---|---|
| TableName1 | Name of table with records to remove from. |
| TableName2 | Name of table from which records will be removed. |

SUBTRACT is equivalent to {Tools} {More} {Subtract} and it works differently on keyed and unkeyed tables. If TableName2 is not keyed, only the records from TableName1 that match all fields exactly will be subtracted. However, if TableName2 is keyed, only the key fields need to match. A bug in Paradox2 versions 2.0 and 2.01 required that keyed tables match exactly across all fields. The space previously occupied by deleted records is not removed, but becomes available for additional records. To fully reclaim the disk space, use one of the techniques outlined in the discussion of the ADD command.

This next example uses SUBTRACT instead of a DELETE query to remove all the records for a given state from the "Customer" table. The use of a tilde variable in the query avoids the state abbreviation that conflicts with the query operator in Paradox3: OR. (We sometimes wonder how users in Oregon feel about the change.)

**Listing 15.12: SUBTRACT.L1**

```
PROC subtractdemo.l()
  ; Returns a True if records are deleted, False otherwise.

  PRIVATE state.a, choice.a, n

  CLEAR
  @1,0 ??"or press [Esc] to cancel"
  @0,0 ??"What state would you like to remove: "
```

```
    ACCEPT "A2" REQUIRED PICTURE "&&"
    TO state.a           ; The state abbreviation.
    IF NOT RETVAL THEN   ; If user pressed [Esc].
      RETURN False       ; So that it might be evaluated later.
    ENDIF
    MESSAGE "Getting records for ", state.a
    MENU {Ask} {Customer}
    CHECK        ; checks all the fields
      ; Now assign a tilde variable to the state field rather than assigning
      ; the field directly because of a potential conflict with reserved query
      ; word "OR" for OREGON.
    [State] = "~state.a"
    DO_IT!
    MOVETO 1
    CLEARIMAGE                    ; remove the query image
    IF ISEMPTY("Answer") THEN
      CLEARIMAGE
      MESSAGE "No records found for ", state.a, " press any key"
      n = GETCHAR()
      RETURN False
    ENDIF
    WHILE True
      WAIT TABLE
        PROMPT "Viewing records for "+state.a,
        "Press [F2] to delete all records, [Esc] to cancel and leave intact"
      UNTIL "F2","Esc","Dos","DosBig"

      SWITCH
        CASE RETVAL="Esc":
          CLEARIMAGE           ; Clear answer table from the workspace.
          RETURN False
        CASE RETVAL="F2" :
          SHOWMENU
            "Delete":"Ok to delete the records from customer",
            "Cancel":"Cancel deletions, leave all records as intact"
          TO choice.a
          IF choice.a = "Delete" THEN
            SUBTRACT "Answer" "Customer"
            CLEARALL           ; Both Customer and Answer.
            RETURN True        ; Actually deleted some records.
          ELSE
            CLEARIMAGE
            RETURN False       ; No records were deleted.
          ENDIF
        OTHERWISE:
          BEEP                 ; For "Dos" and "DosBig."
      ENDSWITCH
    ENDWHILE
ENDPROC

; now use:
l = subtractdemo.l()  ; to run the proc.
```

This avoids a somewhat less safe approach—the use of a DELETE query. With this example, records are not actually deleted from the table until confirmed.

### EMPTY: Remove All Records from a Table

```
EMPTY Tablename
```

Tablename      Name of table (string).

The abbreviated menu command for {Tools} {More} {Empty} deletes all records from a table. EMPTY "INVOICES" is the same as {Tools} {More} {Empty} {Invoices} {Ok}. EMPTY causes a script error if the table is not found.

The following example performs a few error checks before attempting to empty a table. This is an example of an instance in which more code can actually result in overall faster execution. The table is emptied only if it exists and has records:

**Listing 15.13: EMPTY.L1**

```
PROC Empty.u(table.a)
  ; Table.a is the name of table to empty.
  IF ISTABLE(table.a) AND NOT ISEMPTY(table.a) THEN
    EMPTY table.a
  ENDIF
ENDPROC
```

A warning is in order. When a table is emptied, all its records are removed, but Paradox may not physically write the empty table to the disk immediately. After using EMPTY, if you reboot, or if the computer locks up for any reason, you may lose the structure of the table, and, perhaps more critically, all of its family objects will be orphaned. To avoid problems, you need to flush Paradox's memory buffers to disk to assure that the table gets rewritten. There are two known ways of doing this:

1. {Tools} {Info} {Family} SELECT table.a DELETE "List"
2. RESET

That the first method works is hardly intuitive. Paradox physically writes a table to disk when you request information on its family. The second method, issuing a RESET command, flushes all changes to any table to disk. Either technique assures data integrity and that FILESIZE() will return an accurate value. (Keep in mind that issuing a RESET in PDOX386 can take some time because there may be a lot of data stored in memory buffers.)

### SORT: Sort a Table, Optionally Create a New Table

```
SORT Tablename [ON FieldNameList [D]] [TO Table2]
```

TableName      Name of table to sort.
ON      Optionally uses fieldnamelist.

| FieldNameList | List of fields to sort on, in order. |
|---|---|
| D | Sort a field in the list by descending order. |
| TO | The SORT creates a new table. |
| Table2 | Name of new table (a string). |

SORT, an abbreviated menu command for {Modify} {Sort}, works differently in keyed and unkeyed tables. In unkeyed tables, you can either use SORT to change the physical order of records within a table or write the sorted records to a new table. In keyed tables, records are physically maintained in primary key order. Thus records in keyed tables can't be placed in any other order without restructuring the table. The usual need to sort records in keyed tables can usually be accomplished through the placement of Group Bands in report specifications. Each Group placed in a report specification adds an automatic level of sorting.

The default SORTORDER determines the order in which records are sorted.

Sorting records in the desired order is often a problem that can be solved with an extra field and a little PAL. For example, under the default ASCII sort order, [Last name] field values like "d'Angelo" end up at the bottom of the table because the lowercase "d" sorts after all the uppercase letters. The solution is to have an extra, single character field at the end of each record called [Sort code], and to place into it the uppercase first character of the last name. This can be accomplished with a simple scan:

**Listing 15.14: SORT.L1**

```
COEDIT "Customer"
SCAN
  [Sort Code] = UPPER ([Last Name])     ; Will place only the first character
                                        ; because [Sort code] structure is "A1".
ENDSCAN
DO_IT!
```

The report can include Group Bands that define the sort order:

**Listing 15.15: SORT.FG1**

```
-----Group Sort Code--------------------------------
-------Group Last Name------------------------------
---------Group First Name---------------------------
```

Similarly, you can sort an "Answer" table in the same manner:

```
SORT "Answer" ON "Sort Code", "Last Name", "First Name"
```

By sorting records, patterns may emerge. Thus SORT is also an analytical tool. For example, sorting provides an easy way to determine the 20 customers with the highest balance due. Here's an invoice table in which [Tag] is an extra field in the table:

```
"Customer Id" : "A5*",
"Balance Due" : "$",
        "Tag" : "A1"
```

(Footnote: We often recommend adding one or several "A1" fields in your table structure definitions. They come in handy when trying to do things that are a little out of the ordinary.)

**Listing 15.16: SORT.L2**

```
; This example gets the 20 largest invoices from the invoice table.
; It assumes that there is a utility "A1" field called [Tag] in the structure:

MENU {Ask} {Invoice}
CHECKPLUS        ; check all the fields, no sorting of answer table
DO_IT!           ; create the unkeyed answer table

SORT "Answer" ON "BALANCE DUE" D   ; sorts in descending order by [Balance Due]

EDITKEY
SCAN FOR RECNO()<21
  [Tag] = "x"    ; place an x into the utility field of the first 20 records
ENDFOR
DO_IT!
CLEARALL

; Now let's select only those tagged records.
MENU {Ask} {Answer}
CHECKPLUS
[Tag] = "x"      ; or NOT BLANK
DO_IT!
```

Running this script creates an "Answer" table with the top 20 records. See the example in the SHOWMENU command for sorting to a new file.

### SORTORDER: What Is the Current Sort Order?

```
SORTORDER ()
```

Returns:

A String    The current sort order in Paradox3.SOR: "ascii", "intl", "nor-dan", "swedfin".

SORTORDER() always returns a lower case string. The PAL manual is incorrect, showing this function as returning a string with initial capital letters. Paradox lets you choose a default sort order during installation. In the version shipped in the United States, the default sort order is ASCII, that is, sorting and string comparisons are done in the same order as in the ASCII table in the PAL manual. Many Paradox users in the United States designate their sort order as International because uppercase and lowercase letters sort together. Using international sort order, "diMaggio" ends up near "DiMaggio" instead of after "Zenreich."

If your program depends on a particular sort order, you should check SORTORDER() to see if Paradox is correctly set up:

**Listing 15.17: SORTORDE.L1**

```
IF SORTORDER() <> "ascii" THEN  ; note that "ascii" is in lower▾case
  CLEAR
  @4,0
  ?? "This application needs Paradox installed in ASCII order"
  ? "Paradox is currently set up for ", UPPER(SORTORDER())
  SHOWMENU
    "Quit":"Quit to the Paradox main menu",
    "Exit":"Exit Paradox"
  TO choice.a
  IF choice.a = "Exit" THEN
    EXIT
  ELSE
    QUIT
  ENDIF
ENDIF
```

Both keyed and unkeyed tables can often benefit from a secondary index, also known as a query "Speedup" file.

### INDEX: Create a Secondary Index for a Field

```
INDEX [MAINTAINED] Tablename ON Fieldname
```

| | |
|---|---|
| MAINTAINED | Keep up to date in all operations for keyed tables. |
| Tablename | Name of table (String). |
| ON | Which field? |
| Fieldname | Name of field (String). |

INDEX creates a secondary index that may be used by QUERIES, ZOOMS, and LOCATES. A secondary index in Paradox is actually two files, with filename extensions .Xnn and .Ynn, in which nn matches the field number as expressed in hexadecimal notation. The .Ynn file is always much smaller than the .Xnn file. To make a secondary index on the [phone number] field in the "Customer" table:

```
INDEX "Customer" ON "Phone Number"
```

IF [Phone Number] is the fourth field in the table, the files created are "CUSTOMER.X04" and "CUSTOMER.Y04"; if it is the twelfth field, the files created are "CUSTOMER.X0C" and "CUSTOMER.Y0C," since C is the hexadecimal representation of 12.

The MAINTAINED option creates a structurally different index (we explain this in a few pages):

```
INDEX MAINTAINED "Customer" ON "Phone Number"
```

The MAINTAINED option, which works only on keyed tables, keeps the index up to date as modifications are made. Whenever the primary index changes, a MAINTAINED secondary index changes as well. Since by default, INDEXES are not maintained in Paradox, if you want an index to be MAINTAINED, you must create it with that option. You can change this default with the "Custom" script. Nonmaintained indexes are updated only when Paradox needs to make use of them. Once you create a secondary index, no further attention is required.

A secondary index will show up in the "List" table created by {Tools} {Info} {Family} {Customer} as a single file—for example, a "Speedup for Phone Number"—and flagged as [Maintained], [Current], or [Not Current].

A MAINTAINED index is physically different from one that is not maintained. We first discovered this in a table containing 7000 records. Because of the nature of the data, the only appropriate key was on several large fields:

```
"Company name" : "A40*",

   "Last name" : "A25*",

  "First name" : "A15*",

     "Address" : "A40*",

        "City" : "A2",

 ; The rest of the table's 30 fields were not keyed
```

The FILESIZE() of the table was 1.8 megabytes. The primary index was 600K. A nonmaintained secondary index was created on the ninth field in the table, a numeric field. Paradox created an 89K .X09 file and a 4K .Y09 file. When we later MAINTAINED the index on the same field, the .X09 file was 960K and the .Y09 file was 350K! The combined size of a single maintained secondary index was two-thirds the size of the table. The conclusion is easily drawn: a MAINTAINED index stores all the fields of the primary key in each .Xnn file.

If you use tables with large, multifield primary keys, you should be aware that performance gains from a secondary maintained index come at the expense of disk space.

As of this writing there is a rather obscure bug in Paradox2 and Paradox3 (but not in PDOX386): If you attempt to do a MultiEntry or MultiAdd when one of the target tables has more than one maintained index, and one of those maintained fields is an alphanumeric field longer than eight characters, the machine will lock up, requiring a warm boot.

## 15.1.3 Copying, Renaming, and Deleting Paradox Objects

### COPY: Make a Copy of a Table

```
COPY Tablename1 Tablename2
```

Tablename1   Name of source table (string).
Tablename2   Name of target table (string).

COPY is an abbreviated menu command that copies a table and all of its family to a new table without asking for confirmation. If the target table, Tablename2, already exists, the command is the same as:

```
{Tools} {Copy} {Table} {table1} {table2} {Replace}
```

If target table does not exist, the command is:

```
{Tools} {Copy} {Table} {table1} {table2}
```

To duplicate a table called "OldData" to a table in the same directory called "NewData," use:

```
COPY "OldData" "NewData"
```

COPY requires that you have enough disk space to completely copy the file. If you simply need an empty duplicate of the table, use the CREATE command to create a table LIKE the original. If you want the table and all its records, but you want it *without* the family, use:

```
Create "NewData" like "OldData"    ; same structure as OldData
ADD "Newdata" "OldData"
```

### {Tools}{Copy}{JustFamily}: Copy the Family of One Table to Another Table

```
{Tools} {Copy} {JustFamily} {Table1} {Table2} {Replace}
```

{Table1}   Table name with family to be copied, e.g., {Customer} or SELECT "Customer."

{Table2}    Table with same structure as {Table1} that should receive the family.

{Replace}   Lets the family copy continue. If the tables are not of the same structure, the family copy will not occur, and the workspace will stay on the {Replace} choice.

This is one of the most common menu combinations used by PAL programmers, allowing you to copy an entire family (Forms, Reports, ValChecks, Settings) from one table to another.

If the structures of the two tables are not the same, you'll get a script error. The following example checks to make sure two tables are compatible. A word of explanation: We are using the WINDOW() function rather than checking MENU-CHOICE() for "Cancel" because of the slim (however unlikely) chance that the name of the second table is "Cancel" (representing, perhaps, a table of all cancelled orders).

**Listing 15.18: FAMI.L1**

```
PROC CanFamilyCopy.l(table1.a,table2.a)
  ; table1.a  ; Name of first table.
  ; table2.a  ; Name of second table.
  ; RETURNS  True if families can be copied; False otherwise.
  ; Note that this proc does not actually perform any copying.

  PRIVATE ok.l
  MENU {Tools} {Copy} {JustFamily}
  SELECT table1.a
    ; Can't use SELECT for the next statement, because invalid structure.
    ; would cause a script error.
  TYPEIN table2.a
  ENTER
    ; now look ar the WINDOW to see if there is a problem.
  ok.l = WINDOW() = ""     ; If window is blank, Paradox is not complaining.
                           ; In either case, let's cancel the copy justfamily.
  CTRLBREAK                ; Back to whatever you were doing.
  RETURN ok.l
ENDPROC
```

## COPYFORM: Copy a Form within or between Tables

```
COPYFORM Table1 Form1 Table2 Form2
```

Table1    Source table (a string).
Form1     Source form as a string, a number from 1 to 14, or "F."
Table2    Target table (a string).
Form2     Target form as a string, a number from 1 to 14, or "F."

COPYFORM was added to Paradox3 to enable you to copy a form from one table to another (with the same structure) without having to copy an entire family. You can specify that a form be copied to some table by using the same name for both the source and target tables and specifying a different form. Like many abbreviated menu commands. COPYFORM does not ask for confirmation if the target form already exists.

```
COPYFORM "Customer" "F" "NewCust" 2
```

is equivalent to:

```
MENU {Tools} {Copy} {Form} {DifferentTable}
{Customer} {F} {NewCust} {2}
IF MENUCHOICE()="Cancel" THEN
   {Replace}
ENDIF
```

## COPYREPORT: Copy a Report within or between Tables

```
COPYREPORT Table1 Report1 Table2 Report2
```

| | |
|---|---|
| Table1 | Source table as a string. |
| Report1 | Source report as a string, a number from 1 to 14, or "R." |
| Table2 | Target table as a string. |
| Report2 | Target report as a string, a number from 1 to 14, or "R." |

Like COPYFORM, COPYREPORT was added in Paradox3, enabling you to copy a report specification from one table to another (with the same structure) without transferring an entire family. It follows the same syntactical rules as COPY-FORM.

```
COPYREPORT "Customer" 1 "Answer" "R"
```

## RENAME: Change the Name of a Table

```
RENAME Tablename1 Tablename2
```

| | |
|---|---|
| Tablename1 | Original name of table (a string). |
| Tablename2 | New name of table (a string). |

RENAME, an abbreviated menu command, renames the entire table family with all of its objects (forms, reports, etc.). Renaming a script must be done using {Tools} {Rename} {Script}.

The next example executes a simple query that gets all invoices with today's date and renames the resulting "answer" table to "InvToday." Renaming temporary tables, especially "Answer," prevents tables from being written over by the next query or deleted upon changing directories or exiting Paradox.

**Listing 15.19: RENAME.L1**

```
MENU {Ask} {Invoices}
CHECK
[Invoice Date]="TODAY"
DO_IT!
CLEARALL
RENAME "ANSWER" "INVTODAY"   ; Overwrites any existing InvToday table.
```

If you RENAME a table to a reserved Paradox table name, for example, ENTRY or FAMILY, and have a private directory set, Paradox will *physically move* the table to the private directory. This is also true for any tables marked as private through the use of the PRIVTABLES command.

Because of the potential for moving the entire file, RENAME places a Full Lock on the table, assuring that no one else is using the table's files during the renaming process. If a Full Lock cannot be achieved by the end of the RETRY-PERIOD, a script error results.

The Rename.1 procedure is for multiuser environments, and it returns True if renaming is successful and False if it is not. It allows you to override the default RETRYPERIOD by supplying a value in the parameter list.

**Listing 15.20: RENAME.L2**

```
PROC Rename.l(table1.a, table2.a, retryperiods.n, message.l)
  ; table1.a         ; Source table.
  ; table2.a         ; Target table.
  ; retryperiod.n    ; The number of seconds to attempt the rename.
  ; message.l        ; True if message is to display during wait,
                     ; False if no message.
  ; RETURNS True if table was renamed,
  ;         False if time ran out before locks could be placed.
  PRIVATE n
  FOR n FROM 1 TO MAX(retryperiods.n, 1)  ; Because retryperiod.n could be 0.
    LOCK table1.a FL, table2.a FL
    IF RETVAL THEN
      QUITLOOP ; Both tables are locked, even if table2.a doesn't yet exist.
    ENDIF
    IF message.l THEN
      MESSAGE "Waiting for ",ERRORUSER()," to release ",table1.a," or ",table2.a
    ENDIF
    SLEEP 1000 ; Wait 1 second and try lock again.
  ENDFOR
  IF RETVAL THEN                    ; Tables are locked.
    RENAME table1.a table2.a        ; Cannot fail.
    UNLOCK table1.a FL, table2.a FL ; Clean up and release the locks.
  ENDIF
  RETURN RETVAL    ; True if renamed, False if tables could not be locked within
                   ; the retry period.
ENDPROC
```

Examples of its use:

Use the following syntax to RENAME the "Invoice" table to "OldInv" if another user might be using the table. This example displays a message with the name of the user delaying the renaming, and will either try for the default RETRYPERIOD or one designated by SETRETRYPERIOD, with a minimum of one try:

```
l = Rename.l ( "Invoice", "OldInv", RETRYPERIOD(), TRUE )
```

The next approach tries for 60 seconds, and will not display any messages if there are delays.

```
l = Rename.l ( "Invoice", "OldInv", 60, FALSE )
```

## DELETE: Delete a Table and Its Family

```
DELETE Tablename
```

Tablename     Name of table to delete

This abbreviated menu command deletes a table and its family objects. If the named table does not exist, DELETE will generate a script error.

A substitute, the Delete.l procedure below, checks to see if a table exists and if you have the right to delete it before deleting the table. The procedure also assures you that no one else is using the table. Unlike the Rename.1 procedure in the last example, this procedure only makes one attempt to delete the table.

**Listing 15.21: DELETE.L1**

```
PROC delete.l(table.a)
  ; table.a is name of table to delete.
  ; RETURNS True if table is deleted.
  ;         False if table does not exist or cannot be deleted.

  IF NOT ISTABLE(table.a) THEN    ; Check to see if table exists.
    RETURN False
  ENDIF

  IF NOT TABLERIGHTS(table.a,"All") THEN ; Check for master rights.
    RETURN False
  ENDIF

  LOCK table.a FL    ; Make sure no one else is in the table.
  IF NOT retval THEN
    RETURN False
  ENDIF
  DELETE table.a
  UNLOCK table.a FL  ; Remove the lock which remains even though table is gone.
  RETURN True        ; Table found and removed.
ENDPROC
```

Once you've begun a Paradox session, it's important that you delete Paradox objects only by using the {Tools} {Delete} menu choices. That is, don't use DOS commands to delete a form or report if you've suspended your Paradox session with DOS, DOSBIG, RUN, or RUN BIG. Paradox keeps track of the objects associated with a table, and you may cause problems if objects are not deleted under Paradox's control. These Paradox menu commands include:

{Tools} {Delete} {Form}
{Tools} {Delete} {Report}
{Tools} {Delete} {ValCheck}
{Tools} {Delete} {KeepSet}
{Tools} {Delete} {QuerySpeedup}

These two next choices don't deal with family objects, though you can delete graphs and scripts through the menus:

{Tools} {Delete} {Script}
{Tools} {Delete} {Graph}

### 15.1.4 {Tools} {Info} and Related Subjects

The {Tools} {Info} menu enables you to produce tables of special information that may be difficult or impossible to gather any other way. Once Paradox places the resulting "Family," "List," or "Struct" table it creates on the workspace, you can evaluate, query, or print the records as you would with any other table. As with any temporary table, you must rename them if you want to save them. You can make all selections as braced menu choices or by a combination of menu choices and SELECT commands. For example,

```
{Tools} {Info} {Inventory} {Files}
{C:\\Paradox3\\Toolkit\\*.LIB}
```

The SELECT command enables you to easily substitute a variable. For example,

```
{Tools} {Info} {Inventory} {Files}
SELECT "C:\\Paradox3\\Toolkit\\*.LIB"
```

### Get a List of Files That Meet a Specification

```
{Tools} {Info} {Inventory} {Files} SELECT DosSpecification
```

DosSpecification        Any valid Dos file specification.

This command creates a table called "List" with the file names and dates found that meet the specification. The [Name] field in the List table includes file extensions.

### Get a List of All Scripts in a Subdirectory

`{Tools} {Info} {Inventory} {Scripts} SELECT DosPath`

> DosPath      Any valid subdirectory name

This command creates a "LIST" table with the names and dates for scripts found in the specified directory. The [Name] field in the List table does not include the .SC file extension.

### Get a List of All Tables in a Subdirectory

`{Tools} {Info} {Inventory} {Tables} SELECT DosPath`

> DosPath      Any valid subdirectory name

This command creates a "LIST" table with the names and last modification date of tables that Paradox considers to be in a directory. If the directory chosen is your working directory, Paradox also includes tables that are considered private. If appropriate, the "List" table itself will appear as a record in the table, because the table was just created in the private directory. Paradox also searches through memory to find tables that may not have been written to disk.

The [Name] field in the List table *does not* include the .DB file extension.

### Get a List of Family Objects for a Table

`{Tools} {Info} {Family} SELECT Tablename`

> Tablename      Any Paradox table

These menu selections create a table named "Family" which contains two fields, [Name] and [Date] and lists the family objects of the named table. The first record is the name of the table. If the table is in the current directory no path is specified; if the table is in the current drive, no drive specifier is provided. Each subsequent record identifies one of the table's family objects and the date last modified. There may be records for reports, forms, valchecks, settings, and for secondary indexes, which are known as speedups and may be marked as [Maintained] or [Not Current]. It is worth noting that the primary index (.PX) file does not appear in the list; it is not copied during a {JustFamily} copy.

### Get a List of the Structure of a Table

```
{Tools} {Info} {Structure} SELECT Tablename
```

Tablename    Any Paradox table

This command creates a "STRUCT" table with the fields and field types for a table.

### Get a List of User Names on a Network

```
{Tools} {Info} {Who}
```

This command creates a "List" table with the fields for [Username] and (in versions starting with Paradox 2.03) a field for [Product], which lists the type of Paradox running on each user's machine. Note that {Tools} {Info} {Who} will create only the "List" table if you are on a network, or have a NETTYPE() that is not "SingleUser" (for example, it works with multiple sessions of PDOXOS2).

### USERNAME: What Is the Current User Name?

```
USERNAME ()
```

Returns:

A String    Up to 15 characters in length having the user name as known to Paradox.

You do not have to be on a network to test the USERNAME function. USER-NAME determines the value it will return in the following order:

1. from SETUSERNAME name or {Tools} {Net} {UserName}
2. by invoking the program with the -USER command line option (for example: PARADOX3 -USER name)
3. based on the user name as predefined in CUSTOM.SC
4. based on the user name available from certain network environments

The following sample program greets the user, getting his or her name if available:

**Listing 15.22: USERNAME.L1**

```
user.a = USERNAME()    ; Let's get the user name.
IF user.a = "" THEN    ; Paradox doesn't know the user name.
  user.a = "Sir or Madam"
ENDIF
```

```
MESSAGE "Hello ", user.a, ".  Nice to be working with you."
SLEEP 5000
```

### SETUSERNAME: Override the Current User Name

```
SETUSERNAME Name
```

      Name     A string of up to 15 characters.

This command replaces any existing user name with a new string. SETUSER-NAME "Scott" is equivalent to {Tools} {Net} {UserName} {Scott}.

## 15.2 CONTROLLING TABLE ACCESS

### 15.2.1 Controlling IMAGERIGHTS

#### IMAGERIGHTS: Set the Rights to This Image

```
IMAGERIGHTS [{READONLY} | {UPDATE}]
```

      READONLY     Allow viewing only.
      UPDATE     Allow changes to nonkey fields.

This vastly underutilized command allows a simple way of temporarily restricting a user's method of modifying a table. It works even though a table is not encrypted. IMAGERIGHTS by itself resets normal rights to the current image on the workspace. IMAGERIGHTS UPDATE prevents the user from adding or deleting records and allows modification of nonkey fields only. IMAGERIGHTS READONLY prevents the user from typing anything that could modify a table.

    Using IMAGERIGHTS judiciously is a great performance boost, especially if there are many tables on the workspace on a network. Instead of jumping in and out of CoEdit mode, you can go directly into CoEdit and let IMAGERIGHTS READONLY simulate the VIEW mode. This avoids all the work involved in locking and unlocking tables. If the user tries to modify restricted fields, a simple message reports: "Field is not modifiable."

    The WAITPLUS procedures make extensive use of the IMAGERIGHTS commands to simulate some of the restrictions that are otherwise confined to encrypted tables.

    IMAGERIGHTS is useful with the Data Entry Toolkit. You can use the following pair of procedures to allow the user to land on a field, but not change

it, even in one of the edit modes. This avoids creating and using forms with
DisplayOnly fields simply to keep a user from changing the data.

**Listing 15.23: IMAGERIG.L1**

```
; The next proc could be called upon arrival into a field.

PROC imagereadonly.u()
  IMAGERIGHTS READONLY      ; Don't let user change anything.
ENDPROC

; To restore the normal rights upon leaving the field, a depart
; proc could be assigned to a field:

PROC imagenormal.u()
  IMAGERIGHTS
ENDPROC
```

The code fragment below keeps the user in CoEdit mode and prevents him or her
from changing anything until [F9] is pressed.

**Listing 15.24: IMAGERIG.L2**

```
VIEW "Customer"                ; Place the customer and invoice tables on the workspace.
COEDIT "INVOICES"
PICKFORM 1
WHILE True
  IMAGERIGHTS READONLY         ; Simulate a view mode.
  WAIT TABLE
    PROMPT "Viewing Invoices. Press [F2] to exit",
    "[F9]-Edit this record  [F8]-View Customers"
  UNTIL "F2","F8","F9","Dos","DosBig"
  SWITCH
    CASE RETVAL = "F2":
      DO_IT!
      CLEARALL
      RETURN
    CASE RETVAL = "F9":
      LOCKRECORD
      IF NOT RETVAL THEN
        MESSAGE "Record is locked by "+ERRORUSER()+". Press any key."
        n = GETCHAR()
        LOOP
      ENDIF
      IMAGERIGHTS               ; Let the user change the record.
      WHILE True
        WAIT RECORD
          PROMPT "Edit this record.",
          "Press [F2] when done",
        UNTIL "F2", "Dos", "DosBig"
        SWITCH
          CASE RETVAL = "F2":
            UNLOCKRECORD
            IF RETVAL THEN     ; Only if record can be posted.
```

```
              QUITLOOP              ; The IMAGERIGHTS READONLY will get set
            ENDIF                   ; at the top of the WAIT TABLE loop.
          ENDSWITCH
        ENDWHILE
      CASE RETVAL="F8":             ; Want to see, but not change the customer table.
        UPIMAGE
        IMAGERIGHTS READONLY        ; Keep user from changing the table.
        WHILE True
          WAIT TABLE
            PROMPT "Viewing Customers.",
            "Press [Esc] to return to Invoices",
          UNTIL "Esc", "Dos", "DosBig"
          SWITCH
            CASE RETVAL = "Esc":
              IMAGERIGHTS
              DOWNIMAGE              ; Back to invoices.
              FORMKEY               ; Restore the form.
              QUITLOOP              ; The IMAGERIGHTS READONLY will get set at the
                                    ; top of the WAIT TABLE loop.
          ENDSWITCH
        ENDWHILE
    ENDSWITCH
  ENDWHILE
```

## 15.2.2 Controlling Access through Locking

On a network, where tables can be shared, Paradox follows a different set of rules. Activities that modify a table, report, or form on a network create temporary locks that restrict other users' access to these files. When an operation is complete, the lock is removed and the resource is freed. When an object is locked, Paradox creates a lock file (with an extension ".LCK") in the same directory as the object being locked. The file is deleted when the lock is released.

The type of lock placed depends on the command used. For example, {Tools} {Copy} {Table} creates "Write Locks" on the source table, the target table, and all their family objects. A Write Lock restricts others from changing the contents of a file. In contrast, the {Tools} {More} {Add} menu selection places a less restrictive lock on the target table, a "Prevent Write Lock."

With interactive use, these locks are automatic and Paradox informs you about locks only when you vie for a locked resource: "Record locked by Joshua" or "Table in use by Lynn." You are left to take corrective action by yourself.

Under script control, locking is more complex. Every shared resource becomes a possible target of contention. Because many PAL commands create and release locks automatically, your scripts should attempt to place the required lock before executing the operation. Locking a table sets RETVAL to True if it is successful, and to False if not. If a needed resource is locked by another user, your scripts must be designed to take corrective action. Once the operation is complete, you release the lock.

For example, a Changeto or an Insert query will first attempt to place a lock on the target table. If the lock fails, the operation fails. To guarantee that the query executes under script control, your script must place the appropriate type of lock on the table. If the lock is successful, RETVAL is True, and the query can proceed; if RETVAL is False, you can make another attempt at the lock or cancel the query.

### 15.2.2.1 Types of Locks

There are four kinds of table-level "locks" in Paradox.

**Locks that Limit User Access**
Full Lock (FL)      No one else can use the table at all.
Write lock (WL)     No one can write to the table, but others can view it.

The remaining two aren't really locks at all—they are restrictions on another's ability to place locks:

**Locks that Prevent Other Users from Placing Locks**
Prevent Full Lock (PFL)      No other user can place a full lock.
Prevent Write Lock (PWL)     No other user can place a write lock.

In addition, there are two special locks that restrict access to records:

Record Lock     In CoEdit mode, the user has an exclusive right to modify the current record.
Form Lock       Restricts access once a record has been changed when editing a multitable form. On a network, no one can edit records in tables contained in the form except through the current form.

You can attempt to place a lock on a table at any time, regardless of the system mode or even the table's existence. In addition, a table doesn't have to be on the workspace to be locked. A lock is always successful if it hasn't been prevented by another lock. For instance, if you issue the command:

```
LOCK "Customer" FL
```

an attempt will be made to place a Full Lock on the "Customer" table. If the lock fails, someone already has another lock on the table. When the lock succeeds, no one else will be able to even view the "Customer" table until you UNLOCK it. The RESET command releases all explicit locks. Issuing several locks is done with a LockList, a comma separated list pairing table name and lock type:

```
LOCK "Customer" PFL, "Invoices" PFL
```

Paradox takes an "all or nothing" approach to table locking—if any of the locks in a single command fail, they all fail, and RETVAL is set to False. If all tables successfully lock, RETVAL is set to True. Lock types can be mixed and matched in any way you want. Why place two locks on the same table? This guarantees continued access to it. For example, the command:

```
LOCK "Customer" WL, "Customer" PWL
```

says, "Place a Write Lock on the Customer table, and prevent anyone else from placing a Write Lock on it." In this manner, the user that places this combined lock lets other users view the table. Other users, however, cannot do anything that could issue a Write Lock, thus preventing the user who placed the lock from CoEditing the table. See CTRLBACKSPACE for an example of this technique.

## LOCK: Place Locks on One or More Tables

```
LOCK LockList
```

| | |
|---|---|
| LockList | A comma-separated list containing pairs of entries of the table name and the type of lock to place. |
| Tablename | Name of table (a string). |
| FL | Full lock placed on object. |
| PFL | Prevent others from issuing FL. |
| WL | Prevent others from writing. |
| PWL | Prevent others from issuing WL. |

Sets:

| | |
|---|---|
| RETVAL = True | If all locks were successful. |
| RETVAL = False | If all locks could not be completed at one time. If unsuccessful, then none of the locks is placed. This all-or-nothing approach avoids "deadly embrace." |

The LOCK syntax is a bit odd. Although the tablenames must be strings or variables that equate to strings, the lock types must not be quoted.

If you have a Full Lock on the table, you "own" it. A Prevent Full Lock, the least restrictive lock, guarantees that no one but you will be able to place a Full Lock on a table. With it, you can assure that a table remains available for an operation that doesn't involve exclusive use—for example, outputting a report. A Write Lock lets other users view a table, but not change it. A Prevent Write Lock guarantees your ability to modify a table. A Full Lock should be issued before going into Edit mode; a Prevent Write Lock should be attempted before a CoEdit session.

The okReportTable.l procedure below assures that a report can be output from a table. It checks to see that the current user is able to place a Prevent Full Lock on the table, and that the user has at least read only access to the table. The procedure also tells if there are any records to report on. If someone else has placed a Full Lock on the table, a menu allows the user to retry the PFL or cancel the operation. The procedure returns True if it is OK to proceed with the report, and False if the table cannot be locked or there are no records present.

Although this procedure deals only with single table reports, you can also reference a variation which takes lookup tables into account, the OkReport-Rights.l() procedure, listed under REPORTTABLES in the Input/Output chapter.

### Listing 15.25: LOCK.L1

```
PROC okReportTable.l(table.a)
  ; table.a      ; name of report table
  ; RETURNS      True if table has records available for reporting.
  ;              False if unavailable or no records.
  WHILE True
    MESSAGE "Checking table rights for ", table.a
    ; first make sure that we can access the table at all
    LOCK table.a PFL       ; Keep anyone else from locking us out of the table.
    IF RETVAL THEN         ; Table locked ok.
      QUITLOOP             ; PFL was placed, continue.
    ELSE
      BEEP
      MESSAGE ERRORMESSAGE()      ; Show who has locked table.
      WHILE True
        SHOWMENU
          "TryAgain": table.a + " is locked.  Try again to start the operation.",
          "Cancel" : "Don't try again to start the operation right now."
        TO choice.a
        IF choice.a <> "TryAgain" THEN      ; cancelled
          RETURN False                      ; Don't retry lock, cancel operation.
        ENDIF
      ENDWHILE
    ENDIF
  ENDWHILE

  IF NOT TABLERIGHTS(table.a, "ReadOnly") THEN ; check to make sure we have password rights
    MESSAGE "Insufficient rights to read ",table.a
    SLEEP 3000
    UNLOCK table.a PFL     ; Remove the PFL lock that we just placed.
    RETURN False
  ENDIF

  IF ISEMPTY(table.a) THEN
    MESSAGE "No records to report on"
    SLEEP 3000
    UNLOCK table.a PFL     ; No sense reporting.
    RETURN False
  ENDIF
```

```
  RETURN True  ; Got to this point-- table is useable.

ENDPROC


; Remember that after you run the report, you need to explicitly remove the
; Prevent Full Lock placed by the procedure.

; An example of using the procedure to send Customer report #1 to screen:

l = okReportTable.l("Customer")
IF l THEN
  Menu {Report} {Output} {Customer} {1} {Screen}
  UNLOCK "Customer" PFL    ; Must remember to remove lock placed by proc.
ELSE
  Message "Report Cancelled"
  SLEEP 2000
ENDIF
```

**15.2.2.1.1 Semaphore Locking.** One of the challenges in designing and implementing multiuser systems in Paradox, communicating activities between nodes, can be simplified with a technique known as "semaphore-locking."

For example, if a system includes a calculation only one user can perform at a time, you need to prevent all others from even attempting the calculation. What you need is a signal that can be recognized across nodes on the network. Though by design each node on a network functions independently, the status of locks is recognized system-wide. The solution, then, is to place a lock on a nonexistent table and use that lock as a flag for others attempting the calculation.

For another example, here's how you can delay posting a record in Coedit while a query is running on another node so that query restart won't occur:

**Step 1**
Before starting the query, lock a nonexistent table:

```
LOCK "qCust1" FL  ; Creates a lock file called QCUST1.LCK
```

**Step 2**
Perform the query.
**Step 3**
Remove the lock immediately with an

```
UNLOCK "qCust1" FL  ; Removes QCUST1.LCK
```

The procedure below checks to see whether a semaphore lock is active. Whenever a user attempts to post a record, it first checks to see if the query is occurring:

```
l = CheckSemaphor.l ("QCust1", 300)
```

where the procedure's parameters are the name of the semaphore table locked and the maximum number of seconds to wait. You need to include a time-out mechanism in case a rogue lock file accidentally gets left on the disk.

CheckSemaphore.l ("QCust1",300) will stall posting for up to five minutes and return True if the lock file is not present or disappears during waiting, and False if the lock table persisted beyond the maximum time allowed. When it returns True, you can complete your posting routine. When it returns False, you might want to put up a menu to retry or cancel the posting.

**Listing 15.26: LOCK.L2**

```
PROC CheckSemaphore.l(semaphore.a,waitseconds.n)
  ; semaphore.a      the name of semaphore table to check
  ; waitseconds.n    the maximum number of seconds to retry

  PRIVATE n

  FOR n FROM 1 TO MAX (waitseconds.n, 1)  ; Make at least one try.
    IF ISFILE(semaphore.a + ".LCK") THEN   ; Semaphore lock already in place.
      LOCK semaphore.a FL  ; Must fail, but sets ERRORUSER so we can see who
                           ; is doing the query.
      MESSAGE "Waiting ", n, " seconds while ",ERRORUSER(), " queries this table"
      UNLOCK semaphore.a FL  ; just in case our lock snuck in between ISFILE and LOCK
    ELSE
      ; You can add a message here to show that table is available.
      RETURN True  ; Ok to proceed, no semaphor lock is in place.
    ENDIF
    SLEEP 1000      ; Wait one second before trying again (perhaps query is over).
  ENDFOR
  RETURN False      ; The semaphore lock table has held us here for maximum seconds.
ENDPROC
```

Granted, this is a little tricky to implement, but when a table is likely to be queried often by one user while simultaneously being updated by other users, the technique keeps the queries from being interrupted while Paradox tries to get a stable "snapshot" of the query table.

## UNLOCK: Remove Locks from Some or All Tables

```
UNLOCK {LockList | ALL}
```

| | |
|---|---|
| LockList | A comma-separated list containing pairs of entries containing the table name and the type of lock to remove. |
| Lock Types: | |
| FL | Full Lock. |
| PFL | Prevent Full Lock. |
| WL | Write Lock. |

| PWL | Prevent Write Lock. |
| ALL | Removes all explicit table locks. |
| Sets | |
| RETVAL = True | If locks were successfully removed. |
| RETVAL = False | If you attempted to unlock any tables not already explicitly locked. |

Like LOCK, a tablename is a string or string variable. The lock types must not be quoted. UNLOCK has no effect on implicit locks placed by Paradox itself.

You can use UNLOCK to remove an explicit table lock as soon as Paradox has placed a lock of its own. As always, the test for the lock is more important than the lock; UNLOCK simply removes the lock that you gave it. An implicit lock remains in effect for the duration of the Edit. When you finish the edit, Paradox frees the table.

**Listing 15.27: UNLOCK.L1**

```
LOCK "Customer" FL
IF NOT RETVAL THEN
  MESSAGE ERRORUSER()," is using the table.  Try again later"
ENDIF
EDIT "Customer"
UNLOCK "Customer" FL
; Now proceed to do a wait table, or any other code that needs the edit mode.
```

## LOCKSTATUS: How Many Locks Have I Placed on a Table?

```
LOCKSTATUS (Tablename, Locktype)
```

| Tablename | Name of table (a string). |
| Locktype Strings: | |
| "FL" | Full Lock. |
| "PFL" | Prevent Full Lock. |
| "WL" | Write Lock. |
| "PWL" | Prevent Write Lock. |
| "ANY" | Any Locks at All. |

Returns:

| A Number | The number of locks of the locktype specified that *you* have explicitly placed on the table. |

LOCKSTATUS doesn't concern itself with any implicit locks that Paradox may have placed or locks that other users have placed. If you haven't placed any locks at all, or have just issued a RESET, LOCKSTATUS will return a 0. A lock stays in place until you explicitly remove it. Unless you use UNLOCK or RESET to release them, locks keep piling up.

The following example demonstrates the effect of locking tables on the LOCKSTATUS function:

**Listing 15.28: LOCKSTAT.L1**

```
; Start with a clean slate
RESET   ; Clears the workspace and removes all locks explicitly placed by you.

; At this point, there are 0 locks placed.
MESSAGE "Customer has ", LOCKSTATUS("Customer","Any"), " locks placed"
SLEEP 2000

; Now place a prevent write lock on the table.
LOCK "Customer" PWL
MESSAGE "Customer has ", LOCKSTATUS("Customer","PWL"), " PWL locks placed"
; the message will show 1 lock
SLEEP 2000

; Add a few more locks.
LOCK "Customer" PWL, "Customer" wl, "Customer" FL
MESSAGE "Customer has ", LOCKSTATUS("Customer","PWL"), " PWL locks placed"
; the message will show 2 PWL locks placed
SLEEP 2000

; Now for the final message about all the locks.
MESSAGE "Customer has a total of ", LOCKSTATUS("Customer","Any"), " locks placed"
; the message will show a total of 4 locks placed
SLEEP 2000

; Finally remove the locks.
UNLOCK ALL   ; remove all the locks placed
MESSAGE "Customer has a total of ", LOCKSTATUS("Customer","Any"), " locks placed"
  ; The message will show a total of 0 locks placed.
SLEEP 2000
```

## ISSHARED: Is the Table Available for Sharing?

```
ISSHARED (Tablename)
```

Tablename    Name of table (string).

Returns:

| | |
|---|---|
| True | The table is in a shared directory. |
| False | The table is in a private directory or local hard disk. |
| Script Error | If the table does not exist, or is in another user's private directory. |

The ISSHARED() function tests to see if a table is in a shared directory, and is not marked as a private table (by the PRIVTABLES command). Although code like:

**Listing 15.29: ISSHARED.L1**

```
IF ISSHARED( "Customer" ) THEN
  LOCK "Customer" PWL
ENDIF
```

is appropriate, we don't bother with the ISSHARED() and simply attempt to lock the table anyway.

### REFRESH: Refreshes the Workspace to Reflect Changes by Other Users

Simulates pressing the Refresh key, [Alt R]

```
REFRESH
```

REFRESH forces a screen update of all display images on the workspace. Normally, if the default AUTOREFRESH is enabled, the screens automatically refresh every three seconds, showing the current state of the tables and any new records or changes made by other nodes on a network. REFRESH is a workspace command and has no effect on the PAL canvas. So REFRESH is only useful if you need to force a screen update in a WAIT Table, Record, or Field; or when displaying a table with the Echo On.

You can speed up, slow down, or disable the default AUTOREFRESH time with the Custom.SC. Disabling AUTOREFRESH is usually recommended in heavy-transaction environments, where constant screen updating exacts a toll in performance. If you choose to slow down or disable AUTOREFRESH, use the REFRESH command to explicitly update the workspace display.

### SETRETRYPERIOD: How Long Should Paradox Attempt to Get a Resource?

```
SETRETRYPERIOD Number
```

Number    An integer between 0 and 30,000 representing the number of seconds Paradox should continue to attempt to obtain a resource. If the resource is not available within the time specified, an appropriate ERRORCODE() will be set.

With a default retry period of zero, Paradox will make only one attempt to gain access to an object you've requested. If the resource is not available immediately,

Paradox gives up and denies access. A retry period other than zero will allow your script to continuously attempt to gain the resource. For example, SETRE-TRYPERIOD 60 tells Paradox to continually try to access the resource and give up after 60 seconds has elapsed:

**Listing 15.30: SETRETRY.L1**

```
SETRETRYPERIOD 60
MESSAGE "Attempting access to Customer table"
LOCK "Customer" PFL          ; Prevent Full Lock
IF NOT RETVAL THEN
  MESSAGE ERRORUSER(), " has locked the customer table"
  SLEEP 2000
ELSE
  ;For example:
  VIEW "Customer"
  UNLOCK  "Customer" PFL      ; Let the implicit lock take over.
ENDIF
```

If another user has a Full Lock on the "Customer" table and the retry period is set to 0, the error message will appear immediately. However, if you used SETRE-TRYPERIOD 120, the message "Attempting to gain access to the customer table" will stay on the screen for up to two minutes. If time runs out and access has not been gained, RETVAL will be set to False. If the Full Lock is released and you gain access, RETVAL is set to True. As soon as you acquire the resource, the script continues. The last setting for SETRETRYPERIOD remains in effect until you reset it or until the session ends. You can determine the latest setting with the next function, RETRYPERIOD.

### RETRYPERIOD: How Long Will Paradox Attempt to Get a Resource?

```
RETRYPERIOD ()
```

Returns:

A Number    An integer representing the number of seconds that Paradox will try to obtain a requested table or resource that is currently locked or unavailable.

The default Paradox retry period is 0. If RETRYPERIOD() returns 0, Paradox will not attempt to retry the request. The retry period can be altered with a SETRETRYPERIOD of between 0 and 30,000 seconds.

Suppose you wanted to temporarily change the current retry period to three minutes, do something, and then set it back to the original value:

**Listing 15.31: RETRYPER.L1**

```
retry.n = RETRYPERIOD()  ; Get the current retryperiod.
SETRETRYPERIOD 180       ; Now set to 180 seconds.
; Statements go here that require longer (or shorter) retryperiod.
;
; Set it back to the original value.
SETRETRYPERIOD  retry.n
```

### SETRESTARTCOUNT: Specify the Number of Times Paradox Should Attempt to Restart a Query, Report, or Crosstab.

```
SETRESTARTCOUNT {OFF | Number}
```

OFF       Paradox will continuously restart operations until it gets a stable "snapshot" of the tables being queried, reported, or crosstabulated.

Number       Integer value of restart tries, to control the number of restarts due to changes made to the tables during the time the operation is being performed.

Note that the "snapshot" metaphor is simply a way of pointing out that Paradox looks at the table from time to time to see if it has changed from the instant it began the query. Paradox DOES NOT MAKE A COPY of the table.

If the maximum number of retries is exceeded, ERRORCODE will be set to 27 ("Operation not completed"), not 36 as the Paradox 3.0 manual indicates. See the discussion on semaphore locking in this section for a way of keeping users from updating a table while a query is in progress.

## 15.2.3 Controlling Access by Protecting Tables

There are two types of protection available in Paradox. Write-protection keeps any table from being altered or deleted. Encryption allows very detailed controlled access to a table and its family. Although you can combine both types of protection on any one table, it is rarely done.

### 15.2.3.1 Write-Protection

Write-protecting a table is a simple way of preventing inadvertent changes to a table. The table is not encrypted, but no changes can be made as long as the write-protect flag is set. To write-protect a table, you issue the following menu commands:

```
{Tools} {More} {Protect} {WriteProtect} SELECT Tablename {Set}
```

There is a corresponding {Clear} command that replaces {Set} if you want to remove the write-protection. You must take extra care when a table is write-protected. For example, if you have write-protected the "Vendor" table and issue a command like EDIT "Vendor," you'll cause a script error and trigger an ERRORCODE of 22 ("Table is Write-Protected").

You can test for ERRORCODE() = 22 in an error procedure if you have the ERRORPROC variable set, and take the appropriate action to unprotect the table and retry the command. See ERRORPROC for an example of a workaround.

### 15.2.3.2 Encrypting Tables

Paradox allows you to control user access rights at the field level. The discussions that follow assume that you are already familiar with the techniques for protecting tables and assigning master and auxiliary passwords. If you are not, read the Paradox User's guide section about {Tools} {More} {Protect}. The tables and screens below help demonstrate how you can control user access in protected tables with PAL.

There are several commands and functions that restrict and assess rights assigned to password protected tables. When Paradox encrypts a table, it is safe from unauthorized access.

Assigning auxiliary passwords has a side benefit of simplifying PAL code because you can use the passwords to limit access to individual fields without designing special forms and reports that exclude certain information. For example, if a password does not allow the user to view the [Salary] field in a "Customer" table, reports generated by that user will simply leave the field blank.

When you initially password protect a table, you need to create a "Master" password that has all rights to the table. You then are given the opportunity to have any number of auxiliary passwords that control user access to the table. For example, you could encrypt the "Customer" table with a master password of "Secret," which would allow anyone with the password "Secret" to have total control over, and access to, the table.

You can also assign various auxiliary passwords, each with a specified set of rights. The screen that follows shows how to assign an auxiliary password to the "Customer" table. In this example, the password "GHOSTBUSTERS" will have the following rights:

- Cannot add or delete records.
- No changes to any key fields.
- Can modify Forms and Reports, but not Settings and ValChecks.
- Cannot change the [Address] field.
- Cannot even see the [Balance due] field on the screen or report.

We will use this table in examples of FIELDRIGHTS(), FAMILYRIGHTS(), and TABLERIGHTS().

**Listing 15.32: ENCRYPT.FG1**

```
Defining auxiliary password 1 of Customer table Password
[F1] for help with setting password options.  [F7] for table view
```

```
┌─────────────────────────────────────────────────────────────────────┐
│ Auxiliary Password:  GHOSTBUSTERS                            Page 1    │
├─────────────────────────────────────────────────────────────────────┤
│  Table Rights  Update              │  Family Rights   FR              │
│                                    │                                  │
│  Enter one │ Rights conferred      │  Enter all that apply, <┘ for none│
│  ──────────┼─────────────────────  │                                  │
│  All       │ all operations        │  (F)orm     │ change forms       │
│  InsDel    │ change contents       │  (V)alCheck │ change validity checks│
│  Entry     │ data entry and updates │  (R)eport   │ change reports     │
│  Update    │ update nonkey fields  │  (S)ettings │ change image settings│
│  ReadOnly  │ no modifications      │                                  │
│                                    │                                  │
│  Field Rights Enter ReadOnly or None for each field or leave blank for All. │
│                                                                       │
│  Customer ID#                         Contact First Name              │
│  Company name                         Contact Last Name               │
│  Address       ReadOnly               Start date                      │
│  City                                 Last order date                 │
│  State                                Last order amount               │
│  Zipcode                                                              │
│  Balance due   None                                                   │
└─────────────────────────────────────────────────────────────────────┘
```

## PROTECT: Encrypt or Decrypt a Table

```
PROTECT Tablename PasswordString
```

| | |
|---|---|
| Tablename | Name of table (string). |
| PasswordString | String to use as master password for the table, or a blank string if you want to remove all passwords. |

A simple example:

```
PROTECT "Secrets" "shhh"
```

encrypts the "Secrets" table with the master password "shhh," and is syntactically the same as {Tools} {More} {Protect} {Password} {Table} {Secrets} {Master} {shhh} Do_It!

If the table is already encrypted and the valid master password is already in the system, then PROTECT changes the password. If you don't already have master password rights to the table, a script error occurs.

Note that you need to already have master rights to a table before you can encrypt or change the password. You also cannot protect a table called "Password" because it is the name of the table that Paradox creates when it lists auxiliary passwords. Remember too that encrypting is different from locking, which temporarily restricts what a user can do to a table.

If the password specified with the PROTECT command *is not blank*, the table will be encrypted using the supplied password as the master password, no auxiliary passwords will be created, and any existing auxiliary passwords are left unchanged. If the password string *is blank*, all encryption is removed from the table and all auxiliary passwords are deleted.

Although auxiliary passwords are rarely created under PAL control, they could easily be handled by using braced menu selections, as if done interactively. When defining auxiliary passwords, you are actually in a table called "PASSWORD," whose fields can be assigned in the same way as any other table (you can even toggle form view).

The following example encrypts all the tables in a given directory in one fell swoop:

**Listing 15.33: PROTECT.L1**

```
PROC ProtectAll.l(directory.a,master.a)
  ; directory.a ; Name of subdirectory.
  ; master.a    ; String for master password, or "" to decrypt all tables.

  PRIVATE
    n,           ; Used by getchar.
    isnetwork.l,; Are we on a network?
    tables.n,   ; Number of tables found to protect.
    msg.a,       ; Encrypting or decrypting message.
    failed.n    ; Number of tables that failed locks or rights.

  ; First see that a trailing backslash is in place.
  IF not match (directory.a,"..\\") THEN
    directory.a = directory.a + "\\"
  ENDIF

  IF DIREXISTS(directory.a) <> 1 THEN
    Message "Subdirectory ", directory.a, " not found.  Press any key"
    n = GETCHAR()
    RETURN False
  ENDIF
  isnetwork.l = NETTYPE() <> "SingleUser"

  SETDIR DIRECTORY()  ; Gets rid of all temporary tables.

  {Tools} {Info} {Inventory} {tables} SELECT directory.a
  MOVETO [name]
  LOCATE "List"
  IF RETVAL THEN
   EDITKEY
   DEL       ; Remove the list record.
   DO_IT!
```

```
      ENDIF
      tables.n = NRECORDS("list")
      IF tables.n = 0 THEN
        Message "No tables found for ", directory.a, " Press any key"
        n = GETCHAR()
        CLEARALL
        RETURN False  ; Nothing to encrypt.
      ENDIF

      failed.n = 0  ; Initialize variable of tables that failed lock or rights.

      ; Now let's make sure you have the rights to  each table, and that
      ; no one else can stop you from encrypting them.
      MESSAGE "Checking table access"
      SCAN
        IF NOT TABLERIGHTS(directory.a + [name], "All") THEN
          MESSAGE "You have insufficient rights to ",[name],". Press any key"
          n = GETCHAR()
          failed.n = [#]   ; Number of record that failed.
          QUITLOOP
        ENDIF
        IF isnetwork.l THEN
          LOCK directory.a + [name] FL
          IF NOT RETVAL THEN
            MESSAGE [name]," is locked by. ",ERRORUSER()," Press any key"
            n = GETCHAR()
            failed.n = [#]
          ENDIF
        ENDIF
      ENDSCAN
      IF Failed.n = 0 THEN          ; No tables failed the rights or locks.
        IF master.a = "" THEN    ; Decrypting.
          msg.a = "De"
        ELSE
          msg.a = "En"
        ENDIF
        ; Now that all tables are locked, we can proceed to encrypt all the tables.
        SCAN
          MESSAGE msg.a + "crypting ", [name], ", table #", [#], " of ", tables.n
          PROTECT directory.a + [name] master.a
        ENDSCAN
      ENDIF
      IF isnetwork.l THEN ; Now let's remove any and all full locks sucessfully placed.
        SCAN
          UNLOCK directory.a + [name] FL
        ENDSCAN
      ENDIF
      DELETE "list"
      RETURN failed.n = 0
    ENDPROC

    ; Now to demonstrate the procedure and encrypt all tables in the \paradox3\demo
    ; subdirectory with the password "Secret".

    l = ProtectAll.l("\\Paradox3\\demo\\","Secret")

    ; Or conversely, to remove all passwords from all tables:

    l = ProtectAll.l("\\Paradox3\\demo\\","")
```

### PASSWORD: Present Password(s) to Paradox

```
PASSWORD Passwordlist
```

Passwordlist     Comma separated list of passwords to offer to Paradox.

The PASSWORD command offers a password or list of passwords to Paradox to allow access to encrypted tables, or to play protected scripts with Showplay. Passwords stay in effect until one of the following conditions occurs:

- the Paradox session is ended
- the image is cleared *and* another PASSWORD with additional rights to the table is issued, and the new PASSWORD then takes over
- you issue a {Tools} {More} {Protect} {ClearPasswords} to clear the workspace and revoke all passwords
- you issue an UNPASSWORD followed by a RESET command. Note that UNPASSWORD alone is not sufficient to revoke a current PASSWORD. The RESET is necessary, but remember that RESET releases all explicitly placed table locks. To clear a single password, you can use {Tools} {Info} {Family} for the table affected by the withdrawn password.

A few notes are in order about combining password protected scripts and protected tables. All encrypted scripts can be played without issuing a password. However, a common error is to protect a script with a password and use the same password for the underlying tables. For example, a script called "Demo" was encrypted with the password "SKYWALKER" and reads something like:

**Listing 15.34: PASSWORD.L1**

```
; Demo.SC    password demo

AUTOLIB="Utility"
CLEARALL
PASSWORD "SKYWALKER"   ; To give authorization for underlying tables
                      ; that also have "SKYWALKER" as table password.
MainMenu.u()          ; Call the main menu proc from the Utility library.
; Make sure that the user does not return to interactive Paradox with the
; password active.
EXIT
```

The main advantage to protecting a script is to keep the user from pressing a [Ctrl Break] to interrupt script play and see the Cancel/Debug prompt. However, this script issues its own password, which lets the user interrupt it at any time, even though the source code may not be present. So make sure that the password for the main script is not issued as part of the script itself.

Although encrypted scripts can be played without issuing a password, they cannot be played with the SHOWPLAY command until the password is issued.

For example, if the script "Demo.SC" is password protected with the word "shhh" and you issue {Script} {Showplay} {Demo} {Fast}, you'll get a script error if "shhh" has not yet been entered as a password. There is, however, a simple solution. Replace the showplay line with:

```
ECHO FAST      ; you can use ECHO NORMAL or ECHO SLOW
PLAY "Demo"
```

Then sit back and watch the show.

### UNPASSWORD: Withdraw a Previously Offered Password

```
UNPASSWORD PasswordList
```

> PasswordList    A comma-separated list of passwords previously offered to Paradox that you want to "take back."

UNPASSWORD, despite its name, does not remove password protection from a table. Instead, it simply withdraws a password or list of passwords from Paradox. However, when a password is issued to Paradox, either through interactive use or via the password command, it remains active until the password is revoked *and* the buffers are flushed. That is to say that if you have a table called "SECRET" with a master password of "Shhh" (remember that case is specific in passwords), and you run a script like the following without the embedded RESET command, and are not on a network when script play ends, the table would be accessible until the buffers are flushed. The easiest way of flushing the buffers interactively is with the ClearAll key, [Alt-F8]. It is worth noting that ClearAll in PAL does not flush the buffers; only Reset is currently reliable in flushing all buffers.

**Listing 15.35: UNPASSWO.L1**

```
PASSWORD "Shhh"  ; Offer the password so you'll have access to the table.
VIEW "Secret"
WHILE TRUE
  WAIT TABLE
    PROMPT  "Press [F2] when done viewing the Secret table"
  UNTIL "F2", "Dos", "DosBig"
  IF RETVAL="F2" THEN
    CLEARALL
    UNPASSWORD "Shhh"
    RESET    ; Without this reset, the table would still be available
             ; for use when the script ends.
    RETURN
  ENDIF
ENDWHILE
```

Another approach to removing passwords is with the

```
{Tools} {More} {Protect} {ClearPasswords}
```

menu choices. This method clears the workspace, revokes all passwords, and leaves explicit table locks in place. Reset, on the other hand, clears the workspace, but only revokes passwords that have been UNPASSWORDed, and has the unfortunate byproduct of releasing all explicit table locks.

### ISENCRYPTED: Has a Table Been Password Protected?

```
ISENCRYPTED (Tablename)
```

      Tablename     Name of table (string).

Returns:

| | |
|---|---|
| True | The table is password protected. |
| False | The table has no passwords at all. |

ISENCRYPTED() is insensitive to whether or not any passwords have been offered to Paradox. It simply reports whether the table has been encrypted by Paradox and returns True if the table is a password-protected table, and False if the table is not subject to any passwords. Passwords issued to Paradox have no effect on ISENCRYPTED(). Either the table is an encrypted table or it isn't.

To find out if a password that has been entered is sufficient to do a given task, your program needs to evaluate TABLERIGHTS(), FAMILYRIGHTS(), and/or FIELDRIGHTS(), as we'll describe next.

### 15.2.3.3 Testing for Encryption Rights

As mentioned, Paradox lets us use Familyrights, Tablerights, or Fieldrights to test for access to tables. The examples in code that follow use the encrypted "Customer" table example shown at the beginning of this section.

### FAMILYRIGHTS: Do You Have the Right to Change a Family Object?

```
FAMILYRIGHTS (Tablename, String)
```

| | |
|---|---|
| Tablename | Name of table. |
| String | A single letter string that indicates the type of object that you want to inquire about. |
| "F" | Use for forms. |
| "R" | Use for reports. |
| "S" | Use for image settings. |
| "V" | Use for validity checks. |

Returns:

| | |
|---|---|
| True | If user currently has the right to the object. |
| False | The current password does not allow the user to create or modify the object. |

FAMILYRIGHTS is used to determine if the user currently has the right to modify one of the table's family members. Although the PAL User's Guide states the string must be a single *uppercase* letter, lowercase letters also seem to work. If you attempt to use any letter other than F, R, V, or S, a script error occurs.

The following demonstrates the FAMILYRIGHTS() function for the "GHOSTBUSTERS" password (shown at the beginning of this section):

**Listing 15.36: FAMILYRI.L1**

```
MENU {Tools} {More} {Protect} {ClearPasswords}  ; let's start off fresh
PASSWORD "GHOSTBUSTERS"    ; offers the auxiliary password to Paradox
; keep in mind that passwords are case sensitive,
; "GHOSTBUSTERS" is not the same as "Ghostbusters"
CLEAR  ; clear the canvas
@ 0,0
? "Password \"GHOSTBUSTERS\" has the rights to create or change the Customer:"
?
? "   Forms: ", FAMILYRIGHTS ("Customer", "F")    ; would show True
? "  Reports: ", FAMILYRIGHTS ("Customer", "R")    ; would show True
? "  Setting: ", FAMILYRIGHTS ("Customer", "S")    ; would show False
? "ValChecks: ", FAMILYRIGHTS ("Customer", "V")    ; would show False
MESSAGE "Press any key"
n = GETCHAR()
```

## TABLERIGHTS: Do You Have at Least the Specified Rights for Table Changes?

```
TABLERIGHTS (Tablename, String)
```

| | |
|---|---|
| TableName | Name of the table to check for rights. |
| String | One of the following strings representing the minimum rights available to the user (shown in order of increasing rights): |
| "ReadOnly" | User may read, but not change table. |
| "Update" | User may change nonkey fields. |
| "Entry" | User may enter or change data. |
| "InsDel" | User may change data, but not structure. |
| "All" | User can perform all operations (same as having Master password status). |

Returns:

| | |
|---|---|
| True | If rights are at least those specified. |
| False | If rights are not available because of lack of password, or presence of an auxiliary password with lesser rights. |

TABLERIGHTS(Tablename, String) is used to determine whether the user currently has at least the rights to affect the table in the way specified by the string. The table rights below are listed in order of decreasing access rights:

| | |
|---|---|
| "All" | Highest rights, master password status. |
| "InsDel" | Add and delete records. |
| "Entry" | Data entry and updates. |
| "Update" | Update nonkey fields. |
| "ReadOnly" | No modifications allowed. |

If you have any of the first four rights above, you automatically have the right to do any of the functions of the subsequent rights. For example, InsDel also allows Entry, Update, and ReadOnly.

Once again, although the PAL User's Guide states the string must be one of those mentioned above, in fact, PAL disregards the case. So "ALL," is the same as "All" or "all." However, we do not recommend using anything but the proper form, because this flexibility could disappear in a puff of upgrade. The following demonstrates the TABLERIGHTS for any table:

**Listing 15.37: TABLERIG.L1**

```
PROC GetTableRights.a ( table.a )
  ; table.a   name of table
  ; RETURNS the highest level of rights available
  SWITCH
    CASE TABLERIGHTS( table.a, "All") :
      RETURN "All"
    CASE TABLERIGHTS( table.a, "InsDel") :
      RETURN "InsDel"
    CASE TABLERIGHTS( table.a, "Entry") :
      RETURN "Entry"
    CASE TABLERIGHTS( table.a, "Update") :
      RETURN "Update"
    CASE TABLERIGHTS( table.a, "ReadOnly") :
      RETURN "ReadOnly"
    OTHERWISE:
      RETURN "None"
  ENDSWITCH
ENDPROC

; Now a little demonstration which displays a message showing that
; we only have Update rights for the Customer table.
```

```
CLEAR
MESSAGE "Working... Getting Tablerights for Customer"
{Tools} {More} {Protect} {ClearPasswords}  ; let's start off fresh
PASSWORD "GHOSTBUSTERS"                     ; only has Update rights
tablerights.a = GetTableRights.a ("Customer")
@0,0 ?? "Password GHOSTBUSTERS has the Customer Tablerights: ", tablerights.a
MESSAGE "Press any key"
n=GETCHAR()
```

## FIELDRIGHTS: Do You Have at Least the Specified Rights to a Field?

```
FIELDRIGHTS (Tablename, Fieldname, String)
```

| | |
|---|---|
| Tablename | Name of table (string). |
| Fieldname | Name of field to evaluate (string). |
| String | A string representing the rights that you are inquiring about. |
| "ReadOnly" | Can we at least view this field? |
| "All" | Can we make changes to this field? |

Returns:

| | |
|---|---|
| True | If the user currently has at least the rights requested. |
| False | If the user does not have the rights requested. |

FIELDRIGHTS(Tablename, String), like the TABLERIGHTS() function, tells you whether or not you currently have at least the rights specified for a field. Field rights are shown below, in the order of decreasing access:

| | |
|---|---|
| "All" | All rights to the field. |
| "ReadOnly" | Cannot modify the field. |
| "None" | User cannot even see contents of the field. |

Note that there is no provision for "None" as a parameter of FIELDRIGHTS, because if "ReadOnly" returns False, then "None" is implied. If the table rights for the table are "Update" or less, all keyfields are implicitly assigned ReadOnly status, even though they are not explicitly defined on the Password screen.

Now for a demo to display the rights for all fields in the table. This time instead of simply showing the rights on the canvas, we'll place the structure and rights into a table called List.

### Listing 15.38: FIELDRIG.L1

```
; First define a procedure to get the maximum rights for a field.

PROC GetFieldRights.a ( table.a, field.a )
  ; table.a   Name of table.
  ; field.a   Name of field.
```

```
    ; RETURNS    The highest rights available.
    SWITCH
      CASE FIELDRIGHTS(table.a, field.a, "All") :
        RETURN "All"
      CASE FIELDRIGHTS(table.a, field.a, "ReadOnly") :
        RETURN "ReadOnly"
      OTHERWISE:    ; No rights to the field.
        RETURN "None"
    ENDSWITCH
ENDPROC


; Now for the procedure that creates the List table:

PROC ListFieldRights.u (table.a)
  ; table.a   Name of table to evaluate.
  MENU {Tools} {Info} {Structure}
  SELECT table.a
  ; Places "STRUCT" table on the workspace.
  RENAME "STRUCT" "LIST"    ; Necessary because we're going to restructure it.
  MENU {Modify} {Restructure} {List}
  IF MENUCHOICE()="Cancel" THEN   ; In case of existing KeyViol or Problems.
    {Ok}
  ENDIF
  END            ; Move to record for Field Type.
  DEL            ; Delete the fieldtype field.
  DOWN           ; Append a new field.
  "Field Rights" ; New field name.
  ENTER          ;
  "A8"           ; Type for the Field Rights field.
  DO_IT!
  {Delete}       ; Confirm that it is ok to delete the existing Field Type.
  ; now "List" table is on the workspace
  COEDITKEY
  ; Step thru each record of the table and assign [Field Rights] to
  ; the appropriate value.
  SCAN
    a = getfieldrights.a (table.a , [field name] )
    [field rights] = a   ; Assigns field, and allows procedure swapping.
  ENDSCAN
  DO_IT!                      ; Leaves the list table on the workspace.
ENDPROC


; Now that the two procs are defined, let's create the table.

MESSAGE "Working, getting list of field rights for Customer"
{Tools} {More} {Protect} {ClearPasswords}  ; Let's start off fresh.
PASSWORD "GHOSTBUSTERS"                   ; Assign the auxiliary password.
ListFieldRights.u ("Customer")            ; Create and load the List table.
```

When the procedure is run, you see the following screen:

**Listing 15.39: FIELDRIG.FG1**

```
Viewing List table: Record 12 of 12                          Main

LIST─────────────Field Name──────────┬Field Rights┐
    1 │ Customer ID#                  │ ReadOnly
    2 │ Company name                  │ All
    3 │ Address                       │ ReadOnly
    4 │ City                          │ All
    5 │ State                         │ All
    6 │ Zipcode                       │ All
    7 │ Balance due                   │ None
    8 │ Contact First Name            │ All
    9 │ Contact Last Name             │ All
   10 │ Start date                    │ All
   11 │ Last order date               │ All
   12 │ Last order amount             │ All
```

Note that the Customer ID# field is marked as ReadOnly even though no restriction was placed in the field in the Password screen, because the TABLE-RIGHTS for the "GHOSTBUSTERS" password are Update only.

# Chapter 16

# The Workspace

Under script control, though the PAL canvas is usually what a user sees, the Paradox workspace is where the action takes place. This section deals with some of the commands that manipulate and the functions that report on the workspace under script control. Workspace commands perform actions as you would; workspace functions enable your scripts to make informed decisions about what to do. For example, many workspace commands duplicate the effects of keystrokes and a few critically placed keystrokes can save a lot of coding. Yet what a key does always depends on the current system mode, whether or not a menu is on the workspace, the availability of disk and memory resources, etc.—all questions answered by functions.

## 16.1 NAVIGATION AND SHORTCUTS

### ENTER: Press the [Enter] Key

ENTER

Many key commands mimic their namesakes. ENTER does whatever pressing [Enter] does in interactive Paradox. In an image, it moves to the next field or record, or ends FieldView. On the last field of the last record in any editing mode, ENTER opens up a new record. In Report, Form, or Script modes, issuing ENTER moves to the next line in overtype mode and splits the current line in insert mode. You'll see ENTER a lot in recorded scripts. ENTER also accepts the current selection from Paradox menus and type-in prompts. For example, while viewing a table on the workspace, you can display a query form of the current table image with:

**Listing 16.1: ENTER.L1**

```
MENU {Ask}
ENTER ; Brings up a list of available tables
ENTER ; Chooses the current table, which is automatically highlighted by
      ; Paradox if the table is located in the current directory, or in the
      ; user's private directory
```

However, if the table on the workspace is not in the current directory or in the private directory, a better approach doesn't use ENTER—it uses the SELECT command and the TABLE function to grab the full path of the current table:

```
MENU {Ask} Select TABLE()
```

Along the same lines, to clear all temporary tables from the current directory:

**Listing 16.2: ENTER.L2**

```
MENU {Tools} {More} {Directory}
ENTER  ; Select current directory
{Ok}

;Or more simply
SETDIR DIRECTORY()
```

## MENU: Bring up Top Level Menu for Current Sysmode

```
MENU
```

The MENU command displays the main menu of available Paradox choices for the current system mode. If the workspace is empty and you are in Main mode, there is no need to issue the MENU command, since the menu is already displayed. For example, to place a query form for the "Customer" table on a clear workspace:

```
{Ask} {Customer}
```

While viewing an "Invoice" table, the following command sequence places the invoice query form on the workspace:

```
MENU {Ask}
Enter ; brings up selection of tables
Enter ; selects current table
```

Yet the MENU command is rarely necessary; extensive testing has shown that while viewing a table, {Tools} {Copy} {Justfamily} works exactly the same as MENU {Tools} {Copy} {Justfamily}. The main menu choices are always available to PAL whether or not the menu is on screen. Should you leave MENU out of your code? The PAL manual uses MENU on a regular basis, and "undocumented" features of this type may disappear in future releases. Yet issuing the MENU command requires 24 bytes of overhead, and if you are really trying to tweak every last byte out of an application, you might want to consider eliminating it altogether.

Here's a use that isn't superfluous. As it does in interactive Paradox, issuing MENU from within deeply nested menus brings Paradox back to the first menu for that system mode. For example, if you want to display the current lowvalue ValCheck for a field in Edit mode:

```
Menu                          ; Bring up the EDIT menu
{ValChecks} {Define} ENTER    ; Define for the current field
{LowValue}
lowvalue.a = MENUCHOICE()     ; Get the current value
MENU           ; Cancels the choices and brings us back to the EDIT menu
MESSAGE  "Low value for this field is ", lowvalue.a
SLEEP 2000
```

### ESC: Press [Esc]

```
ESC
```

ESC is the PAL command equivalent to pressing [Esc] from the keyboard. In menus, ESC moves up one menu level; at a type-in prompt, ESC cancels the selection. ESC is often confused with "Esc," which is the string that describes the key. "Esc" is returned, for example, when a user presses [Esc] in response to a command like SHOWMENU. The following example uses ESC in a script to display the validity checks for the current field in a table. The script begins in a table in Edit mode (not CoEdit, because ValChecks can only be set from Edit mode), and produces a screen like:

```
Current Valchecks for Student ID#

Low:
High:
Default:
TableLookup: Students
Required: No
Picture: ###-##-####

                    Press any key
```

Listing 16.3: ESC.L1

```
CLEAR                             ; Clear the canvas.
a0,0 ?? "Current ValChecks for "+FIELD()
?                                 ; Advance a line.
MENU
{ValChecks} {Define}
ENTER                             ; Choose current field.
FOR n FROM 1 TO 6                 ; Step through the 6 ValCheck choices.
  ? MENUCHOICE(),": "             ; Display the current choice, "LowValue" etc.
  ENTER
  ?? MENUCHOICE()                 ; Pick up and display value for current field.
  ESC                             ; Back up to the ValCheck menu.
  RIGHT                           ; Move to the next ValCheck.
ENDFOR
CTRLBREAK                         ; Back to the table, cancelling all menu levels.
MESSAGE "Press any key"
n = GETCHAR()
```

See the discussions under SHOWMENU, SHOWFILES, SHOWTABLES, SHOWARRAY, and ACCEPT to let a user back out of a menu you have created.

### KEYPRESS: Simulate Pressing a Key

KEYPRESS KeyCode

KeyCode    Any valid PAL keycode or quoted key name.

The KEYPRESS command creates the effect of any key typed from the keyboard. Many keys have PAL command names and so can be called by name to produce the effect of the key. Yet all keys, even if they don't have a special Paradox key name, can be "pressed" with the KEYPRESS command. The KeyCode is either the numerical code for the key (e.g., [Esc] is 27), or, if available, a string that names a keystroke recognized by Paradox, like "Esc." There is rarely a reason to press a key with a PAL command name—KEYPRESS "Esc" is too much like work; use the ESC command instead.

Listing 16.4: KEYPRESS.L1

```
KEYPRESS "A"              ;
KEYPRESS 65              ; an "A"
KEYPRESS "F2"            ; Do_It!
KEYPRESS -60             ; Do_It!
KEYPRESS "DO_IT!"        ; Do_It!
KEYPRESS "DO_"+"IT!"     ; Do_It!
```

KEYPRESS is simple and powerful, passing a keystroke to Paradox under script control. In a technique similar to that used by the DoWait procedure of the Data

Entry Toolkit, this next example allows the user to type characters until one from a specified list is pressed. The list is made up of numeric keycodes separated by periods. If you invoke the procedure by using:

```
n = PressChar.n(".-60.27.-59.") ;"F2","Esc","F1"
```

the procedure accepts and presses keys from the user until the key is "F2", "Esc," or "F1". The key that ends the procedure is not pressed; it is simply returned to the calling procedure.

**Listing 16.5: KEYPRESS.L2**

```
PROC PressChar.n(UntilList.a)
  ; UntilList.a    ; A list of keycodes that will exit the proc.
  ;                ; UntilList must begin and end with a period and
  ;                ; have periods as separators between keycodes.
  ; Returns        ; The code of the exit key pressed.

  n = GETCHAR()    ; Get the first character pressed.
    ; Now stay in a loop as long as the string value of the key is not
    ; found between periods on the list.
  WHILE SEARCH("." + STRVAL(n) + ".", UntilList.a) = 0
    ; Key pressed was not an exit key.
    KEYPRESS n     ; Type in the key.
    n = GETCHAR()  ; Get the next key.
  ENDWHILE
  RETURN n         ; The character that exited the loop.
ENDPROC
```

There is another example of the ECHO/KEYPRESS combination under the ECHO command that allows the user to type a screen of freeform text.

## SELECT: Makes a Selection from the Paradox Menu or Type-In Prompt

```
SELECT Expression
```

Expression    String representing menu choice or type-in value.

SELECT, one of the most underused PAL commands, is also one of the great workhorses of PAL. We use SELECT throughout this book. SELECT is usually used to make Paradox menu choices based on values stored in a variable. Here's a SHOWMENU prompt that allows the user to SELECT a report to output to the screen.

**Listing 16.6: SELECT.L1**

```
SHOWMENU
  "Client"  : "Output Client report to the screen",
  "Invoice" : "Output Invoice report to the screen",
```

```
    "Order" : "Output a Customer order to the screen"
TO choice.a

IF choice.a <> "Esc" THEN
   MENU {Reports} {Output} SELECT choice.a {1} {Screen}
ENDIF
```

Note that anything in braced menu selections is taken literally. Thus the following will not work:

```
MENU {Reports} {Output} {choice.a} {1} {Screen}
```

Another example of code that works too hard:

```
MENU {Reports} {Output} TYPEIN choice.a ENTER {1} {Screen}
```

Coding in this style comes from paying too much attention to recorded scripts. SELECT choice.a is much more straightforward. Here's another example. To define a picture validity check for a numeric [Customer ID#] field so that the lowest number allowed is 1000, you could write the code in the following example.

**Listing 16.7: SELECT.L2**

```
EDIT "Customer"
MOVETO [Customer Id#]
lowvalue.n = 1000
MENU {ValChecks} {Define} ENTER {LowValue}
CTRLBACKSPACE          ; Clear any existing lowvalue.
TYPEIN lowvalue.n
Enter
DO_IT!
```

However, if you use SELECT, there is no need to clear the value in the prompt.

**Listing 16.8: SELECT.L3**

```
EDIT "Customer"
MOVETO [Customer Id#]
lowvalue.n = 1000
MENU {ValChecks} {Define} ENTER {LowValue}
SELECT lowvalue.a
DO_IT!
```

SELECT works on any Paradox menu or prompt that requires you to type in a value. In addition, although the MENUCHOICE() function returns a string, you can SELECT using any type of expression. Paradox converts the SELECT expression to a string before applying it to the prompt. So SELECT "1000" would work as well as SELECT 1000.

### TYPEIN: Type in an Expression

```
TYPEIN Expression
```

Expression     Any expression that could ordinarily be typed in from the keyboard.

Beginning PAL users often become dependent on the TYPEIN command to simulate interactive Paradox choices. For example, we consistently see code like this used to change the working directory to C:\Paradox3:

```
Menu {Tools} {More} {Directory} CTRLBACKSPACE TYPEIN "C:\\Paradox3" ENTER
```

which is precisely what the user would do from the keyboard. However, there are two easier ways to accomplish the same thing:

```
Menu {Tools} {More} {Directory} SELECT "C:\\Paradox3"
; or most simply
SETDIR "C:\\Paradox3"
```

TYPEIN should be used when variables cannot be used directly (in the Report mode, for example), or to avoid potential run errors (described below). Here are a couple of SETKEY assignments that use TYPEIN to copy a line in Script, Form, or Report mode. The first assignment creates a variable containing the literal screen characters; the second types the variable (if it is assigned) at the cursor position.

```
SETKEY "F11" line.a = CURSORLINE()    ; copies current line to a variable
SETKEY "F12" IF ISASSIGNED(line.a) THEN TYPEIN line.a ENDIF
```

In Report or Form mode, this technique copies only field masks, not their values. The next example uses TYPEIN to place literal text into a report header.

**Listing 16.9: TYPEIN.L1**

```
PROC ReportHeader.u(table.a, report.a, row.n, offset.n, text.v)
  ; table.a    ; Name of table.
  ; report.a   ; Name of report, "R", or "1" - "14".
  ; row.n      ; Report row as shown by vertical ruler.
  ; offset.n   ; Report column offset from the left margin 0 - 1000.
  ;            ; ** Note that offset.n is not the same as COLNO(), it is
  ;            ; simply the number of columns to move right relative to
```

```
;                  ; whatever left hand margin is set in the report.
; text.v           ; String, date, or number to type in.
   MENU {Reports} {Change}
   SELECT table.a
   SELECT report.a
   {}              ; Keeps the current report description.

   ; Now in the left most column on line 1
   ; Move down to the row wanted.
   WHILE ROWNO() < row.n   ; As long as the current row is less than the one
      DOWN                 ; wanted, keep moving down a row.
   ENDWHILE

   FOR n FROM 1 TO offset.n   ; If 0, then RIGHT is not activated.
      RIGHT
   ENDFOR

   TYPEIN text.v            ; Types the value into the report.
   DO_IT!                   ; Saves the report.
ENDPROC
```

A call to the procedure might ask a user for his or her name, and type it into a report header. For example, the call

```
reportheader.u("Answer","3",4,10,lastname.a)
```

opens the Answer.R3 report, moves to row 4, column 10, types in the contents of the variable lastname.a, and saves the report.

TYPEIN can also be used to avoid script run errors that result from direct assignment to a field. For example, attempts to directly assign a value that does not pass a Tablelookup will result in a script error ("Not one of the possible values for this field"). For example:

```
a = "xxxxzzzxxx"  ; or anything else that is not in the lookup table
[] = a            ; assign this value, causing a script error
```

However, if you use TYPEIN, Paradox will test the value's validity only when you attempt to leave the field. If it can't, the cursor simply stays in the field, just as in interactive Paradox.

```
a = "xxxxzzzxxx"
CTRLBACKSPACE    ; clears the field
TYPEIN a         ; as if typed in from the keyboard
ENTER            ; attempt to move off the field
```

In this example, a script error is avoided. You can use the FIELD() function to see if your ENTER moved you off the field successfully. There are other examples of TYPEIN listed in the discussion of {Tools} {Copy} {JustFamily}. Also see the

WaitPlusDitto.u() procedure for comments about TYPEIN's consequences with Picture Valchecks. WaitPlusDitto.u() is found in the WaitPlus chapter's WWPCORE2.SC script.

## MENUCHOICE: What Is the Current Menu Choice or Contents of Type-In Prompt?

```
MENUCHOICE ( )
```

Returns:

| | |
|---|---|
| A String | Equal to the currently highlighted Paradox menu selection or the current Paradox "Type-in" prompt. |
| "Error" | If no menu or type-in prompt is being displayed. |

The MENUCHOICE() function enables you to determine the value of the current Paradox menu selection. This value is always a string, and it includes values that you can change. Here, for example, is a small script that uses MENUCHOICE to display a message showing the current report length while in Report mode.

**Listing 16.10: MENUCHOI.L1**

```
MENU
{Settings}
{PageLayout}
{Length}
length.a = MENUCHOICE()     ; which would return a string "60", "66", "C" etc.
CTRLBREAK                    ; back to the report design.
MESSAGE "Report length is currently: ", length.a, " Press any key"
n = GETCHAR()
RELEASE VARS n
```

MENUCHOICE() can be put to good use to assist you in making menu selections on menus where choices may vary. For instance, when restructuring a table, Paradox presents a menu of {Cancel} {OK} if a "Keyviol" or "Problems" table already exists. So a script to restructure a "Customer" table might include:

**Listing 16.11: MENUCHOI.L2**

```
MENU {Modify} {Restructure} {Customer}
IF MENUCHOICE() = "Cancel" THEN
  {Ok}    ; Okay to overwrite existing KeyViol and Problems tables.
ENDIF
DO_IT!
```

See the related command, SELECT.

### DO_IT!: Press the DO-IT! Key

```
DO_IT!
```

The DO_IT! command activates queries, ends edit sessions, ends report and form design, starts sorting and restructuring . . . the list goes on and on. The form of the command is different from the menu choice, which is DO-IT!; (a hyphen becomes an underscore). Here's a simple use. The following code sorts the "Customer" table in structural field order:

```
MENU {Modify} {Sort} {Customer} DO_IT!
```

An undocumented feature of the SHOWMENU command has a useful side benefit. If you use the string "DO-IT!" as a menu choice in a SHOWMENU, the user will be able to press [F2] when the menu is displayed as an alternate way to select "DO-IT!" The menu choice must have a hyphen instead of being under-scored. A typical menu for an Edit session could look like:

**Listing 16.12: DO-IT.L1**

```
SHOWMENU
  "Undo":"Undo last change made",
  "DO-IT!":"End the edit session, save all changes",
  "Cancel":"Cancel the edit session",
  "Edit":"Continue editing this table"
TO choice.a
SWITCH
  CASE choice.a="DO-IT!" :     ; Note hypen in string.
    DO_IT!                     ; Note underscore in command.
    CLEARIMAGE
    RETURN
  CASE choice.a="Undo":
    UNDO                       ; Undo the last change.
  CASE choice.a="Cancel":
    CANCELEDIT
    CLEARIMAGE
    RETURN
ENDSWITCH
```

### CTRLBREAK: Cancels the Current Task

```
CTRLBREAK
```

The CTRLBREAK command, like pressing [Ctrl Break], cancels form design, edit, report design, password design, etc. If called twice in Edit mode, the first CTRLBREAK cancels Edit, and the second CTRLBREAK clears the workspace. If there is a menu active with at least one image on the workspace, CTRLBREAK cancels the menu and returns to the current image. The CTRLBREAK command is always active; it is not affected by the setting in the CUSTOM script that disables [CtrlBreak] in subsystems for interactive Paradox.

The 3.0 PAL User's Guide is totally incorrect in its discussion of CTRL-BREAK. The CTRLBREAK command *cannot* explicitly enter the debugger or in any way interrupt script play as described. The description actually describes the way the [CtrlBreak] keypress works in interactive Paradox, not the CTRL-BREAK command.

See ESC for examples of CTRLBREAK.

## CANCELEDIT: Select MENU {Cancel} {Yes}

```
CANCELEDIT
```

CANCELEDIT is the exact equivalent of MENU {Cancel} {Yes} and can be used in any mode that presents you with a {No}/{Yes} cancellation choice: Edit, DataEntry, Form, Report, Script, Password, and "Graph." CANCELEDIT will cause a run error if attempted when Paradox does not ask for confirmation of a cancel, or {Cancel} is not an available menu item: e.g., CoEdit, Main, Sort, Create, and Restructure.

The following example of CANCELEDIT's use allows you to print out an InstantReport for the current image with the table name in the page header (instead of "Standard Report"). CANCELEDIT leaves intact an existing standard report when the report finishes printing. To substitute this reporting technique for the regular instant report, attach it to a SETKEY. For example:

```
SETKEY "INSTANTREPORT" PLAY "INSTANTR"
```

### Listing 16.13: CANCELED.L1

```
IF NIMAGES() = 0 OR SYSMODE() <> "Main" THEN
  BEEP
  MESSAGE "No image present, or not in main mode"
  SLEEP 2000
  RETURN
ENDIF
  ; Now design a standard tablular report
MENU {Report} {Design}
SELECT TABLE()                       ; Selects current table name, regardless of directory
{R}                                  ; Select the standard report
  ; If there is an existing report {R}, let's tell Paradox to replace it anyway,
  ; because we'll cancel the report when we are done, and the existing report
  ; will be resurrected.
IF MENUCHOICE() = "Cancel" THEN
  {Replace}
ENDIF
SELECT TABLE()+" Report"   ; Place table name into report description
                           ; and Paradox also places it into the page header
```

```
{Tabular}
INSTANTREPORT  ; Actually outputs report to printer.
               ; Same as MENU {Output} {Printer}.
CANCELEDIT     ; Cancels all changes and reverts back to main mode
```

## 16.2 PARADOX KEYSTROKES AND INFORMATION

### BACKSPACE: Press [Backspace]

BACKSPACE

BACKSPACE deletes the character to the left of the cursor as if the [Backspace] key was pressed. The following example uses BACKSPACE as an alternative to substring manipulation. Suppose you are looking to trim the extended zip codes from a "Customer" table, leaving only the five-digit zip:

**Listing 16.14: BACKSPAC.L1**

```
EDIT "Customer"
MOVETO [Zipcode]
SCAN FOR LEN([]) = 10    ;#####-####  including the dash.
  BACKSPACE
  BACKSPACE
  BACKSPACE
  BACKSPACE
  BACKSPACE
ENDSCAN

;Is the same as:

EDIT "Customer"
MOVETO [Zipcode]
SCAN FOR LEN([]) = 10    ;#####-####  including the dash.
  [] = SUBSTR([],1,5)
ENDSCAN
```

In the "Keep it Simple, Stupid!" school of thought, if you need to remove three characters from a field regardless of field length, the backspace approach is less complicated than the required error trapping using a substring approach.

### CTRLBACKSPACE: Presses [CtrlBackspace]

CTRLBACKSPACE

CTRLBACKSPACE erases the current field or the value at a Paradox prompt, the same as in interactive Paradox. This next example is designed to blank any column in a table regardless of field type. It's a simple approach that is often

much easier than trying to determine the appropriate value to insert, such as """
or BLANKDATE() or BLANKNUM().

**Listing 16.15: CTRLBACK.L1**

```
PROC BlankColumnScan.l(table.a, field.a)
  ; table.a  ; Name of table.
  ; field.a  ; Name of field.
  ; RETURNS  ; TRUE if all changes were made, False if access was denied.

  ; First we need to guarantee exclusive writing to the table to keep anyone
  ; else from locking us out of blanking a record's field. Much the same
  ; as the FULL LOCK placed automatically by a changeto query, except that
  ; other users can view the table.
  LOCK table.a WL, table.a PWL
  IF NOT RETVAL THEN           ; Paradox will set ERRORUSER() to the name of
                               ; the user preventing the locks.
    RETURN FALSE               ; We cannot proceed, so exit the proc.
  ENDIF
  COEDIT table.a
  REQUIREDCHECK OFF            ; Just in case we land on a required field.
  MOVETO FIELD field.a
  SCAN FOR NOT ISBLANK([])     ; Only look at records with value in this field.
    CTRLBACKSPACE              ; Simply blank the field.
  ENDSCAN
  DO_IT!
  CLEARIMAGE
  UNLOCK table.a WL, table.a PWL
  RETURN TRUE
ENDPROC

; A typical call to the proc would be to clear notice dates in a customer table.

l = BlankColumnScan.l ("Customer", "Next Notice Date")
IF NOT l THEN
  MESSAGE "Table is in use by ",ERRORUSER(),". Can't blank field, press any key."
  BEEP
  n = GETCHAR()
ELSE
  MESSAGE "Table updated."
  SLEEP 2000
ENDIF
```

This is functionally very similar to a query approach, which requires the creation
of a "Changed" table:

**Listing 16.16: CTRLBACK.L2**

```
PROC blankcolumnquery.l(table.a, field.a)
  ; table.a  ; Name of table.
  ; field.a  ; Name of field.
  ; RETURNS  ; TRUE if all changes were made, False if access was denied.

  LOCK table.a fl
```

```
; We need to guarantee exclusive writing to the table to keep any
; one else from locking us out of blanking a record's field.
; The changeto query below must be able to place a full lock otherwise
; it won't proceed.
IF NOT RETVAL THEN
   RETURN FALSE   ; Cannot proceed.
ENDIF

   MENU {Ask} SELECT table.a
   MOVETO FIELD field.a
   "NOT BLANK, Changeto BLANK"    ; Types in the changeto value.
   ; same as
   ; []="NOT BLANK, Changeto BLANK"
   DO_IT!
   CLEARALL ; Remove changed table  and query.
   UNLOCK table.a fl
   RETURN TRUE
ENDPROC

;As an example of its use:
; l = blankcolumnquery.l( "Customer" , "Next Notice Date")
```

An advantage to the SCAN approach is that it doesn't need the additional disk space for a "Changed" table. In addition, the SCAN routine doesn't affect other tables on the workspace and other users are allowed to view the table while it is being changed. However, the CHANGETO query's "Changed" table provides an audit trail of the changes. Even with the double duty of creating a "Changed" table, the CHANGETO query can often be dramatically faster than the SCAN approach (particularly on a network). Notice that the locking of the tables guarantees that either all the changes will be made or none will be made at all, thus assuring the process's data integrity. The calling script evaluates this procedure's returned value to see if a CHANGETO query was performed.

CTRLBACKSPACE can also be used to blank a Paradox type-in menu prompt, though the SELECT command is more efficient.

**Listing 16.17: CTRLBACK.L3**

```
length.a = "66"    ; In this case we're using "66", 66 is also ok.
MENU {Setting} {PageLayout} {Length}
CTRLBACKSPACE     ; Clear the existing value.
TYPEIN length.a  ; Place the new value.
ENTER            ; Press enter.

; which is the same as:

length.a = 66     ; Typein prompts convert to strings automatically.
MENU {Setting} {PageLayout} {Length}
SELECT length.a
```

### DEL: Press the [Del] Key

```
DEL
```

Like all keystroke commands, the DEL command does whatever pressing [Del] would do in interactive Paradox. This varies from mode to mode, depending on several circumstances. For example, in Edit mode, it deletes the current record; in FieldView, it deletes the current character. There are examples of DEL scattered throughout the sample code.

### INS: Press the [Ins] Key

```
INS
```

The INS command inserts a new record in any editing mode, or toggles to the insert mode in Form, Report, or Script mode. While in Fieldview, INS toggles between the insert and the overwrite mode, with insert reflected by a blinking cursor and overwrite by only the box cursor.

If used in a table in one of the Edit modes or Create, Password, or Restructure, INS opens a new record *above* the current record. This allows you to create a new record #1 if you are already on the first record. To open a new record after the last record in a table, you would use END and then DOWN, PgDn, or CtrlPgDn, depending on whether you're in TableView or FormView.

Note that on the network in CoEdit mode, a newly inserted record does not exist until you post it to the table. No other user can possibly be in contention for it and so it is not locked, nor does it need to be when adding data to it. Because a record does not actually exist until posted, Paradox lets you open a new record even if another user has placed a write lock on the table. However, you will not be able to post the record until the write lock has been removed. Some write locks come from less than obvious sources. Column statistical functions like CMAX and using an ACCEPT statement with the LOOKUP option both place write locks while they do their work and release the lock when done. See the WaitPlusAdd.v procedure in the WAITPLUS section for examples of code that insert new records into a table.

### ISINSERTMODE: Are We in Insert Mode?

```
ISINSERTMODE ()
```

Returns:

| | |
|---|---|
| True | If Paradox is in insert mode in Form, Report, or Script mode. |
| False | If Paradox is not in insert mode. |
| Script Error | If Paradox is not in one of the three modes. |

INSERTMODE is one of four minor modes (FormView, FieldView, and Help-Mode are the other three). When active, the word "Ins" is displayed in the top right corner of the workspace. To ensure that you are in "Insert" mode when in Report, Form, or Script mode, include:

**Listing 16.18: ISINSERT.L1**

```
IF NOT ISINSERTMODE( ) THEN
   Ins   ; Go to insert mode
ENDIF
```

Note: Paradox3 reports accurately on insert mode within Fieldview. Previous versions would always return False in Fieldview.

### DITTO: Copy Value From Record Above

```
DITTO
```

Like the [Ctrl D] key, DITTO copies the current field's value from the previous record into the current field. DITTO works in Edit, CoEdit, DataEntry, Create, and Restructure modes, as well as in Query images. DITTO duplicates a value even if that value does not conform to the field's ValCheck {Picture} clause. All other ValChecks apply; if a value in the previous field does not meet the current LowValue, HighValue, Required, or TableLookup, using DITTO locks the cursor in the current field until the value is valid. For a DITTO to work, the current field must be empty (if the mode is inappropriate, the command is simply ignored). The following example assigns the "Ditto" key to a command sequence that first clears the current field with CTRLBACKSPACE, then duplicates the field and moves to the right.

**Listing 16.19: DITTO.L1**

```
SETKEY "Ditto" IF NOT ATFIRST( ) THEN CTRLBACKSPACE DITTO RIGHT ENDIF
```

See the SYSMODE function for an example that expands the DITTO functionality to Form, Report, and Script modes.

### SYSMODE: What is The Current Paradox Mode?

```
SYSMODE ( )
```

Returns:

    A String    Representing the current Paradox mode. Note the intraword capitalization: "CoEdit", "Create", "DataEntry", "Edit",

> "Form", "Graph", "Main", "Password", "Report", "Restructure", "Script", "Sort".

Using SYSMODE() helps guard against potential script errors, because many PAL functions and commands are only appropriate in certain Paradox modes. For example, the assignment of the BANDINFO() function:

```
a = BANDINFO()
```

would cause a script error in any mode other than "Report." SYSMODE enables you to change the functionality with the mode. For example, you might want to extend the use of the [Ctrl D] to do different things in different modes:

1. In Password, Create, Restructure, DataEntry, Edit, and CoEdit modes, clear the current field, and copy the contents of the field in the previous record.
2. In Form, Report, and Script modes, copy the character above the cursor.

Here's an example:

**Listing 16.20: SYSMODE.L1**

```
libname.a = "MyProcs"    ; Define the name of the library.

; check to see if MyProcs.lib file exists
IF NOT ISFILE(libname.a + ".lib") THEN   ; library not found, create it.
  CREATELIB libname.a
ENDIF

PROC ditto.u ()
  PRIVATE char.a
  SWITCH
    CASE SEARCH(SYSMODE(),"FormReportScript")>0 AND ROWNO() > 1 THEN
      ; We are in form, report, or script mode, and not on line 1.
      UP   ; Move up one line.
      char.a = CURSORCHAR()
      DOWN ; Back down to where we were.
      TYPEIN char.a
      ; If insertmode was turned on, characters would move to right, otherwise
      ; ditto'd character simply overwrites current character.
    CASE SEARCH(SYSMODE(), "CoEditDataEntryCreateRestructurePassword")
      ; Found an appropriate sysmode().
      AND COLNO() > 1      ; Not in the record number column.
      AND RECNO() > 1 :    ; Not at the first record.
      CTRLBACKSPACE        ; Clear the field.
      DITTO                ; DITTO from the record above it.
    OTHERWISE:
      BEEP                 ; DITTO would be inappropriate.
  ENDSWITCH
```

```
ENDPROC
WRITELIB libname.a ditto.u
RELEASE PROCS     ditto.u
```

You would typically assign a SETKEY as part of an INIT.SC to activate the additional functions:

```
SETKEY "Ditto" autolib = "MyProcs" Ditto.u()
```

This code says, "Whenever I press the Ditto key, look in the MyProcs library for a procedure called Ditto.u, then run the procedure."

Note the use of the SEARCH function on the returned value of SYSMODE(); it is very efficient when compared to the alternative:

```
IF SYSMODE() = "Form" OR SYSMODE() = "Report" or SYSMODE() = "Script"
```

A simple check of SYSMODE can be used to steer a clear course of action and make coding simpler:

```
IF SYSMODE() = "Main" THEN
  COEDITKEY
ENDIF
```

### FIELDINFO: What Information Is Available about the Form or Report Field?

```
FIELDINFO ()
```

Returns:

| | |
|---|---|
| A String | Descriptive information about the current field in a form or report (field name). Includes calculation if applicable. |
| "" | Blank string if the cursor is not on a field. |

While designing a report or form under script control with the cursor resting on a field, FIELDINFO() returns the information displayed in the field indicator in the top right-hand corner of the screen. Some examples of the values that FIELDINFO() returns in Form mode follow.

**Listing 16.21: FIELDINF.L1**

```
Special Paradox field:
  "RecordNumber"

Regular table fields:
  "Regular, Last Name"
  "Regular, Notes, wrap:3"
```

```
Displayonly fields:
  "DisplayOnly, Balance Due"
```

```
Calculated fields:
  "Formula,[Balance Due]*1.0825"
```

If a calculation in a form is  [City]+", "+[State]+"  "+[Zip] and it is to wrap
to two lines, the FIELDINFO() string would be:

```
  "Formula,[City]+\", \"+[State]+\"  \"+[Zip], wrap:2"
```

Note the backslashes denoting the literal quotes. When cursor is on an area
of an embedded form:

```
  "Embedded Lineitem table using form F3, linked"
```

There was a minor change in FIELDINFO() between Paradox2 and Paradox3.
If the cursor is sitting on the [Last name] field in Form mode, there is a
slight difference in the syntax of some fields:

```
  "Regular,Last Name"      Paradox2 version
  "Regular, Last Name"     Paradox3 version added a space after the comma
```

However, calculated fields in forms are consistent between versions:

```
  "Formula,[Balance Due]*1.0825"   Note no space after the comma.
```

Some examples of FIELDINFO() values from fields in Report mode:

**Listing 16.22: FIELDINF.L2**

```
Special Paradox fields:
  "Current date"
  "Current time"
  "Current page number"
  "Current record number"
  "Current record number, per group"
```

```
Regular table fields:
  "Address"
  "[Invoice->Balance Due]"
```

```
Summary of regular fields:
  "Count of Invoice#, per group"
  "Maximum for Date Due"
  "Minimum for Age, per group"
  "Average of Balance Due"
  "Total for Balance Due, per group"
```

```
Summary of Calculated fields:
  "[Age]+10"
  "[Balance due]*1.0825"
  "Total for [Balance Due]*1.0825, per group"
  "Average of [Balance Due]*1.0825"
  "[City]+\", \"+[State]+\"  \"+[Zip], wrap:2"
```

The next two functions, CURSORCHAR and CURSORLINE, are of use in Form, Report and Script modes. In any other mode, they produce a script error. It is important to remember that they deal only with the Paradox workspace, not the PAL canvas (there is no way to read the PAL canvas directly).

## CURSORCHAR: What Is the Current Character in Form, Report, or Script Mode?

CURSORCHAR ( )

Returns:

A String   One character string containing the current character at the cursor position on the workspace in Form, Report, or Script mode.

## CURSORLINE

CURSORLINE ( )

Returns:

A String   The current line at the cursor on the workspace in Form, Report, or Script mode. Trailing spaces will be suppressed. Only the first 255 characters are returned. There is no relationship to PAL canvas.

See examples of using CURSORCHAR in the discussions of SETKEY and SYSMODE and examples of CURSORLINE in the discussions of SETKEY and ECHO.

Both CURSORCHAR() and CURSORLINE() deal with text only. If you are designing a Form or Report and are currently on a field, these functions will always return the string value of the current character or line. What you see is what you get. For example, if the cursor is on an alphanumeric field in a report, which always has a field mask like "AAAAAAA," CURSORCHAR() would simply return an "A." In form design, CURSORCHAR() returns a "_" when in any field. CURSORLINE() also strips all trailing spaces from the result.

CURSORLINE() cannot be used to copy a report line or form line. Only literal characters will copy; the contents of the fields have to be moved or placed explicitly throughout the Paradox menus. CURSORLINE has other limitations. In Paradox, alphanumeric strings have a maximum length of 255 characters. Reports can be up to 2000 characters wide. CURSORLINE will only return the *first 255 characters* of the line.

## HELP: Either ParadoxHelp or LookupHelp

```
HELP
```

Pressing [F1] in interactive Paradox brings up Paradox Help. Pressing [F1] while on a field with a TableLookup validity check will invoke LookupHelp and a table will be put on the workspace for lookup reference. Under script control, Paradox Help is of little or no use. LookupHelp can be critical. If you issue a call to HELP under script control, it should be on a field with LookupHelp. Here's a script that illustrates why.

```
Clearall
Help
{Basics}
{Paradox}
```

This command sequence is perfectly valid, but will not display anything at all. The reason is simple: Paradox help displays only on the workspace and during script play the PAL canvas covers the workspace. Within systems that you design, Paradox's help screens don't usually have relevance. Most important are a few notes about the Help command within WAIT and DoWait sessions.

As might be expected, pressing [F1] during a WAIT table, WAIT record, or WAIT field will bring up tablelookup help if it is available and just beep otherwise. There is no need to trap the "F1" in the UNTIL clause. However, if you want to use [F1] for something else (like a more general help screen) and reassign lookuphelp to another key (say [Shift F1]), a different approach is needed.

**Listing 16.23: HELP.L1**

```
EDIT "Customer"
PICKFORM 1
WHILE TRUE
  WAIT TABLE
    PROMPT "Editing Customer",
    "[F2]-Saves  [F1]-HelpScreen [Shift F1]-FieldHelp"
  UNTIL  "F2","F1","F11", "Dos", "DosBig"

  SWITCH
    CASE RETVAL="F2":
      DO_IT!
      CLEARALL
      RETURN
    CASE RETVAL="F1":
      helpcustomer.u()  ; Might put up some table wide instructions.
    CASE RETVAL="F11":
      HELP  ; press the help key
      IF HELPMODE()<>"LookupHelp" THEN
        ESC  ; back to table
        MESSAGE "No help available for this field"
```

```
            BEEP
            SLEEP 1000
         ELSE  ; must be in lookup help
            ; Now invoke your lookup procedure, for example LookupSelect.n().
            n = LookupSelect.n()  ; Found in Wwputil2.sc or use your lookup procedure.
            IF n = -60 THEN
               DO_IT!  ; Make the help choice.
            ELSE
               ESC      ; Get out of lookuphelp.
            ENDIF
         ENDIF
      ENDSWITCH
   ENDWHILE
```

Although you can do a Lookup as part of a WAIT table, you cannot do another
WAIT TABLE while in Lookuphelp. The next procedure "waits" in any table, but
is used in Lookuphelp to keep the user in the table, and exits the procedure when
[F2] or [Esc] is pressed. The procedure passes back the keycode of the exit key,
which can be evaluated by the calling procedure. The routine also traps for [F1],
[Ctrl 0], and [Alt 0], so the user only sees the table specified.

**Listing 16.24: HELP.L2**

```
PROC LookupSelect.n()
  ; RETURNS the number of the keypress that exits the lookup select.
  PRIVATE  n, lookup.a, a

  lookup.a = UPPER(TABLE())
  ; Enables you to include just the table name in the prompt without
  ; a path. (Often, lookup tables are not in the current directory,
  ; and table names don't necessarily show in table view.)  The
  ; next two lines grab the table name without the path.
  WHILE MATCH(lookup.a, "..\\..", a, lookup.a )
  ENDWHILE

  ECHO NORMAL     ;Display the table to the user
  RETVAL = 0
  ; Replace prompt with custom prompt that includes instructions.
  PROMPT "Viewing " + lookup.a + " lookup table.  [F2]-Select record  [Esc]-Cancel",
         "[Ctrl Z]-Zoom to a field value  [Alt Z]-Zoom to next occurrence"
  WHILE TRUE
    RETVAL = GETCHAR()  ;always returns an integer.
    SWITCH
      CASE RETVAL = -59 OR RETVAL = 15 OR RETVAL = -24: ; pressed [F1], [Ctrl 0] or [Alt 0]
         BEEP
      CASE RETVAL = -60 OR RETVAL = 27 OR RETVAL = 0:    ; [F2], [Esc]
         QUITLOOP
      CASE RETVAL = 26: ; press zoom
        Zoom.l()      ; See Zoom.l() procedure in a discussion of the ZOOM command.
        ECHO NORMAL   ; Because Zoom.l turns it off.
      OTHERWISE: KEYPRESS RETVAL
    ENDSWITCH
  ENDWHILE
  SYNCCURSOR                ; Resynchronize the canvas cursor with that of the workspace
                            ; (when the proc ends, the cursors will not be out of synch.)
```

```
  IF RETVAL = 0 THEN   ; CtrlBreak = 0 which functions the same as Esc. Thus
     RETVAL = 27        ; return the code for Esc unless Do_It! is pressed.
  ENDIF
  PROMPT               ; Assures that your WAIT table can reset its own prompt.
  RETURN RETVAL
ENDPROC
```

Other examples of the use of HELP are in the DataEntry Toolkit scripts LOOKSLCT.SC and LOOKWAIT.SC.

### HELPMODE: What is the Current Help Mode?

```
HELPMODE ()
```

Returns:

| | |
|---|---|
| A String | The current help mode. |
| "Help" | Currently in Paradox help. |
| "LookupHelp" | Currently in table lookup help. |
| "None" | Not in any help mode. |

The example below is a generic procedure that checks to see if there is lookup help available for the current field. Note that this would be useful only in Edit, CoEdit, or DataEntry modes.

**Listing 16.25: HELPMODE.L1**

```
PROC islookuphelp.l ()
  PRIVATE mode.a
  HELP
  mode.a = HELPMODE()
  ESC                          ; Back to the table.
  RETURN mode.a = "LookupHelp"  ; True or False.
ENDPROC
```

The routine presses HELP, looks at the resultant HELPMODE, escapes back to the table, and then reports True if LookupHelp was found.

(Note: "Help" is the only mode in interactive Paradox in which you cannot invoke the PAL menu. This applies to the context-sensitive help screens, help index, and table lookup help. Although users rarely try to access the PAL menu from this mode, it can be a little frustrating to someone who simply wants to try out the HELPMODE() function. The workaround is simple. Before you get into "Help" mode, issue a SETKEY assignment like:

```
SETKEY -35 RETURN "Current HelpMode() = " + HELPMODE()
```

which reassigns the [Alt H] key to display a message about the current help mode. Although the PAL menu is inactive during help, the rest of PAL functions normally.)

See the HELP command and the WaitPluslookup.u() procedure for other examples that use HELPMODE().

# 16.3 QUERY IMAGE MANIPULATION

Query images and Display images have a lot in common. In a query image you can insert and delete rows, rotate fields, use the ditto function and fieldview, and move around as you would within a table. Both abide by a set of rules. Query images constructed in interactive Paradox are by definition syntactically correct—you cannot construct an invalid query (although you'll often construct a query that doesn't give you the answer you intend). But the similarities end there.

Creating and manipulating query images under script control present challenges to any PAL programmer. Tables called by your query statements may no longer exist. Tables may be password protected or corrupted. On networks, tables may have Full Locks on them or be in almost constant use. Field names may have been changed by restructuring subsequent to your using {QuerySave}. Script modifications may make for improper syntax. The list goes on and on.

This section presents commands that help you write and control valid query statements in scripts.

### QUERY: Place a Query on the Workspace

```
QUERY QueryForms ENDQUERY
```

        QueryForms     Text that represents the query layout for all tables involved.

The QUERY command places a query on the workspace. QUERY and ENDQUERY describe a query's boundaries, with representations of tables placed between them. Special query keywords replace familiar symbols representing query operators. Literal strings appear in quotation marks. A query is considered a single PAL statement. For a variety of reasons, the PAL User's Guide encourages you to create this specialized format with the QuerySave command. You then read the saved query script into your application's main script.

To make things easy to read, {Querysave} appends a few extra lines under each query line. The lines that contain only the | (vertical bar) characters can be safely deleted, as can all lines with no fields. However, it is important to make sure that there is a blank line between the word QUERY and the first line of the first table, as well as a blank line between the last line of the query and the word ENDQUERY. The graphical format of query statements makes it easy for us to interpret them, but in the challenge to make code generic, they are often too inflexible. For although you can place variables into field values, with the variable names preceded by the tilde character (so called "tilde variables"), table names are hard-coded and so cannot be changed on the fly.

The following example shows three valid ways of placing a query on the workspace that selects all fields from all records in the "Customer" table:

**Listing 16.26: QUERY.L1**

```
; The first technique is a straight QuerySave.

QUERY

Customer | Customer ID# | Company name | Address | City  | State |
         | Check        | Check        | Check   | Check | Check |


Customer | Zipcode | Balance due | Contact First Name | Contact Last Name |
         | Check   | Check       | Check               | Check             |


Customer | Start date | Last order date | Last order amount |
         | Check      | Check           | Check             |

ENDQUERY

; Now, we'll delete the extra blank lines, the query is still valid.
; It is important to make sure a blank line follows "QUERY" and
; precedes "ENDQUERY".

QUERY

Customer | Customer ID# | Company name | Address | City  | State |
         | Check        | Check        | Check   | Check | Check |
Customer | Zipcode | Balance due | Contact First Name | Contact Last Name |
         | Check   | Check       | Check               | Check             |
Customer | Start date | Last order date | Last order amount |
         | Check      | Check           | Check             |
ENDQUERY


; Although not as intuitive, the next four words place the same query
; on the workspace:
```

```
MENU {Ask} {Customer} CHECK

; Remember that in this case, the table name can be a variable, and used as
; table.a = "Customer"
; MENU {Ask} SELECT table.a CHECK
```

Playing a script in QUERYSAVE format only places the query on the workspace—it does not perform it. Once a QUERY is on the workspace, your script can make modifications to it, then issue a DO_IT! to execute the query. Like a table in any edit mode, you can make field assignments in a number of ways that have the same practical effect (in this case to restrict records to those in New Jersey):

```
1)   [State] = "NJ"


2)   MOVETO [State]

     "NJ"                    ; Implicitly types in string


3)   MOVETO [State]

     TYPEIN "NJ"             ; Explicitly types in string

; Or when dealing with variables

4)   state.a = "NJ"

     MOVETO [State]

     TYPEIN state.a         ; Places the "NJ" into the field

5)   state.a = "NJ"

     MOVETO [State]

     TYPEIN "~state.a"      ; Places the tilde variable into the query
```

A few things are worth noting about assigning values into query fields:

The field value must not conflict with reserved query words. For example, if you need to find records in a [First name] field of someone named Max, you can assign the value enclosed in literal quotes—for example [First name] = "\"Max\"", which assigns "Max", or assign the value to a tilde variable first.

```
firstname.a = "Max"
[First name] = "~firstname.a"
```

The field value must be syntactically correct, with special attention paid to commas separating values. For example, to add a high value in a date field of <=8/22/89, you may need to separate this value and a preexisting value with a comma. The following code evaluates the condition and sees if a comma is necessary:

```
MOVETO [Date]
IF [] <>"" THEN
 TYPEIN ","      ; the necessary comma
ENDIF
TYPEIN "<=8/22/89"
```

Example elements in queries are preceded with an underscore.

**Listing 16.27: QUERY.L2**

QUERY

| Customer | Balance due |
|----------|-------------|
|          | >0, _xbaldue, CHANGETO _xbaldue*1.015 |

| Customer | Last order date |
|----------|-----------------|
|          | <TODAY-30       |

ENDQUERY

When DO_IT! is issued, this query changes the current balance due by adding 1.5% to all outstanding balances in which the last order was more than 30 days ago.

It is often advisable, particularly during development or when getting query restrictions from the user, to evaluate WINDOW() after you issue a DO_IT! If WINDOW() does not return a blank string, then there is a problem, and the query did not execute. You can use the message returned in the window to evaluate the problem and possibly alert the user (or your error routines) to fix the problem. See DOWNIMAGE for additional sample query scripts, and a discussion of the pros and cons of queries vs. direct table editing.

### {Ask} Tablename: Place a Query Image on the Workspace.

{Ask}

This menu choice prompts the user for a table name for a query image.

Using the menu to {Ask} about a table enables you to select the table under script control. Although the QuerySave format is easier to read, table names cannot be changed on the fly. Using MENU {Ask} and then selecting the table can get around the problem. If you need to place additional query forms on the workspace, use {Ask} repeatedly. The name of the table can be most efficiently identified with the SELECT command or as a braced menu selection.

For example,

```
Menu {Ask} {C:\\AR\\INVOICES} CheckPlus
```

can be replaced with

```
table.a = "C:\\AR\\INVOICES"
MENU {Ask} SELECT Table.a CheckPlus
```

There are four kinds of checkmark operators in a query and four equivalent PAL commands. All are ignored if the current image is not a query image. See the section on Paradox fundamentals for a more complete discussion of all the query operators. Checkmark operators are independent of other query field operators, such as literal characters, example elements, and special operators.

### CHECK: Presses the [F6] Key

```
CHECK
```

The CHECK command toggles the checkmark on and off in a query form. In the leftmost column, it places checkmarks in all fields in the form.

Expanding on the technique of building queries in real-time, the example that follows is a generic procedure that gets all records that have a specified value for a specified field.

**Listing 16.28: CHECK.L1**

```
PROC getrecords.u(table.a, field.a, value.v)
  ; table.a    ; Name of table to use.
  ; field.a    ; Name of field to restrict.
  ; value.v    ; Any valid Paradox query field value or pattern.

  PRIVATE ok.l
  MENU {Ask} SELECT table.a
  CHECK
  IF NOT ISBLANK(field.a) THEN
    MOVETO FIELD field.a
    [] = value.v
  ENDIF
  DO_IT!

  ; Now check to see that query syntax is okay.
```

```
      ; Evaluate WINDOW() to see that query did not trip up over a first name
      ; such as "MAX"; Also should clean up after the query.
      ok.l = WINDOW() = ""      ; True of window is blank, False otherwise.
      CLEARALL                  ; Clear the workspace.
      RETURN ok.l               ; Script can tell if query proceeded.
ENDPROC

; Note that this simple version of the procedure merely clears the workspace.


; Typical examples of successful query syntax, would set l = True

l = getrecords.l("Customer", "", "")                 ; Gets all records.
l = getrecords.l("Customer", "State", "CA")          ; Only California records.
l = getrecords.l("Customer", "Zipcode", "BLANK")     ; Only records without zip codes.
l = getrecords.l("Customer", "Balance Due", ">0")    ; Only outstanding balances.
l = getrecords.l("Customer", "Last name", "S..")     ; Only last names starting with S.
l = getrecords.l("Customer", "Last name", "Like Smith") ; All where last name is like Smith.

   ; Potential problems arise where reserved query words could interfere and set
   ; l = False, for example, if you need to find all your customers whose first
   ; name is Max or customers whose state is Oregon, abbreviated "OR".

l = getrecords.l("Customer","First Name","Max")  ; sets l to False because MAX is a reserved word

   ; There are two ways of correcting the situation. First you can surround the
   ; value with literal quotes:

l = getrecords.l("Customer","First Name","\"Max\"")

   ; Another approach is to use a tilde variable:

first.a = "Max"
l = getrecords.l("Customer","First Name","~first.a")
```

## CHECKDESCENDING: Press [Ctrl F6]

```
CHECKDESCENDING
```

The CHECKDESCENDING command toggles the checkdescending mark in a query. A CheckDescending operator reverses the sort order for a particular field.

## CHECKPLUS: Press [Alt F6]

```
CHECKPLUS
```

The third checkmark operator, CHECKPLUS, is used to create an "Answer" table that corresponds to the original record order and includes duplicates. In the leftmost field, CHECKPLUS places CheckPlus operators in every field.

## GROUPBY: Press [Shift F6]

GROUPBY

The final Checkmark command, GROUPBY, is used with SET queries to form the basis for groups based on the current field. Unlike CHECK, the field does not appear in the "Answer" table.

## EXAMPLE: Press [F5]

EXAMPLE

The EXAMPLE command has the same effect as pressing the [F5] key while in a query. It is useful only when constructing a query in real-time (vs. using a Querysave script). You can place examples in one of two ways. First, you can assign an example for a field with the same syntax as Querysave uses, for example,

```
[Customer Id#]="_xcustid"
```

Using the underscore will let the query treat the string xcustid as an example. The second approach uses the EXAMPLE command as a keystroke preceding an example element. To change all balances to reflect an added interest change, use:

```
1 = ChangeNumber.l("AcctRec","Balance due","1.015")
```

### Listing 16.29: EXAMPLE.L1

```
PROC ChangeNumber.l(table.a, field.a, factor.n)
  ;table.a   ; Table to use.
  ;field.a   ; Numeric or currency field to change.
  ;factor.n  ; Multiplication factor  i.e. 1.015 adds 1.5% interest
             ; .40 deducts 60%.
  ; Because this routine does a changeto query, we need to be able to
  ; place a full lock on the table at the time of the change.
  PRIVATE ok.l
  LOCK table.a FL
  IF NOT RETVAL THEN ; Someone is keeping us from placing a full lock on the
                     ; table, so changes won't be able to be made.
     RETURN False
  ENDIF
  CLEARALL             ; Clear the workspace.
  MENU {Ask} SELECT table.a
  MOVETO FIELD field.a
  ; Now place examples for the query and construct the calculation.
  EXAMPLE "xvalue, changeto "
  EXAMPLE "xvalue * "
```

```
TYPEIN factor.n
; same as:
; []="_xvalue, CHANGETO _xvalue * " + STRVAL(factor.n)
DO_IT!
ok.l = WINDOW() = ""      ; True if Paradox is not complaining, False if there
                          ; is a problem with the query syntax.
CLEARALL
; You might want to delete the resultant changed table, or keep it for
; an audit trail.
; This procedure could also be expanded to include other conditions
; (for example only changing balances >0).
UNLOCK table.a FL         ; Clean up lock, release the table for another's use.
RETURN ok.l
ENDPROC
```

## CHECKMARKSTATUS: Returns the Current Type of Check Mark in a Query Image

```
CHECKMARKSTATUS ()
```

Returns:

| | |
|---|---|
| "Check" | Unique values. |
| "CheckDescending" | Descend field in "Answer" table. |
| "CheckPlus" | All values. |
| "GroupBy" | Group without placing field in answer. |
| "" | No check or groupby, or not in query. |

CHECKMARKSTATUS determines if a field in a query has a checkmark operator. It allows you to monitor user interaction in a WAIT TABLE in a Query image. With it, you can test if the user has checked any fields by stepping through and analyzing each field in the image. As part of a routine that describes the current value of a field in a query image, you could include:

**Listing 16.30: CHECKMAR.L1**

```
field.a = FIELDSTR()              ; String of the current field, complete or not.
chk.a = CHECKMARKSTATUS()
IF chk.a <> "" THEN
  field.a = chk.a + " " + field.a
ENDIF
MESSAGE FIELD()," has a value of: ", field.a, ".  Press any key."
n = GETCHAR()
RELEASE VARS n
;  Which might give a message similar to :
; "Last Name has a value of CheckPlus Smith.  Press any key."
```

The next example uses a few little tricks to ditto an entire query row from the one above it:

**Listing 16.31: CHECKMAR.L2**

```
PROC DittoQueryRow.l()
  PRIVATE n,
    field.a,        ; Current field name
    checkstatus.a  ; status of row above

  IF IMAGETYPE() <> "Query" OR ROWNO() = 1 THEN
    BEEP
    RETURN FALSE                          ; Nothing to ditto.
  ENDIF
  field.a = FIELD()                       ; Save the field name, so we can return to it.
  CTRLHOME                                ; Move to the leftmost column.
  FOR n FROM 1 TO NFIELDS(TABLE())        ; Once for each field in the table.
    RIGHT                                 ; Move right one field.
    ; First we need to clear out any existing data in the current field.
    CTRLBACKSPACE
    EXECUTE CHECKMARKSTATUS()             ; If checked, uncheck the field to start clean.
                                         ; If the field isn't checked, EXECUTE "" is simply ignored.
    UP                                    ; go up to the previous row.
    checkstatus.a = CHECKMARKSTATUS()     ; The CHECKMARKSTATUS that we want to ditto.
    DOWN                                  ; Back to the original row.
    EXECUTE checkstatus.a                 ; Does the actual Check, Checkplus etc.
    DITTO                                 ; Copy field value from the row above.
  ENDFOR
  MOVETO FIELD field.a                    ; Go back to the original field.
  RETURN TRUE
ENDPROC

; now test the proc
l = DittoQueryRow.l()                     ; Sets l to True if successful; else False.
```

Paradox3 allows you to change the physical order of fields in "Answer" tables. The default, "TableOrder," creates "Answer" tables, which contain the checked fields in the structural order of the query tables used, starting with the topmost image and moving down. The second method, "ImageOrder," causes the fields in all "Answer" tables to be created according to the order of fields on the query image(s). ImageOrder queries enable you to dictate which columns appear first, thus affecting the automatic sort. As usual, if the query has a "CheckPlus" operator, the "Answer" table is not sorted. You can change the query order two ways:

1. Define the default order in the CUSTOM script.
2. Use the next command, SETQUERYORDER, to change the order to IMAGEORDER or TABLEORDER.

### SETQUERYORDER: Set the Query Order for All Successive Queries

```
SETQUERYORDER {TABLEORDER | IMAGEORDER}
```

TABLEORDER     "Answer" table fields will be displayed in the same order as is the table structure.

IMAGEORDER     "Answer" table fields will be sensitive to rotations in effect at the time of DO-IT!

### QUERYORDER: What is the Current Query Order?

```
QUERYORDER ()
```

Returns:

"TableOrder"     See definition above.
"ImageOrder"

Assuming the default order is "TableOrder", a query form placed on the workspace could look like this, after the Do_It!:

**Listing 16.32: QUERYORD.FG1**

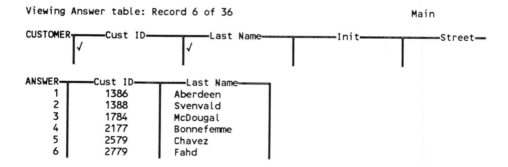

```
Viewing Answer table: Record 6 of 36                          Main

CUSTOMER        Cust ID         Last Name          Init        Street
        √                   √

ANSWER          Cust ID         Last Name
    1           1386            Aberdeen
    2           1388            Svenvald
    3           1784            McDougal
    4           2177            Bonnefemme
    5           2579            Chavez
    6           2779            Fahd
```

If the Query image were rotated so that [Last name] was before the [Cust ID] and the default QUERYORDER was still "TableOrder", the resulting answer table would be the same as before. However, if the default QUERYORDER was "ImageOrder", designated in the CUSTOM configuration program, or if we issued the SETQUERYORDER IMAGEORDER command, the resulting answer table would look like:

**Listing 16.33: QUERYORD.FG2**

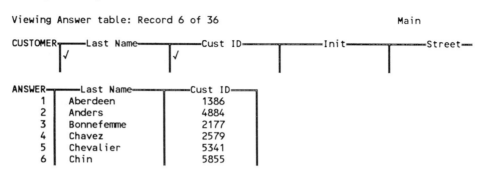

```
Viewing Answer table: Record 6 of 36                        Main

CUSTOMER┬────Last Name──────┬─────Cust ID──────┬────────Init─────────┬───────Street──
        │ √                 │ √                │                     │
        │                   │                  │                     │


ANSWER┬──────Last Name═══════┬═══Cust ID═══┐
    1 │   Aberdeen           │    1386     │
    2 │   Anders             │    4884     │
    3 │   Bonnefemme         │    2177     │
    4 │   Chavez             │    2579     │
    5 │   Chevalier          │    5341     │
    6 │   Chin               │    5855     │
```

## 16.3.1 Rotating and Crosstabbing

### ROTATE: Press [Ctrl R]

ROTATE

   Rotates a column.

You can issue ROTATE to change the order of columns in a display or query image, or a tabular report. The display image must be in TableView. ROTATE is particularly important in Paradox3 because queries can be made sensitive to image rotations with SETQUERYORDER IMAGEORDER. Crosstabs and Graphs are also sensitive to image rotations for sort orders and series definitions. So, if appropriate, use ROTATE to arrange the columns in the proper order. Getting a table in the proper rotation usually takes some trial and error, moving from field to field to get things just right. It is often easiest to use script recording in interactive Paradox. This assures that you will have the order you need.

### CROSSTABKEY: Presses [Alt X]

CROSSTABKEY

   Produces a CrossTab table based on the current table

Paradox3 introduced a cross-tabulation facility. Crosstabbing often reveals otherwise hidden patterns in data and is useful in analysis and graphing. The CROSSTABKEY command makes some assumptions about your data and acts accordingly:

 ● The current field, and all fields to the left of it, become the row labels. They also become the key fields for the Crosstab table produced.

- The data in the next to the last field become the column labels.
- The data in the last field become the values that are totaled (summed) in every row and column. Therefore the field must be numeric, currency, or short number.
- CROSSTAB ignores all other fields.

If all of the conditions are met, the CROSSTABKEY command produces a "Crosstab" table, which like all other temporary tables should be renamed if you intend to keep it. Often you can graph directly from the "Crosstab" table. If you need to do any other type of crosstabbing, you must use the {Image} {Graph} {Crosstab} choices from the main menu. You are given options to select row and column values as well as a variety of crosstab types—Sum, Min, Max, and Count. As with the ROTATE command, it is probably easiest to record these keystrokes interactively and read them into your scripts.

See the Paradox User's guide for examples of crosstabbing.

# 16.4 TABLE MANIPULATION

Though you can change tables that aren't on the workspace with commands like ADD and SORT, most of the time work performed on tables happens when the tables are on the workspace.

The following commands and functions manipulate table images and are grouped according to subtopic. Thus we've listed LOCKRECORD, LOCKKEY, and UNLOCKRECORD under the banner of "CoEdit." Many of the functions covered here also apply to query images.

Main:     User can view, but not change any table on the workspace.
Edit:     User can change table and optionally undo any changes made, all the way back to the beginning of the edit. On a network, only one user may use the table at a time.
CoEdit:     Single or multiple users may change tables and undo the last single change made.
DataEntry:     Users enter data into a temporary Entry table, isolated from the main table. When finished, data can be posted to the main table. There are no command shortcuts for this mode; you must use braced menu selections.

Different modes offer different routes to the same destination. For example, IMAGERIGHTS READONLY provides an alternative to switching between Main and Edit modes. Query images, with few exceptions, behave much in the same manner as do display images. You can, for example, be in Edit or CoEdit mode in a Query image. If you issue a Do_It!, Paradox will revert back to Main mode. If you issue another Do_It!, Paradox will execute the query.

## 16.4.1 Viewing a Table

### VIEW: Places a Table on the Workspace

```
VIEW TableName
```

Tablename      Name of table (string).

VIEW is the abbreviated menu command for Menu {View} SELECT tablename.a. It places a table on the workspace in TableView and remains in Main mode. Multiple tables, or multiple images of the same table can be placed on the workspace concurrently. Keep in mind that if you issue a PICKFORM or FORMKEY command, there must be records in the table or a script error occurs. Once a table is on the workspace, issuing EDITKEY or COEDITKEY is a simple way to switch into an editing mode. However, once a table has been placed in an Edit mode, the entire workspace is in "Edit," and no more tables can be explicitly placed on the workspace until the edit session is ended.

**Listing 16.34: VIEW.L1**

```
; VIEW is used to place one or more tables onto the workspace. i.e.,

View "Customer"    ; Places the table on the workspace.

; It is also necessary if you want to place more than one table on
; the workspace before going into one of the edit modes (because
; images can only be placed while in Main mode).

VIEW "Customer"    ; Place customer on the workspace.
EDIT "Invoices"    ; Places the invoices table on the workspace and then
                   ; puts all tables into edit mode.

;Another way of accomplishing the same thing is:

table1.a = "Customer"
table2.a = "Invoices"
VIEW table1.a
VIEW table2.a
EDITKEY
```

### 16.4.2 Edit Mode

**EDIT: Places a Table on the Workspace and Puts Paradox into Edit Mode**

```
EDIT TableName
```

    TableName    Name of table to place into Edit mode.

The EDIT command places a table on the workspace and puts it and all other tables on the workspace into Edit mode. The EDIT command causes a script error if the table is write protected. No additional tables may be put on the workspace until the edit session is ended. Edit mode creates a transaction log of record changes that allows you to "undo" changes to the table in a record by backward record progression. On networks, because of this undo capability, Edit places a Full Lock on all the tables on the workspace.

    EDIT, an abbreviated menu command for Menu {Modify} {Edit} select table.a, is the functional equivalent of:

```
VIEW table.a
EDITKEY
```

Although many programmers prefer to use CoEdit mode as their normal editing mode, having multiple levels of undo is attractive in many situations.

    If any changes are made to a keyed table in Edit mode, the primary index is temporarily flagged as obsolete. Records can therefore be entered in any order. When the primary index is obsolete, all indexes are obsolete as well. Until the editing session is saved with Do_It! or CANCELEDIT, subsequent ZOOMs or LOCATEs are sequential and cannot use the .PX file. The result, depending on the size of the table, is a much slower performance. Fortunately, with Paradox3, there's a fix with the EDITLOG command.

**EDITLOG: Control the Transaction Log in Edit**

```
EDITLOG [MARK | REVERT | INDEX | PERMANENT]
```

    MARK          Sets a place marker.
    REVERT       Undoes all changes to last marker.
    INDEX        Reindexes primary and secondary indexes.
    PERMANENT  Discards transaction log.

EDITLOG, introduced in Paradox3, can be used in Edit and DataEntry modes only. The EDITLOG MARK command allows you to set "place markers" in the editing transaction log, enabling you to revert to specific points in the edit session. EDITLOG INDEX re-sorts records into key order. Issuing EDITLOG PERMANENT deletes the transaction log, so records entered up to that point are "posted" to the table and cannot be undone.

The code below is a generic table editing routine that lets the user edit a table and use the EDITLOG command via a menu to set markers and reindex.

**Listing 16.35: EDIT.L1**

```
PROC edittable.l(table.a, form.a)
  ; table.a    ; name of table to edit
  ; form.a     ; name of form  "F" or "1" - "14", or "" if table view only
  ; RETURNS    True if edit was ok, False if table was not accessible or canceled
  PRIVATE choice.a, a

  LOCK table.a FL    ; need a full lock
  IF NOT retval THEN
    RETURN FALSE
  ENDIF
  EDIT table.a
  UNLOCK table.a FL   ; the edit now has its own implicit lock
  IF form.a <>"" THEN
    PICKFORM form.a
  ENDIF
  ; now strip out any path for the table, leaving only the name for table.a
  ; so that the prompt line is neater
  WHILE MATCH(table.a, "..\\..", a, table.a)
  ENDWHILE
  WHILE TRUE
    WAIT TABLE
      PROMPT "Editing "+ UPPER (table.a) + " [F2]-Saves  [Esc]-CancelEdit",
             "[Del]-DeleteRecord  [F7]-FormToggle  [Ctrl-F]-FieldView  [F10]-EditLog menu"
    UNTIL  "F2", "Esc", "Del", "F10", "F7", "FieldView", "F35", "Dos", "DosBig", "Zoom"
    SWITCH
      CASE RETVAL = "F2":
        DO_IT!
        CLEARALL
        RETURN TRUE  ; so calling proc can see that all went well
      CASE RETVAL = "Esc":
        SHOWMENU
          "Edit":"Continue with edit session"
          "CancelEdit":"Cancel all changes mad to this table"
        TO choice.a
        IF choice.a = "CancelEdit" THEN
          CANCELEDIT
          CLEARIMAGE
          RETURN FALSE   ; so calling proc could tell how we exited
        ENDIF
      CASE RETVAL = "Del":
        SHOWMENU
          "KeepRecord":"Do not delete this record",
          "Delete":"Ok to delete this record"
        TO choice.a
        IF choice.a = "Delete" THEN
          DEL
```

```
        ENDIF
   CASE RETVAL="F7" AND form.a <>"":   ; ok to toggle form
      FORMKEY
   CASE RETVAL = "F10":
    SHOWMENU
      "Mark":"Sets an EditLog marker at current point, so you can undo up to this point",
      "Revert": "Undo all changes since last EditLog marker",
      "Index":"Reindex table to speed up locates, place into key order, but allow Undo's ",
      "Permanent":"Make changes permanent, delete the transaction log for potential Undo's"
      TO choice.a
      IF choice.a <> "Esc" THEN
        EXECUTE "Editlog " + choice.a
      ENDIF
   CASE RETVAL = "FieldView" or RETVAL = "F35":     ; [Ctrl F] or [Alt F5]
      FIELDVIEW
      WHILE TRUE
        WAIT FIELD
          PROMPT "Edit field and press \017\217 to continue",   ; \017\217 is <┘ sign
                 "Use cursor keys to move around in the field"
        UNTIL "Enter", "Dos" , "DosBig"
        IF REVTAL = "Enter" THEN
          QUITLOOP
        ENDIF
      ENDWHILE
    CASE retval = "Zoom" :
      Zoom.l()      ; see ZOOM command for details about Zoom.l()
    ENDSWITCH
  ENDWHILE
ENDPROC
```

As of this writing, there is an obscure bug in the EDITLOG PERMANENT command that affects Paradox 3.0 and 3.01. If you issue EDITLOG PERMANENT while in a keyed table with no records, Paradox considers the table empty (even though there should be no way for a table to be empty in EDIT mode). The complication is that when you issue DO_IT!, Paradox no longer recognizes the table's primary index, even though the .PX file is present. You must restructure the table to restore the keys by placing asterisks in the appropriate key fields.

### EDITKEY: Press [F9]

```
EDITKEY
```

EDITKEY simulates pressing [F9] from the keyboard, placing Paradox into Edit mode. Issuing EDITKEY while in edit mode has no effect. If you need to ensure that you are in Edit mode, you can issue:

```
IF SYSMODE()="Main" THEN
   EditKey
ENDIF
```

See VIEW for examples.

### UNDO: Press [Ctrl U], the UNDO Key

UNDO

As of this writing, the UNDO command has fallen through the cracks and is not documented in the PAL manual. The command undoes the last change in a table, subject to the restrictions of the Edit mode chosen. CoEdit mode allows only the last change to be undone, whereas Edit and DataEntry modes allow multiple UNDO's all the way back to the table status at the beginning of the edit session (or until the point where an EDITLOG PERMANENT was issued).

    See also CANCELEDIT and CTRLBREAK.

### REQUIREDCHECK: Enable or Disable Required ValChecks

REQUIREDCHECK

    OFF     Required ValChecks are temporarily disabled.
    ON      Required ValChecks enabled on all tables on workspace.

REQUIREDCHECK OFF temporarily disables the REQUIRED ValCheck for a table image.

    Not generally used by experienced PAL programmers because of the limited control it offers, the Required ValCheck is regarded as one of the few obnoxious features of Paradox. For an example, if you enter a field with a {Required} validity check in any edit mode, you cannot leave the field until you make a valid entry. You can't do a Do_It! or even a FormKey. Only an UNDO will let you out. However, if the cursor never reaches the field with the required ValCheck, you can simply move on to the next record. A required field is a field-level check (as are all ValChecks), and not the more generally needed record-level check.

    REQUIREDCHECK OFF gives you the ability to leave a field blank even if it has a {Required} ValCheck. This is especially useful for generic procedures that are not table-specific. There is also a small complication that results from trying to blank a {Required} field. Even if you have set REQUIREDCHECK OFF, and you try to clear a {Required} field by direct field assignment of a blank value, or a COPYFROMARRAY where the array element is blank, a script error results. The way around this is to move to the field and issue a CtrlBackspace, or use a CHANGETO query.

    One common way users encounter the {Required} ValCheck problem is in attempting to toggle to a form from TableView in Edit mode in a required field. Paradox will not even allow you to change views, locking you into the field. See the WaitPlus.v and CopyFromaArray3.u in the WaitPlus section for examples that use REQUIREDCHECK in very generic code.

    A small change made in version 3.01 makes Paradox sensitive to REQUIRED-CHECK status in a way that might affect some generic code. When evaluating the

menu selections for ValChecks, versions prior to 3.01 always reported the
{Required} ValCheck based on the specifications in the .VAL file; however, 3.01
detects whether the field is required at this moment. So if you are trying to step
through all the fields of a table to get the ValChecks, you'll probably want to turn
REQUIREDCHECK OFF so that you can move through blank, yet required fields.
A code fragment that would let 3.01 return the proper menu selection might look
like:

```
; Assuming that REQUIREDCHECK is already OFF
MENU {ValChecks} {Define} ENTER
REQUIREDCHECK ON      ; Necessary to get required status in 3.01, otherwise
                      ; 3.01 will *ALWAYS* show "No" in the menu choice below.
{REQUIRED}
required.a = MENUCHOICE()  ; "Yes" if .VAL says it's required, "No" otherwise.
REQUIREDCHECK OFF          ; Now we can continue on to other fields.
```

### 16.4.3 CoEdit Mode

CoEdit mode was introduced in Paradox2 as a way of letting multiple users edit
access to the same table over a network. Yet because of the way CoEdit keeps
indexes up to date and the way it handles key field violations in real time, many
programmers have adopted CoEdit as their preferred editing mode. The Wait-
Plus procedures, for example, work entirely in CoEdit mode.

Before you start coding with CoEdit, we urge you to spend some time with
CoEdit in interactive mode on a keyed table. Try adding new records, and watch
them "fly away" to their proper position in the table. Try entering records with
conflicting keys, and test out the keylookup and locking mechanisms. Experiment with the workspace to better understand the issues involved in a CoEdit
session. Finally, look at the WaitPlus code. We've supplied code that demonstrates the kinds of things that happen in a multiuser environment, where things
are changing all the time.

COEDIT is indispensable on networks, but extremely useful on single-user
systems as well. It is often good practice to develop single user systems as if they
were network applications, because data integrity and key violation issues span
single and multiuser installations. Coding with CoEdit also makes future
transitions to network applications rather painless.

#### 16.4.3.1 CoEdit and Multiple Images of the Same Table

There is a difference in the way CoEdit works on multiple images of the *same*
table on networks and single-user systems. On a network, multiple images of one
table may remain in CoEdit on the workspace. Consequently, multiple records
can be locked for that table by moving to the various images. However, in single
user systems, as soon as you enter CoEdit mode, duplicate images of a table are

cleared from the workspace and only the topmost image remains. The current record in the topmost image of the table becomes the current record.

Although locking multiple records in CoEdit for a single user on a network is not potentially very useful, this illustrates a small difference in the way the workspace is handled. Unless the user is on a network, Paradox assumes that it doesn't have to bother with record locks and so it doesn't leave multiple images of the same table on the workspace in CoEdit mode.

## COEDIT: Place a Table on the Workspace and Put Paradox in CoEdit Mode

```
COEDIT Tablename
```

The COEDIT command places a table on the workspace and changes the system mode from Main to CoEdit for all images on the workspace. Although Paradox handles file locking automatically, it is a good idea to test for locking rights before CoEditing a table. Typically the least restrictive lock should be attempted. The code below attempts to place a Prevent Full Lock on the selected table. If successful, the procedure places the table on the workspace in CoEdit mode.

**Listing 16.36: COEDIT.L1**

```
PROC coedit.l(table.a)
  LOCK table.a PFL
  IF RETVAL THEN          ; Lock was successful.
    COEDIT table.a
    UNLOCK table.a PFL   ; Let the implicit automatic lock take over.
  ENDIF
  RETURN RETVAL          ; True if table was placed; False if we could not lock.
ENDPROC
```

See the WaitPlus procedures for more examples of using CoEdit mode.

The COEDIT command will cause a script error if the table is write protected.

## COEDITKEY: Press [Alt F9]

```
COEDITKEY
```

The COEDITKEY command places all images currently on workspace into CoEdit mode. It has the same effect as pressing [Alt F9]. On a network, there is always the potential for conflict with another user who is already using a different form to CoEdit the table. The procedure above, called CoEdit.l(), tests the result of a COEDIT command.

See CoEditKey.l() and PickForm.l() in the WAITPLUS section for code that traps for multiuser table and form locking.

### KEYLOOKUP: Press [Alt K] Key Lookup Toggle

KEYLOOKUP

When adding or changing a record in a keyed table in CoEdit mode, the KEYLOOKUP command toggles between the current record and any existing record with conflicting key values. Thus you can use KEYLOOKUP to show the user the original record, and perhaps allow him or her to choose one to keep. There is a full discussion of key violation trapping and the use of KEYLOOKUP in the OkKey3.1 procedure in the WaitPlus section. If you issue KEYLOOKUP and there is no conflicting key, ERRORCODE is set to 56, but no run error occurs.

### LOCKKEY: Press [Alt L] to Toggle Record Lock Status

LOCKKEY

In CoEdit mode, the LOCKKEY command is equivalent to pressing Lock Toggle ([Alt L]) to lock or unlock the current record. LOCKKEY has no effect in any other mode. LOCKKEY attempts to lock an unlocked record or unlock a locked record. LOCKKEY, like LOCKRECORD, attempts to post newly created records to the table. If LOCKKEY cannot be executed successfully, an ERRORCODE() explaining the reason is sent.

LOCKKEY should be used sparingly because LOCKRECORD and UNLOCK-RECORD are more direct.

### LOCKRECORD: Explicitly Lock a Record

LOCKRECORD

Sets:

| | |
|---|---|
| RETVAL = True | If record can be locked. |
| RETVAL = False | If record cannot be locked because it is already locked by you, because it is locked by another user, or because a key violation exists. |

LOCKRECORD allows you to make an explicit attempt to have exclusive control of the current record in CoEdit mode. LOCKRECORD behaves differently in different cases.

- When CoEditing an existing record, a change to a single character locks the record automatically. One reason for issuing a LOCKRECORD is to find out if the record is already locked by someone else. If another user is already working on the record, LOCKRECORD's attempt sets RETVAL to False. If you already have locked the record, RETVAL is set to False and ERRORCODE() is set to 55 (record already locked by you). Otherwise, if no one else is using the record, the record is explicitly locked by your LOCKRECORD.

- If it is a new, unposted record, LOCKRECORD will attempt to post it. If the table is keyed and the posting is successful, the record flies away to its proper place in the file and the cursor stays with the record. If unsuccessful, a key conflict occurs. When a key conflict exists, you can toggle between the new record and the existing record with the same key by pressing [Alt K], KeyLookup. When you find the record you want to keep, issuing LOCKRECORD keeps the current record and throws the other one away.

See OkKey3.1() in the WAITPLUS section for a detailed discussion.

The next example lets users update nonkey fields of existing records in TableView. It prompts the user to press [F9] to edit the current record, and creates a duplicate of the existing record's values with COPYTOARRAY. This memory copy can be used to compare the edited record with the original.

The code, though somewhat rudimentary, should give you an idea of the effort that should be taken to ensure that no one else is editing the record that the user wants to select. To make it more robust, code should be added to check for table access, Zoom, and FieldView problems.

**Listing 16.37: LOCKRECO.L1**

```
COEDIT "Customer"
WHILE TRUE
  IMAGERIGHTS READONLY   ; Don't let them change anything until [F9].
  WAIT TABLE
    PROMPT "Viewing "+STRVAL(RECORDS(TABLE()) + " in the " + TABLE() + " table",
           "[Esc]-when done, [F9]-Update current record"
  UNTIL "Esc", "F9", "Dos", "DosBig", "Zoom"
  SWITCH
    CASE RETVAL="Esc" :
      DO_IT!   ; end the edit
      CLEARIMAGE
      RETURN
    CASE  RETVAL="Zoom":
      Zoom.l()    ; See ZOOM command for discussion of Zoom.l()
    CASE  RETVAL="F9": ; Let user update this record.
      LOCKRECORD        ; Test to see if they can lock the record.
      IF NOT RETVAL AND ERRORCODE()<>55 THEN
        ; Errorcode 55 is that the record is already locked by you.
        MESSAGE "Record is currently locked by ",ERRORUSER(),"." ;Another user.
        BEEP
        SLEEP 2000
        LOOP       ; Back to the WAIT TABLE.
      ENDIF
      COPYTOARRAY oldrecord.r  ; Perhaps you'll want to compare it against the changes.
```

```
WHILE TRUE
    IMAGERIGHTS UPDATE ; Limit user to changing non-key fields.
    WAIT RECORD
        PROMPT "Update this record and press [F2] when done",
               "or [Esc] to cancel changes to record"
        UNTIL "F2","Esc","Dos","DosBig"
    SWITCH
        CASE RETVAL="F2":
            ; If necessary, perform errorchecking here for fields that
            ; must be filled out, etc. Perhaps compare record with
            ; the elements of the oldrecord.r array to see if there
            ; were any changes.  If all was okay then go on to:
            UNLOCKRECORD ; Post the record to the table.
            ; Since this is an update only routine, we don't have to concern
            ; ourselves with key violation conflicts, and the record will not
            ; fly away. Otherwise we might need to do additional checking.
            QUITLOOP
        CASE RETVAL="Esc":
            IMAGERIGHTS
            COPYFROMARRAY oldrecord.r
            ; Used the COPYFROMARRAY rather than UNDO because if nothing was changed
            ; on this record, the UNDO might affect a previously changed record.
            QUITLOOP
    ENDSWITCH
    ENDWHILE
    IMAGERIGHTS  ; reset to default imagerights
ENDSWITCH
ENDWHILE
```

### UNLOCKRECORD: Explicitly Attempt to Unlock the Current Record

```
UNLOCKRECORD
```

Sets:

| | |
|---|---|
| RETVAL = True | If record was unlocked and posted to table. |
| RETVAL = False | If record was not a new record and not already locked; or if unlocking the record resulted in a key conflict. |

UNLOCKRECORD explicitly attempts to unlock and post a record in CoEdit mode. If the table is keyed, the record moves to the position dictated by the key field values; otherwise, it remains where it is. If, for example, you are modifying the key of an existing record and issue UNLOCKRECORD, the record flies away to its appropriate position in the table. In any event, if the UNLOCKRECORD was successful, the cursor remains on the record number that was current when the UNLOCKRECORD command was issued; it does not stay with the record that flew away. Care should be taken if the UNLOCKRECORD fails because of a key conflict—a subsequent UNLOCKRECORD will post the new record, overwriting the existing keyed record. See the example under the LOCKRECORD command as well as the Nextnumber.v() and OkKey3.1() procedures in the WaitPlus section.

## 16.4.4 Workspace Information

Though this section discusses functions and commands that deal mainly with images on the workspace, some of these language elements have uses in Form, Report, and Script modes.

### 16.4.4.1 Table Oriented

### TABLE: What Is the Name of the Current Table?

```
TABLE()
```

Returns:

    A String    The name of the current table on the workspace. If the table is from another directory on the same drive, the path is included. If the table is from another drive, both the drive and path are included.

TABLE() returns the name of the table for the current image as it would be displayed on the top of the menu area (e.g., Viewing "Customer" table). It is particularly useful when writing generic table handling routines. For example, to find the number of fields in the current table, you might use:

```
fields.n = NFIELDS( TABLE() )
```

To get the maximum value in the current numeric field of a table, use:

```
maxval.v = CMAX( TABLE(), FIELD() )
```

where maxval.v is a number, dollar amount, or the word "Error". Note that only the first character of the string TABLE() returns is uppercase; all remaining characters are lowercase. The examples below show the effect of the current directory on the returned value of the TABLE function.

**Listing 16.38: TABLE.L1**

```
SETDIR("C:\\paradox3\\sample\\")    ; Changes directory to C:\Paradox3\Sample.
VIEW "Customer"
MESSAGE "Viewing ",TABLE()
SLEEP 2000
; TABLE() would return "Customer".

SETDIR("C:\\")                      ; Change to the root directory.
VIEW "C:\\Paradox3\\Sample\\Customer"
```

```
MESSAGE "Viewing ",TABLE()
SLEEP 2000
; TABLE() would return "Paradox3\\sample\\customer".
; Note that the C:\ is truncated because it is the current drive.

SETDIR("C:\\Paradox3\\")
VIEW "C:\\Paradox3\\Sample\\Customer"
MESSAGE "Viewing ",TABLE()
SLEEP 2000
; TABLE() would return "Sample\\customer".
; Note that the C:\Paradox3\ is truncated because it is part of the
; current path.

;Now for the tricky part:

SETDIR("C:\\Paradox3\\Samples\\")  ; set a directory on drive C:
SETDIR("D:\\Test\\")               ; now move to drive D:
VIEW "C:\\Paradox3\\Samples\\Customer"
MESSAGE "Viewing ",TABLE()
SLEEP 2000
; TABLE() would return "C:customer"
; Note that the path is truncated because it is the current directory on
; the C drive.
```

### NIMAGERECORDS: How Many Records Does the Current Image Contain?

```
NIMAGERECORDS ()
```

Returns:

| | |
|---|---|
| A Number | In a linked detail table, NIMAGERECORDS returns the number of records contained for the restricted view. Otherwise, it returns the number of records in the entire table. |
| Script Error | If no images are on the workspace. |

In TableView and in the master table of a multitable form, NIMAGERECORDS() is equivalent to NRECORDS(TABLE()). In a detail table of a multitable form, NIMAGERECORDS() performs a count of the number of detail records related to the current master record (the "restricted" view of the table). NIMAGERECORDS disregards any {Image} {Tablesize} setting for the image.

```
Imagerecords.n = NIMAGERECORDS()
```

is equivalent to

```
End
Imagerecords.n = RECNO()
```

The next listing illustrates a simple way of showing the total number of records applicable to a table and a method of moving between a master and a detail table. The code assumes that there are some records in the master table (otherwise issuing a PICKFORM would cause a script error).

**Listing 16.39: NIMAGERE.L1**

```
VIEW "Customer"    ; From the Paradox sample tables disk.
PICKFORM 3         ; Form with BookOrd as an embedded table.
WHILE TRUE
  IF LINKTYPE() = "None" THEN    ; The master customer table.
    WAIT TABLE
      PROMPT "Viewing "+TABLE()+". "+STRVAL(NIMAGERECORDS())+" records on file",
             "Press [F4] for detail records, or [F2] to quit"
    UNTIL "F2", "F4", "Dos", "DosBig"
  ELSE    ; Must be the embedded table.
    WAIT TABLE
      PROMPT "Viewing "+TABLE()+". "+STRVAL(NIMAGERECORDS())+" detail records on file",
             "Press [F3] for Master records, or [F2] to quit"
    UNTIL "F2", "F3", "Dos", "DosBig"
  ENDIF
  SWITCH
    CASE RETVAL="F2":
      CLEARALL
      QUITLOOP
    CASE RETVAL="F3":
      UPIMAGE
    CASE RETVAL="F4":
      DOWNIMAGE
    OTHERWISE:    ; Must be [Ctrl O] or [Alt O].
      BEEP
  ENDSWITCH
ENDWHILE
```

### 16.4.4.2 Record Oriented

The [#] symbol and the RECNO() function both return information about the record number in display images. Before Paradox3, [#] and RECNO() were interchangeable; this is no longer so. Also, keep in mind that in a network environment, record numbers are fleeting. As other users add and delete records, record numbers shift to reflect the changes.

### [#]: What Are the Contents of the Record Number Field?

```
[#]
```

In Paradox3, [#] returns the current value of the record number field. In a Display image, [#] returns the absolute record number—that is, the position of the record in TableView. If used in a Query image, [#] returns a string with the contents of the leftmost query column, possibly "", "Insert," "Delete," "Find," or "Set." If you need to know the row number for the current query line, use ROWNO() or RECNO().

### RECNO: What Is the Relative Record Number?

```
RECNO ( )
```

Returns:

A Number    The record number that the cursor is sitting on with relation to any possible restricted view in effect.

In TableView, RECNO() and [#] return the same value. In a query image, RECNO() returns the row of the query. In a detail table, RECNO() returns the relative record number—that is, the number of the record in the restricted view of the table related to the current master record. See GotoMenu.u in the WaitPlus code for an example that uses RECNO() to let the user move forward or backward in the current image.

### SETRECORDPOSITION: Scroll a Specified Record to a Specified Row in a Multirecord Display Image

```
SETRECORDPOSITION Number Row
```

Number    Record number of the record to position relative to the other records in the image; the value returned by RECNO() for the record. Its minimum value is 1; its maximum, NIMAGERE-CORDS().
Row    Number of the row on the form to scroll the record to. Can be from 1 to NROWS().

In its description of SETRECORDPOSITION, the PAL 3.0 User's Guide states that ROW should be 0 for the first row. This is incorrect; the correct value for the first row is 1. To scroll the last record in the image to the first row (showing only the last record):

```
SETRECORDPOSITION NIMAGERRECORDS( ) 1
```

In a multirecord form, you could use:

```
SETRECORDPOSITION RECNO( ) 1
```

to bring the current record to the top line of the multirecord view.

In the initial release of Paradox3, there was a problem with WAIT RECORD in a multirecord form. The cursor could be inadvertently moved UP to records above it, confusing the display as it went along. The temporary solution was to force the record to line 1 of the form, as just described. Fortunately this was fixed in version 3.01.

### 16.4.4.3 Field Oriented

### FIELD: What Is the Name of the Current Field?

```
FIELD()
```

Returns:

A String     The name of the current field.

The FIELD function returns the structural name of the current field in the current image. FIELD works in both Query and Display images, in Main, Edit, CoEdit, DataEntry, Create, Restructure, and Password modes. If no images are present, or if Paradox is in any other mode, FIELD() causes a script error. If the cursor is in the record number column of a display image, or in the leftmost column of a query image, FIELD() returns "#."

The FIELD name corresponds to the name displayed at the top of the current column in TableView. The value it returns reflects the capitalization present in the structural definition. Thus if your cursor is on a field whose name is [Cust ID#] and you have code that says:

```
IF FIELD()="CUST ID#" THEN
  ; do something
ENDIF
```

The IF condition will not be True, because FIELD() returns "Cust ID#," not "CUST ID#." If you find it difficult to remember the exact case of the field names, try:

```
IF LOWER(FIELD()) ="cust id#" then
  ; do something
ENDIF
```

### ISVALID: Can You Move the Cursor off This Field?

```
ISVALID ()
```

Returns:

| | |
|---|---|
| True | If the current field passes the validity checks in effect for the field or if the system mode is not Edit, CoEdit, or DataEntry. |
| False | If the field will not pass the ValChecks and consequently the cursor cannot leave the field. |

The ISVALID function works in tandem with ValChecks in the Edit, CoEdit, or DataEntry modes. ValChecks are restrictions on what data may currently be entered—they do not place restrictions on data already in a table. There are two types of ValChecks:

1. Those that you *explicitly* place, such as {HighValue} and {TableLookup}
2. Those that Paradox places *implicitly* in date and short number fields that control whether a value will be accepted

Contrary to its name, the ISVALID() function doesn't necessarily tell you if the current field will pass the validity checks—it simply identifies whether or not the cursor can leave the current field.

This is an important distinction. Here's a small test that first requires you to define a SETKEY for [Shift F1] to display whether the data is valid (a SETKEY is necessary because you can't even bring up the PAL menu if the data is invalid):

```
SETKEY "F11" Return ISVALID()
```

Create a one-field table called "List"; enter the following dates and press [DO-IT!].

```
Viewing List table: Record 1 of 2

LIST────────Date──────
    1 │   3/21/89     │
    2 │   4/22/89     │
```

By definition, with no ValChecks in place, pressing [Shift F1] always returns True. After the data has been entered, go into Edit mode and add a {HighValue} ValCheck of 1/1/66.

Value:   1/1/66
Enter the highest acceptable value for this field.

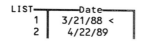

Testing ISVALID on both entries using [Shift F1] returns True. You can still move the cursor through all the records in the file. However, if you then attempt to add a new record or change any existing field, for example, from 3/21/89 to 3/21/88, you will not be allowed to leave the field, because the changed or added data in the current field is invalid.

Editing List table: Record 1 of 2                              Edit

```
LIST┬──────Date──────┐
   1 │   3/21/88  <   │
   2 │   4/22/89      │
```

                        Value no greater than 1/01/66 is expected.

Thus ISVALID() should be thought of more as a function called "CanCursorBe-Moved()". The only two things that will trigger Paradox to take a close look at the actual data in a field are

1.  making any change to the field, and
2.  going into FieldView.

The next example tests for invalid data via a SCAN.

**Listing 16.40: ISVALID.L1**

```
COEDIT "Invoices"
MOVETO [Customer Id#]
SCAN
  FIELDVIEW  ; Forces the ISVALID function to sit up and take notice.
  ENTER      ; Ends fieldview.
  IF NOT ISVALID() THEN
    ; Do something here, realizing that the scan will not be allowed to
    ; continue until the discrepancy is fixed. Perhaps:
    ; PRINT [], " is not valid for record ", RECNO(),"\n" ; Print the error.
    ; UNDO  ; Allows you to move on to the next record.
  ENDIF
ENDSCAN
```

**The Trouble with Dates**    Note that unless there is a {LowValue} or {HighValue} in effect on a date field, it is difficult to get an invalid date, unless the date doesn't exist. That is, a partial date is generally valid and ISVALID returns True. Further testing indicates that partial dates can cause other problems. To demonstrate this, assign another SETKEY:

```
SETKEY "F12" RETURN []
```

Edit the "List" table. Move to a new record and type in a 1. Press [Shift F2] and you'll see that the date returned (for no apparent reason) is 1/1/1070. Press [Shift F1] and ISVALID returns False. However, if you add a slash (your current field value is "1/" instead of the "1"), ISVALID() returns True. For this reason, always place a reasonable value for a {LowValue} ValCheck on a date field. Then, if a user inadvertently types 6/1/8 instead of 6/1/89, Paradox will complain about the attempt to enter 6/1/1908, as 6/1/8 is interpreted.

You can also use FIELDSTR() to evaluate incomplete fields for dates.

**Listing 16.41: ISVALID.L2**

```
PROC iscompletedate.l()
  RETURN DATEVAL( FIELDSTR() ) <> "Error"
ENDPROC
```

The procedure first converts the current field entry to a string, and then sees if a DATEVAL() of the string is a real date. The procedure returns a True if it is O.K., or a False if an invalid or incomplete string is used. See FIELDSTR for some additional information.

### FIELDTYPE: What is the Structural Type of the Current Field?

```
FIELDTYPE ()
```

Returns:

| | |
|---|---|
| A String | The structural type of the current field. |
| "An" | A is an alpha, n is the width of the field. |
| "N" | Number. |
| "$" | Dollar. |
| "D" | Date. |
| "S" | Short number. |

FIELDTYPE returns a string denoting the structural type of the current field. As of this writing, it does not report on the key field status. Note that it does not report on the current field value in which the type can be identified with TYPE([]). Because FIELDTYPE() does not return a key field status, to get the complete structural type for the CURRENT field in Main or CoEdit mode, use the following code:

**Listing 16.42: FIELDTYP.L1**

```
PROC fieldstruct.a ()
  ; RETURNS the field type as it appears in the structure table
  ; complete with an asterisk denoting key field if appropriate.
  ; The word "Error" if not in CoEdit or Main Mode.
  PRIVATE type.a

  ; This proc will not work properly in Edit mode because any changes
  ; to the table will immediately flag the primary index as obsolete
  ; thereby setting NKEYFIELDS() to zero.

  IF SYSMODE() <> "CoEdit" OR SYSMODE() <> "Main" THEN
    RETURN "Error"
  ENDIF
  ; On the other hand, you could modify the code to include Edit mode issue an
  ; EDITLOG INDEX, which would bring the index up to date and let the
  ; rest of the proc work normally.  The procedure would be relatively
  ; useless in DataEntry mode becasue it would return the structure of the
  ; Entry table which is always unkeyed.

  ; Let's get the FIELDTYPE()  "An","S","D","N", or "$"

  type.a=FIELDTYPE()

  ; Now see if the current field number is equal to or less than the
  ; number of key fields in the table.  If so, it must be a key.

  IF FIELDNO(FIELD(), TABLE()) <= NKEYFIELDS(TABLE()) THEN
    type.a = type.a +"*"        ; add the "*" to the end of the string
  ENDIF
  RETURN type.a
ENDPROC
```

If the cursor is on the [Customer ID] field of the sample "Customer" table, a = fieldstruct.a() would set a = "N*".

## FIELDSTR: What Are the Contents of the Current Field?

```
FIELDSTR ()
```

Returns:

A String     Containing the contents of the current field, even if the field is only partially filled in.

The FIELDSTR function always returns a string, regardless of a field's type.

FIELDSTR() is most often used to determine the contents of partially filled fields and is especially useful in keystroke level procedures designed for use with the Data Entry Toolkit. For example, a keystroke procedure might automatically leave the field when it is complete. As described in ISVALID above, determining when a field is complete isn't always straightforward. A safe method of checking valid dates within a keystroke procedure might include:

**Listing 16.43: FIELDSTR.L1**

```
IF FIELDSTR() <> "" AND DATEVAL(FIELDSTR()) = "Error" THEN
  ; Probably want to throw away the keypress that activated this code.
  TKaccept = False   ; Ignore the key pressed.
  TKmessage = "This field does not have a complete date."
  BEEP
ELSE
  ; Go on to do whatever is necessary-- the date value is complete.
ENDIF
```

This code prevents any attempt to move off the field before the date value is completely valid. If, for example, the user entered 5/9, the DATEVAL("5/9") would return "Error." ISVALID() alone should not be used, because 5/9 sets ISVALID() to True, though 5/89 sets ISVALID() to False.

### FIELDVIEW: Press [Alt F5] (Equivalent to [Ctrl F]) to Go Into FieldView

```
FIELDVIEW
```

The FIELDVIEW command simulates pressing the FieldView key. In a Paradox type-in prompt or a Display or Query image, FieldView lets the user move the cursor within existing characters.

While in FieldView, the cursor is an inverse-video, single-character block and several keys have special meanings. Insert mode can be toggled on and off with [Ins]. With insert mode on, the block contains a blinking cursor; in overtype mode, the blinking cursor disappears. In wordwrapped fields on forms, however, this distinction between insert vs. overtype does not show. While in FieldView, [CtrlRight] and [CtrlLeft] move one word at a time; [Home] moves to the first character; [End] to the last character. If the cursor is in a Display image, you need to issue the Enter command to end field view; however, if you are in a Paradox type-in prompt, simply issuing FIELDVIEW turns FieldView on and off.

A side effect of FieldView while CoEditing a table is that it locks the record and leaves the record locked even after exiting FieldView. This occurs even if you have restricted table use with the IMAGERIGHTS READONLY command.

The next example shows a procedure for removing characters from the left or right of a column of values. The procedure works as long as the column is not a "Date" type.

Listing 16.44: FIELDVIE.L1

```
PROC trimcolumn.l(table.a, field.a, characters.n, leftright.a)
  ; table.a       ; Name of table.
  ; field.a       ; Name of field to trim.
  ; characters,n  ; Number of characters to trim.
  ; leftright.a   ; "Right" or "Left", trim from right or left of the value.
  ; RETURNS    True if table could be locked, False otherwise.

  PRIVATE n

  ; Check to see if we can lock the table to make the global changes.
  LOCK table.a fl
  IF NOT RETVAL THEN  ; Someone is using the table.
    RETURN FALSE
  ENDIF
  EDIT table.a
  UNLOCK table.a fl                      ; Let implicit EDIT full lock take over.
  ; We could have used CoEdit, but changes to the key fields could present
  ; problems: To fly away and they might get processed more than once if
  ; changing a record's key moves it down in the file.
  MOVETO FIELD field.a                   ; Move to the specified field.
  SWITCH
    CASE SEARCH(leftright.a,"Right")=1: ; Makes "RIGHT" or "RiGHt" etc ok.
      SCAN FOR NOT ISBLANK([])
        FOR n FROM 1 TO characters.n    ; Extra backspaces will be ignored.
          BACKSPACE
        ENDFOR
      ENDSCAN
    OTHERWISE:                           ; Must be a lefthand trim.
      SCAN FOR NOT ISBLANK([])
        FIELDVIEW                        ; Go into fieldview.
        HOME                             ; Move to first character of the field.
        FOR n FROM 1 TO characters.n
          DEL                            ; Remove current character,
                                         ; extra DEL's are ignored.
        ENDFOR
        ENTER                            ; Get out of fieldview.
      ENDSCAN
  ENDSWITCH
  DO_IT!
  RETURN TRUE
ENDPROC
```

```
; Typical use might be to remove the last five digits from a column
; of values that all have extended zipcodes, to get to the main Zip Code.

l = trimcolumn.l("Customer","Extended Zipcode",5,"Right")

; Another approach would have been to use substring calculations, but this proc
; will work on numbers as well as alphanumeric strings and is meant to demonstrate
; using the Paradox workspace for maximum flexibility.
```

See examples of the WAIT commands for other instances in which FIELDVIEW issues must be considered and dealt with.

### ISFIELDVIEW: Is the Cursor Currently in FieldView?

```
ISFIELDVIEW ()
```

Returns:

| | |
|---|---|
| True | Cursor is currently in field view in a field or type-in prompt. |
| False | Not in FieldView, or in a system mode that is inappropriate for FieldView. |

**Listing 16.45: ISFIELDV.L1**

```
;To explicitly place a user into fieldview:

IF NOT ISFIELDVIEW() THEN
   FIELDVIEW  ; Place user into fieldview.
ENDIF

;To make sure user is not in fieldview:

IF ISFIELDVIEW() THEN
   ENTER       ; End the current fieldview.
ENDIF
```

Before version 3.01, ISFIELDVIEW() always returned False with a Paradox type-in prompt, regardless of current FieldView status. See the VERSION() function for an example of FieldView.

### 16.4.4.4 Forms Oriented

### PICKFORM: Select a Form

```
PICKFORM Formname
```

Formname    The name of the form to use: "F," "1," −"14," or 1 to 14.

The PICKFORM command places the current table into FormView with a prescribed form. (See the related FORMKEY command.) Picking a form temporarily establishes it as the default form, and it remains the default form until the table is cleared from the workspace or another PICKFORM command is issued.

```
PICKFORM "3"
PICKFORM 3
PICKFORM "F"
```

Although it is the abbreviated menu command for {Image} {Pickform}, the

PICKFORM command in version 3.0 is noticeably slower than the menu command sequence. This was remedied in version 3.01.

A few notes about PICKFORM:

- PICKFORM "F" creates a standard form if none exists.
- The current table on the workspace must have at least one record to be viewed in a form; if the table is empty and in Main mode, a PICKFORM causes a script error.
- PICKFORM cannot be used within a form embedded in a master table.
- In any edit mode on a field with a {Required} ValCheck, you cannot pick a form while the field is empty.
- As of this writing, if you attempt to use a PICKFORM with a form that conflicts with a Formlock already placed by a master form on another workstation, a script error results.

The following procedure has three parameters: the name of the table to view, a form name, and the default view. In addition to using PICKFORM, it also performs a bit of error checking, returning a 1, 2, or 3 if an error was found, and a 0 if all went well.

**Listing 16.46: PICKFORM.L1**

```
; This proc limits the user to a WAIT table in a form (it will not
; let the user go into detail records).

PROC ViewMasterForm.n(table.a, form.v, view.a)
  ; table.a   ; Table name.
  ; form.v    ; Form number or "F".
  ; view.a    ; "Table" or "Form" for default initial view.
  ; RETURNS  0 If all went well.
  ;          1 If table already has a full lock placed on it, and you can't access it.
  ;          2 If insufficient password rights.
  ;          3 If empty table.

  LOCK table.a PFL     ; Check if anyone placed a full lock on this table.
  IF NOT RETVAL THEN
    BEEP
    MESSAGE "Table is locked by ",ERRORUSER()
    SLEEP 2000
    RETURN 1
  ENDIF
  IF NOT TABLERIGHTS(table.a, "ReadOnly") THEN
    UNLOCK table.a PFL  ; Release prevent full lock.
    BEEP
    MESSAGE "You have insufficient rights to view ", table.a
    SLEEP 2000
    RETURN 2
  ENDIF
  IF ISEMPTY(table.a) THEN
    UNLOCK table.a PFL  ; Release prevent full lock.
    BEEP
    MESSAGE "No records on file for ", table.a
```

```
    SLEEP 2000
    RETURN 3
  ENDIF
  VIEW table.a
  PICKFORM form.v
  IF UPPER (view.a) = "TABLE" THEN
    FORMKEY  ; Return to table mode, but form has been registered rather
             ; than PICKFORM form.v, because PICKFORM makes a disk read.
  ENDIF
  WHILE True
    WAIT TABLE
      "Viewing " + TABLE() + " no changes permitted",
      "[Esc]-Done  [F7]-FormToggle"
    UNTIL  "F7", "Esc", "Dos", "DosBig", "Zoom"
    SWITCH
      CASE RETVAL = "Esc":
        CLEARIMAGE
        UNLOCK table.a PFL  ; Release prevent full lock.
        RETURN 0
      CASE RETVAL = "F7":
        FORMKEY  ; Toggle the form.
      CASE RETVAL = "Zoom":
        Zoom.l()  ; See ZOOM section for Zoom.l() procedure
    ENDSWITCH
  ENDWHILE
ENDPROC
```

The calling syntax might look like this:

```
n = ViewMasterForm.n("Products", "F", "Table")
```

### ISFORMVIEW: Is the Current Table in Form View?

```
ISFORMVIEW ()
```

Returns:

| | |
|---|---|
| True | If the current Display image is in FormView. |
| False | If the current Display image is in TableView or the current image is a Query image. |
| Script Error | If no images are present, or it is not in Edit, CoEdit, DataEntry, or Main mode. |

The ISFORMVIEW function works as a simple test that determines the current view. It works in a Display image only. The following example ensures that the user is in FormView:

### Listing 16.47: ISFORMVI.L1

```
IF NOT ISFORMVIEW() THEN
  FORMKEY
```

```
 ; Or perhaps specify a PICKFORM
ENDIF
```

### FORMKEY: Press [F7] to Toggle Form View

```
FORMKEY
```

The FORMKEY command is equivalent to pressing [F7], the form toggle key, which toggles between the table view and the "preferred" form. Paradox automatically uses the standard form ("F") as its preferred form unless another has been so designated with PICKFORM or {Image} {PickForm}. If the standard form does not exist, it is created. If a different form has been chosen in the current session, FORMKEY uses that form until another form is chosen, or until the table is cleared from the workspace. When a form is chosen and the {Image} {KeepSet} command is used, the chosen form becomes the preferred form.

As a reminder, FORMKEY cannot be used on an empty table in Main mode, because there are no records to view. FORMKEY is much faster than PICKFORM, which often performs a disk read. Keep in mind that unless you are in a multitable form, every time you move from one image to another on the workspace, you wind up in TableView. If you want to guarantee that you can move back to a table in the proper view, you'll probably want to save the current form state with something like:

```
wasformview.l = ISFORMVIEW()
```

before moving to another table on the workspace. When you return to the table, you can test the wasformview.l variable and restore the previous form status with:

```
IF wasformview.l THEN
  FormKey
ENDIF
```

See examples of FORMKEY in the listings for the WAIT and PICKFORM commands, as well as in the WaitPlus.v and NextNumber.v procedures in the WAITPLUS chapter.

### FORM: What Is the Name of the Current Form?

```
FORM ()
```

Returns:

| | |
|---|---|
| A String | The number of the form currently in use. |
| "F" | Standard form. |

"1" to "14"     Custom form.
"None"          Not in FormView.

The FORM function returns a string containing the letter or number of the current form. The following uses FORM in a procedure that returns the number of tables controlled by the current form.

**Listing 16.48: FORM.L1**

```
PROC tablecount.v ()
  ; RETURNS the number of tables controlled by the current form or table view
  ; including the master table.  If the table is currently Link-Locked, the word
  ; "Error" is returned.  If in a detail form, the proc will always return 1.

  PRIVATE embed.r  ; Array of embedded tables.

  IF NOT ISFORMVIEW() THEN
    IF NOT ISLINKLOCKED() THEN  ; Must be a table view.
      RETURN 1
    ELSE
      RETURN "Error" ; Currently link locked, cannot determine the current form.
    ENDIF
  ELSE
    ; Now get the number of detail tables, if any, and add 1 to the count.
    FORMTABLES TABLE() FORM() embed.r
    RETURN ARRAYSIZE( embed.r ) + 1
  ENDIF
ENDPROC

This can be used in the following manner:


v = tablecount.v () ; Get the number of tables controlled by the current form.

IF v = "Error" THEN
  MESSAGE "Table is link-locked, cannot determine control. Press any key."
ELSE
  form.a = "Form " + FORM()     ; get the form name
  IF form.a = "Form None" THEN
      form.a= "TableView"  ; for the message to follow
  ENDIF
  MESSAGE TABLE(), " ", form.a, " controls ", v, " table(s). Press any key."
ENDIF

n=GETCHAR()

; might display :
; "Customer Form 3 controls 3 tables(s).  Press any key."
```

## FORMTABLES: Create an Array of Tables Corresponding to a Multitable Form

```
FORMTABLES TableName FormName ArrayName
```

Tablename     Name of table as a string.
Formname      Name of form as a string.

ArrayName    Name of array to be created and filled with names of tables embedded in the form.

Introduced in Paradox3, FORMTABLES and its companion REPORTTABLES were designed to provide information about the names of the embedded tables associated with a form or a report. These commands could almost be functions, for they not only set RETVAL but also construct an array if appropriate. The size of the array depends on the number of embedded tables and can be determined with the ARRAYSIZE function. A script error occurs if either the table or the form does not exist or cannot be accessed.

The FORMTABLES command can be used to determine if all the *tables* necessary for a form are available. Unfortunately, there is no easy way to determine if all the *forms* necessary for any embedded tables are available. (With considerable effort, you can go into form design and try to extract the embedded form names.)

The next listing addresses a problem with restructuring tables that contain multitable forms and reports. When you restructure a table, Paradox opens each of the forms and reports for the table and tries to update them. If there are report lookup or embedded form tables involved and for some reason they cannot be located, Paradox drops them from their respective forms and reports. If a lookup table is encrypted and the password is not available, for all intents and purposes the table "cannot be found," and the restructuring system proceeds as if the table were missing and deletes the tables from the forms and reports.

This procedure returns the name of the first table required, but unavailable, to restructure. If all tables are available, the procedure returns a blank string. Though the code might appear odd at first glance, it is rather straightforward—the loops simply shorten the amount of code needed.

**Listing 16.49: FORMTABL.L1**

```
PROC GetMissingLookup.a(table.a)
   ; table.a   ; Name of table to restructure.
   ; RETURNS   "" If all lookup tables are found or the name of the
   ;              first table that you don't have access to.

   PRIVATE
    object.r,    ; Array of object types.
    embedded.r,  ; Array of lookup or embedded tables.
    n1, n2, n3   ; Counters.

   IF NOT ISTABLE(table.a) OR NOT TABLERIGHTS(table.a, "All") THEN
     ; Master table is not available.
     RETURN table.a
   ENDIF
   MESSAGE "Working....."

   ; Set up an array of extension prefixes.
   ARRAY object.r [2]
        object.r [1] = "R"    ; For reports.
        object.r [2] = "F"    ; For forms.
```

```
; Now loop through each object type, and determine if there is a file
; with a valid form or report name.  If so, see if there are any embedded
; or lookup tables, and if so, check the tablerights for each one.

FOR n1 FROM 1 to 2              ; One pass for reports, one pass for forms.
  FOR n2 FROM 0 to 14           ; One pass for each potential object number.
    IF n2 = 0 THEN
      number.a = ""             ; No number, so "F" and "R" will work.
    ELSE
      number.a = strval(n1)     ; e.g. "1"
    ENDIF
    ; Now see if there is an object that needs checking.
    IF ISFILE( table.a + "." + object.r [n1] + number.a ) THEN
      RETVAL = False            ; Initialize retval.
      ; Now prepare part of a message about the table currently being checked.
      msg.a= "Checking " + table.a + "." + object.r[n1] + number.a
      ; Get embedded or lookup tables with the syntax appropriate to the loop counters.
      SWITCH
        CASE n1 = 1  and n2 = 0 :
          REPORTTABLES table.a "R" embedded.r
        CASE n1 = 1 :
          REPORTTABLES table.a number.a embedded.r
        CASE n1 = 2 and n2 = 0 :    ; Must already be into Forms.
          FORMTABLES table.a "F" embedded.r
        CASE n1 = 2 :
          FORMTABLES table.a number.a embedded.r
      ENDSWITCH
      IF RETVAL THEN   ; There were embedded or lookup tables found.
        ; Lets check the arrays for rights to the lookups.
        FOR n3 FROM 1 to ARRAYSIZE(embedded.r)
          ; Display the entire message..
          MESSAGE msg.a , ": " , embedded.r [n3]
          ; Next see if we have master rights to the tables involved.
          RETVAL = (ISTABLE(embedded.r [n3]) and
                      TABLERIGHTS(embedded.r[n3],"All"))
          IF NOT RETVAL THEN
            RETURN embedded.r [n3] ; Name of table not found or encrypted.
          ENDIF
        ENDFOR
      ENDIF
    ENDIF
  ENDFOR
 ENDFOR
 RETURN ""     ; Did not have a problem with any embedded tables.
ENDPROC


; A typical use of the procedure could look like:

table.a = "Invoices"
a = GetMissingLookup.a(table.a)
IF a <> "" THEN   ; Proc found a table it couldn't locate or get rights to.
  MESSAGE "Could not find, or had less than master rights FOR ", a
  n = GETCHAR()
ELSE                ; It's okay to restructure the table.
  MENU {Modify} {Restructure} SELECT table.a
  IF MENUCHOICE() = "Cancel" THEN   ; if problems or keyviol already exist,
    {Ok}                            ; overwrite them.
```

```
ENDIF
  DO_IT!                               ; Pack the table, don't change the structure.
  CLEARIMAGE                           ; Remove the image.
ENDIF
```

See the ISMULTIFORM and FORM for additional examples of FORMTABLES.

## ISMULTIFORM: Does a Form Use Embedded Tables?

```
ISMULTIFORM (Tablename, Formname)
```

Tablename    Name of table (string).

Formname    Name of form as string "F," "1"–"14," or an integer from 1 to 14.

Returns:

True    If the form uses embedded tables.

False    If the form uses only one table.

Script error    If the table does not exist, or the user cannot access it because of limited rights, or if a Full Lock has been placed on it.

The next procedure creates a list of tables embedded in a form:

**Listing 16.50: ISMULTIF.L1**

```
PROC ListMultiForm.l ( table.a, form.a )
  ; table.a     ; Name of table.
  ; form.a      ; Name of form  "F" or "1" - "14".
  ; RETURNS     ; True if list was prepared, False if not a multi-form.

  PRIVATE embed.r  ; Array of embedded tables.
  IF NOT ISMULTIFORM (table.a, form.a) THEN  ; No sense in going any further.
    RETURN FALSE
  ENDIF

  CREATE "List"      ; Create a new list table.
  "Type":"A12",
  "Table":"A40"

  EDIT "List"  ; Since table is empty, we are automatically in the [Type] field.

  ; Place the first record as a master record.
  [Type] = "Form " + STRVAL(form.a) ; STRVAL in case form.a entered as a number.

  [Table]= table.a

  ; Now we can get the embedded tables.
```

```
FORMTABLES table.a form.a embed.r
; We are guaranteed that embed.r will be assigned because we've already
; established that it is a multiform.
FOR n FROM 1 TO ARRAYSIZE (embed.r)
  DOWN  ; appends new record
  [Type] = "Embedded #" + STRVAL(n)   ; e.g. Embedded #1
  [Table] = embed.r [n]
ENDFOR
DO_IT!
RETURN TRUE
ENDPROC
```

```
l = ListMultiForm.l ("\\Paradox3\\Toolkit\\Invoice", "F")
```

would create the following table:

**Listing 16.51: ISMULTIF.FG1**

```
Viewing List table: Record 4 of 4                                    Main

LIST         Type                          Table
      1    Form F            \Paradox3\Toolkit\Invoice
      2    Embedded #1       Carriers
      3    Embedded #2       Cust
      4    Embedded #3       Orders
```

## LINKTYPE: What Kind of Link is Currently in Effect?

```
LINKTYPE ()
```

Returns:

|  |  |
|---|---|
| A String | The type of link between the current detail table and the master table in a multitable form. |
| "1-1 Group" | A one-to-one relationship. |
| "1-M Group" | A one-to-many relationship. |
| "Group" | A many-to-one or many-to-many relationship. |
| "None" | The cursor is currently in the master table, or there is no link between the two tables, or the cursor is not in a multitable form. |

Also introduced with multitable forms in Paradox3, the LINKTYPE function can help you keep your code generic. For example, something as straightforward as the COPYFROMARRAY command does not work in a linked table because you cannot assign values to the linked keys. See WaitPlus's CopyFromArray3.u() procedure in WWPUTIL2.SC, which skirts the problem. Also see WWPCORE.SC for several examples that use LINKTYPE() to determine if actions are necessary or even possible.

Although the example of LINKTYPE on page 437 of the 3.0 PAL User's Guide has the right idea, there are a few typographical errors that can be confusing (F3 and F4 are reversed in the UNTIL clauses). We'll expand on the code fragment a bit to let the user browse through all the records in the "Customer" and "BookOrd" tables.

**Listing 16.52: LINKTYPE.L1**

```
VIEW "Customer"    ; From the sample tables.
PICKFORM 3         ; Form with BookOrd as an embedded table.
WHILE TRUE
  IF LINKTYPE() = "None" THEN
    WAIT TABLE
      PROMPT "Viewing "+TABLE(),
             "Press [F4] for detail records, or [F2] to quit"
    UNTIL "F2", "F4", "Dos", "DosBig"
  ELSE
    WAIT TABLE
      PROMPT "Viewing "+TABLE()+ " detail records",
             "Press [F3] for Master records, or [F2] to quit"
    UNTIL "F2", "F3", "Dos", "DosBig"
  ENDIF
  SWITCH
    CASE RETVAL="F2":
      CLEARALL
      QUITLOOP
    CASE RETVAL="F3":
      UPIMAGE
    CASE RETVAL="F4":
      DOWNIMAGE
    OTHERWISE:    ; Must be [Ctrl O] or [Alt O].
      BEEP
  ENDSWITCH
ENDWHILE
```

## ISLINKLOCKED: Is the Current Table Link Locked?

```
ISLINKLOCKED()
```

Returns:

| | |
|---|---|
| True | If the table is link-locked. |
| False | If the table is not link-locked. |
| Script Error | No images on workspace, or not in a display image. |

Link-locking is at the heart of Paradox's implementation of "referential integrity." A table becomes link-locked when any data is modified through a linked multitable form and then the user (or a PAL script) presses FormKey to toggle to TableView. All tables that are link-locked cannot be edited in tableview, effectively preventing changes to linking fields. Likewise they cannot be edited through any other form (partly because of the potential to place linking fields on that form). If (and only if) you allow editing through only one form at a time, "referential integrity" can be maintained by Paradox.

All unlinked tables may be changed, because they cannot affect the referential integrity of the links. When a table is link-locked, the user may not pick an alternate form to use. In its simplest form:

```
IF ISLINKLOCKED() THEN
  FormKey
ENDIF
```

seems to assure that the user has been placed into the appropriate form. However, if the embedded tables have been explicitly placed on the workspace, you must be careful when you toggle FORMKEY. The following example uses the "Customer" and "BookOrd" Paradox sample tables.

**Listing 16.53: ISLINKLO.L1**

```
VIEW "Bookord"
PICKFORM 1   ; A simple form used as the embedded form in Customer F3.
COEDIT "Customer"
PICKFORM 3   ; Multitable form with a linked BookOrd table.
FORMKEY      ; Back to Tableview in Customer.
UPIMAGE      ; Up to the BookOrd table, now link-locked.
IF ISLINKLOCKED() THEN
  FORMKEY    ; Now in Formview in BookOrd table, however, still link-locked.
ENDIF
```

The last three lines show the difficulty of always assuming that FormKey allows you to change the data. Although the user is now in FormView, all changes must be made through the "Customer" form. Additional code is needed to make sure that all changes are made in the Master form. This example points out the detail necessary when developing generic table handling routines.

### RESYNCKEY: Resynchronize the Images in a Multitable Form

```
RESYNCKEY
```

In a multitable form, RESYNCKEY ([Ctrl L]) updates the links between a master record and its details, changing the linking fields in the detail records to match the new links in the master and forcing a redisplay of the detail records. As of this writing, RESYNCKEY is documented in only the README file on the Paradox installation disk. From that file:

Resynchronizing records

If the linking fields of a master table are changed, the master and detail records are resynchronized when you move to another record or when you move to another image in the form. If you wish to resynchronize the records without moving to another record or another image, you may press the ReSyncKey [Ctrl][L]. Pressing this key will resynchronize the detail records for the new values in the linking fields of the master table.

You can issue a RESYNCKEY command to explicitly force the images to update whenever you feel it is necessary. Otherwise, images resynchronize when you post the current record, move off the record, or move to another table.

Some users are surprised that Paradox does not automatically resynchronize all records in embedded tables, much like a TableLookup validity check works with AllCorrespondingFields. This would be a simple matter if Paradox restricted you to a single field link between tables. Fortunately, Paradox allows many types of links, so a mechanism had to be developed that would prevent all conflicts.

Here's an example. Suppose you have a "Customer" table keyed on [Last name] and [First name] and a form with a one-to-many link to an embedded orders table. You have three customers: John Smith, Mary Smith, and John Jones. Each has orders on file. You want to change the master record for John Smith to Mary Jones.

1. If you change the first name field for John to Mary, the name would read Mary Smith when you attempt to leave the first name field. If Paradox were to resynchronize records automatically, a key conflict would occur before you could complete the change to the last name.
2. If Paradox automatically resynchronized all records after changing only the first name, all the detail records for John Smith would be merged with the records for Mary Smith, possibly with some detail records overwriting others. (This was remedied in Paradox 3.01, which does not allow any master record with detail records to be "absorbed" by another master record.)
3. When you change the last name to Jones, all of Mary Smith's records are changed to Mary Jones'.

You were trying to update only John Smith's records, but poor Mary Smith's records got caught in the crossfire.

This is why paradox does not update links on a field-by-field basis, but instead waits until you try to post the record or manually issue a ReSyncKey.

See the OkKey3.l() procedure in the WAITPLUS section for a use of RESYNCKEY to test for keyviolations in CoEdit mode.

## 16.4.5 Movement Keys

### 16.4.5.1 Workspace Cursor Movement

Cursor movement commands simulate keystrokes pressed in interactive Paradox. They are used to move through the Paradox environment under script control. This book is full of code that demonstrates the use of movement commands in all of the various Paradox modes. To repeat an earlier warning: There is no substitute for knowing what a specific key does in a specific circumstance. When in doubt, test.

Some cursor movement commands are

```
RIGHT
TAB
CTRLRIGHT
CTRLEND
LEFT
REVERSETAB
CTRLLEFT
CTRLHOME
UP
PGUP
CTRLPGUP
HOME
DOWN
PGDN
CTRLPGDN
END
```

### 16.4.5.2 Key Movement

If you use forms with multiple pages, you might want to replace PGDN with CtrlPgDn to move to the next record; otherwise, you wind up on the next page of the current record (if one exists). Note that the decision to use PGDN, PGUP, CTRLPGDN, CTRLPGUP, UP, or DOWN to move within existing records of a Display image can be replaced by a SKIP command, which moves the cursor forward or backward by a specified number of records. SKIP does not append any new records.

END moves the cursor to the last record in a table, the last row on a form, report, or script, the last auxiliary password, or the last Paradox menu choice. To append a new record to the bottom of a current table image while in Edit mode:

**Listing 16.54: END.L1**

```
END
IF ISFORMVIEW() THEN
  CTRLPGDN
ELSE
  DOWN
ENDIF
```

This is, of course, simplified. You should probably check to see whether the table is empty, and whether doing an end-down simply leaves a blank record. Also, keep in mind that you can add a new record with INS, which inserts a new record above the current record position. With keyed tables, records are automatically put in their proper place with Do_It!, or, in CoEdit mode, when moving off the record.

Error checking, often critical on networks, can at times seem to overly complicate a simple request. Here's another example of END, with full error checking in network use, that attempts to get the last value in a table's column:

**Listing 16.55: END.L2**

```
PROC GetLastValue.v(table.a, field.a)
  ; table.a   ; Table name.
  ; field.a   ; Field name.
  ; RETURNS   ; The value found or the logical value FALSE if the
  ;           ; table was not available, or if the table is empty
  ;           ; or has no values in the specified field.

  PRIVATE value.v
  LOCK table.a PFL            ; Prevent full lock.
  IF NOT retval THEN
    RETURN FALSE
  ENDIF
  ; Note the order of the conditions in the next IF statement:
  ; Paradox analyzes the statement from left to right.
  IF NOT ISTABLE(table.a) OR                ; Table doesn't exist.
    NOT TABLERIGHTS(table.a, "ReadOnly) OR   ; Insufficient rights.
     ISEMPTY(table.a) THEN                   ; No records found.
    UNLOCK table.a PFL                       ; Release the lock.
    RETURN FALSE
  ENDIF
  ; Possibly check for table access.
  VIEW table.a
  UNLOCK table.a PFL    ; Let implicit lock placed by View take over.
  MOVETO FIELD field.a
  END
  value.v = []
  CLEARIMAGE
  RETURN value.v
ENDPROC

; In a single user system, a simple way of calculating a next
; check number for a numeric key field might be:
```

```
; lastnumber.n = CMAX("CheckBk","Check#")

; But if the [Check#] field was Alphanumeric (e.g. "A000123") you could use:

lastnumber.v = LastValue.v("CheckBk","Check#")
IF lastnumber.v <> FALSE THEN  ; Note that we did not use NOT LASTNUMBER.V syntax.
  ; Place some code here that does some substring calculations to generate a new
  ; number string.
ENDIF

;Note that in multiuser situations, either technique is risky,
;because more than one user can be trying to evaluate the last number used.
;See the NextNumber.v procedure in the WAITPLUS section for another example.
```

### 16.4.5.3 Moving between Records/Locating Values

### SKIP: Try to Move Up or Down within a Table's Records

```
SKIP [Number]
```

> Number    Number of records to move.

The SKIP command, as mentioned above, is an often-overlooked, simple alternative to many different cursor movement commands. If the number that follows SKIP is positive, Paradox moves forward (down) that number of records; if it is negative, the cursor is moved backward (up) that number of records. If no number is specified, 1 is assumed. A script error occurs if SKIP 0 is used. The cursor always stays in the current field (like CtrlPgUp). Unlike cursor movement keys, however, SKIP cannot append a new record—it only moves within existing records.

SKIP sets EOT() to True if the SKIP attempted to move beyond the end of the table, and BOT() to True if it attempted to move above the first record of the table. If you attempt to move up beyond the first record, the cursor remains on the first record. Similarly, any attempt to move below the last record leaves the cursor on the last record.

See code fragments in the discussions of BOT() and EOT().

### ZOOM: Press [Ctrl Z]

```
ZOOM
```

The ZOOM command presents the user with a prompt that waits for a value to ZOOM for. If a value is typed in and [Enter] is pressed, Paradox moves to the first record that matches the specified value. Unlike LOCATE, a ZOOM does not set RETVAL. However, the user can specify ambiguous values with the pattern operators (.. and @).

PAL programmers often have a few problems with ZOOM because of the way Paradox interprets keystrokes pressed at the ZOOM type-in prompt. Here is an example of a simple WAIT TABLE that waits for the user to press "F7" and "Esc." Pressing [F7] toggles FormView, and [Esc] clears the table.

**Listing 16.56: ZOOM.L1**

```
VIEW "Customer"
PICKFORM 1
WHILE TRUE
  WAIT TABLE
    PROMPT "Viewing Customer table",
           "Press [F7] to toggle FormView, or [Esc] to quit"
  UNTIL  "F7", "Esc"
  SWITCH
    CASE RETVAL="F7":
      FORMKEY             ;-- toggle form view
    CASE RETVAL="Esc":
      CLEARIMAGE          ;-- remove the table from the workspace
      QUITLOOP            ;-- exit the loop
  ENDSWITCH
ENDWHILE
```

Though most keys work as expected, there are notable exceptions. If you press [F1] and are NOT in a field with tablelookup help, Paradox beeps as it should, because Paradox help is not normally available from within a script. Yet problems arise when ZOOM is used. If you press [Ctrl Z], a prompt appears at the top of the screen requesting a value or pattern to search for. Now the fun begins:

1. If you press [Esc] to exit the ZOOM prompt, you satisfy the WAIT UNTIL "Esc" condition, the table is cleared, and you exit the loop (clearly not what you wanted).
2. If you press [F1] while the ZOOM prompt is on-screen, you get Paradox help! In a script this is both unexpected and undesirable.
3. Even worse, if you press [Esc] to exit the Paradox help system, the [Esc] keypress satisfies the WAIT UNTIL condition and clears the table.
4. [Ctrl 0] and [Alt 0] are not disabled (when they really should be).

(Note: if this isn't nasty enough (since your table just got cleared out from under you), in version 2.0, clearing a table while the ZOOM prompt is up and then trying to escape from the ZOOM prompt (which is still on the screen) sends you directly out of Paradox and back to DOS. This was fixed in version 2.01.)

To keep the user from seeing interactive PARADOX help and to toally avoid ZOOM-related problems, we created a substitute procedure called ZOOM.l(). ZOOM.l traps for unwanted function keys and invalid ZOOMs, while allowing Fieldview. If a value is found, ZOOM.l returns True; if not, it returns False. (A value of True only indicates that you *may* have moved off the record). The procedure does not change the canvas. When the ZOOM prompt is displayed, one small side effect is that the current mode is displayed at the upper right of the screen. ZOOM.l could be expanded with a few PROMPT statements to clean this up. Our primary goal was to make the procedure as simple as possible, so it could be easily substituted for the ZOOM command.

**Listing 16.57: ZOOM.L2**

```
PROC Zoom.l()
  ; RETURNS True if match is found,
  ;         False if match not found or user presses [Esc].
  PRIVATE
  n,            ; Used by getchar().
  fieldview.l   ; Keeps track of fieldview status while in zoom prompt.

  IF NIMAGERECORDS() < 2 OR COLNO()=1 THEN
    ; You cannot zoom in the record# column, or in any case where there
    ; are less than 2 records present (as in an empty table, or a 1-1 Group,
    ; or a Many-1 group, or a single record table).
    BEEP
    RETURN False
  ENDIF

  ECHO NORMAL          ; Turn echo on so operator can see keypresses.
  ZOOM                 ; Presses the Zoom key.
  fieldview.l = False
  WHILE True
    n = GETCHAR()      ; Wait for operator's keypress.
    SWITCH
      CASE  n = -108 OR n = 6 :        ; [Alt F5] fieldview or [Ctrl F].

        KEYPRESS n                      ; Press the key.
        fieldview.l = NOT fieldview.l ; Fieldview is started/finished.

      CASE  n = -71 OR   ; Home      ; Accounts for possible FieldView while
            n = -75 OR   ; Left      ; in Zoom prompt.
            n = -77 OR   ; Right
            n = -79 OR   ; End
            n = -82 OR   ; Ins
            n = -83 :    ; Del
        KEYPRESS n                      ; Press the key.

      CASE n < 0 OR n = 15 :            ; Includes unwanted function keys & ^O.
        BEEP                            ; Beep on error.

      CASE fieldview.l AND  n = 13 :   ; User pressed [Enter] while in field view.
        ENTER                           ; End field view.
        fieldview.l = False

      CASE n = 13:                     ; User pressed [Enter].
        KEYPRESS n                      ; Press the key as if the user typed it.
        SWITCH
          CASE WINDOW() = "":          ; Match was found.
            ECHO OFF
            RETURN True
```

```
                CASE WINDOW() = "Match not found":
                   BEEP                    ; Signal user that match was not found.
                   SLEEP 1000              ; Let user see message.
                   ECHO OFF
                   RETURN False
                                   ; Any other window or message would keep us in loop
                                   ; e.g. out of range for a short number field.
                ENDSWITCH

             CASE n = 27:                  ; Pressed [Esc].
                Esc                        ; Get out of zoom with Esc.
                ECHO OFF
                RETURN False               ; keypress n. With RETVAL now set to
                                           ; False instead of "Esc", the "Esc"
                                           ; does not activate a WAIT's UNTIL condition.

             OTHERWISE:                    ; Any legitimate key.
                KEYPRESS n                 ; Press the user's key.
          ENDSWITCH
       ENDWHILE
ENDPROC
```

The following example shows how you could use ZOOM.l. A simple WAIT
TABLE traps for the ZOOM keypress in the UNTIL clause. The example also
avoids problems associated with [Ctrl 0] and [Alt 0] by trapping for them.

**Listing 16.58: ZOOM.L3**

```
VIEW "Customer"
PICKFORM 1
WHILE True
  WAIT TABLE
    PROMPT "Viewing Customer table",
           "Press [F7] to toggle FormView, or [Esc] to quit"
  UNTIL "Esc", "F7", "Dos", "DosBig", "Zoom"

  SWITCH
    CASE RETVAL = "Zoom":
      zoom.l()      ; Eliminates zoom related problems, see zoom.l2 for details.
    CASE RETVAL = "Dos" OR RETVAL = "DosBig" :   ;-- [Ctrl 0] and [Alt 0]
      BEEP          ; Don't want a mistyped character to send us out to DOS.
    CASE RETVAL = "F7":
      FORMKEY       ; Toggle form view.
    CASE RETVAL = "Esc":
      CLEARIMAGE        ; Remove the table from the workspace.
      QUITLOOP          ; Exit the loop.
  ENDSWITCH
ENDWHILE
```

## ZOOMNEXT: Press [Alt Z]

```
ZOOMNEXT
```

The ZOOMNEXT command is equivalent to pressing the ZoomNext key [Alt z] to
locate the next value in the table that matches a previously specified ZOOM

value. Although ZOOM always begins at the top of the table in its search for a matching value, ZOOMNEXT begins its search with the next record. If no ZOOM value has been specified for the field, ZOOMNEXT is ignored.

## LOCATE

```
LOCATE [NEXT] [PATTERN] FieldVal
```

| | |
|---|---|
| NEXT | Start search from the present record. |
| PATTERN | Wildcards @ and .. as in query syntax. |
| FieldVal | Single value to look for or a comma delimited list of values to look for beginning with the first n fields of the table: i.e., val1, val2, val3, valn for the first n fields. |

Returns:

| | |
|---|---|
| True | If value(s) was located. |
| False and EOT() = True | If value cannot be found. |

LOCATE "Smith"
  Locates the first occurrence of "Smith" in the current column.
LOCATE NEXT "Smith"
  Locates the next occurrence of a value starting with the current record. You will probably want to move down one record before using this feature (possibly using the SKIP command).
LOCATE PATTERN "Smi.."
  Locates the first occurrence of a value starting with "Smi". You can also use LOCATE NEXT PATTERN.
LOCATE 1234, "Smith", 1/1/89
  Locates the first record whose first three values match those specified. The field that the cursor is in is not significant.

- If a LOCATE is unsuccessful, the cursor does not move off the current record.
- LOCATE PATTERN cannot be used with a list of values.
- LOCATE NEXT starts with and includes the current record. To find the record beyond the current one, you should use the SKIP command to advance a record.
- If LOCATE is successful, RETVAL is set to True; if unsuccessful, RETVAL is set to False. This favors using LOCATE over ZOOM where possible. ZOOM does not alter RETVAL, so PAL cannot easily be told whether or not a ZOOM was successful.

The next example creates a list of tables in a given directory, while excluding Paradox's temporary tables.

**Listing 16.59: LOCATE.L1**

```
PROC ListDataTables.u(directory.a)
  ; directory.a  ; Name of any valid DOS directory.
 PRIVATE n, temp.r

 ; First make an array of the names of temporary Paradox tables.

 ARRAY temp.r[10]
 temp.r[1] = "List"
 temp.r[2] = "Family"
 temp.r[3] = "Changed"
 temp.r[4] = "Deleted"
 temp.r[5] = "Answer"
 temp.r[6] = "Problems"
 temp.r[7] = "Keyviol"
 temp.r[8] = "Struct"
 temp.r[9] = "Inserted"
 temp.r[10]= "Crosstab"
 ; Next, get a list of all those tables in the specified directory.
 MENU {Tools} {Info} {inventory} {Tables} SELECT directory.a
 ; We're now in the LIST table.
 ; Next delete any temporary table names from the list.
 MOVETO [name]
 EDITKEY  ; No possible conflict with other users because this is a LIST table.
 FOR n FROM 1 TO 10      ; Removes Paradox temporary tables from list.
   LOCATE temp.r[n]     ; Steps through the list of names starting at the top.
   IF RETVAL THEN
     DEL                 ; Remove the temp table from list.
   ENDIF
 ENDFOR
 DO_IT!
 ; Leaves us with a table on the workspace containing names of only active,
 ; permanent data tables, if any.
ENDPROC
```

Although the default syntax for LOCATE calls for an exact match for case, a user is often asked to supply a name, but not to have the name exactly correct. For instance, say you have a table whose keyfield is last name and the user is looking for the name "Smitty" and the value simply does not exist. A smart LOCATE would locate the original value, and if it does not exist, start looking for a pattern, broadening the pattern with each iteration:

**Listing 16.60: LOCATE.L2**

```
PROC DynamicLocate.n(value.v, searches.n, message.l)
    ; value.v    ; Value to search for, no patterns allowed.
    ; searches.n ; Number of search passes to make, each pass being one
                 ; character less specific than the last.
```

```
  ; message.l    ; True or False, should message display while searching?
  ; RETURNS      ; 0 if no value can be found, or a number of the pass that
  ;              ; found a match or partial match.
  PRIVATE n, len.

IF message.l THEN
  MESSAGE "Searching for ",value.v
ENDIF
LOCATE value.v
IF RETVAL THEN   ; Locate was successful.
  RETURN 1       ; Found it on first pass.
ENDIF
value.v = STRVAL(value.v) ; Just in case the value was a number or date.
len.n = LEN(value.v)      ; length of the string
FOR n FROM 1 TO MIN(len.n, searches.n)-1 ; Always leave at least one character.
  IF message.l THEN
    MESSAGE "Searching for ", value.v
  ENDIF
  LOCATE PATTERN value.v + ".." ; Makes it case insensitive.
  IF RETVAL THEN
    RETURN n + 1                     ; Because the straight locate was pass 1.
  ENDIF
  value.v=SUBSTR(value.v,1,LEN(value.v)-1)  ; Remove the last character.
  ; Now try again with one less trailing character.
ENDFOR
RETURN 0   ; If it got this far, no value was found.
ENDPROC
```

To demonstrate, let's assume that the cursor is in the [Last name] field of a "Clients" table:

```
CLIENTS────────Last Name────────Init─
     1  │   Jones <          │  S
     2  │   Smith            │  C
     3  │   Rossi            │  O
     3  │   Kocis            │  T
     3  │   Slick            │  T
```

If you issue:

```
n = DynamicLocate.n("Smothers",255,True)
```

it would first try to locate "Smothers", then failing that, it would try to locate patterns:

Smothers..
Smother..
Smothe..
Smoth..
Smot..
Smo..
Sm..

and finally succeed on pass 8 in locating the Smith record. This is particularly useful when asking a user for an identification number, i.e., a Social Security number, and failing an exact match, providing them with the record that is the most likely match.

Using the LOCATE FieldList option is only helpful in finding a record when you know the first few fields. Patterns cannot be used here. For example:

```
LOCATE "SMITH","JOHN","CA","90012"
```

would find the first occurrence of the name for that zipcode. Now for a little anomaly/feature. The object of the next demonstration is to show that LOCATE will truncate a LOCATE value if the value is longer than the width of the field. We'll create a table with a [Name] field that is "A5," that is, five characters wide. The code then loads the table with a few names and attempts to locate some values.

The code actually demonstrates interesting techniques: creating a table on the fly, loading the table, and synchronizing the canvas cursor with the workspace cursor.

**Listing 16.61: LOCATE.L3**

```
ECHO NORMAL   ; For the demo, echo is turned on so that you can see
              ; the tables created and loaded with values.
CLEARALL
n = 0
CREATE "List"   ; create a new list table
 "Name":"A5"

Edit "List"          ; Create and fill the table     LIST──────Name──
   "Alan"     Down   ; .........................       1 │ Alan
   "David"    Down   ;                                  2 │ David
   "Peter"    Down   ;                                  3 │ Peter
   "Dan"      Down   ;                                  4 │ Dan
   "Steve"    Down   ;                                  5 │ Steve
   "Liz"      Down   ;                                  6 │ Liz
DO_IT!
HOME        ; Back up to the top of the table.
ECHO OFF ; Enough entertainment...

; now locate a few values and give a message about each one
LOCATE "Liz"    ; Finds record 6.
SYNCCURSOR      ; Synchronize the canvas cursor with workspace cursor.
MESSAGE "After Locate Liz, cursor is on: ", [], " Press any key"
n = GETCHAR()

LOCATE "Peter"  ; Finds record 3.
SYNCCURSOR      ; Synchronize the canvas cursor with workspace cursor.
MESSAGE "After Locate Peter, cursor is on: ", [], " Press any key"
n = GETCHAR()

LOCATE "Alan"   ; Finds record 1.
```

```
SYNCCURSOR
MESSAGE "After Locate Alan, cursor is on: ", [], " Press any key"
n = GETCHAR()

LOCATE "Daniel" ; Not found.
SYNCCURSOR
MESSAGE "After Locate Daniel, cursor is on: ", [], " Press any key"
n = GETCHAR()

LOCATE "Steven" ; Finds record 5, "Steve" even though "Steven" is specified.
SYNCCURSOR
MESSAGE "After Locate Steven, cursor is on: ", [], " Press any key"
n = GETCHAR()
CLEARIMAGE
```

The curious thing is that although "Steven" is not a value in the table, LOCATE found "Steve."

This is considered a feature by the Paradox designers, but we're not convinced. A FIND query done the same way would not (and should not) have found "Steve" if "Steven" were specified. Note that this phenomenon only occurs when the LOCATE string is longer than the widest value possible, so locating "Daniel" did not find "Dan." However, for the sake of version compatibility, we suspect that the "feature" will continue as is.

### 16.4.5.4 Moving within and between Images

### MOVETO: Moves to a Specified Area on the Workspace

```
MOVETO {TableName | FieldSpecifier | FIELD Fieldname | RECORD Number| ImageNumber ]
```

| | |
|---|---|
| TableName | String representing the table name. |
| FieldSpecifier | Any valid field specifier enclosed in square brackets. |
| Fieldname | Any valid field name enclosed in square brackets. |
| Number | Record number to move to (respects restricted views). |
| ImageNumber | Number of image on the workspace (as identified by IMAGENO()). |

The MOVETO command has many permutations, and allows you to move around the workspace with relative ease. The listing below shows some examples of MOVETO syntax and the results of each command.

### Listing 16.62: MOVETO.L1

```
;Syntax:               ; MOVES TO:
MOVETO "Customer"      ; the current field in the Customer table.
MOVETO [Customer->]    ; the current field in the Customer table.
MOVETO [Customer ID#]  ; the customer ID# in the current table.
```

```
MOVETO [Customer->Balance Due] ; the balance due field in Customer table.
MOVETO [Customer(Q)->State]    ; the State field in the Customer Query image.
MOVETO [Customer(3)->state]    ; the State field in the third image of the customer table.
MOVETO 3                       ; the third image on the workspace.
MOVETO 2+1                     ; the third image on the workspace.
MOVETO NIMAGES()               ; the last image on the workspace.
MOVETO RECORD 300              ; record # 300 in the current table.
MOVETO RECORD INT(nrecords(table)/2)   ; the record halfway down the table.
MOVETO FIELD "Product 3"       ; [product 3] field in the current table.
MOVETO FIELD "Product "+Strval(sqrt(9)) ; [product 3] field in the current table.
MOVETO [INVOICE->Product 3]    ; [product 3] in invoice table.
MOVETO "INVOICE" MOVETO FIELD "Product "+Strval(sqrt(9)) ; [invoice->product 3].
```

The MOVETO FIELD syntax is particularly useful because in versions before 2.0, moving to a field whose name was a variable needed an execute statement.

**Listing 16.63: MOVETO.L2**

```
; Sample of VERSION 1.1 code
@1,0 ??"or press Esc to cancel"
@0,0 ??"Which quantity field would you like (1-9) :"
ACCEPT "A1" PICTURE "1,2,3,4,5,6,7,8,9" REQUIRED
TO choice.a
IF NOT RETVAL THEN
  RETURN
ENDIF
field.a = "Quantity " + choice.a
EXECUTE "MOVETO [" + field.a + "]"     ; Moveto [Quantity 3].
```

Version 2.0 greatly reduced the need for EXECUTEs, and simplified coding. The last two lines can be replaced with a single

```
MOVETO FIELD "Quantity "+ choice.a
```

Similarly, if both the Table name and Field name are variables,

```
EXECUTE "MOVETO ["+ table.a + "->" field.a + "]"    ; MOVETO [CUSTOMER->BALANCE DUE]
```

can be replaced by

```
MOVETO table.a
MOVETO FIELD field.a
```

Another thing to consider purely from a performance standpoint is whether or not to do explicit table MOVETO's or instead replacing them with UPIMAGE and DOWNIMAGE commands. UPIMAGE and DOWNIMAGE provide the fastest route, but are much less obvious when trying to debug your code.

**Listing 16.64: MOVETO.L3**

```
CLEARALL
VIEW "Customer"
VIEW "VENDOR"
VIEW "Invoice"
```

To move back up to the vendor table from our current position in the "Invoice" table, you could do any one of the following:

**Listing 16.65: MOVETO.L4**

```
MOVETO "VENDOR"
;MOVETO [VENDOR->]
;MOVETO 2
;UPIMAGE
```

See an additional example under CLEARIMAGE.

## UPIMAGE: Press [F3] to Move Up One Image

```
UPIMAGE
```

You can use UPIMAGE to move between tables when you know the exact placement of tables on the workspace. UPIMAGE can be helpful for generalized procedures that don't need to know table names. We generally prefer to use MOVETO commands between images because the code is a little easier to read; however, testing shows that UPIMAGE is often faster if you are moving up only one table. The next example copies the even-numbered records from the "Customer" table and places them into an "Answer" table:

**Listing 16.66: UPIMAGE.L1**

```
CREATE "Answer" LIKE "Customer"  ; Make a new table with the same structure.
VIEW "Answer"
COEDIT "Customer"
SCAN FOR MOD([#],2) = 0     ; For even number records only, record # evenly
                            ; divisible by 2.
  COPYTOARRAY record.r      ; Get all the field information into an array.
  UPIMAGE                   ; Move up to the answer table.
  END                       ; Move to the end of the table.
  DOWN                      ; Append a new record (get rid of blanks later).
  COPYFROMARRAY record.r    ; Place the data into the record.
  DOWNIMAGE                 ; Back to customer table.
ENDSCAN

; Now delete the first blank record because the first END DOWN
```

```
; opened an extra record IF this was not a keyed table (if table
; was keyed, the DOWN would be ignored on a blank record).

IF NKEYFIELDS("Answer") = 0 THEN
  UPIMAGE   ; Back to answer.
  HOME      ; Move to first blank record.
  DEL       ; Delete the blank record.
ENDIF
DO_IT!      ; End the CoEdit.
CLEARALL    ; Clear the workspace.
```

## DOWNIMAGE: Press [F4] to Move Down One Image

```
DOWNIMAGE
```

DOWNIMAGE, like UPIMAGE, is a quick way to move between tables on the workspace or within a multitable form. See the notes in UPIMAGE.

Now let's look at two ways of scanning an "Invoice" table and adding each invoice balance to a [Balance due] field in the correct customer record for each invoice. The first technique is to look at each invoice, move to the "Customer" table, find the customer record, and increment the customer balance due by the amount of the invoice.

### Listing 16.67: DOWNIMAG.L1

```
VIEW "Customer"
MOVETO [Customer ID#]
EDIT "Invoices"
SCAN                  ; Through invoice table.
  UPIMAGE             ; Moves to  [Customer->Customer ID#] field.
  LOCATE [Invoices->Customer ID#]
  IF RETVAL THEN      ; Always a possibility that the Customer record was
                      ; deleted and we don't want to update the wrong record.
    IF ISBLANK([Customer Balance]) THEN
      [Customer Balance] = [Invoices->Invoice Amount]
    ELSE
      [Customer Balance] = [Customer Balance] + [Invoices->Invoice Amount]
    ENDIF
  ENDIF
  DOWNIMAGE           ; Moves back to invoices table so that the scan can continue.
ENDSCAN
DO_IT!
CLEARALL

; Note that if you have installed Paradox to treat blanks as zeros, the
; code to check for a blank balance is not necessary, you can use

;  [Customer Balance] = [Customer Balance] + [Invoices->Invoice Amount]

; directly, and the balance will always increment properly. However if
; blanks are not treated as zeros (the default Paradox installation),
; the previous line would cause a script error if the [Customer Balance] field
; is blank.
```

An alternative approach follows that uses two queries. The first gets the sum of all invoices per customer, the second adds the sums to the current customer balances. The Query approach is easy to set up (and may actually run faster than the SCAN above). You simply place each of the queries on the workspace, save them, and read them into your code, then add a Do_It! where necessary.

**Listing 16.68: DOWNIMAG.L2**

```
; First get the sums of all invoices for each customer id.
CLEARALL
Query

  Invoices | Customer ID# | Invoice Amount |
           | Check        | Calc Sum All   |

Endquery

DO_IT!  ; Execute the query.
CLEARALL

; Now use a changeto Query to increment the customer balance field. Note
; that the querysave format uses underscores to denote example elements.
Query

  Answer | Customer ID# | Sum of Invoice Amount |
         | _xcustid     | _xinvoicesum          |

  Customer | Cust ID   |            Customer Balance                    |
           | _xcustid  | _xbalance, CHANGETO _xbalance + _xinvoicesum   |

Endquery
DO_IT!
CLEARALL
```

### FIRSTSHOW: Make the Current Image the First Image Visible on the Workspace

```
FIRSTSHOW
```

The FIRSTSHOW command puts the current image at the top of the screen. It scrolls all images above the current image off the screen. If images are below the current image, they will only show if the tablesize of the current image is less than 22 records.

The next example allows a user to pick from a list of products, but still allows entries not on the list. This is an alternative to a TableLookup ValCheck, in which you have the benefits of Lookup help but must make an entry that already appears on the list. The example below assumes that there are no TableLookup ValChecks in place on the invoice table. Obviously the code should be refined to add routines to delete records, etc.

Listing 16.69: FIRSTSHO.L1

```
CLEARALL
VIEW "Invoices"  ; Makes this image #1.
VIEW "Products"  ; Makes this image #2.
MOVETO "Invoices"
EDITKEY       ; Might use CoEdit, but would have to add some additional code for
              ; posting added records in the Products table.
PICKFORM 1    ; A single table form.
WHILE True
  WAIT TABLE
    PROMPT "Enter Invoice information",
           "[F1]-Lists products. [F2]-Saves."
  UNTIL  "F2", "F1", "Dos", "DosBig"
  SWITCH
    CASE RETVAL = "F2":
      DO_IT!
      CLEARALL
      RETURN
    CASE RETVAL = "F1":
      MOVETO "Products"  ; Now in table view, possibly showing part of the
                         ; Invoices table above.
      FIRSTSHOW          ; Position the Invoices table so that Products table
                         ; is the only visible.
      WHILE True
        WAIT TABLE
          PROMPT "Select a product and press [F2]",
                 "or Add a product and then press [F2] or press [Esc] to quit"
        UNTIL "F2", "Esc", "Dos", "DosBig"
        IF RETVAL = "F2" OR RETVAL = "Esc" THEN
          QUITLOOP
        ENDIF
      ENDWHILE
      MOVETO "Invoices"
      FORMKEY            ; Reinstates the form.
      IF RETVAL = "F2" THEN
        [Invoice Item#] = [Products->Item#]
      ENDIF
    OTHERWISE : BEEP
  ENDSWITCH
ENDWHILE
```

See also SETRECORDPOSITION to scroll an individual record to a particular position.


## CLEARIMAGE: Clear the Current Image

```
CLEARIMAGE
```

CLEARIMAGE removes the current image, whether Display or Query, from the workspace. Paradox must be in Main mode. Note that CLEARIMAGE does not affect the canvas at all.

Query images always get placed at the top of the workspace, above any Display images. The next example removes all query images from the workspace, and leaves the cursor in the first remaining Display image (if one is present). The code moves to the first image, and as long as it finds a query form, it clears the image, thereby removing any query placed.

**Listing 16.70: CLEARIMA.L1**

```
PROC RemoveQuery.u()
  IF NIMAGES() = 0 THEN       ; No images present.
    RETURN
  ENDIF
  MOVETO 1                    ; The first image on the workspace.
  WHILE IMAGETYPE() = "Query" ; Will continue as long as IMAGETYPE = "Query".
    CLEARIMAGE               ; Remove the query, if present.
  ENDWHILE
ENDPROC
```

## CLEARALL: Clear the Workspace Images

```
CLEARALL
```

The CLEARALL command clears all images from the workspace. Most top-level scripts begin by clearing the canvas and clearing the workspace:

```
CLEAR                   ;clears the canvas
CLEARALL                ;clears the workspace
```

Like its namesake, the ClearAll key [Alt F8], the CLEARALL command clears all Display or Query images from the workspace and can only be used in Main mode; in all other modes it has no effect. Both CLEARALL and the ClearAll key have no effect on the PAL canvas. But that's where the similarity ends.

Pressing the ClearAll key in interactive Paradox flushes all memory buffers to disk, saving changes in tables that have been recorded only in memory.

The CLEARALL command *only clears the workspace*. If you need to explicitly flush all memory buffers, as well as the workspace, you must use RESET. Unfortunately, as outlined below, RESET has additional effects.

## RESET: Reset the Workspace

```
RESET
```

According to the 3.0 PAL User's Guide, the RESET command "is useful for obtaining a clean system state at the beginning of script play, no matter what the user was doing when the script was begun." RESET is a lit powder keg dropped onto your workspace. The RESET command:

- CLEARS the workspace from any mode
- leaves passwords in effect and revokes passwords that were in effect but cancelled with the UNPASSWORD command (See UNPASSWORD for details.)
- flushes memory buffers, writing all changed memory blocks to disk
- removes all explicit table locks
- removes all PRIVTABLES assignments

A RESET is sometimes necessary if problems arise with the SHOWTABLES and SHOWFILES commands. RESET is also necessary if you need to get accurate FILESIZE() values. For another variation on the same theme, the menu command:

```
MENU {Tools} {More} {Protect} {ClearPasswords}
```

clears the workspace, appears to flush the buffers (this is unconfirmed), and releases all passwords, but leaves the table locks intact.

To summarize:

CLEARALL only clears the workspace; it does not affect anything else.

RESET clears the workspace, flushes the memory buffers, and removes all table locks. It does not affect active passwords at all; however, it revokes passwords already released with UNPASSWORD.

MENU {Tools} {More} {Protect} {ClearPasswords} clears the workspace, appears to flush the buffers (this is unconfirmed), releases all passwords, but leaves the table locks intact.

So, if you are on a network *and* do not use encrypted tables, try using the {ClearPasswords} approach instead of a RESET, because it does not affect table locks. If you deal with encrypted tables, perhaps you could keep an array of passwords that the user has entered and reinstate them after each {Clear-Passwords}. This route might be easier than reconstructing all the table locks.

As a by-product of flushing the buffers, RESET also removes the "on chain but not registered" files shown in the [Alt -] screen. This appears to be the only way to keep an obscure "Too many registrations" error from happening when you deal with a large number of tables.

## 16.4.6 Image Information

### NIMAGES: How Many Images Are on the Workspace?

```
NIMAGES ()
```

Returns:

A Number    The number of images currently on the workspace, or a 0 if no images are present.

The NIMAGES function returns the total number of images (both Query and Display) on the workspace. Embedded images in multitable forms are added to the count even if you haven't placed the detail tables on the workspace explicitly. For example, an "Invoice" table with a multitable form that includes a line item table is counted as two images. However, if you press FORMKEY to toggle to TableView, NIMAGES returns 1. This applies even if the table was edited in FormView and is still link-locked. When you are in the Create, Restructure, or Password modes, the image count is incremented by one.

See IMAGENO() for more information.

**Listing 16.71: NIMAGES.L1**

```
SWITCH
  CASE NIMAGES() = 0:
    MESSAGE "There are no images on the workspace"
  CASE NIMAGES() = 1 :
    MESSAGE "There is only one table on the workspace"
  OTHERWISE:
    MESSAGE "There are ",NIMAGES()," tables on the workspace"
ENDSWITCH
SLEEP 2000
```

## IMAGENO: What is the Current Image Number?

```
IMAGENO ()
```

Returns:

   A Number    The position of the current image on the workspace, or 0 if no images are present.

Paradox numbers both Query and Display images from the top of the workspace down. The IMAGENO() function returns the current image's number, its position relative to other images on the workspace. Like record numbers, an image number is dynamic. Placing a query image on the workspace increments every Display image by one; removing a Query image has the opposite effect, but may also change the number of other Query images. Toggling into FormView with a multitable form can increase the number of tables on the workspace by as many as five images.

IMAGENO can be used with the MOVETO command to simplify the process of recreating the current workspace. Without identifying image numbers, you can move between images by naming the tables.

**Listing 16.72: IMAGENO.L1**

```
CLEARALL
VIEW "Employee"
VIEW "Customer"
```

```
table.a = TABLE()  ; "Customer"
 ; Now move to another table, do something there.
MOVETO "Employee"
; Other code might go here.
; When it is time to return to the original table.
MOVETO table.a
; Will return you to the original table.
```

However, the MOVETO tablename command always moves to the first occurrence of the named table. In the following example it moves to a Query image instead of the intended Display image:

**Listing 16.73: IMAGENO.L2**

```
CLEARALL
MENU {Ask} {Customer}    ; Place a query form on the workspace.
VIEW "Customer"
VIEW "Employee"
UPIMAGE ; Back to customer display image.
table.a = TABLE()  ; "Customer"
; Now move to another table, do something there,.
MOVETO "Employee"
; Some other code might go here.
; When it is time to return to the original table.
MOVETO table.a
; Would place you on the QUERY image of the Customer table.
```

Here's an alternative, the MOVETO n command, where n is an image number:

**Listing 16.74: IMAGENO.L3**

```
MENU {Ask} {Customer}
VIEW "Customer"
VIEW "Employee"
UPIMAGE
image.n = IMAGENO()  ; 2
; Now move to another table, do something there,.
MOVETO "Employee"
; Some other code might go here.
; When it is time to return to the original table.
MOVETO image.n      ; MOVETO 2
; Would place you back in the display image for Customer
; where you could continue.
```

IMAGENO combined with IMAGETYPE gives complete information about the position and type of the current image. See the NextNumber.v procedure in the WAITPLUS section for a detailed example of a generic procedure that uses IMAGENO to find its way back to an original image. The values returned by IMAGENO() are more complex in a multitable form, especially when an embedded table is also present as a separate image on the workspace. The rules for embedded tables are:

- If a table has been explicitly placed on the workspace, and is also one of the tables in a multitable form, IMAGENO() returns the image number of the explicitly placed table, whether or not you are in the embedded form.
- If a table is on the workspace only in an embedded form, IMAGENO() counts all the tables on the underlying workspace, and adds 1 for each embedded table. The imageorder in a multitable form (and the order in which UpImage and DownImage move through the tables) is controlled by the order in which the images were placed during form design. This order is the same as that returned by the FORMTABLES command.

### IMAGETYPE: What is the Current Image Type?

```
IMAGETYPE ()
```

Returns:

| | |
|---|---|
| "Query" | Cursor is in a Query form. |
| "Display" | Cursor is in a table image, or in Create, Restructure, or Password mode. |
| "None" | No images are on the workspace. |

The IMAGETYPE function returns one of three strings that describe whether or not an image is present ("None"), and its type ("Query" or "Display"). The example below checks to see if a specified table has already been placed on the workspace.

Although your scripts dictate what happens on the workspace, at times it may seem to get out of control because of queries and restructures creating temporary tables. It pays to evaluate existing conditions before placing a table on the workspace, where it might needlessly duplicate an existing image. The following procedure returns True if the specified image is found on the workspace. No attempt to check embedded tables in the form is made (the code could be extended to look on the form first).

**Listing 16.75: IMAGETYP.L1**

```
PROC Check4Image.l(table.a, type.a )
  ; type.a is the type of image to look for.
  ;  "D" for display, "Q" for query or "" for any image
  ; RETURNS  True if image is already placed, False otherwise

  PRIVATE
    image.n,    ; Current image number
    formview.l, ; Originally in form view?
    n,          ; Counter
    thistable.a, ; Name of table currently being evaluated
    found.l     ; Have we found the table?
```

```
       IF NIMAGES() = 0 THEN    ; Image cannot possibly be on the workspace
         RETURN False
       ENDIF
       table.a = LOWER(table.a)  ; Makes checking easier  by assuring that
       type.a = LOWER(type.a)    ; So that formal parameters need not be case
                                 ; sensitive
       formview.l = ISFORMVIEW() ; Are we in formview
       IF formview.l THEN        ; Could be in a multitable form.
                                 ; Must get back to the tableview workspace.
         FORMKEY
       ENDIF
       image.n = IMAGENO()       ; Save our place on the workspace
       found.l = false           ; Initialize variable
       FOR n FROM 1 TO NIMAGES() ; For all the images on the workspace
         MOVETO n                      ; Moveto the Nth image on the workspace
         thistable.a = LOWER(TABLE()) ; get image name
         SWITCH
           CASE IMAGETYPE() = "Query":
             IF type.a <> "d" THEN
               IF thistable.a = table.a THEN
                 found.l = True
                 QUITLOOP            ; search no further
               ENDIF
             ENDIF
           CASE thistable.a = table.a :   ; Has to be a display image
             IF type.a <> "q" THEN        ; Ok if "d" or "" was specified
               found.l = True
               QUITLOOP
             ENDIF
         ENDSWITCH
       ENDFOR
       MOVETO image.n   ; Back to where we were
       IF formview.l THEN
         FORMKEY
         MOVETO table.a   ; Just in case we were in a detail form
       ENDIF
       RETURN found.l   ; True or False
    ENDPROC

    ; typical syntax might look like:

    l = Check4Image.l("Customer", "D")
    ; which sets l to true if the image already exists on the workspace
    IF NOT l THEN
      ; do whatever is necessary to place the Customer table on the workspace
    ENDIF
```

The procedure also examines the workspace and returns to the starting point, recreating the environment as found. These extra steps are necessary because a multitable form is treated almost as a workspace unto itself. See CLEARIMAGE for an example of code that uses IMAGETYPE() to remove an entire query.

## ATFIRST: Are We at the Top of the Table?

```
ATFIRST ()
```

Returns:

| | |
|---|---|
| True | Current record is first in table. |
| False | Current record is not at the top of the table. |

The ATFIRST function returns the same value as RECNO() = 1. If the current table is an embedded linked table, ATFIRST determines whether or not the cursor is on the first record in the restricted view of the master record. Code often written like:

**Listing 16.76: ATFIRST.L1**

```
IF NOT ATFIRST( ) THEN
   HOME
ENDIF
```

should simply be a HOME command. ATFIRST() can be useful if you are trying to move backwards through a table and want to tell the user that there are no records above the current one.

## BOT: Have We Attempted to Move Above the First Record?

```
BOT ()
```

Returns:

| | |
|---|---|
| True | If Moveto or Skip tried to move past the first record to an impossible record #0. For BOT() to be True, the cursor must be at record 1 (of a master table or detail table). |
| False | No attempt to move past the first record is made. |

BOT stands for "Beginning of Table" and tests to see if an attempt has been made to move up beyond the first record of a table as a result of a MOVETO RECORD or a SKIP command. If MOVETO RECORD has an argument that is less than 1, the cursor moves to record 1 of the table or the restricted view, and BOT() is assigned the value True. Similarly, if a SKIP has a negative value that would attempt to move up beyond the first record, BOT() is also flagged as True.

BOT() is only set by the two cases noted above. PgUp, Up, etc. have no effect on BOT(). If you are currently on record 2 and issue a SKIP -5, the cursor goes to record #1 and BOT() is set to True. To do some tasks, for every record beginning with the current record and proceeding upwards in the file until it runs out of records, BOT() might not be the most obvious choice. For example, without BOT() you might code:

**Listing 16.77: BOT.L1**

```
WHILE TRUE
  ; Do something here
  IF ATFIRST() THEN     ; or optionally  IF RECNO()=1 THEN
    QUITLOOP
  ENDIF
  SKIP -1
ENDWHILE
```

This would work just fine as long as SKIP -1 is issued. However, if you were starting on an even-numbered record and you wanted to affect only even-numbered records with SKIP -2, you would soon run into a problem. When the cursor gets up to record 2, the SKIP -2 would bring the cursor to record 1. There the task would execute before quitting the loop. Therefore, record 1 would have been worked on when you really wanted only the even-numbered records to be affected. The solution is simple.

**Listing 16.78: BOT.L2**

```
WHILE NOT BOT()
  ; do something here
  SKIP -2
ENDWHILE
```

## ATLAST: Is the Current Record the Last Record in the Table?

```
ATLAST ()
```

Returns:

| True | Current record is last in table. |
| False | Not at the bottom of the table. |

The ATLAST function identifies whether or not the cursor is on the last record of the table or the last record in a restricted view of a table. The next code fragment views the "Customer" table and lets the user search for the next record with the same field value as the current record.

**Listing 16.79: ATLAST.L1**

```
VIEW "CUSTOMER"
PICKFORM 1
WHILE TRUE
```

```
WAIT TABLE
  PROMPT "Move to a field in any record, then press [F8] ",
         "to view next record with same field value.  [Esc]-Quits"
UNTIL "F8", "Esc", "Dos", "DosBig", "Zoom"
SWITCH
  CASE RETVAL = "Esc":
    CLEARALL
    RETURN
  CASE RETVAL = "F8":
    IF ATLAST() THEN
      BEEP
      MESSAGE "You are already on the last record"
      SLEEP 2000  ; wait 2 seconds
    ELSE
      MESSAGE "Searching for next: ", []
      SKIP        ; move down to the next record
      LOCATE NEXT []
      IF NOT RETVAL
        SKIP -1  ; move back up one record
        MESSAGE "No more records found for: ", []
        BEEP
        SLEEP 2000
      ENDIF
    ENDIF
  ENDSWITCH
ENDWHILE
; You would probably want to expand this, and all other loops that invoke
; WAIT TABLE to include the Zoom.l() procedure, outlined earlier in this chapter.
```

### EOT: Have We Attempted to Move below the Last Record?

EOT ()

Returns:

False    No attempt was made to move beyond the end of the table.
True    MOVETO, SKIP, or LOCATE attempted to move beyond the last record in the table.

EOT stands for "End of Table" and is the sister command to BOT(). It behaves much the same as BOT(), but it can also be affected by the LOCATE command. EOT() returns True in the following cases:

- When the MOVETO RECORD number is greater than the number of records in the image, EOT() is set to True and the cursor is moved to the last record in the table or in the current restricted view.
- When the argument to the SKIP command is greater than the difference between the current record and the number of records in the table. For example, SKIP 100 at a position 50 records from the bottom of the table makes the last record the current record and sets EOT() to True.
- When a LOCATE was unsuccessful. An unsuccessful LOCATE sets

RETVAL to False and the current record doesn't change. Although some programmers test EOT() to see if LOCATE was successful, most simply test RETVAL.

EOT() is only set by the three cases noted above. PgDn, Down, etc. have no effect on EOT().
See BOT() for a related command.

### NPAGES: How Many Pages Are Present?

```
NPAGES ()
```

Returns: The number of pages in the current form or report spec.

While in the form generator, or in a normal Display form, or in a Master table in FormView, the NPAGES function returns the total number of pages in the current form as indicated in the status line. In a detail table of a Master form, NPAGES always returns 1, because an embedded form can only have one page. In the report generator, NPAGES returns the number of page widths shown by the page width indicator at the top of the screen.
The listing below shows a quick way to delete all but the first page of a report specification. Assigning this code to a SETKEY is useful in cleaning up extra pages produced by Paradox when designing a tabular report.

**Listing 16.80: NPAGES.L1**

```
IF SYSMODE() = "Report" THEN   ; check to make sure we are in report mode
  WHILE NPAGES() > 1
    MENU {Setting} {PageLayout} {Delete} {OK}
  ENDWHILE
ENDIF
```

### PAGENO: What Is the Current Page Number?

```
PAGENO ()
```

Returns:

A Number    The current page number in FormView, form design, or report design.

The PAGENO function simply returns the current page of a form whether designing it in Form mode or viewing data through it in Main, DataEntry, CoEdit, or Edit mode. In Report mode, it reports the horizontal page number.

**Listing 16.81: PAGENO.L1**

```
VIEW "BigForm"
PICKFORM 5    ; a 3 page form
PGDN          ; move to the second page
MESSAGE  "Now viewing page ", PAGENO(), " of ", NPAGES()
SLEEP 2000

; would display:    Now viewing page 2 of 3
```

The next example is called from Form mode and deletes all but the first page of a multipage form. Although this example is not one of the more practical ones in the book, it demonstrates that scripts can be played to manipulate the form generator. The code below can be called as a script by a SETKEY, or by pressing [Alt F10] to bring up the PAL menu, and playing the script.

**Listing 16.82: PAGENO.L2**

```
SWITCH
  CASE SYSMODE() <> "Form":
    BEEP
    MESSAGE "Must be in form mode, press any key"
    n = GETCHAR()
  CASE NPAGES()=1 :
    BEEP
    MESSAGE "There is one page left, delete it manually, press any key."
    n=GETCHAR()
  OTHERWISE:
    SHOWMENU
      "Cancel":"Do not delete the last "+ STRVAL(NPAGES()-1)+ " page(s)"
      "Delete":"Ok to delete the last "+ STRVAL(NPAGES()-1)+ " page(s)"
    TO choice.a
    IF choice.a = "Delete" THEN  ; OK to delete the page(s)
         ; move down to the last page
      WHILE PAGENO() <> NPAGES()   ; while we are not on the last page
        PGDN
      ENDWHILE
      WHILE PAGENO() <> 1
        MENU {Page} {Delete} {OK}     ; delete the current page
      ENDWHILE
    ENDIF
ENDSWITCH
```

### COLNO: What is the Current Workspace Column Number?

```
COLNO ()
```

Returns:    A number representing the current column number of the cursor on the Paradox workspace.

A column is not always a column—a column in a table is a field; in Report, Form, or Script modes, a column is a character. Since the maximum number of fields in a table is 255, COLNO() returns a value of 1 to 255 in a Display or Query image. In either image type, the leftmost column always returns a COLNO() of 1 (in Query images, the leftmost field is named [#]).

In a Display or Query image, the value that COLNO() returns is specific to the image rotations of TableView, and may not reflect the structure. This can be easily overlooked when in FormView. If you want to determine if you are in the leftmost column, you could do the following test:

**Listing 16.83: COLNO.L1**

```
IF COLNO() = 1 THEN
  ; Do something
ENDIF

;or alternately

IF FIELD() = "#" THEN
  ; Do something
ENDIF
```

In the other modes, the value is the current horizontal column, measured in characters. COLNO() returns values based on the workspace, NOT the canvas.

To have [Alt W] activate a message of the current cursor coordinates in Report or Script mode, place the code in the next listing into your INIT.SC. Note that although the code is displayed below in several lines, SETKEY assignments must be typed as a single line not exceeding 132 characters.

**Listing 16.84: COLNO.L2**

```
SETKEY -17
IF SYSMODE()="Report" OR SYSMODE()="Script" THEN
  MESSAGE "< " , ROWNO(), ", " ,COLNO(),">"
  SLEEP 2000
ENDIF
```

In Script mode, COLNO() can have a value from 1 to 132. In Form mode, COLNO() can have a value from 1 to 80. The value COLNO() returns in a report varies.

The COLNO() in a report generally reflects the current position on the ruler line with respect to the current page. The first column on page 1 will return a 1, the third column on page 2 will return a 3. However, if the cursor is on the last column of any page (on the vertical inverse video page divider), COLNO() always returns a 0. To correctly code for the COLNO() phenomenon and get the column relative to the first column on the first report page:

### Listing 16.85: COLNO.L3

```
previouscolumns.n = (PAGENO()-1) * PAGEWIDTH()

; Now add the current COLNO() to the previous value

currentcolumn.n = previouscolumns.n + COLNO()

; Display the message

MESSAGE "Cursor is in physical column: ", currentcolumn.n
SLEEP 2000  ; pause for 2 seconds
```

## NROWS: How Many Rows Are Present?

```
NROWS ()
```

Returns:

    A Number    The number of rows in the current image, report specification, or the number of lines in a script.

In TableView, NROWS() returns the number of records displayed on screen. In tableview or in a multirecord form, NROWS() returns the number of rows displayed, a value from 1 to 22. In a Query image, it returns a minimum of 3 and a maximum of 22. In FormView (not in an embedded multirecord form), it produces a script error. In the report generator and script mode, NROWS returns the total number of lines present. NROWS can be used to simulate a SCAN loop in report or script mode.

The next procedure returns the type of report defined for a table, "Tabular" or "FreeForm":

### Listing 16.86: NROWS.L1

```
PROC reporttype.a ( table.a, rptname.a)
  ; table.a      ; name of table
  ; rptname.a    ; name of report  "R" or "1" through "14"
  ; RETURNS   "Tabular" , "FreeForm" or "Error"

  PRIVATE rpttype.a
  IF SYSMODE()<> "Main" THEN    ; Could also expand this to trap for rights, etc.
   BEEP
   RETURN "Error"
  ENDIF
  MENU {REPORT} {Change}
  SELECT table.a        ; e.g., "Customer"
  SELECT rptname.a      ; e.g., "12"

  IF WINDOW() <> "" THEN  ; There is some error......
   MENU                   ; Go back to main menu
    RETURN "Error"        ; Lookup table must be missing,
```

```
                              ; or for some other reason Paradox will not let
                              ; you into the report
        ENDIF
        ENTER                 ; Confirm the report description, go into report spec
        ; now look at each row until we come to the Form band or Table band
        FOR n FROM 1 TO NROWS() -1
          SWITCH
            CASE MATCH(BANDINFO(),"Table Band.."):   ; Look at the band indicator
              rpttype.a = "Tabular"
              QUITLOOP
            CASE MATCH(BANDINFO(),"Form Band.."):
              rpttype.a = "FreeForm"
              QUITLOOP
          ENDSWITCH
          DOWN                      ; Move down to the next line, try again
        ENDFOR
        RETURN rpttype.a
        CTRLBREAK                   ; Get out of report mode (could have used CANCELEDIT)
      ENDPROC

      ; a = reporttype.a ( "Customer" , "12" )
      ; would return "Tabular", "FreeForm", or "Error"
```

The following example locates the first occurrence of a string of text in the script editor. Although many of us use an external text editor with more features, this example illustrates that even the script mode is programmable (once you're in it). The findfirsttext.1 procedure could be assigned to a setkey, or made part of a menu-driven extension to the script.

**Listing 16.87: NROWS.L2**

```
PROC FindFirstText.l (text.a)
  ; text.a     string of text to search for
  ; RETURNS True if string is found, False otherwise
  ; If the text is found, the cursor moves to it.
  ; If not found the cursor returns to the original cursor position.
  PRIVATE
    n,
    startrow.n,    ; search start row
    startcol.n,    ; search start column
    search.n       ; position found, or 0

  IF SYSMODE()<>"Script" THEN
    QUIT "Must be in script mode"
  ENDIF

  MESSAGE "Searching for ", text.a
  ; First let's save our position
  startrow.n = ROWNO()
  startcol.n = COLNO()
  HOME       ; Start at first line
  CTRLHOME   ; Move to column 1
```

```
FOR n FROM 1 TO NROWS()   ; the total number of rows in the script
  ; Now look at the cursor line and see if the text is found anywhere
  search.n = SEARCH(text.a, CURSORLINE())  ; 0 if not found,
                                           ; or the position # if found

  IF search.n = 0 THEN
    DOWN  ; Move down to the next line
  ELSE  ; the text was found
    ; Now let's position the cursor on the first letter of the word
    IF search.n > 1 THEN
      FOR n FROM 1 TO search.n
        RIGHT
      ENDFOR
    ENDIF
    MESSAGE "Found ", text.a
    BEEP
    SLEEP 1000
    RETURN TRUE
  ENDIF
ENDFOR  ; done for each line

; If we got to this point, the string was not found, so let's go back to our
; original position.  The proc could be expanded to be more intelligent about
; restoring the postion, perhaps scanning up from the bottom if that is the
; shorter route.
MESSAGE text.a, " not found, restoring original position"
BEEP BEEP
SLEEP 1000
HOME  ; move back to the top of the script
FOR n FROM 1 TO startrow.n
  IF ROWNO() = startrow.n  THEN
    QUITLOOP
  ELSE
    DOWN
  ENDIF
ENDFOR
FOR n FROM 1 TO startcol.n
  IF COLNO() = startcol.n THEN
    QUITLOOP
  ELSE
    RIGHT
  ENDIF
ENDFOR
RETURN FALSE  ; never found the text
ENDPROC

; A typical call might look like:
; l = FindFirstText.l ( "ISBLANK" )
```

### ROWNO: What Is the Current Row Number?

```
ROWNO ()
```

Returns: A number representing the current row number on the work-space. The current row in the Image, Script, Report or Form specification.

In a Query or a Display image in TableView, ROWNO() returns the current row number (1–22) relative to the first record displayed. In TableView, ROWNO() returns the number of the line being displayed. For example, if 3 out of 50 records are being displayed, and the cursor is on the second line from the top of the image, ROWNO() returns 2, regardless of the record number. Similarly, in a multirecord form, ROWNO returns the line number within the restricted view. In a regular FormView, it always returns 1.

In Form mode, ROWNO returns the current row of the current page of the form. In Report or Script mode, it returns the current line number. While in Report mode, you can determine if you are at the last row of the report by using:

**Listing 16.88: ROWNO.L1**

```
IF ROWNO()=NROWS() THEN
   MESSAGE "You are on the last line"
ELSE
   MESSAGE "You are currently on row ", ROWNO(), " of ", NROWS()
ENDIF
```

Similarly, when the cursor is on the first row, ROWNO() returns 1. In Form mode, ROWNO() returns the row with respect to the current page. So row 15 on page 2 of the form would have ROWNO() return 15. See NROWS for more information.

## 16.4.7 Report, Form and Script Mode Commands

### DELETELINE: Delete the Remainder of the Current Line from the Current Column to the Right

```
DELETELINE
```

This command presses Ctrl Y to delete the remainder of the line in Report or Script mode. If the cursor is in column one, the entire line is removed.

### VERTRULER: Toggle the Vertical Ruler

```
VERTRULER
```

VERTRULER toggles the vertical ruler that appears on the screen in report and script modes with [Ctrl V]. The command isn't particularly useful except when training others to use Paradox's report generator. It's another reminder that whatever you want to do in interactive Paradox has a corresponding PAL equivalent. To make [Shift F1] go into "Customer" report #1 without changing the title and turn on the vertical ruler, use:

```
SETKEY "F11" {Report} {Change} {Customer} {1} {} VertRuler
```

### BANDINFO: What Is the Current Band in Report Mode?

```
BANDINFO ()
```

Returns:

| | |
|---|---|
| "Report Header" | Cursor in report header. |
| "Page Header" | Cursor in page header. |
| "Group Header for.." | Cursor in a group header. |
| "Table Band.." | Cursor in the table band (tabular report). |
| "Form Band.." | Cursor in form band (freeForm report). |
| "Group Footer for.." | Cursor in group footer. |
| "Page Footer.." | Cursor in page footer. |
| "Report Footer.." | Cursor in report footer. |

See example code under NROWS() that uses BANDINFO to determine report type.

### PAGEWIDTH: What Is the Width of the Current Page?

```
PAGEWIDTH ()
```

Returns:

| | |
|---|---|
| A Number | The page width of the current report specification in Report mode. |

In Report mode, the total width of the report can be calculated by:

```
totalwidth.n = PAGEWIDTH () * NPAGES()
```

To force a report to a Pagewidth of 132, do the following:

**Listing 16.89: PAGEWIDT.L1**

```
IF PAGEWIDTH()<>132 THEN
  MENU {Setting} {PageLayout} {Width}
  SELECT "132"
ENDIF
```

Note that Paradox type-in prompts are converted to string so both

```
SELECT "132"  ;or
SELECT 132
```

work. See COLNO() for more examples of PAGEWIDTH().

# Chapter 17

# Special Functions

PAL provides a rich set of tools for transforming values. The commands and functions discussed in this chapter fall into two classes: those that manipulate strings and those that manipulate numbers. We'll explore some of the techniques that use these special functions, and point out their idiosyncrasies.

## 17.1 STRINGS

PAL provides several string functions. Some will convert nonstring values to strings automatically. These tools provide flexibility in the concatenation, truncation, and display formatting of PAL expressions.

### 17.1.1 Special String Characters

First introduced in the chapter called "Language Elements," the following characters represent special characters in strings.

**Special String Characters**

| | |
|---|---|
| \ " | Literal quote character. |
| \ \ | Literal Backslash character. |
| \ f | Formfeed character [Ctrl L]. |
| \ n | Newline character [Ctrl J]. |
| \ r | Carriage return character [Ctrl M]. |
| \ t | Tab character [Ctrl I]. |
| \ ### | (### = 0 to 255) ASCII character. |

Any character can be represented by its three-digit keycode. For example, instead of displaying a message that says "Press [Enter] to continue," you could substitute "Press \017\027 to continue" where the \017\027 combination displays ◄┘ .

PRINT "\f" is used to explicitly issue a form feed to the printer, whereas "\n" is often used in PRINT and PRINT FILE commands to move to a new line.

### CHR: What is the Character Representation of a PAL Keycode?

```
CHR (Number)
```

    Number      An integer between 1 and 255, representing an ASCII code.

Returns:

    A String     One character string of the ASCII character.

CHR converts a positive ASCII number to its corresponding character:

```
a = CHR(66)    ;sets a ="B"
```

CHR() is often used in combination with GETCHAR() because GETCHAR() returns the number, not the character of the key pressed. To give a message listing the keystrokes pressed and accepted via a GETCHAR():

**Listing 17.1: CHR.L1**

```
n = BLANKNUM()           ; Initialize variable.
MESSAGE "Press any key"
WHILE n <> 27            ; 27 is the ASCII value of [Esc].
  n = GETCHAR()          ; Get the next keystroke.
  MESSAGE "You pressed ", CHR(n), ".  Press [Esc] to quit or any other key to continue"
ENDWHILE
```

### ASC: What Is the ASCII Keycode of a Character?

```
ASC (Char)
```

    Char      An expression that evaluates to a valid PAL Keycode.

Returns:

    A Number    Positive number if ASCII keycode. Negative number for IBM extended keycode.

ASC is the complementary function to CHR.

**Listing 17.2: ASC.L1**

```
n = ASC("B")          ; sets n = 66
n = ASC("F10")        ; sets n = -68
n = ASC("Menu")       ; sets n = -68
n = ASC("Me"+"nu")    ; sets n = -68
```

The next example returns a string that starts with a lowercase character and then alternates between upper- and lowercase. Although it is of little practical use, by varying this technique, you can write procedures that perform simple encryption and decryption of text. This is an example of rudimentary "bit shifting," in which a character is translated to another by simple addition.

**Listing 17.3: ASC.L2**

```
PROC  RollerCoaster.a(string.a)
  ; string.a       ; Any string.
  ; RETURNS        ; A string where the first character is lower case
  ;                ; and then alternates between upper and lower case.
  string.a = LOWER(string.a)      ; Start off in lower case.
  newstring.a = ""                ; Initialize a blank string.
  FOR n from 1 to LEN(string.a)
    a = SUBSTR(string.a, n, 1)  ; Get the next character.
    ; Test if n is an even number and a lower case letter. If the
    ; modulus (remainder) of the number divided by 2 is zero, then
    ; the number is even. Lower case letters have ASCII numbers from
    ; 94 to 122  (a to z).
    IF MOD(n, 2) = 0 and (ASC(a) > 96 and ASC(a) < 123) THEN
      ; If uppercase, subtract 32 from the number and convert back to a string.
      ; If it was a "b" ASC is 98.  subtract 32 yields 66, character 66 is "B".
      a = CHR(ASC(a)-32)
      ; (Sure we know that we could have used UPPER(a) but that wouldn't be
      ;  any fun at all!)
    ENDIF
      ; Odd positioned characters and characters outside of a-z are passed
      ; through normally.
    newstring.a = newstring.a + a
  ENDFOR
  RETURN newstring.a
ENDPROC

; a test
a = RollerCoaster.a("This is a ROLLERCOASTER!!, 25 cents please. Press a key")

MESSAGE a  ; Will display "tHiS Is a rOlLeRcOaStEr!!, 25 cEnTs pLeAsE. pReSs a kEy".

n = GETCHAR()
```

### SPACES: Return a String of Spaces of a Specified Length

```
SPACES (Number)
```

   Number     Number between 0 and 255.

Returns:

   A String     Consisting of the specified number of spaces.

```
a = SPACES(0)    ; sets a = "", the null string
a = SPACES(5)    ; sets a = "     ", a five character string
```

SPACES is commonly used to help print reports without using the Paradox report generator.

Creating a report "on the fly" offers simple solutions to common problems. The following examples show two ways of printing a columnar report while in Edit mode. These examples are simplified, and do not deal with top and bottom margins or form feeds between pages. They simply output two columns of text. They also assume that the printer is online.

**Listing 17.4: SPACES.L1**

```
OPEN PRINTER
PRINT "\f\n"       ; Start with a formfeed to assure a new page,
                   ; followed by a new line.
SCAN
  PRINT
  SPACES(10),                      ; Left hand margin.
  [Customer name],                 ; Name varies in length.
  SPACES(50 - LEN([Customer name])), ; Enough spaces to move to column 50.
  [phone],
  "\n"                             ; New line character sends a line feed.
ENDSCAN
CLOSE PRINTER                      ; Must place Close printer before the
                                   ; final formfeed.

PRINT "\f"                         ; Eject the last page.
```

The alternative uses the FORMAT function to extend the customer name to 50 characters:

**Listing 17.5: SPACES.L2**

```
OPEN PRINTER
PRINT "\f\n"
SCAN
```

```
PRINT
  SPACES(10),
  FORMAT("W50",[Customer name]), ; Will append the proper number of trailing spaces.
  [Phone],
  "\n"
ENDSCAN
CLOSE PRINTER
PRINT "\f"
```

## FILL: Return a String of a Repeating Character

```
FILL (Expression, Number)
```

| | |
|---|---|
| Expression | Automatically converted to a string; only the first character is used. |
| Number | Number of times character is to be repeated (0–255). |

Returns:

| | |
|---|---|
| A String | The length of Number, filled with the character. |

### Listing 17.6: FILL.L1

```
a = FILL("x", 10)      ; Sets a = "xxxxxxxxxx".
a = FILL("x", 0)       ; Sets a = "".

; FILL automatically converts the argument to a string, and only recognizes
; the first character, thus:

a = FILL (96001, 5)      ; sets a = "99999"

;However, if your default date format is set to MM/DD/YY

a = FILL (9/4/89, 5)     ; sets a = "99999"
a = FILL (9-Apr-89, 5)   ; sets a = "44444"

; because paradox converts the date to 4/9/89 before FILL takes over.
```

As with the spaces function, the FILL function can also be used when modifying or building report specifications "on the fly." For example, while changing a report specification, the statement:

```
TYPEIN FILL( ".", 132)
```

creates a dotted line 132 characters long, as if you had typed it in from the keyboard.

### LOWER: What Is the Lowercase Value of an Expression?

LOWER (Expression)

      Expression     Any valid PAL expression.

Returns:

      A String     With all letters converted to lowercase.

LOWER works with all data types, converting the expression to a string if necessary. The same effect can be achieved with the FORMAT("CL",expression).

### Listing 17.7: LOWER.L1

```
a = LOWER ("AbCd")            ; Sets a = "abcd".
a = LOWER ("Para" + "Docs")   ; Sets a = "paradocs".
a = LOWER (2)                 ; Sets a = "2".
a = LOWER (-2)                ; Sets a = "-2".

; As with many other string-based functions, dates are sensitive to the
; current defaults.  If your default date format is mm.dd.yy:

a = LOWER (5-Jan-1983)

; Sets a = "1.05.83" because the date is converted to the default format
; before string conversion.
```

LOWER is also commonly used in combination with the format function. See the FORMAT function for an example that converts strings to proper case.

### UPPER: What Is the Uppercase Value of an Expression?

UPPER (Expression)

      Expression     Any PAL expression.

Returns

      A String     With all characters in uppercase. Nonstrings are automatically treated as strings. Only letters are shifted to uppercase. Returns uppercase of mixed date formats as well.

This command converts an expression into an uppercase string. As with the LOWER function, an equivalent function is FORMAT("CU",expression).

**Listing 17.8: UPPER.L1**

```
A = UPPER ("AbCd")          ; Sets a =  "ABCD".
A = UPPER ("Para" + "Docs") ; Sets a =  "PARADOCS".
A = UPPER (2)               ; Sets a =  "2".
A = UPPER (-2)              ; Sets a =  "-2".

; Like most other string functions, UPPER is sensitive to the date defaults
; If your default date format is dd-Mon-yy:

A = UPPER (1/5/1983)

; Sets a = "1-JAN-83" because the date is converted to the default format
; before string conversion.
```

Many functions return strings with a particular mix of upper- and lowercase letters. For example, in CoEdit, the SYSMODE() function returns the string: "CoEdit." The oddest example is the DIRECTORY() function, which returns a string that reflects the case you used in specifying the directory in the first place. DIRECTORY() returns "c:\\PaRAdoX3\\SAMPles\\" if that's the way you typed it in when you last changed directories. To simplify comparison tests of strings, use the UPPER() function to make them uniform:

**Listing 17.9: UPPER.L2**

```
IF UPPER(DIRECTORY()) = "C:\\PARADOX3\\SAMPLES\\" THEN
  ; do something here
ENDIF
```

See a full description under DIRECTORY() and SETDIR().

The next procedure converts all the alphanumeric fields in a table to uppercase. It places a Full Lock on the table so that no one else can interrupt the changes. Only two things might prevent the procedure from working properly: a key violation resulting from the case conversion, or a field with invalid data.

**Listing 17.10: UPPER.L3**

```
PROC uppertable.l (table.a)            ; Convert entire table to uppercase.
; Table.a    Name of table to convert.
; Returns    True if table was converted, False if no records or locked.
  PRIVATE n
  IF ISEMPTY(table.a) THEN             ; No need to continue.
    RETURN False
  ENDIF
  LOCK table.a FL
  IF NOT RETVAL THEN
    MESSAGE "Table is in use by ",ERRORUSER()
    SLEEP 3000
    RETURN False
  ENDIF
```

```
COEDIT table.a
REQUIREDCHECK OFF                       ; In case there are required fields.
FOR n FROM 1 TO NFIELDS(TABLE())
   RIGHT                                ; Move right one field.
   IF SEARCH("A",FIELDTYPE())=1 THEN    ; It is an alpha field.
      SCAN                              ; Look at each record.
         IF [] <> "" AND [] <> UPPER([]) THEN ; Only shift if not blank and not upper.
            [] = UPPER([])              ; Shift current field to upper case.
         ENDIF                          ;
         IF ERRORCODE()=53 THEN         ; See if there is a keyviol.
            BEEP BEEP
            UNDO                        ; Undo the offending field change from last record.
            ECHO NORMAL                 ; Refresh the canvas.
            ECHO OFF
            @1,0 CLEAR EOL  @0,0 CLEAR EOL
            ??"Changing this record will result in a key conflict "
            ?"Press any key to exit procedure.  Fix the data then try again"
            SYNCCURSOR                  ; Synchronize the cursor on the workspace.
            n=GETCHAR()
            DO_IT!
            UNLOCK table.a FL
            RETURN False
         ENDIF                          ; Keyviol check.
      ENDSCAN
   ENDIF                                ; Field was an alpha.
ENDFOR
DO_IT!
UNLOCK table.a FL
RETURN TRUE
ENDPROC

l = uppertable.l ("Customer")           ; True if all went well, False if keyviol or empty.
```

## FORMAT: Transforms a Value into a String of a Specified Style

```
FORMAT (Formatspec, String)
```

| | |
|---|---|
| String | Value to be formatted. |
| Formatspec | May be concatenated, separated by commas. |

**\*\*Width\*\***

| | |
|---|---|
| Wn | Allowable width. |
| Wn.m | Width and decimal places. |

**\*\*Alignment\*\***

| | |
|---|---|
| AL | Left justify. |
| AR | Right justify. |
| AC | Center within width. |

**\*\*Case\*\***

| | |
|---|---|
| CU | Uppercase. |

| | |
|---|---|
| CL | Lowercase. |
| CC | Initial caps. |

**\*\*Edit\*\***

| | |
|---|---|
| E$ | Floating $ sign. |
| EC | Use separators. |
| EZ | Print leading zeros. |
| EB | Blanks for leading zeros. |
| EI | International format. |
| ES | Scientific notation. |
| E* | Use "*" for leading zeros. |

**\*\*Sign\*\***

| | |
|---|---|
| S+ | Print leading + or −. |
| S− | Print leading −. |
| SP | Print negatives in (). |
| SD | Print DB or CR notation. |
| SC | Print CR after negatives. |

**\*\*Date\*\***

| | |
|---|---|
| D1 | mm/dd/yy. |
| D2 | Month dd, yyyy. |
| D3 | mm/dd. |
| D4 | mm/yy. |
| D5 | dd-Mon-yy. |
| D6 | Mon yy. |
| D7 | dd-Mon-yyyy. |
| D8 | mm/dd/yyyy. |
| D9 | dd.mm.yy. |
| D10 | dd/mm/yy. |
| D11 | yy-mm-dd. |

**\*\*Logical\*\***

| | |
|---|---|
| LY | Yes/No. |
| LO | On/Off. |

Returns:

| | |
|---|---|
| A String | Using the selected format, chosen. |

The FORMAT function allows you to change the appearance of any expression. Expressions of all types are automatically converted to strings. The Formatspecs can be combined into a list (it should really be called a FormatSpecList) by separating entries with commas within a single quoted string:

```
a = FORMAT("CU,W80,AC",[Customer Name]) ;Upper Case, 80 columns, centered
```

FORMAT is often used to create reports. Specifying that data must be printed in columns is relatively easy with the "Wn" (width) option of the FORMAT function as compared to analyzing the length of each string and padding it with spaces (see the example under SPACES). To use special FORMAT features in a report, create a reporting table with only alphanumeric fields and load the table with strings you FORMAT. For example, if you are printing bank checks, you might have an alpha field called [Print Amount] that contains a string put in place with the FORMAT function with leading asterisks and a dollar sign.

### 17.1.1.1 Width

The width parameter lets you specify the length of the returned string. Width formatting is often used in combination with other format options, so there are a few things to remember:

- You can specify a width from 1 to 255 characters.
- When formatting numbers, the width must be wide enough to accommodate any decimal points, commas, signs, etc.
- If the input is a number or date, and a width is chosen that will not display the entire value, a string of asterisks is returned (in much the same way that tables display large or partial columns of numbers).
- If an alphanumeric or logical value is specified that exceeds the width selected, the value is truncated to the selected width.

### 17.1.1.2 Alignment

FORMAT is often used to align (justify) values within a specified width. If no alignment is specified, Date and Number values align to the right, while Alphanumeric and Logical values align left.

**Listing 17.11: FORMAT.L1**

```
a = Format("W11","Paradox")       ; sets a = "Paradox    "
a = Format("W11,AR","Paradox")    ; sets a = "    Paradox"
a = Format("W11,AC","Paradox")    ; sets a = "  Paradox  "
```

The next few lines of code center a string of text on the screen, writing over any existing text on the line:

**Listing 17.12: FORMAT.L2**

```
STYLE REVERSE        ; Set display to inverse video.
@0,0 ?? FORMAT("W80,AC","This is a centered line of reverse text")
```

```
STYLE                   ; Restore default style.
MESSAGE "Press any key"
n = GETCHAR()
```

### 17.1.1.3 Case

Although you can usually use the UPPER and LOWER functions to return a string of the specified case, these capabilities are duplicated in the FORMAT function.

**Listing 17.13: FORMAT.L3**

```
a = FORMAT("CU","PaRaDoX")    ; sets a = "PARADOX"
a = FORMAT("CL","PaRaDoX")    ; sets a = "paradox"
a = FORMAT("CC","paradox")    ; sets a = "Paradox"
```

The "CC" parameter of the FORMAT function shifts the first letter of each word in the string to uppercase. The example in the PAL 2.0 manual is incorrect.

```
? FORMAT("CC","ZZZ AAA")
```

leaves everything in capital letters. The "CC" option shifts the first letter of each word to uppercase; it does not affect any other characters. The intended result is achieved with:

```
? FORMAT("CC",LOWER("ZZZ AAA"))
```

which returns "Zzz Aaa" because the lower function shifts the string to lowercase before it lets the "CC" shift the first letter of each word to uppercase. The example on page 80 of the Paradox2 manual (page 65 in Paradox3) shows the following example:

```
? FORMAT("CC","dOG")    ; outputs "Dog"
```

This simply is not the case (it outputs "DOG"). The function is doing what it says it is supposed to do, "Capitalize the first letter of each word." No more, no less.

The "CC" formatting feature is particularly desirable when trying to "Neaten Up" data imported from other programs (most notably mainframe data bases). You can create a variation of the uppertable.l() procedure outlined in the discussion of the UPPER function to shift columns or entire tables to initial capitalization. The "CC" parameter allows you to do in a few lines of PAL code what is otherwise impossible with a query.

Assuming you are already on a field in Edit or CoEdit mode, the following code converts the entire column to initial caps:

```
SCAN
  []=FORMAT("CC",LOWER([])
ENDSCAN
```

### 17.1.1.4 Edit

The Edit options let you control the way a number appears. You can use several edit options within one "E" prefix. The following example formats a number to be used for printing bank checks. The converted number is a string that is 12 characters wide, has two decimal places, a floating dollar sign, shows number separators, and fills the string with leading asterisks.

**Listing 17.14: FORMAT.L4**

```
n = 1234.56                    ; A positive number.
a = FORMAT("W12.2,E$C*", n)    ; Sets a = "$***1,234.56"
                               ; Which is the same as:
a = FORMAT("W12.2,E$,EC,E*", n) ; sets a = "$***1,234.56"
```

### 17.1.1.5 Sign

You can use FORMAT's sign options to specify the sign of numbers in a variety of ways, including forced signing using +/−, () or CR/DB, or sign negative numbers only.

**Listing 17.15: FORMAT.L5**

```
n1 = 1234.56     ; A positive number.
n2 = -1234.56    ; A negative number.

a = FORMAT("W8.2", n1)          ; sets a = " 1234.56"
a = FORMAT("W8.2,S+", n1)       ; sets a = "+1234.56"     ; Forced sign.
a = FORMAT("W11.2,EC,SP", n2)   ; sets a = "(-1,234.56)"  ; Parentheses and commas.
a = FORMAT("W12.2,E$C*", n2)    ; sets a = "$-**1,234.56" ; Note that - follows the $.
a = FORMAT("W13.2,E$C*,SP", n2) ; sets a = "($**1,234.56)" ; Note () surrounds value.
a = FORMAT("W13.2,E$C*,SD", n2) ; sets a = "$**1,234.56CR" ; Credit.
a = FORMAT("W13.2,E$C*,SD", n1) ; sets a = "$**1,234.56DB" ; Debit.
```

### 17.1.1.6 Date

There are 11 date formats. If you don't specify a format, Paradox uses whatever format you have installed as a default in your custom configuration. If you use a

WIDTH parameter in addition to the date parameter, make sure that the string is wide enough to accommodate the date or FORMAT will return asterisks.

**Listing 17.16: FORMAT.L6**

```
d = 7/3/52
a = FORMAT("D1", d)          ; sets a = "7/03/52"
a = FORMAT("D2", d)          ; sets a = "July  3, 1952"
a = FORMAT("D3", d)          ; sets a = "7/52"
a = FORMAT("D6", d)          ; sets a = "Jul 52"
a = FORMAT("D11", d)         ; sets a = "52-07-03"
a = FORMAT("W5", d)          ; sets a = "*****"
```

### 17.1.1.7 Logical

The default strings for logical values are "True" and "False"; however you can override these strings with the logical parameters:

**Listing 17.17: FORMAT.L7**

```
t.l = True
f.l = False
a = FORMAT("W5", t.l)    ; sets a = "True "    Note trailing space.
a = FORMAT("W5", f.l)    ; sets a = "False"
a = FORMAT("LY", True)   ; sets a = "Yes"
a = FORMAT("LY", False)  ; sets a = "No"
a = FORMAT("LO", 1=1)    ; sets a = "On"
a = FORMAT("LO", 1=2)    ; sets a = "Off"
```

### STRVAL: What Is the String Value of an Expression?

```
STRVAL (Expression)
```

      Expression     Any valid PAL expression.

Returns:

      A String     Containing the expression.

The STRVAL function leaves a string value unchanged and a date value in the currently set date format. If the expression is a number, the value returned is determined by the value and magnitude of the number. If the value is logical, STRVAL returns "True" or "False".
See also NUMVAL().

**Listing 17.18: STRVAL.L1**

```
a = STRVAL("aBcD")           ; Sets a = "aBcD"
a = STRVAL(42)               ; Sets a = "42"
```

```
a = STRVAL(40 + 2)           ; Sets a = "42"
a = STRVAL(40) + STRVAL(2)   ; Sets a = "402"
a = STRVAL( -3 )             ; Sets a = "-3"
a = STRVAL(TRUE)             ; Sets a = "True"
a = STRVAL(3=2)              ; Sets a = "False"

; If you have your date format set to mm/dd/yy.

a = STRVAL(12/25/90)         ; Sets a = "12/25/90"
a = STRVAL(1/1/90)           ; Sets a = "1/01/90"
a = STRVAL(4-jul-1776)       ; Sets a = "7/04/1776"

; However if you wanted to convert 4-jul-1776 TO "4-Jul-1776"  use the
; FORMAT function,

a = FORMAT ("D7", 4-jul-1776)  ; sets a = "4-Jul-1776"
```

Using the "+" operator allows you to concatenate strings. If you need to add nonstring values to a string, use the STRVAL function. For example, the PROMPT parameter of the WAIT command takes two strings—one for each of the top two lines of the screen. If you want to include the number of records for the table in the PROMPT, you need to find the number of records in the table and then convert it to a string to add to the rest of the prompt.

**Listing 17.19: STRVAL.L2**

```
VIEW "CUSTOMER"
WHILE TRUE
  WAIT TABLE
    PROMPT "Viewing Customer " + STRVAL(NRECORDS(TABLE())) + " records on file",
    "Press [Esc] when done"
  UNTIL "Esc", "Dos", "DosBig"
  IF RETVAL = "Esc" THEN
    CLEARIMAGE
    QUITLOOP
  ENDIF
ENDWHILE
```

It is also important to keep in mind that the ?, ??, MESSAGE, and PRINT commands allow you to use a comma-separated list of expressions, and that the expressions may be made up of any combinations of types.

```
MESSAGE "Abcd", 3, 4/22/84, TRUE
```

would display

```
Abcd34/22/84True
```

whereas if you wanted to assign all of that to one string variable you would have to use

```
a = "Abcd" + STRVAL(3) + STRVAL(4/22/84) + STRVAL(TRUE)
```

which sets a to

```
"Abcd34/22/84True"
```

## SUBSTR: Return a Substring of a Given String

```
SUBSTR (String, Number1, Number2)
```

String      Character string.
Number1     Integer of first character position, from 1 to LEN(String).
Number2     Number of characters to extract.

Returns:

A String    Substring of string that starts at position Number1 and continues for Number2 characters.

### Listing 17.20: SUBSTR.L1

```
a = SUBSTR("Paradox", 1, 1)    ; Sets a = "P"
a = SUBSTR("Paradox", 2, 1)    ; Sets a = "a"
a = SUBSTR("Paradox", 2, 3)    ; Sets a = "ara"
a = SUBSTR("Paradox", 5, 3)    ; Sets a = "dox"
a = SUBSTR("aBcD", 2, 2)       ; Sets a = "Bc"
```

SUBSTR, like many other string functions, converts expressions to strings, if necessary. Supplying inappropriate values for Number1 and Number2 will result in a truncated or null string.

### Listing 17.21: SUBSTR.L2

```
a = SUBSTR(123456, 2, 3)    ; Sets a = "234"
a = SUBSTR(109 + 33, 2, 2)  ; Sets a = "42"
a = SUBSTR( -42, 1, 2)      ; Sets a = "-4"
a = SUBSTR("TRue", 1, 2)    ; Sets a = "TR"
a = SUBSTR(TRUE, 1, 4)      ; Sets a = "True"
a = SUBSTR(TRUE, 2, 2)      ; Sets a = "ru"
a = SUBSTR(3=2, 1, 5)       ; Sets a = "False"
```

However, if you want a fixed number of characters returned, you should use the FORMAT command:

**Listing 17.22: SUBSTR.L3**

```
PROC stringfill.a (string.v, length.n)
  ; string.v  ; Any valid PAL expression.
  ; length.n  ; Fixed length of string to return.
  RETURN FORMAT("W"+STRVAL(length.n), string.v)
  ; e.g. FORMAT("W5", "abcdefg")
ENDPROC

; In the procedure above, we are adding the desired length to the "W"
; width parameter of the FORMAT function.

  a = stringfill.a ("Paradox", 5)  ; sets a = "Parad"
  a = stringfill.a (123, 5)        ; sets a = "123  "
```

For example, one way to remove the trailing x's from the "Abcdxxxxxxx" is to look at the last character in the string and explicitly remove it if necessary.

**Listing 17.23: SUBSTR.L4**

```
WHILE string.a <> "" AND SUBSTR(string.a , LEN(string.a), 1) = "x"
  string.a = SUBSTR(string.a, 1, LEN(string.a) - 1 )
ENDWHILE
```

Often there are easier (and faster) ways of doing complicated substring calculations. The same routine could be more simply written with a MATCH function that reassigns the string.a variable.

```
WHILE MATCH(string.a, "..x", string.a)
ENDWHILE
```

The MATCH is also faster than the SUBSTR approach.

The next procedure combines several string functions, letting each do what it does best. The task is to have the procedure determine if a string is a palindrome, a word, or series of words that are spelled the same forwards and backwards, like DEED. Punctuation and case are ignored, so that "a man, a plan, a canal, Panama," returns TRUE.

First, the code shifts the entire string to lowercase and strips out punctuation, leaving only letters and numbers. Then it compares the first and last characters of the string for a match and returns a False if a mismatch is found.

**Listing 17.24: SUBSTR.L5**

```
PROC IsPalindrome.l (string.v)
  ; string.v  ; The string to test, actually any PAL expression can be used.
  ; RETURNS   ; True if a palindrome, otherwise False.
  PRIVATE
```

```
n,            ; Loop counter.
new.a,        ; New string cleaned of punctuation, shifted to lower case.
a,            ; Single character used in substring cleanup.
a1,           ; First letter of string in match function.
a2            ; Last letter of string in match function.

string.v = LOWER(string.v)        ; These 9 lines remove punctuation and case.
new.a = ""                        ; Initialize the string cleaned of punctuation

FOR n FROM 1 TO LEN(string.v)     ; For each character in the original string,
  a = SUBSTR(string.v, n, 1)      ; get substring of string (already lower case),
  IF (a > "`" AND a < "{") OR     ; check for lower case alpha Asc(97)-(122)
    (a > "/" AND a < ":") THEN    ; or number (without use of ASC function).
    new.a = new.a + a             ; Appended to cleaned up string.
  ENDIF
ENDFOR

; Now compare the first and last letters of the string.  If a match is found
; remove the letters and repeat on the remaining string until no match
; is found, or we run out of letters.

WHILE MATCH(new.a, "@ ..@ ", a1, new.a, a2) ; Now actually lookfor Palindrome.

  IF a1 <> a2 THEN                ; Check first and last characters.
    RETURN False                 ; No match? return false.
  ENDIF
ENDWHILE
RETURN True                      ; Passed the test.
ENDPROC

; Now to test the proc

l = ispalindrome.l("Level")              ; sets l = True
l = ispalindrome.l("Evil")               ; sets l = False
l = ispalindrome.l("Madam, I'm Adam")    ; sets l = True
```

## SEARCH: Return the Position of a Substring within a String

```
SEARCH (Substring, String)
```

> Substring    An expression that you are trying to locate within the string.
> String    The string to be searched.

Returns:

> A Number    The position of the character within the string at which the Substring begins.
> 0    If the string is not found.

The SEARCH function returns a positive integer or the value 0. Expressions are automatically converted to strings before evaluation, and are not sensitive to case.

### Listing 17.25: SEARCH.L1

```
n = SEARCH ("ex", "example")        ; Sets n = 1.
n = SEARCH ("ex", "PAL By Example") ; Sets n = 8 , insensitive to case.
n = SEARCH ("ex", "maximum")        ; Sets n = 0 , not found.
n = SEARCH ("Maximum", "Max")       ; Sets n = 0 , not found.

; The search function is totally insensitive to data types, treating
; them all as if they were strings:

n = SEARCH ( 3, 51473)              ; Sets n = 5.
n = SEARCH ( 3, "51473")           ; sets n = 5
n = SEARCH ("3", 51473)            ; sets n = 5

; If your default date format is  mm/dd/yy:

n = SEARCH ("6", 7/04/1776)        ; sets n = 9
n = SEARCH (6, 7/4/1776)           ; sets n = 9  Because date is converted
                                   ;              to 7/04/1776 first.
```

To allow the user to do something while in any one of the editing modes, you might write:

### Listing 17.26: SEARCH.L2

```
IF SYSMODE() = "Edit" OR SYSMODE() = "CoEdit" OR SYSMODE() = "DataEntry" THEN
  ; Do something.
ENDIF

; However, the line can be made slightly shorter by using the SEARCH
; function to determine if the sysmode() is contained within a longer string.

IF SEARCH(SYSMODE(),"CoEditDataEntry") > 0 THEN
  ; Do something.
ENDIF
```

Similarly, if you have a choice on a Main menu that displays the following menu:

### Listing 17.27: SEARCH.L3

```
PROC filemenu.u ()
  PRIVATE choice.a

  WHILE TRUE
    SHOWMENU
      "Customer" : "View the customer table",
      "Invoices" : "View the invoice table",
      "MainMenu" : "Return back to main menu"
    TO choice.a
    SWITCH
      CASE choice.a = "Esc" OR choice.a = "MainMenu" :
        RETURN   ; Leave this proc, go back to procedure that called it.
```

```
      CASE choice.a = "Customer":
        customer.u ()
      CASE choice.a = "Invoice":
        invoice.u ()
    ENDSWITCH
  ENDWHILE
ENDPROC
```

There are two ways to neaten up the SWITCH conditions outlined above. First, you could replace the first CASE statement with:

```
CASE SEARCH(choice.a, "EscMainMenu") > 0 :
```

or, better yet, remove the first case entirely and place an:

```
OTHERWISE:
  RETURN
```

just before the ENDSWITCH.

### MATCH: Does a String Contain a Pattern? Optionally Assign Variables to Match Patterns Found

```
MATCH (String, Patternstring, Varnamelist)
```

| | |
|---|---|
| String | Any valid PAL expression (automatically treated as a string). |
| Patternstring | The string to search for, including wildcard patterns. .. = any number of characters (or no characters), @ = a single character. |
| Varnamelist | Names of variables to assign corresponding to the wildcards in the patternstring. |

Returns:

| | |
|---|---|
| False | If the patternstring is not contained in the string. |
| True | If there is a match. |
| Sets | The varnamelist variable(s) corresponding to the values that the wildcards replaced. |

The MATCH function takes a little getting used to. It has the ability to return a value, and is the only function that can also optionally assign variables directly. MATCH always returns a True or False based on whether a pattern has been found in a string. The optional variables are assigned only if the MATCH returns True; either all the variables are set, or none at all.

Although the MATCH function is not sensitive to case, any variables assigned pick up the case of the original string.

### Listing 17.28: MATCH.L1

```
l = MATCH ("Paradox", "Paradocs")           ; sets l = False
l = MATCH ("Paradox", "Paradox")            ; sets l = True
l = MATCH ("Paradox", "Paradox..")          ; sets l = True
l = MATCH ("Paradox", "P..")                ; sets l = True
l = MATCH ("Paradox", "pa..")               ; sets l = True  not case sensitive.
l = MATCH ("Paradox", "P..", a1)            ; sets l = True  a1="aradox"
l = MATCH ("Paradox", "p..s", a1)           ; sets l = False a1 is not assigned
l = MATCH ("Paradox", "P@..x", a1, a2)      ; sets l = True  a1="a"  a2="rado"
l = MATCH ("Paradox", "..x", a1)            ; sets l = True  a1="Parado"

l = MATCH ("Paradox", "@a@a..", a1, a2, a3) ; sets l = True  a1="P" a2="r" a3="dox"
l = MATCH ("PaRaDox", "@a@a..", a1, a2, a3) ; sets l = True  a1="P" a2="R" a3="Dox"
l = MATCH (1234, "1234")                    ; sets l = True
l = MATCH (1234, "@..@", a1, a2, a3)        ; sets l = True  a1="1" a2="23" a3="4"
l = MATCH (1234, "@..5", a1, a2)            ; sets l = False a1 and a2 are not assigned

; A special case occurs when you need to search for the literal character @.
; For example, the next syntax is incorrect, even though it looks like it
; should work to show that there is an @ sign present as the fourth character:

l = MATCH ("123@56", "..\@ ..")  ; Sets l = True even if there is no @ present
                                 ; in the original string.

; To see if there is an @ sign present in the string, the @ sign must be
; surrounded by literal quotes. The proper syntax is:

l = MATCH ("123@56", "..\"@ \"..")  ; Sets l = True only if there is an @.

; Remember that dates will be converted to your default date format before
; being analyzed. If your date format is set to mm/dd/yy and 7/4/89 is
; converted to 7/04/89

l = MATCH ("7/4/89", "../../@@", month.a, day.a, decade.a, year.a)
l = MATCH (7/4/89, "../../@@", month.a, day.a, decade.a, year.a)
l = MATCH (4-jul-89, "../../@@", month.a, day.a, decade.a, year.a)
 ; Both examples set l = True
 ; month.a = "7"
 ; day.a = "04"
 ; decade.a = "8"
 ; year.a = "9"
```

The ability of the MATCH function to assign variables to the wildcard matches is of particular interest. Examine the next two lines of code:

```
WHILE MATCH(string.a, ".. ", string.a)
ENDWHILE
```

"As long as there is a space as the last character of the string, keep reassigning the variable string.a to the string found before the space."

Though there is no direct PAL function to trim leading or trailing spaces from a string, a simple procedure is demonstrated below. The code uses the MATCH function to truncate the string where needed.

**Listing 17.29: MATCH.L2**

```
PROC trim.a(string.a, where.a)
  ; Where.a =   "L" or "l" to trim the left, or leading, spaces.
  ;             "R" or "r" to trim only the right, or trailing, spaces.
  ;             Any other string will trim both leading and trailing spaces.

  where.a = UPPER(where.a)                    ; Traps for lower case.
  IF where.a <> "R" THEN
    WHILE  MATCH(string.a, " ..", string.a)  ; Is there a leading space?
    ENDWHILE
  ENDIF
  IF where.a <> "L" THEN
    WHILE  MATCH(string.a, ".. ", string.a)  ; Is there a trailing space?
    ENDWHILE
  ENDIF
  RETURN string.a
ENDPROC

; To demonstrate:

test.a = "   This is a test   " ; Three leading and three trailing spaces.

a = trim.a ( test.a, "L")      ; sets a = "This is a test   "
a = trim.a ( test.a, "r")      ; sets a = "   This is a test"
a = trim.a ( test.a, "B")      ; sets a = "This is a test"
a = trim.a ( test.a, "")       ; sets a = "This is a test"
a = trim.a ( test.a, 42)       ; sets a = "This is a test"
```

The example in the PAL User's Guide has the right idea about using the MATCH function to split out a combined last name and first name into separate fields. Unfortunately, there are a few lines of code missing that render it useless. We expand on the example below. The code assumes that there are two tables; one called "OldNames",

```
Viewing Oldnames table: Record 1 of 4
```

```
OLDNAMES            Name
       1 │ Kocis, James
       2 │ Zenreich, Alan
       3 │ Zenreich, Scott Cameron
       4 │ Merlin
```

and a second empty table called "NewNames" that has [Last Name] and [First Name] fields. The object is to load the "NewNames" table with the first and last names, a typical task performed on data imported from other programs. Although most of the data has a comma separating the last name from the first name, the name "Merlin" is an exception. The procedure places any name without a comma into the [Last Name] field of the "NewNames" table.

**Listing 17.30: MATCH.L3**

```
VIEW "NewNames"
COEDIT "OldNames"
SCAN   ; Thru all the records in the oldnames table
  MESSAGE "Working on record ",RECNO(), " of ", NRECORDS("OldNames")
  name.a = [name]
    ; Now look for a comma followed by a space
  l= MATCH( name.a, ".., ..", last.a, first.a)
  UPIMAGE                    ; Move to the NewNames table
    ; the PAL manual forgot to open a new record, so we'll correct that now
  END   ; move to the last record in the table
  IF [last name]<>"" THEN    ; This is not a blank record
    DOWN                     ; Append a new record
  ENDIF
    ; let's see if we sucessfully split the string
  IF l THEN                  ; A match was found
    [last name] = last.a
    [first name] = first.a
  ELSE                       ; No comma and space was found
    [last name] = name.a
    ; or optionally
    ; [oldnames -> Last Name]
  ENDIF
  DOWNIMAGE                  ; Back to the oldnames table
ENDSCAN
DO_IT!                       ; Complete the edit
```

The resultant workspace would look like:

```
Viewing OldNames table: Record 4 of 4
```

```
NEWNAMES┬───────Last Name═══════┬═════First Name═══════┐
     1  │ Kocis                 │ James                 │
     2  │ Zenreich              │ Alan                  │
     3  │ Zenreich              │ Scott Cameron         │
     4  │ Merlin                │                       │

OLDNAMES┬───────────────Name═══════════════┐
     1  │ Kocis, James                      │
     2  │ Zenreich, Alan                    │
     3  │ Zenreich, Scott Cameron           │
     4  │ Merlin                            │
```

Of course, this example doesn't trap for all the possible problems, i.e., "Morse, Lauren" would fail the match because it lacks a space. However, by looking through the data, you can generally recognize exceptions and code accordingly.

## 17.2 TIME AND DATE

Paradox makes it easy to perform date arithmetic as long as the dates are in the range of from 1/1/100 to 12/31/9999. Paradox knows all the valid dates in this range, compensating for leap years.

```
PAL automatically recognizes date values, and you can mix and match
any of the following three formats:

    mm/dd/yy        ; 7/3/90,    7/04/1776
    dd-Mon-yy       ; 3-Jul-90   4-Jul-1776
    dd.mm.yy        ; 3.7.90     4.7.1776

Adding or subtracting a number to or from a date yields a new date:

d = 7/4/1776 + 5            ; sets d = 7/9/1776
d = 7/4/1776 - 5            ; sets d = 6/29/1776

Subtracting one date from another yields the number of days between the two dates:

n = 4/22/90 - 7/3/90        ; sets n = 72, the number of days
n = 22-Apr-90 - 3-Jul-90    ; sets n = 72
n = 22.4.90 - 3-Jul-90      ; sets n = 72
n = 7/3/90 - 4/22/90        ; sets n = -72

n = 3/90                    ; sets n = .03333333..
                            ; because 3/90 is not a date, it is simple division
```

You can create procedures that do time calculations by parsing the string returned by the TIME function into hours, minutes, and seconds, and converting these strings into numbers with NUMVAL. A few of the examples that follow in this chapter use this technique.

Time calculations of this sort are best done by converting elapsed times in seconds. If a new time is needed rather than using elapsed time, care must be taken to trap for carry-over between days. PAL has functions that read the computer's clock to determine the current date and time. Make sure that the clock is set correctly for both.

### TIME: What Time Is It Now?

```
TIME ()
```

Returns:

A String    An eight-character string in military format in the form "hh:mm:ss," hours, minutes and seconds.

**Listing 17.31: TIME.L1**

```
a = TIME()     ; Sets a = "09:30:25" at 9:30:25 AM.
               ; Sets a = "12:00:00" at 12 NOON.
               ; Sets a = "13.30:00" at 1:30 PM.
               ; Sets a = "00:00:00" at MIDNIGHT.
```

To reassign the [Ctrl T] key to display a message about the current time:

```
SETKEY 20 RETURN "The current time is "+ TIME()
```

Note that this uses the RETURN instead of MESSAGE so that the time will stay on the screen. The next procedure returns the time of day for a given time specified in military format.

**Listing 17.32: TIME.L2**

```
PROC timeofday.a ( time.a )
  ; Returns a string  "Morning", "Afternoon" or "Evening".
  PRIVATE v1, v2

  RETVAL=MATCH( time.a ,"..:..",v1, v2)  ;
  ; At this point v1 is a string of the military hours.
  ; v2 is the string of minutes and seconds.

  v1 = NUMVAL(v1)                ; v1 is now a number.
  SWITCH
    CASE v1 > 16 :               ; > = 5:00 PM
      v1 = "Evening"
    CASE v1 > 11 :               ; > = 12:00 PM
      v1 = "Afternoon"
    OTHERWISE:
      v1 = "Morning"
  ENDSWITCH
  RETURN v1
ENDPROC

; test

timeofday.a = timeofday.a ( TIME() )    ; Morning, Afternoon, or Evening
MESSAGE "Good ", timeofday.a, ".  Time is now : ", TIME(), " Press any key"
n = GETCHAR()
```

## TODAY: What Is Today's Date?

```
TODAY ()
```

Returns:

A Date    The current date as set in the computer, returned in the currently used, interactive date format.

### Listing 17.33: TODAY.L1

```
IF TODAY() < 4/1/89 THEN
  MESSAGE "Your system clock must be set incorrectly. Press any key."
  n = GETCHAR()
  ; now, possibly take corrective action
ENDIF
```

## BLANKDATE: Return a Blank Date

```
BLANKDATE ()
```

Returns: A blank date.

The BLANKDATE() function is used to determine if a date field or a variable has a blank value, or to explicitly assign a field or variable as a date, keeping the date blank. See ISBLANKZERO() for a detailed discussion of blank values. The next listing shows two ways of checking whether or not there is a value in the [Invoice Date] field of the current record:

### Listing 17.34: BLANKDAT.L1

```
IF [Invoice date] = BLANKDATE() THEN
  [Invoice date] = TODAY()
ENDIF

; is the same as:

IF ISBLANK( [Invoice date] ) THEN
  [Invoice date] = TODAY()
ENDIF
```

BLANKDATE() is also handy for clearing fields or variables. For example, assume that we want to clear a [Reminder Memo Date] field if there is no outstanding balance:

### Listing 17.35: BLANKDAT.L2

```
IF [Balance due] <= 0 THEN              ; No Balance currently due.
  [Reminder memo date] = BLANKDATE()    ; Clear the memo date field.
ENDIF
```

There is currently (in Paradox 3.01) an error in the way BLANKDATE is handled by the other date functions. As of this writing, you'll have to take some care and make sure that dates are not blank before you try to use these functions:

**Listing 17.36: BLANKDAT.L3**

```
d = BLANKDATE()
n = MONTH(d)       ; sets n = 1          ; Month.
n = DAY(d)         ; sets n = 8          ; Day, getting stranger.
n = YEAR(d)        ; sets n = 18810      ; Year, very strange.
a = DOW (d)        ; causes script error : Expecting non blank value.
a = MOY (d)        ; sets a = "Jan"      ; Month of year.

; So, if you are scanning a table containing blank date entries, you might
; want to use the BLANKDATE function to test the value before proceeding:

EDIT "Invoices"
SCAN
  IF [Last payment date] <> BLANKDATE() THEN
    [Next payment year] = YEAR([last payment date]) + 1
  ENDIF
ENDSCAN
DO_IT!

; Or alternately, use the ISBLANK function:

EDIT "Invoices"
SCAN FOR NOT ISBLANK( [Last payment date] )
  [Next payment year] = YEAR( [Last payment date] ) + 1
ENDSCAN
DO_IT!
```

## DATEVAL: Return the Date Value of a String

```
DATEVAL (String)
```

String    A string evaluating to a valid Paradox date format.

Returns:

A Date    The date equivalent of the string entered.
"Error"    If the string is not a valid date.

The DATEVAL function translates a string into a date, or returns the string "Error" if the date is not legitimate. The following are two examples of the same procedure, which determines the day of the week on which a given calendar day occurs by specifying the number of years forward or backward from that date.

```
a = DOW.a ( 4/22/84, 7 )
```

returns the day of the week on which 4/22 will occur in the year 1991. If the date is 2/29 and the target year is not a leap year, the word "Error" is returned.

### Listing 17.37: DATEVAL.L1

```
PROC dow.a (date.d, yearoffset.n)
  ; date.d        ; date in question.
  ; yearoffest.n  ; the number of years forward or back to move
  ;               ; a positive number moves forward,
  ;               ; a negative number moves backwards
  ;  examples assume date.d = 4/22/84    yearoffset.n = 7
  PRIVATE
  month.a,        ; string of month
  day.a,          ; string of day
  year.a,         ; string of year
  targetdate.v,   ; date, or string of date
  targetyear.n,   ; year of target date
  l               ; used by MATCH function

  IF ISBLANK(date.d) THEN
    RETURN "Error"
  ENDIF

  ; regardless of the original format of the date, let's convert it to a
  ; string with format MM/DD/YYYY

  date.v = FORMAT("D8",date.a)      ; "4/22/1984"
  l = MATCH(date.v, "../../..", month.a, day.a, year.a)
  ; the match implictly assigns the three string variables.
  ; month.v = "4"    day.v = "22"  year.v = "1984"

  targetyear.n = NUMVAL(year.a) + yearoffset.n  ; 1984 + 7 = 1991
  targetdate.v = month.a + "/" + day.a + "/" + STRVAL(targetyear.n)
  ; "4/22/1991"
  targetdate.v = DATEVAL(targetdate.v)

  IF targetdate.v = "Error" THEN
    RETURN "Error"  ; if date does not exist i.e., Feb 29 1991
  ELSE              ; Dateval sucessfully returned a date
    RETURN  DOW(targetdate.v)      ; get the day of week
  ENDIF
ENDPROC
```

### Listing 17.38: DATEVAL.L2

```
PROC dow2.a(date.d, yearoffset.n)
  IF ISBLANK(date.d) THEN    ; Only necessary because of anomalies
    RETURN "Error"           ; in date functions and BLANKDATE().
  ENDIF
  date.d = DATEVAL( STRVAL(MONTH(date.d)) + "/" +
  STRVAL(DAY  (date.d)) + "/" +
  STRVAL(YEAR (date.d) + yearoffset.n)))

  IF date.d = "Error" THEN
    RETURN "Error"           ; If date does not exist e.g., Feb 29 1991.
  ELSE
    RETURN DOW(date.d)       ; Get the day of week.
  ENDIF
ENDPROC
```

The shorter code is preferable, but the first example is more demonstrative of the various techniques of converting to and from dates and is a little easier to follow.

### DAY: On What Day of the Month Does a Date Fall?

```
DAY (Date)
```

    Date          A valid date.

Returns:

    A Number      An integer between 1 and 31 representing the day of the month for the date.

    Script Error   If the date is invalid.

The DAY function returns the day's number (1–31); the DOW function returns the name of the day (e.g., "Mon"). As of this writing, DAY (BLANKDATE()) returns 8. See BLANKDATE().

**Listing 17.39: DAY.L1**

```
d = 3/15/2001      ; Assign a date in any format, or optionally
                   ; use any of the other date formats.
; d = 15.3.2001
; d = 15-Mar-2001
MESSAGE "The Ides of March always falls on March ",DAY(d),".  et tu, Brute!"
SLEEP 3000
```

### MONTH: On What Month of the Year Does a Date Fall?

```
MONTH (Date)
```

    Date          A valid date.

Returns:

    A Number      Between 1 and 12 representing the month.

    Script error    If not a valid date.

**Listing 17.40: MONTH.L1**

```
D = 3/15/2001      ; Assign a date in any format.
                   ; d = 15.3.2001
                   ; d = 15-Mar-2001
MONTH (D)          ; Returns 3.
```

As of this writing, MONTH(BLANKDATE()) returns 1, see BLANKDATE for more information.

## YEAR

```
YEAR (Date)
```

Date                Any valid date.

Returns:

A Number        A 4-digit number if the date is >=1/1/1000, a 3-digit number if the date is >=1/1/100 and <=12/31/999, and an incorrect number if the date is below 1/1/100.

**Listing 17.41: YEAR.L1**

```
d = 3/15/2001        ; Assign a date in any format.
                     ; d = 15.3.2001
                     ; d = 15-Mar-2001
n = YEAR (d)         ; Sets n = 2001.
n = YEAR (3/15/90)   ; Sets n = 1990.
n = YEAR (3/15/250)  ; Sets n = 250.

; If a date less than 1/1/100 is selected, PAL will return an invalid
; answer. In practical terms this may not be significant, but if
; tracking Biblical dates, for example, it would cause problems.

n = YEAR(1/1/100 - 50) ; Sets n = 1999, an incorrect value.
```

As of this writing, YEAR(BLANKDATE()) returns 18810 in Paradox2, Paradox3, and PDOXOS2, and returns 5887424 in PDOX386. See BLANKDATE for further information.

## DOW: On What Day of the Week Does a Date Fall?

```
DOW (Date)
```

Date                A valid date.

Returns:

A String        Three characters representing the day of the week: "Mon", "Tue", "Wed", "Thu", "Fri", "Sat", "Sun".

The example below changes the three letter abbreviation for a weekday returned from the DOW() function to full spelling, i.e., "Wed" becomes "Wednesday".

Since "Mon," "Fri," and "Sun" are simply suffixed with "day," the OTHERWISE command groups them into one calculated line.

**Listing 17.42: DOW.L1**

```
PROC spelldow.a (date.d)
  ;displays greeting, skips line and displays date
  ;beginning on line specified
  PRIVATE day.a, v1, v2
  day.a=DOW(date.d)      ; a three letter string
  SWITCH
    CASE day.a="Tue":
      day.a="Tuesday"
    CASE day.a="Wed":
      day.a="Wednesday"
    CASE day.a="Thu":
      day.a="Thursday"
    CASE day.a="Sat":
      day.a="Saturday"
    OTHERWISE :
      day.a= day.a + "day"      ; Mon, Fri, or Sun
  ENDSWITCH
  RETURN day.a
ENDPROC
```

### MOY: What Is the Month of the Year for a Specific Date?

```
MOY (Date)
```

Date            A valid date.

Returns:

A String        Three characters representing the month: "Jan", "Feb", "Mar", "Apr", "May", "Jun", "Jul", "Aug", "Sep", "Oct", "Nov", "Dec".

As of this writing, MOY(BLANKDATE()) returns "Jan". See BLANKDATE.

**Listing 17.43: MOY.L1**

```
d = 3/15/2001     ; Assign a date in any format.
                  ; d = 15.3.2001
                  ; d = 15-Mar-2001
MOY (d)           ; Returns "Mar".
```

# 17.3 NUMBERS

Paradox has three numeric data types: full precision numbers ("N"); short numbers ("S"); and currency ("$"). Although currency is stored as a full precision number, it always displays two decimal places by default.

## 17.3.1 Blanks

### ISBLANKZERO: Is Paradox Configured to Treat Blanks as Zeros in Arithmetic Calculations not Dealing with Counting?

```
ISBLANKZERO ()
```

Returns:

| | |
|---|---|
| True | If blanks are treated as zeros in arithmetic, noncounting calculations. |
| False | The blank equals zero option has not been chosen in the CUSTOM.SC. |

The ISBLANKZERO() function enables you to determine whether or not Paradox is installed to treat blank values as zeros in certain circumstances. Blank numeric fields are always distinguishable from zeros—a zero is a value and shows in a field, a blank is the absence of a value.

This distinction isn't all that unusual. For example, a final bowling score of zero is different from a blank score. A final score of 0 means the player threw 20 consecutive gutter balls (and is now in hiding from angry teammates). A blank final score means the bowler hasn't completed the game. If you want to perform calculations on the last frame total, you have to decide how to treat blank values. For example, to calculate the score if you had done 10 percent better, you might write:

**Listing 17.44: ISBLANKZ.L1**

```
targetscore.n = [Final Score] * 1.1
; Now, because you can't possibly bowl better than 300, a perfect game:
targetscore.n = MIN ( targetscore.n, 300 )
MESSAGE "Current score is ", [Final Score], ". target score is ", targetscore.n,"."
SLEEP 2000
```

However, if there were blank values in the data, and if Paradox was in its default configuration, a script error would result, because you cannot multiply a number by a blank number. The code should be changed to:

**Listing 17.45: ISBLANKZ.L2**

```
IF ISBLANK([Final Score]) THEN
  MESSAGE "Final score not in."
ELSE
  targetscore.n = [Final score] * 1.1
```

```
targetscore.n = MIN ( targetscore.n, 300 )
    MESSAGE "Current score is ", [Final Score], ".  Target score is ", targetscore.n,"."
ENDIF
SLEEP 2000
```

The default configuration of Paradox2 and Paradox3 treats blanks differently from zeros, though this can be changed with the "Custom" script. Choosing the Blanks = Zero option tells Paradox to treat blanks as zeros in the following cases:

1. calculated fields in forms
2. calculated fields in reports
3. Query calculations not having to do with counting
4. PAL calculations not having to do with counting

Calculations that involve counting nonblank values are not affected at all.

Query calculations: CALC COUNT, CALC AVERAGE
PAL Functions: CCOUNT(), CAVERAGE(), IMAGECCOUNT(), IMAGEC-
AVERAGE()

If blanks are not being treated as zeros, incrementing a numeric field by 1 might look like this:

**Listing 17.46: ISBLANKZ.L3**

```
IF ISBLANK( [Revision number] ) THEN
   [Revision number] = 1
ELSE
   [Revision number] = [Revision number] + 1
ENDIF
```

However, if blanks are being treated as zeros, a simple

```
[Revision Number] = [Revision Number] + 1
```

works fine. If you have to do this a couple of hundred times for various fields in your scripts, it becomes really tedious without the Blanks = Zero turned on. If you have an unkeyed table like:

```
TEST │ Value
1    │  2
2    │  1
3    │          <-- Record #3 is blank
4    │  6
5    │  4
6    │  2
```

if you perform a query that calculates the AVERAGE of [Value], you'll get 3 (15/5, only counting nonblank values). The same goes for the CAVERAGE function. Treating blanks as zeros makes it easier to design reports and forms, as well as simplifying PAL code. However, it's important that you know when calculations would be inappropriate.

### BLANKNUM: Returns a Blank Number

```
BLANKNUM ()
```

Returns: A blank number (Not a zero.)

The BLANKNUM function creates a type that is appropriate for a numeric variable or field, but in fact contains no value. Note that even if blanks are being treated as zeros, BLANKNUM() does not equal zero. In fact, BLANKNUM is less than any and all numbers. This adds a layer of complexity to operations. For example,

```
IF []<=0 THEN
  ; do something
ENDIF
```

should be written:

```
IF NOT ISBLANK([]) AND [] <=0 THEN
  ; do something
ENDIF
```

For example, to clear a balance due, you might want to use [Balance due] = 0, which assigns a zero balance, whereas [Balance due] = Blanknum() or MOVETO [Balance due] CTRLBACKSPACE clears the field of any value.

See ISBLANKZERO for a detailed discussion of blank fields. The next example sets up an array of five elements and loads each element with a blank number:

**Listing 17.47: BLANKNUM.L1**

```
ARRAY numbers.r[5]
FOR n FROM 1 TO 5
  numbers.r[n] = BLANKNUM()
ENDFOR
```

## 17.3.2 Parts of Numbers

### NUMVAL: What Is the Numeric Representation of a String?

```
NUMVAL (String)
```

| | |
|---|---|
| String | A PAL expression that can be converted to a number. |

Returns:

| | |
|---|---|
| A Number | If the string can be converted to a number. |
| A String | "Error" if the string cannot convert to a number. |
| Script Error | If you pass an argument that is not a string. |

The NUMVAL function is used to convert a string to a number. Here are some examples:

**Listing 17.48: NUMVAL.L1**

```
NUMVAL("42")          ; Returns 42
NUMVAL("4"+"2")       ; Returns 42        ; Concatenates string before evaluating.
NUMVAL("4.2E1")       ; Returns 42        ; Scientific notation okay.
NUMVAL("42,424")      ; Returns 42424     ; Accepts comma.
NUMVAL("42,4242")     ; Returns "Error"   ; Comma in the wrong place.
NUMVAL("-42")         ; Returns -42       ; Accepts minus sign.
NUMVAL("(42)")        ; Returns -42       ; Accepts parentheses as negative.
; None of the following evaluate to a number.
NUMVAL("1/1/90")      ; Returns "Error"
NUMVAL("1-5")         ; Returns "Error"
NUMVAL("Forty-Two")   ; Returns "Error"
NUMVAL(123)           ; Causes script error because 123 is not a string.
```

The procedure below, AmPm2Military.a, uses NUMVAL to convert a 12-hour time string to its corresponding military (24-hour) time string. If the string contains a "P" (for p.m.), 12 hours are added and the value converted into a five-character string. If the time does not contain hours and minutes followed by an a.m./p.m. designator, it returns the word "Error". The reason Tenminute.a and Oneminute.a are split out is to eliminate values that don't contain a reference to a.m. or p.m. If the MATCH function is successful, it splits the string into four variables that can be evaluated in the SWITCH.

**Listing 17.49: NUMVAL.L2**

```
PROC ampm2military.a(time.a)
  PRIVATE l, hour.a, tenminute.a, oneminute.a, ampm.a
  l = MATCH(time.a, "..:aaa", hour.a, tenminute.a, oneminute.a, ampm.a)
```

```
SWITCH
  CASE NOT l :
    RETURN "Error"
  CASE UPPER(ampm.a) = "P" AND hour.a <> "12":
    ; Need to add 12 to the numeric value of the string and then convert
    ; back to a string.
    RETURN STRVAL(NUMVAL(hour.a)+12)+ ":" + tenminute.a+ oneminute.a
  CASE UPPER(ampm.a)="A" AND hour.a="12":
    ; 0 hours
    RETURN  "00:"+ tenminute.a+ oneminute.a
  OTHERWISE:
    ; Need to add a 0 to a single character hour.
    IF LEN(hour.a)=1 THEN
      hour.a = "0"+ hour.a
    ENDIF
    RETURN hour.a + ":"+ tenminute.a + oneminute.a
  ENDSWITCH
ENDPROC

a = ampm2military.a ("05:13A")    ; sets a = "05:13A"
a = ampm2military.a ("5:13A")     ; sets a = "05:13A"
a = ampm2military.a ("12:01A")    ; sets a = "00:01A"
a = ampm2military.a ("6:30P")     ; sets a = "18:30"
a = ampm2military.a ("12:22")     ; sets a = "Error"    No am/pm designator.
```

## INT: What Is the Integer Portion of a Number?

```
INT (Number)
```

      Number       A numeric expression.

Returns:

      A Number       The integer portion of the number, removing the decimal portion.

Though the INT function returns the whole number portion of any type of numeric value, the script error message that results from taking an INT of a nonnumeric field is "Expecting a value of s type." This has no effect on the value returned, because INT(1000000.23) returns 1000000.

### Listing 17.50: INT.L1

```
n = INT(42)                     ; Sets n = 42
n = INT(42.99)                  ; Sets n = 42
n = INT(-42.99)                 ; Sets n = -42
n = INT(12345678901234567890)   ; Sets n = 1.23456789E+19
```

The examples below display the number of feet and inches based on input in inches, for example, 64 inches is converted to 5 feet, 4 inches. The two procedures below allow you to split feet and inches into several fields. The first procedure determines the number of whole feet in a given number of inches:

**Listing 17.51: INT.L2**

```
PROC wholefeet.n (inches.n)
  RETURN INT(inches.n / 12)     ; Number of whole feet
ENDPROC
```

The second determines the number of "extra" inches left over:

**Listing 17.52: INT.L3**

```
PROC extrainches.n (inches.n)
  RETURN MOD(inches.n, 12)      ; Number of remaining inches.
ENDPROC
```

**Listing 17.53: INT.L4**

```
PROC inchtest.u()
  PRIVATE n, feet.n, extra.n, total.n
  WHILE TRUE
    CLEAR
    @ 1,0  ?? "or press [Esc] to quit."
    @ 0,0  ?? "How many total inches to convert: "
    ACCEPT "N" REQUIRED TO total.n
    IF NOT RETVAL THEN
      RETURN
    ENDIF
    feet.n =  wholefeet.n (total.n)
    extra.n = extrainches.n (total.n)
    MESSAGE total.n," inches = ", feet.n, "' ", extra.n, "\",  Press any key."
    n = GETCHAR()
  ENDWHILE
ENDPROC

inchtest.u()    ; Do the demo procedure.

;  If you enter 37 inches, the message will read:
;    37 inches = 3' 1", Press any key.
```

## ABS: What Is the Absolute Value of a Number?

```
ABS (Number)
```

Number        A number between $\pm 10^{-307}$ and $\pm 10^{+308}$.

Returns:

A Number    The absolute value of the number, which is always positive.

ABS returns the absolute value of any nonblank number.

### Listing 17.53: ABS.L1

```
n = ABS(1)  ; sets n = 1
n = ABS(-3) ; sets n = 3
n = ABS(0)  ; sets n = 0
n = ABS(BLANKNUM()) ; script error because ABS is expecting a non-blank value
```

## MOD: What Is the Modulus of Two Numbers?

```
MOD (Number1,Number2)
```

Number1    Any numeric expression; the dividend.
Number2    Any numeric expression; the divisor.

Returns:

A Number    The modulus, or remainder, of number1 divided by number2.

The modulus of two numbers is the remainder formula used for the returned value: Number1-(Number2*INT(Number1/Number2)). If you use noninteger values for Number1 and Number2, the result can be noninteger as well. Thus MOD(12,3) = 0 and MOD(12.1,3.1) = 2.8. See INT() for another example of the MOD function.

## 17.3.3 Roots and Exponentials

### SQRT: What Is the Square Root of a Number?

```
SQRT (Number)
```

Number    A nonnegative numeric expression.

Returns:

A Number    The square root of the number.
A String    "Error" if the number is negative.

The SQRT function returns a script error only if a nonnumeric value is being evaluated; it will return the word "Error" if the Number is negative. The PAL 3.0 User's Guide is incorrect in this regard.

**Listing 17.55: SQRT.L1**

```
n = SQRT(9)    ; Sets n = 3
n = SQRT(100)  ; Sets n = 10
n = SQRT(42)   ; Sets n = 6.480740689407
n = SQRT(0)    ; Sets n = 0
n = SQRT(-1)   ; Sets n = "Error"
```

The hypotenuse of a right triangle can be calculated by taking the square root of the sum of the squares of the other two sides.

**Listing 17.56: SQRT.L2**

```
PROC hypotenuse.n( side1.n, side2.n)
  RETURN SQRT( (side1.n * side1.n) + (side2.n * side2.n) )
  ; or alternately use POW to square each number
  ; RETURN SQRT(POW(side1.n,2) + POW(side2.n, 2))
ENDPROC

 ; Now to demonstrate:
n = hypotenuse.n (3, 4)
MESSAGE "A right triangle with sides 3 and 4 has a hypotenuse of ", n
 ; Displays 5
SLEEP 3000
```

## EXP: What Is the Exponential Value of a Number?

```
EXP (Number)
```

Number      A numeric expression.

Returns:

A Number    The exponential of the number. The inverse is LN().

The EXP function returns a value of $e^n$ where e is approximately 2.7182845909. EXP(n) is the same as POW(EXP(1), n).

## POW: Returns a Number Raised to a Power

```
POW (Number1,Number2)
```

Number1     Numeric expression of number to raise.
Number2     Numeric expression of the power to raise Number1 to.

Returns:

| | |
|---|---|
| A Number | Value of Number1 raised to the power of Number2. |
| "Error" | If Number2 is greater than $\pm 10^{308}$ or if Number 2 is less than $\pm 10^{-307}$. |

A little extra care must be taken with the POW() function. Like many other programs, Paradox has difficulty with precision with floating point math operations on a digital computer. The following script prints the first 15 powers of the number 2:

**Listing 17.57: POW.L1**

```
FOR n FROM 1 TO 15
  PRINT "POW(2,",n,")=",POW(2,n),"\n"
ENDFOR
```

The printout shows the following information, with a little surprise at the thirteenth power:

**Listing 17.58: POW.L2**

```
POW(2,1) = 2
POW(2,2) = 4
POW(2,3) = 8
POW(2,4) = 16
POW(2,5) = 32
POW(2,6) = 64
POW(2,7) = 128
POW(2,8) = 256
POW(2,9) = 512
POW(2,10) = 1024
POW(2,11) = 2048
POW(2,12) = 4096
POW(2,13) = 8191.999999999
POW(2,14) = 16384
POW(2,15) = 32768
```

Some complications arise from the POW anomaly. For example, although

```
POW(2,18)        ; returns 262144
INT(POW(2,18))   ; returns 262143
```

This script runs fine until we get to POW(2,37) or so, because we get into fifteen-digit precision, at which point the INT() function has some difficulty with the numbers returned by the POW function. It became so slow in our testing that we originally thought the machine was locked up. INT() appears to work just fine on numbers not generated by the POW() function. The problems demonstrated below arise because the POW() function does not return the correct amount, i.e., POW(2,13) = 8191.999999999:

**Listing 17.59: POW.L3**

```
PROC powtest.u()
  PRIVATE pow.n, int.n
  CLEAR
  FOR n FROM 1 TO 50
    MESSAGE "Working on number ",n," your machine is not locked up"
    pow.n = POW(2,n)
    int.n = INT(pow.n)  ; Be patient, this gets very slow with big numbers.
    IF int.n <> pow.n THEN
      ? "POW(2,",n,")=",pow.n,"   however INT=",int.n
      ; or
      ; PRINT "POW(2,",n,")=",pow.n," however INT=",int.n,"\n"
    ENDIF
  ENDFOR
ENDPROC

;test
powtest.u()
```

Running the procedure demonstrates two things:

1. Some numbers will have decimal points.
2. With some numbers POW.N is not equal to INT.N though the numbers will display the same.

For example, POW(2, 22) returns 4194304, and INT(POW(2, 22)) returns 4194304. But a comparison of the two shows that the INT() is smaller.

## LOG: Returns the Base 10 Logarithm of a Number

```
LOG (Number)
```

      Number      A positive numeric expression.

Returns:

      A Number      The base 10 logarithm of the number.
      "Error"        If the number is 0 or negative.

```
LOG(1)   ; returns 0
LOG(10)  ; returns 1
LOG(100) ; returns 2
LOG(.1)  ; returns -1
LOG(.01) ; returns -2
```

### LN: Returns the Natural Logarithm of a Number

```
LN (Number)
```

> Number      Any positive numeric expression.

Returns:

> A Number      The natural logarithm of the number (the logarithm to base $e$ where $e$ is 2.7182845905).
>
> "Error"      If the number is 0 or a negative number.

For either the LOG or the LN functions, a bug in early versions of Paradox 2 caused the machine to lock up if a 0 or a negative number were evaluated. The bug was fixed in version 3. The workaround for version 2 users is the same for both LOG and LN:

**Listing 17.60: LOG.L1**

```
PROC log.v(number)
  IF number<=0 THEN
    RETURN "Error"
  ELSE
    RETURN LOG(number)
  ENDIF
ENDPROC
```

A similar procedure can be written for the LN function.

## 17.3.4 Comparing Numbers

### MIN: Return the Lesser of Two Numbers

```
MIN (Number1,Number2)
```

> Number1      Any numeric expression.
>
> Number2      Any numeric expression.

Returns:

> A Number      The lesser value of the two numbers.

The MIN function returns the smaller of two numbers. The word MIN is also a special operator in queries that calculates the smallest entry in a column of numeric values. The MIN function requires both parameters to be numbers or a script error results.

```
n = MIN (13, 12)    ; sets n = 12
n = MIN (-13, -12)  ; sets n = -13
```

### MAX: Returns the Larger of Two Numbers

```
MAX (Number1,Number2)
```

Number1    Any numeric expression.
Number2    Any numeric expression.

Returns:

A Number    The larger of the two numbers.

The MAX function simply returns the larger of two numbers. Like MIN, the word MAX is also a special operator in queries. If an expression is used to create Number1 or Number2, the expression must evaluate to a numeric value or a script error results.

```
n = MAX (13, 12)     ; sets n = 13
n = MAX (-13, -12)   ; sets n = -12
n = MAX ("Test",34)  ; trips a run error
```

## 17.3.5 Rounding and Random Numbers

### ROUND: Return a Number Rounded to a Specified Number of Decimal Places

```
ROUND (Number1,Number2)
```

Number1    Number to be rounded.
Number2    Integer between −15 and 15, the number of decimal places to round to.

Returns:

A Number    Of the required precision. If Number2 = 0, then result is integer of Number1, if 1, nearest 0.1, if −1, rounded to nearest multiple.

### Listing 17.61: ROUND.L1

```
n = ROUND(42.42, 0)          ; Sets n = 42
n = ROUND(42.5, 0)           ; Sets n = 43, n = rounded up.
n = ROUND(42.42, 1)          ; Sets n = 42.4
n = ROUND(42.45, 1)          ; Sets n = 42.4, at a halfway point.
n = ROUND(42.4500001, 1)     ; Sets n = 42.5, more than halfway.
n = ROUND(42.5, 1)           ; Sets n = 42.5
n = ROUND(42, 5)             ; Sets n = 42
n = ROUND(424242.42, -1)     ; Sets n = 424240
n = ROUND(42, -1)            ; Sets n = 40
n = ROUND(42, -2)            ; Sets n = 0
```

Rounding is a complicated issue. When a value is on a "threshold" value, it could conceivably round either way, up or down. Rounding is perhaps most critical when dealing with dollars and cents. Adding a very, very small number to the value always assures rounding upwards.

### Listing 17.62: ROUND.L2

```
COEDIT "Customer"
MOVETO [Balance Due]
SCAN
  MESSAGE "Working on record ",[#]," of ",NIMAGERECORDS()
  IF [] > 0  THEN                 ; Needs interest charge.
    []=ROUND([] * 1.015 + .0001, 2)  ; Add 1.5% to field,
                                   ;.0001 assures it will round high.

  ENDIF
ENDSCAN
DO_IT!
```

Although dollar values only display to two decimal places, they carry full precision—two dollar values that may look the same may not actually be the same. The easiest way to compare them, penny for penny, is with ROUND. Assuming that two dollar amounts were found in a table:

### Listing 17.63: ROUND.L3

```
dollar1.c = 25.00325
dollar2.c = 25.00135
MESSAGE dollar1.c = dollar2.c ; Displays false.
MESSAGE ROUND(dollar1.c + .000001, 2) = ROUND(dollar2.c + .000001, 2); Displays true.
```

There seems to be no hard and fast rule to the nature of ROUNDING, as the script below demonstrates:

### Listing 17.64: ROUND.L4

```
CLEAR
@ 0,0
??"When rounding to 0 decimal places, values always round upward"
```

```
?
FOR n FROM 1 TO 8
  ? "ROUND(", n, ".5, 0)= ", ROUND(n + .5, 0)
ENDFOR
?
? "When rounding to 1 decimal place, the rounding is less consistent:"
?
FOR n FROM 1 TO 8
  ? "ROUND(", n, ".25, 1)= ", ROUND(n + .25, 1)
ENDFOR
MESSAGE "Press any key"
n = GETCHAR()
```

When you run the procedure, you'll see this screen:

**Listing 17.65: ROUND.FG1**

```
Full numbers always seem to round up:

ROUND(1.5, 0)= 2
ROUND(2.5, 0)= 3
ROUND(3.5, 0)= 4
ROUND(4.5, 0)= 5
ROUND(5.5, 0)= 6
ROUND(6.5, 0)= 7
ROUND(7.5, 0)= 8
ROUND(8.5, 0)= 9

Partial numbers may vary, rounding up or down:

ROUND(1.25, 1)= 1.3
ROUND(2.25, 1)= 2.2
ROUND(3.25, 1)= 3.2
ROUND(4.25, 1)= 4.2
ROUND(5.25, 1)= 5.2
ROUND(6.25, 1)= 6.3
ROUND(7.25, 1)= 7.2
ROUND(8.25, 1)= 8.2
                            Press any key...
```

## RAND: Return a Random Number

```
RAND ()
```

Returns:

A Number     Randomly selected between 0 and 1.

RAND generates a number uniformly distributed from 0 up to but not including 1:

**Listing 17.66: RAND.L1**

```
n = RAND()                ; Random number between 0 and .9999999...
n = RAND() * 10           ; Random number between 0 and 9.9999999...
n = RAND() * 100          ; Random number between 0 and 99.9999999...
n = INT( RAND() ) * 100   ; Random integer between 0 and 99.
n = INT( RAND() ) * 101   ; Random integer between 0 and 100.
n = ROUND( RAND() * 100, 2) ; Random number between 0 and 100 rounded to two decimal places.
```

To return a random integer in a specified range:

**Listing 17.67: RAND.L2**

```
PROC randinteger.n (min.n, max.n)
  RETURN INT((max.n - min.n + 1) * rand() + min.n)
ENDPROC
```

n = Randinteger.n (200,300), where n would be assigned a number between 200 and 300, perhaps 237. Unlike the RAND() command, Randinteger.n() can return the maximum value. Using 200 as a minimum and 300 as a maximum, let's see what happens:

**Step 1**
Generate the multiplier to use.
$300 - 200 + 1 = 101$
**Step 2**
Multiply RAND by the multiplier.
$101 * RAND()$
would return a number between 0 and 100.999999....,
perhaps returning 37.92345
**Step 3**
Add the minimum number to the random number.
$200 + 37.92345 = 237.92345$
**Step 4**
Return the integer value.
INT(237.92345)
Returns 237.

## 17.3.6 Column Functions

PAL has several functions that let you evaluate numeric data stored in tables. The functions fall into two categories,

Column          Deals with the column values for the entire table. The table does not have to be on the workspace.

ImageColumn     Respects the restricted view of data in detail tables of multitable forms. The cursor must be in the proper field on the workspace.

The Column functions require a stable view of the data and so attempt a Write Lock on the table. If a Write Lock cannot be achieved within the set RETRYPE-RIOD, a script error results. The ImageColumn functions require you to post the current record to return an accurate value. One column function isn't included here. We've listed the CNPV function with the other financial functions later in this chapter.

### 17.3.6.1 Column Functions

We'll use the following table of Little League statistics to demonstrate some of the column-based functions. The table has numeric fields for [Home Runs] and [Age]. The [Dues] column is blank.

**Listing 17.68: COLUMN.FG1**

```
Viewing League table: Record 1 of 6                          Main

LEAGUE─┬─Player#──┬───Name────┬─Home runs─┬──Age──┬────Phone──┬─Dues─┐
    1  │   10     │  Scotty   │     2     │  12   │  555-1111 │      │
    2  │   20     │  Jimmy    │     1     │  13   │  555-2222 │      │
    3  │   30     │  Lauren   │           │   8   │  555-3333 │      │
    4  │   40     │  Slick    │     6     │   9   │           │      │
    5  │   50     │  Andy     │     3     │   7   │  555-8888 │      │
    6  │   60     │  Michael  │     3     │   6   │  555-9999 │      │
```

### CCOUNT: How Many Nonblank Values Are There in a Numeric Field?

```
CCOUNT (Tablename,Fieldname)
```

Tablename     Name of table (string).
Fieldname     Name of NUMERIC field to evaluate (string).

Returns:

A Number     Count of all nonblank entries for the column. The table does not have to be on the workspace.

In the example of the League table:

```
n = CCOUNT("League","Home Runs")   ; sets n = 5
n = CCOUNT("League","Age")         ; sets n = 6
```

```
n = CCOUNT("League","Dues")      ; sets n = 0
n = CCOUNT("League","Phone")     ; causes a script error because field is not numeric
```

To determine the number of blank values in a numeric table field, use:

**Listing 17.69: CCOUNT.L1**

```
PROC cblank.n(table.a, field.a)
   ; table.a   Name of table.
   ; field.a   Name of field to check.
   RETURN NRECORDS(table.a)-CCOUNT(table.a, field.a)
ENDPROC

; where in our example:

n = cblank.n ("League","Home Runs")

; Sets n = 1  because:
;   NRECORDS("League") = 6                ; Total number of records.
;     CCOUNT("League","Home Runs") = 5    ; Total number of non blanks.
;      6 - 5 = 1                          ; Blank values.
```

If you need to get a count of nonnumeric values in a table, you must use a query that simply calculates the count of all the values in the field:

**Listing 17.70: CCOUNT.L2**

```
; This procedure must be run from main mode, and there must not be any other
; query images on the workspace.

PROC queryccount.n(table.a, field.a)
   ; table.a   ; Name of table.
   ; field.a   ; Name of field.
   ; RETURNS   ; Number of non-blank values of any type of field.
   PRIVATE value.n

   MENU {Ask} SELECT table.a
   MOVETO FIELD field.a                ; Move to the correct field.
   [] = "Calc Count All as Qvalue"     ; Counts non blank entries and
                                       ; renames the answer table field.
   DO_IT!
   count.n = [Qvalue]
   DELETE "ANSWER"
   MOVETO 1                            ; To the topmost image, the query image.
   CLEARIMAGE                          ; Remove query image.
   RETURN count.n                      ; The number of entries.

ENDPROC


n = querycount.n("League","Phone")
```

```
message "We have ", n, " phone numbers on file.  Press any key"
n = GETCHAR()

; Will display "We have 5 phone numbers on file.  Press any key"
```

See IMAGECCOUNT for a related function.

### CSUM: What Is the Sum of the Nonblank Numeric Values in a Field?

```
CSUM (Tablename,Fieldname)
```

Tablename    Name of table (string).
Fieldname    Name of NUMERIC field (string).

Returns:

A Number     The sum of all values in the field.
"Error"      If there are no non-blank entries.
Script Error If field is not numeric.

```
n = CSUM("League","Home Runs")    ; sets n = 15
n = CSUM("League","Age")          ; sets n = 55
n = CSUM("League","Dues")         ; sets n = "Error"
n = CSUM("League","Phone")        ; causes a script error because field is not numeric
```

See IMAGECSUM() for a related image function.

### CAVERAGE: What Is the Average of Nonblank Values in a Numeric Field?

```
CAVERAGE (Tablename, Fieldname)
```

Tablename    Name of table (string).
Fieldname    Name of NUMERIC field (string).

Returns:

A Number     Average of all nonblank entries for the column.

```
n = CAVERAGE("League","Home Runs")    ; sets n = 3
n = CAVERAGE("League","Age")          ; sets n = 9.16666...
n = CAVERAGE("League","Dues")         ; sets n = "Error"
n = CAVERAGE("League","Phone")        ; causes a script error because field is not numeric
```

The CAVERAGE returns the average of nonblank values in a column. CAVER-AGE, like many of the functions in this section, can be called without placing the table on the workspace. It can be called from any SYSMODE() as long as you have sufficient rights to access the table. On the other hand, if you needed to treat blanks as if they were zeros to get a per-capita average, you would need to use:

```
n = CSUM("League","Home Runs") / NRECORDS("League")  ; 15 / 6
```

See IMAGECAVERAGE() for a related image function.

### CMIN: What Is the Minimum Nonblank Value in a Numeric Column?

```
CMIN (Tablename,Fieldname)
```

| | |
|---|---|
| Tablename | Name of table (string). |
| Fieldname | Name of NUMERIC field (string). |

Returns:

| | |
|---|---|
| A Number | The smallest nonblank value of the column. |
| "Error" | If no nonblank entries are found. |
| Script Error | If the field is not numeric. |

CMIN returns the minimum nonblank value for a column. Negative numbers are less than zero. Blank values are not counted at all.

```
n = CMIN("League","Home Runs")    ; sets n = 1
n = CMIN("League","Age")          ; sets n = 6
n = CMIN("League","Dues")         ; sets n = "Error", no non-blank values
n = CMIN("League", "Phone")       ; causes a script error because field is not numeric
```

Here's a procedure for getting the lowest value regardless of field type:

**Listing 17.71: CMIN.L1**

```
; This procedure must be run from main mode, and there must not be any other
; query images on the workspace.

PROC QueryCMIN.v(table.a, field.a)
   ; table.a   ; Name of table.
   ; field.a   ; Name of field.
   ; RETURNS   ; Lowest non-blank values of any type of field.
   PRIVATE value.v

   MENU {Ask} SELECT table.a
```

```
    MOVETO FIELD field.a           ; Move to the correct field.
    [] = "Calc MIN as Qvalue"      ; Finds lowest non blank entries and
                                   ; renames the answer table field.
    DO_IT!
    IF ISEMPTY("Answer") THEN
     value.v = "Error"             ; No values found.
    ELSE
     value.v = [Qvalue]
    ENDIF
    DELETE "ANSWER"
    MOVETO 1                       ; To the topmost image, the query image.
    CLEARIMAGE                     ; Remove query image.
    RETURN value.v                 ; The minimum value.
ENDPROC

v = QueryCMIN.v("League","Age")
n = GETCHAR()
; Will display "Minimum Age for League is 6.  Press any key"

v = QueryCMIN.v("League","Phone")
MESSAGE "Minumum ",field.a," for ",table.a," is ", v, ".  Press any key"
n = GETCHAR()
```

## CMAX: What Is the Largest Nonblank Value in a Numeric Column?

```
CMAX (Tablename,Fieldname)
```

|  |  |
|---|---|
| Tablename | Name of table (string). |
| Fieldname | Name of numeric field (string). |

Returns:

|  |  |
|---|---|
| A Number | The largest value in the field. |
| "Error" | If there are no nonblank entries. |
| Script error | If field is not numeric. |

See CMIN for query code that could be modified to return the highest value in any type of field. Although only useful in a single-user environment, a simple way of calculating a next available [Player#] number to use might look like:

```
nextnumber.n = CMAX("League","Player#") + 10    ; increments number by 10
```

On a network, two users looking at the same CMAX at the same time may generate the same new [Player#]. The nextnumber.v() procedure in the WAIT-PLUS section uses a single record table to store the next available number for various fields. The procedure works well in a single or multiuser environment and is fully commented.

### CVAR: What Is the Population Variance of a Numeric Column?

```
CVAR (Tablename,Fieldname)
```

| | |
|---|---|
| Tablename | Name of table (string). |
| Fieldname | Name of numeric field to evaluate (string). |

Returns:

| | |
|---|---|
| A Number | The population variance of a column. |
| "Error" | If there are no nonblank entries. |
| Script Error | If field is not numeric. |

The CVAR function returns the population variance of a set of values in a column, ignoring blank entries even if your configuration treats blanks as zeros. The PAL manual includes an example that describes how to calculate another statistical measure, the *sample variance*.

### CSTD: Return the Standard Deviation for Values in a Numeric Column

```
CSTD (Tablename, Fieldname)
```

| | |
|---|---|
| Tablename | Name of table (string). |
| Fieldname | Name of numeric field (string). |

Returns:

| | |
|---|---|
| A Number | Standard deviation of a column. |
| "Error" | If there are no blank entries. |
| Script Error | If field is not numeric. |

The CSTD function returns the standard deviation of a series of nonblank values in a column. The PAL manual also describes a procedure for calculating a related statistical function—the *sample standard deviation*.

## 17.3.7 Image Column Functions

These functions include: IMAGECAVERAGE, IMAGECCOUNT, IMAGECMAX, IMAGECMIN, and IMAGECSUM. The Image Column functions (we'll refer to them as the IMAGEC functions) work only on the current field in the current table on the workspace. Other column functions (CCOUNT, CMAX, etc.) don't require the table to be on the workspace. If the values are in the restricted view of a table created by a multitable form, the IMAGEC functions only work on the linked values.

### IMAGECCOUNT: Return a Count of Nonblank Numeric Values in This Image Column?

`IMAGECCOUNT ()`

Returns:

| | |
|---|---|
| A Number | The number of non-blank values for the current field in the current image. |
| 0 | If there are no entries. |

### IMAGECAVERAGE: Return the Average of the Nonblank Numeric Values in This Image Column

`IMAGECAVERAGE ()`

Returns:

| | |
|---|---|
| A Number | The average of nonblank values for the current numeric field in the image on the workspace or multitable form. |
| 0 | If there are no nonblank entries. |
| Script Error | If field is not numeric. |

### IMAGECMAX: Return the Highest Nonblank Numeric Values in This Image Column

`IMAGECMAX ()`

Returns:

| | |
|---|---|
| A Number | The largest entry in the current column of the current image. Field must be numeric. |
| "Error" | If there are no nonblank entries. |
| Script Error | If field is not numeric. |

### IMAGECMIN: Return the Lowest Nonblank Numeric Values in This Image Column

```
IMAGECMIN ()
```

Returns:

| | |
|---|---|
| A Number | The smallest entry in the current field of the current image. Field must be numeric. |
| "Error" | If there are no nonblank entries. |
| Script Error | If field is not numeric. |

### IMAGECSUM: Return the Sum of Nonblank Numeric Values in This Image Column

```
IMAGECSUM ()
```

Returns:

| | |
|---|---|
| A Number | The sum of all the values in the current column of the current image. Field must be numeric. |
| "Error" | If there are no nonblank entries. |
| Script Error | If field is not numeric. |

The procedure below is a multipurpose substitute for the IMAGEC functions. It saves the current field in the current table, moves to the target field on the workspace, invokes the specified function, and then moves back to its original place.

**Listing 17.72: IMAGEC.L1**

```
PROC imagec.v (table.a, field.a, type.a)
  PRIVATE oldfield.a, oldtable.a, v
  ; table.a     ; Name of table for image column function.
  ; field.a     ; Name of field for image column function.
  ; counttype.a ;"Average" "Count" "Max" "Min" "Sum"
  ; One proc does it all.

  oldfield.a = FIELD()                     ; Save current place.
  oldtable.a = TABLE()
  MOVETO table.a                           ; Go to the field in question.
  MOVETO FIELD field.a
  EXECUTE "v = ImageC" + type.a +"()"      ; Grab the value needed.
                                           ; e.g., v = ImageCSum().
  MOVETO oldtable.a                        ; Go back to our original field.
  MOVETO FIELD oldfield.a
  RETURN v                                 ; Either a number or the word "Error".
ENDPROC
```

Imagec.v can be used in an "Invoice" table with linked "LineItem" records to calculate the total line items for the current invoice:

**Listing 17.73: IMAGEC.L2**

```
v = imagec.v ( "Lineitem", "Amount", "Sum" )
MESSAGE "Current total for [Amount] is ", v , ". Press any key."
n= GETCHAR()
```

IMAGEC functions only apply to values that have been posted to the table. For instance, on record two of the following table in CoEdit mode:

```
CoEditing Imagec table: Record 2 of 3

IMAGEC——Value—
    1  |   100  |
    2  |   200< |
    3  |   300  |
```

IMAGECSUM() returns 600. However, if the command: []=203 is entered, or the user manually changes the field from 200 to 203, the record is automatically locked.

```
Coediting Imagec table: Record 2 of 3
Record is locked.

IMAGEC——Value—
    1  |   100  |
    2  |   203< |
    3  |   300  |
```

Because the value 203 has not yet been posted to the table, IMAGECSUM still returns 600. You must post the current record (by issuing UNLOCKRECORD, or simply moving off the record) to get values that reflect current entries.

## 17.3.8 Financial

PAL has four financial functions: Present Value, Future Value, Periodic Payment, and Net Present Value. The first three are static, depending only on the parameters supplied. The fourth, CNPV, is dependent on a series of values in a column in a named table. PAL financial functions require consistent parameters. If you use a 12% annualized interest rate and you want a value for a monthly payment, you must use a monthly interest value (0.12/12 = 0.1).

### PV: Returns the Present Value of a Series of Equal Payments

```
PV (Number1,Number2,Number3)
```

| | |
|---|---|
| Number1 | Periodic Payment. |
| Number2 | Interest Rate per Period, as a decimal. |
| Number3 | Number of periods (short number). |

Returns:

| | |
|---|---|
| A Number | The present value of a series of equal payments (the amount of principal paid so far). |

The PV function returns the present value of a series of equal payments. The payments reduce the principal, leaving a balance that continues to generate and compound interest. For example, to determine the loan size you can afford with a monthly payment of $1500 at 12% interest over 30 years, use:

**Listing 17.74: PV.L1**

```
CLEAR  @ 0,0
?? "With a monthly payment of $1200 at 12% over 30 years "
? "Value of loan principal is $", ROUND(PV(1200,.01,360),2)  ; to nearest cent
?
? "After"
FOR n FROM 5 to 30 STEP 5
  ? n," years, principal paid = $ ",ROUND(PV(1200,.01,n*12),2) ,
    " total= $", 1200 * n
  ?
ENDFOR
MESSAGE "Press any key"
n=GETCHAR()
```

### PMT: Returns the Periodic Payment to Pay Off a Loan

```
PMT (Number1,Number2,Number3)
```

| | |
|---|---|
| Number1 | Loan principal. |
| Number2 | Loan interest expressed as a decimal. |
| Number3 | Number of periods in the loan payment plan (short number). |

Returns:

| | |
|---|---|
| A Number | Equal to the constant regular payments necessary to pay off the loan. |

The PMT function is used to determine a periodic payment associated with a loan. The following procedure uses PMT to create a loan comparison table based on input from the user. The procedure first creates an entry screen for a range of potential loans and interest rates.

```
Fill out the information below then press [F2] to continue
[F7]-FormToggle, [Esc]-Cancels
┌──────────────────────────────────────────────────────────────────────┐
│                                                        Entry    #    1 │
│                                                                        │
│   Lowest loan amount $:            195,000.00                          │
│   Highest loan amount $:           201,000.00                          │
│   Loan Amount Increment $:            1000                             │
│   Lowest interest rate %:             10.8                             │
│   Highest interest rate %:            11.2                             │
│   Interest rate increment %:            .1                             │
│   # of payments per year:              12                              │
│   # of years in loan:                  30                              │
│                                                                        │
│                                                                        │
│                                                                        │
│                                                                        │
│                                                                        │
│                                                                        │
│                                                                        │
└──────────────────────────────────────────────────────────────────────┘
```

It then creates a temporary table named "List" with fields that represent the range of possible interest rates.

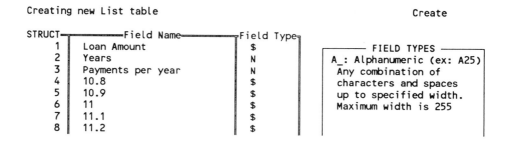

```
Creating new List table                                    Create

STRUCT┬──────────Field Name════════╤Field Type┐
    1 │   Loan Amount              │    $      │    ┌───── FIELD TYPES ─────┐
    2 │   Years                    │    N      │    │A_: Alphanumeric (ex: A25)│
    3 │   Payments per year        │    N      │    │ Any combination of    │
    4 │   10.8                     │    $      │    │ characters and spaces │
    5 │   10.9                     │    $      │    │ up to specified width.│
    6 │   11                       │    $      │    │ Maximum width is 255  │
    7 │   11.1                     │    $      │    └───────────────────────┘
    8 │   11.2                     │    $      │
```

Finally, it steps through each record, placing the proper PMT value into each field, leaving the "Entry" and "List" tables on the workspace.

```
Viewing List table: Record 4 of 7                              Main

ENTRY──┬Lowest loan amount $┬Highest loan amount $┬Loan Amount Increment $┬Lowes
     1 │      195,000.00     │      201,000.00     │        1000           │ ***


LIST┬──Loan Amount──┬Years─┬Payments┬──────10.8──────┬─────10.9─────┬─────11─────┬
   1 │   195,000.00  │  30  │   12   │    1,827.62    │   1,842.31   │  1,857.03  │
   2 │   196,000.00  │  30  │   12   │    1,836.99    │   1,851.76   │  1,866.55  │
   3 │   197,000.00  │  30  │   12   │    1,846.37    │   1,861.21   │  1,876.08  │
   4 │   198,000.00  │  30  │   12   │    1,855.74    │   1,870.65   │  1,885.60  │
   5 │   199,000.00  │  30  │   12   │    1,865.11    │   1,880.10   │  1,895.12  │
   6 │   200,000.00  │  30  │   12   │    1,874.48    │   1,889.55   │  1,904.65  │
   7 │   201,000.00  │  30  │   12   │    1,883.86    │   1,899.00   │  1,914.17  │
```

### Listing 17.75: PMT.L1

```
PROC interestlist.l()

PRIVATE
    lowloan.c,              ; Lowest loan amount $.
    highloan.c,             ; Highest loan amount $.
    incrementloan.c,        ; Loan amount increment $.
    lowinterest.n           ; Lowest interest rate %.
    highinterest.n,         ; Highest interest rate %.
    incrementinterest.n,    ; Interest rate increment %.
    payments.n,             ; # of payments per year.
    years.n,                ; # of years in loan.
    n,                      ; Counter.
    periodrate.n,           ; Rate per period.
    periods.n               ; # of periods.

    MESSAGE "Working, preparing entry table"

    ; First, create an entry table (a private table name).
    CREATE "Entry"
    "Lowest Loan Amount $":"$",
    "Highest Loan Amount $":"$",
    "Loan Amount Increment $":"N",
    "Lowest Interest Rate %":"N",
    "Highest Interest Rate %":"N",
    "Interest Rate Increment %":"N",
    "# of Payments per Year":"N",
    "# of Years in Loan":"N"

    COEDIT "Entry"
    FORMKEY
    WHILE True
      WAIT RECORD
        PROMPT "Fill out the information below then press [F2] to continue",
        "[F7]-FormToggle, [Esc]-Cancels"
      UNTIL "F2","Esc","Dos","DosBig"
      SWITCH
        CASE RETVAL = "Esc":
```

```
            DO_IT!
            DELETE "Entry"
            RETURN False
        CASE RETVAL = "F7":
            FORMKEY
        CASE RETVAL = "F2":
            ; Check to make sure all fields are filled in.
            MOVETO [Lowest loan Amount $]
            RETVAL = True
            for n FROM 1 TO 7
              IF ISBLANK([]) THEN
                MESSAGE "You need to fill in the ",FIELD()," Press any key"
                n = GETCHAR()
                RETVAL = False
                QUITLOOP
              ENDIF
              RIGHT  ; Go on to the next field.
            ENDFOR
            IF RETVAL THEN
              lowloan.c = [Lowest loan Amount $]
              highloan.c = [Highest loan Amount $]
              incrementloan.c = [Loan Amount increment $]
              lowinterest.n = [Lowest interest rate %]
              highinterest.n = [Highest interest rate %]
              incrementinterest.n = [Interest rate increment %]
              payments.n = [# of payments per year]
              years.n = [# of years in loan]
              DO_IT!
              DELETE "ENTRY"
              QUITLOOP                    ; Okay to create the payment table.
            ENDIF
      ENDSWITCH
    ENDWHILE
    CLEAR

MESSAGE "Creating structure of list table"
; Demonstrating an alternate way of creating a temporary table:
MENU {Create} {list}
IF MENUCHOICE() = "Cancel" THEN
  {Replace}
ENDIF
; Now dynamically place field names based on the interest rates wanted.
"Loan Amount"
RIGHT
"$"
RIGHT
"Years"
RIGHT
"N"
RIGHT
"Payments per Year"
RIGHT
"N"
FOR n FROM lowinterest.n TO highinterest.n STEP incrementinterest.n
  RIGHT  ; move to the field name
  TYPEIN ROUND(n,2)   ; Odd things were happening with step without the ROUND.
  RIGHT
  "$"
  IF [#] = 255 THEN   ; Maximum number of fields possible.
```

```
      QUITLOOP
    ENDIF
  ENDFOR
  DO_IT!

  ; Load the table with one record for each loan amount.
  MESSAGE "Loading loan amounts"
  COEDIT "List"

  FOR n FROM lowloan.c TO highloan.c STEP incrementloan.c
    [Loan Amount] = n
    [Years] = years.n
    [Payments per Year] = payments.n
    DOWN
  ENDFOR

  IF n > highloan.c  THEN  ; Could be because step would not actually hit high.
    [Loan Amount] = highloan.c
    [Years] = years.n
    [Payments per Year] = payments.n
  ENDIF

  HOME
  RIGHT                              ; To the year field.
  RIGHT                              ; To the payments field.
  RIGHT                              ; To the first interest field.
  FOR n FROM 1 TO NFIELDS(TABLE())-3  ; Don't need to do the loan amount fields.
    periodrate.n = (NUMVAL (FIELD() )/payments.n) /100
    periods.n = payments.n * years.n
    SCAN                             ; Do for each record in this field.
      MESSAGE "Loading ",FIELD(),"% for $",[Loan Amount]
      [] = PMT([Loan Amount], periodrate.n, periods.n)
    ENDSCAN
    RIGHT
  ENDFOR
  DO_IT!
  RETURN True
ENDPROC
```

## FV: Return the Future Value of a Series of Equal Payments

```
FV (Number1,Number2,Number3)
```

Number1    Periodic payment (number).
Number2    Interest rate per period (number).
Number3    Number of periods (short number).

Returns:

A Number    The future value of the series of equal payments.

The FV function returns the future value of a series of equal periodic payments.

The interest rate and the number of periods must be consistent. If any of the values are non-numeric, a script error will result.

### CNPV: Return the Net Present Value of a Column of Numbers

```
CNPV (Tablename,Fieldname,Number)
```

| | |
|---|---|
| Tablename | Name of table (string). |
| Fieldname | Name of field to evaluate (string). |
| Number | Decimal number representing the interest or discount rate per period. |

Returns:

| | |
|---|---|
| Script Error | If column is not numeric. |
| A Number | Net present value of nonblank entries. |

NPV is a measure of the return on an investment based on a fixed interest rate. The CNPV function returns the net present value of a series of cash flows represented in a single field in a table. The cash flows may be positive or negative. CNPV() works on all the nonblank records in the named table; it does not respect the restricted view of a table created by a multitable form. The field may be numeric, currency, or short number.

All entries in the column create a value and add a period to the NPV calculation. Blank entries do not affect the result. Additionally, all entries of 0 after the last nonzero, nonblank entry have no effect on the result. An NPV of ten numbers, the last five of which are zero, is the same as the NPV of the first five numbers.

## 17.3.9 Trigonometric Functions

PAL provides a full range of trigonometric functions. These are some of the least frequently used of all of PAL's capabilities. Instead of taking space with examples like: "A 20 foot ladder is leaning up against a wall at 30 degrees . . . ," we focus on syntax.

All the trigonometric functions measure angles in radians rather than degrees. Measured in degrees, angles range from 0 to 360. Radians express the size of an angle based on the constant $\pi$. A straight line can also be stated as $\pi$, or 1 radian; a right angle is $\pi/2$, or approximately 1.57 radians; 360 degrees is $\pi * 2$, or approximately 6.2831 radians. The next two procedures convert radians and degrees.

**Listing 17.76: TRIG.L1**

```
;A procedure to convert degrees into radians:

Proc radians.n (degrees.n)
  RETURN  PI() / degrees.n
ENDPROC

;A procedure to convert radians back to degrees

PROC degrees.n (radians.n)
   RETURN  180 / PI() * radians.n
ENDPROC
```

SIN(n): Return the sine of an angle n.
COS(n): Return the cosine of an angle n.
TAN(n): Return the tangent of angle n.

The complementary functions can be remembered with the words "The angle whose . . . ." For example, ASIN(1) can be read "The angle whose sine is 1." ASIN(1) returns the value 1.57. 1.57 radians is the same as PI()/2, or 90 degrees.

ASIN(n): Return the angle whose sine is n.
ACOS(n): Return the angle whose cosine is n.
ATAN(n): Return the angle whose tangent is n.
ATAN2(n1,n2): Return the angle whose cosine is n1 and whose sine is n2

**PI: Return the Value of $\pi$.**

```
PI ()
```

Returns:

A Number    With an approximate value of 3.14159265. The constant $\pi$ is used in calculating the area or circumference of a circle.

To calculate the area of a circle with radius radius.n:

```
area.n = PI() * POW(radius.n, 2)  ; pi R squared
```

To calculate the circumference of a circle with radius radius.n:

```
circumference.n = PI() * 2 * radius.n
```

To calculate the volume of a cylinder with radius radius.n and height height.n:

```
volume.n = PI() * POW(radius.n, 2) * height.n
```

### SIN: Return the Sine of an Angle

```
SIN (Number)
```

Number    Numeric expression representing an angle expressed in radians.

Returns:

A Number    Value between −1 and 1 that represents the sine of the angle.
The inverse function is ASIN ().

```
n = SIN (PI() / 2 )    ; 90 degrees sets n = .999999999.....
n = SIN (PI() * 2 )    ; 360 degrees sets n = -.000035635....
n = SIN (0)            ; sets n = 0
n = SIN (PI())         ; sets n = .0000178.....
```

### COS: Return the Cosine of an Angle

```
COS (Number)
```

Number    An angle expressed in radians.

Returns:

A Number    Value between −1 and 1 representing the cosine of the angle.
Reverse of ACOS.

```
n = COS(0)        ; sets n = 1
n = COS(PI()/2)   ; sets n = 0
```

### TAN: Return the Tangent of an Angle

```
TAN (Number)
```

Number    A numeric expression of an angle expressed in radians.

Returns:

A Number    The tangent of the Number ranging from the smallest negative
to the largest positive Paradox number.

```
n = TAN(0)        ; sets n = 0
n = TAN(PI()/4)   ; sets n = 1
```

TAN diverges at −PI()/2, PI()/2 and every ±PI() radians from those values. The inverse functions are ATAN and ATAN2.

### ASIN: Return the Arc Sine of an Angle

`ASIN (Number)`

> Number      Number between −1 and 1.

Returns:

> A Number     Between −pi/2 and pi/2.
> "Error"        If invalid argument is passed. Returns the arc sine of a number.

### ACOS: Return the Arc Cosine of an Angle

`ACOS (Number)`

> Number      A numeric expression between −1 and 1.

Returns:

> A Number     Between 0 and $\pi$, expressed in radians.
> "Error"        If an illegal argument is passed. Inverse of COS.

### ATAN: Return the Arc Tangent of an Angle

`ATAN (Number)`

> Number      Number representing the tangent of an angle.

Returns:

> A Number     Between −$\pi$/2 and $\pi$/2 expressed in radians. Returns the two quadrant arc tangent of a number.

### ATAN2: Return the Four Quadrant Arc Tangent of a Number

ATAN2 (Number1,Number2)

    Number1     Number representing a cosine of an angle.
    Number2     Number representing a sine of an angle.

Returns:

    A Number     A value expressed in radians. Returns the four quadrant arc
                 tangent of a number.

# Part Three

# Chapter 18

# The Data Entry Toolkit

The Data Entry Toolkit is a collection of utilities written in PAL that:

- lets programmers establish their own rules of data entry
- extends the normal power of interactive Paradox
- aids in the execution of PAL applications.

The "heart and soul" of the toolkit is a special procedure called DoWait, which allows keystroke-by-keystroke control over data entry and table-editing operations. DoWait is a tour-de-force demonstration of the power of PAL. When PAL programmers talk about using the Toolkit, they are usually referring to DoWait.

Unfortunately, there is little about DoWait that is well documented. Late changes about the workings of the Paradox3 Toolkit were included in a file on the Paradox3 installation disk called README. This file is not copied onto your hard disk during installation and so it often goes unread. This information in README corrects information presented in the PAL 3.0 User's Guide. It is reprinted with permission at the end of this chapter.[1] The result is a great deal of confusion over what the Toolkit is and how and when to use it.

DoWait, written entirely in PAL by Mark Pauker and Derc Yamasaki of Borland, is a programmer's tool. By necessity, DoWait violates one of the precepts of Paradox design—hiding complexity from the user. Because the Toolkit procedures are designed to be incorporated into programs you write, they are provided in script form so that you can write them to procedure libraries and debug your code when it fails.

Providing the source code gives the impression that you have to understand these scripts line-by-line to use DoWait—a worthy goal, but unnecessary. Of course, the more understanding you have of DoWait's methods, the more fine-tuned control you can provide. As you will see, the most difficult part of using DoWait is setting it up, and fortunately, that's where you're given the most help. Once a session is set up properly, calling DoWait is like calling any other procedure. Most importantly, setting up DoWait requires a systematic approach.

This chapter is in three parts. The first asks the question "When and why DoWait?" The second part describes the structural design of DoWait—it is an attempt to demystify DoWait by first explaining how it works. The third part is about the use of DoWait, including descriptions of critical procedures, status and control variables, and utilities in the Toolkit that make implementing a DoWait session relatively painless. This chapter finishes with a checklist of the steps necessary to get a DoWait session up and running.

There is no substitute for experience. Learning about the Toolkit firsthand requires that you DO-IT! yourself. On page 499 of the Paradox3 PAL User's Guide is an exercise that allows you to set up a simple DoWait session with the "Cust" table. By following it step-by-step, you will get DoWait running. If you want to step through any Toolkit script in the PAL debugger, though, you'll have to modify your usual habit of simply pressing [Ctrl s]. When you get to the statement:

```
TKChar = GetChar() ;line 502 of the "Kernel" script dated 5/24/89
```

Use [Ctrl s] to step through the statement and then press a key as if you were a user. Continue debugging until this statement repeats, then repeat this technique. A special Toolkit Utility called "TKDebug" helps determine the cause of common DoWait errors.

## 18.1 TOOLKIT INSTALLATION

Installing the files that comprise the Toolkit is an option when you first install Paradox. The script "TKMenu" includes a demonstration of the capabilities of DoWait under Paradox3 with the menu selection {Demo}. This invoice data-entry session is an excellent model of the Toolkit's power.

## 18.2 WHEN AND WHY DOWAIT?

The DoWait procedure is a substitute for the PAL WAIT command. If you are relatively new to PAL programming, WAIT's deficiencies may not be readily apparent. WAIT comes in three variations with an increasingly narrower focus:

WAIT TABLE
WAIT RECORD
WAIT FIELD

These commands all reveal a table already placed on the workspace and allow normal interactive editing and data entry in either edit or coedit mode. Each WAIT statement relies on a single event, the pressing of a specified key, to end its control. You specify the key or keys that end a WAIT:

```
WAIT TABLE UNTIL "F2"
```

The more keys you specify after the word UNTIL, the tighter the control. Unfortunately, the need to trap for both wanted and unwanted keystrokes can border on the absurd:

```
WAIT TABLE PROMPT prompt1.a, prompt2.a.
  UNTIL "Esc", ; End session?
        "Help", ; Lookup help available?
         "F2", ; Do_It! to end session.
         "F3", ; Need to move to another embedded table.
         "F4", ; Need to move to another embedded table.
         "F7", ; Form Toggle.
        "F10", ; Special menu.
        "DOS", ; [Ctrl o].
     "DOSBIG", ; [Alt o].
       "Zoom", ; Zoom works, but it's got problems.
        "Del" ; Prevent user from accidentally deleting record.
```

Any key in the list following the word UNTIL ends the WAIT. The list of these exit keys is usually followed by a SWITCH statement, branching to procedures, menus, or other options appropriate to the key pressed. By using WAIT in a loop, you are continually reinvoking this long statement. The longer the list, the longer the time WAIT takes responding.

## 18.2.1 WAIT and Data Validation

Another major requirement of tightly controlled data entry sessions is data validation: How good is the data that is entered?

Since ValChecks are tacit restrictions on data entered into tables, all Low and High values, Required fields, Defaults, Pictures, and Tablelookups are enforced during a WAIT. One limitation of ValChecks should be obvious—they are restrictions on individual fields. A ValCheck in one field has no sway over information added in another. Even a {Required} field is not truly required if the cursor never gets to it.

Here's an example from the PAL manual: Although you can place a ValCheck in a [Method of Payment] field to select between credit cards (for example {Amex, Visa, Check}), you can't use a ValCheck to assure that a credit card number and expiration date are supplied in other fields. You can, however, accomplish the result with a WAIT RECORD.

```
WHILE True
WAIT RECORD UNTIL "F2"
  IF [Method of Payment] <> "Check" THEN
    IF [Card No.] = "" OR [Exp Date] = "" THEN
      BEEP
      MESSAGE "Credit card info required"
      SLEEP 500
    ELSE
      QUITLOOP
    ENDIF
  ENDIF
ENDWHILE
```

This type of data validation, where a field or several fields in a record rely on the contents of other fields, is quite common. Single and multiple data dependencies may exist, usually requiring a WAIT RECORD to be supplanted by several WAIT FIELDs. The tighter the dependencies, the more complex the WAIT and the slower data entry becomes.

## 18.2.2 Interactive Field Level Events

Moving out of a field that has passed all validity checks is what DoWait refers to as a "field-level event." In addition to ValChecks, there are two other examples of operations in interactive Paradox that force field-level events:

- A calculated field in a form is based on entries in one or more fields in the current table. When you change the value of any field involved in the calculation and move off the field, the calculated field displays a new value.
- Paradox won't allow you to move the cursor off a field in a query image unless it meets certain tests; Paradox always checks that the combination of example elements, special operators, and literals are valid.

These field-level events are built into Paradox and, within their scope, control user interaction. DoWait allows you to control interaction in a data entry session key-by-key.

## 18.2.3 WAIT LOOPS

Within a WAIT statement, the programmer gives up control over events until one of the keys in the UNTIL list—one of the exit keys—is pressed. To make the WAIT appear continuous, you enclose it within a WHILE loop:

```
WHILE True
  WAIT RECORD UNTIL "F2","Esc"
```

```
IF Retval = "Esc" THEN
   QUITLOOP
ELSE
   Ins
ENDIF
ENDWHILE
```

In this example, both "F2" and "Esc" are exit keys—both end the WAIT RECORD. Yet only the "Esc" key appears to end the WAIT. Every time you exit the WAIT RECORD with "F2," the loop forces the WAIT command to be reinvoked, inserting a record, and giving the appearance that the WAIT is continuously in effect. In either case, pressing "F2" or "Esc" causes a special event to occur—the WAIT condition ends.

In contrast, the Toolkit procedure, DoWait, can be called and exited once during a data entry session. All special processing is defined and processed within DoWait.

### 18.2.4 When Not to Use DoWait

DoWait is designed for data entry and editing. We never use the Toolkit to view existing records—WAIT Table works just fine. We also rarely use DoWait if simple data validation can take place on the record level and the number of transactions is modest. We avoid using DoWait during prototyping or while a table's structure is not finalized.

## 18.3 AN EVENT-DRIVEN WAIT

DoWait is referred to by its authors as an "event-driven wait," in which an event is not limited to a key in a list—every keystroke has the potential to cause something to happen. Running under DoWait, you can direct what happens as the result of each keystroke and always retain full control.

This concept requires endowing your application with a higher level of intelligence than WAIT provides. Instead of your program reacting to only exit keys on the table, record, or field level, DoWait watches over every keystroke. What a particular keystroke does may depend on the table, form, and field you are in. Taking it to the extreme, DoWait can also perform actions depending on how long it has been since you last pressed a key. DoWait is highly table- and form-dependent.

## 18.3.1 How DoWait Works

Program Design Criteria: Start with a table on the workspace in either table or form view in Edit, CoEdit, or DataEntry mode. For the duration of the call to DoWait, do not change the layout of the workspace, because a call to DoWait relies on exacting information about this workspace geography. Here's the basic design of the DoWait procedure:

1. Capture a keystroke.
2. Test if it's valid. If it's invalid, go back to 1.
3. Check if the key signalled any special processing. If so, process it. Exit if instructed.
4. Display the result to the user.
5. Return to 1.

## 18.3.2 Capturing Keys

In this section, we'll build a small model of the toolkit's main procedure—DoWait.[2]

The PAL GETCHAR() function captures keystrokes from the keyboard and returns a number, the PAL keycode. A PAL keycode is either a negative integer, one of 95 keys in the range of from −132 to 0; or a positive integer from 1 to 255. You can capture a key and assign its value to a variable named "TKChar"[3] with the following statement:

```
TKChar = GETCHAR()
```

GETCHAR() captures the value of the key typed, and, secondarily, prevents the keystroke from having an effect. If you want the key to function normally, the KEYPRESS command types characters back in:

```
TKChar=GETCHAR()    ; Capture the key.
KEYPRESS TKChar     ; Type the key.
```

Putting this in a loop allows you to execute it continuously, capturing and then pressing every keystroke:

```
WHILE True
 TKChar = GETCHAR() ; Capture the key.
 KEYPRESS TKChar    ; Type the key.
ENDWHILE
```

That this loop is endless is potentially a problem, but this code has a more serious flaw: Because the workspace is hidden from view by the PAL Canvas under script play, the user won't see a thing while typing. Another command is needed to display the effects of each key.

```
ECHO NORMAL              ;Display the workspace.
WHILE True
  TKChar=GETCHAR()       ;Capture the key.
  KEYPRESS TKChar        ;Type the key.
ENDWHILE
```

The ECHO NORMAL command makes the PAL Canvas transparent, revealing the Paradox workspace. With this five line "kernel" of the DoWait procedure, every press of a key has the same effect it had in Paradox. Yet by itself, this fragment of DoWait is essentially useless, serving only to delay keystrokes. However, our first goal has been achieved; every keystroke is captured.

## 18.3.3 Key Types

DoWait begins its work with an assumption that a table is on the workspace in either TableView or Formview, and in Edit, CoEdit, or DataEntry modes. Let us assume the same with our little script. Even though our script will pass through every keystroke, some keys will have no effect. For example, in Edit or CoEdit mode in a display image, [F5] or [F6] have no effect. Other keys, like [Alt F5], behave normally (in this case invoking the special editing function FieldView). For DoWait to be of use, it must act as a filter for keystrokes, allowing regular keys to pass through and preventing illegal keys from having an effect. The way our script is currently written, keystrokes are either accepted or rejected according to the way Paradox works. To exercise more precise control, we must process keys before they reach Paradox.

### 18.3.4 Defining Key Types

Paradox supports 350 keys and key combinations, from simple letters and punctuation to Ctrl, Shift, and Alt combinations of function and cursor movement keys. Though defining what every key does at every juncture seems a monumental task, DoWait uses a "Divide and Conquer" approach that greatly simplifies things. First, every key is assigned a key type. In addition to Illegal and Regular, DoWait adds five classes: Exit, eXit, Special, DepartSpecial, and Movement. These special classes will be explained shortly.

Let's look at the simplest case—Regular Keys. Any key that behaves as would be expected of interactive Paradox while in DoWait is termed a Regular key. For example, the 95 standard keys that display characters should do what is expected of them—display characters. Pressing the key for "A" should produce the letter "A." Tapping a cursor movement key should move the cursor as expected. Using [Ctrl z], Zoom, or [Alt z], ZoomNext, should make things function normally. Additionally, using the Alt key in conjunction with the keypad should produce regular and extended ASCII characters. Keys that perform a function during editing should function normally; keys that have no effect should produce a beep or have no effect.

DoWait uses a single letter to designate a key type. Most keys are regular keys and are designated by the letter "R". Illegal keys (designated by "I") include keys that have no meaning while editing and those that have no Paradox-assigned meaning in any system mode. There are 86 keys that are generally classified as Illegal keys. Examples include:

> [F9] or [Alt F9] ;Already in edit or coedit mode
> [F6] ;Checkmark is irrelevant
> [F8] or [Alt F8] ;No effect
> [Alt 0], [Ctrl @] ;unassigned

Exit keys (designated by "E"), which by default include [F2] and [CtrlBreak], end the editing session. Special keys (designated by "S") include keys that you attach special significance to—for example Menu, ([F10]) can be called at any time. The other two key types are eXit ("X") and DepartSpecial ("D"). The "X" key type was added in Paradox3. If you assign a key as "X", it is interpreted as a request for an immediate exit from DoWait. DepartSpecial, and type "D" are assigned internally. They represent keys assigned to be Special that can cause movement out of a field. Though we will explore in detail how the keys are classified according to type, what is more important is what is done with the key once its type has been determined.

DoWait uses another variable to identify a key's type: TKKeyType. To simplify matters, for the moment we'll use an undefined procedure named GetTKKeyType() to return the type of key that has been pressed:

```
TKKeyType = GetTKKeyType()
```

With this assignment, DoWait can be made to make decisions:

```
PROC DOWAIT()
  ECHO NORMAL                    ; Display the workspace.
  WHILE True
    TKChar = GETCHAR()           ; Capture the key.
    TKKeyType = GetTKKeyType()   ; Get key type.
    SWITCH
      CASE TKKeyType = "R" :
        KEYPRESS TKChar          ; Type the key.
      CASE TKKeyType = "I" :
        BEEP                     ; Don't allow use of the key.
      CASE TKKeyType = "S":
        ExecuteSpecialProcedure()
```

```
      OTHERWISE :
         QUITLOOP
      ENDSWITCH
    ENDWHILE
ENDPROC
```

By simply classifying keys based on key types, we have reduced 350 choices to four. For efficiency, the CASE list is arranged by the number of keys assigned to a category. Thus, because the majority of keys are "R," this CASE statement is tested first, and the least likely, "S," is last.

Assigning and identifying each key's type is critical to DoWait. If a key is assigned the wrong type—for example the letter "A" is designated as "I" for Illegal—DoWait will prevent the letter "A" from being typed in.

## 18.3.5 Movement Keys

For reasons that will become clear, Regular keys must be divided into two subclasses: Keys that type characters and keys that only cause cursor movement. Regular keys that type characters are still classified as "R"; keys that only cause cursor movement are designated as "M."

## 18.3.6 Representing Key Types

The method used by DoWait to designate a type for every key is ingenious.[4] The challenge was representing the key types for 350 keys efficiently. The type of any key had to be identified instantly and accurately based on its key code. Although the natural storage medium in Paradox is a table, looking up values in tables is much, much too slow for our needs here. The solution looks rather odd, but turns out to be very efficient:

```
;              0....+....1....+....2....+....3....+....4....+....5....+....6
    TKNegKey ="EIIIIIIIIIIIIIIIMIIIIIIIIIIIIIIIIIIIIIIIIIIIMIIIIIIIIIIIIIIIIIE" +
              "IIIIIIIIIMMMIMIMIMMMMMIIIIIIIIIIIIIIIIIIIIIIIIIIIIIIIIIIRIIIIIIMMMMMI" +
              "IIIIIIIIIIIIM"
    TKPosKey = "RRRRRRRRMRRRMRIRRIRRMRRRRMRRRRRRRRRRRRRRRRRRRRRRRRRRRRRRRRRRRR" +
              "RRRRRRRRRRRRRRRRRRRRRRRRRRRRRRRRRRRRRRRRRRRRRRRRRRRRRRRRRRRRRRRRRR" +
              "RRRRRRRRRRRRRRRRRRRRRRRRRRRRRRRRRRRRRRRRRRRRRRRRRRRRRRRRRRRRRRRRRR" +
              "RRRRRRRRRRRRRRRRRRRRRRRRRRRRRRRRRRRRRRRRRRRRRRRRRRRRRRRRRRRRRRRRRR" +
              "RRRRRRRRRRRRRRRR"
```

These two statements simply assign two very long variables. The first statement assigns 133 characters to a variable called "TKNegKey." The second assigns 255 characters to the variable "TKPosKey." They are broken in two only because strings in Paradox have a maximum length of 255 characters and there are 350 keys over a range of 388 numbers. Zero begins the negative keys listing and each character corresponds to the assignment for that key. Some keys in the sequence have no meaning.

Once TKChar is accepted and set to a number (e.g., 65 for the letter "A"), DoWait determines the key's type with two steps:

1. checking to see if the key is positive or negative; and
2. using a PAL string function, SUBSTR, to return a value with the key type:

```
IF TKChar > 0 THEN
  TKKeyType = SUBSTR (TKPosKey,TKchar,1)
ELSE
  TKkeyType = SUBSTR (TKNegKey,1-TKchar,1)
ENDIF
```

(Thus for "A", the number is positive, and it is 65 characters into the string. The statement SUBSTR(TKPosKey,65,1) yields a TKKeytype of "R." As another example, [Alt 0], which is character $-24$ yields SUBSTR(TKNegKey,1$-$($-24$),1) elevates to "I" for illegal.)

# 18.4 SETKEYCODES( )

Referring to keys by number is difficult at best ("What is $-124$ anyway?"). Because DoWait relies on the GETCHAR function, TKChar is always a number. To make your life easier, one of the scripts provided in the toolkit is called "Keycodes." We highly recommend that you use it when designing and debugging your toolkit applications.

"Keycodes.sc" contains a single procedure called "SetKeyCodes()", which simply assigns 100 of the most common ASCII keycodes to variables. A portion of it is shown below. The use of SetKeyCodes() makes writing code for the toolkit much simpler.

The naming convention for these 100 variables is easy to use and remember as well: preface the name of the PAL key with the letters "TK." Thus, instead of referring to the RIGHT key as $-77$, by including the procedure SetKeyCodes in your Toolkit applications, you can refer to it as TKRight.[5] Here's how the listing begins:

**Listing 18.1: The SetKeyCodes Procedure Makes DoWait Debugging Easier**

```
PROC SetKeycodes()

TKBackspace = 8    TKDitto  = 4     TKPalMenu  = -113
TKCancel =   0     TKDOS    = 15    TKPgDn     = -81
```

```
TKCheck  =  -64     TKDOSBig = -24     TKPgUp      =  -73

<For the complete listing, see KEYCODES.SC>
ENDPROC
```

We recommend documenting your use of these variables in the following manner. Always place a comment next to the TK variable with the name of the key:

```
IF TKChar = TKPgUp    ; User pressed PgUp
```

This may seem redundant, but here is the reason: The SetKeyCodes script absorbs about 4000 bytes of MEMLEFT(). The Toolkit includes a utility called "PrepareFinal" in the "TKMenu" script that automatically strips out references to the TK variables and replaces them with their keycodes, thus saving 4000 bytes to be used by your applications at run time. The script line above appears as:

```
IF TKChar = -73    ;User pressed PgUp
```

Once these mnemonic variable names are stripped from your scripts, this method allows you to read your code easily. You should use "PrepareFinal" only after extensive testing and debugging of your DoWait scripts.

## 18.4.1 Movement Keys

Thus far, we've classified every keystroke and are able to trap every keystroke. "Movement" keys are a subclass of "Regular" keys. They are distinguished so that you can track when a keystroke moves the cursor out of a field, a record, or a table.[6]

At the most basic level, merely typing and deleting characters causes cursor movement. When you press [Backspace] for example, the character to the left of the cursor, if it exists, is deleted, and the cursor moves into its place. When you type the letter "A," the cursor moves one character to the right—unless an "A" is inappropriate. Under DoWait, every time you press a key, TKChar gets assigned—but is not immediately acted upon. You have the opportunity to accept or reject the keystroke contained in TKChar. Deciding what to do with the keystroke depends, in part, on its acceptability to Paradox:

- Field type validity is checked automatically by Paradox. For example, a letter typed into a numeric field, when passed through to Paradox, will simply beep.

- Validity Checks are implicit. A social security number, for example, may have a picture that restricts entry of only numbers into an alphenumeric field.

Movement keys present an opportunity to leave the field. If you press a movement key with ValChecks in place, the validity of the current field must be tested before the key is processed. This is done with a call to a simple function:

```
IF ISVALID() ; does the current value pass the validity checks?
```

If the field contents are valid, the movement key is also a valid keystroke:

```
IF ISVALID() THEN
  KEYPRESS TKChar
ENDIF
```

## 18.4.2 DoWait Field Level Events

The first level event in DoWait is a keystroke event. The second level is a field level event. Attempting to move out of a field, a field "departure," is a field level event. Leaving a field successfully is termed a "Good Departure." Attempting to leave a field with invalid data is termed a "Bad Departure."

```
Customer ID: _____

            Good Departure →
            Field value is valid.
            If assigned, a "Good Depart" procedure is invoked.

Customer ID: _____ ← Bad Departure

            Field value is invalid.
            If assigned, a "Bad Depart" procedure is invoked.
```

Under DoWait, you can assign procedures to both "Good" and "Bad" field departures. This means that you can take action on invalid or incomplete fields before Paradox recognizes them as invalid.[7] DoWait offers greater control than under a typical WAIT session. Under DoWait, each field is a potential host for one or more procedure assignments. Yet if no special action needs to be taken, no procedures are assigned.

## 18.4.3 Workspace Geography and DoWait

A DoWait session is shaped by the layout of tables and forms on the Paradox workspace. Because of this, a session designed to work with one form rarely works with another. If you set up a DoWait session and then change the placement or number of fields on a form, DoWait almost never performs as expected.

This dependency is in part due to DoWait's use of the COLNO() function to navigate the workspace and determine which field is current.[8] DoWait uses a COLNO() in a procedure called NewField() to help keep track of which field is current:

```
PROC NewField()
   TKFieldVal = []
   TKFieldNum = ColNo()
ENDPROC
```

NewField() simply initializes two variables based on the cursor position. TKFieldVal is assigned the current contents of the field. More importantly, TKFieldNum is assigned the current column number. Unfortunately, the COLNO() function is sensitive to the rotation of fields in the table—if you rotate columns in a table prepared for DoWait and run it, expect disaster.

## 18.4.4 DoWait Procedures Are Called by Array Number

The value assigned to TKFieldNum is critical—it is DoWait's navigator and the key to determining which procedures apply to the field. Even more depends on it—in addition to GoodDepart and BadDepart procedures, DoWait allows you to assign a procedure that executes upon landing in the field, an "Arrive" procedure, and one that is executed with every keystroke, a "Keystroke" procedure.

```
Customer ID: _____
             Arrive Procedure →
             Executes upon arrival to field.


Customer ID: _____
             Keystroke Procedure
             Executes on every keystroke.
```

The names of all these procedures are held in arrays:

    ARRAY TKArrive
    ARRAY TKGoodDepart
    ARRAY TKBadDepart
    ARRAY TKKeystroke

The size of each array is related to the number of fields in the table. The first field in the array corresponds to the first column, the record number column. All calls to field level procedures rely on TKFieldNum as the array element subscript. Another array indexed on the current table's column numbers, called TKAction, holds values that dictate which type of procedures are to be invoked in each field.[9] TKAction is examined first. So, for example, if the third field (the fourth column) in the current table is "Customer ID" and it has an arrival procedure that you've named "GetCustID.n", then:

```
TKAction[4] = "A"
TKArrive[4] = "GetCustID.n"
```

When DoWait's NewField() procedure lands in "Customer ID," COLNO() is set to 4, TKAction is evaluated and found to contain "A," and the arrival procedure "GetCustID.n" is called. This call to a procedure had to be made simple and reliable. The procedure call is made with the help of a substring search and the EXECPROC command:

```
IF SEARCH("A",TKAction[TKFieldNum]) <> 0 THEN
   EXECPROC TKArrive[TKFieldNum]
ENDIF
```

If an "A" is found in an array element of the current column, signalling an arrival procedure assigned to the current field, these statements call the procedure name stored in the array element TKArrive[TKFieldNum]. In this instance, this translates to simply:

```
EXECPROC "GetCustID.n"
```

This highlights an important restriction in DoWait that arises out of the use of EXECPROC: All procedures that you assign DoWait to call must have no formal parameters. This is a limitation of the EXECPROC command. A procedure named:

```
GetCustID.n(Table.a,Field.a)
```

can't be called with EXECPROC because it has formal parameters, and thus it can't be used as a direct procedure call in DoWait.

This method, using the column number as an index into an array of procedure names to execute, is employed for GoodDepart, BadDepart, and Keystroke procedures. These calls are also based on assignments made to TKAction and the array elements in TKGoodDepart, TKBadDepart, and TKKeystroke.

### 18.4.5 Other DoWait Procedure Assignments

With the introduction of multitable forms with Paradox3, DoWait was modified to support both record level and table level events. These occur, as you would expect, upon arrival and departure from records and tables.

```
TKTblArrive     ;Cursor lands in new table.
TKTblDepart     ;Cursor attempts to depart table.
TKRecArrive     ;Cursor lands in new record.
TKRecDepart     ;Cursor attempts to depart record.
```

Since they apply to only one entity, either the current table or the current field, these variables are not arrays—they are set to the names of procedures associated with each event. Like all DoWait procedure assignments, an attempt will be made to execute them only if they are assigned. In addition, there are two procedure assignments that can be assigned once per table:

TKInactiveProc     An "Inactivity" procedure. This procedure watches the keyboard and measures delays between keystrokes.

TKSpclProc     A "Special Key" procedure. Any time this procedure is assigned, a key or list of special keys invokes a single procedure.

In Paradox3, DoWait invokes events in the following order:

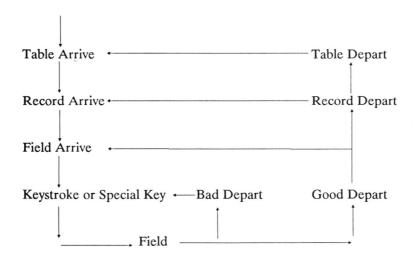

## 18.5 DOWAIT PROCEDURE ASSIGNMENT SETS (DPAS)

All of the variable assignments we have mentioned thus far have applied to one table at a time. With multitable forms, your DoWait sessions will most likely involve calls to multiple tables. Yet DoWait works with only one set of variables at a time. The next design challenge was how to efficiently store and assign the variables for each table.

This was done with a device known as a "DoWait Procedure Assignment Set" (a DPA Set for short), introduced in Paradox3. Here is the DPA Set for the "Cust" table in the "Minidemo" script contained in the Toolkit directory:

**Listing 18.2: MINIDPA.SC**

```
TableName = "Cust"
FormId = "1"
BorrowFile = "Borrow1"

Proc TKCust_1()

    Array TKAction[10]
    TKAction[1] = ""
    TKAction[2] = ""
    TKAction[3] = "K"
    TKAction[4] = "K"
    TKAction[5] = ""
    TKAction[6] = ""
    TKAction[7] = ""
    TKAction[8] = "D"
    TKAction[9] = ""
    TKAction[10] = ""

    Array TKArrive[1]

    Array TKGoodDepart[8]
    TKGoodDepart[8] = "SetDiscount"

    Array TKBadDepart[1]

    Array TKKeystroke[4]
    TKKeystroke[3] = "LeaveName"
    TKKeystroke[4] = "LeaveName"

    TKTblArrive = ""
    TKTblDepart = ""
    TKRecArrive = ""
    TKRecDepart = ""
    TKMvmntProc = "StdMvmnt"
    TKInactiveProc = ""
    TKSpclProc = "EditMenu"

;            0....+....1....+....2....+....3....+....4....+....5....+....6
    TKNegKey ="EIIIIIIIIIIIIIIIIMIIIIIIIIIIIIIIIIIIIIIIIIIIIIIMIIIIIIIIIIIIIIIIIIE" +
```

```
          "IIIIIIISIIMMMIMIMIMMMMMIIIIIIIIIIIIIIIIIIIIIIIIIIIIIIRIIIIIIMMMMMI" +
          "IIIIIIIIIIIM"
TKPosKey = "RRRRRRRMRRRMRIRRIRRMRRRRMRRRRRRRRRRRRRRRRRRRRRRRRRRRRRRRRRR" +
          "RRRRRRRMRRRRRRRRRRRRRRRRRRRRRRRRRRRRRRRRRRRRRRRRRRRRRRRRRRRR" +
          "RRRRRRRRRRRRRRRRRRRRRRRRRRRRRRRRRRRRRRRRRRRRRRRRRRRRRRRRRRRR" +
          "RRRRRRRRRRRRRRRRRRRRRRRRRRRRRRRRRRRRRRRRRRRRRRRRRRRRRRRRRRRR" +
          "RRRRRRRRRRRRRRRR"
```

```
Endproc
```

Fortunately, we aren't left to our own devices to create a DPA set—because no one would ever get them right and DoWait would not be part of Paradox. A DPA set is created for you by running the TKMenu script.

## 18.6 SETUPDOWAIT

A DPA Set is created with the assistance of the main Toolkit Utility script—"TKMenu.sc". If you've installed the Toolkit, TKMenu should be in the \Paradox3\toolkit directory.

Playing TKMenu for the first time creates the Toolkit procedure library. TKMenu contains an excellent demonstration of DoWait in action, using a customer invoicing system with popup help and customer and product lookup tables.

SetupDoWait allows you to define key and procedure assignments and uses them to define DPA variables. Each time you select SetupDoWait, you are asked for the name of a script, the name of a table, and the form you intend to use (if any) in your DoWait session. After analyzing the form, three tables are placed on the workspace for you to make procedure assignments. These tables are the Toolkit Field Level assignment table, "TKFldLvl", the Key level assignment table, "TKKeyLvl", and the Table level assignment table: "TKTblLvl". Assign as few procedures to fields as will do the job.

Through an analysis of the selected table and form, and the resultant table and field "geography," in combination with the procedure assignments you make, a DoWait Procedure Assignment Set is created. Each DPA set is also based on a "Borrow" script, which is referenced with the DPA and resides in the same directory. Each script is named "Borrow#", where the number is a sequential count of from 1 to 99. When you need to modify a DPA set, the corresponding "Borrow" script will be instrumental in keeping your present assignments intact. Don't delete "Borrow" scripts unless you want to rebuild a DPA from scratch when you modify them.

When defining DPA sets, enter specifications into three special toolkit tables:

### 1. TKFLDLVL.DB: Field Level Procedures

The number of records in the first table depends on the number of fields in the table. It's structure is shown. Fill out the "Arrive," "Good Depart," "Bad Depart," and "Keystroke" fields with your own procedure names.

```
"Column No." :   "S*",
"Field No."  :   "S*",
"Field Name" :   "A25*",
"Arrive"     :   "A15",
"Good Depart":   "A15",
"Bad Depart" :   "A15",
"Keystroke"  :   "A15"
```

### 2. TKKEYLVL.DB: Keystroke Assignments

Contains 350 records. The Class assignments permitted are "Exit," "Illegal," "Regular," and "Special." It consists of three fields, only the last of which is modifiable:

```
"ASCII Code":   "S*",
"Function"  :   "A25*",
"Class"     :   "A10"
```

### 3. TKTBLLVL.DB: Table Level Procedures

Contains 6 records in two fields. The procedure types are Table Arrive, Table Depart, Record Arrive, Record Depart, Keyboard Inactivity, and Special Key. You fill out the "Procedure Name" field only if one exists for the table. If you've defined several keys as "Special" in "TkKeyLvl," your special procedure should account for all these special keys and perform the action based on the key pressed.

```
"Procedure Type":   "A20",
"Procedure Name":   "A15"
```

Note: The structures of these tables dictate that the names of the procedures that you use in DoWait must be 15 characters or less.

Adding records to the table level procedure assignment table (TKTblLvl.db) is entirely optional. However, if you reassign a key in TKKeyLvl as "Special," be sure to name it in the [Special Key] field in "TKTblLvl." A TKKeyLvl table allows only Regular, Illegal, Exit, and Special. Regular or Special keys that are classified as Movement keys are assigned through the analysis of the form.

When dealing with multitable forms, you should reassign the UpImage and DownImage keys from the default "Illegal" to "Regular" keys to permit movement between tables. Because of the hazards and special processing required for its use, we always reassign UNDO as an illegal key. In addition, we make it a habit not to assign any key as an exit key—we prefer to have a Special key invoke an exit menu.

When you press DO-IT!, a script containing the DPA set corresponding to the table and form will be created. Within the script (you supplied its name to {SetupDoWait}), a procedure is defined. It follows the naming convention:

```
PROC TK + Tablename + _ + FormNumber
```

Thus a DPA set created from the "Customer" table with form 3 would be:

```
PROC TKCustomer_3
```

You should write all application specific DPA procedures to the application library. You never call these procedures—you simply read them into memory so that they are accessible to DoWait.

## DoWait Requires a DPA Set for Each Table

If you want to run a DoWait session on a master table with three embedded tables, you must make a DPA set for each table that you want to be able to edit. You then must read each DPA set into memory before invoking DoWait (or, if these sets are in a library, let AUTOLIB find them).

## 18.7 PROCEDURES IN DOWAIT

The procedures that you design to be invoked during DoWait should take advantage of variables that DoWait evaluates, monitors, and changes. These are DoWait's status and control variables.

### DoWait Status Variables

| | |
|---|---|
| TKChar | The character typed by the user. |
| TKBuffer | An explicitly assigned key that is acted upon before the next key press. DoWait never assigns TKBuffer—you have to. |
| TKFieldVal | The value of the current field when entered. It is the basis for the next variable, TKChanged. |

| | |
|---|---|
| TKChanged | Logical variable. Is the value in the field the same as when the field was entered? |
| TKKeyType | Type of key assigned in SetupDoWait. Set TKKeyType to "X" to request an immediate exit from DoWait. |
| TKSeconds | The number of elapsed seconds without a keypress if inactivity procedure has been defined. |
| TKLibName | Complete path of DoWait library. |

**DoWait Control Variables**

| | |
|---|---|
| TKAccept | Logical variable. Should DoWait act on the current keypress? This control variable can be set to false and the keystroke will automatically be rejected. |
| TKHoldCanvas | Logical variable. Should DoWait suspend echo normal until user presses key? This temporarily holds the canvas up until the user next presses a key. |
| TKKeyProc | Name of Key Inactivity Procedure. Null string if not assigned. |
| TKMessage | String to display before the next keypress. This should be set as often as necessary to keep the user informed. Important after a BadDepart. |

As long as you let DoWait handle all movement between fields, everything should function as expected. However, if a call to one of your procedures makes an explicit move from the current field to a new field, record, or table, you will have to make explicit calls to some of the Toolkit's procedures to help DoWait keep track of which procedure assignments are current:

| | |
|---|---|
| ArriveField( ) | Inform DoWait that the cursor is in a new field and call the Arrival Procedure if one is assigned. |
| NewField( ) | Inform DoWait that the cursor is in a new field, but do not call an associated Arrival Procedure. |
| ArriveRecord( ) | Inform DoWait that the cursor is in a new record. This procedure should only be called in the event of an explicit move to another record. |
| ArriveTable( ) | Inform DoWait that the cursor is in a new table. Call the arrival procedure for the table if one is assigned. ArriveTable does not call ArriveRecord; it does, however, indirectly call NewField(). To invoke a record arrival procedure, you must make a call to ArriveRecord() explicitly. |
| NewTable( ) | Inform DoWait that the cursor is in a new table. Does not call an associated Table Arrival Procedure. |

## 18.7.1 TKChar

Here's a departure procedure from the "Minidemo" script that leaves a field once the spacebar is pressed:

```
PROC LeaveName()
  IF TKChar = TKSpaceBar THEN
    TKChar = TKRight
  ENDIF
ENDPROC
```

This procedure simply reassigns the value of TKChar. "Ah, you pressed the spacebar, you must be done with the field; I will move you to the next one."

## 18.7.2 TKBuffer

Here's an example of an arrival procedure that makes the field, in effect, a display-only field:

```
PROC DisplayOnly.u()
  IF TKChar = TKLeft OR TKChar = TKReverseTab OR TKChar = TKPgUp THEN
    TKbuffer = TKLeft
  ELSE
    TKBuffer = TKRight
  ENDIF
ENDPROC
```

In this example, there is no need to call the ArriveField() or NewField() procedure. If the Toolkit variable, TKBuffer, is assigned, DoWait processes that keystroke ahead of any other keystroke the user types. This is done by DoWait's main GETCHAR procedure, called "GetKey()," shown below. Notice that TK-Buffer is reinitialized to a blank number as soon as it is processed:

```
PROC GetKey()
  IF ISBLANK(TKBuffer) THEN
    TKChar = GetChar()
  ELSE
    TKChar = TKBuffer
    TKBuffer = BlankNum()
  ENDIF
ENDPROC
```

### 18.7.3 TKCHANGED

TKChanged is set to True if the contents of TKFieldVal, the contents of the current field upon arrival, differ from the current field contents. This can be used, for example, in performing field-dependent calculations. TKChanged is only useful in GoodDepart procedures, because in a BadDepart procedure, the field value has obviously changed.

```
PROC CalcTotal.u()
  IF TKChanged THEN
    [Invoice Amt] = [Quantity] * [Price]
  ENDIF
ENDPROC
```

### 18.7.4 TKACCEPT

The variable TKAccept, by default True, can be explicitly set to False if you want to reject the keystroke entered before it is passed to Paradox. TKAccept is useful only in departing fields, records, and tables and special key procedures.

```
PROC Special.u()
  IF TKChar = TKF10 THEN
    TKAccept = False          ; Don't want keystroke passed on.
                             ; Otherwise, PDOX menu would display.
    EditMenu()
  ENDIF
ENDPROC
```

From the Editmenu script:

> NOTE: The interaction between TKAccept and TKChar is subtle but important. Setting TKAccept to False instructs DoWait not to allow Paradox to act upon the key. Reassigning TKChar to a different key (value) instructs DoWait to act as if a user had actually pressed the new key. Note, however, that setting TKAccept to False takes precedence over changing the value of TKChar, i.e., if you set TKAccept to False, DoWait will ignore the value of TKChar even if you have changed it. In addition, changing the value of TKChar does not guarantee that Paradox will actually act upon the new key. DoWait will reprocess the key exactly as if a user had actually typed it on the keyboard, meaning that it must pass through any event procedures it might activate before being passed on to Paradox.

### 18.7.5 TKMESSAGE

DoWait evaluates and resets the variable TKMessage with every keystroke. If set to anything but a null string, it will be displayed as a message in the lower right-hand corner of the screen until the next keystroke is pressed. TKMessage is particularly useful with departure procedures, enabling you to keep the user informed about the requirements of fields not yet met.

Here's a Good Depart procedure that simulates a required field (without the problems of making the field required with a validity check). It uses both TKMessage and TKAccept:

```
PROC RequiredField.u()
  IF ISBLANK([]) THEN
     TKMessage = "A Value is Required for this Field"
     TKAccept = False        ; Throw away movement keystroke.
  ENDIF
ENDPROC
```

# 18.8 SETTING UP A CALL TO DOWAIT

A call to a special Toolkit procedure called INITWAIT loads DoWait and its supplemental procedures. Before invoking DoWait, you must call InitWait. IF the toolkit variable "TKLibname" is assigned before invoking InitWait, the toolkit procedures will be looked for in the named library.

InitWait has three formal parameters. Its syntax is:

```
InitWait( LastImageNumber, ImageNumberList, TableNameList)
```

This is the final workspace information needed by DoWait, and the call to this procedure is not automatic—you must set it up and get it right. The LastImage-Number is not necessarily the highest image number on the workspace—it is the last image number that DoWait's call will involve. Thus if you have four tables on the workspace and only the first three are involved, the LastImageNumber is 3. See the Examples Section's discussion on the IMAGENO() command. The ImageNumberList is a quoted string representing a sequence of image numbers separated by commas that correspond to the named tables in Table-NameList.

One of the main reasons for the call to InitWait is stated clearly in the comment to the procedure in "Kernel.sc":

> You MUST call InitWait to load DoWait and its supplemental procedures. The Toolkit, like the rest of Paradox, is subject to upgrade. When such upgrades occur, it is possible that the Toolkit may require more procedures, or that undocumented procedure names may change. Calling InitWait rather that loading all of the necessary procedures manually will assure compatibility between Toolkit versions.

## 18.9 DATA ENTRY TOOLKIT CHECKLIST

1. Stabilize Table and Form Design for your application.
2. Determine which events require special processing.
3. Write procedures that include references to TK variables and inform DoWait of explicit field, record, and table arrival.
4. Design your workspace layout. Associate image numbers with table names.
5. Play TKMenu and select {SetupDoWait}; assign the procedures you've named to the appropriate fields in the "TKFldLvl" table. Make key assignments to the "TKKeyLvl" table. Make table level assignments in "TKTblLvl".
6. Repeat step 5 for every table in the DoWait session.
7. Write your DPA sets to the library you've created for the toolkit session.
8. Write a procedure call that makes your call to DoWait.

   - If you've used the TKKeyCode variables, it must call SetkeyCodes.
   - Call InitWait.
   - Read in your DPA sets.
   - Place tables onto the workspace in the proper order in either Edit, CoEdit, or DataEntry modes.
   - Call DoWait.

**Listing 18.3: README.on the installation disk**

```
Record-level events:

    In addition to supporting keystroke, field, and table level events, the
    Data Entry Toolkit now also implements record arrival and record
    departure events.

    If you assign a record departure event for a table, DoWait will
    activate your procedure each time a user presses a key that can cause
    departure from the current record.  Note that DoWait will call your
    record departure procedures upon ANY attempt to leave a record,
    regardless of whether the attempt will be successful or not.  As with
    other kinds of event procedures, DoWait calls record depart procedures
    after a user presses a key that may cause movement out of the current
    record but BEFORE it passes the key to Paradox.  Thus, if a user uses
    ZOOM (or ZOOMNEXT) to locate a value, DoWait will call your record
    departure procedures after the user presses [Enter] (or [Alt][Z]) to
    initiate the ZOOM but before Paradox executes the ZOOM.  DoWait status
    and control variables for field and table departure events are also
    available to your record departure procedures.

    DoWait calls record arrival procedures immediately after a user has
    entered a new record.  Note, however, that if your procedures
    explicitly move a user to a new record, DoWait will not initiate
```

record arrival and departure procedures. As in field and table arrival events, the DoWait control variable TKAccept has no effect since the user has already "arrived in" a new record. You can call the ArriveRecord() procedure to have DoWait execute your arrival procedure or you can execute it yourself.

You assign record-level event procedures through the SetUpDoWait subsystem of TKMenu. To designate a record-level event procedure, simply place its name in the Procedure Name field next to the appropriate "Record Arrive" or "Record Depart" record of the TKTBLLVL table.

Note that DoWait is sensitive to changes in a table's structure and, in applications that use record-level events, the position of fields on a form. If you assign record-level procedures for a table, you MUST rerun SetUpDoWait every time you change the position of fields on a form.

DoWait invokes events in the following order:

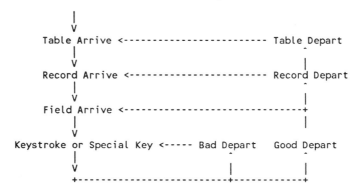

Demo.sc:

DEMO.SC allows you to run the DoWait demonstration from outside TKMenu. If you plan to step through the demonstration in debug mode, you'll need to play Demo since TKMenu is a password-protected script.

LookupSelect and LookupWait:

You can now apply LookupSelect and LookupWait to all types of images, not only lookup help tables. LookupSelect and LookupWait use the ImageRights ReadOnly command to temporarily prevent a user from making changes to the current image. If you have previously issued an ImageRights command on the image, you may need to re-issue the command. See LOOKSLCT.SC and LOOKWAIT.SC for more information.

ReleaseWait:

ReleaseWait, a new procedure, releases DoWait and its supplemental variables and procedures. See RELEASW8.SC for more information.

CHANGES TO THE DOCUMENTATION:

Record-level events:

Because of the implementation of record-level events, all references to movement key procedures and TKMvmntProc are no longer applicable.

In support of record-level events, DoWait now has an additional supplemental procedure: ArriveRecord. ArriveRecord will invoke the record arrival procedure for the current table (if you've assigned one).

RecurseWait and TKDebug:

The RecurseWait and TKDebug procedures, previously in KERNEL.SC, are now in separate script files. RecurseWait is now in RECURSW8.SC. TKDebug is now in TKDEBUG.SC. Note that since DoWait now internally supports multiple table images, existing calls to RecurseWait may no longer be necessary. Refer to the Data Entry Toolkit documentation for more information on removing your calls to RecurseWait.

Closed Toolkit procedures:

The table listing the various Toolkit utility procedures specifies several procedures that are "closed" procedures. NONE of the Toolkit utility procedures are "closed" procedures.

Enhanced Form Editor (Enforme):

To use the Enhanced Form Editor without installing the entire Data Entry Toolkit, copy the following files on to your hard disk from the \TOOLKIT2 directory of the Data Entry Toolkit 2 disk:

```
ENFORME.SC
FORM*.SC     -- FORMMAIN.SC, FORMHOPS.SC, FORMGOTO.SC, FORMBRDR.SC,
                FORMSLCT.SC, FORMHELP.SC, FORMMAKE.SC
```

Playing Enforme.sc will generate a new library, $ENFORME.LIB (if it does not already exist). Once the library is created, you may erase files named FORM*.SC if necessary.

SPECIAL NOTES:

Debugging applications that use inactivity procedures:

If you incorporate inactivity procedures into your applications, pressing [Ctrl][Break] to step through a script will often leave you within the keyboard inactivity loop. To instruct DoWait to continue past the loop, assign the variable TKBuffer to the keycode of the next key you wish to process, press [Ctrl][N] when you encounter the statement "If Charwaiting()", then press [Ctrl][S] to have DoWait act on the keycode saved in TKBuffer.

Using RecurseWait on query images:

> Should you desire to use DoWait on a query image, you'll need to use the RecurseWait variation of DoWait. See RECURSW8.SC for more information.

ArriveTable and ArriveRecord:

> When you explicitly move to another table within an event procedure, you must call ArriveTable or NewTable to alert DoWait that you have switched to another table image. Note that ArriveTable and NewTable do NOT call ArriveRecord. If you wish to invoke a record arrival procedure upon explicit movement to a new table, you must call ArriveRecord or your arrival procedure yourself.

Good Depart and Bad Depart procedures:

> In the previous version of the Toolkit, putting an invalid value in a field within a Good Depart procedure would cause a script error, since Paradox does not allow movement out of an invalid field. In this release, however, DoWait WILL activate the Bad Depart procedure for a field if your Good Depart procedure leaves invalid data in the field.

Interactions with Undo:

> When a user presses Undo within an Edit session (but not CoEdit), Paradox will sometimes move a user out of the current table and into another one. This may occur, for example, when a user is editing a multi-table form. DoWait has no way of knowing whether an Undo will take a user out of the current table until Paradox actually processes the Undo. DoWait WILL activate table, record, and field arrival procedures for the new table, as well as the record departure procedure for the original table. DoWait WILL NOT, however, call the table departure procedure for the original table.

Changing forms of tables with record-level events:

> DoWait requires form-specific information (generated by SetUpDoWait) to determine whether a key will cause movement out of a record. Thus, you MUST rerun SetUpDoWait every time you change the location of fields on a form of a table you use with DoWait. Otherwise, DoWait will not properly activate your record-level procedures.

# NOTES

1. For the inquisitive, the main Toolkit script, Kernel.sc, and various demonstration scripts (Invdemo.sc, Custdemo.sc, Ordrdemo.sc, Help-Demo.sc, Demo.sc and Minidemo) are excellent sources of information on how to program with DoWait.

2. The real DoWait() is in the file in the toolkit directory called "Kernel.sc."

3. We would normally use "n", because GETCHAR() always returns a value with a numeric type—the PAL keycode. The ToolKit has special variables that all begin with "TK".

4. As you will see in the next section, this method requires little work on our part to get these assignments right.

5. Because these are variables, you never refer to them as quoted strings.

6. A special case applies with the mode called "FieldView", which by nature restricts cursor movement within a field. When in FieldView, movement keys are limited to [Right], [Left], [Ctrl Right], [Ctrl Left], [Home], [End], and [Enter]. During FieldView, movement keys should function normally. FieldView is easy to trap for. The main difficulty with movement keys is when not in Fieldview.

7. With the WAIT command, Paradox gives no control over to the programmer if a field value is invalid—Paradox simply won't let the user out of a field that doesn't meet the field type restrictions or the validity checks.

8. The COLNO() function was chosen because it executes about 20 times faster than the FIELDNO() function, which requires access to the table's structure.

9. TKAction may also hold special symbols that relate to record movement.

10. The structures of these tables dictate that names of the procedures that you use in DoWait must be 15 characters or less.

Final note: As of this writing, do not use the "SAVEVARS ALL" command if you are using the Toolkit with record level events because Paradox cannot save the strings assigned to movement keys properly.

# Chapter 19

# WaitPlus

This chapter contains the source code for and the discussion of WaitPlus.

## 19.1 WHAT IS WAITPLUS?

Programming is learned through hard work and discovery. Along the way, though what was new becomes rote, fresh challenges continually appear, leading to new knowledge.

As Paradox has grown more capable, it has become more complex. Paradox3, in its support of multitable forms, is more capable and more complex than ever. Problems which should yield to direct solutions often don't. To those who depend on Paradox and PAL to just get the job done, this can be frustrating.

Fortunately, like other programming languages, PAL lends itself to the creation of standardized routines that can snap into place in larger programming tasks and help speed development, assure consistency, and save work. Programming tools should free the programmer to concentrate on the task at hand.

WaitPlus is a series of PAL procedures that let you control user access to data in Paradox tables in table or form view.

WaitPlus, though not a panacea, is a response both to the need for standardized table editing routines and the complexity of Paradox. Developed over several years, the WaitPlus routines can either be integrated into other systems or used as is. WaitPlus consists of five scripts, Wwputil1 (write WaitPlus Utilities 1), Wwputil2 (the second utility script), Wwpcore1 and Wwpcore2 (write Waitplus Core), and WwpApp (write WaitPlus Application, where much of your customization takes place). All of these scripts are liberally commented on and write procedures to procedure libraries.

A call to WaitPlus is a call to a single procedure that controls record-level processing. In it, the user is placed in a table in a mode that allows only viewing (CoEdit mode with Readonly Imagerights). Depending on the rights selected for a particular table, the user may then add, edit, or delete records. WaitPlus takes care of the routine housekeeping and user interface, but it is easily customized. The code uses WAIT TABLE, WAIT RECORD, and WAIT FIELD extensively, so you can enjoy the depth of programming possible with these familiar Paradox commands.

The WaitPlus procedures are instructional as well as useful in day-to-day coding. They should be of interest to programmers on all levels. The code is presented in a form prepared by ScriptView, FarPoint Systems' Script Documentor. The "Action Diagram" includes line numbers and "Structure" lines that connect logical pairs (PROC and ENDPROC, IF and ENDIF, and all LOOPS). We feel that this makes the code easier to follow, especially in some of the more complex sections.

WaitPlus is copyright, 1989, by Alan Zenreich and James M. Kocis. However, you are granted the right to use the WaitPlus code in your applications. Because of the sheer volume of code and comments involved, we have also decided to make WaitPlus available on disk as a commercial product. In addition to saving you the trouble of typing in the code, the disk includes all the source code, several sample tables demonstrations, and a front-end code generator that writes the calls to WaitPlus for you.

Study WaitPlus; put it through its paces (enjoy the fact that you didn't have to code all of this yourself). You may see features unfold as you work with the code. The examples in WWPAPP.SC are meant to give you insight towards the types of things possible in customized WaitPlus applications.

## 19.2 WHO CAN USE WAITPLUS?

Almost anyone who uses Paradox can put WaitPlus to work.

WaitPlus traps for common data entry errors such as duplicate key fields; keeps users from accidentally deleting records without confirmation; has on-line help for moving around in records, activating menus, and finding records with Zoom or the built-in GoTo menu; traps for obscure back doors to DOS (for example, pressing [Ctrl O] while in FieldView). For most, if not all, purposes, one call to WaitPlus frees the user from the mechanics of programming the data entry session, and "leaves the driving to us."

On the other hand, for those familiar with PAL programming, WaitPlus allows flexible data entry with built-in hooks to customize the code. WaitPlus was built with the needs of application developers in mind. Built-in features include:

- placing the table on the workspace for you, and removing it when done,
- full support for multitable entry forms,
- network locking and access checking,
- easy restriction of access rights without encrypting tables (tables can be marked as "DisplayOnly," ensuring that the cursor won't even land on the table),
- customized table name aliases for the prompt lines (so the user sees, for example, "Orders Placed" instead of "Bookord"),
- intelligent prompts and menus that are sensitive to the rights assigned to the current table image, and
- easy restriction to form view, table view, or both views while specifying whether or not users are allowed to edit in table view (automatically senses link-locking placed by Paradox and responds accordingly).

WaitPlus is provided in five scripts:

| | |
|---|---|
| WWPUTIL1.SC | Utility procedures used by WaitPlus, but generic enough to be used in any PAL code. |
| WWPUTIL2.SC | Additional utility procedures. (The utility procedures are split into two scripts for speedier access.) |
| WWPCORE1.SC | The first part of the WaitPlus engine. |
| WWPCORE2.SC | The second part of the WaitPlus engine. |
| WWPAPP.SC | Script that contains the hooks for customization and decision-making. The script also contains examples of code used by application programmers. |

## 19.3 HOW DOES WAITPLUS DIFFER FROM DOWAIT?

Paradox contains a special set of tools for advanced programming called the Data Entry Toolkit. Its main procedure, DoWait() works very differently than Wait-Plus—they present two different approaches to table access.

DoWait() allows control at the field and keystroke level—DoWait() can do things that are otherwise impossible in PAL code. However, we've found that the overwhelming majority of data entry applications do not demand the features of DoWait(), but can get along quite nicely on a record level, where WaitPlus concentrates its efforts.

If you program with DoWait(), you have to program all the control structures that deal with lookuptables, record locking, link types, key violations, etc. WaitPlus, on the other hand, has extensive errorchecking that takes care of the common, and even rather obscure errors that may occur. WaitPlus knows about the issues that surround multitable forms and network use, and it provides many tools for the application programmer. For example, you can assign rights to the tables involved that mimic some of the features normally found only in encrypted tables with auxiliary passwords (you can easily restrict what the user may do in each table).

As mentioned, WaitPlus operates on a record level. For example, a user moves to a record to edit, presses [F9], edits the record, and when finished, presses [F2] to end the edit of that record. The PAL programmer has complete control over whether or not the record is considered complete.

### 19.3.1 "Events"

There are several procedures that you can customize to make WaitPlus meet the needs of your application. Both DoWait() and WaitPlus let you customize what happens during certain "Events." DoWait() has events that are triggered by:

- individual keystrokes,
- elapsed time,
- attempted field arrival and departure (with both valid and invalid data),
- attempted arrival and departure from records, and
- attempted arrival and departure from tables.

WaitPlus lets you add code that is triggered by a different kind of event that occurs at many strategic points in program flow. The procedures called Wait-PlusAction.l(), WaitPlusLookupAction.l(), WaitPlusMoreMenu.u(), and Help-Data.u() can be customized to let you control events that occur under the following circumstances:

- before the table is placed on the workspace,
- once the table has been put on the workspace in the proper form,
- when arriving on a table by virtue of an [F3] or [F4] keypress,
- when attempting to leave a table because of an [F3] or [F4] keypress,
- when preparing to add a record,
- when arriving at a newly added record,
- when requesting cancellation of the new record,
- after a new record is cancelled,
- when preparing to edit a record,
- before the user is allowed to edit the record,
- when requesting cancellation of the record edit and restoration of the old record,
- when the record edit is cancelled,
- when requesting deletion of a record,
- after deleting a record,
- when pressing [Esc] to end the WaitPlus session,

- when pressing [F1] for field help,
- when arriving in Lookup help,
- when attempting to depart Lookup help,
- upon returning to the data table from Lookup help,
- when making a {More} choice from a WaitPlus menu, and
- when requesting a help screen about the current table.

## 19.4 INVOKING WAITPLUS

WaitPlus is invoked by making a call to a procedure called WaitPlus.v(). The full syntax is:

```
WaitPlus.v(wpTable.a,wpForm.a, wpTableView.l, wpTableViewEdit.l, wpAliasList.a, wpRightsList.a,
wpSetupProc.a, wpConfirmQuit.l)
```

Typically, you should set AUTOLIB to include the library that WAITPLUS is written to so that Paradox takes care of all reading and releasing of the procedures.

The WWPCORE1.SC has a full description of the formal parameters. Here are a few typical calls to WaitPlus.v, and their effects:

Example 1: A single table in table view. ReadOnly (simulating Main mode). No editing, deleting or adding of records permitted. Use the default table name in the prompt. Pressing [Esc] quits without confirmation:

```
WaitPlus.v("Customer",   ; wpTable.a
           "0",          ; wpForm.a
           TRUE,         ; wpTableView.l
           TRUE,         ; wpTableViewEdit.l
                         ;       Could also be FALSE because rights
                         ;       have been designated as ReadOnly.
           "{}",         ; wpAliasList.a    None. Uses table name.
           "R",          ; wpRightsList.a   ReadOnly
           "",           ; wpSetupProc.a.   None.
           TRUE)         ; wpConfirmQuit.l. Must confirm to quit.
```

The top two lines of the screen always reflect the available rights.

### Listing 19.1: WaitPlus.FG1

```
Viewing Customer  (33 records on file)
[Esc]-Quit [F10]-Menu
CUSTOMER╤Cust ID╤═══Last Name══════╤Init╤══════Street═══════╤══════City══╤
      1 │  1386 │  Aberdeen        │ F  │ 45 Utah Street     │ Washington
      2 │  1388 │  Svenvald        │ I  │ Gouvernment House  │ Reykjavik
      3 │  1784 │  McDougal        │ L  │ 4950 Pullman Ave NE│ Seattle
      4 │  2177 │  Bonnefemme      │ S  │ 128 University Drive│ Stanford
```

| 5 | 2579 | Chavez | L | Cypress Drive | Palm Springs |
| 6 | 2779 | Fahd | S | The Palace | Riyadh |
| 7 | 3128 | Elspeth, III | R | 1 Hanover Square | London |
| 8 | 3266 | Hanover | A | 15 State Street | Dallas |
| 9 | 3271 | Massey | C | 29 Aragona Drive | Oxon Hill |

Example 2: A multitable customer form (#3). Table view allowed, but no edit in table view. Two descriptive aliases for the prompt lines. May edit/add only in form view. The assigned rights to the Customer table are "Update"; on the BookOrd table, "Insert/Delete." The user is also asked to confirm the [Esc] keypress to exit WaitPlus.v:

```
WaitPlus.v("c:\\Paradox3\\sample\\Customer",; wpTable.a
          "3",     ; wpForm.a
          TRUE,    ; wpTableView.l
          FALSE,   ; wpTableViewEdit.l
          "{Our Favorite Customers}{Orders Placed}", ; Table aliases.
          "UI",    ; wpRightsList.a
          "",      ; wpSetupProc.a
          TRUE)    ; wpConfirmQuit.l
```

In this case, the prompt lines are different, sensitive to the rights assigned and the functions available at any given time:

**Listing 19.2: WaitPlus.FG2**

```
Viewing Our Favorite Customers  (33 records on file)
[Esc]-Quit [F10]-Menu [F3]-↑Image [F4]-↓Image [F7]-FormKey [F9]-Edit
```
                    LUXURY GIFTS BOOK CLUB
                         ORDER FORM


               ID:    1386
             Name:    F◄ Aberdeen
          Address:    45 Utah Street
                      Washington      DC  20032


          Date     Item # Vol   Quant   Sold by
       ----------- ------ ---   ------- -------
          8/21/87       1 M13   22      146
          10/20/89      1 M18   21      146
          10/20/89      2 M27   11      146

Example 3: No table view. "Entry" rights on the Customer table (i.e., it's O.K. to add and edit records, but no deletions are allowed). Don't even let the cursor rest on the BookOrd table, simulating a "DisplayOnly Table" similar to a "Display-Only Field" in a form. (This differs from setting an embedded or master form to "DisplayOnly" while in FORM mode, because the cursor can't rest on the form.)

```
WaitPlus.v("c:\\Paradox3\\sample\\Customer",; wpTable.a
          "3",      ; wpForm.a
          FALSE,    ; wpTableView.l
          FALSE,    ; wpTableViewEdit.l
          "{Customer List}{}", ; Table aliases.
          "ED",     ; wpRightsList.a
          "",       ; wpSetupProc.a
          TRUE)     ; wpConfirmQuit.l
```

Note: the [F3] and [F4] choices are missing because there is no table to move to. An [Ins] choice is now available.

**Listing 19.3: WaitPlus.FG3**

```
Viewing Customers list  (33 records on file)
[Esc]-Quit [F10]-Menu [F9]-Edit [Ins]-Add
```
---
```
                          LUXURY GIFTS BOOK CLUB
                               ORDER FORM


                     ID:    1386
                   Name:    F. Aberdeen
                Address:    45 Utah Street
                            Washington       DC  20032



               Date      Item #  Vol   Quant    Sold by
            -----------   ------  ---   -------  -------
               8/21/87        1   M13   22       146
              10/20/89        1   M18   21       146
              10/20/89        2   M27   11       146
```

# 19.5 CUSTOMIZING WAITPLUS

There are several places where you can customize WaitPlus to control the way it behaves. This section discusses each procedure and briefly explains the effect of your intervention when each event occurs.

## 19.5.1 WaitPlusAction.l( )

The WaitPlusAction.l() procedure is evaluated at many points in the code. For simple applications, you might want to insert code directly into the procedure itself. However, in larger applications this might be unwieldy, so it is often useful to create your own procedures for the appropriate actions below, and have WaitPlusAction.l() call the appropriate procedures and return the needed values. In this manner, WaitPlusAction.l() can act as a sort of switchboard, controlling the flow of the application. The following is a list of the possible actions that WaitPlusAction.l() controls, and instructions for customizing the routines.

| Decision Point | When Activated, Instructions, and Possible Uses |
|---|---|
| PrepWait | Prepares the WaitPlus session. PrepWait is often used to place other tables on the workspace (for example, a table that holds the next numbers to assign to invoices). It is called by WaitPlusSetup.l before the master table is placed on the workspace. If you return a TRUE, WaitPlus proceeds. If you return a FALSE, you will exit WaitPlus. |
| ArriveWait | Activated just before the user is allowed to view the table. Perhaps you want to issue an END command to take the user to the last record entered instead of the first record in the table as Paradox would normally. The WaitPlusSetup.l procedure sets up many variables and places the master table on the workspace. The proper form is picked (if appropriate). If the master table is marked as DisplayOnly, the cursor will move to the first table available to the user. It is at this point, just before the user sees the table, that ArriveWait takes over. If you return a TRUE, WaitPlus proceeds normally. A FALSE exits WaitPlus immediately. If you want to return a FALSE, you'll need to explicitly remove any tables placed on the workspace, as well as any locks placed. |
| ArriveTable | Activated each time you move between tables in a multitable image and arrive on a new table. Perhaps you want to get some image subtotals and display them to the user, or move to a specific record. It does not matter if you return a TRUE or FALSE. |
| DepartTable | Activated each time you attempt to leave a table in a multitable form. You might want total values that are to be carried over into another table. If you return a TRUE, the user will move to the next table. If you return a FALSE, the user stays in the current table. |
| PrepAdd | Activated when a user presses [Ins] to add a new record. Commonly used to get a new "next number" from another table for automatic assignment or incrementing of field data (e.g., next invoice number). This is also a |

good point at which to implement special code to check access rights of individual users. Allows you to override the normal WaitPlus prompt lines for adding a record. To override the prompts, set variables wwpPrompt1.a and wwpPrompt2.a to the messages that you want to appear at the top of the screen while adding records. If you return a TRUE, WaitPlus inserts a blank record; a FALSE returns the user to "View" mode.

ArriveAdd

Activated after WaitPlus has inserted a new record, but before the user is given access to it. This is the place to assign the value found in the next number table into the appropriate field in the current table. If you return a TRUE, the user continues filling out the record; a FALSE deletes the appended record and returns to "View" mode.

PrepCancelAdd

Activated when the user has chosen to cancel the addition of the current record. You could deny them this privilege if your application is set up so that a record, once started, must be completed or marked void (as with a traffic ticket, you might need to keep an audit trail of all entries, completed or not). On the other hand, you might need to get the information from the current record for use in the CancelAdd condition that follows. A TRUE lets the user Cancel the add record, letting the CancelAdd routine below take place. A FALSE denies the user the right to cancel the record; they are returned to the record in "Add" mode.

CancelAdd

Activated when the user has successfully cancelled adding the record. You might need to update totals in this or other tables. This routine is called after the appended record has been deleted. If you need any information about the record, get it during PrepCancelAdd above. It does not matter whether you return a TRUE or a FALSE.

DepartAdd

Activated when user has successfully added a record. As they return to view mode, any code placed is executed.

PrepEdit

Activated when the user pressed [F9] to edit a record. Perhaps used to check for additional access rights or passwords. You might not want to let certain users edit certain records. This is also the place to override the normal WaitPlus prompt lines for editing a record. To override the prompts, set variables wpPrompt1.a and wpPrompt2.a to the messages that you want to appear at the top of the screen when adding records. If you return a FALSE, the user is returned to "View" mode. If you return a TRUE, WaitPlus attempts to lock the record. If successful, the current record is copied to an array, wpRecord.r, that can be used for comparison later on. It then proceeds to the ArriveEdit routine below.

ArriveEdit
Activated when the user is just about to be allowed to edit this record. Perhaps you'd like to put up a special message. If you return a TRUE, the edit continues. A FALSE unlocks the current record and returns to "View" mode.

PrepCancelEdit
Activated when the user has chosen to cancel the edit of the current record. As above, this can be disallowed. On the other hand, you might need to get the information from the current record for use in the CancelEdit condition that follows. A TRUE lets the user Cancel editing this record, letting the CancelEdit routine below take place. A FALSE denies the user the right to cancel the record; they are returned to the record in "Edit" mode.

CancelEdit
Activated when a user has successfully cancelled the editing of the record. WaitPlus has just restored the original state of the record by copying all the values from the wpRecord.r array. If you return a TRUE, the current record is unlocked and you return to "View" mode. A FALSE keeps the user in "Edit" mode, but the record has been restored to the preedited condition.

DepartEdit
Activated after the user has successfully edited a record and passed the WaitPlusOkRecord.l test. Perhaps you need to update some totals. Returning a TRUE unlocks the record, which posts the changes, and goes back to "View" mode. A FALSE keeps the user in "Edit" mode.

PrepDelete
Activated when the user chooses {Delete} from the WaitPlus menu. You might want to verify that there are no records in other tables that are dependent on this record. Returning a TRUE, this command lets the user see a menu of {Cancel} {OkDelete} for verification. A FALSE returns the user to "View" mode.

OkDelete
Activated after the user has answered "OK" to the {Delete} menu, but before any attempt to delete the record. This is used when you are trying to delete a master record that has detail records. Since Paradox won't let you delete a master record when details in a 1-M group depend on it, WaitPlus normally presents the user the {Cancel} {Ok} menu, but then is unable to delete the master because of the independent details.

You can use the OkDelete action to move to the detail table, delete all the detail records, then move back to the master table and return a TRUE, so that WaitPlus will be able to delete the master record. This avoids having the user manually delete the detail records before deleting the master.

Obviously, this technique should be used with caution, for the effects are irreversible. If OkDelete returns a FALSE, the record is not deleted and you are returned to "View" mode. If OkDelete returns TRUE, the record is deleted and WaitPlus goes on to the Depart-Delete action.

DepartDelete
After a user confirms a deletion with {OkDelete}, Wait-Plus attempts to delete the current record. If this is possible (it might not be possible if this is a master record with dependent detail records), the current record is removed. At this point, the DepartDelete routine is called. Once again, you might need to update totals somewhere based on information gathered in PrepDelete. It does not matter if you return a TRUE or a FALSE.

DepartWait
Activated when a user attempts to exit WaitPlus. The normal way to exit WaitPlus is when the user presses [Esc] while in "View" mode. However, if you set a variable called wpQuit.l to TRUE, WaitPlus acts as if the user has pressed [Esc] and triggers the DepartWait routine. Normally it clears the current image from the workspace and removes the explicit table locks. If you return a TRUE, WaitPlus is exited. A FALSE puts the user back in "View" mode.

## 19.5.2 WaitPlusLookupAction.l( )

In WaitPlus, the [F1] key is treated as a "special" key. When the user presses [F1] for help, a procedure named WaitPlusLookup.u() is called. It in turn calls WaitPlusLookupAction.l(). There are several points at which you can insert your own code here. Normally, WaitPlus issues the HELP command and sees if there is tablelookup help available for the field. If so, the user is presented with the lookup table, where they may select a record. If no lookup help is available, the program beeps once.

**Decision Point** | **When Activated, Instructions, and Possible Uses**
PrepLookup | When the user presses [F1], this is the first place that is analyzed. This is also the place to intercept the [F1] call

with any special help routines for particular fields. For example, you might want [F1] to present a SHOWMENU of available choices, or you may need to use an ACCEPT statement. Or you can use this point to show a special help screen that is sensitive to the field or username. If the call returns a TRUE, WaitPlusLookup.u() tries to determine if there is a lookup table assigned to this field. If you return a FALSE, you are returned to whatever you were doing before pressing [F1]. Typically any special help routines would simply return a FALSE when they are finished, telling WaitPlusLookup.u() that it need go no further.

ArriveLookup
Activated when the user arrives in the lookup table. Perhaps you'd like to locate the record with the value that was currently in the data table. Or maybe you simply want to move to the end of the table. You might simply change the prompt lines presented to the user while in the lookup table. If you return a TRUE, the user is allowed access to the table. A FALSE brings the user directly back to the data table.

DepartLookup
Activated when the user is in a lookup table and has pressed [F2]. You might want to confirm that the record selected is valid. For example, if the lookup table is a list of inventory items, you might not want to let the user select an item that is currently out of stock. If you return a TRUE, the lookup table is removed from the screen. If you return a FALSE, the user remains in the lookup table.

LookupReturn
Activated when the user returns to the data table from the lookup table. You might want to issue a RESYNCKEY to update all the images in a form based on the current field value. For example, in a field for a customer ID# with a linked customer table on the workspace, issuing a RE-SYNCKEY would force the customer data to appear in the embedded table. It does not matter if this routine returns a TRUE or a FALSE.

## 19.5.3 WaitPlusOkRecord.l( )

The WaitPlusOkRecord.l() routine is called in a few places, but typically where a user is editing or adding a record and has pressed [F2] to complete the entry. This is the juncture at which to check that the fields necessary for the record have been filled in, or at which to verify the contents of the field. If you use this procedure to examine the current record, you need to set two additional variables, incomplete.l and error.a. If the record fails your inspection, then set incomplete.l to TRUE and optionally set error.a to a message that you want to display to the user. For example, if you want to make sure that the name fields in the record are filled in, you might code something like

```
incomplete.l = ISBLANK([last name]) OR ISBLANK([First name])
error.a = "You need to enter a value in the last name field"
```

If incomplete.l is set to TRUE, the error message will be presented to the user and they will remain editing or adding the current record. If incomplete.l is set to FALSE, WaitPlus goes on to check out key conflicts (if appropriate), and then goes on to the departadd or departedit routines.

This approach has many advantages over using a Required ValCheck in Paradox. If you never reach the required field, the validity check never activates. WaitPlus turns REQUIREDCHECK OFF because required fields are too restrictive when used in forms.

### 19.5.4 WaitPlusMoreMenu.u( )

When the user presses [F10], WaitPlus presents a menu of available options. Each menu has a {More} choice that links to a procedure called WaitPlusMoreMenu.u(). You can insert code that is specific to the particular table, user, or field value. Some programmers have used it to change forms in single-user systems. You can make the {More} choice as flexible as you like, or use the default "No more menu choices currently available" message.

### 19.5.5 HelpData.u( )

When the user presses [F10], there is always a {Help} choice on the menu. WaitPlus has built-in help screens that describe the functions of the Paradox movement keys, how to make menu selections, and how to find records with Zoom and the WaitPlus {GoTo} menu. It includes a choice called {Data} that calls HelpData.u(), with which you call custom help screens. You can make the help specific to the current table, and even make it sensitive to the current mode (View, Add, or Edit) or user name.

### 19.5.6 WaitPlus Variables

There are also several variables that can be overridden to help with decision making, or create "special effects:"

wpTablename.a      Name of current table, no path, initial capitalization. Useful for determining the actions of help screens, menus, and when the user presses [F1].

| | |
|---|---|
| wpTableDesc.a | Description for current table as defined in the table aliases. If there is no table alias assigned, the table-desc.a variable is set to the same description as table-name.a as shown above. |
| wpTableRights.a | The rights assigned to the current table ("I", "E", "U", "R" or "D"). You might want to temporarily override the rights. For example if your code generates an invoice number which is the key field for the record, an ArriveAdd routine might change Tablerights.a from "I" to "U" so that the user cannot modify the key field. Remember to set it back to normal in DepartAdd and CancelAdd if you use this feature. |
| wpPromptProc.a | Name of an alternate prompt procedure for view mode. By default, the procedure is called "WaitPlus-Prompt.u," which analyzes the rights associated with the current table, as well as the number of records for the image. If you set promptproc.a to another string, WaitPlus will use EXECPROC to use your procedure instead. Make sure that your procedure sets the variables wwpPrompt1.a and wwpPrompt2.a. Because we are using EXECPROC, it is also important that your procedure not take any formal parameters. |
| wpMode.a | The current WaitPlus mode: "View," "Add," or "Edit". Often useful in making help context sensitive. |
| wpQuit.1 | If this variable is set, the DepartWait routine will be executed, and if successful, WaitPlus is exited. Sometimes it is useful to have a {More} menu set WaitQuit.1 to true. Some users in non-network installations use this technique to present the user with a menu of alternate forms. If the user selects a form, the programmer sets WaitQuit.1 to TRUE, then passes and assigns the form number to WaitRetval.v. When WaitPlus is exited, the programmer often has the call to WaitPlus.v in a loop, so that if a form number is returned by WaitPlus.v, the code simply reinvokes another Wait-Plus session with the new form. If an "Esc" is passed back to the calling program, the session ends. |
| wpRetval.v | Value returned by the WaitPlus.v. Normally "Esc," but it can easily be overridden at any point, preferably by WaitPlusAction.1("departwait"). |
| wpUntilBuffer.v | A special variable that lets you override some of the WAIT conditions, generally used by experienced WaitPlus programmers. If the variable is set to anything other than a null string (""), WaitPlus will not pause for user input at the WAIT TABLE or WAIT |

RECORD point in "View," "Add," or "Edit" modes. If a WAIT has been overridden, the variable is reinitialized to "" immediately after transferring the value to RETVAL. This deliberately set RETVAL value is used in place of the RETVAL ordinarily gathered by the UNTIL clause of the WAIT condition.

Consider the wwpUntilBuffer.v variable a one-keystroke buffer with which the programmer can simulate a user keypress. For example, when a user finishes adding a record, you might want to set wwpUntilBuffer.v="Ins" to append another record and keep the user in "Add" mode, rather than returning the user to the "View" mode. This technique actually returns the user to "View" mode behind the scenes, but then acts as if the user chose to add a new record. Returning to "View" mode gets around potential stack problems that can occur when procedures call themselves recursively.

Another example of a wwpUntilBuffer.v assignment involves having the user edit a record, and when complete, set wwpUntilBuffer.v="F9", jump to another table with a sister record, and call WaitPlusInfo() to initialize the variables for that table. The user will automatically be placed into "Edit" mode on the record.

Combining the wwpUntilBuffer.v variable with custom prompts can lead to finely controlled access of "logical records" spread across several tables. It is important to note that wwpUntilBuffer.v must match the retval it is meant to replace *exactly*, and that WaitPlus.v is expecting "Ins" to add a new record, not "INS." So look at WWPCORE1.SC for the UNTIL parameters of the WAIT conditions in "View," "Add," and "Edit" modes.

## 19.5.7 WaitPlusInfo.u( )

There is one additional procedure that is handy for advanced users: WaitPlusInfo.u(). Whenever WaitPlus implicitly arrives at a new table, WaitPlusInfo.u() is automatically called to evaluate two variables: tablename.a and tablerights.a. If you code to explicitly move to another table, be sure to call WaitPlusInfo.u() to reinitialize those variables; otherwise WaitPlus will not know that the table has been changed. You might also want to call WaitPlusAction.l("ArriveTable") if you have code there that should be activated.

### WWPUTIL1

```
1   ;****************************** WWPUtil1.SC ******************************
2   ; First script of Utility procedures used by WaitPlus.v.  The procedures
3   ; in this script are also of use in general Paradox code.
4   ;
5   ;  WWPUTIL1.SC
6   ;--------------------------------------------------------------------
7   ;  Working.u(message.v)                  ; General purpose message.
8   ;  Beeper.u(delay.n)                     ; Beeps until key is pressed.
9   ;  TopMsg.u(line1.a, line2.a, delay.v)   ; Centered two line message
10  ;                                        ; with optional beeps.
11  ;  Zoom.l()                              ; Substitute for ZOOM
12  ;  LookupSelect.n()                      ; Returns key that ended LOOKUP
13  ;  HelpTable.u()                         ; Menu for Help selections.
14  ;  HelpText.u(type.a)                    ; Text for help topics.
15  ;  GoToMenu.u()                          ; Record movement menu.
16  ;  MoveToRecno.l(type.a)                 ; Explicit move to a record.
17  ;  StripPath.a(string.a)                 ; Strips path off file spec.
18  ;  NextNumber.v(table.a, field.a,        ; Auto-incrementing routine
19  ;               embedded.l, increment.n, ; for advancing numeric IDs.
20  ;               working.a)
21  ;
22  ;--------------------------------------------------------------------
23  ; WaitPlus uses two scripts that contain general purpose utilities.
24  ; These scripts are WWPUtil1.SC and WWPUtil2.SC. They are commented
25  ; liberally and contain examples of each procedure's use. They are
26  ; separated because together they would result in a script over 1000
27  ; lines long and Paradox takes a long time between steps in the
28  ; debugger in scripts over 1024 lines.
29
30  ;--------------------------------------------------------------------
31  ; Working.u()
32  ; Proc puts "Working...." on the first line and an optional prompt on
33  ; the second line of the screen. It usually serves as an attempt to
34  ; try to keep the user informed of what is expected of them or what
35  ; the program is doing.  No blank screens at any time!!
36  ;
37  ;    Examples:  Working.u("Printing report")
38  ;               Working.u("")                    ; No message.
39
40  ┌─PROC Working.u(message.v)
41  │   ; message.v   ; Any message to display on the second line of the screen.
42  │   ;               It can be a string, or any other value type.
43  │   @1,0 CLEAR EOL ?? message.v   ; Display the message.
44  │   @0,0 CLEAR EOL ??"Working"    ; Display working.
45  │   STYLE BLINK                   ; And a few blinking dots.
46  │   ??"...."
47  │   STYLE
48  │   @0,0
49  └─ENDPROC
50  WRITELIB libname.a  Working.u
51  RELEASE PROCS       Working.u
52
53  ;--------------------------------------------------------------------
54  ; Beeper.u()
55  ; Beeper.u clears the keyboard buffer and beeps at the user until any
```

```
56   ; key is pressed.  The delay between beeps may vary between 1 and
57   ; 30000 milliseconds.
58   ;
59   ;  Example:  Beeper.u(1000)
60   ;               Sounds a beep every second until a key is pressed.
61
62  ┌PROC Beeper.u(delay.n)
63  │   ; delay.n   ; Number of milliseconds between beeps, 1 - 30000
64  │   PRIVATE n                       ; Any characters in the buffer.
65  │  ┌─WHILE CHARWAITING()            ; User might be typing ahead of the program.
66  │  │   n = GETCHAR()                ; Grab keystroke from buffer assign to n.
67  │  └─ENDWHILE
68  │  ┌─IF delay.n > 30000 THEN
69  │  │   delay.n = 1000               ; If more than 30000, set delay.n to one second.
70  │  └─ENDIF
71  │  ┌─WHILE NOT CHARWAITING()        ; Waits for keystroke from operator.
72  │  │   BEEP BEEP                    ; Two quick beeps.
73  │  │   SLEEP delay.n                ; Pauses for the amount specified by delay.n.
74  │  └─ENDWHILE
75  │   n = GETCHAR()                   ; Retrieves the operator keystroke.
76  └ENDPROC
77   WRITELIB libname.a Beeper.u
78   RELEASE PROCS Beeper.u
79
80   ;--------------------------------------------------------------
81   ; TopMsg.u()
82   ; Procedure to place two lines of text centered at the top of screen.
83   ; The user can easily get accustomed to looking to the top of screen for all
84   ; instructions, errormessages and menus.  Messages never obscure data.
85   ; This proc uses the one above, Beeper.u(), to sound a tone at regular
86   ; intervals. Varying the delay.n parameter allows you to adjust the
87   ; "urgency" of the message.
88   ;
89   ; Example: TopMsg.u("This is an error", "Press any key...",1000)
90
91  ┌PROC TopMsg.u(line1.a, line2.a, delay.v)
92  │   ; line1    ; Text to display at the top of the screen'
93  │   ; line2    ; Text to display on the second line of the screen
94  │   ; Three shortcuts have been implemented, when evaluating line2.a
95  │   ; If line2.a = "" second line will read "Press any key".
96  │   ; If "X", second line will read "Press any key to exit".
97  │   ; If "C", second line will read "Press any key to continue".
98  │   ; So if you want a blank second line make line2.a = "  ".
99  │   ; delay.v  ; Amount of delay between beeps.
100 │   ; If 0, it beeps once and waits for a key.
101 │   ; If a number between 1 and 30000, beeps until a key is pressed,
102 │   ; Using the delay.v as the pause between beeps.
103 │   ; If "", it simply puts up the message, relying on the calling
104 │   ; program to get keystrokes and clean up display.
105
106 │   PRIVATE
107 │   n,        ; Used to get keyboard character
108 │   pak.a     ; String for "Press any key"
109
110 │  ┌─IF VERSION() <3 THEN
111 │  │   STYLE REVERSE                    ; Use inverse video.
112 │  ├─ELSE
113 │  │   STYLE ATTRIBUTE SYSCOLOR(3)      ; Use same color as Paradox messages.
```

```
114  └ENDIF
115    @ 0,0 ?? FORMAT("W80,AC",line1.a)  ; Center the first line.
116  ┌IF LEN(line2.a) <= 1 THEN
117  │   pak.a = "Press any key"
118  │ ┌SWITCH
119  │ ├──CASE line2.a = "":
120  │ │    line2.a = pak.a
121  │ ├──CASE UPPER(line2.a) = "X":
122  │ │    line2.a = pak.a + " to exit"
123  │ ├──CASE UPPER(line2.a) = "C":
124  │ │    line2.a = pak.a + " to continue"
125  │ └ENDSWITCH
126  └ENDIF
127    ?? FORMAT("W80,AC", line2.a)      ; Center the second line.
128    STYLE
129  ┌SWITCH
130  ├──CASE delay.v = "":               ; Return to calling program.
131 ◄─────RETURN
132  ├──CASE delay.v = 0 :
133  │    BEEP BEEP                       ; Beep twice and get a character.
134  │    n = GETCHAR()
135  ├──OTHERWISE :                       ; Most often used, this beeps at the user
136  │    Beeper.u(delay.v)               ; until a key is pressed.
137  └ENDSWITCH
138    @1,0 CLEAR EOL                     ; Clean up after messages, except for
139    @0,0 CLEAR EOL                     ; delay.v = "".
140  └ENDPROC
141  WRITELIB libname.a TopMsg.u
142  RELEASE PROCS      TopMsg.u
143
144  ;-------------------------------------------------------------------
145  ; Zoom.l()
146  ; The problem:  ZOOM is not enough of a world unto itself.
147  ;
148  ; Example 1:
149  ;
150  ;     View "Customer"
151  ;     PICKFORM 1
152  ;     WHILE TRUE
153  ;       WAIT TABLE
154  ;       PROMPT "Viewing Customer table",
155  ;             "Press [F7] to toggle FormView, or [Esc] to quit"
156  ;       UNTIL  "F7","Esc"
157  ;       SWITCH
158  ;         CASE retval = "F7":
159  ;           FORMKEY             ; Toggle form view.
160  ;         CASE retval = "Esc":
161  ;           CLEARIMAGE          ; Remove the table from the workspace.
162  ;           QUITLOOP            ; Exit the loop.
163  ;       ENDSWITCH
164  ;     ENDWHILE
165  ;
166  ; This example shows a simple WAIT TABLE. Pressing [F7] toggles
167  ; formview, and [Esc] clears the table. Though most keys work as
168  ; expected, there are some notable exceptions.  If you press [F1] and
169  ; are NOT in a field with a tablelookup help, the computer beeps as
170  ; it should, because PARADOX help is not normally available to the
171  ; user from within a script.
```

```
172   ;
173   ; The problem arises when Zoom is used. If you press [Ctrl Z] (Zoom),
174   ; a prompt appears at the top of the screen asking you for the Zoom
175   ; value.
176   ; 1) If you press [Esc] to exit the Zoom prompt you will satisfy the
177   ;      WAIT UNTIL condition, clear the table, and exit the loop (CLEARLY
178   ;      not what you wanted)!
179   ;
180   ; 2) If you press [F1] while the Zoom prompt is on screen, you will get
181   ;      PARADOX help!  Not helpful to user under script control.
182   ;
183   ; 2) To further complicate the problem, if you press [Esc] to exit the
184   ;      PARADOX help system, the [Esc] keypress will satisfy the WAIT UNTIL
185   ;      condition, and clear the table.
186   ;
187   ;      If this isn't nasty enough (since your table just got cleared out from
188   ;      under you), in version 2.0, clearing a table while the Zoom prompt is up
189   ;      and then trying to escape from the ZOOM prompt (which is still on the
190   ;      screen) will send you directly out of Paradox and back to DOS.
191   ;      (The problem was fixed in version 2.01.  If you View a table,
192   ;      Press [Ctrl Z], and press [F8] to clear the image, the ZOOM
193   ;      prompt also clears.  At least the error won't dump you out of Paradox.)
194   ;
195   ; Zoom.l was written in order to keep the user from seeing interactive
196   ; PARADOX help and avoiding ZOOM related problems.
197   ;
198   ;   Zoom.l traps for function keys (except FieldView) and for invalid zooms.
199   ;   It also traps for invalid ZOOMS in inappropriate LinkTypes in Paradox 3.01.
200   ;
201   ;
202   ; =======
203   ; Example 2: This script allows the WAIT condition to trap for the
204   ;            ZOOM keypress.
205   ;
206   ;    VIEW "customer"
207   ;    PICKFORM 1
208   ;    WHILE TRUE
209   ;      WAIT TABLE
210   ;      PROMPT "Viewing Customer table",
211   ;            "Press [F7] to toggle FormView, or [Esc] to quit"
212   ;      UNTIL "Esc", "F7", "Dos", "DosBig","Zoom"
213   ;
214   ;      SWITCH
215   ;        CASE RETVAL = "Zoom":
216   ;          Zoom.l()            ; Eliminate zoom related problems.
217   ;        CASE RETVAL = "Dos" OR RETVAL="DosBig":   ; [Ctrl O] and [Alt O]
218   ;          BEEP               ; Don't want a Typo to send us out to DOS.
219   ;        CASE RETVAL = "F7":
220   ;          FORMKEY            ; Toggle form view.
221   ;        CASE RETVAL = "Esc":
222   ;          CLEARIMAGE          ; Remove the table from the workspace.
223   ;          QUITLOOP            ; Exit the loop.
224   ;      ENDSWITCH
225   ;    ENDWHILE
226   ;
227
228   ; Note that this procedure uses ECHO NORMAL, and will not run under Paradox
229   ; Runtime.  The optional source code listing disk contains a library with an
```

```
230   ; alternate variation of this proc that works with Runtime.
231
232 ┌─PROC Zoom.l()
233 │   ; RETURNS True if match is found,
234 │   ;          False if match not found or user presses [Esc].
235 │   PRIVATE
236 │   n,              ; Used by GETCHAR().
237 │   fieldview.l  ; Keeps track of fieldview status while in zoom prompt.
238
239 │ ┌─IF NIMAGERECORDS() < 2 OR COLNO() = 1 THEN
240 │ │   ; You cannot zoom in the record# column, or in any case where there
241 │ │   ; are less than 2 records present (as in an empty table, or a 1-1 Group,
242 │ │   ; or a Many-1 group, or a single record table).
243 │ │   BEEP
244 ◄─│────RETURN False
245 │ └─ENDIF
246
247 │   ECHO NORMAL         ; Turn echo on so operator can see keypresses.
248 │   ZOOM                ; Presses the Zoom key.
249 │   fieldview.l = False
250 │ ┌─WHILE True
251 │ │   n = GETCHAR()     ; Wait for operator's keypress.
252 │ │ ┌─SWITCH
253 │ │ ├──CASE  n = -108 OR n = 6 :      ; [Alt F5] fieldview or [Ctrl F].
254
255 │ │ │    KEYPRESS n                   ; Press the key.
256 │ │ │    fieldview.l = NOT fieldview.l ; Fieldview is started/finished.
257
258 │ │ ├──CASE  n = -71 OR   ; Home   ; Accounts for possible FieldView while
259 │ │ │        n = -75 OR   ; Left   ; in Zoom prompt.
260 │ │ │        n = -77 OR   ; Right
261 │ │ │        n = -79 OR   ; End
262 │ │ │        n = -82 OR   ; Ins
263 │ │ │        n = -83 :    ; Del
264 │ │ │    KEYPRESS n                   ; Press the key.
265
266 │ │ ├──CASE n < 0 OR n = 15 :       ; Includes unwanted function keys & ^O.
267 │ │ │    BEEP                         ; Beep on error.
268
269 │ │ ├──CASE fieldview.l AND  n = 13 : ; User pressed [Enter] while in fieldview.
270 │ │ │    ENTER                        ; End field view.
271 │ │ │    fieldview.l = False
272
273 │ │ ├──CASE n = 13:                  ; User pressed [Enter].
274 │ │ │    KEYPRESS n                   ; Press the key as if the user typed it.
275 │ │ │ ┌─SWITCH
276 │ │ │ ├──CASE WINDOW() = "":         ; Match was found.
277 │ │ │ │    ECHO OFF
278 ◄─│─│─│────RETURN True
279 │ │ │ ├──CASE WINDOW() = "Match not found":
280 │ │ │ │    BEEP                      ; Signal user that match was not found.
281 │ │ │ │    SLEEP 1000                ; Let user see message.
282 │ │ │ │    ECHO OFF
283 ◄─│─│─│────RETURN False
284 │ │ │ │    ; Any other window or message would keep us in loop
285 │ │ │ │    ; e.g. out of range for a short number field.
286 │ │ │ └─ENDSWITCH
287
```

```
288 │ │   ┌──CASE n = 27:                      ; Pressed [Esc].
289 │ │   │   ESC                              ; Get out of zoom with Esc.
290 │ │   │   ECHO OFF
291 ◄─────────RETURN False                     ; With RETVAL now set to False instead
292 │ │   │                                    ; of "Esc", the "Esc" does not activate
293 │ │   │                                    ; a WAIT's UNTIL condition.
294 │ │   │
295 │ │   ├──OTHERWISE:                        ; Any legitimate key.
296 │ │   │   KEYPRESS n                       ; Press the user's key.
297 │ │   └─ENDSWITCH
298 │ └──ENDWHILE
299 └─ENDPROC
300   WRITELIB libname.a Zoom.l
301   RELEASE PROCS      Zoom.l
302
303   ;-------------------------------------------------------------------
304   ; LookupSelect.n()
305   ; This procedure lets you simulate a WAIT TABLE.  Though it is generally
306   ; used after the cursor has been moved to a table lookup as a result of
307   ; issuing the HELP command in an appropriate field, it can be used in any
308   ; table.
309   ;
310   ; In the WaitPlus Add and Edit procedures, we have UNTIL "F1" which calls
311   ; WaitPlusLookup.u()
312   ;
313   ; This is a variation of LookUpSelect() found in the DataEntry Toolkit.
314   ; It has been expanded to disable [Ctrl O] , [Alt O], and [F1], and it also
315   ; calls Zoom.l if necessary to trap for similar keypresses while in Zoom.
316   ; LookupSelect.n() was written because although you can do a lookup from
317   ; within a WAIT TABLE, you cannot do a WAIT TABLE while in a lookup table.
318   ; In addition, it's often useful to know which of the two keystrokes the
319   ; user pressed to exit the lookup session ([F2] or [Esc]).
320   ;
321   ; Note that this procedure uses ECHO NORMAL, and will not run under Paradox
322   ; Runtime.  The optional source code listing disk contains a library with an
323   ; alternate variation of this proc that works with Runtime.
324
325 ┌─PROC LookupSelect.n()        ;Adapted from Toolkit proc.
326 │   ECHO NORMAL               ;Display the table to the user.
327 │   IMAGERIGHTS READONLY      ;Prevent user from making changes to image.
328 │ ┌─WHILE True
329 │ │   RETVAL = GETCHAR()
330 │ │ ┌─SWITCH
331 │ │ ├──CASE MENUCHOICE() = "Error" AND  ; Could be in HELP, HELP INDEX, or ZOOM.
332 │ │ │   (RETVAL = -60 OR RETVAL = 27 OR RETVAL = 0 ): ;F2, Esc, CtrlBreak
333 ◄───────QUITLOOP
334 │ │ │
335 │ │ │   ;The next case statement disables keys that allow a user to leave:
336 │ │ ├──CASE (RETVAL < -60 AND RETVAL > -71)
337 │ │ │   OR RETVAL = -110 OR RETVAL = -111 OR RETVAL = -100
338 │ │ │   OR RETVAL = 15 OR RETVAL= -24  OR RETVAL=-59 :
339 │ │ │   BEEP
340 │ │ ├──CASE RETVAL= 26:    ; User pressed [Ctrl Z]
341 │ │ │   Zoom.l()
342 │ │ │   ECHO NORMAL        ; Zoom.l turns echo back off.
343 │ │ ├──OTHERWISE: KEYPRESS RETVAL
344 │ │ └─ENDSWITCH
345 │ └─ENDWHILE
```

```
346 |   ECHO OFF
347 |   SYNCCURSOR
348 |  ┌IF RETVAL = 0
349 |  │  THEN
350 |  │    RETVAL = 27          ; [Ctrl][Break] functions as an [Esc].
351 |  └ENDIF                     ; from lookup help.
352 |   IMAGERIGHTS              ; Restore image status of table.
353 ◄────RETURN RETVAL
354 └ENDPROC
355   WRITELIB libname.a LookupSelect.n
356   RELEASE PROCS       LookupSelect.n
357
358   ;------------------------------------------------------------------
359   ; HelpTable.u()
360   ; This procedure presents the user with a menu of available help.
361   ; It is usually called while viewing or editing a table. When a
362   ; help menu choice is made, the appropriate text is displayed, and
363   ; the menu is repeated, highlighting the current choice.
364   ; If the user selects "Data" from the menu, the proc calls helpdata.u(),
365   ; a procedure that *you* customize in WWPAPP.SC.
366
367 ┌PROC HelpTable.u()
368 │  PRIVATE
369 │  choice.a  ; Menu choice.
370 │
371 │  choice.a = "Data"     ; Initialize default menu choice.
372 │ ┌WHILE True
373 │ │  SHOWMENU
374 │ │    "Data"   : "Help about the information needed for this table",
375 │ │    "Find"   : "Help about locating records quickly",
376 │ │    "Keys"   : "Help about moving around in the table",
377 │ │    "Menus"  : "Help about moving around in menus",
378 │ │    "Return" : "Return to table"
379 │ │    DEFAULT choice.a    ; Highlights the last choice the use made.
380 │ │  TO choice.a
381 │ │ ┌SWITCH
382 │ │ ├──CASE SEARCH(choice.a,"Esc,Return") > 0 :
383 │ │◄──────QUITLOOP
384 │ │ ├──CASE choice.a = "Data" :
385 │ │ │    HelpData.u()    ; Show the appropriate help for this table.
386 │ │ ├──OTHERWISE :
387 │ │ │    HelpText.u(choice.a)     ; Show help for keys, menus, etc.
388 │ │ └ENDSWITCH
389 │ └ENDWHILE
390 │   CLEAR
391 │   Working.u("")                ; Display working... message.
392 └ENDPROC
393   WRITELIB libname.a  HelpTable.u
394   RELEASE PROCS       HelpTable.u
395
396   ;------------------------------------------------------------------
397   ; HelpText.u()
398   ; This procedure displays help information about menus, keys, and finding
399   ; records using Paradox keys and features. It is usually called by
400   ; helptable.u(), but is generic enough for other use. The proc simply
401   ; displays the text.  The calling program controls clearing the canvas.
402
403 ┌PROC HelpText.u(type.a)
```

```
404    ; type.a        ; String designating the type of help screen to present:
405    ;                  "Menus", "Keys", or "Find".  It is case independent.
406
407    CLEAR
408    @2,0 ??FILL("\196",80)    ; Draw a line across the third line of the screen.
409    type.a = LOWER(type.a)    ; Make it case independent.
410  ┌─SWITCH
411  │
412  │  ┌──CASE  type.a = "menus" :
413  │  │    TEXT
414  │  │    A menu presents you with a list of options available at any given point.
415  │  │    Each menu choice has a descriptive line attached to it.
416  │  │    ─────────────────────────────────────────────────────────────────────
417  │  │    There are two ways to select a menu choice:
418  │  │
419  │  │        1) Press the first letter of the menu selection.
420  │  │           If there is more than one choice beginning with the first letter,
421  │  │           you will be asked to select from those that begin with that letter.
422  │  │
423  │  │        2) Use [Left] and [Right] arrow keys to highlight the menu choice,
424  │  │           then press [Enter]. (When a menu choice is highlighted, it displays
425  │  │           a descriptive help line).
426  │  │
427  │  │    To escape from the menu, returning to whatever you were doing before you asked
428  │  │    for it, press [Esc].
429  │  │    ─────────────────────────────────────────────────────────────────────
430  │  │    Special keys:
431  │  │           [Home]   Moves to first menu selection.
432  │  │            [End]   Moves to last menu selection.
433  │  │           [Down]   Moves right one screen (if available).
434  │  │             [Up]   Moves left one screen (if available).
435  │  │    ENDTEXT
436  │  │
437  │  ┌──CASE type.a = "keys" :
438  │  │    TEXT
439  │  │           [Left] Previous field left.          [Home] First record.
440  │  │          [Right] Next field right.       [Ctrl Home] First field of form or table.
441  │  │             [Up] Next field up.                 [End] Last record.
442  │  │         [Down] Next field down.           [Ctrl End] Last field of form or table.
443  │  │          [PgDn] Next screen down.            [PgUp] Next screen up.
444  │  │     [Ctrl PgDn] Next record, same field.  [Ctrl PgUp] Previous record, same field.
445  │  │    [Ctrl Right] Next screen right.        [Ctrl Left] Previous screen left.
446  │  │    ─────────────────────────────────────────────────────────────────────
447  │  │    Special keys: [Esc] Exits table or menu.    [F10] Gets menu if available.
448  │  │                      [F1] Field help if available
449  │  │                      [F3] UpImage     [F4] DownImage     [F7] FormToggle
450  │  │        [Ctrl Backspace] Delete field.     [Backspace] Deletes char left of cursor.
451  │  │               [Ctrl D] Usually Dittos (copies field from previous record).
452  │  │               [Ctrl Z] Zoom to first occurrence of value.  [Alt Z] ZoomNext.
453  │  │                [Alt L] Lock/Unlock record.
454  │  │    ─────────────────────────────────────────────────────────────────────
455  │  │    To allow cursor movement within a field (FieldView) press [Ctrl F] or [Alt F5].
456  │  │    Cursor pad keys while in FieldView:
457  │  │           [Left]   Previous character      [Home]  First character in field
458  │  │          [Right]   Next character          [End]   Last character in field
459  │  │     [Ctrl Right]   Next word right         [Del]   Deletes character at cursor
460  │  │      [Ctrl Left]   Prev word left          [Ins]   Toggles insert mode on/off
461  │  │    ENDTEXT
```

```
462  |    |
463  |    |----CASE type.a = "find" :
464  |    |       TEXT
465  |    |       There are several ways to search for data.
466  |    |       _____
467  |    |       While in a table:
468  |    |          1) [Home] moves to the first record in the table, [End] moves to the last one.
469  |    |          2) [Ctrl Z] Zooms to the first occurrence of a value for the field that you
470  |    |             are in.  You will be asked for a search value.  When Zooming you may:
471  |    |                a) Enter the EXACT value (case sensitive) or
472  |    |                b) Use wildcards (not case sensitive).
473  |    |                   The wildcards are:   @  For any one character.
474  |    |                                       ..  For any string of characters.
475  |    |                      Examples:   ..new..  In a city field would find the first field
476  |    |                                           that has the word "new" in it.
477  |    |                                  @..  Finds first field that is not blank.
478  |    |                                  * Note: leave zoom blank for first blank value.
479  |    |          3) [Alt Z] finds the next occurrence of the last zoom value specified.
480  |    |          _____
481  |    |       While at a GoTo MENU select you may locate a record with:
482  |    |          1) =# Goes to a record number that you specify.
483  |    |          2) +# Goes forward a specified number of records.
484  |    |          3) -# Goes backward a specified number of records.
485  |    |          4) Zooming to the first or next occurrence of a value.
486  |    |       ENDTEXT
487  |    |--ENDSWITCH
488  |    |
489  |--ENDPROC
490       WRITELIB libname.a  HelpText.u
491       RELEASE PROCS       HelpText.u
492
493     ;-------------------------------------------------------------------
494     ; GoToMenu.u()
495     ; This procedure presents a menu of options that quickly locate a record.
496     ; This procedure must be called while in a display image.
497
498  |--PROC GoToMenu.u()
499  |      PRIVATE
500  |      choice.a     ; Showmenu choice
501  |
502  |    |--WHILE True
503  |    |     SHOWMENU
504  |    |        "Zoom" : "Zoom to the first occurrence a value for the current field",
505  |    |        "NextZoom" : "Go to the next occurrence of the last value Zoomed in this field",
506  |    |        "=#" : "Go directly to a specified record number",
507  |    |        "+#" : "Go forward in table by # of records",
508  |    |        "-#" : "Go backward in table by # of records",
509  |    |        "Help" : "Get help about locating information"
510  |    |     TO choice.a
511  |    |    |--SWITCH
512  |    |    |----CASE choice.a = "Esc" :
513  |  <-|    |--------RETURN
514  |    |    |----CASE choice.a = "Zoom" :
515  |    |    |       Zoom.l()
516  |    |    |----CASE choice.a = "NextZoom" :
517  |    |    |       MESSAGE "Searching"
518  |    |    |       ZOOMNEXT
519  |    |    |    |--IF WINDOW() <> "" THEN
```

```
520  | |      |    BEEP
521  | |      |    MESSAGE WINDOW()
522  | |      |    SLEEP 1500                    ; Let user see the message.
523  | |      └─ENDIF
524  | |    ──CASE choice.a = "Help" :
525  | |         HelpText.u("find")
526  | |         SHOWMENU
527  | |           "GoTo-Menu" : "Return to the GoTo menu",
528  | |           "Return" : "Return to the table"
529  | |         TO choice.a
530  | |       ┌─IF choice.a = "GoTo-Menu" THEN
531  | ▲────────────LOOP
532  | |       └─ENDIF
533  | |    ──OTHERWISE :
534  | |         MoveToRecno.l(choice.a)
535  | └─ENDSWITCH
536  ◄─────RETURN                           ; Don't want to keep user in the loop.
537  | └─ENDWHILE
538  └─ENDPROC
539   WRITELIB libname.a  GoToMenu.u
540   RELEASE PROCS       GoToMenu.u
541
542   ;--------------------------------------------------------------------
543   ; MoveToRecno.l()
544   ; This procedure asks the user for a record number to move to, or the
545   ; number of records to move forward or back.
546  ┌─PROC MoveToRecno.l(type.a)
547  |   ; type.a    ; How we move in the file:
548  |   ; "=#"   Asks for a specific record number.
549  |   ; "+#"   Asks for a number of records to move forward.
550  |   ; "-#"   Asks for a number of records to move backward.
551  |   ; RETURNS True if user made a selection, False otherwise.
552  |   PRIVATE
553  |   choice.n,  ; ACCEPT choice.
554  |   records.n, ; Number of records in image.
555  |   maxmove.n  ; Maximum records possible to move forward.
556  |
557  |   records.n = NIMAGERECORDS()      ; Get the number of records in the table.
558  |
559  |   @ 1,0 CLEAR EOL
560  |   ?? "Currently on Record ", RECNO(), " of ", records.n, ". [Esc] quits."
561  |   @ 0,0 CLEAR EOL
562  |   CURSOR NORMAL
563  |   ; Ask the user to supply information about the move:
564  |  ┌─SWITCH
565  |  ├─CASE type.a = "=#" :        ; Move to a record #
566  |  |     ?? "Move to record number :  "
567  |  |     ACCEPT "N" MAX records.n MIN 1 PICTURE "#[*#]" REQUIRED
568  |  |     TO choice.n
569  |  |    ┌─IF RETVAL THEN
570  |  |    |  MOVETO RECORD choice.n
571  |  |    └─ENDIF
572  |  ├─CASE type.a = "+#" :
573  |  |    ┌─IF ATLAST() THEN       ; No where to move down.
574  |  |    |  CURSOR OFF
575  |  |    |  TopMsg.u("Already on the last record", "C", 0)
576  |  |    ├─ELSE
577  |  |    |  maxmove.n = records.n - RECNO() ; The number of records we can move forward
```

```
578              ?? "How many records to move forward? (MAX ", maxmove.n, "): "
579              ACCEPT "N" MAX maxmove.n PICTURE "*#" REQUIRED    ; Whole numbers only
580              TO choice.n
581             ┌IF RETVAL THEN
582                MOVETO RECORD RECNO() + choice.n
583                ; Could have used SKIP choice.n,
584                ; but we'd have to trap for SKIP 0, an illegal call.
585             └ENDIF
586            └ENDIF
587         ──CASE type.a = "-#" :
588            ┌IF ATFIRST() THEN
589               CURSOR OFF
590               TopMsg.u("Already on the first record", "C", 0)
591            ├ELSE
592               ?? "How many records to move backward? (MAX ", RECNO()-1, "): "
593               ACCEPT "N" MAX RECNO()-1 PICTURE "*#" REQUIRED
594               TO choice.n
595              ┌IF RETVAL THEN
596                 MOVETO RECORD RECNO() - choice.n
597              └ENDIF
598            └ENDIF
599        └ENDSWITCH
600        CURSOR OFF
601  ◄──RETURN RETVAL  ; FALSE if user pressed Esc, TRUE otherwise.
602  └ENDPROC
603  WRITELIB libname.a  MoveToRecno.l
604  RELEASE PROCS        MoveToRecno.l
605
606  ;------------------------------------------------------------------
607  ; StripPath.a()
608  ; This procedure strips the drive specifier and DOS path from a string.
609  ; It is used to get just the name of a table even if a full path has
610  ; been specified. The returned value is often used in WAIT TABLE prompt
611  ; lines. Note that it does not change the case of the string found.
612  ; Examples:
613  ;    a = StripPath.a("\\Paradox3\\toolkit\\invoices") ; Sets a = "invoices"
614  ;    a = StripPath.a("C:invoices")                    ; Sets a = "invoices"
615  ;    a = StripPath.a("Invoices")                      ; Sets a = "Invoices"
616
617 ┌PROC StripPath.a(string.a)
618    ; string.a      ; Usually a full table name.
619    ; RETURNS       ; the string with drive and path specifiers removed.
620    PRIVATE a1
621
622    ; First, remove anything prior to the last backslash:
623   ┌WHILE MATCH(string.a,"..\\..",a1,string.a)
624   └ENDWHILE
625
626    ; Next, in event there was no backslash, but string.a had a drive spec.
627    ; (e.g., "C:User" as a result of a logged directory on another drive):
628   ┌WHILE MATCH(string.a, "@:..", a1, string.a)
629   └ENDWHILE
630  ◄──RETURN string.a
631 └ENDPROC
632  WRITELIB libname.a StripPath.a
633  RELEASE PROCS       StripPath.a
634
635  ;------------------------------------------------------------------
```

```
636   ; NextNumber.v()
637   ; Increments a counter.
638   ; This procedure assumes that a single record table is on the workspace,
639   ; with a structure something like:
640   ;
641   ; [Next Invoice#]
642   ; [Next Employee ID#]
643   ; [Next Project #]
644   ;
645   ; and that we are in CoEdit mode along with the table that we are entering
646   ; data into.
647   ;
648   ; We use this procedure to store a variety of "next numbers", including dates.
649   ; When a request for a next number is made, this procedure jumps to the
650   ; next-number table, moves to the appropriate field, grabs the number,
651   ; increments it for next use, moves back to the data table, and drops in
652   ; the value. If NextNumber.v() is unable to lock the record within 5 seconds,
653   ; it will return "Error".  If it returns Error, consider putting Erroruser()
654   ; into the error prompt.
655   ;
656   ; *** In the form below, it assumes the system mode is already "CoEdit."*****
657
658   ; In a DeToolkit application, sample code may look like:
659   ;   v = NextNumber.v("Nextnum","Next Invoice#",FALSE,1,"Getting next invoice #")
660   ;   IF v <> "Error" THEN
661   ;     [Invoice#] = v
662   ;   ELSE            ; perhaps do some other errorchecking or tk code
663   ;     TKACCEPT = False
664   ;   ENDIF
665   ;
666   ; You might use it in a WaitPlusAction.l("PrepAdd") procedure
667   ; to get a next number *before* inserting a new record.  Then, in
668   ; WaitPlusAction.l("ArriveAdd"), the number (or date) is placed into
669   ; the target field in the table.
670   ;
671   ; A common technique is to embed the table that contains the next
672   ; numbers as an unlinked embedded table on the main form. This
673   ; embedded table can be made invisible by matching the foreground
674   ; and background colors or attributes (for example Blue on Blue)
675   ; and in WaitPlus, setting the TableRights to DisplayOnly for the image.
676   ;
677   PROC NextNumber.v(table.a, field.a, embedded.l, increment.n, working.a)
678      ; table.a      ; Name of next number table.
679      ; field.a      ; Name of field containing next number.
680      ; embedded.l   ; True if table is embedded in the current form.
681      ;              ; False if next number table is elsewhere on the workspace.
682      ; increment.n  ; Amount to increment number by.
683      ; working.a    ; Message to display while getting next number.
684
685      PRIVATE n,    ; Loop counter.
686      v,            ; Incrementor and error flag.
687      oldtable.a,   ; Original table name.
688      oldimage.n ,  ; Master image if any.
689      formview.l ,  ; Original form status.
690      recno.n ,     ; Current record number.
691      detail.l      ; Is this an embedded detail table?
692
693      MESSAGE working.a      ; Or some other proc that displays a message like:
```

```
694  ;                        Working.u(working.a)
695  oldtable.a = TABLE()   ; Find the original table name
696  detail.l = LINKTYPE() <> "None"
697  recno.n = RECNO()
698  formview.l = ISFORMVIEW()    ; Lets us put it back.
699  ┌IF NOT ISVALID() THEN
700  │   CTRLBACKSPACE              ; Clear the field.
701  └ENDIF
702  ; This next statement applies only if nextnumb table is explicitly
703  ; on workspace, not embedded in form.
704  ┌IF NOT embedded.l AND formview.l THEN
705  │   ; Otherwise you can't get to the next number if in a multitable form.
706  │   FORMKEY
707  └ENDIF
708  oldimage.n = IMAGENO()
709  MOVETO table.a
710  MOVETO FIELD field.a
711  ┌FOR n FROM 1 TO 10    ; Attempt to lock the record up to 10 times.
712  │   LOCKRECORD
713  │  ┌IF RETVAL THEN        ; No one else is doing this at the same time.
714  ◄──────QUITLOOP
715  │  └ENDIF
716  │   SLEEP 500             ; Someone else is using the record, wait 1/2 second.
717  └ENDFOR
718  ┌IF NOT RETVAL THEN    ; 10 attempts.
719  │   TopMsg.u(ERRORUSER() + " has locked " + table.a + ".",
720  │           "Press any key to return.",1000)
721  │   ; or whatever your technique for telling your user that something is amiss.
722  │   v= "Error"
723  ├ELSE
724  │   v = []                     ; Grab the current field.
725  │   [] = [] + increment.n      ; Increment or decrement the field.
726  └ENDIF
727  UNLOCKRECORD                   ; Free it up for others.
728  ┌SWITCH
729  ├──CASE NOT embedded.l AND formview.l :
730  │     MOVETO oldimage.n        ; The master table in table view.
731  │     FORMKEY
732  │     MOVETO oldtable.a
733  │    ┌IF detail.l THEN         ; Cursor is now at the top of the table.
734  │    │  MOVETO RECORD recno.n  ; Find the old position in the table even
735  │    │  ;                      ; if someone else has added or deleted records.
736  │    └ENDIF
737  ├──OTHERWISE :
738  │     MOVETO oldtable.a        ; Back to the original table.
739  └ENDSWITCH
740  @1,0 CLEAR EOL                 ; Clean up the message.
741  @0,0 CLEAR EOL
742 ◄──RETURN v
743 └ENDPROC
744  WRITELIB libname.a NextNumber.v
745  RELEASE PROCS    NextNumber.v
```

### WWPUTIL2

```
1    ;***************************** WWPUtil2.SC *******************************
2    ; Second script of Utility procedures used by WaitPlus.v.
3    ; The procedures in this script are also of use in general Paradox code.
4    ;
5    ; Contents
6    ;-------------------------------------------------------------------------
7    ; CoEditKey.l()                      ; Can workspace go into CoEdit?
8    ; PickForm.v(form.v)                 ; Can form be picked?
9    ; SetView.u(viewtype.a)              ; Change to "form" or "table" view.
10   ; RecordLock.l(type.a)               ; Lock or unlock a record successful?
11   ; IsBlankMasterKey.l(table.a)        ; Does master record contain blank
12   ;                                    ; values in key fields?
13   ; OkKey35.l(requiredcheck.l)         ; Ok Key procedure that is sensitive
14   ;                                    ; to features in Paradox 3.5.  It is
15   ;                                    ; typically called by OkKey3.l()
16   ; OkKey3.l(requiredcheck.l)          ; Does current record pose a key
17   ;                                    ; conflict? Calls OkKey35 if appropriate.
18   ; CopyFromArray3.u(arrayname.a,      ; Copies array to table.  Works with
19   ;               requiredcheck.l)     ; detail tables and avoids several problems
20   ;                                    ; arising from invalid data
21   ;                                    ; Substitute for COPYFROMARRAY
22   ; InvalidArrayRecover.u(arrayname.a) ; Special error procedure to handle
23   ;                                    ; COPYFROMARRAY errors when array
24   ;                                    ; contains invalid data.
25   ; OkKey2.l()                         ; Key Violation proc for unlinked
26   ;                                    ; tables.  See notes in OkKey3.l()
27   ; OopsPrint.u()                      ; Error handling procedure.
28
29
30   ;-------------------------------------------------------------------------
31   ; CoEditKey.l()
32   ; This procedure tests to see if the workspace can be put into
33   ; CoEdit mode with a press of the CoEditKey.  If another user
34   ; is using the table in a form that is inconsistent with the current
35   ; view of the table, or if the table has a Full or Write Lock on it,
36   ; the procedure returns FALSE, otherwise it returns TRUE.
37  ┌PROC CoEditKey.l()
38  │   ; RETURNS TRUE if successful, FALSE otherwise
39  │   COEDITKEY
40  │  ┌SWITCH
41  │  ├─CASE ERRORCODE() = 3 OR ERRORCODE() = 62 :
42  │  │    TopMsg.u(ERRORUSER()+" is using this table in another form","X",1000)
43 ◄──────────RETURN FALSE
44  │  ├─OTHERWISE:
45 ◄──────────RETURN TRUE
46  │  └ENDSWITCH
47  └ENDPROC
48   WRITELIB libname.a  CoEditKey.l
49   RELEASE PROCS       CoEditKey.l
50
51   ;-------------------------------------------------------------------------
52   ; Pickform.l()
53   ; There are a few problems with determining if executing a PICKFORM
54   ; would be successful or if it would bump into a Form Lock problem.
55   ; We thought that a simple way to check for a successful PICKFORM
```

```
56   ; would be simply to issue the command and check the resultant errorcodes,
57   ; in the way we do in CoEditKey.l():
58   ;
59   ; PROC pickform.l(form.a)
60   ;    PICKFORM form.a
61   ;    IF ERRORCODE() = 3 OR ERRORCODE() = 62 THEN
62   ;      RETURN FALSE
63   ;    ELSE
64   ;      RETURN TRUE
65   ;    ENDIF
66   ; ENDPROC
67   ;
68   ; The problem is that in Paradox 3.0, a conflict would cause a run error.
69   ; We don't think this is intentional, as it should probably be treated more
70   ; like trying to lock a record that is already locked by someone else (the
71   ; errorcode should be set so you can test it, but no run error). The odd
72   ; thing is that while stepping through the debugger, a run error is not
73   ; tripped, and the code above works just fine.  However, the real world
74   ; beckons, so the procedure below should help solve the problem.
75
76 ┌─PROC PickForm.v(form.v)
77 │   ; form.v      ; the form name,  "F", "1"-"14"  or  1-14
78 │   ; RETURNS     ; TRUE if PICKFORM was successful, or
79 │   ;             ; a string containing the errormessage if the form is
80 │   ;             ; incompatible with another user, or table is locked.
81 │   ;             ; A run error is tripped if you have insufficient rights,
82 │   ;             ; or the table is otherwise unavailable.
83 │
84 │   PRIVATE
85 │   okform.l,    ; Was the form ok?
86 │   error.a,     ; Errormessage found.
87 │   ERRORPROC    ; Name of special error handling procedure.
88 │
89 │   ; Define a proc that will trip if a Form Lock conflict exists.
90 │ ┌─PROC PickFormError.n()
91 │ │    PRIVATE ERRORPROC   ; So that any error in this code will not call
92 │ │    ; itself recursively.  In the event that a
93 │ │    ; PICKFORM is unsuccessful because of a conflict
94 │ │    ; with another user's use of a table (or Rights),
95 │ │    ; this ERRORPROC *may* kick in.
96 │ │    error.a = ERRORMESSAGE()
97 │ │    okform.l = FALSE
98 ◄─────RETURN 1
99 │ └─ENDPROC
100│   ERRORPROC = "PickFormError.n"
101│   okform.l = TRUE
102│   MENU {Image} {PickForm} SELECT form.v
103│   ; We used the braced menu selections instead of a simple PICKFORM because
104│   ; in the first version of Paradox 3.0, the menu selections were faster
105│   ; than the abbreviated menu command, PICKFORM.
106│   RELEASE PROCS PickFormError.n   ; Release the memory used by the error proc.
107│   ; If errorproc was tripped, okform.l would return FALSE.
108│ ┌─IF okform.l THEN
109◄─────RETURN TRUE
110│ ├─ELSE
111◄─────RETURN error.a                 ; The errormessage that Paradox presented.
112│ └─ENDIF
113└─ENDPROC
```

```
114    WRITELIB libname.a PickForm.v
115    RELEASE PROCS       PickForm.v
116
117    ;------------------------------------------------------------------------
118    ; SetView.u()
119    ; The SetView.u procedure below forces the current table into either
120    ; tableview or formview.  It looks at the current view, and if necessary,
121    ; presses Formkey toggle.
122  ┌─PROC SetView.u(viewtype.a)
123  │    ; viewtype.a  ; Either "Form" or "Table", independent of case.
124  │  ┌─IF (NOT ISFORMVIEW() AND LOWER(viewtype.a) = "form") OR
125  │  │    (ISFORMVIEW() AND LOWER(viewtype.a) = "table") THEN
126  │  │    FORMKEY
127  │  └─ENDIF
128  └─ENDPROC
129    WRITELIB libname.a  SetView.u
130    RELEASE PROCS        SetView.u
131
132    ;------------------------------------------------------------------------
133    ; RecordLock.l()
134    ; There are times when you want to lock or unlock a record, *and* also
135    ; need to know if the action was successful.  Although rarely used in
136    ; WaitPlus code, we thought that it would be useful to have a proc that
137    ; captures whatever message comes up in the Paradox WINDOW() and
138    ; displays it to the user with another of the utility procedures,
139    ; TopMsg.u() (found in wwputil1.sc). This procedure also uses
140    ; WaitPlusError.v (found in WWPCORE2.SC) for special error trapping
141    ; when a LockRecord or  UnlockRecord is attempted in a DisplayOnly
142    ; form.  If this occurs, it resets the tablerights for WaitPlus so
143    ; that the error will not repeat. See the code below for details.
144
145  ┌─PROC RecordLock.l(type.a)
146  │    ; type.a   ; Type of action, "Lock" or "Unlock".
147  │    ; RETURNS  ; TRUE if record can be locked, FALSE otherwise.
148  │    PRIVATE
149  │    window.a,               ; Paradox window message.
150  │    error.a                 ; Errormessage.
151  │    RETVAL = FALSE          ; Initialize.
152  │    type.a = LOWER(type.a)  ; Make case independent.
153  │  ┌─SWITCH
154  │  ├──CASE type.a = "lock":
155  │  │    LOCKRECORD           ; Record possibly locked by LookUpHelp or
156  │  │                         ; Default ValCheck.
157  │  ├──CASE type.a = "unlock":
158  │  │    UNLOCKRECORD
159  │  └─ENDSWITCH
160  │    window.a = WINDOW()
161  │    error.a = ERRORMESSAGE()
162  │  ┌─SWITCH
163  │  │    ; In case the WaitPlusError.n proc was triggered while trying to
164  │  │    ; lock a display only record, it would reset RETVAL to 1.
165  │  │    ; You may remove the next two lines if not called by WaitPlus,
166  │  │    ; though they do no harm if left in.
167  │  ├──CASE RETVAL = 1:                      ; Retval was set by the errorproc.
168 ◄│  │───RETURN FALSE
169  │  ├──CASE NOT RETVAL AND ERRORCODE() <> 55 : ;"Record is already locked by you"
170  │  │    ; Must be locked by someone else.
171  │  │  ┌─IF window.a <> "" THEN
```

```
172  │  │      │    TopMsg.u(window.a, "C", 1000)       ; Show window message.
173  │  │      ├─ELSE
174  │  │      │    TopMsg.u(error.a, "C", 1000)        ; Show errormessage.
175  │  │      └─ENDIF
176 ◄─────────RETURN FALSE
177  │  ├──────OTHERWISE:
178 ◄─────────RETURN TRUE
179  │  └─ENDSWITCH
180  └─ENDPROC
181  WRITELIB libname.a  RecordLock.l
182  RELEASE PROCS       RecordLock.l
183
184
185
186   ;-------------------------------------------------------------------------
187   ; IsBlankMasterKey.l()
188   ; This proc is an attempt to keep the user from getting into trouble
189   ; when trying to edit or add a record when the master record has blank keys.
190   ; Paradox would eventually return an errorcode 60 when trying to modify
191   ; fields, but this proc can be used to avoid letting the user make
192   ; changes in the first place. It is used by WaitPlusAdd.u() and
193   ; WaitPlusEdit.u().
194   ;
195   ; A performance note:
196   ; If your application uses WaitPlus, and is coded in such a way that there
197   ; can never be master records with blank keys, you can set the WaitPlus
198   ; variable called  wpCheckBlankKeys.l = FALSE  and WaitPlus will bypass
199   ; its normal call to IsBlankMasterKey.l().  This is particularly useful on
200   ; local area networks because the IsBlankMasterKey.l() proc makes
201   ; some disk access as it attempts to get the number of key fields for each
202   ; table.
203
204
205  ┌─PROC IsBlankMasterKey.l(table.a)
206  │    ; table.a    ; The name of the master table.
207  │    ; RETURNS    ; FALSE if master record has non-blank keys.
208  │    ;           ; TRUE if master record has all blank keys.
209  │    PRIVATE
210  │    keys.n,     ; Number of keys to check.
211  │    empty.r,    ; Array of the current record.
212  │    n          ; Counter.
213  │
214  │  ┌─IF LINKTYPE()="None"  THEN
215  │  │    ; We can't have an error, no linked keys.
216 ◄─────────RETURN FALSE
217  │  └─ENDIF
218  │    COPYTOARRAY empty.r  ; Put the current record into a temporary array.
219  │
220  │    ; The next command compares the number of fields in the master
221  │    ; table (table.a) with the number of keys in the current table.
222  │    ; We only need to check the lower of the two:
223  │
224  │    keys.n = MIN (NKEYFIELDS(table.a), NKEYFIELDS (TABLE()) )
225  │  ┌─IF keys.n = 0 THEN   ; The master must not be keyed
226 ◄─────────RETURN FALSE
227  │  └─ENDIF
228  │    ; Now let's look at the values in empty.r for blank values.
229  │  ┌─FOR n FROM 1 TO keys.n
```

```
230 |  | ┌─IF NOT ISBLANK(empty.r[n+1]) THEN  ; n+1 uses the correct array element.
231 ◄─────────RETURN FALSE
232 |  |  └─ENDIF
233 |  └─ENDFOR
234 |    TopMsg.u("Detail records cannot be changed when the master record has empty keys",
235 |            "Press any key",0)
236 ◄──RETURN TRUE ; The keys in the master record must be empty, we cannot add or
237 |               ; edit this record.
238 └─ENDPROC
239   WRITELIB libname.a IsBlankMasterKey.l
240   RELEASE PROCS      IsBlankMasterKey.l
241
242   ;-------------------------------------------------------------------------
243   ;
244   ; These following procedures were developed to trap for key violations
245   ; in Coedit mode in real time.
246
247   ; First a little background on why this is necessary. In interactive
248   ; Paradox in CoEdit mode, a user is made aware of key violations with
249   ; a message:
250   ;
251   ;"Key exists -- press [Alt] [L] to confirm [Alt] [K] to see existing record"
252
253   ; A key conflict may only occur when trying to post the record. This
254   ; can happen either when the user adds a new record or edits an existing
255   ; record. Key violation checking under script control in real time is a
256   ; somewhat more complicated matter. Here are some considerations:
257   ;
258   ; Newly posted records in a keyed table "fly away" from the cursor to
259   ; their proper location in the table. Unless you are at the proper
260   ; location when adding the record (or changing its key), the record
261   ; just changed appears to disappear. Better would be to to remain on
262   ; the record, and not let it fly away (to "travel" with it).
263   ;
264   ; Other situations:
265   ;
266   ;     A record is posted with a valid key and it is edited and
267   ;     replaced with a conflicting key.
268   ;
269   ;     A record, not yet posted to the table (a new record) should
270   ;     stay unposted until you are ready to commit the changes.
271   ;
272   ;     If editing an existing record changes the key, how does
273   ;     this affect other records that depend on it (should the user
274   ;     be allowed to change the key in the first place?)
275   ;
276   ;     If it is okay to change a key and the user accidentally changes
277   ;     it to an existing key, then we have to deal with it immediately,
278   ;     Do you want to show the user the offending key, and have them
279   ;     toggle? Do you want to tell the user that the key is already on
280   ;     file, and reject the change?
281   ;
282   ;     What happens if the user wants to "UNDO" his or her changes?
283   ;     When does the record disappear from other nodes on the network?
284   ;     If another user attempts to edit the record on their node, do
285   ;     they get a "Record deleted by another user" message?
286   ;
287   ; Obviously we would prefer new PAL functionality (perhaps a new
```

```
288   ; function, ISKEYVALID() or a POSTRECORD command.
289
290   ; There are three key violation checking procedures here.
291   ; OkKey35.l() uses features of Paradox 3.5 where available.
292   ; It is the fastest version, and is the safest one when confronted by
293   ; invalid data (possible when editing an existing record where the data no
294   ; longer passes the validity checks).  The other two procedures need to
295   ; attempt to delete the record and reinsert it.  At that point the key
296   ; violation can be evaluated.  If you study the 3.5 technique below, and
297   ; compare it to the older techniques, you'll see some of the issues raised.
298
299
300   ; When you use the OkKey2.l() or OkKey3.l() procedures, if a key conflict
301   ; exists, the record is deleted and then reinserted to make it an unposted
302   ; record.
303   ; The OkKey procedures are used to return a TRUE or FALSE
304   ; to inform the calling program whether or not the proposed key is "OK".
305   ; It is useful just about any time you need to see if there is a
306   ; duplicate key (for example, in a DEToolkit Good Depart field
307   ; procedure).
308   ;
309   ; CopyFromArray3.u(arrayname.a, requiredcheck.l) is another necessary
310   ; evil. It simulates a COPYFROMARRAY but will work on an embedded
311   ; linked detail table in a multitable form, where the linked fields
312   ; cannot be placed explicitly.  It also takes care of some less obvious
313   ; problems.  New to version 1.5 is error trapping to deal with invalid data
314   ; found in the array.  The errorchecking is extensive and commented in the
315   ; code.
316   ;
317   ; At this writing everything appears to work, as it has undergone
318   ; extensive testing under a variety of LinkTypes.
319   ;-------------------------------------------------------------------------
320
321   ; OkKey35.l() Checks for key violation in coedit mode for Paradox 3.5.
322   ; Note: It is OkKey35 because it uses Paradox 3.5 commands.
323   ; In WaitPlus, OkKey35.l() is called by OkKey3.l() if appropriate.
324   ;
325   ; The proc returns a TRUE if the key is okay, and a FALSE if not.
326   ; Because we can determine the RECORDSTATUS(), the record's status is not
327   ; changed (unlike the OkKey3.l proc that deletes and reinserts a record),
328   ; except for the fact that the record is locked at the end of the key violation
329   ; checking.  The procedure also goes to great lengths to avoid conflicts
330   ; with existing invalid data.
331   ;
332   ; Paradox 3.5 specific features are coded with EXECUTE statements so they
333   ; can be compiled into a 3.0 library yet still take advantage of the
334   ; 3.5 feature set (very useful in a network with mixed Paradox versions)
335   ;
336   ;Examples  l = OkKey35.l(TRUE)    ; Make sure REQUIREDCHECK is turned back on.
337   ;          l = OkKey35.l(FALSE)   ; REQUIREDCHECK will remain off.
338   ;          l = OkKey35.l("")      ; REQUIREDCHECK will be turned back ON.
339   ;
340
341  ┌─PROC OkKey35.l(requiredcheck.l)
342  │   ; requiredcheck.l  ; Determines if required fields should be
343  │   ;                  ; reinstated when leaving the proc.
344  │   ; Should be TRUE if you want to make sure that
345  │   ; REQUIREDCHECK ON is in effect when exiting
```

```
346    ; Copyfromarray3.u, which is called by this proc.
347    ; If requiredcheck.l is any value other than FALSE,
348    ; REQUIREDCHECK will be set back to the normal
349    ; ON status.
350    ; RETURNS TRUE if key is okay, FALSE if key already exists
351
352    PRIVATE
353    field.a,        ; Current field name.
354    r,              ; Temporary array.
355    a,              ; Window() message.
356    ok.l,           ; Is record okay (no key conflict)?
357    error.n,        ; Errorcode for keyviolation or write lock.
358    keys.n,         ; Number of key fields.
359    maxkeys.n,      ; Maximum number of keys to check for.
360    fields.n,       ; Number of fields.
361    newkey.l,       ; Has the key changed?
362    values.a,       ; Used to locate record in the event that it flies away.
363    n,              ; Counter
364    old.r,          ; Values in unedited record, used for comparison.
365    proc.a          ; Name of procedure
366
367    proc.a = "OkKey35.l"
368
369    ; The next few lines allow you to specify an alternate OkKey procedure,
370    ; perhaps necessary under special circumstances, for example when an
371    ; embedded table is also explicitly place on the workspace. To invoke
372    ; an alternate key violation procedure, assign a variable called
373    ; OkKeyproc.a to the name of the alternate procedure prior to invoking
374    ; the OkKey3.l procedure. The alternate procedure must return a TRUE
375    ; if the key is okay, or FALSE if there is a keyviolation.
376    ;
377    ; This can be handy for performance gains by making the key checking
378    ; more specific to the particular needs of the table. Remember
379    ; to release or reassign OkKeyproc.a = "" when no longer needed.
380
381   ┌─IF ISASSIGNED (OkKeyproc.a) AND OkKeyproc.a <> "" THEN
382   │    EXECPROC OkKeyproc.a    ; Do the special procedure and return its value.
383 ◄─│────RETURN RETVAL
384   └─ENDIF
385    ; If no special keyfield proc has been assigned, we continue from this point
386    keys.n = NKEYFIELDS(TABLE())
387   ┌─IF keys.n = 0 OR LINKTYPE()="1-1" THEN
388   │    ok.l = true        ; Cannot possibly be a key conflict.
389   └─ELSE                  ; There must be key fields.
390   │    ; Now on to the keyviolation checking...
391   │    REQUIREDCHECK OFF       ; Helps deal with required valcheck and empty fields.
392   │    IMAGERIGHTS             ; Make sure that we have rights to do this.
393   │    field.a = FIELD()   ; Just in case RESYNCKEY manages to jump you to
394   │
395   │   ┌─IF ISFORMVIEW() THEN   ; We need to see if this is a master form
396   │   │    RESYNCKEY      ; Shows a key conflict without unlocking-- records won't fly away.
397   │   │    window.a = WINDOW()
398   │   │   ┌─IF window.a = "Only relevant when editing master table in a multi-table form" THEN
399   │   │   │    master.l = FALSE     ; This is not a master form
400   │   │   └─ELSE
401   │   │   │    master.l = TRUE
402   │   │   │    error.n = ERRORCODE()    ; Get the errorcode
403   │   │   │    ok.l = error.n <> 53 AND error.n <> 3
```

```
404          L   ; Error.n 53 is set if key exists, error.n 3 if a Write Lock is on table
405        LENDIF
406      ELSE
407        master.l =false   ; If not in form view, we can't possibly be in a master
408      LENDIF
409     IF NOT master.l THEN   ; Let's see if this is a new unposted record
410        EXECUTE "new.l = RECORDSTATUS(\"New\")"
411        EXECUTE "modified.l = RECORDSTATUS(\"Modified\")"
412       SWITCH
413         CASE new.l :   ; A new unposted record.
414           KEYLOOKUP   ; Attempt to toggle to possible offending key.
415           error.n = ERRORCODE()
416           ok.l = error.n = 56  ; If it can't find lookup, then key is okay.
417          IF ok.l THEN        ; Lookupkey not found or another user locked
418                             ; the offending key (which means it exists).
419             LOCKRECORD      ; Record posts, and cursor remains with it.
420          ELSE
421             KEYLOOKUP          ; Return to record values as operator entered.
422          LENDIF
423         CASE (NOT new.l) AND (NOT modified.l):
424           ; The record exists, and has not been modified, therefore it must be ok
425           ok.l = true
426         OTHERWISE:
427           ; Existing, modified record (therefore obviously locked.)
428           ; We will unlock the record and try to locate it again after it "flies away"
429           ; Granted, there is a remote possiblity that another user can lock the record
430           ; or even delete the record before we get to it, but it probably has about
431           ; the same possibility as someone sucessfully posting a conflicting record
432           ; between the "lookupkey" and lockrecord statements in the new record routine
433           ; posted above.  We'll check for the possible multi-user conflict below.
434
435           ; We are going to try to UNLOCK (which posts) the record and then
436           ; re-lock it.
437           ; When the record is unlocked, we need to be able to find it again.
438           ; First we'll copy the values to an array.
439           COPYTOARRAY r      ; Save the edited state of the record.
440           ; Now we'll construct a string to execute that will find the record in
441           ; the event that it flies away.
442           ; For example, let's assume there are 3 keys.  To find the records
443           ; we'd have to issue LOCATE r[2],r[3],r[4] which will find the
444           ; unique record.  Remember that the first element of the array is the
445           ; table name so it is not used.
446           ; The second element is the first key field.
447
448           ; Now let's construct the search string to be EXECUTE'd
449           values.a=""  ; initialize string
450           ; Now let's make sure that we don't have more than 20 keys
451           ; because the EXECUTE string below would be too long.
452           maxkeys.n = MIN(keys.n, 21)
453          FOR n FROM 1 TO maxkeys.n
454           IF n >1 THEN
455              values.a = values.a +","      ; add a comma before the next value
456           LENDIF
457             values.a = values.a + "r["+STRVAL(n+1)+"]"
458          LENDFOR
459           ; We now have a string that might look like
460           ; "r[2],r[3],r[4]"
461
```

```
462        ; Now we have to check to see if there is only one key.  If so,
463        ; we'll have to move to the key field because LOCATE r[2] would only
464        ; locate the current column.  If we have more fields, we can append
465        ; another value
466       ┌─IF keys.n = 1 AND ARRAYSIZE(r)>2 THEN  ; there are more fields
467       │   values.a = values.a+",r[3]"
468       │   ; so we can locate regardless of current field
469       └─ENDIF
470        ; Now, the logic that follows is
471        ; 1) If the non key fields have been modified and the key fields haven't
472        ;    been touched, KEYLOOKUP will never show a conflicting key.
473        ; 2) If the key field has been touched, KEYLOOKUP will attempt to
474        ;    find the existing key.
475        fields.n=NFIELDS(TABLE())  ; Get the number of fields in the table
476
477        ; Now we have to determine if the keys have changed.
478        ; (The record is at this point unquestionably locked)
479        UNDO    ; Return the record to an unchanged, unlocked state.
480        LOCKRECORD  ; Let's not lose control of the record
481        COPYTOARRAY old.r  ; The unedited version of the record
482        newkey.l = FALSE   ; Let's assume that the key has not been changed
483        changed.l= FALSE   ; Let's assume that the record has not been changed
484       ┌─FOR n FROM 2 TO fields.n + 1
485       │ ┌─IF r[n] <> old.r[n] THEN
486       │ │   changed.l = true
487       │ │   ; There has been a change.  Let's see if a key has been changed
488       │ │ ┌─IF n <= keys.n + 1 THEN
489       │ │ │   newkey.l=true
490       │ │ └─ENDIF
491   ◄───────QUITLOOP
492       │ └─ENDIF
493       └─ENDFOR
494        ; If any fields have been changed, we'll replace changed values that were undone
495       ┌─IF changed.l THEN
496       │   MENU {Image} {Zoom} {Field}
497       │ ┌─FOR n FROM 1 TO fields.n
498       │ │ ┌─IF r[n+1] <> old.r[n+1] THEN
499       │ │ │   EXECUTE "[" + MENUCHOICE() + "]= r[n+1]"
500       │ │ └─ENDIF
501       │ │   RIGHT
502       │ └─ENDFOR
503       │   ; For example, if the first field is [Cust#] the execute would prepare:
504       │   ; [Cust#] = r[2]     ; The second element of the array.
505       │   CTRLBREAK                ; Back out of the zoom/field.
506       │   ; Now we have the original record restored
507       └─ENDIF
508        ok.l = true   ;Let's assume that the key is ok
509
510       ┌─IF newkey.l THEN   ; We have to try to see if there is a conflicting key
511       │   KEYLOOKUP          ; Attempt toggle to possible offending key.
512       │   error.n = ERRORCODE()
513       │   ok.l = error.n = 56  ; If it can't find a conflicting lookup,
514       │ ┌─IF NOT ok.l THEN    ; Lookupkey found; return to record values
515       │ │   KEYLOOKUP          ; as operator entered them.
516       │ ├─ELSE                 ; The lookup key has not been found, or another
517       │ │                      ; user has locked the offending key (which means it exists).
518       │ │   UNLOCKRECORD        ; Record posts, and can fly away.
519       │ │ ┌─IF ARRAYSIZE(r) = 2 THEN  ; We must have only one field
```

```
520                              ; Make sure we move to the field for LOCATE, whether in table or form view
521                              CTRLEND
522                           ─ENDIF
523                              EXECUTE "LOCATE " + values.a
524                           ┌─IF NOT RETVAL THEN
525                              TopMsg.u("The modified record posted correctly but cannot be located now",
526                                       "Your cursor may wind up on an incorrect record",1000)
527                           ─ELSE    ; we found the record
528                              LOCKRECORD  ; let's regain control over the record
529                           ┌─IF NOT RETVAL AND ERRORCODE()<>55 THEN
530                                ; Another user grabbed the record
531                                TopMsg.u("The modified record posted correctly but cannot be locked now",
532                                         "You no longer have control over the record",1000)
533                           ─ENDIF; If we couldn't lock record
534                        ─ENDIF  ; If we located record
535                     ─ENDIF     ; If key is ok
536                  ─ENDIF        ; If it is a new key
537               ─ENDSWITCH
538            ─ENDIF
539            MOVETO FIELD field.a ; Paradox3 sometimes jumps to another field or page.
540         ─ENDIF
541
542      ┌─IF NOT ok.l THEN
543         ; Place whatever error message or procedure you like to use here.
544      ┌─SWITCH
545      ├──CASE error.n = 3 :      ; Possible Write Lock.
546            TopMsg.u("Table locked by: "+ERRORUSER()+ ". Cannot verify key.","c",1000)
547      ├──OTHERWISE:
548            TopMsg.u("A record with this key already exists.", "C", 1000)
549      ─ENDSWITCH
550      ─ENDIF
551      ┌─IF requiredcheck.l <> false THEN
552         REQUIREDCHECK ON
553      ─ENDIF
554  ◄──RETURN ok.l
555  ─ENDPROC
556   WRITELIB libname.a OkKey35.l
557   RELEASE PROCS      OkKey35.l
558
559
560   ;-------------------------------------------------------------------------
561   ; OkKey3.l()
562   ; Purpose: Checks for key violation in coedit mode.
563   ; Note: It is OkKey3 because it uses Paradox 3.0 and 3.01 commands.
564   ; If you are using Paradox 3.5, this proc will automatically invoke the
565   ; OkKey35.l() procedure, which takes advantage of the newer environment.
566   ;
567   ; The proc returns a TRUE if the key is okay, and a FALSE if not.
568   ;
569   ; If the record is a Master record, with dependent detail records,
570   ; and a key conflict exists, that is the state that will remain.
571   ; It is safe, because subsequent calls to OkKey3.l will *NOT*
572   ; overwrite any existing record because it does not use a LOCKRECORD
573   ; to test for ability to post.
574   ;
575   ; If not in a Master record with active detail records, the proc
576   ; deletes the record and then reinserts it, returning it to a
577   ; "not yet posted" state.  This avoids a potential problem when
```

```
578   ; a record is locked and the next attempt to lock or unlock the
579   ; record results in a "key already exists" situation. If this occurs,
580   ; the next LOCKRECORD or UNLOCKRECORD will automatically post
581   ; the offending record, overwriting the record with the valid
582   ; key.  This is not usually what you want, so this proc keeps
583   ; the record as not yet posted, to make it relatively harmless.
584   ;
585   ; A byproduct of the delete and reinsert technique is that UNDO
586   ; becomes dangerous, as it would remove the recently reinserted
587   ; record.  This proc gets around this by always keeping a copy
588   ; of the record (with COPYTOARRAY) being edited. When the user
589   ; wants to "Undo" changes, it issues a COPYFROMARRAY to restore
590   ; the record's original state.
591   ;
592   ; Note that this routine ONLY works with Paradox version 3, as it
593   ; uses the RESYNCKEY command to pseudo-post the record without letting
594   ; it fly away.
595   ;
596   ; This current incarnation also traps for the way Paradox 3.01 handles
597   ; the KEYLOOKUP command in master tables (KeyLookup has been disabled, and a
598   ; new ERRORMESSAGE has been instated).  The procedure is backwards compatible
599   ; with Paradox 3.0.
600   ;
601   ;Examples l = OkKey3.l(TRUE)    ; Make sure REQUIREDCHECK is turned back on.
602   ;          l = OkKey3.l(FALSE)   ; REQUIREDCHECK will remain off.
603   ;          l = OkKey3.l("")      ; REQUIREDCHECK will be turned back ON.
604   ;
605
606  ┌─PROC OkKey3.l(requiredcheck.l)    ; version 3.10
607  │    ; requiredcheck.l  ; Determines if required fields should be
608  │    ;                  ; reinstated when leaving the proc.
609  │    ; Should be TRUE if you want to make sure that
610  │    ; REQUIREDCHECK ON is in effect when exiting
611  │    ; Copyfromarray3.u, which is called by this proc.
612  │    ; If requiredcheck.l is any value other than FALSE,
613  │    ; REQUIREDCHECK will be set back to the normal
614  │    ; ON status.
615  │    ; RETURNS TRUE if key is okay, FALSE if key already exists
616  │
617  │    PRIVATE
618  │    field.a,          ; Current field name.
619  │    r,                ; Temporary array.
620  │    a,                ; Window() message.
621  │    ok.l,             ; Is record okay (no key conflict)?
622  │    error.n,          ; Errorcode for keyviolation or write lock.
623  │    proc.a            ; Name of procedure
624  │
625  │    proc.a = "OkKey3.l"
626  │
627  │    ; The next few lines allow you to specify an alternate OkKey procedure,
628  │    ; perhaps necessary under special circumstances, for example when an
629  │    ; embedded table is also explicitly place on the workspace. To invoke
630  │    ; an alternate key violation procedure, assign a variable called
631  │    ; OkKeyproc.a with the name of the alternate procedure, prior to invoking
632  │    ; the OkKey3.l procedure. The alternate procedure must return a TRUE
633  │    ; if the key is okay, or FALSE if there is a keyviolation.
634  │    ;
635  │    ; This can be handy for performance gains by making the key checking
```

```
636  |    ; more specific to the particular needs of the table. Remember
637  |    ; to release or reassign OkKeyproc.a = "" when no longer needed.
638  |
639  |  ┌IF ISASSIGNED (OkKeyproc.a) AND OkKeyproc.a <> "" THEN
640  |  |   EXECPROC OkKeyproc.a      ; Do the special procedure and return its value.
641 ◄──────RETURN RETVAL
642  |  └ENDIF
643  |
644  |  ┌IF VERSION()>=3.5 THEN      ; Let's do the procedure that is sensitive to 3.5
645  |  |   OkKey35.l(requiredcheck.l)
646 ◄──────RETURN RETVAL      ; Send the value back to the calling procedure
647  |  └ENDIF
648  |
649  |    ; If no special okkeyproc.a proc has been assigned, we continue from this point
650  |  ┌IF NKEYFIELDS(TABLE()) = 0 THEN
651  |     ok.l = true      ; No key fields, cannot possibly be a key conflict.
652  |  ┌ELSE               ; There must be key fields.
653  |     ; Now on to the keyviolation checking...
654  |     REQUIREDCHECK OFF      ; Helps deal with required valcheck and empty fields.
655  |     COPYTOARRAY r          ; For safekeeping.
656  |     IMAGERIGHTS            ; Make sure that we have rights to do this.
657  |     DEL                    ; Attempt to remove the current record.
658  |    ┌SWITCH
659  |    ┌─CASE SEARCH("Can't delete master", WINDOW()) = 1 : ; Must be a master table.
660  |        field.a = FIELD()   ; Just in case RESYNCKEY manages to jump you to
661  |                            ; another page in a multi page form.
662  |        RESYNCKEY               ; Shows a key conflict without unlocking-- records
663  |                            ; won't fly away.
664  |        error.n = ERRORCODE()
665  |        ok.l = error.n <> 53 AND error.n <> 3  ; Error.n 53 is set if key exists;
666  |                                            ; error.n 3 if a Write Lock is
667  |                                            ; on table.
668  |        MOVETO FIELD field.a ; Paradox3 sometimes jumps you to another field or page.
669  |    ┌─OTHERWISE:                 ; Detail record, or not a master with details.
670  |        INS                 ; Insert a blank, unposted record.
671  |        ; Copy from the array to create a complete
672  |        ; unposted record.
673  |        CopyFromArray3.u("r", requiredcheck.l) ; checks for possible problems
674  |        KEYLOOKUP           ; Attempt toggle to possible offending key.
675  |        error.n = ERRORCODE()
676  |        a = ERRORMESSAGE()
677  |       ┌IF MATCH(a,"keylookup can not..") THEN
678  |          ; 3.01 doesn't allow KEYLOOKUP in master.
679  |          RESYNCKEY
680  |          error.n = ERRORCODE()
681  |          ok.l = error.n <> 53 AND error.n <> 3 ; error.n 53 is set if key exists;
682  |          ; error.n 3 if a Write Lock is
683  |          ; on table.
684  |       ┌ELSE
685  |          ok.l = error.n = 56    ; If it can't find lookup,
686  |                              ; then key is okay.
687  |       └ENDIF
688  |       ┌IF ok.l THEN           ; Lookupkey not found.
689  |          LOCKRECORD          ; Record posts, and cursor remains with it.
690  |       ┌ELSE
691  |          KEYLOOKUP           ; Return to record values as operator entered.
692  |       └ENDIF
693  |    └ENDSWITCH
```

```
694  └ENDIF
695  ┌IF NOT ok.l THEN
696  │  ; Place whatever error message or procedure you like to use here.
697  │  ┌SWITCH
698  │  ├──CASE error.n = 3 :      ; Possible Write Lock.
699  │  │    TopMsg.u("Table locked by: "+ERRORUSER()+ ". Cannot verify key.","C",1000)
700  │  ├──OTHERWISE:
701  │  │    TopMsg.u("A record with this key already exists.", "C", 1000)
702  │  └ENDSWITCH
703  └ENDIF
704  ┌IF requiredcheck.l <> false THEN
705  │   REQUIREDCHECK ON
706  └ENDIF
707 ◄──RETURN ok.l
708 └ENDPROC
709  WRITELIB libname.a OkKey3.l
710  RELEASE PROCS      OkKey3.l
711  ;=======================================================================
712
713  ;=======================================================================
714  ; CopyFromArray3.u()
715  ; Version 1.5. This revision supercedes all previous versions.
716  ;
717  ; This procedure simulates a COPYFROMARRAY that will work in
718  ; all table images whether master, linked, or unlinked. It uses
719  ; ErrorProc to specify a procedure to handle errors that would
720  ; normally occur when using the COPYFROMARRAY command. For those
721  ; who have used prior versions, the syntax is the same, but
722  ; there are some new features of CopyFromArray3.u :
723
724  ; 1) Faster than previous versions.
725  ; 2) Works with all forms of linked embedded tables.
726  ; 3) Works in all edit modes, not just CoEdit.
727  ; 4) Lets Paradox version 3.0 place blank required fields
728  ;     (this caused a script error in Paradox 3.0, but was fixed
729  ;     in Paradox 3.01).
730  ;
731  ; 5) If an unanticipated error occurs, the OopsPrint.u()
732  ;     proc user is presented with a
733  ;     Cancel/Debug prompt (just as COPYFROMARRAY would).
734  ; 6) In the event of an error caused by invalid data, a procedure called
735  ;     InvalidArrayRecover.u() is invoked to document the error and try to
736  ;     recover any potentially lost data.
737
738 ┌PROC CopyFromArray3.u(arrayname.a, requiredcheck.l)
739 │   ; arrayname.a      ; A string representing the name of the array to copy from.
740 │   ; requiredcheck.l  ; If you set requiredcheck.l to FALSE, REQUIREDCHECK
741 │   ;                     will remain OFF.
742 │   ;                     If requiredcheck.l is any other value, REQUIREDCHECK
743 │   ;                     will be turned back to its normal ON status.
744 │   ; linkedkeys.n      Optional global variable. If set, tells CopyFromaArray3.u
745 │   ;                   how many keys to avoid placing.  This is necessary only in
746 │   ;                   one odd circumstance described below.
747 │   PRIVATE
748 │   fields.n,   ; Number of fields in table.
749 │   n ,         ; Field counter.
750 │   linked.n,   ; Number of linked keys specified by optional variable
751 │               ; called linkedkeys.n   ; see notes for explanation
```

```
752   ERRORPROC,  ; Name of error procedure.
753   proc.a      ; Name of procedure
754
755   proc.a = "CopyFromArray3.u"
756
757   ; Requires you to define an error procedure to handle link and required
758   ; field errors. We've tried to make the proc as small as possible because
759   ; it is only called when an EXECUTE fails in the code below.
760
761   PROC copyerror.n()
762      PRIVATE n   ; Used by GETCHAR() in case of error.
763      SWITCH
764         ; The first case statement traps for linked fields, empty master records
765         ; and required fields.
766         CASE (ERRORCODE() = 60 AND
767            MATCH (ERRORMESSAGE(),"..linked fields in ..") OR
768            MATCH (ERRORMESSAGE(),"..master record is blank..")) OR
769            (ERRORCODE() = 23 AND MATCH(ERRORMESSAGE(),"..value must be provided..")):
770            RETURN 1
771         CASE ERRORCODE() = 23 AND MATCH(ERRORMESSAGE(),"..not one of the possible value.."):
772            ; Do the recovery for invalid data
773            InvalidArrayRecover.u(arrayname.a)
774            RETURN 2    ; The Cancel/Debug prompt
775         OTHERWISE: ; An unanticipated script error.
776            ; This could occur, for example, if another user has locked the
777            ; current record
778            MESSAGE "CopyFromArray3.u has found Errorcode() =",
779            ERRORCODE(), " ", ERRORMESSAGE()+"   Press any key."
780            n = GETCHAR()
781            RETURN 2    ; Causes Cancel/Debug prompt to appear after key is pressed.
782            ; In Runtime, it would simply end script play and exit to DOS.
783      ENDSWITCH
784   ENDPROC
785
786   REQUIREDCHECK OFF             ; You might not even be allowed to issue
787                                 ; MENU otherwise.
788   ERRORPROC = "CopyError.n"     ; Set name of error handler
789
790   IF VERSION() >= 3.5 THEN
791      ; Linked problems with COPYFROMARRAY were fixed in 3.5
792      ; however the invalid data problems could still be present
793      EXECUTE "COPYFROMARRAY " + arrayname.a
794   ELSE
795      ; let's trap for potential problems with Paradox 3.0 and 3.01
796      fields.n = NFIELDS(TABLE())
797
798      ; The next few lines allow you to specify the number of linked keys on an
799      ; embedded form.  Normally this is not necessary. However, there is a bug
800      ; in Paradox3 whereby if a table is present as an embedded form and *also*
801      ; is elsewhere on the workspace, attempting to assign a linked key field
802      ; moves the cursor out of the embedded form and onto the tableview image.
803      ; This also happens with the COPYFROMARRAY command.  So, if you have set up
804      ; the workspace so that this becomes a problem, set a variable called
805      ; linkedkeys.n to the number of key fields to ignore during the copyfromarray
806      ; process.  Remember to release or reset the linkedkeys.n variable to 0 if
807      ; it doesn't apply to the table.
808      IF NOT ISASSIGNED (linkedkeys.n) THEN
809         linked.n = 0
```

```
810          ┌─ELSE
811          │    linked.n = linkedkeys.n
812          └─ENDIF
813
814            ; Use the {Image} {Zoom} menu to find out field names and place the
815            ; values into the record. Luckily, the menu choices presented are not
816            ; sensitive to column rotations.
817
818            MENU {Image} {Zoom} {Field}
819            ; Now, make an attempt to place all available fields. If no linked keys
820            ; have been specified with the linkedkeys.n variable, the errorproc will
821            ; handle linked fields and ignore them.
822
823            ; Note that all fields will be filled, even if they are not different from
824            ; the array element.  This is done because there might be some fill-in fields
825            ; that are sensitive to the order in which the values are placed.  That is,
826            ; Field 1 may fill in field 2, but field 2 may need to fill in field 3.  If
827            ; we did not explicitly assign the fields when unchanged, the subsequent
828            ; fill-ins would not work the same as the COPYFROMARRAY command.
829            ; Granted, it's an obscure point, but one worth mentioning.
830
831          ┌─FOR n FROM 1 TO fields.n         ; Step through the field names one at a time.
832          │  ┌─IF n > linked.n THEN
833          │  │    EXECUTE "[" + MENUCHOICE() + "]=" + arrayname.a + "[n+1]"
834          │  │    ; For example, if the first field is [Cust#] the execute would prepare:
835          │  │    ; [Cust#]=record.r[2]      ; The second element of the array.
836          │  └─ENDIF
837          │    RIGHT                         ; Go on to the next field name.
838          └─ENDFOR
839            CTRLBREAK                        ; Back out of the zoom/field.
840          └─ENDIF
841          ┌─IF requiredcheck.l <> false THEN
842          │    REQUIREDCHECK ON
843          └─ENDIF
844            RELEASE PROCS copyerror.n        ; Remove the error proc from memory.
845        └─ENDPROC
846        WRITELIB libname.a CopyFromArray3.u
847        RELEASE PROCS     CopyFromArray3.u
848
849        ;------------------------------------------------------------------
850        ; InvalidArrayRecover.u()
851        ;
852        ; This proc is only invoked when there has been an invalid field assignment
853        ; through a COPYFROMARRAY.  It is called by CopyFromarray3.u() whenever
854        ; invalid data causes a script error while attempting to update a field.
855        ; Existing data that does not pass the validity checks can be invalid due to
856        ; several factors.
857        ;  1) A LowValue or HighValue valcheck was changed after the data was entered,
858        ;     causing the current data to be out of range.
859        ;  2) The field has a TableLookup valcheck, and the current value no longer
860        ;     exists in the lookup table.
861        ;
862        ; Obviously it is much better never to run into this case in the first place,
863        ; but sometimes we come across data that was not entered through script control
864        ; and the invalid data should not simply be ignored.
865        ;
866        ; This procedure attempts to recover from the error, and document all
867        ; the values in the array.  Because of some quirks in Paradox, it is impossible
```

```
868    ; to determine just where the cursor will end up in the event of the run error,
869    ; so we cannot simply recover and continue.
870    ;
871    ; We will note the error in the ErrorLog.Sc (or create the script if necessary).
872    ; It will document all the values in the offending array and the postion of
873    ; the cursor at the time of the error (this is not necessarily the
874    ; offending field).
875    ; Next it will attempt to force the data back into the table by creating a
876    ; temporary table and issuing an ADD command to override the valchecks.
877
878   ┌PROC InvalidArrayRecover.u(arrayname.a)
879    │  PRIVATE
880    │  ERRORPROC,       ; This is an error procedure, so we keep ErrorProc private
881    │  Oldtable.a,      ; Current table name
882    │  TempTable.a,     ; Name of temporary table
883    │  Recno.n,         ; Current record number
884    │  Formview.l,      ; Are we in form view?
885    │  Field.a,         ; Current field name
886    │  Sysmode.a,       ; Sysmode at time of error
887    │  zzzxzzzz.r       ; Values of current record
888    │
889    │  ; First let's alert the user that there is a problem
890    │  TopMsg.u("Error: There is invalid data in an array",
891    │          "Press any key and wait while a copy of the data is written to the ErrorLog.",
892    │          1000)
893    │
894    │  TopMsg.u("Writing contents of array" + arrayname.a ,
895    │          "to ErrorLog.sc.  Please wait.","")
896    │
897    │  Oldtable.a = TABLE()   ; Find the original table name
898    │  Recno.n = RECNO()
899    │  Formview.l = ISFORMVIEW()   ; Lets us put it back.
900    │  Field.a = FIELD()
901    │  Sysmode.a = SYSMODE()
902    │
903    │  ; Let's create a holding array
904    │  EXECUTE "size.n = ARRAYSIZE(" + arrayname.a +")"
905    │  PRINT FILE "ErrorLog.sc"
906    │  "\n**Error** Invalid Data while attempting CopyFromArray ", arrayname.a,
907    │  "\n      Date: ", TODAY(),
908    │  "\n      Time: ", TIME(),
909    │  "\n      User: ", USERNAME(),
910    │  "\n     Table: ", TABLE(),
911    │  "\n     Recno: ", RECNO(),
912    │  "\n     Field: ", FIELD(),
913    │  "\n ErrorCode: ", ERRORCODE(),
914    │  "\n ErrorMess: ", ERRORMESSAGE(),
915    │  "\n\n  ARRAY ", arrayname.a, "[", size.n, "]\n"
916    │
917    │ ┌FOR n FROM 1 TO size.n
918    │ │   ; get the value
919    │ │   EXECUTE "v = " + arrayname.a +"[n]"
920    │ │   PRINT FILE "ErrorLog.sc"
921    │ │   "   ", arrayname.a, "[", n, "] = ", v, "\n"
922    │ └ENDFOR
923    │
924    │  PRINT FILE "ErrorLog.sc"
925    │  "\n  Current field values in ", TABLE(), ".db record at time of error:"
```

```
926
927        COPYTOARRAY zzzxzzzz.r    ; The current record
928      ┌─FOR n FROM 2 TO ARRAYSIZE(zzzxzzzz.r)
929      │    ; get the value
930      │    PRINT FILE "ErrorLog.sc"
931      │    "\n  Field #", n-1, " = ", zzzxzzzz.r[n]
932      └─ENDFOR
933
934        ; Now let's try a DO_IT! to get out of our editing mode
935        TopMsg.u("Attempting to recover data and add it to the table",
936              "Please wait","")
937        DO_IT!
938      ┌─IF SYSMODE() <> "Main" THEN   ; the DO_IT was unsuccessful
939      │   UNDO   ; Either deletes new record, or restores original unedited record
940      │   DO_IT!
941      └─ENDIF
942        image.n = IMAGENO()
943        ; To get the invalid data back into the table we will create a temporary
944        ; table like the current table.  Then copy the data into the new table, and
945        ; finally ADD the new table to the old table, skirting the ValChecks.
946        TempTable.a = PRIVDIR() + "ZZZXZZZZ"
947        CREATE TempTable.a LIKE Oldtable.a
948        COEDIT TempTable.a
949        EXECUTE "Copyfromarray " + arrayname.a
950        DO_IT!
951        ADD TempTable.a OldTable.a
952        ; Updates the existing table with record information
953      ┌─IF TABLE() = "Changed" THEN
954      │   DELETE "Changed"
955      └─ENDIF
956        DELETE TempTable.a
957        MOVETO image.n
958      ┌─IF SEARCH(sysmode.a,"CoEdit")>0 THEN
959      │   EXECUTE sysmode.a +"Key"   ; EditKey   or CoEditKey
960      └─ENDIF
961      ┌─IF formview.l THEN
962      │   FORMKEY
963      └─ENDIF
964        MOVETO oldtable.a  ; Could have been a detail table
965        TopMsg.u("All possible attempts have been made to recover the data",
966              "Examine data when possible to verify recovery.  Press any key." , 0)
967        TopMsg.u("Error conditon makes it impossible to continue program because the ",
968              "data may have been affected.  Press any key for Debug prompt", 0)
969        ; The procedure that calls this one is responsible for final action,
970        ; which is normally presenting the Cancel/Debug prompt
971      └─ENDPROC
972        WRITELIB libname.a InvalidArrayRecover.u
973        RELEASE PROCS      InvalidArrayRecover.u
974
975        ;-------------------------------------------------------------------
976
977        ; This routine can only be used when there are no linked forms involved.
978        ; It is potentially faster than OkKey3.l() because it does less error
979        ; checking .   See notes about Key Violation checking under OkKey3.l()
980        ; The procedure also does not check for invalid data, so use it only when
981        ; appropriate.
982
983      ┌─PROC OkKey2.l()      ;assumes coedit mode and returns a true or false
```

```
984  |   PRIVATE
985  |   conflict.r, ; Temporary array
986  |   proc.a      ; Name of procedure
987  |
988  |   proc.a = "OkKey2.l"
989  |
990  |   ECHO OFF
991  |   COPYTOARRAY conflict.r
992  |   DEL
993  |   INS             ; need an unposted record to
994  |   COPYFROMARRAY conflict.r
995  |   KEYLOOKUP      ; attempt lookup toggle to possible offending key
996  | ┌─IF ERRORCODE()=56 THEN   ; lookupkey not found
997  | │    LOCKRECORD
998  ◄─┼───RETURN true
999  | └─ENDIF
1000 |   KEYLOOKUP  ; return to record values as operator entered
1001 |   ; Place whatever error proc you use to alert your user here
1002 |   TopMsg.u("A record with this key is already on file.",
1003 |            "Press any key to continue",1000)
1004 ◄──RETURN false
1005 └─ENDPROC
1006   WRITELIB libname.a OkKey2.l
1007   RELEASE PROCS     OkKey2.l
1008
1009
1010   ;----------------------------------------------------------------
1011   ; OopsPrint.u()
1012   ; We have found that this procedure saves time and eliminates a great
1013   ; deal of confusion.
1014   ;
1015   ; Paradox 2 and 3 allow for the setting of a special system variable
1016   ; called ERRORPROC. ERRORPROC contains the name of a procedure that was
1017   ; read in from a library that will execute when a run error occurrs.
1018   ; This variation of OopsPrint.u is used to document UNANTICIPATED errors.
1019   ;
1020   ; Appearances are deceptive. This procedure was developed to accurately
1021   ; document the Paradox environment when an unanticipated run error causes
1022   ; a script to fail. Usually there is a dramatic difference between what
1023   ; an operator thought happened and what really happened.
1024   ;
1025   ; For example, suppose your script was controlling several tables on
1026   ; the workspace in CoEdit mode. A MOVETO "tablename" was ignored
1027   ; because of an unexpected key violation (resulting in errors in
1028   ; subsequent field assignments). The odds are that the user would not
1029   ; be viewing the table where the trouble was occurring (instead
1030   ; perhaps, the last table before the PAL canvas was dropped).
1031   ;
1032   ; This procedure should be put into place after all known bugs have
1033   ; been found. When an unknown bug (or table corruption) is found,
1034   ; script play stops, and the complete status of the system is
1035   ; output to the printer (if online), and appended to a script called
1036   ; ERRORLOG.SC in the current directory. You might want to change the
1037   ; name of the script, or its location, to suit the application.
1038   ;
1039   ; When the client calls with a problem, we usually ask them to read
1040   ; the piece of paper that was just ejected from the printer.  We also
1041   ; ask them what they were doing just before the error occurred.  The
```

```
1042   ; ERRORLOG lets you see a history of errors, (many of which your clients
1043   ; will not admit to), and lets you get a feel of any pattern that is
1044   ; developing (whether or not it is script based, or errors in the
1045   ; integrity of the data or indexes).
1046   ;
1047   ; OopsPrint.u() gets all appropriate information about the system status,
1048   ; but must be read in at the beginning of the application. This allows
1049   ; Paradox to find it when necessary (even though it will be swapped out of
1050   ; memory later).
1051   ;
1052   ;   Example:     READLIB libname.a OopsPrint.u, working.u, beeper.u
1053   ;
1054   ; Alternately, OopsPrint.u() may be called from another errorproc specific
1055   ; to your application when the errorproc cannot deal with the error found.
1056   ; For example:
1057   ; PROC Oops.n()
1058   ;   PRIVATE Errorproc        ; So any errors in this proc won't be recursive.
1059   ;   SWITCH
1060   ;     CASE ERRORCODE() = 41:; "Not enough disk space to complete operation."
1061   ;       ;statements          ; Do something to free up some disk space.
1062   ;       RETURN 0             ; To retry the statement that caused the error.
1063   ;     OTHERWISE:
1064   ;       OopsPrint.u()        ; Print the errors.
1065   ;   ENDSWITCH
1066   ; ENDPROC
1067   ;
1068   ; You'll may notice that one thing that OopsPrint.u *DOES NOT* do is
1069   ; to issue a SAVEVARS ALL. There are several reasons. First, your code
1070   ; might make use of a SAVEVARS.SC, and we did not want to overwrite it.
1071   ; Second, there there was a bug involving SAVEVARS in all Paradox versions
1072   ; prior to release 3.0. The bug mainfests itself by locking up the machine
1073   ; when the the SAVEVARS command attempts to write a line in SAVEVARS.SC
1074   ; that is longer than 132 characters.  This presents a problem with long
1075   ; alphanumeric variables (such as TkNegKey and TkPosKey used in the
1076   ; DataEntry Toolkit) as well as long text fields assigned with COPYTOARRAY
1077   ; statements. The bug was *almost* fixed in Paradox version 3, so you might
1078   ; want to include some code like:
1079   ;           IF VERSION() > = 3.0 THEN
1080   ;               SAVEVARS ALL
1081   ;           ENDIF
1082   ; It will still cause a problem if you are using long variables that contain
1083   ; many characters with ASCII values below 30.  This is of particular
1084   ; importance to those who use the Data Entry Toolkit with record level
1085   ; movement procedures.
1086   ;
1087   ; This procedure uses a lot of variables and functions, so it consumes about
1088   ; 9kb of memory.  If you are working within very limited memory, you
1089   ; might not even have enough memory to load this procedure in the event of a run
1090   ; error.  You might consider splitting the procedure into two parts, the first
1091   ; part could get all the variables, and the second part could record them to
1092   ; disk and printer.
1093
1094   PROC OopsPrint.u ()   ; error procedure
1095     PRIVATE
1096     ERRORPROC,                 ; Private in case there is error in this proc. We
1097     ; would not want the errorproc to call itself.
1098     sysmode.a,              ; System mode  (Edit, Main, etc).
1099     drivespace.n,           ; Amount of free space on disk.
```

```
1100 |    date.d,                    ; Current date.
1101 |    time.a,                    ; Current time.
1102 |    version.n,                 ; Paradox Version (even though accurate to only 1 decimal).
1103 |    errorcode.n,               ; Paradox error code.
1104 |    errormessage.a,            ; Paradox error message.
1105 |    erroruser.a,               ; Network user who caused the error (e.g., locked record).
1106 |    username.a,                ; Current network user.
1107 |    memleft.n,                 ; Bytes of free memory for procs and variables.
1108 |    nimages.v,                 ; # of images on the workspace.
1109 |    table.a,                   ; Table name (if applicable).
1110 |    imagetype.a,               ; Image type (if applicable).
1111 |    field.a,                   ; Field name (if applicable).
1112 |    nrecords.v,                ; Number of table records (if applicable).
1113 |    nimagerecords.v,           ; Number of image records (if applicable).
1114 |    form.a,                    ; Form name (if applicable)
1115 |    recno.v,                   ; Current record # (if applicable).
1116 |    fieldvalue.v,              ; Current field value (if applicable).
1117 |    menuchoice.a,              ; Current Paradox menuchoice or "Error"
1118 |    isvalid.a,                 ; Is the current field valid?
1119 |    runtime.a,                 ; Is this paradox runtime? (converted to string).
1120 |    printerstatus.a,           ; Is printer online and ready?
1121 |    directory.a,               ; Current directory.
1122 |    privdir.a,                 ; Private directory.
1123 |    isshared.l,                ; Is current table shared?
1124 |    n,                         ; Used to remove keys from keyboard buffer.
1125 |    procname.a                 ; Used to display Proc.a variable (if assigned)
1126 |
1127 |    BEEP
1128 |    SLEEP 200  BEEP
1129 |    SLEEP 200  BEEP
1130 |    MESSAGE "Error has occurred, please wait while it is logged"
1131 | ┌─WHILE CHARWAITING()   ; Clear keyboard buffer, so user does not inadvertently.
1132 | │   ; Press Cancel if the {Cancel}/{Debug} prompt is displayed.
1133 | │   n = GETCHAR()
1134 | └─ENDWHILE
1135 |    directory.a = DIRECTORY()
1136 |    privdir.a = PRIVDIR()
1137 |    sysmode.a = SYSMODE()
1138 |    drivespace.n = DRIVESPACE (SUBSTR (directory.a, 1, 1) )
1139 |    ;-- First character of current directory is drive
1140 |    date.d = TODAY()
1141 |    time.a = TIME()
1142 |    version.n = VERSION()
1143 |    errorcode.n = ERRORCODE()
1144 |    errormessage.a = ERRORMESSAGE()
1145 |    erroruser.a = ERRORUSER()
1146 |    username.a = USERNAME()
1147 |    memleft.n = MEMLEFT()
1148 |    runtime.a = FORMAT("LY",ISRUNTIME())
1149 |    printerstatus.a = FORMAT("LO",PRINTERSTATUS())  ; "On" or "Off"
1150 | ┌─IF NIMAGES()<>0 THEN        ; Occurred on image on workspace
1151 | │   nimages.v = NIMAGES()
1152 | │   table.a = TABLE()
1153 | │   imagetype.a = IMAGETYPE()
1154 | │   field.a = FIELD()
1155 | │ ┌─SWITCH
1156 | │ ├──CASE imagetype.a = "Query":
1157 | │ │ ┌─IF CHECKMARKSTATUS()<>"" THEN  ; Place checkmark if appropriate
```

```
1158              fieldvalue.v = CHECKMARKSTATUS()+" "+[]
1159           -ELSE
1160              fieldvalue.v = []
1161           -ENDIF
1162        -CASE NIMAGERECORDS() > 0 : ; Cannot get value from empty table
1163           fieldvalue.v = FIELDSTR()
1164        -OTHERWISE:          ; Must be an empty table
1165           fieldvalue.v = ""
1166        -ENDSWITCH
1167       isshared.l = ISSHARED(table.a)
1168       nrecords.v = NRECORDS(TABLE())
1169       nimagerecords.v = NIMAGERECORDS()
1170      -IF imagetype.a ="Display" AND SEARCH(SYSMODE(),"MainCoEditDataEntry")>0 THEN
1171         form.a = FORM()
1172         recno.v = RECNO()
1173      -ELSE ; Could be in restructure subsystem where Formview is inappropriate.
1174         form.a = "N/A"
1175         recno.v = RECNO()
1176      -ENDIF
1177    -ELSE                    ; Not in an image.
1178       nimages.v = "N/A"
1179       table.a = "N/A"
1180       imagetype.a = "N/A"
1181       isshared.l = "N/A"
1182       field.a = "N/A"
1183       nrecords.v = "N/A"
1184       nimagerecords.v = "N/A"
1185       form.a ="N/A"
1186       recno.v = "N/A"
1187       fieldvalue.v = "N/A"
1188    -ENDIF
1189    menuchoice.a = MENUCHOICE()   ; The current Paradox menu choice or "Error"
1190    ; Now we're checking to see if a variable called Proc.a is assigned.  Many
1191    ; programmers set this variable in all their procedures in order to have the
1192    ; procedure name available in the event of a run error.
1193   -IF ISASSIGNED(proc.a) THEN
1194      procname.a = proc.a
1195   -ELSE
1196      procname.a = ""
1197   -ENDIF
1198
1199    PRINT FILE "ERRORLOG.SC"      ; In the current directory (appends if one exists).
1200    "\n\n" ,                      ; "\n" is linefeed  "\f"  is formfeed.
1201    "         Date: ", date.d, "\n",
1202    "         Time: ", time.a, "\n",
1203    "      Version: ", version.n, "\n",
1204    "    Errorcode: ", errorcode.n, "\n",
1205    " Errormessage: ", errormessage.a, "\n",
1206    "    Erroruser: ", erroruser.a, "\n",
1207    "         User: ", username.a, "\n",
1208    "       Proc.a: ", procname.a, "\n",
1209    "  Memory left: ", memleft.n, "\n",
1210    "      Sysmode: ", sysmode.a, "\n",
1211    "      Nimages: ", nimages.v, "\n",
1212    "        Table: ", table.a, "\n",
1213    "       Shared: ", isshared.l, "\n",
1214    "   Image Type: ", imagetype.a, "\n" ,
1215    "   Field name: ", field.a, "\n",
```

```
1216          "      Nrecords: ", nrecords.v, "\n",
1217          " NImageRecords: ", nimagerecords.v, "\n",
1218          "          Form: ", form.a, "\n",
1219          "      Record #: ", recno.v, "\n",
1220          "   Field value: ", fieldvalue.v, "\n",
1221          "    MenuChoice: ", menuchoice.a, "\n",
1222          "       Runtime: ", runtime.a, "\n",
1223          "    Drivespace: ", drivespace.n, "\n",
1224          "     Directory: ", directory.a, "\n",
1225          "       Privdir: ", privdir.a, "\n",
1226          " Printer Status: ", printerstatus.a ,"\n\n"
1227
1228    ┌─IF PRINTERSTATUS() THEN    ; Print out status if printer is available.
1229    │    open PRINTER
1230    │    ; Keeps [Crtl Z] from printing as right arrows on each line,
1231    │    ; if you have Paradox2 on a HP LaserJet II in IBM character set mode.
1232    │    PRINT
1233    │    "\f",    ; a form feed
1234    │    "** Error occured in program **", "\n\n",
1235    │    "\n\n" ,
1236    │    "          Date: ", date.d, "\n",
1237    │    "          Time: ", time.a, "\n",
1238    │    "       Version: ", version.n, "\n",
1239    │    "     Errorcode: ", errorcode.n, "\n",
1240    │    "  Errormessage: ", errormessage.a, "\n",
1241    │    "     Erroruser: ", erroruser.a, "\n",
1242    │    "          User: ", username.a, "\n",
1243    │    "        Proc.a: ", procname.a, "\n",
1244    │    "   Memory left: ", memleft.n, "\n",
1245    │    "       Sysmode: ", sysmode.a, "\n",
1246    │    "       Nimages: ", nimages.v, "\n",
1247    │    "         Table: ", table.a, "\n",
1248    │    "        Shared: ", isshared.l, "\n",
1249    │    "    Image Type: ", imagetype.a, "\n" ,
1250    │    "    Field name: ", field.a, "\n",
1251    │    "      Nrecords: ", nrecords.v, "\n",
1252    │    " NImageRecords: ", nimagerecords.v, "\n",
1253    │    "          Form: ", form.a, "\n",
1254    │    "      Record #: ", recno.v, "\n",
1255    │    "   Field value: ", fieldvalue.v, "\n",
1256    │    "    MenuChoice: ", menuchoice.a, "\n",
1257    │    "       Runtime: ", runtime.a, "\n",
1258    │    "    Drivespace: ", drivespace.n, "\n",
1259    │    "     Directory: ", directory.a, "\n",
1260    │    "       Privdir: ", privdir.a, "\n",
1261    │    " Printer Status: ", printerstatus.a ,
1262    │    "\f"   ; a form feed
1263    │    close PRINTER
1264    └─ENDIF
1265  └─ENDPROC
1266    WRITELIB libname.a OopsPrint.u
1267    RELEASE PROCS     OopsPrint.u
```

### WWPCORE1

```
1    ;*************************** WWPCore1 ********************************
2    ; WWPCORE1.SC and WWPCORE2.SC comprise the "core" of WaitPlus.
3    ;
4    ; (The core is broken up into two scripts because their combined length
5    ; would be longer than 1000 lines, and stepping through scripts of
6    ; this length is slow.)
7    ;
8    ; WWPCORE1.SC contains procedures that let the user view, edit, add,
9    ; and delete records. WWPCORE2.SC contains auxilary procedures that
10   ; handle image movement, dittoing, menus, prompts, lookups, and errors,
11   ; as well as procedures for setting up the workspace.
12   ;
13   ; Contents WwpCore1.SC    version 1.5
14   ;------------------------------------------------------------------
15   ;  WaitPlus.v(wpTable.a, wpForm.a, wpTableView.l, wpTableViewEdit.l,
16   ;            wpAliasList.a, wpRightsList.a, wpSetupProc.a,
17   ;            wpConfirmQuit.l)   ; The main WaitPlus call.
18   ;
19   ;  WaitPlusAdd.u()               ; Controls adding of records.
20   ;  WaitPlusEdit.u()              ; Controls editing of records.
21   ;  WaitPlusDelete.l()            ; Controls deleting of records.
22   ;
23   ;------------------------------------------------------------------
24   ; Both core scripts also refer to procedures that can be specific to
25   ; your application, usually contained in WWPAPP.SC. Required also are
26   ; the procedures found in WWPUTIL1.SC and WWPUTIL2.SC.
27   ;------------------------------------------------------------------
28   ; WaitPlus.v()
29   ;
30   ; WaitPlus.v() is the main WaitPlus procedure. It calls other procedures
31   ; to verify and set up the session, and if successful, places the user
32   ; into a "View" mode (actually CoEdit with IMAGERIGHTS READONLY).
33   ;
34   ;
35   ; The WaitPlus.v procedure syntax is:
36   ;
37   ;    WaitPlus.v (wpTable.a,        ; Master table name.
38   ;                wpForm.a,         ; Form to use. (0) if none.
39   ;                wpTableView.l,    ; TRUE if tableview is allowed.
40   ;                wpTableViewEdit.l, ; TRUE if editing tableview is allowed.
41   ;                wpAliasList.a,    ; List of aliases for available tables.
42   ;                wpRightsList.a,   ; Rights associated with each table.
43   ;                wpSetupProc.a,    ; If assigned, the name of a setup procedure
44   ;                                  ; that overrides the default,
45   ;                                  ; WaitPlusSetup.l(), found in "wwpcore2.sc".
46   ;                wpConfirmQuit.l)  ; Need to select {Ok} to confirm exit?
47   ;
48   ; Example 1: A single table ("Customer") displayed in table view,
49   ;            ReadOnly (simulating Main mode). We'll use the default
50   ;            table name in the prompt, and pressing [Esc] quits
51   ;            without confirmation:
52   ;
53   ;    WaitPlus.v("Customer",  ; wpTable.a
54   ;               "0",         ; wpForm.a
55   ;               TRUE,        ; wpTableView.l
```

```
56    ;              TRUE,         ; wpTableViewEdit.l
57    ;                            ;         Could also be FALSE because rights
58    ;                            ;         have been designated as ReadOnly.
59    ;              "{}",         ; wpAliasList.a.   None. Uses table name.
60    ;              "R",          ; wpRightsList.a   ReadOnly
61    ;              "",           ; wpSetupProc.a.   None.
62    ;              FALSE)        ; wpConfirmQuit.l. No confirm.
63    ;
64    ; Example 2: A multitable form ("Customer.F3"). Viewable in table view,
65    ;            but not editable in table view. The tables are referenced
66    ;            by two aliases that show in the prompt line. The "Customer"
67    ;            table can only be updated in non-key fields ("U" for Update);
68    ;            the user has "Insert/Delete" rights on the BookOrd table. {Ok}
69    ;            will need to be selected to confirm the [Esc] keypress to exit
70    ;            WaitPlus.v:
71    ;
72    ;    WaitPlus.v("c:\\Paradox3\\sample\\Customer",; wpTable.a
73    ;              "3",          ; wpForm.a
74    ;              TRUE,         ; wpTableView.l
75    ;              FALSE,        ; wpTableViewEdit.l
76    ;              "{Our Favorite Customers}{Orders Placed}", ; Table aliases.
77    ;              "UI",         ; wpRightsList.a
78    ;              "",           ; wpSetupProc.a
79    ;              TRUE)         ; wpConfirmQuit.l
80    ;--------------------------------------------------------------------------
81
82
83   ┌PROC WaitPlus.v(wpTable.a, wpForm.a, wpTableView.l, wpTableViewEdit.l,
84   │  wpAliasList.a, wpRightsList.a, wpSetupProc.a, wpConfirmQuit.l)
85   │  ;wpTable.a          Name of table or master table.
86   │
87   │  ;wpForm.a,          Form to use "F", "1" - "14",
88   │  ;                   or "0" (for table view).
89   │
90   │  ;wpTableView.l      TRUE if okay to view master in table view,
91   │  ;                   FALSE user is restricted to FormView.
92   │
93   │  ;wpAliasList.a      Names/alias of tables to display for prompt.
94   │  ;                   Must be in order that cursor would move in a
95   │  ;                   multitable form and each name enclosed in braces
96   │  ;                   "{Customer}{Orders}". If a table has no alias,
97   │  ;                   use "{}" as in a three table form where the
98   │  ;                   middle table is to use the default table name:
99   │  ;                   "{Customer}{}{Orders}". The names themselves must
100  │  ;                   not contain braces, e.g. "{{Customer}}{Orders}"
101  │  ;                   will not work properly.
102  │  ;
103  │  ;wpRightsList.a     The Rights associated with each table. A string
104  │  ;                   that includes a character for each table in the
105  │  ;                   order in which the cursor would move between
106  │  ;                   tables when [F4] is pressed.
107  │  ;
108  │  ;                   "IEURD" would mean that this is a five table form and
109  │  ;                   that the tables counting from 1 to 5 would have:
110  │  ;
111  │  ;                   I - InsDel = Full Insert and delete rights.
112  │  ;                   E - Entry = Add new records, edit existing, but no deletes.
113  │  ;                   U - Update = Update non key fields.
```

```
114  |   ;                    R - ReadOnly = No changes allowed.
115  |   ;                    D - DisplayOnly = User cannot move to table.
116  |   ;
117  |   ;wpSetupProc.a        Name of alternate setup procedure to initialize all the
118  |   ;                    variables necessary for WaitPlus.v(). If
119  |   ;                    wpSetupProc.a = "", the default WaitPlusSetup.l will
120  |   ;                    be activated.  If any other string is assigned, the
121  |   ;                    procedure with that name will execute instead.  Because
122  |   ;                    it uses EXECPROC, the procedure must not have any
123  |   ;                    formal parameters and it must return TRUE if the setup
124  |   ;                    was successful, or a FALSE if WaitPlus should terminate.
125  |   ;                    This variable is only of use to advanced programmers who
126  |   ;                    thoroughly understand (and can duplicate) all the variables
127  |   ;                    and arrays that normally get initialized by WaitPlusSetup.l.
128  |   ;
129  |   ; wpConfirmQuit.l     TRUE if {Cancel}/{Ok} menu should be presented with
130  |   ;                    an attempt to quit the table. FALSE lets [Esc] quit
131  |   ;                    immediately.
132  |   ;
133  |   ; RETURNS     The value of wpRetval.v, typically "Esc", or anything you set
134  |   ;             to the wpRetval.v variable.
135  |   PRIVATE
136  |   ERRORPROC,            ; "WaitPlusError.v" handles incorrectly assigned DisplayOnly.
137  |   v,                   ; Utility variable.
138  |   l,                   ; Logical variable.
139  |   wpChoice.a,          ; Menu choices for various WaitPlus menus.
140  |   wpForms.r,           ; Array of embedded forms/tables.
141  |   wpMultiForm.l,       ; Is this a multitable form?
142  |   wpAlias.r,           ; Array of table descriptions.
143  |   wpNames.r,           ; Array of table names, no path, init capitalization.
144  |   wpRights.r,          ; Array of table rights.
145  |   wpTables.n,          ; Number of tables including embedded tables for this form.
146  |   wpStations.n,        ; Number of tables the cursor can land on.
147  |   wpTableDesc.a,       ; Description for current table.
148  |   wpTable.n,           ; Number of current image, with respect to multitable form.
149  |   wpTableRights.a,     ; From wpRightsList.a, the rights assigned to current table.
150  |   wpTableName.a,       ; Name of current table, no path, init capitalization.
151  |   wpUntilView.v,       ; The key pressed to satisfy the until condition in "View" mode.
152  |   wpPromptProc.a,      ; Name of prompt procedure.
153  |   wpViewTable.l,       ; Should WaitPlus place the table on the workpace?  Default : TRUE.
154  |   wpCheckBlankKeys.l,; Should we check for records with all blank keys? Default : TRUE.
155  |   wpPrompt1.a,         ; First line of wait prompt.
156  |   wpPrompt2.a,         ; Second line of prompt, sensitive to tablerights.
157  |   wpQuit.l,            ; If this variable is set to TRUE, the wait will be terminated.
158  |   wpMode.a,            ; Current wait mode, "View" "Add" or "Edit".
159  |   wpUnlockRecord.l,    ; Lets you override WaitPlus's unlocking of a record
160  |   ;                    ; when Add or Edit is complete.  Resets to TRUE after use.
161  |   ;                    ; It is of use when jumping to another table in a "DepartAdd".
162  |   wpUntilBuffer.v,     ; Variable that lets you override some of the Wait loops
163  |   ;                    ; by making WAIT TABLE or WAIT RECORD choices for the user.
164  |   wpRetval.v           ; Value returned by the WaitPlus.v, normally "Esc", but can
165  |   ;                    ; be easily overridden at any point preferably by
166  |   ;                    ; WaitPlusAction.l("departwait").
167  |   CANVAS ON      ; Just in case previous code turned it off.
168  |   Working.u("")
169  |   ERRORPROC = "WaitPlusError.v"
170  |   wpViewTable.l = TRUE
171  |   ; WaitPlus will attempt to place table on workspace unless a "PrepWait"
```

```
172      ; resets the wpViewTable.l to FALSE.
173
174      wpCheckBlankKeys.l = TRUE
175      ; Blank key values in a master record prevent you from adding/editing/
176      ; deleting records in embedded details. Setting wpCheckBlankKeys.l
177      ; to TRUE always checks to see if detail records have blank keys.
178      ; This can occur when the records are added or edited outside of the
179      ; form. If this will never be the case in your system, you can set
180      ; wpCheckBlankKeys.l to FALSE for slightly increased performance.
181
182      wpUnlockRecord.l = TRUE          ; By default, WaitPlus unlocks a record when
183      ;                                ; finished adding or editing.
184      wpPromptProc.a = "WaitPlusPrompt.u" ; Name of default procedure for prompt lines.
185
186    ┌─IF wpSetupProc.a = "" THEN       ; No alternate setup proc specified.
187    │    WaitPlusSetup.l()            ; Initilizes most of the variables,
188    ├─ELSE
189    │    EXECPROC wpSetupProc.a  ; A special setup procedure has been specified
190    │    ; in the initial call. The procedure must accurately set up all the
191    │    ; necessary WaitPlus variables and place the table on the workspace.
192    │    ; It should return a value of TRUE if all is okay, or a FALSE if
193    │    ; WaitPlus.v is to terminate and go on to "DepartWait", which can
194    │    ; evaluate the error and exit gracefully.
195    └─ENDIF
196
197    ┌─IF NOT RETVAL THEN
198    │    WaitPlusAction.l("DepartWait")  ; Probably need to release the locks.
199 ◄──────RETURN FALSE                    ; Setup was unsuccessful.
200    └─ENDIF
201
202   ┌─WHILE NOT wpQuit.l        ; This lets you out of the wait quickly if necessary
203   │    ; if you set wpQuit.l to TRUE.
204   │    wpTableDesc.a = wpAlias.r[wpTable.n]  ; Pick up the description for the prompt.
205   │    IMAGERIGHTS READONLY   ; Simulates view mode.
206   │    wpMode.a = "View"      ; Could be useful in conditional errorchecking in action procs.
207   │
208   │    ; Normally the user is placed into a Wait table here. However, if you
209   │    ; want to force a specific mode, for example ADD, you'd have one of the
210   │    ; action procs set wpUntilBuffer.v = "Ins". This overrides the need for
211   │    ; the WAIT TABLE. This should be used in conjunction with WaitPlusInfo.u
212   │    ; to get the proper table information. If wpUntilBuffer.v = "", the Wait
213   │    ; table works normally. This feature should only be used once you become
214   │    ; very familiar with WaitPlus.
215   │
216   │  ┌─IF wpUntilBuffer.v = "" THEN ; No assigned buffer key to act on?
217   │  │    ; Build an intelligent prompt line, which
218   │  │    EXECPROC wpPromptProc.a    ; sets two variables, wpPrompt1.a and
219   │  │    ; wpPrompt2.a, for the WAIT TABLE below.
220   │  │    WAIT TABLE
221   │  │      PROMPT wpPrompt1.a, wpPrompt2.a
222   │  │      UNTIL "F10", "Esc", "Zoom", "Dos", "DosBig", "F35", 6, -103,  ; -103 is "ToQpro"
223   │  │      "F2", "F3", "F4", "F1", "Ins", "F9", "F7", "Del", "Undo", 22
224   │  ├─ELSE
225   │  │    RETVAL = wpUntilBuffer.v  ; As if the user pressed it from the keyboard.
226   │  │    wpUntilBuffer.v = ""       ; Reinitialize it to a null string.
227   │  └─ENDIF
228   │    wpUntilView.v = RETVAL ; Capture current RETVAL (as RETVAL is too fleeting)
229   │    ; in the event we want to do something later based
```

```
230    ; on the key that ended the WAIT.
231   ┌SWITCH
232   ├──CASE wpUntilView.v = "Esc" or wpUntilView.v = "F2":  ; [Esc] or [F2] gets out.
233        wpChoice.a = "Ok"
234      ┌IF wpConfirmQuit.l THEN        ; Confirmation menu specified.
235         SHOWMENU
236           "Cancel" : "Continue viewing the table",
237           "Ok" : "Done with the table"
238         TO wpChoice.a
239      └ENDIF
240        wpQuit.l = wpChoice.a = "Ok"  ; If TRUE, will attempt to exit WaitPlus.
241   ├──CASE wpUntilView.v = "Zoom" :
242        Zoom.l()
243   ├──CASE wpUntilView.v = 6 OR wpUntilView.v = "F35" :
244      ┌SWITCH
245      ├──CASE ISBLANK([]):
246           ; The reason for trapping FieldView in "View" mode is that there is
247           ; a potential for locking, thereby creating a new record in an empty
248           ; detail table by simply invoking FieldView.
249           MESSAGE "Field is empty"
250           BEEP SLEEP 2000
251      ├──CASE FIELD() = "#" and RECNO() > 65535:
252           ; There is also a bug in Paradox that will not allow you to exit
253           ; FieldView while in the record number column for any record whose
254           ; number is higher than 65535.
255           MESSAGE "Record# ", RECNO(), " FieldView unavailable for this field"
256           BEEP SLEEP 2000
257      ├──OTHERWISE:
258           FIELDVIEW
259         ┌WHILE TRUE
260           WAIT FIELD
261             PROMPT "Viewing in FieldView.  Press [Enter] when done.",
262                    "Cursor keys move through field."
263             UNTIL "Enter", "Dos", "DosBig", -103
264          ┌IF RETVAL = "Enter" THEN
265      ◄────────QUITLOOP
266          └ENDIF
267         └ENDWHILE
268      └ENDSWITCH
269   ├──CASE wpUntilView.v = "F7" :
270      ┌SWITCH
271      ├──CASE wpForm.a = "0" OR NOT wpTableView.l OR wpTable.n >1 :
272           BEEP  ; No form view allowed.
273      ├──OTHERWISE :
274           FORMKEY
275           ; Check to see if the master record is locked due to editing
276           ; one of the detail tables.
277         ┌IF WINDOW() <> "" THEN  ;
278           UNLOCKRECORD
279           FORMKEY
280         └ENDIF
281      └ENDSWITCH
282   ├──CASE wpUntilView.v = "F3" OR wpUntilView.v = "F4" :
283      ┌IF wpStations.n < 2 THEN
284        BEEP
285      ├ELSE
286        l = WaitPlusAction.l("DepartTable")
287       ┌IF l THEN        ; If l = FALSE we don't move anywhere.
```

```
288  │  │      │       WaitPlusImageMove.u(wpUntilView.v)  ; Moves in the proper direction.
289  │  │      │       l = WaitPlusAction.l("ArriveTable") ; Do any action for arriving
290  │  │      └──ENDIF                                    ; on a table.
291  │  │   └──ENDIF
292  │  ├──CASE wpUntilView.v = "F9" :
293  │  │    WaitPlusEdit.u()  ; Do the Edit procedure (checks for rights first).
294  │  ├──CASE wpUntilView.v = "Ins" :
295  │  │    WaitPlusAdd.u()
296  │  ├──CASE wpUntilView.v = "Del" :
297  │  │    WaitPlusDelete.l()
298  │  ├──CASE wpUntilView.v = "F10" :     ; Display a menu.
299  │  │    WaitPlusMenu.u()
300  │  ├──CASE wpUntilView.v = 22 :        ; [Ctrl v]
301  │  │    MESSAGE "WaitPlus Version 3.01"
302  │  │    SLEEP 2000
303  │  ├──OTHERWISE : BEEP
304  │  └──ENDSWITCH
305  │  ┌──IF wpQuit.l THEN
306  │  │    wpQuit.l = WaitPlusAction.l("DepartWait")
307  │  │    ; Will exit loop if wpQuit.l is still TRUE.
308  │  └──ENDIF
309  │  └──ENDWHILE
310 ◄──RETURN wpRetval.v
311 └──ENDPROC
312    WRITELIB libname.a WaitPlus.v
313    RELEASE PROCS      WaitPlus.v
314
315
316    ;-------------------------------------------------------------------
317    ; WaitPlusAdd.u()
318    ; This procedure is invoked when the user presses [Ins] or when you've set
319    ; wpUntilBuffer.v = "Ins".
320    ; Unlike interactive Paradox, it appends a new record *BELOW*
321    ; the current record, allowing users to ditto the record they just left.
322    ;
323  ┌─PROC WaitPlusAdd.u()
324  │   PRIVATE
325  │   wpRecord.r,     ; Copied array of the record currently on the screen.
326  │   l,
327  │   new.l,          ; Is this a new unposted record?
328  │   wpAtLast.l,     ; Cursor on the last record when attempting to add new record?
329  │   wpUntilAdd.v,   ; Keypress that satisfies the WAIT RECORD condition.
330  │   wpMode.a,       ; "Add"
331  │   wpPrompt1.a,    ; First "add record" prompt line.
332  │   wpPrompt2.a     ; Second "add record" prompt line.
333  │
334  │  ┌─IF SEARCH(wpTableRights.a,"IE") = 0 THEN   ;Insert/Entry Rights?
335  │  │   TopMsg.u("You may not add records to this table", "C", 1000)
336 ◄──────RETURN
337  │  └──ENDIF
338  │   wpMode.a = "Add"
339  │   wpPrompt1.a = "Adding new record to " + wpTableDesc.a + ".  Press [F2] when done."
340  │   wpPrompt2.a = "[F1]-Field help (if available)  [Esc]-CancelAdd  [F10]-Menu"
341  │   ; If you want to override the prompt lines above, specify new wpPrompt1.a
342  │   ; and wpPrompt2.a variables in the WaitPlusAction "PrepAdd" or "ArriveAdd"
343  │   ; routines in the "wWPApp" script.
344  │  ┌─IF wpCheckBlankKeys.l THEN
345  │  │   l = IsBlankMasterKey.l(wpTable.a)
```

```
346 |  |  ┌─IF l THEN   ; If l then the master record has blank keys, we cannot edit.
347 ◄──────RETURN
348 |  |  └─ENDIF
349 |  └─ENDIF
350 |    IMAGERIGHTS
351 |    COPYTOARRAY wpRecord.r   ; Gets info from last record viewed on screen.
352 |    l = WaitPlusAction.l("PrepAdd")
353 |  ┌─IF NOT l THEN
354 ◄──────RETURN
355 |  └─ENDIF
356 |  ┌─IF NOT ISFORMVIEW() AND (NOT wpTableViewEdit.l OR ISLINKLOCKED()) THEN
357 |     FORMKEY  ; Need to return to form view.
358 |  └─ENDIF
359 |    wpAtLast.l = ATLAST()   ; Are we on the last record?
360 |    new.l = FALSE   ; Let's assume that the current record is not a new and unposted
361 |  ┌─IF VERSION() >= 3.5 THEN
362 |     ; Now if this is Paradox 3.5 we can also check to see if this is an unposted
363 |     ; record, if so we don;t have to open a new record at all
364 |     EXECUTE "new.l = RECORDSTATUS(\"New\")"
365 |     ; Used EXECUTE to maintain 3.0 compatibility.  For 3.5 only, you could use:
366 |     ; new.l = RECORDSTATUS("New")
367 |  └─ENDIF
368 |  ┌─SWITCH
369 |  ├──CASE new.l or LINKTYPE() = "1-1 Group" :
370 |     ; If this is a new record, we are ready to receive data.
371 |     ; If the LINKTYPE() is "1-1 Group" a few special considerations are in order.
372 |     ; There should never be any more than the one record that we are currently on.
373 |     ; This is an attempt to overcome a bug in Paradox 3.0 that was fixed in 3.01.
374 |     ; In 3.0 you could inadvertantly append a second record in a 1-1 group.
375 |     ; In 3.01 this first case statement isn't really necessary.
376 |     ; If this were a 1-1 or M-1 group, any of the subsequent case statements would
377 |     ; be rendered useless anyway because 3.01 won't let you append a second record
378 |     ; where 3.0 inadvertently did.
379 |
380 |  ├──CASE NOT wpAtLast.l :
381 |     SKIP
382 |     INS     ; Inserts a new record BELOW the current one.
383 |  ├──OTHERWISE :
384 |     ; At the last record. Append a new record, whether form or tableview.
385 |     CTRLEND  ; Go to the last field
386 |     RIGHT RIGHT
387 |     ; Force to append a record. If in tableview, moves to the first
388 |     ; field of new record.
389 |  └─ENDSWITCH
390 |  ┌─IF ERRORCODE() = 3 or ERRORCODE() = 9 THEN
391 |     ; Another user has locked this or a master table.
392 |     Topmsg.u(ERRORMESSAGE(), "Cannot add records to this table.  Press any key",1000)
393 |   ┌─IF NOT wpAtLast.l THEN  ; Move back up to the previous record.
394 |   │   SKIP -1
395 |   └─ENDIF
396 ◄──────RETURN
397 |  └─ENDIF
398 |    CTRLHOME   ; Moves to first field on form, or record # column.
399 |  ┌─IF NOT ISFORMVIEW() THEN
400 |     RIGHT   ; Move to the first field.
401 |  └─ENDIF
402 |    l = WaitPlusAction.l("ArriveAdd")
403 |  ┌─IF NOT l THEN    ; If it returned a FALSE.
```

```
404  | |   DEL              ; Remove it.
405  ◄────────RETURN
406  | └─ENDIF
407  | ┌─WHILE TRUE
408  |   ┌─IF wpTableRights.a = "U" THEN
409  |   |   IMAGERIGHTS UPDATE  ; Disallow changing key field(s) that
410  |   |   ; have been assigned.
411  |   ├─ELSE
412  |   |   IMAGERIGHTS
413  |   └─ENDIF
414  |   ┌─IF wpUntilBuffer.v = "" THEN
415  |   |   WAIT RECORD
416  |   |     PROMPT wpPrompt1.a, wpPrompt2.a
417  |   |     ; Unless otherwise specified, the prompt will be:
418  |   |
419  |   |     ;"Adding new record to "+ wpTableDesc.a +".  Press [F2] when done",
420  |   |     ;"[F1]-Field help (if available)  [Esc]-CancelAdd  [F10]-Menu"
421  |   |
422  |   |     UNTIL "F2", "F1", "F10", "Ditto", "Dos", "DosBig", "LockKey", "Undo", "KeyLookup",
423  |   |           "Del", "Esc", 6, "F35", -103  ; 6 is [Ctrl F], "F35" is [Alt F5] fieldview.
424  |   ├─ELSE
425  |   |   RETVAL = wpUntilBuffer.v  ; As if the user pressed it from the keyboard.
426  |   |   wpUntilBuffer.v = ""      ; Reinitialize the variable to a null string.
427  |   └─ENDIF
428  |     wpUntilAdd.v = RETVAL
429  |   ┌─SWITCH
430  |   ├───CASE wpUntilAdd.v = 6 OR wpUntilAdd.v = "F35" :    ; [Ctrl F] or [Alt F5].
431  |   |   ┌─IF FIELD() = "#" and RECNO() > 65535 THEN
432  |   |   |   ; Workaround bug described in Waitplus.v
433  |   |   |   MESSAGE "Record# ", RECNO(), " FieldView unavailable for this field"
434  |   |   |   BEEP SLEEP 2000
435  |   |   ├─ELSE
436  |   |   |   FIELDVIEW
437  |   |   | ┌─WHILE TRUE
438  |   |   | |   WAIT FIELD
439  |   |   | |     PROMPT "Edit this field then press [Enter].  Cursor keys move through field.",
440  |   |   | |     "[Ins]-Toggle Insert/OverWrite  [Del]-Delete Character"
441  |   |   | |     UNTIL "Enter", "Dos", "DosBig", -103
442  |   |   | |   ┌─IF RETVAL = "Enter" THEN
443  |   |   | ◄──────QUITLOOP
444  |   |   | |   └─ENDIF
445  |   |   | └─ENDWHILE
446  |   |   └─ENDIF
447  |   ├───CASE wpUntilAdd.v = "Ditto" :
448  |   |     ; Copy from field of record that was on the screen just before you
449  |   |     ; appended the new record.  A regular DITTO command is of little
450  |   |     ; use in a network environment in a master record in formview,
451  |   |     ; as you never really know what the record above you looks like
452  |   |     ; (another user may have changed or inserted a record above).
453  |   |     WaitPlusDitto.u() ; Procedure to handle special cases.
454  |   ├───CASE wpUntilAdd.v = "F1" :
455  |   |     WaitPlusLookup.u()
456  |   ├───CASE wpUntilAdd.v = "F2" :
457  |   |     l = WaitPlusOkrecord.l()   ; Could check record for blank fields.
458  |   |   ┌─IF l THEN                 ; Record was okay, let's check keyviol
459  |   |   |   ; and do depart routines.
460  |   |   |   Working.u("")
461  |   |   |   l = OkKey3.l(FALSE)      ; Checks for a record with this key.
```

```
462 │ │ │      ┌IF l THEN                    ; There was no key violation.
463 │ │ │      │  l = WaitPlusAction.l("DepartAdd")
464 │ │ │      │  ┌IF l THEN
465 │ │ │      │  │  ┌IF wpUnlockRecord.l THEN   ; The default setting for wpUnlockRecord.l.
466 │ │ │      │  │  │  UNLOCKRECORD
467 │ │ │      │  │  ┌ELSE
468 │ │ │      │  │  │  ; Programmer doesn't want to unlock record this time, perhaps we
469 │ │ │      │  │  │  ; been moved to another table.  Reset wpUnlockRecord.l to TRUE
470 │ │ │      │  │  │  ; for the next time.
471 │ │ │      │  │  │  wpUnlockRecord.l = TRUE
472 │ │ │      │  │  └ENDIF
473 ◄─────────────────RETURN
474 │ │ │      │  └ENDIF
475 │ │ │      └ENDIF
476 │ │ └ENDIF
477 │ ├CASE wpUntilAdd.v = "F10" or wpUntilAdd.v = "Del" or wpUntilAdd.v = "Esc":
478 │ │  ┌IF wpUntilAdd.v = "F10" THEN    ; Show the Add menu.
479 │ │  │  SHOWMENU
480 │ │  │    "Add" : "Continue working on this record",
481 │ │  │    "Help" : "Get help information",
482 │ │  │    "CancelAdd" : "Delete this record, return to viewing table",
483 │ │  │    "More" : "Additional choices"
484 │ │  │  TO wpChoice.a
485 │ │  ┌ELSE
486 │ │  │  wpChoice.a = "CancelAdd"  ; Go directly to CancelAdd menu.
487 │ │  │  BEEP
488 │ │  └ENDIF
489 │ │  ┌SWITCH
490 │ │  ├─CASE wpChoice.a = "More" :
491 │ │  │    WaitPlusMoreMenu.u()
492 │ │  ├─CASE wpChoice.a = "Help" :
493 │ │  │    HelpTable.u()
494 │ │  ├─CASE wpChoice.a = "CancelAdd" :
495 │ │  │    SHOWMENU
496 │ │  │      "ContinueAdd" : "Do not delete this record, continue entry",
497 │ │  │      "OkDelete" : "Okay to delete this record"
498 │ │  │    TO wpChoice.a
499 │ │  │  ┌IF wpChoice.a = "OkDelete" THEN
500 │ │  │  │  l = WaitPlusAction.l("PrepCancelAdd")
501 │ │  │  │  ┌IF l THEN       ; Okay to cancel the add.
502 │ │  │  │  │  IMAGERIGHTS   ; May be restricted by special rights,
503 │ │  │  │  │                ; so we need to assure IMAGERIGHTS.
504 │ │  │  │  │  DEL
505 │ │  │  │  │  ┌IF NOT ATLAST() THEN
506 │ │  │  │  │  │  SKIP -1    ; Move back up one record because we appended
507 │ │  │  │  │  │             ; below existing record.
508 │ │  │  │  │  └ENDIF
509 │ │  │  │  │  WaitPlusAction.l("CancelAdd")  ; Possibly resets rights.
510 ◄────────────────────RETURN
511 │ │  │  │  └ENDIF
512 │ │  │  └ENDIF
513 │ │  └ENDSWITCH
514 │ ├─OTHERWISE :
515 │ │    BEEP  ; DOS, DOSBIG, etc.
516 │ └ENDSWITCH
517 │ └ENDWHILE
518 └ENDPROC
519  WRITELIB libname.a WaitPlusAdd.u
```

```
520    RELEASE PROCS      WaitPlusAdd.u
521
522
523    ;--------------------------------------------------------------------
524    ; WaitPlusEdit.u()
525    ; This procedure is invoked when the user is allowed to edit the current
526    ; record. It uses the IMAGERIGHTS command to control the user's editing
527    ; of key fields. We cannot pass the wpTableRights.a a formal parameter
528    ; of this proc because of errorchecking implemented in WaitPlusError.v().
529    ; If the rights are inappropriate to a display-only, the errorproc
530    ; resets the wpTableRights.a for future use. This could not be done if
531    ; wpTableRights.a was a formal parameter of the procedure.
532    ;
533    ; The edit procedure copies the original unedited version of the record to
534    ; an array called wpRecord.r, so you can undo any changes, and also gives
535    ; you values to compare the edited record against.  This allows you to
536    ; take action based on whether or not values were changed.
537
538  ┌─PROC WaitPlusEdit.u()
539  │   PRIVATE
540  │   wpRecord.r,      ; Original record is copied to array
541  │   l,
542  │   wpUntilEdit.v,   ; Keystroke pressed to leave edit WAIT RECORD
543  │   wpMode.a,        ; Current waitplus mode, "Edit"
544  │   wpPrompt1.a,     ; First edit prompt line
545  │   wpPrompt2.a      ; Second edit prompt line
546  │
547  │   ┌─IF SEARCH(wpTableRights.a, "IUE") = 0 THEN  ; Does not have proper rights to edit.
548  │   │   TopMsg.u("You may not edit records in this table", "C", 1000)
549 ◄├───────RETURN
550  │   └─ENDIF
551  │   wpMode.a = "Edit"
552  │   wpPrompt1.a = "Edit this record, press [F2] when done. "
553  │   wpPrompt2.a = "[F1]-Field help (if available)  [Esc]-CancelEdit  [F10]-Menu"
554  │   ; If you want to override the prompt lines above, specify new wpPrompt1.a
555  │   ; and wpPrompt2.a variables in the WaitPlusAction.l "PrepEdit" or
556  │   ; "ArriveEdit" routines.
557  │   l = WaitPlusAction.l("PrepEdit")  ; Any special processing.
558  │   ┌─IF NOT l THEN
559 ◄├───────RETURN
560  │   └─ENDIF
561  │   ┌─IF NOT ISFORMVIEW() AND (NOT wpTableViewEdit.l OR ISLINKLOCKED()) THEN
562  │   │   FORMKEY      ; Make sure that they are back in the form.
563  │   └─ENDIF
564  │   ┌─IF wpCheckBlankKeys.l THEN
565  │   │   l = IsBlankMasterKey.l(wpTable.a)
566  │   │   ┌─IF l THEN  ; If True, the master record has blank keys and we cannot edit.
567 ◄├│───────RETURN
568  │   │   └─ENDIF
569  │   └─ENDIF
570  │   IMAGERIGHTS
571  │   l = RecordLock.l("Lock")    ; Test to see if we can lock this record.
572  │   ┌─IF NOT l THEN
573 ◄├───────RETURN                  ; WaitPlus.v will reassign IMAGERIGHTS READONLY.
574  │   └─ENDIF
575  │   COPYTOARRAY wpRecord.r      ; So you can replace the fields if necessary.
576  │   l = WaitPlusAction.l("ArriveEdit")  ; Any special processing.
577  │   ┌─IF NOT l THEN
```

```
578 | |     UNLOCKRECORD
579 ◄────────RETURN
580 |    └ENDIF
581 |     ; Stay in a WAIT RECORD loop until the user is finished.
582 ┌─WHILE TRUE
583 |    ┌─SWITCH
584 |    ├──CASE wpTableRights.a = "U" : IMAGERIGHTS UPDATE
585 |    ├──OTHERWISE : IMAGERIGHTS          ; Could be "I" or "E".
586 |    └─ENDSWITCH
587 |    ┌─IF wpUntilBuffer.v = "" THEN
588 |       WAIT RECORD
589 |         PROMPT  wpPrompt1.a, wpPrompt2.a
590 |         ; Unless otherwise specified the prompt is:
591 |         ; "Edit this record, press [F2] when done.",
592 |         ; "[F1]-Field help (if available) [Esc]-CancelEdit  [F10]-Menu"
593 |
594 |         UNTIL "F2", "F1", "LockKey", "Undo", "KeyLookup", "Dos", "DosBig", "F10",
595 |         "F35", 6, "Esc", -103  ; [Alt F5], [Ctrl F], [Alt K] and [Alt L] are locked out.
596 |    ├─ELSE
597 |       RETVAL = wpUntilBuffer.v   ; As if the user pressed it from the keyboard.
598 |       wpUntilBuffer.v = ""       ; Reinitialize the variable to a null string.
599 |    └─ENDIF
600 |     wpUntilEdit.v = RETVAL  ; In case any other special processing needs to use it.
601 |    ┌─SWITCH
602 |    ├──CASE wpUntilEdit.v = 6 OR wpUntilEdit.v = "F35" :
603 |       ┌─IF FIELD() = "#" and RECNO() > 65535 THEN
604 |          ; Workaround bug described in Waitplus.v
605 |          MESSAGE "Record# ", RECNO(), " FieldView unavailable for this field"
606 |          BEEP SLEEP 2000
607 |       ├─ELSE
608 |          FIELDVIEW
609 |          ┌─WHILE TRUE
610 |          |  WAIT FIELD
611 |          |    PROMPT "Edit this field then press [Enter].  Cursor keys move through field.",
612 |          |    "[Ins]-Toggle Insert/OverWrite  [Del]-Delete Character"
613 |          |    UNTIL "Enter", "Dos", "DosBig", -103
614 |          | ┌─IF RETVAL = "Enter" THEN
615 |          ◄─────QUITLOOP
616 |          | └─ENDIF
617 |          └─ENDWHILE
618 |       └─ENDIF
619 |    ├──CASE wpUntilEdit.v = "F1" :
620 |       WaitPlusLookup.u()
621 |    ├──CASE wpUntilEdit.v = "F10" or wpUntilEdit.v = "Esc" :
622 |       ┌─IF wpUntilEdit.v = "F10" THEN  ; Show a menu.
623 |          SHOWMENU
624 |          "Edit" : "Return to editing this record",
625 |          "Help" : "Help about tables and the workspace",
626 |          "CancelEdit" : "Undo all changes made to this record",
627 |          "More" : "More choices"
628 |          TO wpChoice.a
629 |       ├─ELSE
630 |          wpChoice.a = "CancelEdit"   ; As if the user mad the menu choice.
631 |       └─ENDIF
632 |       ┌─SWITCH
633 |       ├──CASE wpChoice.a = "More" :  ; Attach more choices in this proc
634 |          WaitPlusMoreMenu.u()        ; located in "wwpapp.sc".
635 |       ├──CASE wpChoice.a = "Help" :
```

```
636              HelpTable.u()
637          ──CASE wpChoice.a = "CancelEdit" :
638              SHOWMENU
639                "ContinueEdit" : "Resume editing this record",
640                "OkCancel" : "Cancel all changes made to this record"
641              TO wpChoice.a
642          ──IF wpChoice.a = "OkCancel" THEN
643              l = WaitPlusAction.l("PrepCancelEdit") ; Is it is okay to cancel Add?
644            ──IF l THEN         ; Okay to cancel the add.
645                Working.u("Cancelling changes made to this record")
646                IMAGERIGHTS   ; Make sure we can undo the record.
647                ; The reason we are not using a simple UNDO
648                ; here is that we cannot be absolutely sure
649                ; what is being undone.
650                CopyFromArray3.u("wpRecord.r",TRUE)  ; Restore the record to
651                ; its original state.
652              ──IF wpTableRights.a = "U" OR LINKTYPE() = "1-1 Group" THEN
653                  ; Key couldn't possibly have been changed.
654                  ; (Unfortunately there is no way to test for Many to 1 Group).
655                  l = TRUE
656              ──ELSE
657                  l = OkKey3.l(FALSE)  ; Make sure that old key is still valid.
658              ──ENDIF
659              ──IF l THEN
660                  l = WaitPlusAction.l("CancelEdit")  ; Possibly resets rights.
661                ──IF l THEN
662                    UNLOCKRECORD  ; So that the record doesn't fly away.
663 ◄──────────────────────────RETURN
664                  ──ENDIF
665              ──ELSE
666                  ; This message will probably never come up in normal use,
667                  ; but it is here to demonstrate the kind of checking necessary
668                  ; on a network. While this user was possibly trying to change
669                  ; the key to this record and failed because the new key already
670                  ; existed, the record became an unposted record and by wild
671                  ; coincidence, someone else posted a record with the original
672                  ; key, rendering the original version of this record invalid
673                  ; because of a key conflict.
674                  TopMsg.u("Current key is invalid.  Another user has placed this key",
675                          "C", 1000)
676              ──ENDIF
677            ──ENDIF
678          ──ENDIF
679        ──ENDSWITCH
680      ──CASE wpUntilEdit.v = "F2" :
681          l = WaitPlusOkrecord.l()    ; Checks record for blank fields.
682        ──IF l THEN                  ; Record was okay, let's verify the
683          ; keys and do depart routines.
684          Working.u("")
685        ──IF wpTableRights.a = "U" OR LINKTYPE() = "1-1 Group" THEN
686          ; Key couldn't possibly have been changed.
687          l = TRUE
688        ──ELSE
689          l = OkKey3.l(FALSE)            ; Assure that old key is still valid.
690        ──ENDIF
691        ──IF l THEN   ; Okay to leave this record
692          l = WaitPlusAction.l("DepartEdit")
693          ──IF l THEN
```

```
694            ┌IF wpUnlockRecord.l THEN  ; The default setting for wpUnlockRecord.l.
695               UNLOCKRECORD
696            ┤ELSE
697               ; If you set wpUnLockRecord.l to False, then the record is
698               ; left locked.
699               wpUnlockRecord.l = TRUE ; Reset for the next time.
700            └ENDIF
701 ◄────────────RETURN  ; Quits the proc.
702          └ENDIF
703         └ENDIF
704        └ENDIF
705       ┤OTHERWISE :
706          BEEP  ; Must be "Dos" or "DosBig", or Lockkey.
707      └ENDSWITCH
708     └ENDWHILE
709 └ENDPROC
710   WRITELIB libname.a WaitPlusEdit.u
711   RELEASE PROCS      WaitPlusEdit.u
712
713   ;--------------------------------------------------------------------
714   ; WaitPlusDelete.l()
715   ; This procedure deals with deleting any one reference record. It checks
716   ; with WaitPlusAction.l("PrepDelete") before allowing deletion.
717
718 ┌PROC WaitPlusDelete.l()
719   PRIVATE
720   l,
721   wpChoice.a,
722   wpError.n,
723   wpWindow.a
724
725   ┌IF NOT TABLERIGHTS( TABLE(),"Insdel" ) OR wpTableRights.a <> "I" THEN
726   │ TopMsg.u("You may not delete this record", "C", 1000)
727 ◄────────RETURN FALSE
728   └ENDIF
729     l = WaitPlusAction.l("PrepDelete")   ; Okay to delete record?
730     ; Any special processing would go there
731   ┌IF NOT l THEN
732 ◄────────RETURN FALSE                      ; Return to WaitPlus.v.
733   └ENDIF
734     SHOWMENU
735     "Cancel" : "Do not delete this record",
736     "OkDelete" : "Okay to delete this record"
737     TO wpChoice.a
738   ┌IF wpChoice.a <> "OkDelete" THEN
739 ◄────────RETURN FALSE
740   └ENDIF
741     IMAGERIGHTS
742   ┌IF ISLINKLOCKED() THEN              ; Might be linklocked.
743   │ FORMKEY
744   └ENDIF
745     l = WaitPlusAction.l("OkDelete")  ; Perhaps an additional menu, or delete details
746   ┌IF NOT l THEN
747 ◄────────RETURN FALSE
748   └ENDIF
749     DEL
750     wpError.n = ERRORCODE()
751     wpWindow.a = WINDOW()
```

```
752  | ┌─SWITCH
753  | ├──CASE wpError.n = 9 or wpError.n = 3 :
754  | |    ; Another user has locked the master table or record, implicitly or explicitly.
755  | |    TopMsg.u(ERRORMESSAGE(), "Cannot delete this record.  Press any key.", 1000)
756  ◄────────RETURN FALSE
757  | ├──CASE wpWindow.a <> "" : ; Could be cannot delete master record if details are present.
758  | |    TopMsg.u(wpWindow.a, "Press any key.", 1000)
759  ◄────────RETURN FALSE
760  | └─ENDSWITCH
761  |   Working.u("")
762  |   WaitPlusAction.l("DepartDelete") ; Check if any subtotals, etc. need to be recalculated.
763  ◄──RETURN TRUE
764  └─ENDPROC
765    WRITELIB libname.a  WaitPlusDelete.l
766    RELEASE PROCS       WaitPlusDelete.l
```

### WWPCORE2

```
1    ;*************************** WWPCore2 *******************************
2    ; This the second core script.
3    ;
4    ; WWPCORE2.SC contains the auxilary procedures that handle image movement,
5    ; dittoing, menus, prompts, lookups, and errors.  It also contains the code
6    ; for setting up the workspace. WWPCORE1.SC contains the procedures that
7    ; let the user view, edit, add, and delete records.
8    ;
9    ; Contents
10   ;-------------------------------------------------------------------
11   ; WaitPlusSetup.l()                   ; Setup procedure for WaitPlus.
12   ; WaitPlusPrompt.u()                  ; Prompt line definition. Called
13   ;                                     ; whenever current table changes.
14   ; WaitPlusInfo.u()                    ; Set info for current table.
15   ; WaitPlusImageMove.u(wpKeyPress.v)   ; Moves between tables with [F3]
16   ;                                     ; or [F4] keypress.
17   ; WaitPlusError.v()                   ; The main WaitPlus Errorproc.
18   ; WaitPlusDitto.u()                   ; Smart "ditto" proc.
19   ; WaitPlusMenu.u()                    ; [F10] menu in WaitPlus.
20   ; WaitPlusLookup.u()                  ; [F1] (Help) definition.
21   ;-------------------------------------------------------------------
22   ; Both core scripts also refer to procedures that are specific to your
23   ; application, typically contained in WWPAPP.SC. All scripts also
24   ; need procedures found in WWPUTIL1.SC and WWPUTIL2.SC.
25   ;
26   ;
27   ;-------------------------------------------------------------------
28   ; WaitPlusSetup.l()
29   ; The default setup procedure for WaitPlus.  It defines all necessary
30   ; arrays, reads the error procedure, and checks to make sure the table
31   ; is available and can be placed into CoEdit mode in the appropriate form.
32   ; You can specify an alternate setup procedure by assigning the
33   ; wpSetupProc.a formal parameter when invoking WaitPlus.v. If you do,
34   ; you must make sure that your alternate procedure sets all the necessary
35   ; variables.
36
37  ┌PROC WaitPlusSetup.l()
38   │   ; Returns TRUE if setup went well, FALSE if there was a problem.
39   │   PRIVATE
40   │   a1,             ; Used in match function.
41   │   n,
42   │   v,              ; Used by pickform.v procedure.
43   │   wpError.a,      ; Error message if something goes wrong.
44   │   wpReadError.l,  ; Flag to explicitly read the error procedure.
45   │   wpMultiForm.l   ; Is the form specified a multi- form?
46   │
47   │   wpReadError.l = TRUE    ; Used by errorproc to determine if the errorproc is
48   │                           ; being read explicitly, or tripped by a run error.
49   │   WaitPlusError.v()       ; Forces the errorproc into memory.
50   │   wpReadError.l = FALSE   ; Reset so that errorproc will behave normally.
51   │
52   │   ; If the table about to be locked has a Form Lock on it, Paradox treats it
53   │   ; as a special kind of write lock. The next lines tend to this:
54   │  ┌IF wpForm.a = "0" AND wpRightsList.a <> "R" THEN
55   │  │   ; In attempting to allow editing in tableview, we must try to
```

```
56   │     ; place a PWL to test for contention with a Form Lock (which is
57   │     ; seen by Paradox as a Write Lock).
58   │     LOCK wpTable.a PWL
59   │   ─ELSE
60   │     ; The user has specified a form, or specified tableview with ReadOnly
61   │     ; rights. If the case is tableview with ReadOnly, the user will be
62   │     ; allowed to view the table, but cannot go into fieldview if another
63   │     ; user has placed a form lock on the table.
64   │     LOCK wpTable.a PFL
65   │   └ENDIF
66   │   ┌IF NOT RETVAL THEN
67   │   │   TopMsg.u(ERRORMESSAGE(),"Cannot continue until table is released",1000)
68 ◄─┼───RETURN FALSE         ; Lock failed.
69   │   └ENDIF
70   │   ┌IF wpForm.a <> "0" THEN  ; Need the form info to go into form view.
71   │   │   FORMTABLES wpTable.a wpForm.a wpForms.r   ; Check if this is a multiform.
72   │   ─ELSE
73   │     ; No form view.
74   │     wpTableViewEdit.l = TRUE  ; Any allowed modifications must be in table view.
75   │     ; Hard coded in event parameter came in as FALSE.
76   │     RETVAL = FALSE            ; Used by wpMultiForm.l.
77   │   └ENDIF
78   │   wpMultiForm.l = RETVAL      ; FALSE if tableview, or if FormTables found no
79   │                              ; embedded tables.  TRUE if there are embedded
80   │                              ; tables.
81   │   ; Get the number of tables involved.
82   │   wpTables.n = ARRAYSIZE(wpForms.r) + 1   ; If wpForms.r has not been assigned,
83   │                                          ; ARRAYSIZE returns 0, so
84   │                                          ; wpTables.n = 1
85   │   wpStations.n = wpTables.n              ; Initialize the number of stations
86   │                                          ; (tables) that cursor will be allowed
87   │                                          ; allowed to rest on.
88   │
89   │   ; Check to see that there are enough characters for rights for each table.
90   │   ┌IF LEN(wpRightsList.a) < wpTables.n THEN  ; There are not enough listings
91   │   │                                         ; for each table.
92   │   │   TopMsg.u("There have not been rights assigned for each table", "X", 1000)
93 ◄─┼───RETURN FALSE                                 ; Incomplete rights list.
94   │   └ENDIF
95   │
96   │   ;Make sure that all tables have not been flagged as display only.
97   │   ┌IF UPPER(wpRightsList.a) = FILL("D", wpTables.n) THEN
98   │   │   TopMsg.u("Cannot have all tables as display only", "X", 1000)
99 ◄─┼───RETURN FALSE  ; All DisplayOnly
100  │   └ENDIF
101  │
102  │   ; Parse the aliaslist, rightslist and table names into arrays.
103  │   ARRAY  wpNames.r[wpTables.n]    ; Table names, stripped of path
104  │   ARRAY  wpAlias.r[wpTables.n]    ; Table aliases
105  │   ARRAY wpRights.r[wpTables.n]    ; Table rights
106  │
107  │   ; Loop through the aliaslist and place aliases into alais.r array
108  │   ┌FOR n FROM 1 TO wpTables.n
109  │   │   ┌IF MATCH(wpAliasList.a,"..{..}..", a1, wpTableDesc.a, wpAliasList.a) THEN
110  │   │   │   ; Used a1 in case of spaces.
111  │   │   │   wpAlias.r[n] = wpTableDesc.a
112  │   │   ─ELSE
113  │ ◄─┼───QUITLOOP
```

```
114  |  └─ENDIF
115  └─ENDFOR
116
117     ; Place table names into array.  The array elements do not have drive or
118     ; path specifiers, but do have the first letter of the table name in upper
119     ; case, while the rest of the letters are in lower case.
120  ┌─FOR n FROM 1 TO wpTables.n      ; Set up array elements for each table.
121     ; Get the table name.
122  ┌─IF n = 1 THEN                   ; Use stripped table name of the master table.
123  |    wpNames.r[1] = StripPath.a(wpTable.a)
124  └─ELSE
125       wpNames.r[n] = StripPath.a(wpForms.r[n-1]) ; Get the table name from wpForms.r.
126  └─ENDIF
127     ; Makes sure that it is initial caps.
128     wpNames.r[n] = FORMAT("CC", LOWER(wpNames.r[n]))
129
130     ; If there is no alias for the table, use the table name.
131  ┌─IF NOT IsAssigned(wpAlias.r[n]) OR IsBlank(wpAlias.r[n]) THEN
132  |    wpAlias.r[n] = wpNames.r[n]
133  └─ENDIF
134     ; Now get the rights for this table and evaluate the number of table
135     ; that the cursor can land on.
136     wpRights.r[n] = UPPER(SUBSTR(wpRightsList.a, n, 1))  ; Get the substring.
137  ┌─IF wpRights.r[n] = "D" THEN
138  |    wpStations.n = wpStations.n -1    ; Subtract 1 from the number of stations
139  |    ;                                 ; that the cursor can land on.
140  └─ENDIF
141     ; Perform a little errorchecking to see that a valid imagerights are
142     ; assigned. The errorchecking can of course be removed, but it was worth
143     ; coding for demonstrative purposes of how to handle such an error.
144  ┌─IF SEARCH(wpRights.r[n],"IERUD") = 0 THEN  ; Not a valid imagerights parameter
145  |    TopMsg.u( "Invalid table rights in rights list", "Press any key.", 1000)
146 ◄──────RETURN FALSE  ; Invalid TableRights.
147  └─ENDIF
148  └─ENDFOR              ; End of the loop that steps through each table name.
149
150     ; Check if there is any action pending before we get into the main
151     ; wait session.  This could involve placing other tables on the workspace
152     ; or asking for passwords, etc.  If the procedure returns TRUE, proceed.
153     l = WaitPlusAction.l("PrepWait")  ; Perhaps place a next number table
154                                       ; on the workspace.
155  ┌─IF NOT l THEN
156 ◄────RETURN FALSE                     ; PrepWait Failed.
157  └─ENDIF
158
159     ; Place the table on the workspace.  If the table is already on the
160     ; workspace, you can set wpViewTable.l =FALSE in your "PrepWait" code,
161     ; and WaitPlus will use the image already present.
162  ┌─IF wpViewTable.l THEN
163  |    VIEW wpTable.a    ; Put main table on the workspace.
164  └─ENDIF
165     WaitPlusInfo.u()        ; Get information about this table.
166     l = CoEditKey.l()       ; Attempt to go into coeditmode.
167  ┌─IF NOT l THEN            ; Error, perhaps someone editing a table in a
168  |                          ; different form.
169 ◄────RETURN FALSE           ; CoEditKey Failed.
170  └─ENDIF
171  |
```

```
172     ; Go into the selected form (if applicable).
173   ┌─IF wpForm.a <> "0" AND FORM() <> wpForm.a THEN
174   │   REQUIREDCHECK OFF
175   │   ; Need to do this in the case where the table is empty and the
176   │   ; first field is REQUIRED.  Otherwise, we would not be able to issue
177   │   ; the PICKFORM without filling in a value.
178   │
179   │   ; The next line attempts to pick the form. If it is successful and no
180   │   ; formlock conflict exists, the table will be in form view and v
181   │   ; is set to TRUE.
182   │   v = PickForm.v(wpForm.a)
183   │   ; Returns TRUE if form is okay or a string with error if a
184   │   ; pickform cannot be performed.
185   │
186   │
187   │   ┌─IF v <> TRUE THEN    ; Some error was flagged by PickForm.v.
188   │   │    TopMsg.u( v, "Unable to access table in FormView.  Press any key.", 1000)
189 ◄─┼────────RETURN FALSE     ; PickForm Failed.
190   │   └─ENDIF
191   └─ENDIF
192     ; Determine if the cursor can settle on the master table or
193     ; if the rights to the master table has been flagged as DisplayOnly.
194   ┌─WHILE wpTableRights.a = "D"
195   │   DOWNIMAGE
196   │   WaitPlusInfo.u()     ; Get the new info.
197   └─ENDWHILE
198     wpUntilBuffer.v= ""   ; This will let the main WAIT TABLE proceed normally.
199     wpQuit.l = FALSE      ; Initialize variable.
200     wpRetval.v = "Esc"    ; Initialize variable.
201     l = WaitPlusAction.l("ArriveWait")
202 ◄──RETURN l
203 └─ENDPROC
204   WRITELIB libname.a  WaitPlusSetup.l
205   RELEASE PROCS       WaitPlusSetup.l
206
207   ;-------------------------------------------------------------------
208   ; WaitPlusPrompt.u()
209   ; This procedure sets up the two prompt lines for the Wait Table.
210   ; It is the default procedure called by WaitPlus.v unless wpPromptProc.a
211   ; has been set to a procedure name.  If wpPromptProc.a has been altered,
212   ; then that procedure will be called with EXECPROC.  Any alternate prompt
213   ; procedure must set wpPrompt1.a and wpPrompt2.a.
214
215 ┌─PROC WaitPlusPrompt.u()
216 │   PRIVATE nrecords.a, a
217 │   nrecords.a = STRVAL(NIMAGERECORDS()) + " record"
218 │ ┌─IF NIMAGERECORDS() <> 1 THEN
219 │ │    nrecords.a = nrecords.a + "s"
220 │ └─ENDIF
221 │   wpPrompt1.a =  "Viewing " + wpTableDesc.a + "  (" + nrecords.a + " on file)"
222 │   wpPrompt2.a =  "[Esc]-Done [F10]-Menu"    ; Beginning of second line.
223 │
224 │ ┌─IF wpStations.n > 1 THEN                  ; Are [F3], [F4] allowed?
225 │ │    wpPrompt2.a = wpPrompt2.a + " [F3]-\024Image [F4]-\025Image"
226 │ └─ENDIF
227 │   ; Is form toggle allowed?, If so, show.
228 │ ┌─IF wpForm.a <> "0" AND wpTable.n = 1 AND wpTableView.l THEN
229 │ │ ┌─IF ISFORMVIEW() then
```

```
230  |  |      a = "Table"                          ; Show [F7]-Table.
231  |  └─ELSE
232  |  |      a = "Form "                          ; Show [F7]-Form.
233  |  └─ENDIF
234  |      wpPrompt2.a = wpPrompt2.a + " [F7]-" + a
235  └─ENDIF
236  ┌─SWITCH    ; Display in the prompt only the options that are
237  |           ; appropriate for the assigned rights.
238  |
239  ├──CASE SEARCH(wpTableRights.a, "IE") <> 0: ; Show add and edit.
240  |      wpPrompt2.a = wpPrompt2.a + " [F9]-Edit [Ins]-Add"
241  |
242  ├──CASE wpTableRights.a = "U":               ; Show edit.
243  |      wpPrompt2.a = wpPrompt2.a + " [F9]-Edit"
244  └─ENDSWITCH
245  └─ENDPROC
246  WRITELIB libname.a WaitPlusPrompt.u
247  RELEASE PROCS      WaitPlusPrompt.u
248
249  ;------------------------------------------------------------------
250  ; WaitPlusInfo.u()
251  ; This procedure gets information about the current table and sets the
252  ; variables that are used by waitplus.v and other procedures.
253  ; Normally, WaitPlus.v knows when to invoke this procedure when it lands
254  ; on a table.  However, if *YOU* write code in any of the WaitPlusAction
255  ; procedures that *EXPLICITLY* moves the cursor to another table, and you want
256  ; WaitPlus to continue from that point, you *MUST* invoke WaitPlusInfo.u()
257  ; so WaitPlus can get the table name and rights associated with the new table.
258  ; One way of avoiding this is to let WaitPlus do an *IMPLICIT* move by setting
259  ; wpUntilBuffer.v to "F3" or "F4", as if the user pressed the key interactively.
260  ; For those of you who have used the DataEntry Toolkit, this technique is
261  ; similar to placing a movement into the TKBuffer variable, rather than
262  ; having to use the toolkit's ArriveField() procedure.
263
264  ┌─PROC WaitPlusInfo.u()
265  |    ;SETS wpTableName.a   ; Name of current table, stripped of path, in init caps.
266  |    ;     wpTable.n       ; Table number.
267  |    ;     wpTableRights.a ; Rights for this table.
268  |
269  |    wpTableName.a = StripPath.a(LOWER(TABLE()))
270  |    wpTableName.a = FORMAT("CC", wpTableName.a) ; Shift wpTableName.a to init caps.
271  |
272  |    ; Step through each array value until we find the table name.
273  |    ; Set wpTable.n to the array element that finds a match on the table name.
274  ┌─FOR wpTable.n FROM 1 TO wpTables.n
275  |  ┌─IF wpNames.r[wpTable.n] = wpTableName.a THEN  ; This sets the wpTable.n to
276  |  |    ; the number and exits.
277  ◄──────QUITLOOP
278  |  └─ENDIF
279  └─ENDFOR
280  |    wpTableRights.a = wpRights.r[wpTable.n]
281  |    REQUIREDCHECK OFF                    ; There are potential problems if
282  |                                         ; we cannot move from a field.
283  └─ENDPROC
284  WRITELIB libname.a  WaitPlusInfo.u
285  RELEASE PROCS       WaitPlusInfo.u
286
287  ;------------------------------------------------------------------
```

```
288     ; WaitPlusImageMove.u()
289     ; This procedure traps for possible problems when moving between
290     ; images with [F3] or [F4]. It calls WaitPlusInfo.u() to initialize
291     ; wpTableName.a and wpTableRights.a.
292
293     PROC WaitPlusImageMove.u(wpKeyPress.v)
294       WHILE TRUE                    ; In case we come across a DisplayOnly image.
295         SetView.u("form")           ; Returns to formview in case we are in tableview.
296                                     ; (Contained in "wwputil2.sc").
297         IMAGERIGHTS                 ; Reinvoke imagerights to make movement possible.
298         ; Skirts "LINK RANGE" anomaly, where moving from a
299         ; blank master record with IMAGERIGHTS READONLY
300         ; to open up a blank record in a detail table.
301         KEYPRESS wpKeyPress.v   ; Upimage or Downimage.
302         WaitPlusInfo.u()        ; Get the table name and rights.
303         IF wpTableRights.a <> "D" THEN  ; If wpTableRights.a is "D", it will
304                                         ; loop back and try the next table.
305
306           IF wpTable.n = 1 AND wpTableRights.a <> "R" THEN  ; Cannot unlock a
307                                                            ; DisplayOnly.
308             UNLOCKRECORD  ; In case this is record is a master record that
309                           ; was implicitly locked by editing a detail record.
310           ENDIF
311           ; If current table is not the master table, and you have assigned
312           ; the current table ReadOnly rights, any changes to detail tables
313           ; will have locked the master. This is okay because it only affects
314           ; FormKey, and we trap for it. We have left LockKey active in
315           ; WaitPlus.v in view mode, so that the user may explicitly lock
316           ; or unlock a record at any time.
317           RETURN TRUE       ; Must not be in a display only image.
318         ENDIF
319       ENDWHILE
320     ENDPROC
321     WRITELIB libname.a  WaitPlusImageMove.u
322     RELEASE PROCS       WaitPlusImageMove.u
323
324     ;------------------------------------------------------------------
325     ; WaitPlusError.v()
326     ; This is the main WaitPlus error handling procedure. It can be invoked
327     ; in two ways:
328     ;
329     ; 1) As the result of a run error.
330     ;
331     ; 2) If you set the variable wpReadError.l to TRUE. This enables you to
332     ;    invoke the errorproc without an explicit READLIB command, placing
333     ;    its location in memory so that Paradox can call it in the event of
334     ;    a run time error.
335     ;    wpReadError.l = TRUE  ; Simply read the errorproc into memory.
336     ;    WaitPlusError.v()     ; Proc will load, and exit immediately
337     ;    wpReadError.l = FALSE ; Next time, if a run error occurs, the
338     ;                            errorproc will be called from its now
339     ;                            known location.
340
341     ;    This is particularly useful if WaitPlus does not know the name of the
342     ;    library in which this procedure is found. Or, you might be using an
343     ;    autolib that searches several libraries, so that using:
344     ;       READLIB autolib WaitPlusError.v
345     ;    would cause a script error if autolib = "Util,Waitplus".
```

```
346
347  ┌─PROC WaitPlusError.v()
348  │    PRIVATE ERRORPROC
349  │  ┌─SWITCH
350  │  ├──CASE ISASSIGNED(wpReadError.l) AND wpReadError.l = TRUE: ;Inits errorproc.
351  ◄──────RETURN 0 ; Simply continue the script.
352  │  │
353  │  ├──CASE SEARCH("Can't lock record in display only form",ERRORMESSAGE())>0 :
354  │  │      ; The user forgot to specify a display only form as ReadOnly only, so
355  │  │      ; we'll ignore the lock or unlock command. PAL currently has no way of
356  │  │      ; knowing if you are in a Display only form, so perhaps you'd want to put
357  │  │      ; a message up here. Keep this from happening again by reassigning
358  │  │      ; the wpRights.r array element
359  │  │      wpRights.r[wpTable.n] = "R"
360  │  │      wpTableRights.a = "R"
361  ◄──────RETURN 1                  ; Step over the offending command.
362  │  │
363  │  ├──OTHERWISE:
364  │  │    OopsPrint.u()  ; Log the error to the ERRORLOG.SC file and the printer.
365  │  │    TopMsg.u("An error occurred in this program","Press any key for debug prompt",1000)
366  ◄──────RETURN 2
367  │  │
368  │  └─ENDSWITCH
369  └─ENDPROC
370    WRITELIB libname.a WaitPlusError.v
371    RELEASE PROCS      WaitPlusError.v
372
373    ;------------------------------------------------------------------
374    ; WaitPlusDitto.u()
375    ; This procedure traps for potential problems with dittoing from the
376    ; wpRecord.r array.  Run errors could be caused by a value out of range,
377    ; or a value that does not conform to a lookup ValCheck.  We took this
378    ; approach rather than a simple CTRLBACKSPACE TYPEIN wpRecord.r[FIELD()]
379    ; because of potential conflicts with PICTURE ValChecks, particularly
380    ; with date values that have pictures to fill in the slashes. For instance,
381    ; if you have a date with a picture "##/##/##", and the value to ditto is
382    ; 1/2/30, a TYPEIN approach would leave the field with the incomplete
383    ; value: 12/30, clearly a problem. (This also points out why we generally
384    ; avoid putting pictures in date fields, although we do suggest LowValue
385    ; validity checks so that a user doesn't enter 1/1/9 when they really meant
386    ; to type 1/1/90.)
387
388  ┌─PROC WaitPlusDitto.u()
389  │    ; Dittos from the wpRecord.r array element of the same field name.
390  │    PRIVATE ERRORPROC
391  │  ┌─IF COLNO() = 1 THEN
392  │  │    BEEP
393  ◄──────RETURN FALSE
394  │  └─ENDIF
395  │    ERRORPROC = "wpDittoError.n"
396  │  ┌─PROC wpDittoError.n()        ; Define a temporary errorproc.
397  │  │    PRIVATE a
398  │  │    a = WINDOW()                ; Pick up the message being displayed.
399  │  │    TopMsg.u("You cannot ditto " + STRVAL(wpRecord.r[FIELD()]),
400  │  │            a + ".  Press any key", 0)
401  ◄──────RETURN 1                  ; Ignore the field assignment that caused the error.
402  │  └─ENDPROC
403  │    [] = wpRecord.r[FIELD()]   ; Uses errorproc to trap for invalid data.
```

```
404  |    RELEASE PROCS wpDittoError.n
405  └─ENDPROC
406    WRITELIB libname.a WaitPlusDitto.u
407    RELEASE PROCS      WaitPlusDitto.u
408
409    ;-------------------------------------------------------------------
410    ; WaitPlusMenu.u()
411    ; This is the main WaitPlus menu procedure.  It is called from "View" mode.
412    ; The reason we split it out as a separate proc is to try to keep the size
413    ; of WaitPlus.v down to a minimum, so it can be kept in memory.
414
415  ┌─PROC WaitPlusMenu.u()
416  |    PRIVATE wpChoice.a
417  | ┌─IF wpTableRights.a = "I" THEN   ; Only let them delete if imagerights are "I"
418  | |    SHOWMENU
419  | |      "GoTo" : "Locate record" ,
420  | |      "Help" : "Get help information",
421  | |      "Delete" : "Remove this record",
422  | |      "More" : "Additional menu choices"
423  | |    TO wpChoice.a
424  | ├─ELSE
425  | |    SHOWMENU
426  | |      "GoTo" : "Locate record" ,
427  | |      "Help" : "Get help information",
428  | |      "More" : "Additional menu choices"
429  | |    TO wpChoice.a
430  | └─ENDIF
431  | ┌─SWITCH
432  | ├──CASE wpChoice.a = "More" :
433  | |     WaitPlusMoreMenu.u()   ; Found in "wwpapp.sc".
434  | ├──CASE wpChoice.a = "GoTo" :
435  | |     GoToMenu.u()
436  | ├──CASE wpChoice.a = "Help" :
437  | |     HelpTable.u()
438  | ├──CASE wpChoice.a = "Delete" :
439  | |     WaitPlusDelete.l()
440  | └─ENDSWITCH
441  └─ENDPROC
442    WRITELIB libname.a WaitPlusMenu.u
443    RELEASE PROCS      WaitPlusMenu.u
444
445    ;-------------------------------------------------------------------
446    ; WaitPlusLookup.u()
447    ; This proc determines what happens during and after an "F1" is pressed.
448    ; It traps for [Ctrl O] and [Alt O], as well as mapping out [F1] which
449    ; could invoke Paradox help.  The proc also evaluates WaitPlusLookupAction.l
450    ; (found in WWPAPP.SC) to see if it is okay to make a lookup selection
451    ; (departlookup).  You can also issue commands to execute when the
452    ; cursor returns to the data table (e.g. RESYNCKEY) by coding logic
453    ; into WaitPlusLookupAction.l("LookupReturn").
454
455  ┌─PROC WaitPlusLookup.u()
456  |    PRIVATE l, wpPrompt1.a, wpPrompt2.a
457  |    ; Check if you have a custom help routine for this field.
458  |    l = WaitPlusLookupAction.l("preplookup")
459  | ┌─IF NOT l THEN
460 ◄├──────RETURN
461  | └─ENDIF
```

```
462 │  ; Check if there is assigned lookup help for this field.
463 │  HELP
464 │ ┌IF HELPMODE() <> "LookupHelp" THEN
465 │ │   BEEP
466 │ │   ESC                     ; Back to the main data table.
467 ◄─────RETURN
468 │ └ENDIF
469 │  wpPrompt1.a= "Use cursor keys to move to the record you want to select."
470 │  wpPrompt2.a= "[F2]-Select  [Esc]-Cancel  [Ctrl Z]-Zoom  [Alt Z]-ZoomNext"
471 │  l = WaitPlusLookupAction.l("ArriveLookup") ; Perhaps move to a specific record
472 │ ┌IF NOT l THEN
473 │ │   ESC                     ; Back to the main data table.
474 ◄─────RETURN
475 │ └ENDIF
476 │ ┌WHILE TRUE                ; Now in the lookup table.
477 │ │   PROMPT  wpPrompt1.a, wpPrompt2.a
478 │ │   LookupSelect.n()        ; Lets user view and optionally select from table.
479 │ │   ; LookupSelect.n is found in WWPUTIL1.SC.
480 │ │ ┌SWITCH
481 │ │ ├───CASE RETVAL = -60 : ;User selected a record with [F2]
482 │ │ │     l = WaitPlusLookupAction.l("DepartLookup")
483 │ │ │     ; Departlookup might, for example, check to see that an inventory
484 │ │ │     ; item is currently in stock before letting user select it.
485 │ │ │   ┌IF NOT l THEN      ; Keep the user in the lookup table
486 ◄───────────LOOP
487 │ │ │   └ENDIF
488 │ │ │     DO_IT!               ; Return to data table and fill in lookup value.
489 │ │ │     WaitPlusLookupAction.l("LookupReturn") ;
490 │ │ │     ;                    ; Perhaps moves to next field, possibly issue a
491 │ │ │     ;                    ; RESYNCKEY.
492 │ │ ├───CASE RETVAL=27 :
493 │ │ │     ESC                  ; Return to data table without fill in.
494 │ │ └ENDSWITCH
495 ◄─────QUITLOOP
496 │ └ENDWHILE
497 │   PROMPT                  ; Cancel lookup prompt.
498 │   ECHO OFF
499 └ENDPROC
500  WRITELIB libname.a WaitPlusLookup.u
501  RELEASE PROCS    WaitPlusLookup.u
```

## WWPAPP

```
1    ; ******************* WWPApp.SC ***************************
2    ; The procedures in this script are the ones that you would modify
3    ; to customize WaitPlus.v.  WaitPlus uses the following
4    ; procedures that can be specific to your application:
5    ;
6    ; Contents
7    ;--------------------------------------------------------------
8    ; WaitPlusAction.l()          ; The traffic cop. Controls program flow.
9    ; WaitPlusLookupAction.l()    ; Controls actions when [F1] is pressed.
10   ; WaitPlusMoreMenu.u()        ; Presents additional menus.
11   ; WaitPlusOkRecord.l()        ; Controls whether or not user can end
12   ;                             ; "Add" or "Edit".
13   ; HelpData.u()                ; Customized help screens.
14   ;--------------------------------------------------------------
15   ;
16   ; If an application is relatively small, you might want to add your code
17   ; directly to the body of these procedures. If your routines become
18   ; complicated, you can split the program flow into a series of smaller
19   ; procedures calls.
20
21   ; You will find coding examples in these listings along with comments
22   ; about what each is trying to accomplish. Some of the code runs
23   ; in conjunction with the "Customer" table from the sample tables
24   ; provided on the Paradox source disks; other code provided is purely
25   ; hypothetical. In either case, none of the example code referencing
26   ; the "Customer" or "Orders" tables is necessary for your application.
27   ; Copy this script and modify or delete these examples.
28
29   ; There are currently 36 procedures in WaitPlus in five scripts. When
30   ; creating and writing the WaitPlus library, you'll probably want
31   ; to set up a script like:
32
33   ; Libname.a = "WaitPlus"
34   ; CREATELIB Libname.a
35   ; Play "wwpapp"
36   ; Play "wwpcore1"
37   ; Play "wwpcore2"
38   ; Play "wwputil1"
39   ; Play "wwputil2"
40   ; INFOLIB "WAITPLUS"
41
42   ;--------------------------------------------------------------
43   ; WaitPlusAction.l()
44   ;
45   ; This is the main procedure that lets you direct the flow of your
46   ; application running under WaitPlus. Within this procedure,
47   ; WaitPlusAction.l(), you define actions that occur before and
48   ; after "critical" events.
49   ;
50   ; WaitPlusAction.l covers 18 critical events and each of them
51   ; by default return the value True.
52   ;
53   ;PROC WaitPlusAction.a(action.a)
54   ; action.a = LOWER(action.a)  ; Shifts to lower case so Case statements are easier
55   ; SWITCH
```

```
56   ;    CASE action.a = "prepwait":        ; Prep for initial view of master table.
57   ;    CASE action.a = "arrivewait":      ; Arrived at first viewable table.
58   ;    CASE action.a = "arrivetable":     ; Arriving on a table.
59   ;    CASE action.a = "departtable":     ; Departing a table.
60   ;    CASE action.a = "prepadd":         ; Prepare to add record.
61   ;    CASE action.a = "arriveadd":       ; Arrived in the add mode.
62   ;    CASE action.a = "prepcanceladd": ; Prepare to cancel the adding of a record.
63   ;    CASE action.a = "canceladd":       ; Add was cancelled.
64   ;    CASE action.a = "departadd":       ; About to depart add mode.
65   ;    CASE action.a = "prepedit":        ; Prepare to edit record.
66   ;    CASE action.a = "arriveedit":      ; Arrived in the edit mode.
67   ;    Case action.a = "prepcanceledit":; Prepare to cancel the edit.
68   ;    CASE action.a = "canceledit":      ; Edit was cancelled.
69   ;    CASE action.a = "departedit":      ; About to depart from edit.
70   ;    CASE action.a = "prepdelete":      ; Prepare to delete a record.
71   ;    CASE action.a = "okdelete":        ; Delete was okayed.
72   ;    CASE action.a = "departdelete":    ; Record was deleted.
73   ;    CASE action.a = "departwait":      ; Depart WaitPlus.
74   ; ENDSWITCH
75   ;ENDPROC
76
77   ;  WaitPlusAction.l is called before and after these critical events
78   ;  by the core procedures of WaitPlus. For example, prior to adding
79   ;  a record, these core procedures call both:
80   ;
81   ;  WaitPlusAction.l("PrepAdd")  and
82   ;
83   ;  WaitPlusAction.l("ArriveAdd").
84   ;
85   ;  The first is called prior to inserting a record, the second
86   ;  is called after inserting the record but prior to the user being
87   ;  allowed to enter information into the record. If you don't add
88   ;  code to their corresponding case statements in WaitPlusAction.l,
89   ;  it simply returns the value True and nothing special occurs. However, if
90   ;  you place code after statements in WaitPlusAction.l that dictate
91   ;  pre- and post processing, you can exercise a great deal of control
92   ;  over how and what WaitPlus does:
93
94   ;  CASE action.a = "prepadd" :
95   ;    IF TABLE() = "Customer" THEN
96   ;       MOVETO "Idtable"      ; A one record embedded table.
97   ;       IMAGERIGHTS
98   ;       [] = []+1             ; Increment after coming in.
99   ;       Newid.s = []
100  ;       MOVETO "Customer"
101  ;    ENDIF
102  ;    RETURN True
103  ;  CASE action.a = "arriveadd"
104  ;  IF TABLE() = "Customer" THEN
105  ;    [Cust Id] = Newid.s
106  ;    RELEASE VARS Newid.s
107  ;    wpTableRights.a = "U"    ; Assigns IMAGERIGHTS UPDATE to keep the user
108  ;                            ; from changing key field values.
109  ;  ENDIF
110  ;  RETURN True
111  ;
112  ;
113  ; You never **have** to call WaitPlusAction.l()-- the procedures in the
```

```
114   ; WaitPlus core automatically call it (in scripts "wWPCore1" and
115   ; "wWPCore2").  However, the procedures you write can reference
116   ; variables already assigned (e.g. wpMode.a, which tells which
117   ; WaitPlus mode you're in, or wpUntilView.v, which contains the
118   ; keypress that exited the WAIT table.).
119   ;
120   ; At times the code necessary to control the program flow can get quite
121   ; complicated.  If for example there are a lot of tables involved,
122   ; the size of this procedure can easily become unwieldy.  As with all
123   ; the procedures in this script, you can use WaitPlusAction.l() to call
124   ; subordinate procedures that return a result to WaitPlusAction.l(),
125   ; which then, in turn, passes the result back to the WaitPlus procedure
126   ; that called it.
127   ;
128   ; It is up to you keep it as simple, or make it as complicated, as the
129   ; situation demands.
130   ;
131   ; However you choose to add code WaitPlusAction.l, it must have the case
132   ; statements listed above and return an appropriate True or False
133   ; for each case. By default, all of these case statements return True
134   ; and (with the one exception) WaitPlusAction.l does NOTHING
135   ; unless you add code to it. The last case, "departwait," performs
136   ; clean up duty, clearing tables, etc. The way it is coded below
137   ; should handle most exits of a WaitPlus session.
138   ;
139   ; Now for the real thing...
140   ;
141   ;-----------------------------------------------------------------------
142   ; The sample code in this procedure is meant to be instructive and
143   ; representative of code that YOU would place in each case statement.
144   ; It references some of the sample tables Paradox provides. You should
145   ; examine it to familiarize yourself with the way WaitPlus uses
146   ; WaitPlusAction.l, but then copy this script, and delete or modify
147   ; this sample code from your applications. As a final reminder, with
148   ; the exception of the last case statement, all statements need only
149   ; return the value True for WaitPlus to run.
150
151  ┌─PROC WaitPlusAction.l(action.a)
152  │   PRIVATE v
153  │   action.a = LOWER(action.a)
154  │ ┌─SWITCH
155  │ │
156  │ ├──CASE action.a = "prepwait":  ; Prepare for initial view of master table.
157  │ │ │   ; The table and form are chosen but not yet placed on the workspace.
158  │ │ │   ;
159  │ │ │   ; You might change the wpPromptProc.a variable to use another
160  │ │ │   ; method of determining the two prompt lines.
161  │ │ │   ;
162  │ │ │   ; Another example is to include statements that puts a "next number"
163  │ │ │   ; table on the workspace. The following code fragment puts
164  │ │ │   ; up a table that holds the current value of a sequential id
165  │ │ │   ; number on the workspace before placing the Customer table into
166  │ │ │   ; form F3.  This allows you to reference this value during the
167  │ │ │   ; call to WaitPlus and increment ID numbers in your tables when
168  │ │ │   ; adding new records. The alternative is to place this auxiliary
169  │ │ │   ; table on the workspace before you invoke WaitPlus.v().  You will
170  │ │ │   ; need to remember to clear the additional images either in
171  │ │ │   ; "DepartWait", or after you exit WaitPlus.v.
```

```
172  │   │       ;
173  │   │    ┌─IF wpTable.a="Customer" and wpForm.a = "3" THEN
174  │   │    │   VIEW "Nextnumb"   ;Puts table on workspace before formview invoked.
175  │   │    └─ENDIF
176  │   │
177  ◄───┼──────RETURN TRUE
178  │   │
179  │   ├──CASE action.a = "arrivewait":    ; Prepare for initial view of first
180  │   │      ; viewable table.
181  │   │      ; The table is on the workspace (and in the form, if one was
182  │   │      ; chosen) in CoEdit mode. An example might be to move to the
183  │   │      ; last record in the table with an "END" command.
184  │   │
185  ◄───┼──────RETURN TRUE
186  │   │      ; If you return FALSE, remember that WaitPlusSetup.a has placed
187  │   │      ; the table on the workspace in CoEdit mode and you are specifying
188  │   │      ; that the call to WaitPlus.v should not execute. You must then
189  │   │      ; do a cleanup routine like the one supplied in "DepartWait".
190  │   │
191  │   ├──CASE action.a = "arrivetable":   ; Anything appropriate when landing on a table.
192  │   │      ; You have just moved to a table.
193  │   │      ; This ONLY activates when an [F3] or [F4] is pressed to move
194  │   │      ; between tables. It does not activate when you originally arrive
195  │   │      ; in the master table. There you would use "ArriveWait" for any
196  │   │      ; preprocessing.
197  ◄───┼──────RETURN TRUE
198  │   │
199  │   ├──CASE action.a = "departtable":   ; Anything appropriate when departing a table.
200  │   │      ; You have just moved from a table.
201  │   │      ; This ONLY activates when an [F3] or [F4] is pressed to move
202  │   │      ; between tables.
203  │   │
204  ◄───┼──────RETURN TRUE
205  │   │
206  │   ├──CASE action.a = "prepadd":       ; Prepare to add a record.
207  │   │      ; You are preparing to add, but have not yet added, a record.
208  │   │
209  │   │      ; An example that assigns a next customer number follows.
210  │   │      ; This must be done prior to inserting a new record. Once you
211  │   │      ; insert a record in a multitable form, Paradox doesn't let you
212  │   │      ; leave the record to get to the next number table.  This proc
213  │   │      ; gets the number, but doesn't place it into a record because
214  │   │      ; the record hasn't yet been inserted. We'll place it into the
215  │   │      ; new record when we get to "ArriveAdd."
216  │   │    ┌─SWITCH
217  │   │    ├──CASE TABLE() = "Customer" AND wpForm.a = "3" :
218  │   │    │      ; The "NextNumb" table must be on the workspace.
219  │   │    │      SHOWMENU
220  │   │    │        "GetNextID#" : "Automatically increment the Cust ID number",
221  │   │    │        "ManualEntry" : "Leave field blank, so you can fill it in"
222  │   │    │       TO choice.a
223  │   │    │    ┌─SWITCH
224  │   │    │    ├──CASE choice.a="Esc":
225  ◄───┼──┼──┼──────RETURN FALSE
226  │   │    │    ├──CASE choice.a = "GetNextID#":
227  │   │    │    │      NextNumber.v = NextNumber.v("nextnumb","next cust id",FALSE,1,"Getting next cust id")
228  │   │    │    │      ;This procedure is found in the "wwputil1" script.
229  ◄───┼──┼──┼────────RETURN NextNumber.v <> "Error"   ; TRUE if nextnumber.v is not "Error"
```

```
230 │  │    │    ┌─OTHERWISE:
231 │  │    │    │    NextNumber.v = BLANKNUM()
232 ◄──────────────────RETURN TRUE
233 │  │    │  └─ENDSWITCH
234 │  │    └─ENDSWITCH
235 ◄────────RETURN TRUE
236 │
237 │    ┌─CASE action.a = "arriveadd":    ; Arrived in the add mode.
238 │    │    ;You have inserted, but not attempted to post, a new record.
239 │    │
240 │    │    ; This example continues the previous and illustrates how
241 │    │    ; these procedures can contain branches that are table specific.
242 │    │    ; The first inserts the next customer number into the new customer
243 │    │    ; record. The second example increments a line item number
244 │    │    ; automatically in an embedded invoice item table ("Invitem").
245 │    ├─SWITCH
246 │    ├─CASE TABLE() = "Customer" AND wpForm.a= "3":  ; If nextnumber table is present
247 │    │    ┌─IF NextNumber.v <> "Error" THEN
248 │    │    │    [Cust ID] = NextNumber.v          ; Place the field value.
249 │    │    │   ┌─IF NOT ISBLANK([Cust ID]) THEN    ; Number was filled in.
250 │    │    │   └   MOVETO [Init]                   ; Move off the field.
251 │    │    │   └─ENDIF
252 │    │    ├─ELSE
253 ◄───────────────RETURN FALSE
254 │    │    └─ENDIF
255 │    │        ; At times you may want to keep the user from changing the [Cust ID]
256 │    │        ; number once it has been assigned.  If so, issue the next command:
257 │    │        ;
258 │    │        ;              wpTableRights.a = "U"
259 │    │        ;
260 │    │        ; to override the "I" or "E" previously assigned. If you do this,
261 │    │        ; remember to set the rights back to normal in both the "DepartAdd"
262 │    │        ; and "CancelAdd" case statements or else the user will not be
263 │    │        ; allowed to add any other new records.
264 │    │
265 │    ├─CASE TABLE() = "Invitem" : ; Increment the line number for new record.
266 │    │        MOVETO [line #]
267 │    │        v = IMAGECMAX()
268 │    │    ┌─IF v = "Error" THEN
269 │    │    │    v = 1                    ; No line items.
270 │    │    ├─ELSE
271 │    │    │    v =INT(v)+1              ; Just to be sure it's an integer.
272 │    │    └─ENDIF
273 │    │        [] = v                    ; Make the assignment.
274 │    │        ; If you are using the original release of Paradox 3.0 in a
275 │    │        ; *MULTIRECORD* form, you'll need to include the following
276 │    │        ; statement due to a problem with WAIT RECORD that was fixed
277 │    │        ; in release 3.01:
278 │    │        ; SETRECORDPOSITION RECNO() 1
279 │    └─ENDSWITCH
280 ◄────────RETURN TRUE
281 │  │
282 │  ├─CASE action.a = "prepcanceladd":  ; Cancel the adding of a record.
283 │  │    ; You have inserted a new record and you are about to delete it.
284 │  │
285 ◄──────RETURN TRUE
286 │  │
287 │  ├─CASE action.a = "canceladd":        ; Add was cancelled.
```

```
288 |   |   ; You have deleted the record.
289 |   |   ; Return TRUE if it is okay to return to view mode,
290 |   |   ; FALSE if you need to keep the user in Add mode.
291 ◄──────RETURN TRUE
292 |   |
293 |   ┌──CASE action.a = "departadd":      ; About to depart add mode.
294 |   |   ; You have inserted and posted a new record.
295 |   |   ;
296 |   |   ; If you would like to have another blank record appear after
297 |   |   ; the current record is saved, you can set
298 |   |   ;
299 |   |   ;   wpUntilBuffer.v="Ins"     ; case sensitive
300 |   |   ;
301 |   |   ; here, so that when this procedure returns to WaitPlus.v, it acts
302 |   |   ; as if the user pressed the [Ins] key from the keyboard to open a
303 |   |   ; new record. This can be used when the user has many records
304 |   |   ; to enter at one time (without having to press [Ins] for each one).
305 |   |   ; When the user wants to stop adding records, he or she would simply
306 |   |   ; press [F10] {CancelAdd} {Yes}, and the current blank record is
307 |   |   ; removed.
308 ◄──────RETURN TRUE
309 |   |
310 |   ┌──CASE action.a = "prepedit":     ; Prepare for edit.
311 |   |   ; You have selected an existing record to edit.
312 |   |
313 |   |   ; Here you might want to change wpTableRights.a to "U" so that only
314 |   |   ; non-key fields can be edited.
315 ◄──────RETURN TRUE
316 |   |
317 |   ┌──CASE action.a = "arriveedit":   ; Arrived in the edit mode.
318 |   |   ; You are editing the current record.
319 |   |
320 ◄──────RETURN TRUE
321 |   |
322 |   ┌──CASE action.a = "prepcanceledit":
323 |   |   ; You have chosen to cancel the edit.
324 |   |
325 |   |   ; This action can be disallowed with a RETURN FALSE. Thus
326 |   |   ; the user would be required to add the record once entry
327 |   |   ; was begun.
328 ◄──────RETURN TRUE
329 |   |
330 |   ┌──CASE action.a = "canceledit":   ; Edit was cancelled.
331 |   |   ; You have cancelled the changes (if any) made to the
332 |   |   ; current record.
333 |   |
334 |   |   ; Return TRUE if it is okay to return to view mode,
335 |   |   ; FALSE if you need to keep the user in Edit mode.
336 ◄──────RETURN TRUE
337 |   |
338 |   ┌──CASE action.a = "departedit":   ; About to depart from edit.
339 |   |   ; You have completed the editing of a record.
340 |   |
341 |   |   ; Record level validity can be checked prior to the depart.
342 |   |   ; For example, you can cross-check and recalculate values
343 |   |   ; on the entire record, displaying messages and returning FALSE
344 |   |   ; if the appropriate fields are not valid.
345 ◄──────RETURN TRUE
```

```
346
347     ┌──CASE action.a = "prepdelete":    ; Prepare for delete.
348     │    ; You are about to delete a record.
349
350     │    ; For example, you might copy the current record to an array
351     │    ; and rework calculations based on the values in "departdelete."
352     │    ; You might also check to see that the record is not in use
353     │    ; by another table.
354 ◄───────RETURN TRUE
355
356     ┌──CASE action.a = "okdelete":     ; Delete has been okayed.
357     │    ; You have authorized the current record to be deleted.
358
359     │    ; If the master record has dependent details, they should be
360     │    ; deleted first.
361 ◄───────RETURN TRUE
362
363     ┌──CASE action.a = "departdelete":  ; Record has been deleted.
364     │    ; You have just deleted a record.
365
366     │    ; If the master record maintains a calculated total of detail
367     │    ; values, the total should be updated.
368 ◄───────RETURN TRUE
369
370     ┌──CASE action.a = "departwait":    ; Processing that occurs after user
371     │    ; presses [Esc] from view mode, or if
372     │    ; the setup procedure reported an error.
373     │    ; You are about to leave this call to WaitPlus.v.
374
375     │    ; The code below is typical of a "DepartWait" routine. You may want to
376     │    ; add some other code if special processing is needed. If a TRUE is
377     │    ; returned, WaitPlus.v is exited. With the following code, we are also
378     │    ; attempting to account for any problems that may have occurred in
379     │    ; WaitPlusSetup.l
380     │    Working.u("")
381     ┌─IF LOCKSTATUS(wpTable.a,"Any") > 0 THEN  ; The table lock was successful.
382     │  ┌─IF wpForm.a = "O" AND wpRightsList.a <> "R" THEN
383     │  │    UNLOCK wpTable.a PWL
384     │  ├─ELSE
385     │  │    UNLOCK wpTable.a PFL
386     │  └─ENDIF
387     └─ENDIF
388     ┌─IF IMAGETYPE() = "Display" THEN   ; So that if the table was never placed,
389     │  ;                                ; we won't get a script error.
390     │    IMAGERIGHTS                    ; Make sure Do_It! is possible.
391     └─ENDIF
392     ┌─IF SYSMODE() = "CoEdit" THEN      ; Traps for a possible problem with
393     │  ;                                ; CoEditkey not being available.
394     │    DO_IT!
395     └─ENDIF
396     ┌─IF ISASSIGNED(wpTableName.a) THEN
397     │    ; The table must be on the workspace because wpTableName.a is set by
398     │    ; WaitPlusInfo.u, which means WaitPlus actually arrived on the table.
399     │    CLEARIMAGE
400     └─ENDIF
401 ◄───────RETURN TRUE
402     ├──OTHERWISE:  ; Call to WaitPlus action was NOT one of the case statements.
403     │    ; Return a message.
```

```
404  | |          TopMsg.u("Call to WaitPlusAction.l(\""+action.a+"\") unknown",
405  | |                    "Press any key",1000)
406 ◄————————RETURN TRUE
407  |  └ENDSWITCH
408  └ENDPROC
409
410    WRITELIB libname.a  WaitPlusAction.l
411    RELEASE PROCS       WaitPlusAction.l
412
413    ;--------------------------------------------------------------------------
414    ; WaitPlusLookupAction.l()
415    ;
416    ; Normally, when [F1] is pressed, "preplookup" below simply returns
417    ; True. However, you can easily have the "preplookup" case statement
418    ; run another proc that does something special.  For example, you might
419    ; move to another table already placed on the workspace and call
420    ; LookupSelect.n (found in wwputil1.sc) to select from a table that is
421    ; not linked by a TableLookup ValCheck.  If you don't want
422    ; WaitPlusLookup.u to continue with its normal routine, return FALSE
423    ; and you'll be returned to the data table.
424  ┌PROC WaitPlusLookupAction.l(action.a)
425  |    action.a=LOWER(action.a)
426  |  ┌SWITCH
427  |  ├—CASE action.a="preplookup":
428  |  |     ; You might, for example, need to some special field level help
429  |  |     ; for certain fields in an "Invoice" table.  You can create a
430  |  |     ; procedure called InvoiceHelp.l() that checks the current field
431  |  |     ; name, and invokes an alternate help procedure (perhaps performing
432  |  |     ; calculations).  If InvoiceHelp.l() returns a FALSE to the example
433  |  |     ; below, WaitPlusLookup.u() (found in the WWPCore.SC) will simply
434  |  |     ; return to the table.  If you want normal table help to occur
435  |  |     ; (if available), make sure that "preplookup" returns a value of TRUE.
436  |  |   ┌SWITCH
437  |  |   ├—CASE wpTableName.a="Invoice":
438  |  |   |     l = InvoiceHelp.l()
439 ◄—————————————RETURN l
440  | |      └ENDSWITCH
441 ◄————————RETURN TRUE
442  | ├—CASE action.a = "arrivelookup":  ; Perhaps move to a certain record value.
443 ◄————————RETURN TRUE
444  | ├—CASE action.a = "departlookup" :  ; Any processing before returning to data
445  | |     ;                             ; table and filling in lookup value(s).
446 ◄————————RETURN TRUE
447  | ├—CASE action.a = "lookupreturn" :
448  | |     ; Back in data table...possibly issue a movement or resync command.
449 ◄————————RETURN TRUE
450  |  └ENDSWITCH
451  └ENDPROC
452    WRITELIB libname.a WaitPlusLookupAction.l
453    RELEASE PROCS       WaitPlusLookupAction.l
454
455    ;--------------------------------------------------------------------------
456    ; WaitPlusOkRecord.l()
457    ; This next procedure is called when a user presses [F2] to either
458    ; end the edit of an existing record or to finish adding a new record.
459    ; With it, you can decide if the user has completed all the necessary
460    ; fields.  If it returns TRUE, then the [F2] is accepted and the calling
461    ; procedure goes on to check for duplicate key fields (if appropriate).
```

```
462   ; If WaitPlusOkRecord.l returns FALSE, the user is returned to the record
463   ; to fix any problems. You should inform them through messages.
464   ;
465   ; Although you might change the body of the procedure to reflect your
466   ; programming style, the example below uses two variables, incomplete.l
467   ; and Error.a, to control decision making.  The reason we used
468   ; incomplete.l rather than ok.l, is that you typically would want to see
469   ; if certain fields were left blank. Thus code like:
470   ;
471   ;     incomplete.l = ISBLANK([Customer#]) OR ISBLANK([Phone#])
472   ;
473   ; is easier to write than
474   ;
475   ;     ok.l = NOT ISBLANK([Customer#]) AND NOT ISBLANK([Phone#])
476   ;
477   ; In addition, it allows you to easily attach an error message and
478   ; move to the field that is missing.
479   ;
480   ; This procedure is also a good place to add record level calculations.
481   ; For example, if the record is an invoice line item, and all the fields
482   ; were filled in properly, you might want to calculate:
483   ;
484   ;         [Extended Price] = [Quant]*[Price]
485   ;
486   ; Record level calculations can also be done at "departadd" or "departedit"
487   ; in the WaitPlusAction.l procedure, but placing them here has a few
488   ; advantages. You might need, for example, to calculate extended price and
489   ; compare it to the customer's credit limit. If it exceeeds the limit, you
490   ; might put up a menu for authorization, or return them to the record to
491   ; correct the error.
492   ;
493  ┌PROC WaitPlusOkrecord.l()
494  │   ; RETURNS     True  If record is okay, False otherwise.
495  │   PRIVATE incomplete.l, Error.a
496  │   incomplete.l = FALSE   ; Initialize variable. Assume record is okay.
497  │   error.a=""
498  │  ┌SWITCH
499  │  ├──CASE wpTableName.a="Bookord":
500  │  │    ; In this case, if [Quant] or [Item #] is blank, we'll reject the
501  │  │    ; [F2] and put up the standard message that the record is not yet
502  │  │    ; complete.
503  │  │    incomplete.l = IsBlank([Quant]) OR IsBlank([Item #])
504  │  │
505  │  ├──CASE wpTableName.a="Customer":
506  │  │    ; In this case, if the [Cust ID] field is empty, we'll put up a
507  │  │    ; custom message and move the cursor to the [Cust ID] field.
508  │  │    incomplete.l = IsBlank([Cust ID])
509  │  │    Error.a = "You need to enter a Customer ID"
510  │  │   ┌IF incomplete.l THEN
511  │  │   │  MOVETO [Cust ID]   ; So that the user can make corrections.
512  │  │   └ENDIF
513  │  ├──OTHERWISE: incomplete.l = FALSE
514  │  └ENDSWITCH
515  │
516  │  ┌IF NOT incomplete.l THEN  ; The record is okay.
517 ◄├──RETURN TRUE
518  │  ├ELSE
519  │  │  ┌IF error.a = "" THEN    ; Use the standard error message
```

```
520  │ │ │    TopMsg.u("The record is not yet complete", "C", 0)
521  │ │ ├─ELSE                    ; Put custom error message on the screen.
522  │ │ │    TopMsg.u(error.a, "", 0)
523  │ │ └─ENDIF
524  ◄─────────RETURN FALSE        ; The record is not okay.
525  │ └─ENDIF
526  └─ENDPROC
527  WRITELIB libname.a WaitPlusOkRecord.l
528  RELEASE PROCS      WaitPlusOkRecord.l
529
530  ;--------------------------------------------------------------------
531  ; WaitPlusMoreMenu.u()
532  ; When the user presses [F10], all three WaitPlus modes
533  ; ("View", "Edit", "Add") present a menu whose last choice is {More}.
534  ; This is where you might add subordinate menus.
535  ;
536  ; This menu does not have to be static, but can be controlled by
537  ; a switch which evaluates special conditions (quite often
538  ; based on wpMode.a and wpTableName.a). This allows you to present
539  ; different menus of available tasks.
540  ;
541  ; You might use these menus to allow users to:
542  ;
543  ;           1) Perform extensive calculations.
544  ;           2) Fill in fields not normally accessible on the form.
545  ;           3) Print the current record.
546  ;
547  ; You might have want to make the current menu reflect the current
548  ; FIELD() or USERNAME().
549
550  ┌─PROC WaitPlusMoreMenu.u()
551  │   PRIVATE choice.a
552  ├─SWITCH
553  ├──CASE wpMode.a = "View" AND wpTableName.a = "Customer":
554  │     ; A subordinate Customer menu that only appears in "View" mode.
555  │     SHOWMENU
556  │       "StatusChange"  : "Mark this customer as Active or Inactive",
557  │       "PrintCustomer" : "Print the current record"
558  │     TO choice.a
559  │   ┌─SWITCH
560  │   ├──CASE choice.a = "StatusChange":
561  │   │     ; For example, place code to fill in whether or not the client
562  │   │     ; is "active."
563  │   ├──CASE choice.a = "PrintCustomer":
564  │   │     ; Output a report based on the current record. You might first
565  │   │     ; insert some code here to make sure that the printer is ready
566  │   │     ; and then use one of the following techniques:
567  │   │     ;
568  │   │     ; 1) Create an Answer table with the proper report:
569  │   │     ;    COPYTOARRAY temp.r  ; Save the current record values.
570  │   │     ;    DO_IT!              ; End the CoEdit Session.
571  │   │     ;    CREATE "Answer" LIKE "Customer"
572  │   │     ;    isformview.l = ISFORMVIEW()
573  │   │     ;    CoEdit "Answer"     ; Place the table on the workspace.
574  │   │     ;    COPYFROMARRAY temp.r
575  │   │     ;    DO_IT!              ; End Coedit mode.
576  │   │     ;    CLEARIMAGE          ; Remove the answer table from the workspace.
577  │   │     ;    MOVETO "Customer"
```

```
578  |  |  |       ;       COPYREPORT "Customer" "1" "Answer" "1"
579  |  |  |       ;       REPORT "Answer" "1"
580  |  |  |       ;       COEDITKEY           ; This is CRITICAL because you need to reinstate
581  |  |  |       ;                           ; CoEdit mode for WaitPlus.v to work properly
582  |  |  |       ;                           ; when this procedure is over.
583  |  |  |       ;       IF isformview.l THEN
584  |  |  |       ;           FORMKEY
585  |  |  |       ;       ENDIF
586  |  |  |       ;
587  |  |  |       ; 2) Use a technique similar to the one described above, except
588  |  |  |       ;       issue a QUERY to create the answer table with the record
589  |  |  |       ;       to use for report.  This technique is especially useful when you
590  |  |  |       ;       don't want to print a report for a single record, but instead
591  |  |  |       ;       want to print all records with the same ZipCode as the current
592  |  |  |       ;       record.  You'll have all the capabilities of the query mechanism
593  |  |  |       ;       at your disposal.  Remember to remove the query image and return
594  |  |  |       ;       to Coedit mode in the proper form when you are done.
595  |  |  |       ;
596  |  |  |       ; 3) Use a COPYTOARRAY, combined with PRINT staements to send
597  |  |  |       ;       the report to the printer.  This technique allows you to stay
598  |  |  |       ;       in CoEdit mode, and although sometimes the code may be difficult,
599  |  |  |       ;       the technique allows you to do very sophisticated print formatting.
600  |  |  └ENDSWITCH
601  |  ├OTHERWISE :
602  |  |       MESSAGE "No more choices currently available..."
603  |  |       BEEP
604  |  |       SLEEP 2000
605  |  └ENDSWITCH
606  └ENDPROC
607  WRITELIB libname.a WaitPlusMoreMenu.u
608  RELEASE PROCS      WaitPlusMoreMenu.u
609
610  ;--------------------------------------------------------------------------
611  ; HelpData.u()
612  ; This procedure is usually customized by the programmer to provide help
613  ; screens for individual tables.  It is called by the HelpTable.u()
614  ; procedure found in the WWPUTIL.SC, when the user makes the {Data} choice
615  ; from the Help menu.
616  ;
617  ; Although one way to use the proc is to make the help screen sensitive to
618  ; the table name, it is often useful to make the switch more specific,
619  ; using other variables (e.g. to wpMode.a or USERNAME()).
620  ;
621  ; The examples below demonstrate both single and multi-screen help text
622  ; using a variety of factors to determine what screen should be presented.
623  ; You can modify the code to change the color of the screens presented,
624  ; or use any other technique you've developed for displaying information
625  ; to the user.
626
627  ┌PROC HelpData.u()
628  |   ; You place any logic necessary to determine the help text to show.
629  |   PRIVATE choice.a
630  |   CLEAR
631  |   @2,0 ?? FILL("\196",80)        ; A divider line across the screen at row 2.
632  ├SWITCH
633  ├CASE LOWER(wpTableDesc.a) = "our favorite customers":   ; Picked up from the alias.
634  |   ┌WHILE TRUE                                          ; Need more than one screen.
635  |   |    @3,0 CLEAR EOS
```

```
636  │  │      TEXT
637  │  │      This would be the help screen for the customer table
638  │  │      ENDTEXT
639  │  │      SHOWMENU
640  │  │        "Next-Screen":"Show the next help screen",
641  │  │        "Return":"Return to the help menu"
642  │  │      TO choice.a
643  │  │  ┌─IF choice.a = "Return" OR choice.a = "Esc" THEN
644  │  ◄─────QUITLOOP
645  │  │  └─ENDIF
646  │  │      @3,0 CLEAR EOS
647  │  │      TEXT
648  │  │
649  │  │              Second screen of help for the customer table.
650  │  │
651  │  │      ENDTEXT
652  │  │      SHOWMENU
653  │  │        "Previous-Screen" : "Show the previous help screen",
654  │  │        "Return" : "Return to the help menu"
655  │  │      TO choice.a
656  │  │  ┌─IF choice.a = "Return" OR choice.a = "Esc" THEN
657  │  ◄─────QUITLOOP
658  │  │  └─ENDIF
659  │  └─ENDWHILE
660  ├──CASE TABLE() = "Bookord":
661  │      TEXT
662  │
663  │              Help screen for bookord table.
664  │
665  │      ENDTEXT
666  ├──CASE UserName() = "Scott" :   ; Ignore wpTableDesc.a.
667  │      ; Put up special message.
668  │      TEXT
669  │
670  │              Hello Scott, nice to see you again.
671  │              Too bad there is no more help.
672  │
673  │      ENDTEXT
674  ├──OTHERWISE:                    ; Proc can't find an appropriate CASE.
675  │      TEXT
676  │
677  │              No help currently available
678  │
679  │      ENDTEXT
680  └─ENDSWITCH
681 └─ENDPROC
682  WRITELIB libname.a  HelpData.u
683  RELEASE PROCS       HelpData.u
```

# Part Four

# Chapter 20

# Paradox 3.5 Features

## 20.1 ALL PC's ARE NOT CREATED EQUAL

In September 1990, Borland released Paradox 3.5 and an entirely new product, Paradox SQL Link, which provides access to data in SQL Databases.

On the surface, Paradox 3.5 appears to add little to Paradox. The limit on the number of embedded tables in a form has been increased from five to nine; you can place variables and a restricted set of PAL functions in calculated fields in forms and reports; you can now recall and edit a {MiniScript} or {Value} selection in the PAL Menu. Error procedures no longer need to be explicitly read–they can be acccessed via AUTOLIB. There are nice additions that affect interactive use, like incremental letter menu selections. Yet these changes are minor compared to improvements made behind the scenes.

Release 3.5 improved the underlying core code of Paradox, greatly affecting the results of both interactive use and PAL programming. Two new Borland technologies, VROOMM and TURBODRIVE, are incorporated in this release. First introduced in Quattro Pro, Virtual Run-Time Object Oriented Memory Manager (VROOMM) enables Paradox 3.5 to swap code and data space in memory. TURBODRIVE employs a DOS extender that lets Paradox recognize and use the type of processor and available memory installed. On 286, 386 or 486 PCs with one megabyte or more of extended memory, Paradox will run in the 16Mb contiguous address space provided by the CPU's protected mode. The performance differences can be dramatic with the use of large tables.

The increased memory available with Paradox 3.5 allowed Borland to implement Paradox SQL Link, which installs into the existing Paradox menu structure. Paradox SQL Link requires from 1Mb to 1.5Mb of extended memory to run.

## 20.2 DOCUMENTATION

With this new release, the Paradox documentation has been revised to correct all known or reported typos. If you have upgraded from an earlier release, we recommend you reread certain sections of the manuals. Here are a few important changes:

- The Performance and Resource Tuning chapter of the PAL User's Guide has been rewritten to better explain the control you have over memory management.
- The explanation of the swapping mechanism now falls in line with the explanation in this book.
- The Advanced Topics chapter of the Paradox User's Guide contains a particularly valuable section entitled "How Paradox Uses Memory." Read it to help understand the difference between real and protected mode operation.
- The Paradox 3.5 documentation also contains a more complete explanation of the command line options.

## 20.3 NEW OR CHANGED PAL COMMANDS & FUNCTIONS

Paradox 3.5 made relatively few changes to PAL. In total, two commands and three new functions were added. In addition, seven existing commands and two functions were changed. See Table 20-1 for a complete listing of these commands and functions. Some of the changes to the manuals simply document previously inadequately documented features such as the UNDO and the RESYNCKEY commands. Other changes legitimized the use of undocumented features of Paradox 3.0.

---

**Table 20-1    Paradox 3.5 PAL Changes & Additions**

COPYFROMARRAY    CALCDEBUG
RUN              SAVETABLES
SETSWAP
SHOWARRAY
SHOWFILES
SHOWMENU
SHOWTABLES
ERRORCODE
MEMLEFT()
FORMTYPE()
RECORDSTATUS()
RMEMLEFT()

---

## PAL Commands

### CALCDEBUG: Assign A Value To Display For Invalid Calculated Data

```
CALCDEBUG {ON | OFF} String
```

If you have entered a calculated field in a form or report, and for some reason the calculation is incomplete or invalid, Paradox allows you to fill the field with a message. For instance, if your calculation is

```
"Your name is " + UserName.a
```

and you have not yet assigned UserName.a, you could issue

```
CALCDEBUG ON "User name not assigned yet"
```

Unless you've specified otherwise in the CUSTOM script, the default value is

```
CALCDEBUG OFF ""
```

Which does not display any message if the calculation contains invalid (or missing) data; it leaves the field blank.

### COPYFROMARRAY: Copy Array Values Into The Current Record

```
COPYFROMARRAY ArrayName
```

Paradox 3.5 now allows the use of COPYFROMARRAY while in a linked detail table in a multitable form, provided that you don't attempt to change the linked key field values. If you attempt to change the linked key values, a run error is tripped. Paradox 3.0 did not allow COPYFROMARRAY at all in linked tables. See the CopyFromArray3.u() procedure in wwpUtil2.sc in the WaitPlus code listings.

### RUN: Run A Dos Program

```
RUN [BIG] [SLEEP Number] [NOREFRESH] [NORESTORE] [NOSHELL]
DOSCommand
```

With Paradox 3.5, RUN has an NOSHELL option. RUN normally loads a copy of COMMAND.COM to run an external program. If you use the NOSHELL option, COMMAND.COM is not loaded. This can be helpful in two ways:

- More memory is available to the called program.
- If your external program sets the DOS ERRORLEVEL, the ERROR-LEVEL value is assigned to RETVAL. By evaluating RETVAL on returning to Paradox, you can determine how your program terminated and how best to proceed.

The only disadvantage to the NOSHELL approach is that you cannot use it to run batch files. If you need to run a batch file, don't use NOSHELL, and Paradox will load the needed COMMAND.COM.

Because of the way Paradox 3.5 uses memory, RUN will sometimes automatically execute the RUN BIG command. Unfortunately, though Paradox will always free as much memory as it did under Paradox 3.0, you may have no way of knowing how long it will take to actually run your command line. Don't be surprised if Paradox gives you more memory than you've asked for. Refer to page 265 for a fuller explanation of the RUN command.

## SAVETABLES: Flush The Table Buffers To Disk

SAVETABLES

The Swap Manager's table buffers are used to read and write table data. Because the buffers are not write-through, some data often exists only in memory and hasn't been written out to disk. The SAVETABLES command is used to explicitly flush all buffers currently in the Swap Manager's table buffers (it does not flush the cache, which is automatically write-through).

Like the RESET command, SAVETABLES will force all the buffers out to disk. Unlike RESET, SAVETABLES does not release locks, and retains all PRIVTABLES settings.

On networks, SAVETABLES is less necessary because tables are written to disk immediately. On single user installations, you might use SAVETABLES after an EMPTY command to make sure that the empty table is forced out of memory to disk. In the event of an unforeseen error (like a power failure) a table thus cleared from memory will not be lost.

## UNTIL..KEYTO And The SHOW Commands

The SHOW commands (SHOWARRAY, SHOWMENU, SHOWFILES, and SHOWTABLES) had an option called UNTIL...KEYTO that was (nearly) removed from the documentation in Paradox 3.0. Although its syntax was present in the help screens, UNTIL..KEYTO was officially "unsupported" until Release 3.5.

UNTIL...KEYTO adds a clause to the SHOW commands which allows a user to press keys that do not represent one of the choices on the menu. UNTIL...KEYTO is similar to the UNTIL list in the WAIT command, allowing any one of a set of specified keys to exit the menu. Unlike the WAIT command, however, the UNTIL feature of the SHOW commands is optional.

UNTIL...KEYTO can be used for conditional branching on menus, or to hide special menu choices. A typical use might be to assign the [F1] key to give an explanation of the currently highlighted menu choice. A detailed discussion of each of the SHOW commands is in the examples section on page 183.

```
SHOWARRAY Array1 Array2 [UNTIL KeyCodeList  [KEYTO VarName1] ]
[DEFAULT choice] TO VarName2

SHOWFILES [NOEXT] DOSPath Prompt
[UNTIL KeyCodeList [KEYTO VarName1] ] [DEFAULT choice] TO VarName2

SHOWMENU MenuItemList [UNTIL KeyCodeList  [KEYTO VarName1] ]
[DEFAULT choice] TO VarName2

SHOWTABLES DOSPath Prompt [UNTIL KeyCodeList  [KEYTO VarName1] ]
[DEFAULT choice] TO VarName2
```

Using the UNTIL...KEYTO clause for the first time can be confusing. The SHOWMENU example below presents three menu choices and displays a special help screen for each of the choices when the user presses [F1] while the choice is highlighted. The UNTIL...KEYTO clause also hides a special utility menu accessed by with [Ctrl U].

### Listing 20.1 SHOWMENU.L7

```
CLEAR
WHILE TRUE
  @ 24,0 CLEAR EOL
  STYLE REVERSE
  ?? FORMAT("W80,AC", "[F1] gets help for highlighted choice")
  SHOWMENU
  "Files" : "Menu of available tables",
  "Reports" : "Menu of available reports",
  "Quit" : "Exit this menu"
  UNTIL "F1", 21  ;  21 is [Ctrl U]
  KEYTO Key.v
  TO choice.a
    ; First we have to see if the user pressed a key on the UNTIL list.
```

```
IF Key.v = FALSE THEN
  ; No key on the keycode list was pressed, normal switch
  SWITCH
    CASE choice.a = "Esc" or choice.a ="Quit" :
      RETURN
    CASE choice.a = "Files":   ; The user selected Files
      MESSAGE "This choice normally brings up a file menu"
    CASE choice.a = "Reports":  ; The user selected Reports
      MESSAGE "This choice normally brings up a report menu"
ELSE
  ; Key.v is not FALSE, so a key on the UNTIL's KeyCodeList
  ; list must have been pressed
  SWITCH
    CASE Key.v = "F1":
      SWITCH
        CASE choice.a = "Files":  ; [F1] while highlighting "Files"
          MESSAGE "This choice could invoke a help proc for Files"
        CASE choice.a = "Reports":  ;[F1] while highlighting "Reports"
          MESSAGE "This choice would invoke a help proc for Reports"
      ENDSWITCH
    CASE Key.v = 21:  [Ctrl U]
      MESSAGE "[Ctrl U] could bring up the hidden utility menu"
  ENDSWITCH
ENDIF
ENDWHILE
```

You need to pay attention to a few things when using the UNTIL...KEYTO feature of the SHOW commands:

- If the user presses a key in the KeyCodeList, the variable defined in the UNTIL...KEYTO clause (Key.v) gets set to the value of the key pressed. Also, RETVAL is set to FALSE because the user did not make a selection from one of the choices on the list. The variable assigned to the TO menu choice variable (in this case, choice.a) is given the value of the currently highlighted menu choice when the key was pressed.

- If the user ends the menu by making a selection that is not on the KeyCodeList then the UNTIL...KEYTO variable (Key.v) is set to FALSE and there two additional things to consider:

  1) If the user had pressed [Esc] then choice.a is set to "Esc" and RETVAL is set to FALSE

  2) If the user made a menu selection, then choice.a is set to the selection and RETVAL is set to TRUE.

Now let's change the code slightly by adding a few more keys to the UNTIL list and a few more messages:

### Listing 20.2 SHOWMENU.L8

```
CLEAR
WHILE TRUE
 @ 24,0 CLEAR EOL
 STYLE REVERSE
 ?? FORMAT("W80,AC", "[F1] gets help for highlighted choice")
 SHOWMENU
 "Files" : "Menu of available tables",
 "Reports" : "Menu of available reports",
 "Quit" : "Exit this menu"
 UNTIL "F1", 21, "Esc", "F"  ;  21 is [Ctrl U]
 KEYTO Key.v
 TO choice.a
  ; First we have to see if the user pressed a key on the UNTIL list.
 IF Key.v = FALSE THEN
   ; No key on the keycode list was pressed, normal switch
   SWITCH
     CASE choice.a = "Esc" or choice.a ="Quit" :
       RETURN
     CASE choice.a = "Files":
       MESSAGE "This choice normally brings up a file menu"
     CASE choice.a = "Reports":
       MESSAGE "This choice normally brings up a report menu"
   ENDSWITCH
 ELSE
 ; Either "F1" or [Ctrl U] was pressed
   SWITCH
     CASE Key.v = "F1":
       SWITCH
         CASE choice.a = "Files":
           MESSAGE "This choice would invoke a help procedure for Files"
         CASE choice.a = "Reports":
           MESSAGE "This choice would invoke a help proc for Reports"
         OTHERWISE:
           MESSAGE "You pressed [F1] on the ",choice.a, " selection"
       ENDSWITCH
     CASE Key.v = 21:
       MESSAGE "You pressed [Ctrl U] which could invoke a utility menu"
     OTHERWISE:   ; demonstration purposes only
       MESSAGE "Choice.a= ",choice.a, " Key.v=", Key.v," RETVAL=",RETVAL
   ENDSWITCH
 ENDIF
ENDWHILE
```

If the user presses [Esc], while highlighting "Files", a message will come up that says

```
Choice.a=Files  Key.v=Esc  RETVAL=FALSE
```

because we placed "Esc" on the UNTIL list, and the list is searched before the menu choices. If the user presses a lower case "f" to select the file menu we'll get the message

```
"This choice normally brings up a file menu"
```

because Paradox is taking that as a normal menu selection (which is not case sensitive). However, if the user presses an upper case "F" (which is on the UNTIL list) we'll see:

```
Choice.a=Files  Key.v=F  RETVAL=FALSE
```

The normal "Files" selection has not been made because the UNTIL list's "F" took precedence. The choice.a variable will be set to the current menu choice.

So, although some programmers like to put "Esc" in the KeyCodeList, we don't find it particularly necessary. Keep in mind that if you put alphabetic characters in the UNTIL's keycode list, they are case sensitive (as they are in the WAIT command).

### TOQPRO: Invoke Quattro Pro version 2.0 from Paradox

```
TOQPRO
```

If you have started Paradox with the -QPRO option enabled, the TOQPRO command will switch out of Paradox and load Quattro Pro. In order to use the TOQPRO command, Paradox must be started with

PARADOX -QPRO [FileName MacroName /Options]

Note that in this case the square brackets are part of the call syntax.

# PAL Functions

### ERRORCODE

The error mechanism has been updated in 3.5 so that it can take advantage of some of the Code Pool memory. See the 3.5 memory management discussions for additional information about the low memory warning and code pool invasion.

```
ERRORCODES new to 3.5
   44   Low Memory warning
```

```
ERRORCODES possible if SQL Link is installed
1000  General SQL Error, use SQLERRORMESSAGE to return the error
1001  Network error
1002  Deadlock on server
1003  User abort  [Ctrl Break]
1004  Not enough memory to complete operation
1005  Communication error
1006  Connection failed
1007  Insufficient access privileges or incompatible locks
1008  Object already exists
1009  Object name invalid
1010  General create error
1011  Database or disk full
1012  Object does not exist
1013  Column type or usage invalid
1014  Remote key violations (SQL...ENDSQL only)
1015  Syntax error (SQL...ENDSQL only)
1016  Copy failed
1017  Number of authorized users exceeded
1018  Replica inconsistent with remote table
```

## FORMTYPE: What Kind Of Form Is This?

```
FORMTYPE (String)
```

| Form type | MultiRecord | Linked | Detail | DisplayOnly |
|---|---|---|---|---|
| Standard form or Multi table master | False | False | False | False |
| Multi-record or single | True | False | False | False |
| Unlinked detail | False | False | True | False |
| Display only master | False | False | False | True |
| Unlinked-Multi-record detail | True | False | True | False |
| Linked detail | False | True | True | False |
| Display-Only unlinked detail | False | False | True | True |
| Multi-record linked detail | True | True | True | False |
| Multirecord unlinked detail, displayonly | True | False | True | True |
| Linked detail, display only | False | True | True | True |

You'll note that there is no way to determine if you are in a multitable master with linked detail records (as opposed to a master with unlinked detail forms). If you need to only know if the form has any embedded forms, use:

```
ISMULTIFORM(TABLE(),FORM())
```

If this statement returns TRUE, then the current form is a multitable master. However, at this point you still don't know if the detail tables are linked or unlinked. To determine if the detail tables are linked, you can issue a RESYNCKEY and evaluate WINDOW() to see if Paradox is complaining about not being in a linked form. For example:

```
RESYNCKEY
LinkedMaster.l=WINDOW()="Only relevant when editing master table in a multitable form"
```

which sets LinkedMaster.l to TRUE if the RESYNCKEY was appropriate or FALSE if it was inappropriate because the cursor is not in a linked master form.

## RECORDSTATUS: What Is The Current Record Status?

```
RECORDSTATUS (String)
```

String is the type of condition you want to test for: "New", "Locked", "Modified", or "KeyViol".

This function only works in CoEdit mode. The following table shows the possible RECORDSTATUS() values for each option, for typical record states.

| Record Status | New | Locked | Modified | KeyViol |
|---|---|---|---|---|
| New, blank record | True | False | False | False |
| New record after input | True | False | True | False |
| New record with key-violation after attempting to post | True | True | True | True |
| Existing record, unchanged | False | False | False | False |
| Existing record, locked but unchanged | False | True | False | False |
| Existing record modified | False | True | True | False |
| Existing record, modified, key-violation while attempting to post | False | True | True | True |

When you insert a new record. Paradox doesn't consider it to be part of the table until it is posted. Until posted, RECORDSTATUS("New") is always TRUE. As soon as you enter data into the new record it s considered "Modified". This occurs even if you blank the fields that you entered, so that the record appears to be blank. Therefore, RECORDSTATUS("Modified") returns TRUE.

Under no circumstance is a locked record considered "New"; if it is locked, it must already exist in the table, so "Locked" and "New" are mutually exclusive. If an existing record has been locked, it does not necessarily mean that it has been modified. However, if it has been modified, it must be locked (either explicitly by you, or automatically by Paradox).

The tricky part comes with the "KeyViol" option. To state it simply: RECORDSTATUS("KeyViol") will return TRUE only when you are in the key conflict state. That is, only when Paradox is reporting that there is currently a conflicting key, and you can press [Alt K] to see the conflicting key or [Alt L] to lock and keep the current record. RECORDSTATUS("KeyViol") does not tell you if your key is unique and that the record will be able to post; it simply reports the current status of the record. If you are in the key violation state, RECORDSTATUS("KeyViol") returns TRUE whether you are on the record you've just entered (or changed the key of) or viewing the conflicting existing record. You have to keep track of where you are.

## Another Source Of Confusion

If the cursor is in a master record with linked detail records, RECORDSTATUS("KeyViol") will always return FALSE. This is because Paradox 3.01 and 3.5 do not let you get into the "KeyViol" state for a 1:1 or 1:Many form in the master record, and will not let you view or accept a conflicting key. This restriction prevents orphaning detail records if you attempt to overwrite a conflicting master's records. With these restrictions, Paradox simply informs you that there is a conflicting key, but does not put you into the "Key-Viol" state. RECORDSTATUS() is therefore working consistently, but perhaps not as you would expect.

Key violation checking under script control is a very complicated task in Paradox. Take a look at the OkKey35.l() procedure for examples of how to use RECORDSTATUS() and RESYNCKEY to safely determine if a key is unique. Although RECORDSTATUS() has no way of determining if the key values for the record have changed, the OkKey35.l() procedure demonstrates a workaround.

## RMEMLEFT: How Much Memory Is Available To PAL In The Code Pool?

```
RMEMLEFT()
```

The RMEMLEFT() function returns a number, the amount of memory available to be borrowed from the code pool. This reserved memory is 67Kb at startup, the difference between the 167Kb available in the code pool and the point slightly above the 96Kb resource limit point. You really only need to know the current RMEMLEFT() if you are in an ERRORPROC trying to deal with low memory. If you need to know the amount of code pool invasion from point to point, you could store RMEMLEFT() to a variable when you start your application and have your ERRORPROC check the current MEMLEFT() and RMEMLEFT() to decide how best to proceed. Sometimes, if there is still enough RMEMLEFT() available, it is best to call a subordinate procedure to handle an error. In other cases you might use SETSWAP or RELEASE VARS to gain some memory and take the strain off the code pool.

See the section on Paradox 3.5 memory management later in this chapter for a detailed explanation of code pool invasion.

## 20.4 PARADOX, PAL, & SQL LINK

The SQLINST.EXE program installs Paradox SQL Link and makes the folowing additions to the Paradox menu structure.

{Report} The Report menu allows a SQL Replica table to store a report. The report cannot be a multitable report; it must be single table based.

{Create} The CREATE command has an additional choice, either {Local} or {Remote}.

{Form} Although you can create a form for a replica table, it must be a single table form.

{Modify} {DataEntry} This selection can be done against a remote table but only with a single table form.

{Tools} The {Tools} menu contains the most additions. When you use {Tools} {Copy} to copy or {Tools} {Delete} to delete a table and its family, you specify whether the table is {Local} or {Remote}. The {Tools} {SQL} menu choices:

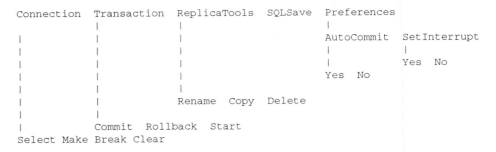

```
Connection  Transaction  ReplicaTools  SQLSave  Preferences
                 |            |                          |
     |           |            |            AutoCommit  SetInterrupt
     |           |            |                |            |
     |           |            |                |         Yes   No
     |           |            |             Yes   No
     |           |            |
     |           |         Rename  Copy  Delete
     |           |
     |        Commit  Rollback  Start
     |
 Select  Make  Break  Clear
```

In addition, the {Add}, {Empty} and {Protect} choices all work with replicas. Abbreviated menu commands that apply to SQL are

| | |
|---|---|
| ADD | Tools \| More \| Add |
| COPY | Tools \| Copy \| Table |
| CREATE | Create |
| DELETE | Tools \| Delete \| Table |
| EMPTY | Tools \| More \| Empty |
| PROTECT | Tools \| More \| Protect |
| QUERY..ENDQUERY | |
| REPORT | Report \| Output \| |

There are several functions that are normally used by Paradox's SQL Link program that are useable when SQL link is not available. If SQL Link is not available, all other SQL commands and functions will cause a script error that tells you that Paradox SQL is inactive.

## ISSQL: Is SQL Link Currently Running?

ISSQL()

Returns TRUE if SQL Link is installed and running, FALSE otherwise.

## SQLISREPLICA: Is The Specified Table A SQL Replica Table?

SQLISREPLICA(TableName)

TableName is a string with the name of the table to check. Returns TRUE if the table is a remote table, FALSE if it is a regular (local) Paradox table. Paradox SQL link can create local versions of remote tables. These *replica* tables are used to hold forms and reports as well as used for DataEntry mode.

If you have a mixture of local and replica tables, it is important to test for the existence of replicas. For example, you cannot enter View, CoEdit or Edit on a replica table. Many PAL functions cannot be used on replica tables at any time (they cause a script error). These include CMAX(), CMIN(), CAVERAGE(),

CSUM(), and NRECORDS(). However, if SQL Link is installed, you can use NFIELDS() and NKEYFIELDS() without causing a script error.

## SQLERRORCODE: What Was The Last SQL Errorcode?

```
SQLERRORCODE()
```

Returns the number 0 is SQL Link is not active.

## SQLERRORMESSAGE: What Was The Last SQL Error Message?

```
SQLERRORMESSAGE()
```

Returns a blank string ("") if SQL Link is inactive.

Here is a complete listing of the special Paradox SQL Link commands and functions. All of the following except those mentions above will cause a script error when used when SQL Link is not active.

### SQL Link Commands

| | |
|---|---|
| SQL - ENDSQL | Embedded SQL statements. |
| SQLAUTOCOMMIT | Sets default for AUTOCOMMIT. |
| SQLBREAKCONNECT | Breaks connections with the server. |
| SQLCLEARCONNECT | Clears connection, workspace, and all remote user name and passwords. |
| SQLCOMMIT | Commits all open changes to the database server. |
| SQLFETCH | Fetches one record at a time and copies it to an array. |
| SQLMAKECONNECT | Attempts to reconnect to the server specified in the current connection. |
| SQLRELEASE | Releases the pending query. |
| SQLRESTORECONNECT | Attempts to reconnect to the server specified in the current connection. |
| SQLROLLBACK | Rolls back changes on the database server. |
| SQLSAVECONNECT | Temporarily saves the current connection. |
| SQLSELECTCONNECT | Selects a server connection. |
| SQLSETINTERRUPT | Determines whether Paradox interrupts a remote PAL operation with [CtrlBreak]. |
| SQLSTARTTRANS | Starts a transaction on the database server. |

### SQL Link Functions

| | |
|---|---|
| ISSQL | Determines whether SQL Link is running. |

| | |
|---|---|
| SQLCONNECTINFO | Returns connection information from a remote table or from the current connection. |
| SQLERRORCODE | Returns the server code of the most recent error on the database server. |
| SQLERRORMESSAGE | Returns a string containing the messge text of the most recent runtime error condition on the database server or a blank string ("") if no error has occurred. |
| SQLISCONNECT | Determines whether Paradox is currently connected to a server. |
| SQLISREPLICA | Determines whether a table ia a local table or a replica. |
| SQLMAPINFO | Returns structural information about a remote table. |
| SQLVAL | Translates any embedded PAL expression to a valid SQL expression (for use in SQL queries). |

# 20.5 PARADOX 3.5 MEMORY MANAGEMENT

Paradox 3.5 is a house rewired. During the work there were holes chopped in the walls, floors and ceilings, and new wires strung everywhere. With the rewiring finished, it's almost as if nothing was done– the holes are now patched, the ceilings and walls are painted and wallpapered. The first obvious change may be that you no longer blow a fuse when you turn on the air conditioner and the dishwasher at the same time. It takes more to overload the system. When you do, it's easier to reset the new circuit breaker than it was to replace the old fuse.

## What Is VROOMM?

Like many large and complex programs, Paradox 3.0 uses overlay files to make efficient use of memory. Overlays allowed Paradox 3.0, a program that consumed over a megabyte of disk space, to run on a PC equipped with only 512K of conventional memory by putting only a portion of the program in memory at any time. Overlay files generally store less-frequently used parts of a program. When you use a feature that isn't in memory, a portion of available memory is freed and the appropriate overlay read from disk. Unfortunately, this conventional overlay scheme has several limitations:

- Code in the overlays has a predetermined arrangement in memory. Only specific portions of overlays can be in memory at a time.
- There is a fixed barrier between code and data.

VROOMM added flexibility by breaking the code into smaller chunks that can be loaded when needed. Code fragments from different overlays can reside in memory at the same time; there is no predetermined order in memory. VROOMM uses algorithms that retain recently used code in memory, keeping disk activity to a minimum. In addition, although a portion of the code is in memory at all times, the line between data and code space can vary. With limited memory, code space can be swapped for data space. In addition to managing the memory for Paradox program code, VROOMM also manages expanded memory (EMS) and extended memory (as a caching device).

## TurboDrive

Paradox 3.5 introduces TurboDrive to support both real and protected mode operation. Real mode works within 640K of RAM, the only operating mode of an 8086 series processor. If your PC uses an 80286, 80386 or 80486 microprocessor and is equipped with 1Mb or more of extended memory, Paradox can make use of up to 16Mb of extended memory not only for disk caching, but for direct program use as well. Protected mode operation can improve performance dramatically with large tables.

For PAL developers accustomed to conserving memory, tweaking every last bit of MEMLEFT() available, Paradox 3.5 is welcome relief. It is a pleasure to have several megabytes of MEMLEFT(). Paradox 3.5 is one of the first applications to use extended memory effectively. Fortunately too, Paradox 3.5 came at a time when memory prices have fallen dramatically.

Paradox 3.5 can use up to 16 megabytes of memory directly for code and data. Disk intensive operations, such as sorting, may be able to be done in protected mode entirely in memory, resulting in dramatic performance gains. Although your PAL code might not do much sorting, sorting is an integral part of the query and report mechanism, with Paradox sorting data behind the scenes.

Paradox 2.0 and 3.0 use expanded memory as a swap device with two purposes:
- Hold procedures that would don't fit in active memory
- Act as a disk cache.

Paradox 3.5's new caching scheme is more intelligent and interacts better with the rest of the Paradox environment.

## Memory Consumers

There are many parts of Paradox that share available memory. Let's take a look at these memory consumers and what their jobs are.

The diagram below represents how Paradox uses memory. The bottom of the diagram is the lowest area of DOS memory. The dotted horizontal lines represent boundaries that can be moved dynamically, while solid horizontal lines cannot be moved.

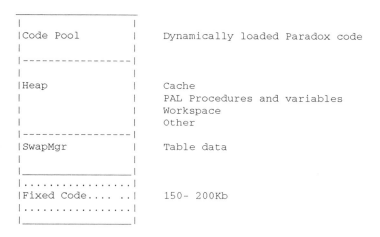

```
|                 |
|Code Pool        |        Dynamically loaded Paradox code
|                 |
|-----------------|
|                 |
|Heap             |        Cache
|                 |        PAL Procedures and variables
|                 |        Workspace
|                 |        Other
|-----------------|
|SwapMgr          |        Table data
|                 |
|_____|
|.................|
|Fixed Code.... ..|        150- 200Kb
|.................|
|_____|
```

## The Fixed Paradox Code

When Paradox is started, it must load a certain amount of its own code directly into memory to get itself up and running. This fixed code stays in place for the rest of the session.

## The Code Pool

The VROOM mechanism dynamically loads portions of the rest of the Paradox program code as needed. The "objects" are actually small pieces of code that Paradox requires for the task at hand.

## The Swap Manager

Some memory is set aside to act as an input/output buffer. This Swap Manager (abbreviated SwapMgr, and nicknamed the Swap Mugger) is not to be confused with the mechanism that controls procedure swapping. The SwapMgr is used to pass blocks of table data from the workspace to Paradox and back out to disk. As you page down through a table on the workspace, Paradox reads the disk to get the data, places it into the SwapMgr and then onto the workspace. As the SwapMgr fills up, the overflow can be directed into the cache device.

## The Cache

The cache memory is used to store table data, forms, libraries and other Paradox objects previously read from disk (even its own overlays). In earlier versions of Paradox, cache memory was taken from expanded memory (or extended memory in PDOX386). You had to predetermine how much of the memory was to be used for a cache, and set it aside. Paradox 3.5 on the other hand, can dynamically resize the cache as needed. That is, when you first start up Paradox, there is very little in the cache (because you haven't done anything yet). However, the cache is considered "free" memory because it can be given back to Paradox whenever it is needed. So when evaluating MEMLEFT() it will always include the memory used by the cache because that memory is available for the next command.

## PAL Procedures and Variables

Procedures defined on the fly or read from procedure libraries take memory. Variables remain in memory until released, but procedures can be swapped out if necessary to free some additional memory. If you are running Paradox 3.5 in protected mode, and there is no memory designated solely as a swap device (like Paradox3's use of expanded memory), the swapped procedures don't actually get moved to a new location in memory. Excess procedures are simply discarded and then looked for in the cache or reread from the procedure library. The amount of procedure swapping is subject to the overall amount of memory and how high you've set your SETSWAP point.

## The Workspace

Paradox needs a small amount of memory for formatting and displaying each image on the workspace.

## What else?

There are other memory consumers that are by and large transient. For example, Paradox needs some memory to display and keep track of its menus. Similarly, each time you are prompted to type in a response, some memory is allocated. These other memory consumers come and go, so don't be concerned if it's a bit difficult to account for all memory all the time.

# 20.6 ERROR PROCEDURES AND CODE POOL INVASION

Although one of the joys of using Paradox 3.5 is the ability to exploit vast amounts of memory, there are a few fundamental differences between the way Release 3.0 dealt with low memory situations and the implementation in Release 3.5.

With Paradox 3.0, when MEMLEFT() reached zero and there were no procedures to swap out, a script simply ran out of memory and stopped. Paradox 3.0 could not even trip an ERRORPROC because it had no memory left to do so. Paradox 3.5 has a safety net. When MEMLEFT() equals zero and you need more memory, Paradox can use memory that is normally used by the Code Pool. When this happens, the Code Pool is said to have been invaded. The PAL User's Guide gives an overview of code pool invasion, but it leaves a few things unsaid.

To use the checking account analogy from the User's Guide, you can think of the Code Pool as overdraft protection. It's not a particularly good idea to invade the code pool because overall Paradox performance will suffer. In general, setting a SETSWAP point will avoid code pool invasions—if MEMLEFT() is never allowed to get to zero, then you cannot possibly invade the code pool. However, if you do invade the code pool, here's what happens:

## Code Pool Diagram

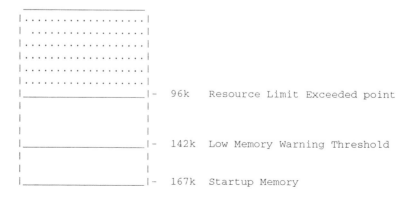

At startup, the code pool is a 167Kb area of memory. If your PAL program invades the code pool, and Paradox needs to take less than 25Kb of memory (it will not trip a run error), nothing will happen. However, if your program needs more than 25Kb, it will cross the 142Kb threshold and trigger a script error. If you have an ERRORPROC in place, Paradox will set the ERRORCODE() to 44 (Low Memory Warning), and let your ERRORPROC take over. This gives you the opportunity to take some corrective action (typically freeing some memory by releasing procedures, variables or images).

When the ERRORPROC is finished, Paradox will retry the statement that flagged the ERRORPROC in the first place (even if you set RETURN 1 to attempt to skip over the problem). Once you are below the threshold, low memory warnings no longer exist. That is, the warning only comes when you actively cross over the threshold because once you're in a low memory situation and have been warned, additional invocations of the ERRORPROC would be useless and tie up memory. Once you've crossed the threshold, you have a maximum of about 46Kb of additional memory available before reaching the point where you'll get a "Resource Limit Exceeded" error.

The RMEMLEFT() function returns the amount of memory available to be borrowed from the code pool. This reserved memory is 67Kb at startup, the difference between the 167Kb available in the code pool and a point slightly above the 96Kb resource limit point. You really only need to know the current RMEMLEFT() if you are in an ERRORPROC trying to deal with a low memory situation. If you need to know the amount of code pool invasion from point to point, you could store RMEMLEFT() to a variable when you start your application and have your ERRORPROC check the current MEMLEFT() and RMEMLEFT() to decide how best to proceed. Sometimes, if there is still enough RMEMLEFT() available, it is best to call a subordinate procedure to handle an error. In other cases you might use SETSWAP or RELEASE VARS to gain some memory and take the strain off the code pool.

Remember that MEMLEFT() is the amount of memory above the code pool and that a code pool invasion won't happen until MEMLEFT() is allowed to go to zero. Setting SETSWAP will usually avoid this condition in the first place (unless you've really run out of memory altogether). If you don't set a SETSWAP point explicitly, it is likely that the default SETSWAP 0 will eventually intrude on the code pool.

## More about Error Procedures

Most Paradox run errors can be handled by error procedures. There have been some changes in the way the 3.5 version works.

- In Paradox 3.0 you have to explicitly read in an error procedure prior to a run error. Release 3.5 allows Paradox to search the libraries contained in the AUTOLIB for the location of the specified ER-RORPROC.
- Because of the availability of the code pool, a 3.5 ERRORPROC can use up to 46k more memory before triggering a resource limit error.
- In the event of a low memory warning, an ERRORCODE() of 44, you should try to back out of the code pool because the offending statement will always be retried.

## The Swap Manager

As mentioned earlier, the SwapMgr handles blocks of data for tables on the workspace. It should not be confused with the cache which resides in a different area of memory. The cache feeds data to and accepts data from the SwapMgr. The SwapMgr is not a direct write-through device, that is, it does not automatically write data to disk immediately. If you empty a table, the table is removed from disk, but the new empty copy of the table may not be written to disk unless you're on a network. In standalone use, Paradox will write data to disk from time to time as part of the autosave feature.

Though keeping disk access to a minimum improves performance, if you need to explicitly flush the data in the SwapMgr to disk, use SAVETABLES or RESET.

Though the SwapMgr is allocated approximately 25Kb to 100Kb of memory by default (depending on how much memory is available), you can explicitly control the amount of memory assigned to it with the -TABLEK command line option. It is usually better to let Paradox handle memory allocation, because the amount available can be expanded and contracted dynamically by Paradox depending on the operation.

## The Cache

Although Paradox 3.5 improves on the use of memory as a disk cache, there are still many good reasons to use a commercial disk cache, like SuperPCKwik from MultiSoft, along with Paradox's built-in cache. Here are some reasons:

- Single-purpose caches are usually more effective.
- They can be used by other programs, generally speeding up all disk operations.
- They can generally do full track reads.
- They usually cannot cache network drives (but the Paradox 3.5 cache can).

In our testing, SuperPCKwik coexists well with Paradox 3.5's cache when we allocate 500Kb to 1000Kb of memory to the external cache. Our tests also show that overall Paradox performance improves when an external cache is in place; providing, of course, that you don't steal too much memory away from Paradox.

You can think of Paradox's cache as an overflow device for the SwapMgr. In addition to storing table data recently read from disk, it can also hold forms, procedure libraries, and (if memory permits in protected mode) the overlays for Paradox program code. Unlike the SwapMgr, the cache is write-through, so that all changed data written to the cache also goes to the disk immediately.

Paradox 3.0 cache memory was split into two sections: one to cache data, and one to swap procedures. Cache memory could not be used for anything else. The cache worked at a disk sector level, and could not be used on network drives or drives larger than 32 megabytes.

Paradox 3.5, on the other hand, integrates the cache as part of the overall memory scheme. In this way, the cache is considered a very low priority user of memory. All memory used by the cache is considered available to the next PAL statement. If Paradox needs memory, it will throw data out of the cache to make room. Because the 3.5 cache knows that a table is an object, it can also know that if a table is changed by another user, it can flag the cache memory as immediately available. Paradox also keeps track of the whether data in the cache is current and can therefore cache network drives.

With Paradox 3.5 running in protected mode, there is no area in memory for swapping procedures. An active procedures stays in memory, and when it gets swapped out, it is simply discarded. There is a good chance, however, that the area of the library that contains the procedure remains in the cache.

## Procedure Swapping and Swap devices

When using Paradox 3.5 in real mode with additional Expanded (EMS) or extended memory available, Paradox will use the additional memory as a swap device. This area of memory is used to store recently used procedures and as a disk cache. As in Paradox 3.0, code does not execute directly from a swap device, but must be copied from the device into the more limited active memory. The swap device can be further divided to allocate amounts for the area used to store swapped procedures and table data (with the -CACHEK command line option).

If you use Paradox 3.5 in protected mode, memory is handled quite differently. There is no swap device–all memory is treated as active. Procedures are kept *in* and executed directly *from* the central pool of memory, which is shared among all memory "consumers." As procedures are called from libraries, they are put into the central pool, and if necessary, push cached data out of the way to make room. This brings up a fundamental difference between the use of SETSWAP in Paradox 3.0 and Paradox 3.5.

In Paradox 3.0 the general rule of thumb is that you should keep SETSWAP to the lowest possible value that still allows Paradox to execute your scripts. A script always needs enough free memory to step through the next single PAL statement. If you assign the swap point too high, procedures are swapped out of memory needlessly, and Paradox can't use the available memory for anything else. For example, a query doesn't run any faster with a swap point at 30,000 than it would with a swap point of 100,000; the query either runs or it doesn't.

Paradox 3.5 changes the rules in protected mode. With a PC equipped with 2 megabytes of extended memory running in protected mode, Paradox will begin with a MEMLEFT() value of about 1,200 Kb. When you start an application, procedures are read from libraries and placed into memory. As you work with tables, they too are placed in memory, in the cache. As you continue using the application, more and more procedures get read in, with each one potentially taking memory away from the cache.

Eventually you must come to a decision: Which is more important, the PAL code or the data?

The answer is not simple. If you have small procedure libraries and lots of data, it probably doesn't matter very much. But if you have a lot of PAL code, performance may suffer if you have a low SETSWAP because as a session goes on, procedures are loaded at the expense of the cache. It is likely that you could fill memory with procedures and leave no memory for caching at all, at which point table access will bog down. In this instance, it is better to try to decide how much memory should be reserved for non-procedure use.

With Paradox 3.5, you control caching by assigning the SETSWAP point. In the example above, if you assign a SETSWAP of 500,000 bytes, you guarantee this memory for holding tables and other cached objects. On the other hand, if you want a lot of procedures to remain in memory, you can assign a low swap point.

As was true with a low SETSWAP in Paradox 3.0, there seem to be no hard and fast rules for assigning a high SETSWAP in Paradox 3.5. Evaluating memory at the start of the application can tell you the highest SETSWAP setting. A little experimentation can help fine-tune performance. You might consider not hard-coding a SETSWAP into your applications, but instead using a variable assignment, either picked up from a table or an initialization script. By changing the variable, you can change SETSWAP for conditions found on different PCs.

One last note about procedure swapping. The 3.5 PAL User's guide states that both EXECPROC and scripts that call other scripts inhibit procedure swapping. Our testing shows that this is not the case.

It is fortunate that EXECPROC does run correctly, for if it disabled swapping, the DoWait procedure from the Data Entry Toolkit, which depends heavily on the use of EXECPROC, would grind to a halt.

# Chapter 21

# Problems & Solutions

"No good deed goes unpunished."

Improving software is a risky business. While users clamor for new features, every change adds potential for conflicts or unintended results. Simple changes often have profound effects. It's not surprising to encounter a well-intentioned change that slows an existing application to a crawl or grinds it to a halt. Changes in Paradox may force changes to code that was working just fine under a prior release.

During your PAL application development or subsequent performance tuning, you're likely to run into things that cause a bit of head scratching. This section presents some of the most common problems we encounter with Paradox development.

## 21.1 ERRORS, BUGS, WADS AND ANOMALIES

- Errors are things you did wrong.
- Bugs are Paradox errors that were not intended by the Paradox designers.
- Anomalies are things that don't work the way you expect, but are not really bugs.
- WAD stands for Works-As-Designed, where features are working the way they are supposed to, but you disagree with the results.

### Errors - {Cancel}/{Debug}

Like it or not, getting the {Cancel}/{Debug} prompt usually means you did something wrong. Simple errors are easily fixed, but quite often errors aren't simple and finding out what you did wrong takes an analysis of the workspace and a bit of back-tracking through code.

Fortunately, the PAL debugger allows you to step through your procedures statement by statement. While debugging, the workspace is active, and if need arises, you can modify the workspace, assign variables, or copy objects. With the Pal Menu's {Value} choice, you can interrogate values of variables. The {Where} selection shows the calling chain, so you know where you are and how you got there and also shows the current values of all PRIVATE variables. Though the PAL debugger lacks a trace facility, if you know approximately where an error occurs, you can run your program to a point just before the error, and break into the script where appropriate. When the {Cancel}/{Debug} menu appears, you can step through statements with [Ctrl S], skip to the next statement with [Ctrl N], find your location with [Ctrl W], or continue script play with [Ctrl G]. Putting the DEBUG command in your code takes you to the debugger directly.

We have learned that it rarely pays to remove offending or seemingly superfluous code from a script we're debugging—usually we'll just comment it out. Too often we found out too late that a section of code had been put there for a reason long ago forgotten. Removing semicolons is a lot easier than recreating complex code. Only after exhaustive testing do we remove outdated code from our scripts entirely. Murphy's Law at work: when your auto mechanic fixes your brakes, it won't be long before your tailpipe falls off.

Though problems are usually the result of something you did, there are some things you can blame on others.

## Bugs

It is axiomatic that any program as large and as complex as Paradox has bugs. Some bugs are more annoying than harmful. Others can be catastrophic. As Paradox has evolved, many of the reported bugs have been fixed. Yet with each revision, new bugs are introduced. It's hard to get too annoyed at this, because the bugs that do slip by got past the Paradox R&D team, Quality Assurance, and most, if not all, beta testers. At times bugs are reported too late to fix without jeopardizing the rest of the program. Other bugs may not emerge until the new release has been out in the field for a while.

### Square Brackets

Paradox has always had problems dealing with literal square brackets in calculated fields in reports. A calculated field using square brackets might look like:

```
"This is customer [" + [Customer ID#] + "]."
```

which (for customer ID# 1234) should print

```
This is customer [1234].
```

In fact, this works just fine when the report is designed. However, if you use {Modify} {Restructure} on the table with this report, even if there are no structural changes, Paradox updates the report. Unfortunately, it changes the calculated field, removing the literal brackets and substituting the name of the first field in the table. As any script that attempts to runs an invalid report trips a run error, this unintended change can bring an application to a quick stop. As noted, this bug goes back a long time, but it was rarely encountered. After all, how many users place values in square brackets in reports?

Enter Paradox version 3.5, where you can use variables and arrays in forms and reports. Array elements are referenced by subscripts, which are enclosed in square brackets. The result is that any array element in a report or form will be rendered invalid after a table restructure. Here's a workaround in the event that you're not changing the names or structure of a table during a {Modify} {Restructure}.

The technique is pretty simple:

1) Create a temporary table like the one you're about to restructure.

2) Copy {JustFamily} from the data table to the temporary table.

3) Restructure the data table (this might cause the invalid calculations).

4) Copy {JustFamily} from the temporary table to the data table.

Here are a few more Paradox 3.5 bugs and their workarounds:

## SAVEVARS

Another bug that goes back a long way is a problem with the SAVEVARS ALL command. Although it was improved in version 3.0, it can still lock up your PC when attempting to save long string variables that have special ASCII characters in them. Paradox attempts to write some of the lower characters as four character strings (for example "\002") and the mechanism that updates the SAVEVARS.SC file can crash. Although you're not likely to come across it in everyday use, anyone using the DataEntry Toolkit with record level procedures must avoid the SAVEVARS ALL command because the movement variables will cause the error.

## General Protection Errors

With Paradox in protected mode, when restructuring tables or modifying reports, Paradox may stop suddenly with an "Unexpected Condition" message and an internal (not PAL) error code that contains the letters ...GP... (" General Protection"). This is a protected mode error. The current wisdom seems to be that you should place the table on the workspace before doing the restructure or modifying the report.

## PRINT Statements

There is also currently a problem with the PRINT command. On 3Com networks (and perhaps PC-LAN) there is a bug that issues a form feed after every value. That is, PRINT "This ", "That ", "The other" outputs these strings on three separate pages. The current workaround is to print these strings to a file first, then output the file to the printer.

# WADs

Software design is a subjective art. It's easy to disagree with some of the design decisions that went into making Paradox what it is. Here's a complicated example:

The EDIT mode creates a transaction log that records changes to records. With keyed tables, the order in which records are processed in this transaction log has an effect on what records are saved. To demonstrate this, create a table called "List" with one key field.

```
;Create keyed table called "List"
;List is a temporary table
CREATE "List"
  "KeyField"    :  "A1*",
  "SecondField" :  "A1"

; Load the table with data
Edit  "List"
"1"  Enter  "A" Enter   ; moves to the next record
"2"  Enter  "B" Enter
"3"  Enter  "C" Enter
"4"  Enter  "D" Enter
"5"  Enter  "E" Enter
"6"  Enter  "F" Enter
Do_It!
```

You should now have a table that looks something like this

```
Viewing List table: Record 6 of 6

LIST═══╦KeyField╦SecondField╗
    1  ║    1   ║     A     ║
    2  ║    2   ║     B     ║
    3  ║    3   ║     C     ║
    4  ║    4   ║     D     ║
    5  ║    5   ║     E     ║
    6  ║    6   ║     F     ║
```

So far so good. Now go into Edit mode and make the following changes in interactive Paradox. Change the 1 to a 2, change the 2 to a 3, and so forth until the table looks like this:

```
Editing List table: Record 6 of 6

LIST═══╦KeyField╦SecondField╗
    1  ║    2   ║     A     ║
    2  ║    3   ║     B     ║
    3  ║    4   ║     C     ║
    4  ║    5   ║     D     ║
    5  ║    6   ║     E     ║
    6  ║    7◄  ║     F     ║
```

Now press [F2] and watch what happens. You'll wind up with this:

```
Viewing List table: Record 1 of 1

LIST═══╦KeyField╦SecondField╗
    1  ║    7   ║     F     ║
```

Surprised? Paradox is just doing what you told it to do. You said "Change number 1 to a 2." Okay, Paradox says, done. The original record called 1 now no longer exists– it has been absorbed by 2. Now you said, "Let's go on to the next step, change the 2 to a 3." Here we go again, the 2 is removed and absorbed by 3. This continues until only the lone 7 remains–all the others have been absorbed by the key conflicts. Although you might not expect this outcome, it is exactly what should happen. Paradox is doing its job, working as designed.

This example is another compelling reason to use CoEdit mode, where key violations are trapped in real time.

## Form Lock And Its Workarounds

Almost everyone who uses multi-table forms on a network runs into some problems with Paradox's Form Lock mechanism. A Form Lock is a special kind of Write Lock. With a Form Lock in effect, Paradox insists that any time a table is used in a 1-1 or 1-Many link, all users must use the same form when in CoEdit mode.

This is Paradox's way of trying to maintain the referential integrity of the relationship between master and detail tables. Unfortunately, the general consensus is that the current implementation of the Form Lock mechanism is too restrictive. A simple case might be an invoice master table that is keyed on one field [Invoice#]. It has a form that has an embedded line-item table that's is keyed on [Invoice#] and [Line#]. The detail form has been linked to the [Invoice#] field in the master table, defining a classic 1-many relationship. Any master record may have many detail records (line items), but any particular line item can have only one master record.

The idea behind this is pretty powerful. As you scroll through the master table, Paradox automatically shows you only those detail records that apply to the current invoice. If you create a new invoice, and then add line items, the line items will automatically be given the invoice# of the master. If you then change the invoice# of an existing master, Paradox will automatically change the invoice#'s of any appropriate line items. All these features that Paradox handles with such ease was a major PAL programming effort before Paradox 3.0 was released. So we applaud the tool, but it causes some real headaches. The biggest problem is that there is no explicit way to turn off FormLock. That is, unlike the REQUIREDCHECK OFF command which lets you override the Required Field validity check, there is no way of getting around a Form Lock once placed (the Form Lock stays in effect as long as you're in an editing mode; it has no effect on Main mode).

In its simplest case, let's assume that you have two almost identical multi-table forms, with the only difference being the color of the form. If a user goes into one of the edit modes, all other users must use the same form if they too want to be in an edit mode. Even though the links and integrity rules are the same for both forms, Paradox insists that the first form registered is the only one permitted. This extends not only to forms, but ALL updating of ANY of the tables involved must be made through the form. So if someone is coediting a table in a linked form, no one can update it in table view.

The Form Lock should not be confused with its close cousin, the Link Lock. When you get a message saying that a table is Link Locked, Paradox is telling you that you've picked a multitable linked form, but now you're in table view, and you need to go back to the form before changing a record. You are also prevented from picking another form (even to one that enforces exactly the same integrity rules). The only way to remove a Link Lock is to issue a DO_IT!, which takes you back to Main mode, where you can pick another form.

## The Many-To-Many Solution

Is there anything we can do to get around the Form Lock problem? Yes, but at a cost. The old joke goes:

> Patient: "Doctor, it hurts when I do this!"
> Doctor: "So don't do this!"

As mentioned, Paradox enforces referential integrity of 1-1 and 1-Many relationships. The way to avoid Form Locks is to avoid those relationships. The main concern is making sure that Paradox sees the potential for many master records for any given detail record.

There are three different (but similar) scenarios that can accomplish this:

* UnKeying the master table
* Adding an additional key to the master and not linking to it
* Adding an additional unkeyed field to the master, and linking to that field.

## Unkeying the Master Table

Let's again use the Invoice and Line Item tables. However, this time, the invoice table is unkeyed.

The detail form is still linked to the [Invoice#] field, but as far as Paradox is concerned, there are many potential Invoices with the same invoice number. This is possible because in an unkeyed table you can have any number of duplicate records. In this scenario, as you page down through invoices in the master, you'll see the proper detail records for the current invoice; and in this way it works just like the 1-Many link. However, the main difference is that

Paradox has not placed a Form Lock on any of the tables, they can be updated in other forms (that don't try to impose a Form Lock) or in table view.

## Adding An Extra Key Field And Not Linking To It

The second approach is to add a second key field to the master (but not to the detail). Let's assume that the new version of the invoice table has two key fields: [Invoice#], and a one-character field called [Extra Key]. We link the detail table only to the [Invoice#] field. This way, Paradox considers that there are several potential invoices for any given detail. For example, there could be [Invoice#]=1000 and [Extra Key]="A", and another record that has [Invoice#]=1000 and [Extra Key]="B". Nonetheless, all detail records are still keyed on [Invoice#] and [Line#]. Although there is the potential for many master records. Your PAL code must assure that there is only one master for each invoice#.

One way of doing this is to make sure that the user is never allowed to enter data into the [Extra key] field–it is always blank. Invoices will be unique because of their number. Once again, Paradox thinks that there is a potential for many masters. It doesn't know that you will be enforcing the single master per invoice# by programming, and the Form Lock is avoided. Adding an extra key field is probably the most efficient and fastest method of avoiding form-locks, and is the one we prefer.

Among other reasons for not wanting to use unkeyed tables is that accessing unkeyed tables is usually slower than keyed tables. However, there may be cases where you don't want an additional key; for example if you need to use the Invoice table's [Invoice#] field as a lookup validity check for other tables. Lookup ValChecks can only access tables with no more than one key field.

## Adding An Additional Unkeyed Field To The Master, And Linking To That Field.

This brings us to the third scenario. In this case, the Invoice table is still keyed on only the [Invoice#] field, but we'll add an extra field at the end of the table called [Invoice# Link] which has the same field type as [Invoice#]. This time, instead of linking to the key field, we'll link the detail form to the [Invoice# Link]. Now the programmer has an additional responsibility: Every time a new master is added or edited, the programmer must place an exact copy of the [Invoice#] field into the [Invoice# Link] field. Because invoice numbers are unique, the link will be unique, simulating a 1-Many relationship where actually a many-many relationship exists. Paradox sees the Many-many relationship because it has no way of knowing that you are keeping the linked field unique (as far as it's concerned, all the links could have the same value, since it is just a regular data field). Again, it is up to the you to assure that [Invoice# Link] = [Invoice#] at all times.

### The Many-To-Many Overhead

As in most good things, there is a cost to avoiding form-locks. If you are not depending on Paradox to enforce the referential integrity, you have to do it. Let's look at what happens to details records in a Many-Many relationship. If you add detail records (which must be keyed), the linked keys are automatically assigned by Paradox. That is, any details entered while invoice# 1000 is the master will give the detail's [Invoice#] field the value 1000. So far, so good; it works just like a 1-Many situation.

The difference is what happens when you change the invoice# of the master? Let's assume that in a Many-Many link, you are looking at Invoice# 1000, and it has 5 detail line item records. If you change the invoice# to 2000 and post the invoice record, what happens to the detail records? They appear to disappear! Unlike the result of such a change in a 1-Many relationship, the linked keys are not changed to reflect the new invoice#, they stay at 1000. The reason is simple: As far as Paradox is concerned, there may be other masters with the same invoice number, so changing the detail records would be inappropriate. What happens on screen is that the detail records disappear from the display because as soon as the Invoice# 2000 is posted, the line items with the 1000 number are not appropriate to the restricted detail view for that master, but they still exist in the detail table. In fact, if you add a new Invoice# 1000 record, and post it, the old detail records will appear in the line item detail form.

So in a Many-Many relationship, if you'll be likely to change keys on the master table, you'll probably need to place a standalone image of the detail table on the workspace so that you can access and change any orphaned details to synchronize their keys with the updated master. Fortunately, there is no Form Lock in place, so you are free to manipulate the table in this way.

The issue of Form-Locks is pretty involved, and hopefully we'll get some less restrictive tools in the future. For now, the scenarios outlined above might help you out of a very bad situation, or greatly improve performance by freeing you from updating only through the same form as that which imposed a Form Lock.

## Anomalies

Anomalies are just about everything else. At times things happen that are caused by Paradox interacting with other programs (often collisions with TSRs and ill-behaved programs). For example, the ARRAYSIZE() function sometimes returns an absurdly high number when evaluating an undefined array instead of reporting a zero. We've been able to cure Paradox of this by changing parameters in the CONFIG.SYS file, but we've seen it happen after merely shelling out to QEDIT (a popular shareware editor).

Then again, when examining some of the environments that Paradox runs under, it's a wonder that it runs at all. Some CONFIG.SYS and AUTOEXEC.BAT files we've seen make us marvel that upon bootup the computer doesn't burst into flames. In the event that you run across an anomaly, there are a few things you can do:

- Start with a clean CONFIG.SYS and AUTOEXEC.BAT. You can always add features back one at a time, and try to see what is causing the complication.
- Ask other devlopers for help. The BORDB forum on CompuServe is an excellent place to get help and advice. The forum members take special interest in impossible problems. New to you may be old hat to someone who's already tripped over it.
- If you don't have access to CompuServe, Contact Borland Technical Support.

# 21.2 Common PAL Problems and Solutions

## Library Maintenance

When you make changes to code, don't forget to write the changes back to the library. During development, recreate your library from scratch from time to time so that outdated procedures will be removed.

It's easy to write a small script that creates the library from scratch and plays all scripts to load the libraries with procedures. When you install a new system, recreate the libraries on the client's PC.

## The Number Of Procedures In Libraries And Procedure Size

In release 2 of Paradox, using a library that had more than 50 procedures required large chunks of contiguous memory. This was fixed in Paradox 3.0.

With Paradox 3.0, many programmers got into the habit of breaking up larger procedures into many tiny procedures for the wrong reasons. One reason was that their applications were running out of memory. However, in many cases, the applications were running out of memory because the code used techniques that disabled the Paradox procedure swapping mechanism. Another reason was that there was a widely-circulated recommendation to keep procedure size between 6 and 8Kb. This was and is an unnecessary restriction.

If you split your routines into many small procedures, Paradox may try to swap procedures at every turn (depending on your SETSWAP point). Yet procedures that are "too large" might take up valuable memory when they should be swapped. It's mostly up to you to determine the "right" size. We try to keep our procedures under about 12Kb (as reported by INFOLIB) but it's not a hard and fast rule. The size of the proc should be determined by the task at hand, the resources available, and the maintainability of the code. Large procedures are sometimes hard to follow, but a maze of smaller procedures can be equally confusing. We recommend that you liberally comment your code, as comments are not written into a library and consume no space or memory.

With Paradox 3.5 in protected mode and lots of memory available, your procedures may never get swapped out.

## Script Size

Although there is no specific rule, the PAL debugger seems to slow to a crawl when stepping through large scripts. Paradox 3.5 seems to be more sensitive to this phenomenon than before. As a general rule, keep scripts down to a maximum of 700 lines. In scripts with a file size of 64Kb or greater the debugger cursor can actually "get lost" and seemingly point to the wrong line while executing the correct statements.

## Error Procedures That Eat Memory

Error procedures called by a run error while within a loop will eat memory on each invocation, and only return memory when the loop is exited.

## Recursive Calls

A common programming error is to have script "A" call script "B" which in turn calls script "A". This will eventually cause a "Not enough stack space" error. To avoid this, you should use the RETURN command from script "B" when you want to leave and automatically return to script "A". This is also true for procedures.

Another common cause of a stack space error is when an ERRORPROC itself contains an error. This causes the ERRORPROC to keep calling itself until the stack runs out. The solution is to simply make the ERRORPROC variable PRIVATE to the error procedure. If you have a run error within the error procedure, you'll simply return to the {Cancel}/{Debug} menu.

## Decimal Precision: Rounding & FieldView

All digital computers have difficulty at times with decimal numbers. When comparing values, you might find that numbers that look alike don't actually match. We've also found that going into FieldView on a number can change the precision of the number in some cases. Using PAL's ROUND function is often helpful in comparing numbers. The usual technique involves adding a very small number to the target number and rounding to a predetermined number of places. This assures that numbers will always "round up." For example to compare an outstanding balance with a payment you might want to code something like:

```
IF ROUND([Balance] + .0001, 2)<> ROUND([Payment] + .0001,2) THEN
   MESSAGE "There is still an outstanding balance, press any key."
   n = GETCHAR()
ENDIF
```

## Left-over Images And Variables

Housekeeping is important. Anything that you use, you should put away or discard after use. Be aware of images you've placed on the workspace and clear them after use as each image uses memory. Yet to avoid unnecessay locking, leave images on the workspace until you're sure you're done with them. Pay particular attention to left over query images.

Variables should be made PRIVATE to the procedures that need them. PRIVATE variables are released when the procedure is finished. If you need global variables in your application (for example, a password), either make a top level procedure that declares the variables PRIVATE, or make your top level procedure CLOSED. When script play ends, there shouldn't be any global variables left in interactive Paradox.

## Workspace

Visualizing the workspace takes practice:

- Know when Paradox creates tables as a byproduct of an action. For example, a CHANGETO query creates a CHANGED table and places it on the workspace. Knowing this will help you anticipate where the workspace cursor will end up after the query.
- Know when Paradox is going to ask you for additional menu choices. For example, when you restructure a table, if a "KeyViol" or

"Problems" table exists, you will be presented with the menu choices {Ok} {Cancel}.

- Know when your movements will be restricted. In particular, get to know CoEdit mode, and experiment with those things that will keep you on a record until the record is posted. For example, in an empty, linked detail table, you cannot issue FORMKEY because the record is unposted. You can, however, move back to the master table, UNLOCK the record and then issue FORMKEY. This is not a problem when there are posted records in the detail image, but a new record is considered unposted, and in CoEdit mode there is always at least one record.

## Key Violations Will Restrict Cursor Movement

One of the most complex issues in PAL application development is how to assure unique keys. Multitable forms and dealing with invalid data make for some very involved code. See the OkKey35.l(), OkKey3.l(), OkKey2.l(), CopyFrom-Array3.u(), InvalidArrayRecover.u(), and OopsPrint.u() procedures supplied in the wwpUtil2.SC file for a detailed analysis and sample code.

## Invalid Data

Invalid data can wreak havoc on an application. Data that will no longer pass the validity checks for LowValue, HighValue, or TableLookup is considered invalid, and the cursor cannot leave the field if the value has been changed, or if FieldView has been invoked.

### How It Gets There

Data can become invalid if a validity check has been changed or added after data has been entered. Also, deleting records in a lookup table has the same effect on a data table that verifies against the lookup table. Another way to get invalid data into a table is via an ADD statement, or an INSERT or CHAN-GETO query.

### How It Affects You

Aside from locking the cursor into the field, run errors will occur if you try to assign invalid data into a field. This is particularly problematic when an array contains invalid data, and you're attempting to update a record with the COPYFROMARRAY command. See the CopyFromArray.u() and InvalidArray-Recover.u() procedures for more details.

## Additional Tips

### Make Sure You Have Resources Before You Attempt A Task

This is a general rule, but is particularly important on networks where there may be contention for file control. Verify that files exist and are available to you before acting on them. For example, make sure that you can place a FULL LOCK on a table before restructuring it.

### Verify That What You Wanted Done Has Actually Happened

Watch the WINDOW() function to make sure that a query has actually occurred. There are many factors that can prevent a query such as invalid syntax, or another user's locks could prevent a changeto query.

### Avoid Table Names That Are The Same As Directory Names

Paradox will trip a run error if you try to select a table that has the same name as a subdirectory. Borland considers this a "Feature", so be careful when naming tables and directories.

### Field Names That Contain Special Characters Or Arithmetic Operators

Although Paradox will allow you to create field names that contain special characters, it is not advisable. For example, you could name a field: "Sex (M/F)". You cannot explicitly move to it with the statement

```
MOVETO [Sex (M/F)]
```

because the parentheses are part of field specifier syntax. When PAL sees parentheses, it assumes that you are referring to a specific image of the table on the workspace and so expects a Q, for query image, or a number denoting the display image number wanted. Similarly you could not assign

```
[Sex (M/F)] = "Male"
```

### Determining Blanks=Zero Status

Paradox allows you to determine how blank values are to be treated in arithmetic calculations that do not involve counting. Your startup procedures should check the ISBLANKZERO() function to assure that the current Paradox configuration is correct for your application. If the setting is incorrect, it is best to trap the error before you need the calculations and have the user or an administrator run the CUSTOM script to reinstall Paradox.

## 21.3 Performance Tuning

This section discusses some of the issues that surround application performance. In our travels, we get to see systems designed by many people. Programmers' styles vary widely and their approaches to tasks are diverse. Sometimes we're asked to help with the design of a new system. More often than not, the reason we're asked to look at an existing application is because it isn't working properly, or is performing sluggishly. It's not unusual to have administrators ready to throw Paradox out the door because of poor performance. Fortunately, virtually every system we've looked at had room for improvement, and some speed increases have been rather dramatic.

### How Fast is Fast?

It is often said that perception of speed is more important than speed itself. Many spreadsheets use background recalculation, which shows on-screen calculations first, and continues with the rest of the calculations behind the scenes. If a single user selection has many parts, it's a good idea to bombard the user with messages that show progress at each step. In this manner, the user gets an idea of the steps involved and is not simply looking at a "Working, please wait..." message. In fact, if messages come so fast and furious that the user cannot even read them, the perception of speed is even greater.

Another benefit to keeping users informed and entertained is that if the program slows down or crashes, they can relate what was going on at the time of a crash by noting the current message. Keeping screen activity high not only keeps users informed of progress but also assures users that their PC isn't locked up. Applications with blank screens or those that don't give immediate feedback to user selections are cause for alarm. Panicked users sometimes reboot their computers when all was in fact going well. Keep the user informed.

Sometimes the reasons for poor performance are obvious; at other times, obscure. It's not unusual to hear a programmer complain "It worked fine until I put it on the network." Sometimes well intentioned techniques intended to help performance actually slow things down, for example, excessive use of CLOSED procedures.

## Use Procedures, Libraries, and AUTOLIB

The most efficient and fastest PAL code is stored in procedure libraries. Normally, there should be only one driver script that sets the AUTOLIB variable and calls the top level procedure. With AUTOLIB set, Paradox handles the memory management and procedure swapping. Don't clutter up and slow down your code with explicit READLIB and RELEASE PROCS statements. Code in libraries is pre-parsed, tokenized, and ready for Paradox's immediate use when needed.

## Inhibiting Or Disabling Procedure Swapping

Many memory problems are due to code that inhibits or disables Paradox's procedure swapping mechanism. This isn't surprising, since the Personal Programmer writes code that also inhibits swapping. This is frustrating to programmers who use these scripts for foundations to their application development. For a complete discussion of what permits and inhibits procedure swapping, see section 11.6, "Procedure Swapping."

## Unnecessary Use Of Closed Procs

The CLOSED option of the PROC command was introduced in Paradox 3.0 as a means to conserve and recover memory used in an application. A CLOSED procedure is oblivious to all that came before it and removes all traces of its having been invoked. Within a CLOSED procedure, all variables are automatically PRIVATE. Needed variables must be declared with the USEVARS option. The USEVARS list should include variables that you want to remain in memory once the CLOSED procedure completes. CLOSED procedures may be helpful when memory is low, but we tend to use them only under duress.

- Many of our systems depend on variables that are set at the beginning of an application. These variables contain information about printer strings, starting memory, user customizations, etc. Having to pass USEVARS parameters through every CLOSED proc is oppressive.
- CLOSED procedures take longer to load and longer to release than normal procedures. At times we've seen a 386 computer appear to hang for a few seconds the first time a CLOSED proc is finished.

- The very nature of a CLOSED proc poses significant performance problems. Its ability to isolate itself from the rest of the application also means that every time it is called the CLOSED procedure has to be read from the disk (or perhaps from the cache) because all traces of its use and anything it learned were eradicated after each use. Anything learned means any procedures that the CLOSED proc called, and any subordinate procedures that were called.

Putting a CLOSED procedure in a loop, where it is called over and over again, will cause a tremendous performance degradation because the subordinate procs will have no way of staying in memory. In Paradox 3.0, this delay included the overhead of having to explicitly read in an error procedure every time you entered a CLOSED proc (fortunately this has been fixed in 3.5).

In addition, you can only nest up to six levels of CLOSED procs. Therefore, CLOSED procedures are probably best used as upper- level procedures for control of major subsections. For example, you might want to keep a payroll section as a CLOSED proc to separate it from an invoice section. However, if the two sections will be using procedures common to both, you'll run into the same performance problem as you move from section to section. Remember that one of the main reasons that CLOSED procedures were developed was to regain every bit of memory possible when memory is low with Paradox 3.0 (particularly in network use). With more memory available in Paradox 3.5, there is much less need for CLOSED procedures.

## CLOSED PROCS and Duplicate Procedure Names

One case where you might need CLOSED procedures is when you have multiple libraries and the same procedure name is in more than one library. Though not good programming style, you may encounter the need to do this. In writing generic procedures you may have no way of knowing what procedures Paradox has used before it gets to your code. Normally, once Paradox uses a procedure it knows where to find it, and will ALWAYS refer to the first occurrence of the procedure. Even if you explicitly do a READLIB later in your program to get a different procedure with the same procedure name from another library, Paradox will ignore the request because it already knows where to find it–in the first library. The only way to have Paradox temporarily "forget" the first occurrence of the proc is to make the call to the second version of the procedure from within a CLOSED procedure–any CLOSED procedure. Keep in mind that this is a rare case. This is what we mean by using CLOSED procs under duress.

## Let Paradox Do The Work

At the beginning of this book, we emphasized that the "Paradox Way" of programming requires intimate knowledge of Paradox. Programmers coming to Paradox from other databases quite often presume too much and either don't take the time to understand or simply ignore this advice. PAL code in this style is easily recognizable, with looping constructs that seem endless. Most notably absent is the use of QUERY/ENDQUERY. Paradox 3.5 has changed nothing in this regard. Reread the first chapter in this book.

## Evaluate Conditions Before Taking Action

It pays to determine if you need to make a change to a record before you make the change. For example, let's say you're scanning a table to convert all [City] values to upper case. You could write:

```
CoEdit "Customer"
SCAN
  [City] = UPPER([CITY])
ENDSCAN
DO_IT!
```

Unfortunately, this will cause every record to be changed regardless of whether or not it needs to be. With several thousand records, if only a few need changing, changing every record creates overhead, locking, posting and releasing each record in turn. A better way is:

```
CoEdit "Customer"
SCAN FOR [City] <> UPPER([CITY])
  [City] = UPPER([City])
ENDSCAN
DO_IT!
```

Use similar evaluations in queries. With the DoWait() of the Data Entry Toolkit, use the tkChanged variable to determine what actions need to be done.

## Use Queries Whenever Possible

In general, queries run faster than the explicit PAL code necessary to accomplish the same task. Paradox's query mechanism is highly optimized and efficiently uses memory and disks. Performance gains of queries over PAL code can be spectacular.

There are times when queries are not the best approach. An example is when a query requires exclusive access to a table and you simply cannot provide it. For example, say you have an INVOICE table that is actively being updated by multiple workstations. Once a day, you print outstanding invoices and update a [Date Printed] field. On a single user machine, you might use a CHANGETO query that changes the records to reflect current date. On a network, a CHANGETO query requires a FULL LOCK on the table at the time of the DO_IT!

Another restriction is that queries and reports can only by issued from Main mode. If you need to remain in CoEdit mode (for locking reasons) you might develop explicit PAL routines that do what would normally be done in the query or report domain.

### Report Pre-processing

The reporting capability of Paradox is both powerful and somewhat limited. It is often much easier to take the burden of complex calculations out of a report, and pre-process the data, using queries or SCAN loops to load the table with data. It's convenient to have extra fields in a report table to hold the results of these calculations, letting the report generator simply print the fields. Although this technique is obvious for complex record calculations it can also be useful for complex summary data.

### Copy Reports—Don't Empty Tables

Along these lines, a common mistake is as follows:

```
;RptTable contains data from the last printing
EMPTY "RptTable"
ADD "Answer" "RptTable"    ;Add records to reporting table
REPORT "RptTable" "1"      ;Print the report
```

The technique has two problems:
- On a network, there will be a collision when two users need to empty and load the same report table (which is in a shared directory).
- It takes much longer to add the Answer records to the report table than it does to copy the report file to the Answer table.

The solution is to simply bring the report to the data, not the other way around.

```
COPYREPORT "RptTable" "1" "Answer" "1"
REPORT "Answer" "1"
```

## Multitable Reports

Paradox developers seem to fall into two camps when asked about multi-table reports: those who hate them, and those who love them. Those who are against them argue that it is better to pre-load the report table with data with queries because reports appear to do no optimization. When the report table is complete, it contains fields from all necessary tables and prints quickly. With this method, all necessary queries must be completed before the report can be printed. This pre-processing takes time up front that is compensated later by the faster speed of printing a single-table report.

Those in favor of using multi-table reports point out that letting Paradox lookup records on an as-needed basis starts printing as soon as the first group is complete. Printing the entire report may actually take a little longer because the lookup information is added on the fly. However, this is usually offset by two factors:

- You didn't need to take the time to do queries to pre-load (often redundant) lookup data.
- Reports are printer-bound, that is, they're waiting for the printer to catch up, so the lookup time is pretty much "free" anyway.

Once the first grouping is complete, the report starts printing. Here again the perception of speed may be more important than actual speed. Users like it when printing starts almost immediately.

A word of caution: With linked reports, the table structure should be fairly stable. Because Paradox links lookup tables based on field numbers (not field names), changes to the structure of the report table that effect the field numbers can have unexpected results on report lookup links. In general we use multi-table reports quite extensively. When handled with care they are a valuable tool.

## Give Paradox Plenty of Room

VROOMM actually allows Paradox 3.5 to work better within conventional memory than its predecessors. Because there are usually other things to address first, we don't usually advocate throwing hardware at performance problems. Yet computer memory is cheap again, and a modest investment pays off through better performance in a very short time.

Additional EXTENDED or EXPANDED memory can be put to good use and in some cases dramatically improve performance. For example, if you are working with a two megabyte table and you have 6Mb or more of extended memory, it is likely that Paradox 3.5 will be able to sort the table entirely in memory, with little disk access. This can have a substantial impact on performance, reducing a task that normally takes minutes to one that takes seconds. Because databases rely heavily on sorting (in the background) for queries and reports, this can be critical.

### Use A Good Memory Manager And Cache

Even if you use Paradox 3.5 in protected mode on a 386 or 486 machine, it's a good idea to use a memory manager like Quarterdeck's QEMM386 or Qualitas' 386-To-The-Max. Both use the VCPI interface for protected mode programs, and supply EXPANDED memory when protected mode is not actively requested. This way, you can have it both ways: your spreadsheets and disk cache can make use of EXPANDED memory, and you still can run Paradox 3.5 in protected mode.

Although Paradox 3.5 has a good disk cache, it's generally no match for the top-end commercial caches. We regularly use MultiSoft's SuperPCKwik cache in combination with Paradox's default cache. The reason for keeping the two caches in place (they don't seem to conflict) is that Paradox can cache data on network drives. There are several advantages to using an external cache:

- It improves performance for all your programs, not only Paradox.
- PCKwik, for example also has a print spooler available that shares the same memory as the cache. Print spoolers accept data from the computer faster than a printer would, consequently the user doesn't have to wait for an entire report to be printed before continuing their work.

### Hard Disk Storage

As applications become more complex, and their tables larger, you'll need plenty of disk space. Paradox needs room to process as well as store data. On networks, this involves PRIVATE directory disk space for each user, whether local or server-based. The faster these drives are, the less time spent waiting.

### Microprocessors

On networks, because Paradox runs on the workstation (not on the file servers), upgrading the microprocessor of the workstation will speed up calculations. 80286 (AT Class), 80386, and 80486 machines with sufficient memory run Paradox 3.5 in protected mode (8088 and 8086 based machines run in real mode, but make use of EXPANDED memory). Many companies are standardizing on the 386 SX chip as their entry-level machines, and use 386DX or 486 machines for their power users.

### Play "Custom" And Select {Tune}

If Paradox does not automatically use your 286, 386, or 486 PC's protected mode, try invoking Paradox with the command

```
PARADOX -REAL
```

Then run Paradox's CUSTOM script found in the \PDOX35 subdirectory and select {Tune} from the menu. Follow the instructions and if possible Paradox will determine the memory configuration for your machine.

### Effect on data

Applications run in protected mode generally accomplish overall tasks faster than when running in real mode, but there are some exceptions. The major speed benefit has to do with Paradox's ability to manipulate large blocks of data entirely in memory.

### Effect on PAL

One of the major effects of having a large amount of memory available is that you'll rarely ever see "Not enough memory to complete operation" messages. In real mode, there is typically a range of 50Kb to 250Kb of memory (as measured by the MEMLEFT() function). This memory is available for images, variables, and procedures. When running in protected mode, you can often have several megabytes of MEMLEFT() available. Having memory of this magnitude lying around might tempt you to become less than diligent (pronounced "sloppy") about your use of resources. Remember that good, tight code will always run faster. With large amounts of memory available, procedures stay in memory longer (if there is sufficient room to hold procedures, there is no need to swap), so there is less disk access.

## Speed of Operations: Real vs. Protected Mode

Although most data-intensive procedures run faster in protected mode, PAL appears to run faster in real mode. For example, the simple FOR loop below takes about 15% more time in protected mode.

```
CLEAR
?? "Processing ....... Please wait"
?? "Start time: ", TIME()
FOR n FROM 1 TO 5000
    a = "X"    ; so as to give the loop a simple thing to do
ENDFOR
? "End time for 5000 counts: ", TIME()
MESSAGE "Press any key"
n = GETCHAR()
```

Try running this in the different modes. protected mode takes longer to move bytes between memory segments, and Paradox is treating the protected memory as the lowest common level: as if it is 286 memory.

SCAN appears to take longer in protected mode. As of this writing, we've seen some SCANs take twice as long under protected rather than under real mode and we've not been able to narrow down the cause.

Protected mode will be slightly slower if your program does a lot of screen updating. DOS forces Paradox to resort to real mode to make DOS calls such as screen input/output or disk access and then Paradox can jump back to protected mode. This is not so much a limitation of protected mode as it is a limitation of DOS. OS/2 on the other hand knows how to exploit protected mode directly.

Although pure PAL constructs may be slower in protected mode, the increase in speed of table manipulation and the ability to keep procedures in memory more than compensate for these few delays. If you're not running into protection errors, running in protected mode will give you better, and in many instances much better, overall performance than real mode.

## Limit The Number Of Files In A Subdirectory

On a single user machine, or on an uncached DOS-based network, DOS file allocation can slow down performance.

A subdirectory is a file that lists the starting points of other files. If the size of the current subdirectory itself is larger than the available BUFFERS, DOS may have to make several disk reads in order to fulfill a file request. Unfortunately, deleting files from a subdirectory does not reduce its size. If a directory once contained 500 files and you deleted 450 of them, the directory size is unchanged. With each file name requested, DOS may have to search the entire directory. This directory remains bloated until you either recreate the directory or run a disk optimizing utility that removes unused space. Raising the BUF-FERS in the CONFIG.SYS file is an inefficient use of memory. Using a good disk cache helps, but it's better not to let the number of files grow past 120 in the first place.

So, how do you keep the number of files in a directory to a minimum?

## The PRIVATE Directory

Paradox creates and erases dozens of temporary files during the course of nor-mal operations. These files are created in the user's PRIVATE directory, if assigned. On a standalone machine, if no PRIVATE directory has been specified, Paradox uses the current directory. Temporary files can cause the directory size to swell and this adversely affects performance. Even on a single user machine, it is worthwhile to set a PRIVATE directory in any one of three ways:

- Via the Custom script
- Using the {Tools} {Net} {SetPrivate} choices
- Using the SETPRIVDIR command

The last two could be part of an application, or included in an INIT.SC so Paradox will do this when invoked. Where should the PRIVATE directory be located?

On a standalone machine, a PRIVATE directory can be any subdirectory on the hard disk, but it's preferable that the directory is used only for this purpose. For a network installation, the answer is more involved. If the PRIVATE direc-tory on a network is kept on the local hard disk, then most input/output (I/O) processing will be kept at the workstation level where it can be easily cached. On the other hand, many installations send and retrieve data to the file server faster than they do to the local hard disk.

Put your PRIVATE directory on the fastest hard disk. Most networks allow a PRIVATE area of the disk for each user, so that is a likely place for the PRIVATE directory. Another consideration is data security. Although temporary tables are erased when no longer needed, erased files on local disks might be fairly easy to resurrect with the available un-erase utilities on the market. If your data contains highly sensitive information, that may weigh very heavily in favor of placing the PRIVATE directory on the network drive, and possibly using a diskless workstation in the first place.

## Split Your Application Into Several Directories

Rather than lumping an entire application into one directory, you might consider splitting it into several directories. You might have one directory for data tables, another for lookup tables, another for report tables, yet another has scripts and libraries. There are several ways of implementing this. One popular method is called Relative Directory Addressing (RDA), which uses a home directory that contains only the driver script and little else. Subdirectories under the home directory have single letter names and contain related parts of an application.

| | |
|---|---|
| V | ValCheck  Lookup Tables |
| D | Data Directory |
| S | Scripts |
| L | Libraries |
| E | Empty Reporting Tables |

All tables, forms and reports are created from the home directory. All references to Paradox objects are also relative to the home directory.

## Reduce Locking Whenever Practical

On a network, Paradox needs to control access to all shared tables and it does so with a series of lock files (with the extension .LCK). There are two kinds of locks, those placed implicitly by Paradox, and those placed explicitly by you.

When moving a single user application to a network, the overhead of maintaining these lock files should be kept to a minimum, to keep performance to a maximum. Try not to work any harder than necessary! This may sound a bit obvious, but take an example of a routine we've seen over and over again.

```
1) Start a loop
2) Clear the workspace
3) Ask the user for a customer# to update. If the user selects a
   number, proceed with the next step, otherwise quit the loop,
   we're done.
4) Put the customer table on the workspace
5) Locate the record by customer#
6) Go into CoEdit mode
7) Pick a form
```

```
 8) Do a WAIT RECORD so user can update the customer
 9) When done, issue a DO_IT!
10) Continue to the top of the loop which clears the image and
    starts over for the next customer#
```

To novice programmers, this might look very reasonable, after all, it's pretty much the way some users work in interactive mode. In fact, it's not too oppressive on a single user machine. Unfortunately there are some significant performance flaws here that are aggravated when you go to a network.

## Keep Tables On The Workspace Until You're Done With Them

If you are going to be using a table on a regular basis, try to keep it on the workspace. Placing tables *on* and removing tables *from* the workspace involve writing lock files. In the routine above, you'd simply place the customer table on the workspace once, and keep the table there until the user decides to quit the loop. Only remove the table when the routine is over.

## Avoid Jumping In And Out Of Coedit Mode.

Along the same lines, once you're in CoEdit mode, try to stay in CoEdit mode. This is particularly true if you have many lookup tables. When in Main mode, Paradox does not need the lookups, but as soon as you jump to CoEdit mode, Paradox must write Prevent Full Locks on each of the lookup tables and this takes time. So a more appropriate routine might look like:

```
 1) Put the customer table on the workspace
 2) Go into CoEdit mode
 3) Pick a form
 4) Start a loop
 5) Ask the user for a customer# to update. If the user selects a
    number, proceed with the next step, otherwise quit the loop,
    go on to the cleanup.
 6) Locate the record by customer#
 7) Do a WAIT RECORD so user can update the customer
 8) Continue to the top of the loop which clears the image and
    starts over for the next customer#
 9) End the loop
10) If the user is finished, then clean up with:
11) DO_IT!
12) CLEARALL
```

## Avoid Overusing The PickForm Command

One command that is often overlooked when evaluating performance is PICK-FORM. You generally need a PICKFORM to select a form when you place a table on the workspace. However, if you issue a FORMKEY to toggle back to table view, don't issue another PICKFORM to get back to form view, simply use FORMKEY again. The reason is pretty simple, PICKFORM is exactly the same as issuing

```
MENU {Image} {Pickform}
```

At which point Paradox has to go to disk and try to find out which forms are available and get the form descriptions for every form for the table to display on the {Pickform} menu choice lines. Even though you might expect that the explicit PICKFORM command wouldn't go through all this work and simply get the form you've specified, it nonetheless does. From a performance standpoint it's best to initialize a form once the table is on the workspace and let FORMKEY do the work because FORMKEY does not go back out to disk, it simply toggles the existing form on and off.

## Keep The Number Of Lookup Tables To A Minimum

On a network, every time you change to Edit or CoEdit mode, Paradox needs to place implicit locks on the tables on the workspace and on the associated lookup tables. If you find that it is taking an extraordinarily long time to get into CoEdit mode, check if there are any validity check table lookups that are unnecessary and remove them.

## Effect Of Implicit Locks Caused By Pal Commands And Functions

Assume that you have a customer table with 20 fields. Take a look at the following code:

```
CLEARALL
FOR n FROM 1 TO (NFIELDS("Customer") * 100)
    MESSAGE "Now n = ", n
ENDFOR
```

Though not the most useful code in the world, it will illustrate a point. On a single user machine, this code will execute pretty quickly. On a network it will crawl. The reason is simple, but not obvious. On a network, when Paradox needs to get the number of fields in a table, it needs to place a Prevent Full Lock on the table to make sure that no one else has current exclusive use of the table. Paradox then removes the lock as soon as it gets the information it needs. On each and every pass of the loop Paradox will write and remove a lock file! This creates an extraordinary amount of overhead and bogs down the network while this is done 2,000 times. One solution is to evaluate the number of loops needed once, and proceed with the loop:

```
CLEARALL
Total.n = NFIELDS("Customer") * 100   ;get the number of loops
FOR  n FROM 1 TO  Total.n
  MESSAGE "Now n = ", n
ENDFOR
```

Although the method above is preferred, there is another way to eliminate the massive amount of locking. Put the table on the workspace first, so Paradox can get the information from the memory needed to store the image. Because the table is actively on the workspace, Paradox does not need to go to the disk to get the number of fields, and no extra locks will be created.

```
VIEW "Customer"
FOR n FROM 1 TO (NFIELDS("Customer")* 100)
  MESSAGE "Now n = ", n
ENDFOR
```

Keep in mind that there are PAL functions that will place implicit locks on table if they are not on the workspace, among those that do are NFIELDS(), NRECORDS(), NKEYFIELDS(), TABLERIGHTS(), ISEMPTY(), CMAX(), etc. Just about any function that needs to look at a table is prone to excessive implicit locking.

## Private Directories Are Always Locked

Whenever you update a shared table, Paradox locks the record(s) to be updated. It does so even if you've placed a FULL LOCK on the table. One technique is to explicitly create or use a query to create a table in the PRIVATE directory. Any processing done to the table while in the PRIVATE directory is exempt from all locking. You can then copy the table back to the shared directory. This little trick can save an enormous amount of time when the target file needs to end up on a network drive, but you need exclusive use of it.

## Use CoEdit Instead Of Edit Mode

Since the debut of CoEdit mode, Edit mode is generally of little use. Edit mode not only requires a full lock on the table, but also produces a transaction log so you can undo all changes back to the beginning of the edit session. Creating and maintaining this edit log takes time. In addition, as soon as one field has been modified, the primary index is flagged as obsolete and it is not used. Once a change has been made to a table in edit mode, performance is crippled by lack of access to indexes of any type.

## Updating Records In A Shared Table Without A Changeto Query

Here's a variation on a previous example that avoids the use of a CHANGETO query to update records while other users have access to it in CoEdit mode. Say that you need to update records in an invoice table to flag invoices as having been printed. Since other users need access, you can't get the FULL LOCK necessary for a changeto query. For this example, lets assume that you need to update every invoice entered yesterday:

```
CoEdit "Invoice"
SCAN FOR [Invoice date] = TODAY() -1
  WHILE TRUE
    LOCKRECORD  ;attempt to lock the record found
    IF RETVAL THEN
      ; If ok, then update the record and continue, which unlocks it
      [date printed] = TODAY()
      QUITLOOP     ; continues the SCAN loop
    ELSE     ; can't lock the record
      ; Put up some sort of menu giving the user the opportunity
      ; to loop back and try the record again, or pass this one up
    ENDIF
  ENDWHILE
ENDSCAN
DO_IT!
```

This technique is satisfactory for a limited number of records, but on a network, the amount of locking and network refreshing can make this oppressively slow. An alternate technique is as follows:

```
;The invoice table is keyed on [Invoice#].
Menu {Ask} {Invoice}
CheckPlus  ; get all the fields
[Invoice date] = "Today -1"
DO_IT!
```

```
;We now have an Answer table with the invoices from yesterday
CLEARALL
Menu {Ask} {Answer}
[date printed] = "Changeto TODAY"
DO_IT! ;Now the Answer table has the correct printed date.
;Finally, ADD the records in the Invoice table.
ADD "Answer" "Invoice"
; We now have a Changed table
CLEARALL
```

This will attempt to update all the invoice records. There is one final thing you must check: if the number of records in the resulting "Changed" table is not equal to the number of records in the "Answer" table, it means that someone had locked one or more of the records when the ADD took place. Those records did not get updated. In this case, it is unlikely, but possible that someone would be working on an invoice dated yesterday. Were this likely to occur, you can run a DELETE query to remove the successfully updated records from the Answer table, attempt the ADD again with just the records that didn't make it through the first time.

```
Menu {Ask} {Answer}
"Delete"
[Invoice#] = "_x"    ; an example element
Menu {Ask} {Changed}
[Invoice#] = "_x"
DO_IT!
; creates a Deleted table
CLEARALL
```

Now you can try the ADD "Answer" "Invoice" again. It's probably best to keep this in a loop that keeps on trying until there are no records left in "Answer", which means that all records have been successfully posted.

The Moral: Don't overlook the ADD command as a way of making global changes on shared, keyed tables.

# 21.4 Conclusions

There are many areas where problems can be avoided with a little forethought and preparation. Performance tuning is a natural extension of problem solving/avoidance, and depends on an intimate understanding of the tools at hand and the environment. You might be surprised just how fast a Paradox system can be when you help it along, or at least keep from getting in its way.

# Appendix

This is an alphabetical listing of the commands, functions, menuchoices, and variables found in the EXAMPLES section of this book.

# Index

WaitPlus Pro

We often get asked about the differences between the the code for WaitPlus included in the book and WaitPlus Pro. Here are the basics:

- WaitPlus Pro has more features than the base WaitPlus and is therefore more powerful. For example it supports "special keys" in addition to the default function key set.
- WaitPlus Pro comes with several sample applications and tables to help you see how WaitPlus can be integrated in an application.
- WaitPlus Pro includes a menu driven front end that provides on-line help and a "script generator" that lets you fill out a form to create an accurate call to WaitPlus.
- A user's manual is included and registered WaitPlus Pro users are eligible for technical support.

WaitPlus Pro is evolving and will be updated from time to time. Registered users will be notified of changes and enhancements as both Paradox and Wait-Plus Pro evolve.

## Diskette Offer

Save time, worry, and frustration by purchasing the listings to PAL by Example on diskette. This includes the latest source listings to all example code and the code listings for WAITPLUS. Also included is a library with special versions of procedures that would otherwise not run under Paradox Runtime.

A second form of WaitPlus, called WaitPlus PRO, is also available. WaitPlus PRO includes all the source code for WaitPlus (and through this special offer, all source code for the book). In addition, WaitPlus PRO includes sample tables, application examples, documentation, and a copy of a front-end generator that writes the calls to WaitPlus for you (of special interest to novice programmers). WaitPlus PRO purchasers are entitled to technical support.

---

### Order Form

Shipping information (please print)

Name _____

Company Name _____

Street _____

City _____ State _____ Zip Code _____

Country _____ Telephone Number _____

**Please send me:**

_____ copies of WaitPlus PRO @ $249.95 each                    _____

_____ copies PAL by Example code listings @ $34.95 each        _____

_____ Shipping and handling                              $5.00

Add $10.00 for orders outside U.S.                                  _____

Add $5.00 for C.O.D. orders                                        _____

(NJ Residents add applicable sales tax)                            _____

Total Order                                        _____

Format:        _____ 5.25" disk        _____ 3.5" disk

### Check method of payment

_____ Check _____ Money Order _____ Visa _____ M/C_____ C.O.D.

Credit Card Number _____ Expiration Date _____

Signature        _____

**Send order to:**       **PAL by Example**                 **Fax orders to:** (201) 795-9237
                    **P. O. Box 810**
                    **Hoboken, New Jersey 07030**
                    **U.S.A.**

All payments shall be in U.S. dollars. Make checks payable to "PAL by Example." For special handling on international orders, please call (201) 795-5144. Price and availability subject to change without notice.